WEBSTER'S
New Explorer
Rhyming
Dictionary

WEBSTER'S
New Explorer
Rhyming
Dictionary

Created in Cooperation with
the Editors of
MERRIAM-WEBSTER

FEDERAL
STREET
PRESS

A Division of Merriam-Webster, Incorporated
Springfield, Massachusetts

This 2002 edition published by
Federal Street Press
A Division of Merriam-Webster, Incorporated
P.O. Box 281
Springfield, MA 01102

Federal Street Press books are available for bulk purchase for sales promotion and premium use. For details write the manager of special sales, Federal Street Press, P.O. Box 281, Springfield, MA 01102

ISBN 1-892859-35-1

Library of Congress Control Number: 2001096833

Printed in the United States of America

02   03   04   05   06   5   4   3   2   1

PREFACE

Webster's New Explorer Rhyming Dictionary is a listing of words grouped according to the way they rhyme. In selecting words for entry, the editors have focused on words that are most likely to be used in poetry; highly technical or otherwise obscure words are generally not included. However, some words that are restricted in their applications (such as slang words and words that are stigmatized) as well as words that are likely to be unfamiliar to many users have been included. Thus, not every word listed in this book will be appropriate in every context and *it is essential that the rhyming dictionary be used in conjunction with an adequate dictionary*.

The editors have assigned words to rhyming groups on the basis of pronunciations that are in standard and widespread use. However, many words have more than one standard pronunciation, and these variants often produce alternate rhyming sounds. Thus, some words may appear in more than one list, and not every word on every list will rhyme for every person.

Users of this book who are uncertain about any aspect of meaning, usage status, or pronunciation of any word listed here should consult their dictionary.

The rhyming sound   Words in this book are gathered into entries on the basis of their rhyming sound. The rhyming sound is the terminal part of the word — from the vowel sound in the last stressed syllable to the end of the word. In this book, the rhyming sound may have one, two, or three syllables. One-syllable rhyming sounds are found in one-syllable words and in words in which primary or secondary stress falls on the final syllable. For example, **wide** \'wīd\, **appeal** \ə-'pēl\, **mongoose** \'män-ˌgüs\, and **undergrad** \'ən-dər-ˌgrad\ all have one-syllable rhyming sounds. For *wide*, the rhyming sound is \īd\, as in *bedside* and *qualified*. For *appeal*, it is \ēl\, as in *heal* and *cockatiel*. For *mongoose*, it is \üs\, as in *juice* and *introduce*. For *undergrad*, it is \ad\, as in *plaid* and *comrade*.

Two-syllable rhyming sounds are found in words in which the last syllable with primary or secondary stress is the next-to-last syllable in the word (often called the penultimate syllable or penult). For example, *cola* \'kō-lə\ and *remover* \rē-'mü-vər\ have two-syllable rhyming sounds. For *cola*, the rhyming sound is \ō-lə\, as in *granola* and *Gorgonzola*. For *remover*, it is \ü-vər\, as in *louver* and *maneuver*.

Three-syllable rhyming sounds are found in words in which the syllable before the penult (the antepenultimate syllable or antepenult) carries primary or secondary stress. For example, *mutable* \'müt-ə-bəl\ and *frivolity* \friv-'äl-ət-ē\ have three-syllable rhyming sounds. For *mutable*, it is \üt-ə-bəl\, as in *suitable* and *unscrutable*. For *frivolity*, it is \äl-ət-ē\, as in *jollity* and *equality*.

Using this book   *Webster's New Explorer Rhyming Dictionary* is designed to be used with a minimum of instruction. In order to use this book successfully, the reader needs to understand the following four points:
1. All of the words in this book are gathered into main entries on the basis of their rhyming sounds.
2. All of the main entries are arranged according to the way the rhyming sound is most often spelled, represented by the boldface form that begins each main entry.
3. Alternate spellings of the rhyming sound are entered as cross-reference entries that direct the user to the appropriate main entry. The alternate spelling is the boldface form that begins each cross-reference entry.
4. All main entries and cross-reference entries, whether for one-, two-, or three-syllable rhyming sounds, are alphabetized by the boldface form in a single sequence.

To find a rhyme for a given word, then, you need to know only the spelling of the word and its rhyming sound. If, for instance, you wanted to find a word to rhyme with *deep*, you would look up *eep*, because that is the way the rhyming sound is spelled. When you look up *eep*, you will find the following entry:

> **eep** \ēp\ beep, bleep, cheap, cheep,
>   clepe, creep, deep, heap, jeep,
>   Jeep, keep, . . .

If the word you wanted to find a rhyme for had been *cheap*, you might have looked up *eap*, because that is how the rhyming sound is spelled in that word. If you had done so, you would have found the following cross-reference entry:

eap \ēp\ see EEP

In some cases (explained in more detail later in this Preface), you may find two or more entries for the same spelling. If, for instance, you wanted a rhyme for *give*, you would have found the following entries at *ive*:

> ¹**ive** \īv\ chive, dive, drive, five,
>   gyve, hive, I've, jive, . . .
> ²**ive** \iv\ give, live, sheave, shiv,
>   sieve, spiv, forgive, . . .
> ³**ive** \ēv\ see ¹EAVE

In cases like this, you would look at the pronunciation given in the entry. The rhyming sound in *give* is \iv\, and the pronunciation given at *²ive* is \iv\; therefore the entry *²ive* is the appropriate one.

The following sections of this Preface discuss in detail the major features of this book. A careful reading of these sections will ensure that the user gets the maximum benefit from this book.

Main entries   Main entries consist of three principal elements: an entry form, a pronunciation, and a list of words that rhyme:

> **arten** \ärt-ᵊn\ Barton, carton,
>   hearten, marten, martin, Martin,
>   smarten, Spartan, tartan, baum
>   marten, dishearten, Dumbarton,
>   freemartin, Saint Martin, Sint
>   Maarten, kindergarten

The main entry form in this entry is **arten**. It represents the way the rhyming sound is most often spelled. When two or more spellings are used with virtually equal frequency, the editors have chosen one arbitrarily to be the main entry form.

The rhyming sound itself is \ärt-ᵊn\, as shown in pronunciation symbols which appear within reversed virgules following the entry word. These symbols are listed and explained beginning on page xii. The pronunciations include no stress marks; the reader is meant to understand that the first syllable in the pronunciation is the last stressed syllable in the word. The pronunciation is given for identification purposes only; that is, it is meant to help the user confirm that the entry includes words with the desired rhyming sound. Each entry includes only one pronunciation even though there may be more than one way to pronounce the main entry form. Following the pronunciation is the list of words that share the rhyming sound. The words are arranged by the number of syllables: the words with the fewest syllables are listed first, followed by groups of words with successively more syllables. Groups of words having the same number of syllables are arranged alphabetically. In the list in the sample entry shown above, *Barton, carton, hearten, marten, martin, Martin, smarten, Spartan*, and *tartan*, each with two syllables, come first. They are followed by *baum marten, dishearten, Dumbarton, freemartin, Saint Martin*, and *Sint Maarten*, with three syllables, and *kindergarten*, with four syllables.

Cross-reference entries   Main entries in this book are supplemented by cross-reference entries. Like main entries, cross-reference entries have an entry form and a pronunciation, but in place of a list of rhyming words, cross-reference entries provide a note that directs the user to a main entry where the list of rhyming words can be found. The following cross-reference entries, for instance, send the reader to the entry **arten** shown as a sample earlier:

> **artin** \ärt-ᵊn\ see ARTEN
> **aarten** \ärt-ᵊn\ see ARTEN

The entry form in a cross-reference entry represents an alternate spelling of the rhyming sound. In the sample entries above, the cross-reference entries **artin** and **aarten** have been included because the spellings *-artin* and *-aarten* are represented by the words *freemartin* and *Sint Maarten*, respectively. A cross-reference entry has been included for every alternate spelling of a rhyming sound that is represented by one or more words in the list at the main entry.

The pronunciation in the cross-reference entry matches the pronunciation shown at the main entry. The pronunciation is provided to help the user confirm that the cross-reference leads to the desired main entry, which is shown in small capital letters.

Identification numbers   In some cases, the same spelling has been used to represent more than one rhyme and therefore appears as a main entry form more than once.

¹age \äj\ dodge, lodge, raj, stodge,
    wodge, barrage, collage, corsage,
    dislodge, garage, hodgepodge,
    Karaj, massage, swaraj,
    camouflage, espionage,
    counterespionage
²age \äzh\ plage, assuage, barrage,
    collage, corsage, dressage,
    frottage, gavage, lavage,
    massage, ménage, mirage,
    montage, moulage, . . .
³age \āj\ age, cage, gage, Gage,
    gauge, mage, page, rage, sage,
    stage, swage, wage, assuage,
    backstage, birdcage, broad-gauge,
    downstage, . . .
⁴age \āg\ see ¹EG
⁵age \āzh\ see ¹EIGE
⁶age \äg-ə\ see ¹AGA

In order to alert users whenever this situation occurs, identification numbers (in the form of small raised numerals that precede the entry form) have been added to all identically spelled entry forms. In order to assist readers in following cross-references, identification numbers also appear as part of the cross-reference when necessary.

aj \äj\ see ¹AGE
itey \īt-ē\ see ²ITE

Inflected and derived forms   In order to save space, most regular inflected forms of words have not been included in the lists of rhymes. For example, there is no entry **eaks** to cover words such as *beaks, cheeks, cliques,* and *antiques.* In order to find a rhyme for these words, the user needs to go to the entry for the base word (in this case **¹eak** \ēk\) and look for words on the list that will take the inflection that creates the desired rhyming sound.

In some cases, both inflected and noninflected forms share the same rhyming sounds. For example, the uninflected forms *lox* and *paradox* share the same rhyming sound with the inflected forms *docks* and *socks.* In such cases, all of the uninflected forms are listed at the entry for the rhyming sound. At the end of the list, an italicized note appears telling the user that additional rhymes exist and giving directions to the entry where the base words can be found:

> **ox** \äks\ box, cox, fox, . . . —*also*
> *plurals and possessives of nouns*
> *and third person singular pres-*
> *ents of verbs listed at* ¹OCK

Such notes have been added whenever two or more rhyming words could be created by adding inflections to the base words at the entry. If only one such rhyme could be created, it has simply been added to the list.

The particular inflected forms that are covered by these notes are plurals and possessives of nouns, comparatives and superlatives of adjectives, and past tense and third person present tense forms of verbs. In addition, present participles of verbs are covered at entries where the spelling of the entry form (after the *-ing* ending has been removed and any elided *e* or doubled consonant has been taken into account) does not match the spelling of the entry for the base words:

> **aining** \ā-niŋ\ veining, complaining,
> sustaining, . . . —*also present*
> *participles of verbs listed at* ¹ANE

The treatment of words derived by adding a suffix to another word is somewhat similar. There is no entry for a rhyming sound if all of the words that would be on the list are regular derived words formed by adding a suffix to words drawn from another list. This treatment applies mostly to adverbs ending in *-ly*, nouns ending in *-ness* or *-ment*, and adjectives ending in *-less*. For instance, there is no entry for **arkly** \ärk-lē\, because the only words on the list would be *darkly* and *starkly*, and they are both formed by adding an *-ly* ending to the adjectives found at the entry **ark** \ärk\. If, however, any of the words on the list are not derived forms, a complete list is entered. There is an entry at **¹eanly** \ēn-lē\, for instance, because among the adverbs at the entry there is also the adjective *queenly*; and, for the purposes of this book, adjectives ending in *-ly* are not treated as regular derived forms.

WEBSTER'S
New Explorer
Rhyming
Dictionary

PRONUNCIATION SYMBOLS

ə . . . . . . banana, collide, abut

ᵊ . . . . . . immediately preceding \l\ and \n\, as in battle, mitten, and eaten; immediately following \l\, \m\, \r\, as often in French table, prisme, titre

ər . . . . . . further, merger, bird

a . . . . . . mat, map, mad, gag, snap, patch

ā . . . . . . day, fade, date, aorta, drape, cape

ä . . . . . . bother, cot

aů . . . . . . now, loud, out

b . . . . . . baby, rib

ch . . . . . . chin, nature \'nā-chər\ (actually, this sound is \t\ + \sh\)

d . . . . . . did, adder

e . . . . . . bet, bed, peck

ē . . . . . . fee, easy

f . . . . . . fifty, cuff

g . . . . . . go, big, gift

h . . . . . . hat, ahead

i . . . . . . tip, banish, active

ī . . . . . . site, side, buy, tripe (actually, this sound is \ä\ + \i\)

j . . . . . . job, gem, edge, join, judge (actually, this sound is \d\ + \zh\)

k . . . . . . kin, cook, ache

k̲ . . . . . . German ich, Buch; one pronunciation of loch

l . . . . . . lily, pool

m . . . . . . murmur, dim, nymph

n . . . . . . no, own

ⁿ . . . . . . indicates that a preceding vowel or diphthong is pronounced with the nasal passages open, as in French un bon vin blanc \œⁿ-bōⁿ-vaⁿ-bläⁿ\

ŋ . . . . . . sing \'siŋ\, singer \'siŋ-er\, finger \'fiŋ-ger\, ink \'iŋk\

ō . . . . . . bone, know, beau

Pronunciation Symbols

ȯ ...... saw, all, gnaw, caught

ȯi ...... coin, destroy

p ...... pepper, lip

r ...... red, car, rarity

s ...... source, less

sh ...... as in shy, mission, machine, special (actually, this is a single sound, not two); with a hyphen between, two sounds as in *grasshopper* \'gras-ˌhäp-ər\

t ...... tie, attack, late, latter

th ...... as in thin, ether (actually, this is a single sound, not two); with a hyphen between, two sounds as in *knighthood* \'nīt-ˌhu̇d\

<u>th</u> ...... then, either, this (actually, this is a single sound, not two)

ü ...... rule, youth, union \'yün-yən\, few \'fyü\

u̇ ...... pull, wood, book, curable \'kyu̇r-ə-bəl\, fury \'fyu̇(ə)r-ē\

v ...... vivid, give

w ...... we, away

y ...... yard, young, cue \'kyü\, mute \'myüt\, union \'yün-yən\

z ...... zone, raise

zh ...... as in vision, azure \'azhər\ (actually, this is a single sound, not two); with a hyphen between, two sounds as in *hogshead* \'hȯgz-ˌhed, 'hägz-\

\ ...... slant line used in pairs to mark the beginning and end of a transcription: \'pen\

ˈ ...... mark preceding a syllable with primary (strongest) stress: \'pen-mən-ˌship\

ˌ ...... mark preceding a syllable with secondary (medium) stress: \'pen-mən-ˌship\

- ...... mark of syllable division

a

¹a \ä\ aah, ah, baa, bah, blah, bra, dah, droit, fa, Fra, ha, Jah, Kwa, la, ma, na, nah, pa, pas, qua, Ra, rah, schwa, shah, ska, spa, à bas, aba, Accra, aha, Allah, Armagh, blah-blah, Borgia, bourgeois, brava, Casbah, chamois, Chang-sha, Chita, Degas, Dumas, éclat, fa la, faux pas, fellah, fetah, foie gras, gaga, galah, Galois, grandma, grandpa, ha-ha, halvah, Hama, hoo-ha, hoopla, Hsia, hurrah, huzzah, isba, Issa, Luda, Marat, markka, mudra, Oita, opah, orgeat, Oujda, quinoa, pai-hua, paisa, Para, pasha, patois, pooh-bah, prutah, pya, San'a, sangfroid, selah, Shema, sola, supra, tola, Tonghua, Ufa, Utah, Valois, Vaudois, viva, voilà, whoopla, abaca, Adana, agora, ahimsa, Akita, aloha, assignat, Aymara, baccarat, baklava, Bogotá, brouhaha, cervelat, Chippewa, coup d'état, Cumanà, Delacroix, entrechat, feria, habdalah, haftarah, haniwa, Kashiwa, koruna, Kostroma, la-di-da, Libera, ma-and-pa, Machida, Malinois, Mardi Gras, Modena, moussaka, Omaha, Oshawa, Ottawa, padishah, pakeha, panama, Panama, Paraná, parashah, pas de trois, persona, picara, pietà, podesta, polenta, polynya, port de bras, Quebecois, reseda, rufiyaa, Shangri-la, tempura, ulema, usquebaugh, Ahvenanmaa, Alma-Ata, ayatollah, Baha' Allah, caracara, con anima, coureur de bois, hispanidad, hors de combat, je ne sais quoi, Karaganda, ménage à trois, phenomena, res publica, sursum corda, tamandua, Alto Paraná, Haleakala, Katharevusa, Makhachkala, mousseline de soie, Nishinomiya, Isthmus of Panama, pâté de foie gras, Utsunomiya, Afars and the Isas, exempli gratia, Novaya Zemlya, Tokorozawa

²a \ā\ see ¹AY

³a \ȯ\ see ¹AW

¹aa \a\ see ³AH

²aa \ä\ see ¹A

aachen \ä-kən\ Aachen, lochan

aag \äg\ see ¹OG

¹aal \āl\ see AIL

²aal \ȯl\ see ALL

³aal \äl\ see ¹AL

aam \äm\ see ¹OM

aan \an\ see ⁵AN

¹aans \äns\ see ²ANCE

²aans \änz\ see ONZE

aard \ärd\ see ¹ARD
aari \är-ē\ see ¹ARI
aaron \ar-ən\ see ²ARON
aarten \ärt-ᵊn\ see ARTEN
aas \äs\ see ¹OS
aatz \ätz\ see OTS
¹ab \äb\ see ¹OB
²ab \äv\ see ²OLVE
³ab \ab\ blab, cab, crab, dab, drab, flab, gab, grab, jab, lab, Lab, Mab, nab, scab, slab, stab, tab, Ahab, Moab, baobab, Cantab, confab, prefab, Rajab, rehab, smack-dab, astrolabe, minilab, pedicab, taxicab
aba \äb-ə\ Kaaba, Labe, PABA, Saba, Sabah, casaba, djellaba, indaba, Ali Baba, Orizaba, Sorocaba, jaboticaba, Pico de Orizaba
abah \äb-ə\ see ABA
abala \ab-ə-lə\ cabala, cabbalah, parabola
abalist \ab-ə-ləst\ cabalist, diabolist
abard \ab-ərd\ clapboard, scabbard, tabard—also pasts of verbs listed at ²ABBER
abatis \ab-ət-əs\ abatis, habitus
abbalah \ab-ə-lə\ see ABALA
abbard \ab-ərd\ see ABARD
abbas \ab-əs\ see ABBESS
abbat \ab-ət\ see ABIT
¹abbed \ab-əd\ crabbed, rabid
²abbed \abd\ blabbed, stabbed—also pasts of verbs listed at ³AB
¹abber \äb-ər\ see OBBER
²abber \ab-ər\ blabber, clabber, crabber, dabber, drabber, gabber, grabber, jabber, slabber, stabber, yabber, rehabber, bonnyclabber
abbess \ab-əs\ abbess, Barabbas
abbet \ab-ət\ see ABIT
abbey \ab-ē\ see ABBY
¹abbie \äb-ē\ see OBBY
²abbie \ab-ē\ see ABBY
abbin \ab-ən\ see ABIN
abbit \ab-ət\ see ABIT
abbitry \ab-ə-trē\ see ABBITTRY
abbitt \ab-ət\ see ABIT
abbittry \ab-ə-trē\ Babbittry, rabbitry
¹abble \äb-əl\ bauble, bobble, cobble, gobble, hobble, Kabul, nobble, obol, squabble, wabble, wobble
²abble \ab-əl\ Babel, babble, brabble, dabble, drabble, gabble, grabble, habile, rabble, scrabble, bedabble, hardscrabble, psychobabble, technobabble
abblement \ab-əl-mənt\ babblement, rabblement
abbler \ab-lər\ babbler, dabbler, gabbler, grabbler, rabbler, scrabbler
abbly \ab-lē\ see ABLY
abbot \ab-ət\ see ABIT
abby \ab-ē\ abbey, Abby, blabby, cabbie, crabby, flabby, gabby, grabby, scabby, shabby, tabby, kohlrabi, Panjabi, Punjabi
¹abe \āb\ babe, mabe, nabe, astrolabe
²abe \ab\ see AB
³abe \ä-bə\ see ABA
abel \ā-bəl\ see ABLE
aben \äb-ən\ see OBIN
¹aber \ā-bər\ see ABOR

²**aber** \äb-ər\ see OBBER
abes \ā-bēz\ see ABIES
¹**abi** \äb-ē\ see OBBY
²**abi** \əb-ē\ see UBBY
³**abi** \ab-ē\ see ABBY
abia \ā-bē-ə\ Arabia, labia,
  Swabia, Bessarabia, Saudi
  Arabia
abian \ā-bē-ən\ Fabian, gabion,
  Arabian, Bessarabian
abid \ab-əd\ see ABBED
abies \ā-bēz\ rabies, scabies,
  tabes—*also plurals and*
  possessives of nouns listed at
  ABY
abile \ab-əl\ see ²ABBLE
abilis \äb-ə-ləs\ obelus, annus
  mirabilis
abin \ab-ən\ cabin, rabbin
abion \ā-bē-ən\ see ABIAN
abit \ab-ət\ abbot, babbitt,
  Babbitt, Cabot, habit, rabbet,
  rabbit, sabbat, cohabit,
  inhabit, jackrabbit
abitant \ab-ət-ənt\ habitant,
  cohabitant, inhabitant
abitus \ab-ət-əs\ see ABATIS
able \ā-bəl\ Abel, able, Babel,
  cable, fable, Froebel, gable,
  label, Mabel, sable, stable,
  table, disable, enable,
  instable, pin-table, retable,
  round table, timetable,
  turntable, unable, unstable,
  worktable
abled \ā-bəld\ fabled, gabled—
  also pasts of verbs listed at
  ABLE
ablis \ab-lē\ see ABLY
ably \ab-lē\ chablis, drably,
  scrabbly
abo \ab-ō\ abo, sabot

abola \ab-ə-lə\ see ABALA
abolist \ab-ə-ləst\ see ABALIST
abor \ā-bər\ caber, labor,
  neighbor, saber, tabor,
  belabor, von Weber, zeitgeber
aborer \ā-bər-ər\ laborer,
  taborer
¹**abot** \ab-ō\ see ABO
²**abot** \ab-ət\ see ABIT
abra \äb-rə\ sabra, Sabra,
  candelabra
abre \äb\ see ¹OB
abul \äb-əl\ see ¹ABBLE
abular \ab-yə-lər\ fabular,
  tabular, vocabular, acetabular
abulous \ab-yə-ləs\ fabulous,
  fantabulous
abulum \ab-yə-ləm\ pabulum,
  acetabulum, incunabulum
aby \ā-bē\ baby, gaby, maybe,
  crybaby, grandbaby
¹**ac** \ak\ see ²ACK
²**ac** \äk\ see ¹OCK
³**ac** \ȯ\ see ¹AW
¹**aca** \äk-ə\ see ¹AKA
²**aca** \ak-ə\ Dacca, Dhaka, paca,
  alpaca, malacca, Malacca,
  sifaka, portulaca, Strait of
  Malacca
acable \ak-ə-bəl\ see ACKABLE
acao \ō-kō\ see OCO
acas \ak-əs\ Bacchus, fracas,
  Gracchus, Caracas
¹**acca** \ak-ə\ see ACA
²**acca** \äk-ə\ see ¹AKA
accent \ak-sənt\ accent, relaxant
acchanal \ak-ən-ᵊl\ see ACONAL
acchic \ak-ik\ bacchic, halakic,
  stomachic, tribrachic,
  amphibrachic
acchus \ak-əs\ see ACAS
accid \as-əd\ see ACID

accio \ä-chē-ō\ bocaccio,
Bocaccio, carpaccio

¹acco \ak-ə\ see ACA

²acco \ak-ō\ see ²AKO

acculus \ak-yə-ləs\ sacculus,
miraculous

¹ace \ās\ ace, base, bass, brace,
case, chase, dace, face, grace,
Grace, lace, mace, Mace,
pace, place, plaice, prase,
race, res, space, Thrace, trace,
vase, abase, airspace, Alsace,
ambsace, apace, backspace,
best-case, biface, birthplace,
blackface, boldface, bookcase,
bootlace, braincase, briefcase,
crankcase, debase, deface,
disgrace, displace, dogface,
doughface, efface, embrace,
emplace, encase, enchase,
enlace, erase, firebase,
fireplace, footpace, footrace,
foreface, gyrase, half-space,
hard case, headspace, Jerez,
lightface, manes, millrace,
milreis, misplace, notecase,
null-space, outface, outpace,
outrace, paleface, postface,
Quilmes, replace, retrace,
scapegrace, shoelace,
showcase, showplace,
slipcase, smearcase,
someplace, staircase, subbase,
subspace, suitcase, surbase,
tailrace, tenace, typeface,
ukase, unbrace, unlace,
watchcase, wheelbase, whey-
face, whiteface, workplace,
worst-case, about-face,
aerospace, anyplace, boniface,
bouillabaisse, carapace,
commonplace, contrabass,
double-space, everyplace,
interface, interlace, kilobase,
lemures, lowercase,
marketplace, pillowcase,
Samothrace, single-space,
steeplechase, thoroughbass,
thoroughbrace, triple-space,
uppercase, rarae aves, beta-
lactamase, in medias res,
Aguascalientes, Goya y
Lucientes, superoxide
dismutase, litterae humaniores

²ace \ā-sē\ see ACY

³ace \äs\ see ¹OS

⁴ace \as\ see ³ASS

⁵ace \äch-ē\ see OTCHY

⁶ace \äs-ə\ see ¹ASA

aceable \ā-sə-bəl\ placeable,
traceable, displaceable,
effaceable, embraceable,
erasable, persuasible,
replaceable, ineffaceable,
irreplaceable

acean \ā-shən\ see ¹ATION

aced \āst\ based, baste, chaste,
faced, geest, haste, laced,
mayest, paste, taste, waist,
waste, bald-faced, barefaced,
bold-faced, distaste, dough-
faced, foretaste, impaste,
lambaste, lightfaced,
moonfaced, pie-faced, po-
faced, posthaste, rad waste,
self-paced, shamefaced,
shirtwaist, snail-paced,
slipcased, stone-faced,
straight-faced, straitlaced,
toothpaste, two-faced,
unchaste, unplaced, white-
faced, aftertaste, brazen-faced,
double-faced, Janus-faced,
hatchet-faced, pantywaist,

poker-faced, thorough-
paced—*also pasts of verbs
listed at* ¹ACE
aceless \ā-sləs\ baseless,
faceless, graceless, laceless,
placeless, spaceless, traceless
aceman \ā-smən\ baseman,
placeman, spaceman
acement \ā-smənt\ basement,
casement, placement,
abasement, debasement,
defacement, displacement,
effacement, embracement,
emplacement, encasement,
enlacement, misplacement,
outplacement, replacement,
self-effacement
acence \ās-ᵊns\ see ¹ASCENCE
acency \ās-ᵊn-sē\ adjacency,
complacency, subjacency
acent \ās-ᵊnt\ nascent, adjacent,
complacent, complaisant,
subjacent, circumjacent,
superjacent
aceor \ā-sər\ see ¹ACER
aceous \ā-shəs\ see ACIOUS
¹**acer** \ā-sər\ baser, bracer,
chaser, facer, pacer, placer,
racer, spacer, tracer, defacer,
disgracer, effacer, embraceor,
embracer, eraser, replacer,
subchaser, steeplechaser
²**acer** \as-ər\ see ASSER
acery \ās-rē\ tracery, embracery
¹**acet** \ā-sət\ hic jacet, nonplacet
²**acet** \as-ət\ asset, facet, tacet,
tacit
acewalking \ās-wȯ-kiŋ\
racewalking, spacewalking
acey \ā-sē\ see ACY
¹**ach** \ä̱k\ Bach, saugh, Pesach,

pibroch, Offenbach,
Mönchengladbach
²**ach** \äk\ see ¹OCK
³**ach** \ak\ see ²ACK
⁴**ach** \ach\ see ⁴ATCH
acha \äch-ə\ cha-cha, dacha,
kwacha, viscacha
achary \ak-ə-r-ē\ see ²ACKERY
¹**ache** \āk\ see ¹AKE
²**ache** \ash\ see ³ASH
³**ache** \äch-ē\ see OTCHY
⁴**ache** \ach-ē\ see ATCHY
acheal \ā-kē-əl\ brachial,
tracheal
ached \acht\ attached, detached,
unattached, semidetached—
also pasts of verbs listed at
⁴ATCH
acher \ā-kər\ see ¹AKER
achet \ach-ət\ see ATCHET
achi \äch-ē\ see OTCHY
achial \ā-kē-əl\ see ACHEAL
achian \ā-shən\ see ¹ATION
achic \ak-ik\ see ACCHIC
aching \ā-kiŋ\ see ¹AKING
¹**achio** \ash-ō\ mustachio,
pistachio
²**achio** \ash-ē-ō\ mustachio,
pistachio
achm \am\ see ²AM
achment \ach-mənt\ see
ATCHMENT
achne \ak-nē\ see ACNE
acho \äch-ō\ muchacho,
quebracho
achou \a-shü\ see ASHEW
achsen \äk-sən\ see OXEN
acht \ät\ see ¹OT
achtsman \ät-smən\ see
OTSMAN
achy \ā-kē\ see AKY
acia \ā-shə\ Dacia, fascia,

geisha, acacia, Croatia, Dalmatia, ex gratia, Galatia, prima facie, exempli gratia

acial \ā-shəl\ facial, glacial, racial, spatial, abbatial, bifacial, biracial, englacial, palatial, primatial, subglacial, interfacial, interglacial, interracial, multiracial

acian \ā-shən\ see ¹ATION

acias \ā-shəs\ see ACIOUS

acid \as-əd\ acid, Chasid, flaccid, Hasid, jassid, placid, Abbasid, antacid

acie \ā-shə\ see ACIA

acient \ā-shənt\ see ATIENT

¹acier \ā-shər\ see ¹ASURE

²acier \ā-zhər\ see AZIER

acile \as-əl\ see ²ASSEL

acing \ā-siŋ\ bracing, casing, facing, lacing, racing, spacing, tracing, catfacing, effacing, all-embracing, interfacing, letterspacing, self-effacing

acious \ā-shəs\ gracious, spacious, audacious, bodacious, capacious, ceraceous, cretaceous, crustaceous, curvaceous, edacious, fallacious, flirtatious, fugacious, herbaceous, Horatius, Ignatius, loquacious, mendacious, mordacious, pomaceous, predaceous, pugnacious, rapacious, sagacious, salacious, sebaceous, sequacious, setaceous, tenacious, testaceous, ungracious, veracious, vexacious, vinaceous, vivacious, voracious, alliaceous, arenaceous, argillaceous, carbonaceous, contumacious, coriaceous, disputatious, efficacious, farinaceous, foliaceous, ostentatious, pectinaceous, perspicacious, pertinacious, saponaceous, scire facias, stercoraceous, violaceous, inefficacious, fieri facias

acis \as-ē\ see ASSY

acist \ā-səst\ see ASSIST

acit \as-ət\ see ²ACET

¹acity \as-tē\ see ²ASTY

²acity \as-ət-ē\ audacity, capacity, fugacity, loquacity, mendacity, opacity, rapacity, sagacity, tenacity, veracity, vivacity, voracity, efficacity, incapacity, overcapacity

acive \ā-siv\ see ASIVE

¹ack \äk\ see ¹OCK

²ack \ak\ back, black, clack, claque, crack, flack, flak, hack, jack, Jack, knack, lac, lack, mac, Mac, Mack, pack, plaque, quack, rack, sac, Sac, sack, sacque, shack, slack, smack, snack, stack, tach, tack, thwack, track, Wac, whack, wrack, yak, aback, ack-ack, alack, amtrac, Anzac, Arak, attack, backpack, backtrack, Balzac, bareback, blackjack, blue-black, bootblack, bootjack, brushback, bushwhack, buyback, callback, calpac, champac, cheapjack, Coalsack, coatrack, cognac,

come back, comeback,
cookshack, cossack,
crackback, crookback, cut
back, cutback, Dayak,
dieback, draw back,
drawback, fall back, fallback,
fastback, fast-track, fatback,
feedback, finback, fireback,
flapjack, flareback, flashback,
fullback, gimcrack,
graywacke, greenback,
gripsack, guaiac, halfback,
half-track, hardback,
hardhack, hardtack,
hatchback, hayrack, haystack,
hijack, hogback, hold back,
holdback, hopsack, horseback,
humpback, hunchback, Iraq,
jam-pack, jet-black, kayak,
Kazak, Kazakh, kickback,
knapsack, knickknack, Kodak,
kulak, kyack, laid-back,
lampblack, leaseback, linac,
macaque, man jack, manpack,
Micmac, mossback, muntjac,
Muzak, notchback, offtrack,
outback, packsack, payback,
pitch-black, play back,
playback, plow back,
plowback, Polack, pullback,
quillback, racetrack, ransack,
rickrack, roll back, rollback,
roorback, rucksack, runback,
scatback, serac, set back,
setback, shellac, shellback,
shoeblack, shoepac, sidetrack,
six-pack, skewback, skipjack,
skyjack, slapjack, slotback,
Slovak, smokejack,
smokestack, snap back,
snapback, snowpack,
softback, sumac, swayback,

sweepback, swept-back,
switchback, tailback, tarmac,
thornback, throw back,
throwback, thumbtack,
ticktack, tieback, tie tack,
tombac, touchback, tow sack,
trictrac, tripack, unpack,
Welsbach, wetback,
whaleback, wingback,
wisecrack, woolpack,
woolsack, yashmak, Yurak,
zwieback, almanac,
amberjack, anorak, antiblack,
applejack, Arawak,
Armagnac, birdyback,
bivouac, bric-a-brac,
camelback, canvasback,
cardiac, carryback, celiac,
coeliac, cornerback, Cousin
Jack, crackerjack, cul-de-sac,
diamondback, fiddleback,
fishyback, Frontenac,
gunnysack, hackmatack,
haversack, high-low-jack,
huckaback, hydrocrack, iliac,
ipecac, Kodiak, ladder-back,
leatherback, lumberjack,
maniac, medevac, minitrack,
moneyback, nunatak, otomac,
paperback, Pasternak,
pickaback, piggyback,
Pontiac, portapak,
quarterback, razorback,
retropack, running back,
sandarac, Sarawak, Sazerac,
silverback, single-track,
Skaggerak, snapper-back,
solonchak, steeplejack,
stickleback, supplejack,
Syriac, tamarack, tenure-track,
theriac, tokamak, turtleback,
umiak, zodiac, Adirondack,

ammoniac, amnesiac,
Aniakchak, biofeedback,
celeriac, counterattack,
demoniac, elegiac, insomniac,
Monterey Jack, paranoiac,
simoniac, tacamahac,
aphrodisiac, coprophiliac,
Dionysiac, dipsomaniac,
egomaniac, hemophiliac,
hypochondriac, intracardiac,
kleptomaniac, melancholiac,
monomaniac, mythomaniac,
necrophiliac, neophiliac,
nymphomaniac, pedophiliac,
pyromaniac, Rhodesian
Ridgeback, sacroiliac, sal
ammoniac, megalomaniac,
Cyrano de Bergerac

ackable \ak-ə-bəl\ packable,
placable, stackable,
implacable

ackage \ak-ij\ package,
trackage, prepackage,
repackage

ackal \ak-əl\ see ACKLE

acked \akt\ see ACT

acken \ak-ən\ blacken, bracken,
flacon, slacken, Arawakan

ackened \ak-ənd\ blackened—
also pasts of verbs listed at
ACKEN

acker \ak-ər\ backer, clacker,
cracker, hacker, jacker,
knacker, lacquer, packer,
sacker, slacker, smacker,
stacker, tacker, tracker,
whacker, attacker,
backpacker, bushwacker,
firecracker, hijacker, kayaker,
linebacker, nutcracker,
racetracker, ransacker,
safecracker, shellcracker,

skyjacker, unpacker,
wisecracker, simulacre,
counterattacker

ackeray \ak-ə-rē\ see ACKERY

ackerel \ak-rəl\ see ACRAL

ackery \ak-ə-rē\ flackery,
quackery, Thackeray,
Zachary, gimcrackery

acket \ak-ət\ bracket, jacket,
packet, placket, racket,
bluejacket, straitjacket,
yellowjacket

ackey \ak-ē\ see ACKY

ackguard \ag-ərd\ see AGGARD

ackie \ak-ē\ see ACKY

acking \ak-iŋ\ backing,
blacking, cracking, packing,
sacking, smacking, tracking,
whacking, bushwacking,
kayaking, linebacking,
meatpacking, nerve-racking,
nerve-wracking, safecracking,
skyjacking

ackish \ak-ish\ blackish,
brackish, quackish

ackle \ak-əl\ cackle, crackle,
grackle, hackle, jackal, macle,
rackle, shackle, spackle,
tackle, debacle, gang-tackle,
ramshackle, unshackle,
tabernacle

ackly \ak-lē\ blackly, crackly,
hackly, abstractly, compactly,
exactly, inexactly

ackman \ak-mən\ hackman,
packman, trackman

ackney \ak-nē\ see ACNE

ackneyed \ak-nēd\ see ACNED

acko \ak-ō\ see ²AKO

acksman \ak-smən\ see AXMAN

ackson \ak-sən\ see AXON

acky \ak-ē\ hackie, Jackie,

Jacky, khaki, lackey, Paki,
tacky, wacky, ticky-tacky
¹**acle** \ik-əl\ see ICKLE
²**acle** \äk\ see ¹OCK
³**acle** \äk-əl\ see OCKLE
⁴**acle** \ak-əl\ see ACKLE
acne \ak-nē\ acne, hackney,
Hackney, Arachne
acned \ak-nēd\ acned,
hackneyed
aco \äk-ō\ see OCCO
¹**acon** \ā-kən\ see ¹AKEN
²**acon** \ak-ən\ see ACKEN
aconal \ak-ən-ªl\ bacchanal,
diaconal, archidiaconal
¹**acque** \ak\ see ²ACK
²**acque** \äk\ see ¹OCK
acquer \ak-ər\ see ACKER
acques \äk\ see ¹OCK
acral \ak-rəl\ mackerel, sacral
¹**acre** \ā-kər\ see ¹AKER
²**acre** \ak-ər\ see ACKER
acrum \ak-rəm\ sacrum,
simulacrum
act \akt\ act, backed, bract,
cracked, fact, packed, pact,
stacked, tact, tracked, tract,
abstract, attract, coact,
compact, contact, contract,
crookbacked, detract, didact,
diffract, distract, enact,
entr'acte, epact, exact, extract,
half-tracked, humpbacked,
hunchbacked, impact, infract,
intact, mossbacked, playact,
protract, react, redact, refract,
subtract, swaybacked,
transact, unbacked, abreact,
artifact, cataract, chain-react,
counteract, cross-react,
inexact, interact, overact,
paperbacked, precontact,
razor-backed, reenact,
subcompact, subcontract,
underact, vacuum-packed,
ventifact, autodidact, matter-
of-fact, overreact,
semiabstract, underreact—
also pasts of verbs listed at
²ACK
actable \ak-tə-bəl\ actable,
tractable, abstractable,
attractable, compactible,
contractible, distractable,
extractable, intractable
actance \ak-təns\ attractance,
reactance
actant \ak-tənt\ attractant,
reactant, surfactant,
interactant
¹**acte** \äkt\ see OCKED
²**acte** \akt\ see ACT
acted \ak-təd\ fracted,
abstracted, impacted—*also
pasts of verbs listed at* ACT
acter \ak-tər\ see ACTOR
actery \ak-trē\ see ACTORY
actible \ak-tə-bəl\ see ACTABLE
actic \ak-tik\ lactic, tactic,
atactic, climactic, didactic,
galactic, syntactic, ataractic,
chiropractic, parallactic,
paratactic, prophylactic,
anaphylactic, anticlimactic,
autodidactic, extragalactic,
intergalactic, intragalactic,
stereotactic
actical \ak-ti-kəl\ practical,
tactical, didactical,
impractical, syntactical
actice \ak-təs\ cactus, practice,
malpractice, cataractous
actics \ak-tiks\ tactics,
didactics, syntactics,

phonotactics—*also plurals
and possessives of nouns
listed at* ACTIC

actile \ak-t°l\ dactyl, tactile,
contractile, protractile,
refractile, retractile,
polydactyl, pterodactyl

acting \ak-tiŋ\ acting, exacting,
self-acting—*also present
participles of verbs listed at*
ACT

action \ak-shən\ action, faction,
fraction, taction, traction,
abstraction, attraction, bolt-
action, coaction, compaction,
contraction, detraction,
diffraction, distraction,
exaction, extraction,
impaction, inaction,
infraction, olfaction,
protraction, reaction,
redaction, refraction,
retraction, subtraction,
transaction, benefaction,
counteraction, interaction,
liquefaction, malefaction,
overaction, petrifaction,
putrefaction, rarefaction,
retroaction, satisfaction,
single-action, stupefaction,
tumefaction, dissatisfaction,
photoreaction, self-satisfaction

actional \ak-shnəl\ factional,
fractional, tractional,
abstractional, contractional,
redactional, transactional,
interactional, rarefactional

actious \ak-shəs\ factious,
fractious

active \ak-tiv\ active, tractive,
abstractive, attractive,
coactive, contractive,

detractive, distractive,
extractive, impactive,
inactive, proactive, reactive,
refractive, subtractive,
bioactive, counteractive,
hyperactive, interactive,
overactive, psychoactive,
putrefactive, retroactive,
unattractive, radioactive

actly \ak-lē\ see ACKLY

actor \ak-tər\ actor, factor,
tractor, abstractor, attractor,
cofactor, compactor,
contractor, detractor, enactor,
exactor, extractor, g-factor,
impactor, infractor, protractor,
reactor, redactor, refractor,
retractor, subtracter,
transactor, benefactor,
chiropractor, malefactor,
subcontractor, bioreactor,
campylobacter

actory \ak-trē\ factory,
olfactory, phylactery,
refractory, calefactory,
manufactory, satisfactory,
dissatisfactory, unsatisfactory

actous \ak-təs\ see ACTICE

actress \ak-trəs\ actress,
benefactress

actual \ak-chəl\ actual, factual,
tactual, artifactual,
counterfactual

acture \ak-chər\ facture,
fracture, contracture,
manufacture, remanufacture

actus \ak-təs\ see ACTICE

actyl \ak-t°l\ see ACTILE

acular \ak-yə-lər\ macular,
oracular, spectacular,
spiracular, tentacular,
vernacular, tabernacular

aculate \ak-yə-lət\ maculate, ejaculate, immaculate

aculous \ak-yə-ləs\ see ACCULUS

acy \ā-sē\ Basie, lacy, pace, précis, racy, spacey, Stacey, Stacy, Tracey, Tracy, O'Casey, prima facie, Sulawesi, Veronese

acyl \as-əl\ see ²ASSEL

¹ad \ä\ see ¹A

²ad \äd\ see ¹OD

³ad \ad\ ad, add, bad, bade, brad, cad, chad, Chad, clad, dad, fad, gad, Gad, glad, grad, had, lad, mad, pad, plaid, rad, sad, scad, shad, tad, Thad, trad, Akkad, aoudad, Baghdad, Belgrade, Carlsbad, caudad, comrade, Conrad, crawdad, doodad, dorsad, dryad, dyad, egad, farad, footpad, forbade, gonad, granddad, heptad, hexad, horn-mad, ironclad, keypad, launchpad, maenad, Mashad, monad, naiad, nicad, nomad, notepad, pentad, pleiad, Sinbad, Sindbad, tetrad, thinclad, triad, triclad, Troad, armor-clad, Ashkhabad, cephalad, chiliad, ennead, Galahad, hebdomad, helipad, Hyderabad, laterad, mediad, oread, overplaid, Pythiad, undergrad, Volgograd, superadd, Trinidad, Allahabad, bromeliad, gesneriad, hamadryad, hispanidad, Kaliningrad, Kirovograd, olympiad, seminomad, Upanishad, Voroshilovgrad

¹ada \äd-ä\ Dada, Dhu'l-Qa'dah, aficionada

²ada \äd-ə\ nada, sadhe, tsade, Agada, Agade, Aggada, armada, cicada, gelada, Granada, Haggadah, Jumada, Nevada, panada, posada, tostada, autostrada, empanada, enchilada, Ensenada, Theravada, aficionada, Ponta Delgada, Vijayawada, cascara sagrada, Sierra Nevada

³ada \ād-ə\ Ada, Veda, armada, cicada, Grenada, alameda, Avellaneda

adable \ād-ə-bəl\ gradable, tradable, wadable, abradable, degradable, evadable, persuadable, biodegradable

a'dah \äd-ä\ see ¹ADA

adah \äd-ə\ see ²ADA

adal \ad-ᵊl\ see ADDLE

adam \ad-əm\ Adam, madam, macadam, tarmacadam

adams \ad-əmz\ Adams—*also possessives and plurals of nouns listed at* ADAM

¹adan \ad-n\ see ADDEN

²adan \äd-n\ see ODDEN

adant \ād-ᵊnt\ cadent, abradant

add \ad\ see ³AD

adden \ad-ᵊn\ gladden, madden, sadden, Aladdin, Ibadan

adder \ad-ər\ adder, bladder, gadder, ladder, madder, stepladder—*also comparatives of adjectives listed at* ³AD

addie \ad-ē\ see ADDY

addik \äd-ik\ see ODIC

addin \ad-ᵊn\ see ADDEN

adding \ad-iŋ\ cladding, madding, padding

¹**addish** \äd-ish\ see ODDISH

²**addish** \ad-ish\ see ADISH

addison \ad-ə-sən\ Addison, Madison

addle \ad-ᵊl\ addle, paddle, raddle, saddle, staddle, straddle, astraddle, foresaddle, gonadal, packsaddle, sidesaddle, skedaddle, unsaddle, fiddle-faddle

¹**addler** \äd-lər\ see ODDLER

²**addler** \ad-lər\ saddler, paddler, straddler, skedaddler

addo \ad-ō\ see ADOW

¹**addock** \ad-ik\ see ²ADIC

²**addock** \ad-ək\ haddock, paddock, shaddock

¹**addy** \ad-ē\ baddie, caddie, caddy, daddy, faddy, laddie, paddy, Paddy, forecaddie, granddaddy, finnan haddie

²**addy** \äd-ē\ see ¹ODY

¹**ade** \ād\ aid, aide, bade, blade, braid, cade, clade, fade, glade, grade, jade, lade, laid, made, maid, paid, raid, rayed, shade, spade, stade, staid, suede, they'd, trade, wade, Wade, abrade, afraid, aggrade, arcade, Band-Aid, barmaid, Belgrade, blockade, bondmaid, bridesmaid, brigade, brocade, cascade, Cascade, charade, clichéd, cockade, corrade, cross-trade, crusade, decade, degrade, dissuade, downgrade, evade, eyeshade, fair-trade, forebade, gainsaid, glissade, grenade, handmade, handmaid, homemade, housemaid, inlaid, invade, limeade, low-grade, man-made, mermaid, milkmaid, navaid, nightshade, nursemaid, outlaid, parade, persuade, pervade, plain-laid, pomade, postpaid, repaid, sacheted, scalade, sea-maid, self-made, shroud-laid, souffléed, stockade, sunshade, switchblade, tirade, torsade, twayblade, twice-laid, unbraid, unlade, unmade, unpaid, upbraid, upgrade, waylaid, accolade, Adelaide, ambuscade, aquacade, autocade, balustrade, barricade, bastinade, cable-laid, cannonade, carronade, cavalcade, centigrade, chambermaid, chiffonade, colonnade, countertrade, custom-made, dairymaid, defilade, enfilade, escalade, escapade, esplanade, everglade, fusillade, gallopade, gasconade, grant-in-aid, hawser-laid, intergrade, lemonade, marinade, marmalade, masquerade, medicaid, motorcade, orangeade, orthograde, overtrade, palisade, pasquinade, plantigrade, promenade, ready-made, renegade, retrograde, serenade, stock-in-trade, tailor-made, underlaid, fanfaronade, harlequinade, overpersuade, rodomontade

²**ade** \äd\ see ¹OD

³**ade** \ad\ see ³AD
⁴**ade** \äd-ə\ see ²ADA
aded \ād-əd\ bladed, arcaded,
  brocaded, cockaded,
  colonnaded—*also pasts of
  verbs listed at* ¹ADE
adeless \ād-ləs\ fadeless,
  gradeless, shadeless
adely \ad-lē\ see ADLY
¹**aden** \ād-ᵊn\ Aden, laden,
  maiden, handmaiden,
  menhaden
²**aden** \äd-ən\ Aden, Wiesbaden
adent \ād-ᵊnt\ see ADANT
ader \ād-ər\ aider, braider,
  cheder, fader, grader, heder,
  nadir, raider, seder, shader,
  spader, trader, wader,
  blockader, crusader,
  dissuader, evader, persuader,
  masquerader, serenader
¹**ades** \ād-ēz\ ladies, Hades,
  quaker-ladies
²**ades** \ādz\ AIDS, Glades,
  Cascades, antitrades,
  Everglades, jack-of-all-
  trades—*also plurals and
  possessives of nouns and
  third singular presents of
  verbs listed at* ¹ADE
adge \aj\ badge, cadge, Madge,
  hajj
adger \aj-ər\ badger, cadger
adh \äd\ see ¹OD
¹**adhe** \äd-ə\ see ²ADA
²**adhe** \äd-ē\ see ¹ODY
adia \ād-ē-ə\ stadia, Acadia,
  arcadia, Arcadia, palladia
adial \ād-ē-əl\ radial, biradial,
  interstadial
adian \ād-ē-ən\ Acadian,
  Akkadian, arcadian, Arcadian,

Barbadian, Canadian,
  circadian, Orcadian, Palladian
adiant \ād-ē-ənt\ gradient,
  radiant
¹**adic** \ād-ik\ Vedic, tornadic
²**adic** \ad-ik\ Braddock,
  haddock, paddock, balladic,
  dyadic, faradic, haggadic,
  hexadic, maenadic, monadic,
  nomadic, sporadic, tetradic,
  tornadic, triadic, Iliadic,
  seminomadic
adie \ād-ē\ see ADY
adient \ād-ē-ənt\ see ADIANT
adies \ād-ēz\ see ¹ADES
ading \ād-iŋ\ braiding, lading,
  shading, arcading, degrading,
  downgrading, unfading
adir \ād-ər\ see ADER
adish \ad-ish\ caddish, faddish,
  radish, horseradish
adison \ad-ə-sən\ see ADDISON
¹**adist** \òd-əst\ broadest,
  sawdust, haggadist
²**adist** \äd-əst\ see ODEST
adium \ād-ē-əm\ radium,
  stadium, caladium, palladium,
  vanadium
adle \ād-ᵊl\ cradle, dreidel,
  ladle, wedel
adley \ad-lē\ see ADLY
adly \ad-lē\ badly, Bradley,
  gladly, madly, sadly,
  comradely
adness \ad-nəs\ badness,
  gladness, madness, sadness
¹**ado** \äd-ō\ bravado, camisado,
  carbonado, cruzado, Manado,
  mikado, passado, stoccado,
  strappado, avocado,
  bastinado, Colorado,
  Coronado, desperado, El

Dorado, hacendado,
amontillado, zapateado,
aficionado, incommunicado,
Llano Estacado

²**ado** \äd-ō\ dado, credo,
crusado, gambado, strappado,
teredo, tornado, barricado,
bastinado, camisado,
carbonado, desperado, El
Dorado, fettuccine Alfredo

ados \ā-dəs\ see ADUS

adow \ad-ō\ Caddo, shadow,
foreshadow, overshadow

adrate \äd-rət\ see ODERATE

adre \ad-rē\ see ADERY

adrian \ā-drē-ən\ Adrian,
Adrienne, Hadrian

adrienne \ā-drē-ən\ see ADRIAN

adt \ät\ see ¹OT

adual \aj-əl\ see AGILE

adus \ā-dəs\ Padus, Barbados—
*also possessives and plurals
of nouns listed at* ³ADA

ady \ād-ē\ cedi, glady, lady,
Sadie, shady, forelady,
landlady, milady, saleslady

¹**ae** \ā\ see ¹AY

²**ae** \ē\ see ¹EE

³**ae** \ī\ see ¹Y

aea \ē-ə\ see ¹IA

aean \ē-ən\ see ¹EAN

aedal \ēd-ᵊl\ see EEDLE

aedile \ēd-ᵊl\ see EEDLE

aedra \ē-drə\ see EDRA

¹**aegis** \ā-jəs\ see AGEOUS

²**aegis** \ē-jəs\ see EGIS

ael \āl\ see AIL

aeli \ā-lē\ see AILY

¹**aelic** \äl-ik\ see ¹OLIC

²**aelic** \al-ik\ see ALLIC

aemon \ē-mən\ see ¹EMON

aen \äⁿ\ see ¹ANT

¹**aena** \ā-nä\ scena, faena

²**aena** \ē-nə\ see ²INA

¹**aenia** \ē-nē-ə\ see ¹ENIA

²**aenia** \ē-nyə\ see ²ENIA

aens \äⁿs\ see ¹ANCE

aeon \ē-ən\ see ¹EAN

aera \ir-ə\ see ²ERA

¹**aere** \er-ē\ see ¹ARY

²**aere** \ir-ē\ see EARY

¹**aerial** \er-ē-əl\ see ARIAL

²**aerial** \ir-ē-əl\ see ERIAL

¹**aerie** \ā-rē\ aerie, aery, faerie,
fairy

²**aerie** \er-ē\ see ¹ARY

³**aerie** \ir-ē\ see EARY

¹**aero** \er-ō\ see ²ERO

²**aero** \ar-ō\ see ²ARROW

¹**aeroe** \ar-ō\ see ²ARROW

²**aeroe** \er-ō\ see ²ERO

¹**aery** \ā-rē\ see ¹AERIE

²**aery** \er-ē\ see ¹ARY

aesar \ē-zər\ see ²EASER

aese \ā-zə\ see ²ESA

aestor \ē-stər\ see EASTER

aestus \es-təs\ see ESTIS

aet \āt\ see ¹ATE

aetor \ēt-ər\ see ¹EATER

aeum \ē-əm\ see ¹EUM

aeus \ē-əs\ see ¹EUS

af \af\ see APH

¹**afe** \āf\ chafe, safe, strafe, waif,
fail-safe, vouchsafe,
bathyscaphe

²**afe** \af\ see APH

afel \äf-əl\ offal, waffle, falafel,
pantofle, rijsttafel

afer \ā-fər\ chafer, safer, strafer,
wafer, cockchafer

aff \af\ see APH

affable \af-ə-bəl\ affable,
laughable

affe \af\ see APH

affed \aft\ see ²AFT

¹affer \äf-ər\ see ¹OFFER

²affer \af-ər\ chaffer, gaffer, Kaffir, kafir, Kafir, laugher, staffer, zaffer, paragrapher, polygrapher

affia \af-ē-ə\ raffia, agraphia

affic \af-ik\ see APHIC

affick \af-ik\ see APHIC

affir \af-ər\ see ²AFFER

affish \af-ish\ raffish, giraffish

¹affle \äf-əl\ see AFEL

²affle \af-əl\ baffle, raffle, snaffle

affron \af-rən\ saffron, Biafran

affy \af-ē\ chaffy, daffy, taffy

afic \af-ik\ see APHIC

afir \af-ər\ see ²AFFER

afran \af-rən\ see AFFRON

¹aft \äft\ toft, waft, gemeinschaft, gesellschaft— *also pasts of verbs listed at* ¹OFF

²aft \aft\ aft, craft, daft, draft, graft, haft, kraft, raft, shaft, Taft, waft, abaft, aircraft, campcraft, camshaft, crankshaft, engraft, handcraft, indraft, kingcraft, rockshaft, scoutcraft, seacraft, spacecraft, stagecraft, statecraft, updraft, witchcraft, woodcraft, countershaft, fore-and-aft, handicraft, Hovercraft, overdraft, rotorcraft, turboshaft, understaffed, watercraft, antiaircraft

aftage \af-tij\ graftage, waftage

after \af-tər\ after, dafter, drafter, grafter, laughter, rafter, hereafter, thereafter, fore-and-after, handicrafter, hereinafter, thereinafter

aftness \af-nəs\ daftness, Daphnis, halfness

aftsman \af-smən\ craftsman, draftsman, raftsman, handcraftsman, handicraftsman

afty \af-tē\ crafty, drafty

ag \ag\ bag, brag, crag, dag, drag, fag, flag, gag, hag, jag, lag, mag, nag, quag, rag, sag, scag, scrag, shag, slag, snag, sprag, stag, swag, tag, wag, YAG, zag, beanbag, blackflag, chin-wag, dirtbag, dishrag, fleabag, gasbag, greylag, handbag, hangtag, mailbag, postbag, ragbag, ragtag, ratbag, sandbag, schoolbag, scumbag, seabag, sleazebag, washrag, wigwag, windbag, workbag, zigzag, ballyrag, bullyrag, carpetbag, litterbag, lollygag, saddlebag, scalawag, tucker-bag

¹aga \äg-ə\ quagga, raga, saga, anlage, vorlage's gravenhage

²aga \ā-gə\ Vega, bodega, omega, rutabaga

³aga \eg-ə\ see ¹EGA

⁴aga \ȯ-gə\ see AUGA

agan \ā-gən\ see AGIN

¹agar \ā-gər\ Hagar, jaeger

²agar \äg-ər\ see ¹OGGER

³agar \əg-ər\ see ¹UGGER

agary \ag-ə-rē\ see AGGERY

agate \ag-ət\ see AGGOT

¹age \äj\ dodge, lodge, raj, stodge, wodge, barrage, collage, corsage, dislodge, garage, hodgepodge, Karaj,

massage, swaraj, camouflage,
espionage, counterespionage
²**age** \äzh\ plage, assuage,
barrage, collage, corsage,
dressage, frottage, gavage,
lavage, massage, ménage,
mirage, montage, moulage,
portage, potage, treillage,
triage, arbitrage, assemblage,
badinage, bon voyage,
bricolage, cabotage,
camouflage, colportage,
curettage, decoupage,
empennage, enfleurage,
entourage, fuselage,
Hermitage, maquillage,
persiflage, repechage,
sabotage, vernissage,
décolletage, espionage,
photomontage, rite de
passage, counterespionage
³**age** \āj\ age, cage, gage, Gage,
gauge, mage, page, rage, sage,
stage, swage, wage, assuage,
backstage, birdcage, broad-
gauge, downstage, encage,
engage, enrage, forestage,
front-page, greengage,
offstage, onstage, Osage,
outrage, presage, rampage,
restage, soundstage, space-
age, substage, teenage,
uncage, upstage, disengage,
multistage, ossifrage, overage,
saxifrage, underage
⁴**age** \āg\ see ¹EG
⁵**age** \äzh\ see ¹EIGE
⁶**age** \äg-ə\ see ¹AGA
ageable \ā-jə-bəl\ gaugeable,
stageable, unassuageable
aged \ājd\ aged, gauged, broad-
gauged, engaged, unpaged,

middle-aged—*also pasts of
verbs listed at* ³AGE
agel \ā-gəl\ bagel, Hegel,
plagal, finagle, inveigle,
wallydraigle
ageless \āj-ləs\ ageless,
wageless
¹**agen** \ā-gən\ see AGIN
²**agen** \ä-gən\ see OGGIN
agenous \aj-ə-nəs\ see AGINOUS
ageous \ā-jəs\ aegis,
ambagious, courageous,
contagious, outrageous,
rampageous, umbrageous,
advantageous,
disadvantageous
¹**ager** \ā-jər\ gauger, major,
Major, pager, stager, wager,
teenager, Canis Major,
golden-ager, middle-ager,
Ursa Major
²**ager** \äg-ər\ see ¹OGGER
agey \ā-jē\ see AGY
agga \äg-ə\ see ¹AGA
aggar \äg-ər\ see ¹OGGER
aggard \ag-ərd\ blackguard,
haggard, laggard
agged \ag-əd\ cragged, jagged,
ragged
agger \ag-ər\ bagger, bragger,
dagger, dragger, gagger,
jagger, lagger, nagger, sagger,
stagger, swagger, wagger,
foot dragger, four-bagger,
one-bagger, sandbagger,
three-bagger, two-bagger,
carpetbagger
aggery \ag-ə-rē\ jaggery,
staggery, vagary, waggery,
carpetbaggery
aggie \ag-ē\ see ²AGGY
agging \ag-iŋ\ bagging,

flagging, lagging, nagging, brown bagging, foot-dragging, unflagging, carpetbagging

aggish \ag-ish\ haggish, waggish

aggle \ag-əl\ draggle, gaggle, haggle, raggle, straggle, waggle, bedraggle, raggle-taggle

aggly \ag-lē\ scraggly, straggly, waggly

aggot \ag-ət\ agate, faggot, fagot, maggot

¹aggy \äg-ē\ see ¹OGGY

²aggy \ag-ē\ aggie, baggy, braggy, craggy, draggy, jaggy, quaggy, ragi, scraggy, shaggy, snaggy, staggy, swaggy

agh \ä\ see ¹A

¹agi \äg-ē\ see ¹OGGY

²agi \ag-ē\ see ²AGGY

agian \ā-jən\ see AJUN

agic \aj-ik\ magic, tragic, choragic, pelagic

agile \aj-əl\ agile, fragile, gradual, vagile

agin \ā-gən\ fagin, pagan, Reagan, Copenhagen

aginal \aj-ən-ᵊl\ paginal, vaginal, imaginal

aging \ā-jiŋ\ aging, raging, staging, unaging

aginous \aj-ə-nəs\ collagenous, farraginous, plumbaginous, viraginous, cartilaginous, mucilaginous, oleaginous

agion \ā-jən\ see AJUN

agious \ā-jəs\ see AGEOUS

¹aglia \äl-yə\ see ¹AHLIA

²aglia \al-yə\ see ALUE

aglio \al-yō\ intaglio, seraglio

agm \am\ see ²AM

agma \ag-mə\ magma, syntagma

agman \ag-mən\ bagman, flagman, swagman

agna \än-yə\ see ¹ANIA

agne \ān\ see ¹ANE

agnes \ag-nəs\ Agnes, Albertas Magnus

agnum \ag-nəm\ magnum, sphagnum

agnus \ag-nəs\ see AGNES

¹ago \äg-ō\ lago, Chicago, farrago, galago, virago, Asiago, Calinago, Santiago, solidago

²ago \ā-gō\ dago, sago, farrago, galago, imago, lumbago, plumbago, sapsago, Tobago, virago, solidago, San Diego, Tierra del Fuego

ago \äŋ-gō\ see ONGO

agon \ag-ən\ dragon, flagon, lagan, wagon, bandwagon, jolt-wagon, Pendragon, snapdragon, battlewagon

agonal \ag-ən-ᵊl\ agonal, diagonal, heptagonal, hexagonal, octagonal, pentagonal, tetragonal

agora \ag-ə-rə\ agora, mandragora

agoras \ag-ə-rəs\ Protagoras, Pythagoras

agot \ag-ət\ see AGGOT

agrance \ā-grəns\ flagrance, fragrance

agrancy \ā-grən-sē\ flagrancy, fragrancy, vagrancy

agrant \ā-grənt\ flagrant, fragrant, vagrant, conflagrant

agster \ag-stər\ dragster, gagster

agua \äg-wə\ majagua, Managua, piragua, Aconcagua, Nicaragua

¹ague \āg\ see ¹EG

²ague \äg\ see ¹OG

aguey \eg-ē\ see EGGY

agus \ā-gəs\ magus, Tagus, choragus, Las Vegas, Simon Magus

agy \ā-jē\ cagey, Meiji, stagy

¹ah \ä\ see ¹A

²ah \ȯ\ see ¹AW

³ah \a\ baa, nah, pas de chat

aha \ä-hä\ Baja, Naha, Praha

aham \ā-əm\ see AHUM

ahd \äd\ see ¹OD

ahdi \äd-ē\ see ¹ODY

ahdom \äd-əm\ see ODOM

ahib \äb\ see ¹OB

ahl \äl\ see ¹AL

ahler \äl-ər\ see OLLAR

¹ahlia \äl-yə\ dahlia, passacaglia

²ahlia \al-yə\ see ALUE

³ahlia \ā-lē-ə\ see ¹ALIA

¹ahma \ā-mə\ see ³AMA

²ahma \äm-ə\ see ²AMA

³ahma \am-ə\ see ⁴AMA

¹ahman \äm-ən\ see OMMON

²ahman \am-ən\ see AMMON

ahn \än\ see ¹ON

ahms \ämz\ see ALMS

ahnda \än-də\ see ONDA

ahr \är\ see ³AR

ahru \ä-rü\ see ARU

aht \ät\ see ¹OT

ahua \ä-wə\ see ¹AWA

ahum \ā-əm\ Graham, mayhem, Nahum, Te Deum

ahveh \ä-vā\ see ¹AVE

¹ai \ā\ see ¹AY

²ai \ē\ see ¹EE

³ai \ī\ see ¹Y

⁴ai \ȯi\ see OY

⁵ai \ä-ē\ see AII

a'i \ī\ see ¹Y

¹aia \ā-ə\ Freya, Aglaia, cattleya, Hosea, Isaiah, Nouméa, Himalaya, Kilauea, Mauna Kea, Meghalaya

²aia \ī-ə\ see ¹IAH

¹aiad \ā-əd\ naiad, pleiad

²aiad \ī-əd\ see YAD

aiah \ā-ə\ see AIA

aias \ā-əs\ see ¹AIS

aic \ā-ik\ laic, alcaic, Altaic, archaic, Chaldaic, deltaic, Hebraic, Incaic, Judaic, Mishnaic, Mithraic, mosaic, Mosaic, prosaic, Romaic, spondaic, stanzaic, trochaic, voltaic, algebraic, Aramaic, Cyrenaic, faradaic, formulaic, pharisaic, Ptolemaic, apotropaic, paradisaic, photomosaic, Ural-Altaic

aica \ā-ə-k-ə\ Judaica, Cyrenaica

aical \ā-ə-kəl\ laical, pharisaical, paradisaical

aice \ās\ see ¹ACE

aich \āk̲\ see AIGH

aiche \esh\ see ¹ESH

aicos \ā-kəs\ see ECAS

¹aid \ād\ see ¹ADE

²aid \ed\ see ¹EAD

³aid \ad\ see ³AD

aida \ī-də\ see ²IDA

¹aide \ād\ see ¹ADE

²aide \īd-ē\ see IDAY

aiden \ād-ᵊn\ see ADEN

aider \ād-ər\ see ADER

aiding \ād-iŋ\ see ADING
aido \ī-dō\ see ¹IDO
aids \ādz\ see ²ADES
aiety \ā-ət-ē\ see AITY
aif \āf\ see ¹AFE
aig \āg\ see ¹EG
aiga \ī-gə\ taiga, Auriga
aigh \āk̲\ laigh, quaich
aight \āt\ see ¹ATE
aighten \āt-ⁿn\ see ¹ATEN
aightly \āt-lē\ see ¹ATELY
aign \ān\ see ¹ANE
aigne \ān\ see ¹ANE
aignment \ān-mənt\ see
  AINMENT
aii \ä-ē\ Hawaii, Tubuai
aiian \ä-yən\ zayin, Hawaiian
aijin \ī-jēn\ gaijin, hygiene
aik \īk\ see ²IKE
aika \ī-kə\ see ¹ICA
ail \āl\ ail, ale, baal, bail, bale,
  brail, braille, Braille, dale,
  Dale, drail, fail, flail, frail,
  Gael, gale, Gale, Gayle, grail,
  hail, hale, Hale, jail, kale,
  mail, male, nail, pail, pale,
  quail, Quayle, rail, sail, sale,
  scale, shale, snail, stale,
  swale, tael, tail, taille, tale,
  they'll, trail, vail, vale, veil,
  wail, wale, whale, Yale,
  abseil, airmail, assail, avail,
  bangtail, bewail, blackmail,
  blacktail, bobtail, broadscale,
  broadtail, bucktail, canaille,
  cattail, Clydesdale, coattail,
  cocktail, contrail, curtail,
  derail, detail, doornail,
  dovetail, downscale, ducktail,
  E-mail, entail, exhale, fantail,
  female, fishtail, folktale,
  foresail, foxtail, full-scale,
  Glendale, greenmail,
  guardrail, Hallel, handrail,
  hangnail, headsail, hightail,
  hobnail, horntail, horsetail,
  impale, inhale, Longueuil,
  lugsail, mainsail, oxtail, pass-
  fail, percale, pigtail, pintail,
  pinwale, portrayal, prevail,
  rattail, regale, resale, rescale,
  retail, ringtail, Sangreal, sei
  whale, shavetail, shirttail,
  skysail, small-scale,
  springtail, spritsail, staysail,
  surveil, swordtail, taffrail,
  telltale, thumbnail, timescale,
  toenail, topsail, travail,
  treenail, trysail, unnail,
  unveil, upscale, ventail,
  wagtail, wassail, whitetail,
  wholesale, abigail, Abigail,
  aventail, betrayal, bristletail,
  Chippendale, Corriedale,
  cottontail, countervail,
  defrayal, disentail, draggle-
  tail, farthingale, fingernail,
  flickertail, forestaysail, gaff-
  topsail, galingale, martingale,
  monorail, montadale,
  nightingale, Nightingale,
  overscale, ponytail,
  romeldale, scissortail,
  swallowtail, tattletale,
  tripletail, trundle-tail,
  yellowtail, self-betrayal, Fort
  Lauderdale, Oregon Trail,
  Santa Fe Trail
ailable \ā-lə-bəl\ bailable,
  mailable, sailable, salable,
  scalable, assailable, available,
  resalable, unassailable
ailand \ī-lənd\ see IGHLAND
ailant \ā-lənt\ see ALANT

aile \ī-lē\ see YLY

ailed \āld\ mailed, nailed, sailed, scaled, tailed, veiled, detailed, engrailed, hobnailed, pigtailed, ring-tailed, unveiled, ponytailed, swallow-tailed—*also pasts of verbs listed at* AIL

ailer \ā-lər\ alar, bailer, bailor, baler, hailer, jailer, mailer, malar, nailer, sailer, sailor, scalar, scaler, tailer, tailor, Taylor, trailer, wailer, waler, whaler, blackmailer, curtailer, derailleur, detailer, entailer, inhaler, loud-haler, retailer, wassailer, wholesaler, semitrailer—*also comparatives of adjectives listed at* AIL

ailey \ā-lē\ see AILY

ailful \āl-fəl\ see ALEFUL

ailie \ā-lē\ see AILY

ailiff \ā-ləf\ bailiff, caliph

ailing \ā-liŋ\ failing, grayling, mailing, paling, railing, sailing, tailing, veiling, whaling, boardsailing, prevailing, retailing, self-mailing, unfailing, parasailing, unavailing

¹aille \āl\ see AIL

²aille \ī\ see ¹Y

³aille \īl\ see ¹ILE

⁴aille \ä-yə\ see ¹AYA

ailles \ī\ see ¹Y

ailleur \ā-lər\ see AILER

ailment \āl-mənt\ ailment, bailment, curtailment, derailment, entailment, impalement

ailor \ā-lər\ see AILER

ails \ālz\ see ALES

ailsman \ālz-mən\ see ALESMAN

aily \ā-lē\ bailey, Bailey, bailie, daily, gaily, grayly, paly, scaly, shaley, wally, Bareilly, Bareli, Disraeli, Israeli, shillelagh, triticale, ukulele

aim \ām\ see ¹AME

aima \ī-mə\ see YMA

aimable \ā-mə-bəl\ see AMABLE

aiman \ā-mən\ see ¹AMEN

aimant \ā-mənt\ see AYMENT

aiment \ā-mənt\ see AYMENT

aimer \ā-mər\ blamer, claimer, framer, gamer, tamer, declaimer, defamer, disclaimer, exclaimer—*also comparatives of adjectives listed at* ¹AME

aimless \ām-ləs\ see AMELESS

¹ain \ā-ən\ see ¹AYAN

²ain \ān\ see ¹ANE

³ain \en\ see ¹EN

⁴ain \in\ see ¹IN

⁵ain \īn\ see ¹INE

⁶ain \aⁿ\ see ⁴IN

aina \ī-nə\ see ¹INA

ainable \ā-nə-bəl\ stainable, trainable, attainable, containable, explainable, maintainable, restrainable, retrainable, sustainable, inexplainable

ainder \ān-dər\ attainder, remainder

¹aine \ān\ see ¹ANE

²aine \en\ see ¹EN

ained \ānd\ brained, caned, craned, drained, grained, maned, pained, paned, stained, strained, vaned,

veined, birdbrained,
bloodstained, close-grained,
coarse-grained, crackbrained,
cross-grained, edge-grained,
harebrained, ingrained,
lamebrained, mad-brained,
membraned, restrained,
tearstained, unfeigned,
featherbrained, rattlebrained,
scatterbrained, self-contained,
unrestrained—*also pasts of
verbs listed at* ¹ANE

ainer \ā-nər\ caner, drainer,
feigner, gainer, planar, planer,
seiner, stainer, strainer,
trainer, veiner, campaigner,
complainer, container,
coplanar, cordwainer,
detainer, lupanar, maintainer,
ordainer, profaner, restrainer,
retainer, sustainer, Trakehner,
entertainer—*also
comparatives of adjectives
listed at* ¹ANE

ainful \ān-fəl\ baneful, gainful,
painful, disdainful

aininess \ā-nē-nəs\ braininess,
graininess

aining \ā-niŋ\ veining,
complaining, sustaining, self-
sustaining, uncomplaining—
*also present participles of
verbs listed at* ¹ANE

ainish \ā-nish\ brainish, Danish,
swainish

ainless \ān-ləs\ brainless,
painless, stainless

ainly \ān-lē\ mainly, plainly,
thegnly, vainly, humanely,
insanely, profanely, ungainly,
inhumanely

ainment \ān-mənt\ arraignment,

attainment, containment,
detainment, detrainment,
enchainment, entrainment,
ordainment, refrainment,
entertainment, preordainment,
self-containment

aino \ī-nō\ see ¹INO

ains \ānz\ Keynes, reins,
cremains, Great Plains, Mains
Plains, remains—*also plurals
and possessives of nouns and
third person singular presents
of verbs listed at* ¹ANE

ainsman \ānz-mən\ plainsman,
reinsman

aint \ānt\ ain't, faint, feint,
mayn't, paint, plaint, quaint,
saint, taint, 'tain't, acquaint,
attaint, bepaint, complaint,
constraint, distraint,
greasepaint, impaint, restraint,
unconstraint, unrestraint

ain't \ānt\ see AINT

ainting \ān-tiŋ\ underpainting—
*also present participles of
verbs listed at* AINT

aintly \ānt-lē\ faintly, quaintly,
saintly

ainy \ā-nē\ brainy, grainy,
meiny, rainy, veiny, zany,
Allegheny

ainz \īnz\ see ³INES

aipse \āps\ see APES

¹air \er\ see ⁴ARE

²air \īr\ see ¹IRE

aira \ī-rə\ see YRA

aird \erd\ see AIRED

¹aire \er\ see ⁴ARE

²aire \ir\ see ²EER

³aire \īr\ see ¹IRE

aired \ard\ caird, haired, laird,
merde, fair-haired, impaired,

long-haired, misleared,
prepared, shorthaired,
unpaired, wirehaired,
multilayered, underprepared,
unimpaired—*also pasts of
verbs listed at* [4]ARE

airer \er-ər\ see [3]EARER

[1]aires \er\ see [4]ARE

[2]aires \ar-ēs\ see [2]ARES

[1]airess \er-əs\ see ERROUS

[2]airess \ar-əs\ see [2]ARIS

airie \er-ē\ see [1]ARY

airing \ar-iŋ\ see [1]ARING

airish \er-ish\ see [1]ARISH

airist \er-əst\ see ARIST

airly \er-lē\ fairly, ferlie, rarely,
squarely

airn \ern\ see [1]ERN

airo \ī-rō\ see [1]YRO

airs \erz\ theirs, backstairs,
downstairs, nowheres,
somewheres, upstairs,
unawares—*also plurals and
possessives of verbs listed at*
[4]ARE

[1]airy \er-ē\ see [1]ARY

[2]airy \ā-rē\ see [1]AERIE

[1]ais \ā-əs\ dais, Laius, Isaias,
Menelaus

[2]ais \ā\ see [1]AY

[1]aisal \ā-zəl\ see [2]ASAL

[2]aisal \ī-səl\ see [1]ISAL

aisance \ās-°ns\ see [1]ASCENCE

aisant \ās-°nt\ see ACENT

[1]aise \āz\ see [1]AZE

[2]aise \ez\ see [1]AYS

aisement \āz-mənt\ see
AZEMENT

[1]aiser \ā-zər\ see AZER

[2]aiser \ī-zər\ see IZER

aisian \ā-zhən\ see ASION

aisin \āz-°n\ see AZON

aising \ā-ziŋ\ braising, glazing,
hazing, phrasing, appraising,
fund-raising, hair-raising,
hell-raising, house-raising,
stargazing, trailblazing—*also
present participles of verbs
listed at* [1]AZE

aisle \īl\ see [1]ILE

aisley \āz-lē\ paisley, nasally

aisne \ān\ see [1]ANE

aisse \ās\ see [1]ACE

aisson \ās-°n\ see [1]ASON

[1]aist \ā-əst\ see AYEST

[2]aist \āst\ see ACED

[3]aist \äst\ see [1]OST

aisy \ā-zē\ see AZY

[1]ait \ā\ see [1]AY

[2]ait \āt\ see [1]ATE

[3]ait \īt\ see [1]ITE

[4]ait \at\ see [5]AT

aite \īt\ see [1]ITE

aited \āt-əd\ see ATED

aiten \āt-°n\ see [1]ATEN

aiter \āt-ər\ see ATOR

aith \āth\ eighth, faith, Faith,
saithe, scathe, wraith, unfaith,
interfaith

aithe \āth\ see AITH

aithless \āth-ləs\ faithless,
natheless

aiti \āt-ē\ see ATY

aitian \ā-shən\ see [1]ATION

aiting \āt-iŋ\ see ATING

aitly \āt-lē\ see [1]ATELY

aitor \āt-ər\ see ATOR

aitorous \āt-ə-rəs\ see ATERESS

aitour \āt-ər\ see ATOR

aitress \ā-trəs\ traitress,
waitress, aviatress

aity \ā-ət-ē\ deity, gaiety, laity,
corporeity, spontaneity,
synchroneity, diaphaneity,

contemporaneity,
extemporaneity
¹aius \ā-əs\ see ¹AIS
²aius \ī-əs\ see ¹IAS
aiva \ī-və\ see ¹IVA
aive \āv\ see ²AVE
aix \ā\ see ¹AY
aize \āz\ see ¹AZE
aj \äj\ see ¹AGE
¹aja \ä-hä\ see AHA
²aja \ī-ə\ see ¹IAH
ajan \ā-jən\ see AJUN
ajj \aj\ see ADGE
ajor \ā-jər\ see ¹AGER
ajos \ā-əs\ see ¹AIS
ajun \ā-jən\ Cajun, Trajan,
   contagion, Pelagian, reagin
¹ak \äk\ see ¹OCK
²ak \ak\ see ²ACK
¹aka \äk-ə\ Dacca, Dhaka, kaka,
   paca, taka, Lusaka, maraca,
   medaka, Oaxaca, Osaka,
   pataca, Mbandaka,
   saltimbocca, Toyonaka, Lake
   Titicaca, Higashiosaka
²aka \ak-ə\ see ²ACA
akable \ā-kə-bəl\ breakable,
   makable, shakable,
   mistakable, unslakable,
   unmistakable
¹akan \äk-ən\ see ²AKEN
²akan \ak-ən\ see ACKEN
akar \äk-ər\ see OCKER
¹ake \āk\ ache, bake, Blake,
   brake, break, cake, crake,
   drake, Drake, fake, flake,
   hake, jake, Jake, lake, make,
   quake, rake, sake, shake,
   sheikh, slake, snake, spake,
   stake, steak, strake, take,
   wake, Wake, awake,
   backache, beefcake, beefsteak,

betake, blacksnake,
canebrake, caretake,
cheesecake, clambake,
corncrake, cupcake, daybreak,
earache, earthquake, firebreak,
firedrake, forsake, friedcake,
fruitcake, grubstake,
handshake, headache,
heartache, heartbreak,
hoecake, hotcake, housebreak,
intake, jailbreak, keepsake,
lapstrake, mandrake,
Marsquake, mistake,
moonquake, muckrake,
namesake, newsbreak,
oatcake, opaque, outbreak,
outtake, Pan-Cake, pancake,
partake, remake, retake,
rewake, seaquake, seedcake,
sheldrake, shortcake,
snowflake, sweepstake,
toothache, unmake, uptake,
windbreak, youthquake,
bellyache, give-and-take,
halterbreak, johnnycake,
kittiwake, make-or-break,
microquake, overtake, pat-a-
cake, patty-cake, put-and-take,
rattlesnake, stomachache,
undertake, wapentake,
wideawake, semiopaque
²ake \ak\ see ²ACK
³ake \äk-ē\ see OCKY
aked \ākt\ awaked, half-baked,
   ringstraked, sunbaked—*also
   pasts of verbs listed at* ¹AKE
akeless \ā-kləs\ brakeless,
   wakeless
¹aken \ā-kən\ bacon, Bacon,
   Macon, waken, shaken, taken,
   awaken, partaken, retaken,
   betaken, forsaken, mistaken,

rewaken, well-taken,
godforsaken, overtaken,
undertaken
²**aken** \äk-ən\ kraken,
Arawakan
¹**aker** \ā-kər\ acre, baker,
breaker, faker, laker, maker,
nacre, quaker, Quaker, raker,
saker, shaker, taker, waker,
backbreaker, bookmaker,
caretaker, carmaker, comaker,
dressmaker, drugmaker,
earthshaker, filmmaker,
glassmaker, groundbreaker,
grubstaker, hatmaker,
haymaker, heartbreaker,
homemaker, housebreaker,
icebreaker, jawbreaker,
kingmaker, lawbreaker,
lawmaker, mapmaker,
matchmaker, mistaker,
muckraker, mythmaker,
noisemaker, oddsmaker,
pacemaker, peacemaker,
phrasemaker, platemaker,
playmaker, printmaker,
rainmaker, saltshaker,
shirtmaker, shoemaker,
snowmaker, stavesacre,
steelmaker, strikebreaker,
tastemaker, tiebreaker,
toolmaker, trailbreaker,
watchmaker, windbreaker,
wiseacre, automaker,
bellyacher, boilermaker,
merrymaker, moneymaker,
moviemaker, papermaker,
simulacre, troublemaker,
undertaker, cabinetmaker,
holidaymaker, policymaker
²**aker** \ak-ər\ see ACKER
akery \ā-krē\ bakery, fakery

akes \āks\ jakes, cornflakes,
Great Lakes, sweepstakes—
*also plurals and possessives
of nouns and third person
singular presents of verbs
listed at* ¹AKE
ake-up \ā-kəp\ break-up,
breakup, make-up, makeup,
shake-up, shakeup, take-up,
wake-up
akey \ā-kē\ see AKY
¹**akh** \äk\ see ¹OCK
²**akh** \ak\ see ²ACK
¹**aki** \äk-ē\ see OCKY
²**aki** \ak-ē\ see ACKY
akian \äk-ē-ən\ see OCKIAN
akic \ak-ik\ see ACCHIC
¹**aking** \ā-kiŋ\ aching, making,
waking, bookmaking,
breathtaking, caretaking,
dressmaking, earthshaking,
filmmaking, glassmaking,
groundbreaking,
heartbreaking, housebreaking,
lawbreaking, lawmaking,
leave-taking, lovemaking,
mapmaking, matchmaking,
mythmaking, noisemaking,
pacemaking, painstaking,
pathbreaking, peacemaking,
phrasemaking, printmaking,
rainmaking, snowmaking,
stocktaking, strikebreaking,
toolmaking, watchmaking,
world-shaking, merrymaking,
moneymaking, moviemaking,
papermaking, undertaking,
cabinetmaking, policymaking
²**aking** \ak-iŋ\ see ACKING
¹**ako** \äk-ō\ see OCCO
²**ako** \ak-ō\ shako, wacko,
tobacco

aku \äk-ü\ Bunraku, gagaku, nunchaku

akum \ā-kəm\ vade mecum, shalom aleichem

aky \ā-kē\ achy, braky, cakey, flaky, laky, shaky, snaky, headachy

¹al \äl\ Bâle, col, dahl, dal, doll, loll, moll, nal, pol, sol, Sol, Taal, toile, Algol, atoll, austral, Baikal, Bhopal, cabal, Chagall, chorale, grand mal, gun moll, hamal, jacal, mistral, narwhal, Natal, nopal, Pascal, petrol, quetzal, real, rial, riyal, Shawwal, tical, timbale, Transvaal, à cheval, aerosol, Emmenthal, falderal, femme fatale, folderol, Heyerdahl, parasol, pastoral, pastorale, protocol, Provençal, Simmental, urial, Wuppertal, entente cordiale, Neanderthal, procès-verbal, sublittoral, succès de scandale

²al \el\ see ¹EL

³al \ȯl\ see ALL

⁴al \al\ Al, gal, Hal, pal, rale, sal, Val, banal, cabal, canal, Chagall, chorale, copal, corral, decal, fal-lal, grand mal, joual, La Salle, Laval, locale, mescal, moral, morale, nopal, pall-mall, pascal, percale, quetzal, salal, serval, vinal, bacchanal, caracal, chaparral, femme fatale, musicale, pastoral, pastorale, pedocal, rationale, retinal, Seconal, Guadalcanal, kilopascal, sublittoral

¹ala \äl-ä\ à la, Allah, gala

²ala \äl-ə\ Allah, olla, tala, wallah, cabala, cantala, Chapala, chuckwalla, cicala, corolla, Douala, halala, Kampala, koala, Lingala, marsala, nyala, tambala, Tlaxcala, Valhalla, Walhalla, ayotollah, Guatemala, Gujranwala

³ala \ā-lə\ ala, gala, Venezuela, zarzuela

⁴ala \al-ə\ see ALLOW

alaam \ā-ləm\ Balaam, golem, Salem, Winston-Salem

alable \ā-lə-bəl\ see AILABLE

alace \al-əs\ see ²ALIS

alad \al-əd\ see ²ALID

alam \äl-əm\ see OLUMN

alamine \al-ə-mən\ allemande, calamine

alan \al-ən\ see ALLON

alance \al-əns\ balance, valance, imbalance, outbalance, unbalance, counterbalance, overbalance

alant \ā-lənt\ assailant, bivalent, covalent, exhalent, inhalant, multivalent, pentavalent, quadrivalent, surveillant, tetravalent, trivalent, univalent

alap \al-əp\ see ²ALLOP

alar \ā-lər\ see AILER

¹alary \al-rē\ see ALLERY

²alary \al-ə-rē\ calorie, gallery, Mallory, Malory, salary, Valerie, Valery, kilocalorie

alas \al-əs\ see ²ALIS

alate \al-ət\ see ²ALLET

¹alcon \ȯ-kən\ see ¹ALKIN

²alcon \al-kən\ falcon, gyrfalcon, grimalkin

¹ald \ȯld\ bald, scald, skald,

walled, close-hauled,
keelhauled, kobold, piebald,
ribald, skewbald, so-called,
sunscald, Archibald,
coveralled, overalled—*also
pasts of verbs listed at* ALL
²ald \ȧlt\ see ALT
alder \ȯl-dər\ alder, balder,
Balder
aldi \ȯl-dē\ Bartholdi, Vivaldi,
Garibaldi
aldron \ȯl-drən\ aldron,
caldron, cauldron, chaldron
¹ale \ā-lē\ see AILY
²ale \āl\ see AIL
³ale \äl\ see ¹AL
⁴ale \al\ see ⁴AL
⁵ale \äl-ē\ see ¹OLLY
⁶ale \al-ē\ see ⁴ALLY
alea \ā-lē-ə\ see ¹ALIA
¹aleck \el-ik\ see ²ELIC
²aleck \al-ik\ see ALLIC
aled \āld\ see AILED
aleful \āl-fəl\ baleful, wailful
¹aleigh \äl-ē\ see ¹OLLY
²aleigh \ȯl-ē\ see AWLY
alem \ā-ləm\ see ALAAM
alement \āl-mənt\ see AILMENT
alen \ä-lən\ see ⁵OLLEN
alence \ā-ləns\ valence,
surveillance
alends \al-ənz\ see ALLANS
¹alent \al-ənt\ see ALLANT
²alent \ā-lənt\ see ALANT
alep \al-əp\ see ²ALLOP
¹aler \ā-lər\ see AILER
²aler \äl-ər\ see OLLAR
alerie \al-ə-re\ see ²ALARY
alery \al-ə-rē\ see ²ALARY
¹ales \ālz\ sales, Wales, entrails,
Marseilles, New South Wales,
Prince of Wales, cat-o'-nine-

tails—*also plurals and
possessives of nouns listed at*
AIL
²ales \äl-əs\ see OLIS
alesman \ālz-mən\ bailsman,
dalesman, salesman, talesman
alet \al-ət\ see ²ALLET
alette \al-ət\ see ²ALLET
aley \ā-lē\ see AILY
alf \af\ see APH
alfa \al-fə\ see ALPHA
alfness \af-nəs\ see AFTNESS
algia \al-jə\ neuralgia, nostalgia
¹ali \äl-ē\ see ¹OLLY
²ali \al-ē\ see ⁴ALLY
³ali \ȯ-lē\ see AWLY
⁴ali \ā-lē\ see AILY
¹alia \ā-lē-ə\ dahlia, Australia,
azalea, battalia, realia, regalia,
vedalia, Westphalia,
bacchanalia, genitalia,
glossolalia, inter alia,
Lupercalia, marginalia,
Orientalia, paraphernalia,
penetralia, saturnalia
²alia \al-yə\ dahlia, battalia, et
alia, passacaglia
¹alian \ā-lē-ən\ alien,
Australian, Daedalian,
Deucalion, Hegelian,
mammalian, Pygmalion,
Uralian, bacchanalian,
Lupercalian, saturnalian,
Episcopalian, sesquipedalian,
tatterdemalion
²alian \al-yən\ see ALLION
alic \al-ik\ see ALLIC
alice \al-əs\ see ²ALIS
¹alid \äl-əd\ see OLID
²alid \al-əd\ ballad, pallid,
salad, valid, invalid
alie \äl-yə\ see ¹AHLIA

alien \ā-lē-ən\ see ¹ALIAN
aling \ā-liŋ\ see AILING
alinist \äl-ə-nəst\ see OLONIST
alinn \al-ən\ see ALLON
¹alion \ā-lē-ən\ see ¹ALIAN
²alion \al-yən\ see ALLION
aliph \ā-ləf\ see AILIFF
¹alis \ā-ləs\ see AYLESS
²alis \al-əs\ Alice, balas,
  callous, callus, chalice,
  Dallas, gallus, malice, palace,
  Pallas, phallus, talus, thallous,
  thallus, oxalis, digitalis,
  hemerocallis, aurora borealis,
  Corona Borealis
alist \al-əst\ ballast, callused,
  gallused, cabalist, sodalist
¹ality \äl-ət-ē\ jollity, polity,
  quality, equality, frivolity,
  coequality, inequality
²ality \al-ət-ē\ anality, banality,
  brutality, carnality, causality,
  centrality, duality, extrality,
  fatality, feudality, finality,
  formality, frontality, frugality,
  legality, locality, mentality,
  modality, morality, mortality,
  nasality, natality, neutrality,
  nodality, orality, plurality,
  primality, rascality, reality,
  regality, rurality, sodality,
  tonality, totality, venality,
  vitality, vocality, abnormality,
  actuality, amorality,
  animality, atonality, axiality,
  bestiality, bimodality,
  bipedality, cardinality,
  classicality, coevality,
  comicality, commonality,
  communality, conjugality,
  cordiality, corporality,
  criminality, criticality,
  ethicality, externality,
  factuality, farcicality,
  fictionality, functionality,
  generality, geniality,
  hospitality, ideality, illegality,
  immorality, immortality,
  informality, integrality,
  internality, irreality, lexicality,
  liberality, lineality, literality,
  logicality, musicality,
  mutuality, nationality,
  notionality, nuptiality,
  optimality, partiality,
  personality, physicality,
  principality, punctuality,
  rationality, seasonality,
  sexuality, sociality, spaciality,
  speciality, subnormality,
  technicality, temporality,
  topicality, triviality,
  unmorality, unreality,
  verticality, virtuality,
  whimsicality, asexuality,
  atypicality, bisexuality,
  collaterality, collegiality,
  colloquiality, commerciality,
  conceptuality, conditionality,
  congeniality, connaturality,
  conventionality, conviviality,
  corporeality, dimensionality,
  directionality, effectuality,
  emotionality, ephemerality,
  equivocality, essentiality,
  ethereality, eventuality,
  exceptionality, extensionality,
  fantasticality, grammaticality,
  illiberality, illogicality,
  impersonality, impracticality,
  inhospitality, instrumentality,
  irrationality, materiality,
  microtonality, monumentality,
  municipality, originality,

orthogonality, pansexuality, paranormality, polytonality, potentiality, provinciality, self-partiality, sentimentality, spirituality, substantiality, theatricality, transexuality, triaxiality, universality, veridicality, ambisexuality, artificiality, circumstantiality, confidentiality, consequentiality, constitutionality, homosexuality, hypersexuality, immateriality, individuality, ineffectuality, insubstantiality, intellectuality, internationality, intersexuality, paradoxicality, psychosexuality, referentiality, superficiality, supranationality, territoriality, tridimensionality, two-dimensionality, uncongeniality, unconventionality, ungrammaticality, unisexuality, unsubstantiality, exterritoriality, heterosexuality, inconsequentiality, unconstitutionality, unidimensionality, extraterritoriality

alium \al-ē-əm\ see ALLIUM

alius \ā-lē-əs\ alius, Sibelius

alk \ȯk\ auk, balk, calk, caulk, chalk, gawk, hawk, Koch, Salk, Sauk, squawk, stalk, talk, walk, Bartok, Black Hawk, bemock, boardwalk, cakewalk, catwalk, chalktalk,

cornstalk, crosswalk, duckwalk, eyestalk, fast-talk, goshawk, jaywalk, langue d'oc, leafstalk, Mohawk, nighthawk, Norfolk, outtalk, ropewalk, shoptalk, sidewalk, skywalk, sleepwalk, Suffolk, sweet-talk, belle epoque, catafalque, double-talk, Swainson's hawk, tomahawk

alkan \ȯl-kən\ see ¹ALKIN

alker \ȯ-kər\ balker, caulker, gawker, hawker, squawker, stalker, walker, cakewalker, deerstalker, floorwalker, jayhawker, jaywalker, nightwalker, ropewalker, sleepwalker, spacewalker, streetwalker, trackwalker, double-talker

alkie \ȯ-kē\ balky, chalky, gawky, gnocchi, pawky, stalky, talkie, talky, Milwaukee, Handie-Talkie, walkie-talkie, Winnipesaukee

¹alkin \ȯ-kən\ Balkan, falcon, malkin, grimalkin, gyrfalcon

²alkin \al-kən\ see ²ALCON

alking \ȯ-kiŋ\ caulking, walking, racewalking, spacewalking, streetwalking

alkland \ȯk-lənd\ see AUCKLAND

alky \ȯ-kē\ see ALKIE

¹all \ȯl\ all, awl, ball, bawl, brawl, call, caul, crawl, doll, drawl, fall, Gall, Gaul, hall, Hall, haul, kraal, mall, maul, moll, pall, Paul, pawl, Saul, scall, scrawl, shawl, small, Sol, spall, sprawl, squall, stall, tall, thrall, trawl, wall,

y'all, yauld, yawl, Algol,
ALGOL, appall, argol, air
ball, ashfall, at all, atoll,
AWOL, baseball, Baikal,
beanball, befall, Bengal, best-
ball, birdcall, blackball,
Bokmål, bookstall, boxhaul,
bradawl, broomball, catcall,
catchall, COBOL, cornball,
Cornwall, cure-all, curveball,
deadfall, de Gaulle, dewfall,
dodgeball, downfall,
downhaul, drywall, enthrall,
eyeball, fastball, fireball,
floodwall, football, footfall,
footstall, footwall, forestall,
forkball, four-ball, free-fall,
gadwall, goofball, googol,
grease ball, guildhall, hair
ball, handball, hardball,
headstall, heelball, highball,
holdall, icefall, install,
keelhaul, know-all, landfall,
Landsmål, line-haul, lowball,
meatball, menthol, Metol,
miscall, mothball, naphthol,
Nepal, nightfall, nutgall,
oddball, outfall, outhaul,
pitfall, plimsoll, pratfall, pub-
crawl, puffball, punchball,
pushball, rainfall, rainsquall,
recall, rial, Riksmål, riyal,
rockfall, rorqual, Saint Paul,
save-all, screwball, seawall,
short-haul, shortfall, sidewall,
sleazeball, slimeball,
snowball, snowfall, softball,
speedball, spitball, Stendhal,
stickball, stonewall, stoopball,
T-ball, tell-all, three-ball,
trackball, Tyrol, Walsall,
waterfall, what all, Whitehall,
whitewall, windfall, windgall,
withal, withdrawal, you-all,
aerosol, alcohol, barbital,
basketball, bucky ball,
butterball, buttonball,
cannonball, carryall,
caterwaul, cover-all, coverall,
Demerol, disenthrol, Donegal,
entresol, evenfall, free-for-all,
gasohol, girasole, Grand
Guignol, haute école, know-
it-all, knuckleball, Komsomol,
methanol, minié ball,
Montreal, Nembutal, overall,
overcall, overhaul, paddleball,
parasol, Parsifal, Pentothal,
protocol, racquetball, Seconal,
Senegal, superball, tattersall,
tetherball, therewithal,
timolol, volleyball,
wherewithal, cholesterol,
Costa del Sol, Mariupol,
Massif Central, Neanderthal,
Sevastopol, Transalpine Gaul,
Vincent de Paul, be-all and
end-all

²all \äl\ see ¹AL

³all \al\ see ⁴AL

¹alla \äl-ə\ see ²ALA

²alla \al-ə\ see ⁴ALLOW

allable \ȯ-lə-bəl\ callable,
spallable

allace \äl-əs\ see OLIS

allacy \al-ə-sē\ fallacy, jalousie

allad \al-əd\ see ²ALID

allage \al-ə-jē\ see ²ALOGY

¹allah \äl-ä\ see ¹ALA

²allah \äl-ə\ see ²ALA

³allah \al-ə\ see ⁴ALLOW

allan \al-ən\ see ALLON

allans \al-ənz\ calends,
Lallans—*also plurals and*

possessives of nouns listed at
ALLON

allant \al-ənt\ callant, gallant, talent, topgallant, fore-topgallant

allas \al-əs\ see ²ALIS

allasey \äl-ə-sē\ see OLICY

allast \al-əst\ see ALIST

¹**alle** \al\ see ⁴AL

²**alle** \al-ē\ see ⁴ALLY

³**alle** \äl-ē\ see OLLY

alled \öld\ see ALD

allee \al-ē\ see ⁴ALLY

allemande \al-ə-mən\ see ALAMINE

¹**allen** \ö-lən\ fallen, stollen, befallen, chapfallen, chopfallen, crestfallen, downfallen, tarpaulin, unfallen

²**allen** \al-ən\ see ALLON

¹**aller** \ö-lər\ bawler, brawler, caller, drawler, faller, hauler, mauler, scrawler, squaller, trawler, fireballer, footballer, forestaller, installer, stonewaller, knuckleballer

²**aller** \al-ər\ caller, pallor, valor, high yaller

alles \ī-əs\ see ¹IAS

¹**allet** \äl-ət\ see OLLET

²**allet** \al-ət\ ballot, callet, mallet, palate, palette, pallet, sallet, shallot, valet

alley \al-ē\ see ⁴ALLY

alli \al-ē\ see ⁴ALLY

alliard \al-yərd\ galliard, halyard

allic \al-ik\ Gaelic, Gallic, malic, phallic, salic, Salic, thallic, cephalic, italic, mandalic, medallic, metallic, smart aleck, Uralic, Vandalic, vocalic, genitalic, intervallic, ithyphallic, nonmetallic, postvocalic, prevocalic, intervocalic

allid \al-əd\ see ²ALID

allie \al-ē\ see ⁴ALLY

alling \ö-liŋ\ balling, calling, drawling, falling, galling, hauling, infalling, mauling, name-calling, Pauling, stalling

alinn \al-ən\ see ALLON

allion \al-yən\ scallion, stallion, battalion, Italian, medallion, rapscallion, tatterdemalion

¹**allis** \al-əs\ see ²ALIS

²**allis** \al-ē\ see ⁴ALLY

³**allis** \äl-əs\ see OLIS

allish \ö-lish\ Gaulish, smallish, tallish

allit \ä-lət\ see OLLET

¹**allith** \äl-əs\ see OLIS

²**allith** \äl-ət\ see OLLET

allium \al-ē-əm\ allium, gallium, pallium, thallium, Valium

allment \öl-mənt\ enthrallment, forestallment, installment

allo \äl-ō\ see ¹OLLOW

allon \al-ən\ Alan, Allan, Allen, Allyn, gallon, lallan, Talinn, talon

¹**allop** \äl-əp\ see OLLOP

²**allop** \al-əp\ gallop, galop, jalap, salep, Salop, scallop, shallop, escallop

allor \al-ər\ see ²ALLER

¹**allory** \al-re\ see ALLERY

²**allory** \al-ə-rē\ see ²ALARY

allot \al-ət\ see ²ALLET

allous \al-əs\ see ²ALIS

¹**allow** \el-ō\ see ELLO

²**allow** \äl-ə\ see ²ALA
³**allow** \äl-ō\ see ¹OLLOW
⁴**allow** \al-ə\ Allah, callow,
  fallow, gala, Galla, hallow,
  sallow, shallow, tallow,
  cavalla, impala, unhallow,
  Valhalla
⁵**allow** \al-ō\ aloe, callow,
  fallow, hallow, mallow,
  sallow, shallow, tallow,
  unhallow
allowed \al-ōd\ hallowed,
  unhallowed
allows \al-ōz\ gallows,
  Allhallows—*also plurals and
  possessives of nouns listed at*
  ⁴ALLOW
alls \olz\ Angel Falls, Niagara
  Falls—*also possessives and
  plurals of nouns, third person
  singular presents of verbs
  listed at* ALL
allsy \ol-zē\ see ALSY
allus \al-əs\ see ²ALIS
allused \al-əst\ see ALIST
¹**ally** \ā-lē\ see AILY
²**ally** \äl-ē\ see ¹OLLY
³**ally** \o-lē\ see AWLY
⁴**ally** \al-ē\ alley, bally, challis,
  dally, galley, gally, mallee,
  pally, rally, sallie, sally, Sally,
  tally, valley, Aunt Sally,
  bialy, crevalle, Death Valley,
  finale, Nepali, tomalley,
  dillydally, Mexicali, shilly-
  shally, teocalli, Great Rift
  Valley
allyn \al-ən\ see ALLON
alm \äm\ see ¹OM
alma \al-mə\ Alma, halma
almar \äm-ər\ see ¹OMBER
almer \äm-ər\ see ¹OMBER

almily \äm-ə-lē\ see OMALY
almish \äm-ish\ see ¹AMISH
almist \äm-əst\ palmist,
  psalmist, Islamist
almody \äm-əd-ē\ see OMEDY
almon \am-ən\ see AMMON
almoner \äm-ə-nər\ see
  OMMONER
alms \ämz\ alms, Brahms,
  Psalms—*also plurals and
  possessives of nouns and
  third singular presents of
  verbs listed at* ¹OM
almy \äm-ē\ see ¹AMI
alo \äl-ō\ see ¹OLLOW
aloe \al-ō\ see ⁵ALLOW
¹**alogist** \äl-ə-jəst\ see OLOGIST
²**alogist** \al-ə-jəst\ analogist,
  dialogist, mammalogist,
  genealogist
¹**alogy** \äl-ə-jē\ see OLOGY
²**alogy** \al-ə-jē\ analogy,
  hypallage, mammalogy,
  tetralogy, mineralogy
alom \äl-əm\ see OLUMN
alon \al-ən\ see ALLON
alop \al-əp\ see ²ALLOP
¹**alor** \äl-ər\ see OLLAR
²**alor** \al-ər\ see ²ALLER
¹**alorie** \al-rē\ see ¹ALLERY
²**alorie** \al-ə-rē\ see ²ALARY
¹**alory** \al-rē\ see ALLERY
²**alory** \al-ə-rē\ see ²ALARY
alousie \al-ə-sē\ see ALLACY
alp \alp\ alp, salp, scalp
alpa \al-pə\ salpa, catalpa,
  Tegucigalpa
alpal \al-pəl\ palpal, scalpel
alpel \al-pəl\ see ALPAL
alpha \al-fə\ alpha, alfalfa
¹**alque** \ok\ see ALK

²**alque** \alk\ calque, talc,
catafalque

als \älz\ see OLS

alsa \ȯl-sə\ balsa, salsa

alse \ȯls\ false, waltz

alsey \ȯl-zē\ see ALSY

alsy \ȯl-zē\ ballsy, Halsey,
palsy

alt \ȯlt\ fault, gault, halt, malt,
salt, smalt, vault, volt, Walt,
asphalt, assault, basalt, cobalt,
default, desalt, exalt,
footfault, gestalt, Great Salt,
Schwarzwald, stringhalt,
double-fault, somersault,
pepper-and-salt

alta \äl-tə\ Malta, Salta, Volta,
Yalta

altar \ȯl-tər\ see ALTER

alter \ȯl-tər\ altar, alter, falter,
halter, palter, Psalter, salter,
vaulter, Walter, defaulter,
desalter, exalter, Gibraltar,
pole-vaulter

altery \ȯl-trē\ see ALTRY

¹**alti** \əl-tē\ Balti, difficulty

²**alti** \ȯl-tē\ see ALTY

altic \ȯl-tik\ Baltic, asphaltic,
cobaltic, systaltic, peristaltic

alting \ȯl-tiŋ\ halting, salting,
vaulting

altless \ȯlt-ləs\ faultless, saltless

alto \al-tō\ alto, contralto, rialto

alton \ȯlt-ᵊn\ Alton, dalton,
Dalton, Walton

altry \ȯl-trē\ paltry, psaltery,
psaltry

alty \ȯl-tē\ Balti, faulty, malty,
salty, vaulty

altz \ȯls\ see ALSE

alu \äl-ü\ Yalu, Tuvalu

alue \al-yü\ value, devalue,
disvalue, misvalue, revalue,
transvalue, overvalue,
undervalue

¹**alus** \ā-ləs\ see AYLESS

²**alus** \al-əs\ see ²ALIS

¹**alve** \äv\ see ²OLVE

²**alve** \alv\ salve, valve, bivalve,
univalve, inequivalve

³**alve** \av\ calve, halve, have,
salve

alver \al-vər\ salver, salvor,
quacksalver

alvin \al-vən\ Alvin, Calvin

alvor \al-vər\ see ALVER

aly \al-ē\ see ⁴ALLY

alyard \al-yərd\ see ALLIARD

alysis \al-ə-səs\ analysis,
dialysis, paralysis,
cryptanalysis, metanalysis,
self-analysis

¹**am** \äm\ see ¹OM

²**am** \am\ am, cam, cham, clam,
cram, dam, damn, damned,
drachm, dram, DRAM, flam,
gam, Graham, gram, ham,
Ham, jam, jamb, lam, lamb,
Lamb, ma'am, Pam, pram,
ram, RAM, Sam, SAM, scam,
scram, sham, slam, swam,
tam, tram, wham, yam,
Annam, ashram, Assam,
dirham, Edam, ngram, exam,
flimflam, goddamn, grandam,
iamb, logjam, madame,
mailgram, milldam, nizam,
Priam, program, quondam,
tam-tam, thiram, trigram,
whim-wham, ziram,
Abraham, aerogram,
Amsterdam, anagram,
Birmingham, Boulder Dam,
cablegram, centigram,

Christogram, chronogram,
cofferdam, cryptogram,
decagram, deprogram,
diagram, diaphragm,
dithyramb, epigram, fluid
dram, hexagram, histogram,
Hohokam, hologram, Hoover
Dam, kilogram, logogram,
mammogram, milligram,
Minicam, monogram,
nomogram, oriflamme,
pentagram, phonogram,
pictogram, reprogram,
Rotterdam, scattergram,
skiagram, Smithfield ham,
sonogram, subprogram,
Surinam, telegram,
tetradrachm, thank-you-
ma'am, Uncle Sam, ad
nauseam, cardiogram,
heliogram, ideogram, in
personam, microprogram,
New Amsterdam, Omar
Khayyam, parallelogram

¹ama \äm-ə\ Brahma, comma,
drama, Kama, lama, llama,
mama, momma, squama,
Rama, Bahama, pajama,
Toyama, Atacama, cyclorama,
Dalai Lama, diorama,
docudrama, Fujiyama,
Fukuyama, Matsuyama,
melodrama, monodrama,
Mount Mazama, Okayama,
panorama, photodrama,
psychodrama, Suriname,
Wakayama, Yokohama,
Fujinoyamia, Puna de
Atacama

²ama \am-ə\ Brahma, drama,
gamma, grama, mamma, da
Gama, Manama, Miami,

pajama, Alabama, anadama,
cyclorama, diorama,
docudrama, melodrama,
monodrama, panorama,
photodrama, psychodrama

amable \ā-mə-bəl\ blamable,
claimable, framable,
nameable, tamable,
irreclaimable

amah \äm-ä\ see ¹AMA

¹aman \ā-mən\ see ¹AMEN

²aman \äm-ən\ see OMMON

¹amant \ā-mənt\ see AYMENT

²amant \am-ənt\ see ²AMENT

amas \am-əs\ see AMICE

amash \äm-ish\ see ¹AMISH

amateur \am-ət-ər\ see AMETER

amatist \am-ət-əst\ dramatist,
epigrammatist, melodramatist

amba \äm-bə\ gamba, mamba,
samba, Zomba, Cochabamba,
viola da gamba

¹ambar \äm-bər\ see ²OMBER

²ambar \am-bər\ amber,
Amber, camber, sambar,
timbre, liquidambar

ambe \am-bē\ see AMBY

ambeau \am-bō\ see AMBO

¹amber \am-bər\ see ²AMBAR

²amber \am-ər\ see AMMER

ambia \am-bē-ə\ Gambia,
Zambia

ambit \am-bət\ ambit, gambit

¹amble \äm-bəl\ see ¹EMBLE

²amble \am-bəl\ amble,
bramble, gamble, gambol,
ramble, scramble, shamble,
preamble, unscramble,
skimble-skamble

ambler \am-blər\ ambler,
gambler, rambler, scrambler,
unscrambler

ambo \am-bō\ crambo,
jambeau, sambo, Ovambo
ambol \am-bəl\ see ²AMBLE
ambray \am-brē\ see AMBRY
ambry \am-brē\ ambry,
chambray
ambulant \am-byə-lənt\
ambulant, somnambulant
amby \am-bē\ crambe,
Dushanbe, namby-pamby
¹ame \ām\ aim, blame, came,
claim, dame, fame, flame,
frame, game, hame, kame,
lame, maim, name, same,
shame, tame, wame, A-frame,
acclaim, aflame, airframe,
became, byname, cross-claim,
declaim, defame, disclaim,
endgame, enframe, exclaim,
forename, freeze-frame,
grandame, inflame,
mainframe, misname,
nickname, place-name,
prename, proclaim, quitclaim,
reclaim, selfsame, surname,
counterclaim, overcame,
Niflheim
²ame \äm\ see ¹OM
³ame \am\ see ²AM
⁴ame \äm-ə\ see ¹AMA
ameable \ā-mə-bəl\ see
AMABLE
amed \āmd\ famed, named,
ashamed, forenamed,
unashamed—*also pasts of
verbs listed at* ¹AME
ameful \ām-fəl\ blameful,
shameful
amel \am-əl\ see AMMEL
ameless \ām-ləs\ aimless,
blameless, nameless,
shameless, tameless

amely \ām-lē\ gamely, lamely,
namely, tamely
¹amen \ā-mən\ bayman,
Bremen, caiman, Cayman,
Damon, drayman, flamen,
Haman, layman, shaman,
stamen, Yemen, examen,
gravamen, highwayman
²amen \äm-ən\ see OMMON
ameness \ām-nəs\ gameness,
lameness, sameness, tameness
¹ament \ā-mənt\ see AYMENT
²ament \am-ənt\ ament, clamant
amer \ā-mər\ see AIMER
ames \āmz\ James—*also
possessives and plurals of
nouns, third person singular
presents of verbs listed at*
¹AME
ameter \am-ət-ər\ amateur,
decameter, diameter,
heptameter, hexameter,
octameter, parameter,
pentameter, tetrameter
¹amfer \am-pər\ see ²AMPER
²amfer \am-fər\ camphor,
chamfer
¹ami \äm-ē\ balmy, commie,
mommy, palmy, pommy,
qualmy, swami, Tommy,
gourami, pastrami, Sagami,
salami, tatami, tsunami,
origami
²ami \am-ə\ see ⁴AMA
³ami \am-ē\ see AMMY
amia \ā-mē-ə\ lamia, zamia,
Mesopotamia
¹amic \ō-mik\ see ²OMIC
²amic \am-ik\ gamic, Adamic,
agamic, balsamic, ceramic,
dynamic, adynamic,
cleistogamic, cryptogrammic,

cycloramic, dioramic,
exogamic, panoramic,
phonogrammic, polygamic,
aerodynamic, biodynamic,
hydrodynamic, hypothalamic,
ideogramic, thermodynamic,
magnetodynamic

amice \am-əs\ amice, camas,
chlamys, Lammas

amics \äm-iks\ see OMICS

¹amie \ā-mē\ Amy, Jamie,
Mamie, ramie, cockamamie,
cockamamy

²amie \am-ē\ see AMMY

¹amil \äm-əl\ see ¹OMMEL

²amil \am-əl\ see AMMEL

amily \am-lē\ family,
profamily, stepfamily

amin \am-ən\ see AMMON

amina \am-ə-nə\ lamina,
stamina

aminal \am-ən-ᵊl\ laminal,
foraminal

aminant \am-ə-nənt\
contaminant, examinant

aminar \am-ə-nər\ see ²AMINER

amine \am-ən\ see AMMON

¹aminer \äm-ə-nər\ see
OMMONER

²aminer \am-ə-nər\ laminar,
gewurztraminer

aming \ā-miŋ\ flaming,
framing, gaming

¹amish \äm-ish\ Amish,
qualmish, quamash,
schoolmarmish

²amish \am-ish\ Amish, famish

amist \am-əst\ see ALMIST

amity \am-ət-ē\ amity, calamity

amlet \am-lət\ camlet, hamlet,
Hamlet, samlet

amlets \am-ləts\ Tower

Hamlets—*also possessives
and plurals of nouns listed at*
AMLET

amma \am-ə\ see ⁴AMA

ammable \am-ə-bəl\
flammable, programmable,
diagrammable

ammal \am-əl\ see AMMEL

ammany \am-ə-nē\ see
AMMONY

ammar \am-ər\ see AMMER

ammas \am-əs\ see AMICE

ammatist \am-ət-əst\ see
AMATIST

amme \am\ see ²AM

ammel \am-əl\ camel, mammal,
stammel, Tamil, trammel,
enamel

ammer \am-ər\ clamber,
clammer, clamor, clamour,
crammer, dammar, gammer,
glamour, grammar, hammer,
jammer, lamber, rammer,
shammer, slammer, stammer,
yammer, clawhammer,
enamor, flimflammer,
jackhammer, programmer,
sledgehammer, trip-hammer,
windjammer, katzenjammer,
monogrammer, ninnyhammer,
yellowhammer

ammes \äm-əs\ see OMISE

ammie \am-ē\ see AMMY

ammies \am-ēz\ jammies—*also
possessives and plurals of
nouns listed at* AMMY

amming \am-iŋ\ damning,
programming

ammock \am-ək\ drammock,
hammock, mammock

ammon \am-ən\ Brahman,
famine, gamin, gammon,

mammon, salmon,
backgammon, examine, cross-
examine

ammony \am-ə-nē\ scammony,
Tammany

ammy \am-ē\ chamois,
clammy, gammy, Grammy,
hammy, mammy, ramie,
Sammie, Sammy, shammy,
whammy, Miami

amn \am\ see ²AM

amned \am\ see ²AM

amning \am-iŋ\ see AMMING

amois \am-ē\ see AMMY

¹**amon** \ā-mən\ see ¹AMEN

²**amon** \am-ən\ see OMMON

amor \am-ər\ see AMMER

amorous \am-rəs\ amorous,
clamorous, glamorous

amos \ā-məs\ see AMOUS

amour \am-ər\ see AMMER

amous \ā-məs\ Amos, famous,
shamus, squamous, biramous,
mandamus, ignoramus,
Nostradamus

¹**amp** \ämp\ see ¹OMP

²**amp** \äⁿ\ see ¹ANT

³**amp** \amp\ amp, camp, champ,
clamp, cramp, damp, gamp,
gramp, guimpe, lamp, ramp,
samp, scamp, stamp, tamp,
tramp, vamp, blackdamp, C-
clamp, chokedamp, decamp,
encamp, firedamp, headlamp,
off-ramp, on-ramp, preamp,
revamp, sunlamp, unclamp,
afterdamp, aide-de-camp,
minicamp

¹**ampean** \äm-pē-ən\ pampean,
tampion

²**ampean** \am-pē-ən\ see
²AMPION

¹**amper** \äm-pər\ see OMPER

²**amper** \am-pər\ camper,
chamfer, damper, hamper,
pamper, scamper, stamper,
tamper

amphor \am-fər\ see ²AMFER

¹**ampi** \äm-pē\ see OMPY

²**ampi** \am-pē\ see AMPY

ampian \am-pē-ən\ see
²AMPION

¹**ampion** \äm-pē-ən\ see
¹AMPEAN

²**ampion** \am-pē-ən\ campion,
champion, Grampian,
pampean, rampion, tampion

ample \am-pəl\ ample, sample,
trample, ensample, example,
subsample, counterexample

ampler \am-plər\ sampler,
trampler

ampo \äm-pō\ see OMPO

ampos \am-pəs\ see AMPUS

ampsia \am(p)-sē-ə\ eclampsia,
preeclampsia

ampton \am-tən\ Hampton,
Easthampton, Northampton,
Southampton,
Wolverhampton

ampus \am-pəs\ Campos,
campus, grampus,
hippocampus

ampy \am-pē\ campy, scampi

ams \amz\ Jams—*also
possessives and plurals of
nouns and third person
singular presents of verbs
listed at* ²AM

amson \am-sən\ damson,
Samson

amster \am-stər\ hamster,
lamster

amsun \äm-sən\ Hamsun,
Thompson
amulus \am-yə-ləs\ famulus,
hamulus
¹**amus** \ā-məs\ see AMOUS
²**amus** \äm-əs\ see OMISE
amy \ā-mē\ see ¹AMIE
amys \am-əs\ see AMICE
¹**an** \äⁿ\ see ¹ANT
²**an** \än\ see ¹ON
³**an** \ən\ see UN
⁴**an** \aŋ\ see ²ANG
⁵**an** \an\ an, Ann, Anne, ban,
bran, can, clan, crayon, Dan,
fan, Fan, flan, Jan, Klan, man,
Mann, nan, Nan, pan, Pan,
panne, plan, ran, scan, San,
Shan, span, Stan, tan, van,
Van, adman, Afghan, aidman,
ape-man, ashcan, Bataan,
bedpan, began, Bhutan,
birdman, boardman, brainpan,
brogan, caftan, caiman,
cancan, capstan, captan,
caveman, Cayman, Cèzanne,
chessman, Cheyenne,
chlordan, Chopin, claypan,
clubman, Cohan, cooncan,
corban, cowman, Cruzan,
cyan, deadpan, deskman,
Dian, Diane, Diann, Dianne,
dishpan, divan, doorman,
dustpan, fancy-dan, fan-tan,
fibranne, flyman, foreran,
FORTRAN, freedman,
freeman, frogman, G-man,
gagman, Georgeann, glucan,
Gosplan, hardpan, he-man,
iceman, inspan, Iran, japan,
Japan, jazzman, Joann,
Joanne, Kazan, kneepan,
Koran, Kurgan, leadman,

Leanne, legman, liftman,
loran, Luanne, madman,
Mandan, Marfan, mailman,
merman, Milan, milkman,
newsman, oilcan, oilman,
outran, pavane, pecan,
plowman, postman, preman,
pressman, propman, Queen
Anne, Qur'an, ragman, rattan,
reedman, reman, rodman,
Roseanne, routeman,
Roxanne, Ruthann, Saipan,
sampan, sandman, Saran,
saucepan, scalepan,
schoolman, sedan, sideman,
snowman, soundman, soutane,
spaceman, Spokane, stewpan,
stickman, stockman,
strongman, stuntman, Sudan,
suntan, Susanne, Suzanne, T-
man, TACAN, taipan, Tarzan,
tisane, toucan, trainman,
trashman, trepan, Tristan,
unman, vegan, Walkman,
wingspan, yardman, yes-man,
Alcoran, allemande, also-ran,
Ameslan, anchorman,
Andaman, astrakhan,
Astrakhan, ataman, Athelstan,
attackman, automan,
balmacaan, Baluchistan,
Bantustan, bartizan,
Belmopan, black-and-tan,
bogeyman, boogeyman,
businessman, Caliban,
cameraman, caravan, catalan,
cattleman, Civitan, colorman,
cornerman, counterman,
counterplan, countryman,
courtesan, dairyman,
defenseman, everyman,
exciseman, expressman,

fellowman, funnyman, gamelan, garageman, garbageman, Hamadan, handyman, harmattan, Hindustan, hotelman, Isle of Man, jerrican, Juliann, Julianne, Kazakhstan, Ku Klux Klan, Kurdistan, Kyrgyzstan, man-for-man, man-to-man, Marianne, Maryann, Maryanne, middleman, minuteman, Monaghan, moneyman, Occitan, ombudsman, Omdurman, overman, overran, Pakistan, Parmesan, partisan, pattypan, Peter Pan, pivotman, plainclothesman, Port Sudan, Powhatan, Ramadan, repairman, rewrite man, Ryazan, safetyman, selectman, serviceman, shandrydan, Shantyman, shovelman, signalman, spick-and-span, superman, tallyman, tamarin, Teheran, teleman, teleran, triggerman, trimaran, turbofan, weatherman, workingman, yataghan, Yucatan, Afghanistan, arrière-ban, bipartisan, catamaran, catch-as-catch-can, cavalryman, committeeman, deliveryman, Kalimantan, newspaperman, orangutan, radioman, salary man, Tajikistan, Turkmenistan, Uzbekistan

⁶an \än-yə\ see ¹ANIA

⁷an \äng\ see ¹ONG

⁸an \änt\ see ²ANT

¹ana \än-ə\ ana, anna, Anna, bwana, Dona, donna, Donna, fauna, Ghana, Kana, Lana, Lonna, mana, Botswana, chicana, gymkhana, iguana, jacana, lantana, liana, Madonna, mañana, nagana, nirvana, piranha, Purana, ruana, Tijuana, Tirane, Toscana, zenana, Africana, belladonna, epifauna, French Guiana, Guadiana, Haryana, Hinayana, hiragana, ikebana, Ludhiana, Mahayana, marijuana, parmigiana, pozzolana, prima donna, Rajputana, Rosh Hashanah, Tatiana, Americana, fata morgana, Lincolniana, Ljubljana, nicotiana, Shakespeareana, Victoriana, Ciuda Guyana

²ana \ā-nə\ ana, Dana, Lana, Africana, cantilena, Cartagena, nicotiana, Shakespeareana

³ana \an-ə\ ana, Anna, canna, manna, Ghana, Hannah, Lana, nana, banana, bandanna, cabana, Deanna, Diana, Dianna, Fermanagh, goanna, Guiana, Guyana, gymkhana, Havana, hosanna, Joanna, Johanna, Montana, savanna, Savannah, sultana, Susanna, Susannah, Africana, Indiana, Juliana, Mariana, Marianna, poinciana, Pollyanna, Santa Ana, Americana, fata morgana, Louisiana, nicotiana, Shakespeareana, Victoriana

aña \än-yə\ see ¹ANIA

anacle \an-i-kəl\ see ANICAL

anage \an-ij\ manage, tannage, stage-manage, micro manage

anagh \an-ə\ see ³ANA

¹anah \ō-nə\ see ¹ONA

²anah \än-ə\ see ¹ANA

anal \ān-ᵊl\ anal, banal

analyst \an-ᵊl-əst\ analyst, annalist, panelist, cryptanalyst, psychoanalyst

anan \an-ən\ see ANNON

anape \an-ə-pē\ see ANOPY

¹anary \ān-rē\ see ANERY

²anary \an-rē\ see ²ANNERY

anate \an-ət\ see ANNET

anative \an-ət-iv\ sanative, explanative

anbe \am-bē\ see AMBY

¹anc \aⁿ\ see ¹ANT

²anc \aŋ\ see ²ANG

³anc \aŋk\ see ANK

anca \aŋ-kə\ barranca, Kanka, Casablanca, lingua franca, Salamanca

¹ance \äⁿs\ Reims, nuance, outrance, séance, à outrance, Provence, Saint-Saëns, diligence, Fort-de-France, ordonnance, renaissance, mésalliance, par excellence, concours d'elegance, pièce de résistance

²ance \äns\ Hans, nonce, ponce, sconce, brisance, ensconce, faience, nuance, response, seance, Afrikaans, complaisance, fer-de-lance, nonchalance, provenance, renaissance, pièce de résistance

³ance \ans\ chance, dance, France, glance, lance, Lance, manse, nance, Nantes, prance, stance, trance, trans, Vance, advance, askance, bechance, enhance, entrance, expanse, finance, mischance, perchance, romance, Romance, side-glance, sweatpants, circumstance, complaisance, contredanse, country-dance, fer-de-lance, happenchance, happenstance, Liederkranz, Port-au-Prince, refinance, smarty-pants, underpants—*also plurals and possessives of verbs listed at* ⁵ANT

anceable \an-sə-bəl\ see ANSIBLE

anced \anst\ canst, circumstanced, underfinanced—*also pasts of verbs listed at* ³ANCE

ancel \an-səl\ cancel, chancel, handsel, expansile, precancel

anceler \an-slər\ canceler, chancellor, vice-chancellor

ancellor \an-slər\ see ANCELER

ancement \an-smənt\ advancement, enhancement

ancer \an-sər\ answer, cancer, dancer, glancer, lancer, prancer, advancer, enhancer, free-lancer, merganser, romancer, ropedancer, anticancer, geomancer, necromancer, rhabdomancer

ances \an(t)-səs\ see ANCIS

ancet \an-sət\ lancet, Narragansett

¹anch \änch\ see ¹AUNCH

²anch \önch\ see ²AUNCH

³anch \anch\ blanch, Blanche,

branch, ranch, rebranch,
avalanche

¹anche \änsh\ tranche, carte
blanche, revanche

²anche \anch\ see ³ANCH

³anche \an-chē\ see ANCHY

¹ancher \ȯn-chər\ see AUNCHER

²ancher \an-chər\ ceinture,
rancher

anchi \an-chē\ see ANCHY

anchion \an-chən\ see ANSION

anchor \aŋ-kər\ see ANKER

anchoress \aŋ-krəs\ see
ANKEROUS

anchy \an-chē\ branchy,
Ranchi, Comanche

ancial \an-chəl\ see ANTIAL

ancis \an(t)-səs\ Frances,
Francis, Aransas—*also third
person singular presents of
verbs and plurals of nouns
listed at* ANCE

anck \äŋk\ see ¹ONK

anco \äŋ-kō\ see ONCO

ancolin \aŋ-klən\ see ANKLIN

ancor \aŋ-kər\ see ANKER

ancorous \aŋ-krəs\ see
ANKEROUS

ancre \aŋ-kər\ see ANKER

ancrous \aŋ-krəs\ see
ANKEROUS

anct \aŋt\ see ANKED

ancy \an-sē\ chancy, fancy,
Nancy, unchancy,
chiromancy, geomancy,
hydromancy, necromancy,
pyromancy, rhabdomancy,
sycophancy, oneiromancy

¹and \än\ see ¹ANT

²and \änd\ see ¹OND

³and \and\ and, band, bland,
brand, canned, gland, grand,
hand, land, manned, NAND,
rand, Rand, sand, Sand, stand,
strand, armband, backhand,
backland, badland, bandstand,
benchland, blackland,
broadband, brushland,
bushland, cabstand,
cloudland, coastland,
command, cowhand, crash-
land, cropland, deckhand,
demand, disband, dockhand,
dockland, downland,
dreamland, dryland, duneland,
expand, farmhand, farmland,
fenland, filmland, firebrand,
firsthand, flatland, forehand,
four-hand, free hand,
freehand, gangland, glad-
hand, Gotland, grandstand,
grassland, handstand,
hardstand, hatband, headband,
headstand, heartland,
heathland, homeland, Iceland,
inkstand, inland, Inland,
kickstand, Kokand, Lapland,
left-hand, longhand,
mainland, marshland,
misbrand, newsstand,
nightstand, northland,
noseband, offhand, outland,
outstand, parkland, pineland,
playland, proband,
Queensland, quicksand,
rangeland, remand, repand,
Rheinland, Rhineland,
ribband, right-hand, rimland,
roband, Saarland, scabland,
screenland, scrubland,
seastrand, shorthand,
sideband, softland, southland,
spaceband, stagehand,
summand, swampland,

sweatband, Thailand,
thirdhand, tideland, trainband,
unhand, unmanned,
waistband, washstand,
wasteland, watchband,
wetland, wildland, withstand,
wristband, ampersand,
beforehand, behindhand,
bellyband, belly-land,
borderland, bottomland,
confirmand, contraband,
countermand, Damavand,
Dixieland, fairyland,
fatherland, Ferdinand,
forestland, four-in-hand,
graduand, hand-to-hand, hand
to hand, hinterland,
Krugerrand, lotusland,
meadowland, motherland,
Nagaland, narrowband, no-
man's-land, operand,
ordinand, overhand, overland,
pastureland, reprimand, Rio
Grande, Samarkand, saraband,
secondhand, Swaziland,
tableland, Talleyrand,
timberland, Togoland,
underhand, undermanned,
understand, wonderland,
Zululand, analysand,
Bechuanaland, cloud-cuckoo-
land, fantasyland,
misunderstand, multiplicand,
Prince Rupert's Land,
Somaliland, Sudetenland,
vacationland, videoland,
Witwatersrand, Matabeleland,
Alice-in-Wonderland—*also*
pasts of verbs listed at ⁵AN
⁴**and** \än\ see ¹ON
⁵**and** \änt\ see ²ANT
¹**anda** \an-də\ Ganda, panda,

Amanda, Luanda, Luganda,
Miranda, Uganda, veranda,
jacaranda, memoranda,
nomina conservanda,
propaganda
²**anda** \än-də\ see ONDA
andable \an-də-bəl\ mandible,
commandable, demandable,
expandable, understandable
andaed \an-dəd\ see ANDED
andal \an-dᵊl\ see ANDLE
andaled \an-dᵊld\ handled,
sandaled, well-handled—*also*
pasts of verbs listed at ANDLE
andall \an-dᵊl\ see ANDLE
andalous \an-dləs\ see
²ANDLESS
andam \an-dəm\ see ANDUM
andant \an-dənt\ see ANDENT
andar \ənd-ər\ see UNDER
andarin \an-drən\ mandarin,
alexandrine, salamandrine
¹**ande** \ən\ see UN
²**ande** \an\ see ⁵AN
³**ande** \an-dē\ see ANDY
⁴**ande** \and\ see ³AND
⁵**ande** \än-də\ see ONDA
anded \an-dəd\ banded,
branded, candid, handed,
landed, stranded, backhanded,
bare-handed, cleanhanded,
forehanded, four-handed,
freehanded, ham-handed,
hardhanded, high-handed,
ironhanded, left-handed, light-
handed, offhanded, one-
handed, red-handed, right-
handed, shorthanded,
sure-handed, three-handed,
two-handed, unbranded,
verandaed, empty-handed,
evenhanded, heavy-handed,

openhanded, overhanded,
singlehanded, underhanded—
also pasts of verbs listed at
³AND
andel \an-dᵊl\ see ANDLE
andem \an-dəm\ see ANDUM
andent \an-dənt\ candent,
scandent, demandant
¹ander \en-dər\ see ENDER
²ander \än-dər\ see ¹ONDER
³ander \an-dər\ bander, brander,
candor, dander, gander,
grandeur, lander, pander,
sander, slander, strander,
zander, auslander,
backhander, blackhander,
bystander, commander,
demander, expander,
flatlander, germander, glad-
hander, goosander,
grandstander, inlander,
Leander, left-hander,
mainlander, meander,
outlander, philander,
pomander, right-hander,
scrimshander, soft-lander,
Uitlander, Africander,
alexander, Alexander,
calamander, coriander,
gerrymander, oleander,
salamander, single-hander—
also comparatives of
adjectives listed at ³AND
anderous \an-drəs\ see
ANDROUS
anders \an-dərz\ Flanders,
Bouvier des Flandres, golden
alexanders—*also plurals and*
possessives of verbs listed at
³ANDER
andery \an-drē\ see ANDRY
andes \an-dēz\ Andes—*also*

possessives and plurals of
nouns and third person
singular presents of verbs
listed at ANDY
¹andeur \an-dər\ see ³ANDER
²andeur \an-jər\ see ⁴ANGER
andhi \an-dē\ see ANDY
andi \an-dē\ see ANDY
andible \an-də-bəl\ see
ANDABLE
andid \an-dəd\ see ANDED
anding \an-diŋ\ standing,
commanding, crossbanding,
freestanding, hardstanding,
long-standing, outstanding,
upstanding, mind-expanding,
notwithstanding,
understanding
andish \an-dish\ blandish,
brandish, standish, Standish,
outlandish
andist \an-dəst\ contrabandist,
propagandist—*also*
superlatives of adjectives
listed at ³AND
andit \an-dət\ bandit, pandit
andle \an-dᵊl\ candle, dandle,
Handel, handle, Randall,
sandal, scandal, vandal,
footcandle, manhandle,
mishandle, panhandle,
stickhandle, coromandel,
Coromandel
andled \an-dᵊl\ see ANDALED
andler \an-lər\ candler,
chandler, handler, panhandler,
stickhandler
andless \an-ləs\ see ANLESS
andly \an-lē\ see ²ANLY
andment \an-mənt\
commandment, disbandment
ando \an-dō\ Fernando, Orlando

andom \an-dəm\ see ANDUM

andor \an-dər\ see ³ANDER

andra \an-drə\ Sandra, Cassandra, Alexandra, pachysandra

andrea \an-drē-ə\ see ANDRIA

andrel \an-drəl\ mandrel, mandrill, spandrel

andres \an-dərz\ see ANDERS

andria \an-drē-ə\ Andrea, Alexandria

andrill \an-drəl\ see ANDREL

andrine \an-drən\ see ANDARIN

andros \an-drəs\ see ANDROUS

androus \an-drəs\ Andros, slanderous, gynandrous, meandrous, polyandrous

andry \an-drē\ commandery, monandry, polyandry

ands \anz\ Badlands, Lowlands, Canyonlands

andsel \an-səl\ see ANCEL

andsman \anz-mən\ bandsman, clansman, Klansman, landsman

andsome \an-səm\ see ANSOM

andum \an-dəm\ fandom, grandam, random, tandem, memorandum, nomen conservandum, subpoena ad testificandum

andy \an-dē\ Andy, bandy, brandy, Brandy, candy, dandy, handy, Handy, pandy, randy, Randy, sandhi, sandy, Sandy, shandy, jim-dandy, unhandy, Rio Grande, modus operandi

¹ane \ān\ ain, Aisne, ane, bane, blain, Blaine, brain, Cain, cane, chain, crane, Crane, Dane, deign, drain, Duane, Dwain, Dwayne, fain, fane, feign, gain, grain, Jane, Jayne, lane, Lane, main, Maine, mane, pain, Paine, pane, plain, plane, quean, rain, reign, rein, sain, sane, seine, Seine, skein, slain, Spain, sprain, stain, stane, strain, swain, thane, thegn, train, twain, Twain, vain, vane, vein, wain, wane, Wayne, Zane, abstain, again, airplane, amain, arcane, arraign, attain, Bahrain, Bassein, Beltane, biplane, birdbrain, Biscayne, bloodstain, bugbane, campaign, champagne, champaign, Champlain, checkrein, chicane, chilblain, chow mein, cinquain, cocaine, Cockaigne, coxswain, complain, constrain, contain, cordwain, cowbane, crackbrain, demesne, deplane, destain, detain, detrain, devein, disdain, distain, distrain, dogbane, domain, drivetrain, Duane, dumbcane, edge-grain, Elaine, emplane, enchain, engrain, enplane, entrain, explain, eyestrain, fleabane, floatplane, floodplain, Fort Wayne, Gawain, germane, grosgrain, Helaine, Helene, henbane, house-train, humane, Hussein, Igraine, immane, inane, ingrain, insane, lamebrain, lightplane, lo mein, Loraine, Lorraine, maintain, marchpane, membrane, migraine, Montaigne,

montane, moraine, mortmain,
Moulmein, mundane, neck-
rein, obtain, octane, ordain,
pertain, plain-Jane, profane,
ptomaine, purslane, quatrain,
refrain, remain, restrain,
retain, retrain, romaine,
sailplane, sea-lane, seaplane,
seatrain, sustain, tearstain,
terrain, terrane, triplane,
Touraine, Ukraine, unchain,
urbane, vervain, vicereine,
villein, volplane, warplane,
wolfsbane, aeroplane,
appertain, aquaplane,
Aquitaine, ascertain, avellane,
Bloemfontain, cellophane,
Charlemagne, Charles's Wain,
chatelain, chatelaine,
counterpane, de Montaigne,
entertain, featherbrain,
foreordain, frangipane,
gyroplane, hurricane,
hydroplane, hyperplane,
inhumane, Kwajalein, La
Fontaine, marocain, Mary
Jane, mise-en-scène,
monoplane, Novocain,
neutercane, novocaine,
overlain, paravane, paper-
train, peneplain, Port of
Spain, port-wine stain,
preordain, rattlebrain,
scatterbrain, shaggymane,
Spanish Main, sugarcane,
suzerain, Tamburlaine,
Tamerlane, terreplein,
tramontane, transmontane,
windowpane, Alsace-Lorraine,
auf Wiedersehen,
balletomane, convertiplane,
demimondaine, elecampane,

extramundane, intermontane,
Lake Pontchartraine,
legerdemain, ultramontane,
trichalomethane
²ane \an\ see ⁵AN
³ane \än-ə\ see ¹ANA
⁴ane \än\ see ¹ON
anea \ā-nē-ə\ see ²ANIA
anean \ā-nē-ən\ see ²ANIAN
aned \ānd\ see AINED
anee \an-ē\ see ANNY
aneful \ān-fəl\ see AINFUL
anel \an-ᵊl\ see ANNEL
anelist \an-ᵊl-əst\ see ANALYST
aneous \ā-nē-əs\ cutaneous,
extraneous, spontaneous,
coetaneous, consentaneous,
instantaneous, miscellaneous,
porcelaneous, simultaneous,
succedaneous,
contemporaneous,
extemporaneous
¹aner \ā-nər\ see AINER
²aner \än-ər\ see ¹ONOR
anery \ān-rē\ granary, chicanery
anet \an-ət\ see ANNET
aneum \ā-nē-əm\ see ANIUM
aney \ȯ-nē\ see ¹AWNY
anford \an-fərd\ Sanford,
Stanford
¹ang \äŋ\ see ¹ONG
²ang \aŋ\ bang, bhang, clang,
dang, fang, Fang, gang,
gangue, hang, pang, prang,
rang, sang, slang, spang,
sprang, stang, tang, twang,
whang, yang, cliff-hang,
defang, ginseng, harangue,
linsang, meringue, mustang,
orang, parang, Pinang, press-
gang, probang, shebang, slam-
bang, straphang, trepang,

whizbang, boomerang,
charabanc, overhang,
parasang, siamang,
interrobang, orangutan

³ang \ȯŋ\ see ²ONG

anga \äŋ-gə\ see ONGA

angar \aŋ-ər\ see ²ANGER

¹ange \äⁿzh\ blancmange,
mélange

²ange \ānj\ change, grange,
mange, range, strange,
arrange, derange, downrange,
estrange, exchange, free-
range, gearchange, long-
range, outrange, short-range,
shortchange, counterchange,
disarrange, interchange,
omnirange, Great Dividing
Range

³ange \anj\ flange, phalange

angel \aŋ-gəl\ see ANGLE

angell \aŋ-gəl\ see ANGLE

angement \ānj-mənt\
arrangement, derangement,
estrangement, disarrangement

angency \an-jən-sē\ plangency,
tangency

angent \an-jənt\ plangent,
tangent

¹anger \ān-jər\ changer, danger,
granger, manger, ranger,
stranger, bushranger,
endanger, estranger,
exchanger, shortchanger,
interchanger

²anger \aŋ-ər\ banger, clanger,
clangor, clangour, ganger,
hangar, hanger, languor,
Sanger, twanger, cliff-hanger,
straphanger, haranguer,
paperhanger

³anger \aŋ-gər\ anger, clangor

⁴anger \an-jər\ flanger,
grandeur, phalanger

angi \aŋ-ē\ see ²ANGY

angible \an-jə-bəl\ frangible,
tangible, infrangible,
intangible, refrangible

angie \aŋ-ē\ see ²ANGY

¹anging \ān-jiŋ\ bushranging,
unchanging, wide-ranging

²anging \aŋ-iŋ\ hanging, cliff-
hanging, paperhanging

angle \aŋ-gəl\ angle, bangle,
dangle, jangle, mangel,
mangle, spangle, strangle,
tangle, wangle, wrangle,
embrangle, entangle, Mount
Wrangell, pentangle,
quadrangle, rectangle,
triangle, untangle, wide-angle,
disentangle

angled \aŋ-gəld\ angled,
tangled, newfangled,
oldfangled, right-angled, star-
spangled—*also pasts of verbs
listed at* ANGLE

anglement \aŋ-gəl-mənt\
tanglement, embranglement,
entanglement,
disentanglement

angler \aŋ-glər\ angler, dangler,
jangler, mangler, strangler,
wangler, wrangler, entangler

angles \aŋ-gəlz\ Angles,
strangles—*also plurals and
possessives of nouns and
third singular presents of
verbs listed at* ANGLE

anglian \aŋ-glē-ən\ Anglian,
ganglion

angling \aŋ-gliŋ\ angling,
gangling

anglion \aŋ-glē-ən\ see
ANGLIAN
angly \aŋ-glē\ gangly, jangly,
tangly
ango \aŋ-gō\ mango, tango,
Durango, fandango
¹**angor** \aŋ-ər\ see ²ANGER
²**angor** \aŋ-gər\ see ³ANGER
angorous \aŋ-ə-rəs\ clangorous,
languorous
angour \aŋ-ər\ see ²ANGER
angster \aŋ-stər\ gangster,
prankster
anguage \aŋ-gwij\ language,
slanguage, metalanguage,
paralanguage, protolanguage
angue \aŋ\ see ²ANG
anguer \aŋ-ər\ see ²ANGER
anguish \aŋ-gwish\ anguish,
languish
anguor \aŋ-ər\ see ²ANGER
anguorous \aŋ-ə-rəs\ see
ANGOROUS
angus \aŋ-gəs\ Angus, Brangus
¹**angy** \ān-jē\ mangy, rangy
²**angy** \aŋ-ē\ tangy, twangy,
Ubangi, collieshangie
anha \än-ə\ see ¹ANA
anhope \an-əp\ see ANNUP
¹**ani** \än-ē\ Bonnie, bonny,
Connie, Donnie, fawny,
johnny, Ronnie, tawny,
afghani, Fulani, chalcedony,
Kisangani, maharani,
Nuristani, quadriphony,
Rajasthani, mulligatawny
²**ani** \an-ē\ see ANNY
¹**ania** \än-yə\ Agana, España,
lasagna, Titania, Emilia-
Romagna
²**ania** \ā-nē-ə\ mania, titania,
Titania, Urania, Acarnania,

Anglomania, Aquitania,
collectanea, dipsomania,
egomania, hypomania,
kleptomania, Lithuania,
Mauretania, Mauritania,
miscellanea, monomania,
mythomania, nymphomania,
Oceania, Pennsylvania,
Pomerania, pyromania,
Transylvania, balletomania,
bibliomania, decalcomania,
megalomania—*see also* ³ANIA
³**ania** \ān-yə\ Campania,
Catania, Hispania, Titania,
Aquitania, malaguena,
Tripolitania—*also words
listed at* ²ANIA
¹**anian** \än-ē-ən\ Kiwanian,
Araucanian, Turanian
²**anian** \ā-nē-ən\ Albanian,
Dardanian, Iranian,
Romanian, Rumanian,
Sassanian, Turanian,
Ukrainian, Uranian,
vulcanian, Lithuanian,
Pennsylvanian, Pomeranian,
Ruritanian, subterranean,
Indo-Iranian, Mediterranean
aniard \an-yərd\ lanyard,
Spaniard
anic \an-ik\ manic, panic,
tannic, Brahmanic, Britannic,
cyanic, firemanic, galvanic,
Germanic, Hispanic, Koranic,
mechanic, melanic, organic,
Romanic, satanic, shamanic,
Sudanic, titanic, tympanic,
volcanic, aldermanic,
Alemannic, councilmanic,
epiphanic, inorganic,
messianic, oceanic, Ossianic,
pre-Hispanic, talismanic,

theophanic, Indo-Germanic,
megalomanic, Rhaeto-
Romanic, suboceanic,
transoceanic

anical \an-i-kəl\ manacle,
panicle, sanicle, botanical,
mechanical, tyrannical,
puritanical

anice \an-əs\ see ANISE

anicle \an-i-kəl\ see ANICAL

anics \an-iks\ annex,
mechanics—*also plurals and
possessives of nouns listed at*
ANIC

¹**anid** \ā-nəd\ ranid, tabanid

²**anid** \an-əd\ canid, ranid,
Sassanid

¹**aniel** \an-ᵊl\ see ANNEL

²**aniel** \an-yəl\ see ANUAL

anigan \an-i-gən\ see ANNIGAN

anikin \an-i-kən\ see ANNIKIN

animous \an-ə-məs\ animus,
magnanimous, unanimous,
pusillanimous

animus \an-ə-məs\ see
ANIMOUS

¹**anion** \än-yən\ see ¹ONYON

²**anion** \an-yən\ banyan, canon,
canyon, fanion, companion,
Grand Canyon, Hells Canyon

anis \an-əs\ see ANISE

anise \an-əs\ anise, Janice,
Janis, stannous, johannes,
Johnannes, pandanus,
titanous, Scipio Africanus

¹**anish** \ā-nish\ see AINISH

²**anish** \an-ish\ banish, clannish,
mannish, planish, Spanish,
tannish, vanish, Pollyannish,
Judeo-Spanish

anist \än-əst\ see ONEST

anister \an-ə-stər\ canister,
ganister

anite \an-ət\ see ANNET

anity \an-ət-ē\ sanity, vanity,
humanity, inanity, insanity,
profanity, urbanity,
Christianity, churchianity,
inhumanity, superhumanity

anium \ā-nē-əm\ cranium,
geranium, uranium,
succedaneum

ank \aŋk\ bank, blank, brank,
clank, crank, dank, drank,
flank, franc, frank, Frank,
hank, lank, plank, prank,
rank, sank, shank, shrank,
spank, stank, swank, tank,
thank, yank, Yank, Burbank,
claybank, embank, foreshank,
gangplank, greenshank,
nonbank, outflank, outrank,
pickthank, point-blank,
redshank, sandbank,
sheepshank, snowbank,
mountebank, riverbank,
clinkety-clank

¹**anka** \äŋ-kə\ concha, tanka,
Sri Lanka

²**anka** \aŋ-kə\ see ANCA

ankable \aŋ-kə-bəl\ bankable,
frankable

anked \aŋt\ shanked, tanked,
spindle-shanked, sacrosanct—
also pasts of verbs listed at
ANK

ankee \an-kē\ see ANKY

anken \aŋ-kən\ flanken,
Rankine

anker \aŋ-kər\ anchor, banker,
canker, chancre, flanker,
franker, hanker, rancor,
ranker, spanker, tanker,

thanker, co-anchor,
unanchor—*also comparatives
of adjectives listed at* ANK
ankerous \aŋ-krəs\ anchoress,
cankerous, chancrous,
rancorous, cantankerous
ankh \äŋk\ see ¹ONK
ankie \an-kē\ see ANKY
ankine \aŋ-kən\ see ANKEN
ankish \aŋ-kish\ Frankish,
prankish
ankle \aŋ-kəl\ ankle, crankle,
rankle
ankly \aŋ-klē\ blankly, dankly,
frankly
anks \aŋs\ see ANX
ankster \aŋ-stər\ see ANGSTER
anky \aŋ-kē\ cranky, hankie,
lanky, swanky, Yankee,
hanky-panky
anless \an-ləs\ handless,
manless, planless
anley \an-lē\ see ²ANLY
anli \an-lē\ see ²ANLY
¹anly \än-lē\ fondly, thrawnly,
wanly
²anly \an-lē\ blandly, grandly,
manly, Stanley, Osmanli,
unmanly
¹ann \an\ see ⁵AN
²ann \än\ see ¹ON
¹anna \än-ə\ see ¹ANA
²anna \an-ə\ see ³ANA
annage \an-ij\ see ANAGE
annah \an-ə\ see ³ANA
annalist \an-ᵊl-əst\ see
ANALYST
annan \an-ən\ see ANNON
anne \an\ see ⁵AN
anned \and\ see ³AND
annel \an-ᵊl\ channel, Channel,
Daniel, flannel, panel,

scrannel, spaniel, impanel,
English Channel
annequin \an-i-kən\ see
ANNIKIN
anner \an-ər\ banner, canner,
fanner, lanner, manner,
manor, planner, scanner,
spanner, tanner, vanner,
deadpanner, japanner,
caravanner
¹annery \än-rē\ ornery,
swannery
²annery \an-rē\ cannery,
granary, tannery
annes \an-əs\ see ANISE
anness \än-nəs\ fondness,
wanness
annet \an-ət\ gannet, granite,
Janet, planet, pomegranate
annexe \an-iks\ see ANICS
annibal \an-ə-bəl\ cannibal,
Hannibal
annic \an-ik\ see ANIC
annie \an-ē\ see ANNY
annigan \an-i-gən\ brannigan,
shenanigan
annikin \an-i-kən\ cannikin,
manikin, mannequin, pannikin
annin \an-ən\ see ANNON
annish \an-ish\ see ²ANISH
annon \an-ən\ cannon, canon,
Shannon, tannin, Buchanan,
Clackmannan, colcannon
annous \an-əs\ see ANISE
anns \anz\ see ⁴ANS
annual \an-yəl\ see ANUAL
annular \an-yə-lər\ annular,
cannular, granular
annulate \an-yə-lət\ annulate,
annulet, campanulate
annulet \an-yə-lət\ see
ANNULATE

annum \an-əm\ see ²ANUM
annup \an-əp\ sannup, stanhope
anny \an-ē\ Annie, canny,
cranny, Danny, fanny, granny,
Lanny, nanny, afghani,
ca'canny, kokanee, uncanny,
frangipani, Hindustani,
hootenanny
¹**ano** \än-ō\ guano, Kano, llano,
mano, mono, Chicano,
Marrano, Nagano, piano,
Romano, Serrano, soprano,
altiplano, boliviano, fortepiano, mezzo piano, mezzo-
soprano, Città del Vaticano
²**ano** \ä-nō\ ripieno, volcano
³**ano** \an-ō\ Hispano, piano,
soprano, fortepiano, mezzo-
soprano
¹**anon** \an-ən\ see ANNON
²**anon** \an-yən\ see ²ANION
anopy \an-ə-pē\ canape, canopy
anor \an-ər\ see ANNER
anous \an-əs\ see ANISE
anqui \än-kē\ see ONKY
¹**ans** \äns\ see ²ANCE
²**ans** \änz\ see ONZE
³**ans** \ans\ see ³ANCE
⁴**ans** \anz\ banns, Hans, sans,
trans, Sextans—*also plurals
and possessives of nouns and
third singular presents of
verbs listed at* ⁵AN
⁵**ans** \aⁿ\ see ¹ANT
ansard \an-sərd\ see ANSWERED
¹**ansas** \an(t)-səs\ see ANCIS
²**ansas** \an-zəs\ Kansas,
Arkansas
anse \ans\ see ³ANCE
ansea \än-zē\ see ANZY
anser \an-sər\ see ANCER
anset \an-sət\ see ANCET

ansett \an-sət\ see ANCET
ansible \an-sə-bəl\ danceable,
expansible
ansile \an-səl\ see ANCEL
ansing \an-siŋ\ Lansing—*also
present participles of verbs
listed at* ³ANCE
ansion \an-chən\ mansion,
scansion, stanchion,
expansion
ansk \änsk\ Bryansk, Gdansk,
Murmansk, Saransk
ansman \anz-mən\ see
ANDSMAN
ansom \an-səm\ handsome,
hansom, ransom, transom,
unhandsome
anst \anst\ see ANCED
answer \an-sər\ see ANCER
answered \an-sərd\ answered,
mansard, unanswered
ansy \an-zē\ pansy, tansy,
chimpanzee
¹**ant** \äⁿ\ Caen, Gant, arpent,
beurre blanc, croissant, en
banc, Mont Blanc, riant,
roman, Rouen, Tátouan,
savant, versant,
accouchement, aide-de-camp,
au courant, battement,
cidevant, contretemps,
debridement, denouement, en
passant, Maupassant,
Mitterand, Orléans,
Perpignan, rapprochement,
revenant, se tenant, soi-disant,
vol-au-vent, arrondissement,
chateaubriand, Chateaubriand,
Clermont-Ferrand, de
Maupassant, idiot savant,
ressentiment, sauvignon blanc
²**ant** \änt\ aunt, can't, daunt,

flaunt, font, fount, gaunt,
taunt, vaunt, want, wont,
avant, avaunt, bacchant,
bacchante, Balante,
Beaumont, bouffant, brisant,
courante, détente, entente,
Fremont, gallant, grandaunt,
piedmont, Piedmont, piquant,
romaunt, Rostand, savant,
sirvente, Vermont, bon vivant,
commandant, complaisant,
confidant, debridement,
debutant, debutante,
dilettante, John of Gaunt,
intrigant, nonchalant, poste
restante, restaurant, symbiont,
dicynodont, subdebutante,
Montcalm de Saint Veran,
sinfonia concertante
³**ant** \ənt\ see ¹ONT
⁴**ant** \ȯnt\ see ¹AUNT
⁵**ant** \ant\ ant, aunt, brant, cant,
can't, chant, grant, Grant,
hant, Kant, pant, plant, rant,
scant, shan't, slant, aslant,
bacchant, bacchante, bezant,
courante, decant, descant,
discant, displant, eggplant,
enceinte, enchant, explant,
extant, formant, gallant,
grandaunt, houseplant,
implant, incant, leadplant,
levant, Levant, pieplant,
pissant, plainchant, pourpoint,
preplant, rampant, recant,
replant, savant, supplant,
transplant, adamant,
commandant, complaisant,
confidant, cormorant,
corposant, Corybant,
covenant, demipointe,
dilettante, disenchant,

gallivant, hierophant,
interplant, sycophant
anta \ant-ə\ anta, manta,
Atlanta, infanta, vedanta,
Atalanta
antage \ant-ij\ vantage,
advantage, coign of vantage,
disadvantage
antain \ant-ᵊn\ see ²ANTON
¹**antal** \änt-ᵊl\ see ¹ONTAL
²**antal** \ant-ᵊl\ see ANTLE
antam \ant-əm\ bantam,
phantom
antar \ant-ər\ see ²ANTER
antasist \ant-ə-səst\ see
ANTICIST
¹**ante** \än-tā\ Brontë, Dante,
andante, Asante, volante, Belo
Horizonte
²**ante** \änt\ see ²ANT
³**ante** \ant\ see ⁵ANT
⁴**ante** \änt-ē\ see ¹ANTI
⁵**ante** \ant-ē\ ante, canty,
chantey, pantie, scanty,
shanty, slanty, andanti,
Asante, Ashanti, Chianti,
infante, non obstante, penny-
ante, vigilante, pococurante,
status quo ante
antean \ant-ē-ən\ Dantean,
Atlantean, post-Kantian
anteau \an-tō\ see ²ANTO
anted \an-təd\ disenchanted—
also pasts of verbs listed at
⁵ANT
antel \ant-ᵊl\ see ANTLE
antelet \ant-lət\ mantelet,
plantlet
¹**anter** \änt-ər\ see ¹AUNTER
²**anter** \ant-ər\ antre, banter,
canter, cantor, chanter,
granter, grantor, plantar,

planter, ranter, scanter,
decanter, implanter, instanter,
levanter, transplanter,
trochanter, covenanter,
covenantor, disenchanter

¹antes \an-tēz\ Cervantes—*also
possessives and plurals of
nouns and third person
singular presents of verbs
listed at* ⁵ANTE

²antes \ans\ see ³ANCE

antey \ant-ē\ see ⁵ANTE

anth \anth\ amaranth,
coelacanth, perianth,
tragacanth

antha \an-thə\ Samantha,
polyantha, pyracantha

anthemum \an-thə-məm\
chrysanthemum,
mesembryanthemum

anther \an-thər\ anther, panther

anthropy \an-thrə-pē\
lycanthropy, misanthropy,
philanthropy

anthus \an-thəs\ acanthus,
ailanthus, dianthus,
agapanthus, amianthus,
polyanthus, Rhadamanthus

¹anti \änt-ē\ Brontë, jaunty,
monte, Monte, Monty,
vaunty, andante, Asante,
Ashanti, Chianti

²anti \ant-ē\ see ⁵ANTE

antial \an-chəl\ financial,
substantial, circumstantial,
consubstantial, insubstantial,
transsubstantial, unsubstantial,
supersubstantial

¹antian \änt-ē-ən\ see ONTIAN

²antian \ant-ē-ən\ see ANTEAN

¹antic \änt-ik\ see ONTIC

²antic \ant-ik\ antic, frantic,

mantic, Atlantic, bacchantic,
gigantic, pedantic, romantic,
semantic, Vedantic,
corybantic, geomantic,
hierophantic, necromantic,
sycophantic, transatlantic

anticist \ant-ə-səst\ fantasist,
Atlanticist, romanticist,
semanticist

antid \ant-əd\ mantid,
Quadrantid—*also pasts of
verbs listed at* ⁵ANT

antie \ant-ē\ see ⁵ANTE

antine \ant-°n\ see ²ANTON

¹anting \ant-iŋ\ anting, canting,
disenchanting

²anting \ənt-iŋ\ see UNTING

antis \ant-əs\ cantus, mantis,
Santos, Atlantis

antish \ant-ish\ dilettantish,
sycophantish

antle \ant-°l\ cantle, mantel,
mantle, quintal, dismantle,
quadrantal, consonantal,
covenantal, overmantel,
determinantal

antlet \ant-lət\ see ANTELET

antling \ant-liŋ\ bantling,
scantling

¹anto \än-tō\ Squanto, Toronto,
Esperanto, bel canto

²anto \an-tō\ canto, panto,
coranto, Otranto,
portmanteau, Esperanto, Strait
of Otranto

antom \ant-əm\ see ANTAM

¹anton \änt-°n\ see ONTON

²anton \ant-°n\ Anton, canton,
Canton, plantain, Scranton,
Stanton, adamantine

antor \ant-ər\ see ²ANTER

¹antos \an-təs\ see ANTIS

²**antos** \än-təs\ Santos,
    Propontis

antra \ən-trə\ tantra, yantra

antre \ant-ər\ see ²ANTER

antry \an-trē\ chantry, gantry,
    pantry

ants \ans\ see ³ANCE

antua \anch-wə\ mantua,
    Gargantua

antus \ant-əs\ see ANTIS

anty \ant-ē\ see ⁵ANTE

¹**anual** \an-yəl\ Daniel, spaniel,
    Nathaniel

²**anual** \an-yə-wəl\ annual,
    manual, Manuel, biannual,
    bimanual, Emanuel,
    Emmanuel, Immanuel, semi-
    annual, Victor Emmanuel

anuel \an-yəl\ see ²ANUAL

anular \an-yə-lər\ see
    ANNULAR

anulate \an-yə-lət\ see
    ANNULATE

¹**anum** \ā-nəm\ paynim,
    arcanum

²**anum** \an-əm\ per annum,
    solanum

¹**anus** \ā-nəs\ see AYNESS

²**anus** \an-əs\ see ANISE

anx \aŋs\ Manx, thanks, Grand
    Banks, phalanx—*also plurals*
    and possessives of nouns and
    third singular presents of
    verbs listed at ANK

¹**any** \ā-nē\ see AINY

²**any** \en-ē\ see ENNY

anyan \an-yən\ see ²ANION

anyard \an-yərd\ see ANIARD

anyon \an-yən\ see ²ANION

anz \ans\ see ³ANCE

¹**anza** \än-zə\ kwanza, Kwanza,
    Kwanzaa, Sancho Panza

²**anza** \an-zə\ stanza, zanza,
    bonanza, organza, Sancho
    Panza, extravaganza

anzaa \än-zə\ see ¹ANZA

anzee \an-zē\ see ANSY

anzer \än-sər\ see ONSOR

anzo \än-zō\ gonzo, garbanzo

anzy \än-zē\ bronzy, Ponzi,
    Swansea

¹**ao** \ā-ō\ see ¹EO

²**ao** \ō\ see ¹OW

³**ao** \au̇\ see ²OW

⁴**ao** \ä-ō\ Caliao, Mindanao

aoedic \ēd-ik\ see ¹EDIC

aoighis \āsh\ see ¹ECHE

aole \au̇-lē\ see ²OWLY

aône \ōn\ see ¹ONE

aori \au̇r-ē\ see OWERY

¹**aos** \au̇s\ see ²OUSE

²**aos** \ā-äs\ chaos, Laos

aotian \ō-shən\ see OTION

aow \au̇\ see ²OW

¹**ap** \äp\ see ¹OP

²**ap** \əp\ see UP

³**ap** \ap\ cap, chap, clap, crap,
    flap, frap, gap, gape, hap, Jap,
    JAP, knap, lap, Lapp, map,
    nap, nape, nappe, pap, rap,
    sap, scrap, slap, snap, strap,
    tap, trap, wrap, yap, Yap, zap,
    backslap, backwrap, blackcap,
    bootstrap, burlap, catnap,
    claptrap, dewlap, dognap,
    earflap, entrap, enwrap,
    firetrap, flatcap, foolscap,
    giddap, heeltap, hubcap,
    jockstrap, kidnap, kneecap,
    lagniappe, livetrap, madcap,
    mantrap, mayhap, mishap,
    mobcap, mousetrap, nightcap,
    pinesap, rattrap, recap, redcap,
    remap, riprap, satrap, shiplap,

shrink-wrap, skullcap, skycap,
snowcap, steel-trap, stopgap,
unsnap, unstrap, unwrap, verb
sap, whitecap, wiretap,
afterclap, gingersnap,
handicap, overlap, rattletrap,
thunderclap, verbum sap,
wentletrap, Venus's-flytrap

¹apa \äp-ə\ grappa, Joppa, papa,
poppa, tapa, Jalapa, jipijapa

²apa \ap-ə\ kappa, tapa, Phi
Beta Kappa

apable \ā-pə-bəl\ capable,
drapable, shapable, escapable,
incapable, inescapable

apal \ā-pəl\ see APLE

apas \äp-əs\ Chiapas—*also
possessives and plurals of
nouns listed at* ¹APA

apboard \ab-ərd\ see ABARD

¹ape \āp\ ape, cape, chape,
crape, crepe, drape, gape,
grape, jape, nape, rape, scape,
scrape, shape, tape, agape,
broomrape, cloudscape, duct
tape, escape, landscape,
moonscape, North Cape,
reshape, seascape, shipshape,
snowscape, streetscape,
townscape, transshape,
undrape, waveshape,
cityscape, masking tape,
waterscape, Xeriscape,
audiotape, stereotape,
videotape

²ape \ap\ see ³AP

³ape \äp-ē\ see OPPY

⁴ape \ap-ē\ see APPY

aped \āpt\ bell-shaped—*also
pasts of verbs listed at* ¹APE

apel \ap-əl\ see APPLE

apelin \ap-lən\ see APLAIN

apen \ā-pən\ capon, shapen,
unshapen

aper \ā-pər\ caper, draper,
gaper, paper, scraper, shaper,
taper, tapir, vapor, vapour,
curlpaper, endpaper, flypaper,
glasspaper, landscaper,
newspaper, notepaper,
sandpaper, skyscraper,
wallpaper, wastepaper, run-of-
paper

aperer \ā-pər-ər\ paperer,
taperer, vaporer

apery \ā-prē\ drapery, japery,
napery, papery, vapory,
sandpapery

apes \āps\ traipse, jackanapes—
*also plurals and possessives
of nouns and third singular
presents of verbs listed at*
¹APE

apey \ā-pē\ crepey, drapy,
grapey, grapy, kepi, scrapie

aph \af\ caff, calf, chaff, daff,
gaff, gaffe, graph, half, laugh,
quaff, raff, sclaff, staff, staph,
Waf, waff, agrafe, behalf,
carafe, chiffchaff, cowlstaff,
digraph, distaff, Falstaff,
flagstaff, giraffe, half-staff,
horselaugh, kenaf, mooncalf,
paraph, pikestaff, riffraff,
tipstaff, autograph, barograph,
bathyscaphe, cenotaph,
chronograph, cryptograph,
epigraph, epitaph, half-and-
half, hectograph, holograph,
homograph, hygrograph,
kymograph, lithograph,
logograph, micrograph,
monograph, pantograph,
paragraph, phonograph,

photograph, pictograph, polygraph, quarterstaff, seismograph, serigraph, shadowgraph, shandygaff, spectrograph, sphygmograph, telegraph, thermograph, typograph, understaff, cardiograph, choreograph, heliograph, ideograph, mimeograph, oscillograph, pseudepigraph, radiograph, chromolithograph, cinematograph, encephalograph, photomicrograph, radiotelegraph, electrocardiograph, electroencephalograph

aphael \af-ē-əl\ see APHIAL

¹aphe \āf\ see ¹AFE

²aphe \af\ see APH

apher \af-ər\ see ²AFFER

aphia \af-ē-ə\ see AFFIA

aphial \af-ē-əl\ Raphael, epitaphial

aphic \af-ik\ graphic, maffick, sapphic, traffic, digraphic, edaphic, serafic, triaphic, allographic, autographic, barographic, biographic, calligraphic, cartographic, cosmographic, cryptographic, demographic, epigraphic, epitaphic, ethnographic, geographic, hectographic, homographic, hydrographic, lithographic, logographic, mammographic, monographic, orthographic, pantographic, paragraphic, petrographic, phonographic, photographic, pictographic, polygraphic, pornographic, reprographic, stenographic, stratigraphic, telegraphic, tomographic, topographic, typographic, xerographic, bibliographic, choreographic, crystallographic, hagiographic, homolographic, iconographic, ideographic, lexicographic, oceanographic, stereographic, autobiographic, cinematographic, echocardiographic, historiographic, electroencephalographic

aphical \af-i-kəl\ graphical, biographical, cartographical, cosmographical, cryptographical, epigraphical, ethnographical, geographical, orthographical, petrographical, topographical, typographical, bibliographical, choreographical, hagiographical, iconographical, lexicographical, oceanographical, autobiographical, historiographical

aphics \af-iks\ graphics, demographics, micrographics, supergraphics

aphnis \af-nəs\ see AFTNESS

aphora \a-fə-rə\ anaphora, cataphora

api \äp-ē\ see OPPY

apid \ap-əd\ rapid, sapid, vapid

apie \ā-pē\ see APEY

apin \ap-ən\ see APPEN

apine \ap-ən\ see APPEN

apir \ā-pər\ see APER

apis \ā-pəs\ Apis, Priapus, Serapis

apist \ā-pəst\ papist, rapist, escapist, landscapist

aplain \ap-lən\ capelin, chaplain, chaplin, sapling

aple \ā-pəl\ maple, papal, staple

aples \ā-pəlz\ Naples—*also plurals and possessives of nouns and third person singular presents of verbs listed at* APLE

apless \ap-ləs\ hapless, napless, sapless, strapless

aplin \ap-lə-n\ see APLAIN

aply \ap-lē\ see APTLY

apnel \ap-nᵊl\ grapnel, shrapnel

apo \äp-ō\ capo, da capo, gestapo, Mount Apo

apolis \ap-ə-ləs\ Annapolis, Minneapolis, Indianapolis

apon \ā-pən\ see APEN

apor \ā-pər\ see APER

aporer \ā-pər-ər\ see APERER

apory \ā-prē\ see APERY

apour \ā-pər\ see APER

app \ap\ see ³AP

¹appa \äp-ə\ see ¹APA

²appa \ap-ə\ see ²APA

appable \ap-ə-bəl\ flappable, mappable, recappable, unflappable

appalli \äp-ə-lē\ see OPOLY

appe \ap\ see ³AP

apped \apt\ see APT

appen \ap-ən\ happen, lapin, rapine

¹apper \äp-ər\ see OPPER

²apper \ap-ər\ capper, clapper, crapper, dapper, flapper, knapper, rapper, sapper, scrapper, snapper, strapper,

tapper, wrapper, zapper, backslapper, catnapper, didapper, kidnapper, knee-slapper, petnapper, wiretapper, handicapper, snippersnapper, understrapper, whippersnapper

appet \ap-ət\ lappet, tappet

apphic \af-ik\ see APHIC

appie \äp-ē\ see OPPY

appily \ap-ə-lē\ happily, scrappily, snappily, unhappily

appiness \ap-ē-nəs\ happiness, sappiness, scrappiness, snappiness, unhappiness

apping \ap-iŋ\ capping, mapping, strapping, trapping, wrapping, kneecapping, petnapping

apple \ap-əl\ apple, chapel, dapple, grapple, scrapple, antechapel, mayapple, pineapple

apps \aps\ see APSE

appy \ap-ē\ crappy, flappy, gappy, happy, nappy, pappy, sappy, scrappy, snappy, zappy, satrapy, serape, slaphappy, unhappy, triggerhappy

aps \aps\ see APSE

apse \aps\ apse, chaps, craps, lapse, schnapps, taps, traps, collapse, elapse, perhaps, prolapse, relapse, synapse, time-lapse—*also plurals and possessives of nouns and third singular presents of verbs listed at* ³AP

apt \apt\ apt, napped, rapt, adapt, black-capped, coapt, dewlapped, enrapt, inapt, snowcapped, unapt, untapped, periapt—*also pasts of verbs listed at* ³AP

apter \ap-tər\ captor, chapter, raptor, adapter

aption \ap-shən\ caption, adaption, contraption

aptive \ap-tiv\ captive, adaptive, maladaptive, preadaptive

aptly \ap-lē\ aptly, haply, raptly, inaptly, unaptly

aptor \ap-tər\ see APTER

apture \ap-chər\ rapture, enrapture, recapture

apular \ap-yə-lər\ papular, scapular

apus \ā-pəs\ see APIS

¹apy \ā-pē\ see APEY

²apy \ap-ē\ see APPY

¹aq \äk\ see ¹OCK

²aq \ak\ see ²ACK

aqi \äk-ē\ see OCKY

¹aque \āk\ see ¹AKE

²aque \ak\ see ²ACK

aqui \äk-ē\ see OCKY

¹ar \er\ see ⁴ARE

²ar \ȯr\ see ¹OR

³ar \är\ ar, are, bar, barre, car, carr, char, charr, czar, far, gar, gnar, guar, jar, Lar, mar, moire, noir, our, par, parr, R, quare, Saar, scar, spar, SPAR, star, tar, tahr, Thar, tsar, tzar, yare, Adar, afar, ajar, all-star, armoire, attar, bazaar, beaux arts, Bihar, bizarre, boudoir, boxcar, boyar, briard, bulbar, Bulgar, bursar, canard, catarrh, Cathar, chukar, cigar, clochard, cougar, couloir, crossbar, crowbar, Dakar, daystar, debar, decare, devoir, dinar, disbar, drawbar, Dunbar, durbar, earthstar, Elgar, eschar, eyebar, feldspar, five-star, flatcar, four-star, fulmar, gazar, guitar, Gunnar, Hagar, handcar, Hoggar, horsecar, hussar, Invar, Ishtar, Kolar, Loire, Iyar, jack-tar, jowar, Khowar, lahar, Lamar, lekvar, lodestar, Magyar, memoir, Mizar, Mylar, Navarre, nightjar, paillard, peignoir, petard, Pindar, pissoir, planar, plantar, polestar, pourboire, pulsar, qintar, quasar, radar, railcar, rebar, Renoir, Safar, Samar, sandbar, scalar, shikar, shofar, sidebar, sidecar, sirdar, sitar, sofar, solar, sonar, streetcar, Svalbard, tramcar, trocar, unbar, volar, voussoir, Weimar, abattoir, acinar, Ahaggar, Aligarh, aide-memoire, au revoir, avatar, bete noire, beurre noir, bolivar, Bolivar, café noir, caviar, cinnabar, commissar, communard, coplanar, Côte d'Ivoire, cultivar, deciare, deodar, Dreyfusard, escolar, escritoire, exemplar, fluorspar, handlebar, insofar, isobar, Issachar, jacamar, jaguar, Kandahar, Kashgar, kilobar, Krasnodar, Malabar, megabar, megastar, millibar, minicar, montagnard, motorcar, Mudejar, muscle car, Myanmar, Nicobar, objet d'art, pinot noir, Qiqihar,

registrar, rent-a-car,
repertoire, reservoir, ricercar,
samovar, scimitar, seminar,
simular, steak tartare,
subahdar, superstar, tutelar,
turbocar, VCR, Veadar,
zamindar, Zanzibar,
budgerigar, conservatoire,
Gulf of Mannar, Hubli-
Dharwar, kala-azar,
Kathiawar, proseminar
¹**ara** \är-ə\ Kara, Laura, Mara,
Nara, para, vara, Asmara,
Bambara, begorra, Bukhara,
Camorra, Ferrara, Gomorrah,
saguaro, Samara, samsara,
tantara, tiara, capybara,
carbonara, Connemara,
deodara, Gemarara,
Guadalajara, Guanabara,
solfatara, tuatara, Ogasawara,
Sagamihara, Tarahumara,
Timisoara
²**ara** \er-ə\ see ¹ERA
³**ara** \ar-ə\ Clara, jarrah, Kara,
Sara, Sarah, Tara, Bukhara,
cascara, mascara, Sahara,
Samara, Tamara, tantara,
tiara, capybara, caracara,
marinara, Santa Clara
⁴**ara** \òr-ə\ see ²ORA
arab \ar-əb\ Arab, Carib, carob,
scarab, shatt-al-Arabk
arable \ar-ə-bəl\ arable,
bearable, parable, shareable,
spareable, wearable,
declarable, unbearable,
inenarrable
aracen \ar-ə-sən\ see ARISON
aracin \ar-ə-sən\ see ARISON
arad \ar-əd\ see ARID

araday \ar-əd-ē\ faraday,
parody
arage \ar-ij\ see ARRIAGE
aragon \ar-ə-gən\ paragon,
tarragon
¹**arah** \er-ə\ see ¹ERA
²**arah** \ar-ə\ see ¹ARROW
¹**aral** \ar-əl\ see ²ARREL
²**aral** \ər-əl\ see ERRAL
¹**aralee** \ar-ə-lē\ Marilee,
Saralee
²**aralee** \er-ə-lē\ see ARILY
¹**aran** \er-ən\ see ¹ARON
²**aran** \ar-ən\ see ²ARON
¹**arant** \er-ənt\ see ¹ARENT
²**arant** \ar-ənt\ see ²ARENT
¹**araoh** \er-ō\ see ²ERO
²**araoh** \ar-ō\ see ²ARROW
araph \ar-əf\ see ARIFF
aras \är-əs\ see ¹ORRIS
arass \ar-əs\ see ²ARIS
arat \ar-ət\ Barrett, carat, caret,
carrot, claret, garret, Garrett,
karat, parrot, disparate
arate \ar-ət\ see ARAT
¹**arative** \er-ət-iv\ declarative,
imperative
²**arative** \ar-ət-iv\ narrative,
comparative, declarative,
preparative, reparative
arator \ar-ət-ər\ barrator,
apparitor, comparator,
preparator
arb \ärb\ barb, barbe, carb,
darb, garb, bicarb, rhubarb
arbel \är-bəl\ see ¹ARBLE
arber \är-bər\ see ARBOR
arbered \är-bərd\ see ARBOARD
arbin \är-bən\ see ARBON
¹**arble** \är-bəl\ barbel, garble,
marble
²**arble** \òr-bəl\ see ORBEL

arboard \är-bərd\ barbered,
larboard, starboard,
astarboard, unbarbered
arbon \är-bən\ carbon, Harbin
arbor \är-bər\ arbor, barber,
harbor, Pearl Harbor
¹arc \äk\ see ¹OCK
²arc \ärk\ see ¹ARK
arca \är-kə\ see ¹ARKA
¹arce \ers\ scarce, Nez Percé
²arce \ärs\ see ¹ARSE
arcel \är-səl\ see ARSAL
arcener \ärs-nər\ larcener,
parcener, coparcener
arch \ärch\ arch, larch, march,
March, parch, starch,
cornstarch, frog-march,
countermarch
archal \är-kəl\ darkle, sparkle,
exarchal, monarchal,
hierarchal, matriarchal,
patriarchal
archate \är-kət\ see ARKET
arche \ärsh\ see ARSH
arched \ärcht\ arched,
parched—*also pasts of verbs
listed at* ARCH
archer \är-chər\ archer,
marcher, departure
arches \är-chəz\ Arches,
Marches
archic \är-kik\ anarchic,
autarchic, autarkic,
monarchic, tetrarchic,
hierarchic, oligarchic
archical \är-ki-kəl\ autarchical,
autarkical, monarchical,
oligarchical
archon \är-kən\ see ARKEN
archy \är-kē\ barky, charqui,
darky, larky, snarky, anarchy,
autarchy, autarky, dyarchy,

eparchy, exarchy, heptarchy,
malarkey, menarche,
monarchy, pentarchy,
squirearchy, tetrarchy,
triarchy, trierarchy, hierarchy,
matriarchy, patriarchy,
oligarchy
arck \ärk\ see ¹ARK
arco \är-kō\ arco, narco
arct \ärkt\ see ARKED
¹arctic \ärk-tik\ arctic, Arctic,
antarctic, Antarctic, Holarctic,
Nearctic, subarctic, Palearctic,
subantarctic
²arctic \ärt-ik\ see ¹ARTIC
arcy \är-sē\ farcy, Parsi
¹ard \ärd\ bard, barred, card,
chard, Dard, fard, guard, hard,
lard, nard, pard, sard, shard,
yard, Asgard, backyard,
bankcard, barnyard, Bernard,
blackguard, blowhard,
boatyard, bombard, boneyard,
brassard, brickyard, canard,
churchyard, courtyard,
deeryard, die-hard, diehard,
discard, dockyard, dooryard,
farmyard, filmcard, fireguard,
foreyard, foulard, Gerard,
graveyard, ill-starred,
jacquard, junkyard, lifeguard,
Lombard, mansard, Midgard,
milliard, mudguard,
noseguard, petard, placard,
postcard, poularde, rear guard,
rearguard, regard, retard,
ritard, safeguard, scorecard,
shipyard, spikenard, steelyard,
stockyard, switchyard, tabard,
tanyard, tiltyard, unbarred,
unguard, vanguard, vizard,
avant-garde, Beauregard,

bodyguard, boulevard,
disregard, goliard, Hildegard,
interlard, Kierkegaard,
Langobard, leotard,
Longobard, no-holds-barred,
lumberyard, Saint Bernard,
Savoyard, Scotland Yard,
self-regard, undercard,
unitard, camelopard—*also
pasts of verbs listed at* ³AR
²ard \är\ see ³AR
³ard \ȯrd\ see OARD
ardant \ärd-ᵊnt\ ardent,
guardant, regardant, retardant
arde \ärd\ see ¹ARD
¹arded \ärd-əd\ guarded,
mansarded, retarded,
unguarded—*also pasts of
verbs listed at* ¹ARD
²arded \ȯrd-əd\ corded, sordid,
swarded, warded—*also pasts
of verbs listed at* ²OARD
ardee \ȯrd-ē\ see ¹ORDY
¹arden \ärd-ᵊn\ Arden, Dardan,
garden, harden, pardon,
bombardon, caseharden, face-
harden, Kincardine
²arden \ȯrd-ᵊn\ cordon, Gordon,
Jordan, warden, churchwarden
ardener \ärd-nər\ gardener,
hardener, pardner, pardoner,
partner
ardent \ärd-ᵊnt\ see ARDANT
¹arder \ärd-ər\ ardor, carder,
guarder, harder, larder,
discarder, green-carder
²arder \ȯrd-ər\ see ORDER
ardi \ärd-ē\ see ARDY
¹ardian \ärd-ē-ən\ guardian,
Edwardian, Lombardian
²ardian \ȯrd-ē-ən\ see ORDION
ardic \ärd-ik\ bardic, Dardic,

Lombardic, Sephardic,
goliardic, Longobardic
ardine \ärd-ⁿ\ see ¹ARDEN
arding \ȯrd-iŋ\ see ¹ORDING
ardingly \ȯrd-iŋ-lē\ see
ORDINGLY
ardom \ärd-əm\ czardom,
stardom, superstardom
ardon \ärd-ᵊn\ see ¹ARDEN
ardoner \ärd-nər\ see ARDENER
ardor \ärd-ər\ see ¹ARDER
ardy \ärd-ē\ hardy, Hardy,
lardy, tardy, foolhardy,
Lombardy, Sephardi
¹are \er-ē\ see ¹ARY
²are \är\ see ³AR
³are \är-ē\ see ¹ARI
⁴are \er\ air, Ayr, bare, bear,
Blair, blare, chair, chare,
Claire, Clare, dare, Dare, e'er,
ere, err, eyre, fair, fare, flair,
flare, glair, glare, hair, hare,
Herr, heir, lair, mare, ne'er,
pair, pare, pear, prayer, quare,
rare, rear, scare, share, snare,
spare, square, stair, stare,
swear, tare, tear, their, there,
they're, vair, ware, wear,
weir, where, yare, affair,
aglare, airfare, Ajmer, Altair,
armchair, au pair, aware,
barware, Basseterre,
Baudelaire, beachwear,
beware, bricklayer, bugbear,
caneware, carfare, clayware,
cochair, coheir, compare,
compere, confrere, cookware,
corsair, courseware,
creamware, cudbear, day-care,
daymare, decare, declare,
delftware, despair, dishware,
éclair, elsewhere, enclair,

ensnare, eyewear, fanfare,
fieldfare, firmware, flatware,
Flaubert, footwear, forbear,
forebear, forswear,
foursquare, funfair, galère,
giftware, glassware, Great
Bear, Gruyère, hardware,
hectare, horsehair, impair,
infare, Khmer, Kildare,
knitwear, Lake Eyre, life-care,
longhair, loungewear,
menswear, meunière, midair,
mohair, Molière, neckwear,
nightmare, outstare, outwear,
Pierre, playwear, plein air,
plowshare, Poor Clare,
portiere, premiere, prepare,
pushchair, rainwear, redware,
repair, Saint Pierre, Sancerre,
shorthair, skiwear, sleepwear,
slipware, software,
somewhere, spongeware,
sportswear, stemware,
stoneware, swimwear,
threadbare, tinware, torchère,
tracklayer, trouvère, tuyere,
unfair, unhair, unswear,
Voltaire, warfare, welfare,
wheelchair, wirehair,
workfare, aftercare, air-to-air,
antiair, anywhere, bayadere,
bêche-de-mer, billionaire,
boutonniere, Camembert,
chinaware, crackleware,
cultivar, debonair, deciare, de
la Mare, Delaware, derriere,
dinnerware, disrepair,
doctrinaire, earthenware,
étagère, everywhere, Cape
Finisterre, fourragère,
Frigidaire, graniteware,
hollowware, ironware,

jasperware, kitchenware,
laissez-faire, Lake Saint Clair,
laquerware, legionnaire,
luminaire, lusterware,
maidenhair, mal de mer,
medicare, metalware,
millionaire, minaudière,
minelayer, Mon-Khmer,
Mousquetaire, nom de guerre,
otherwhere, outerwear,
overbear, overwear, potty-
chair, porte cochere,
questionnaire, rivière,
Robespierre, Santander, savoir
faire, self-aware, self-despair,
silverware, solitaire,
tableware, thoroughfare,
unaware, underwear,
vaporware, Venushair,
vivandière, willowware,
woodenware, yellowware,
zillionaire, chargé d'affaires,
chemin de fer,
commissionaire,
concessionaire, couturiere,
Croix de guerre, devil-may-
care, enamelware, memoriter,
pied-à-terre, ready-to-wear,
son et lumière, vin ordinaire,
cordon sanitaire

area \er-ē-ə\ see ARIA
¹areable \er-ə-bəl\ see
　　¹EARABLE
²areable \ar-ə-bəl\ see ARABLE
areal \er-ē-əl\ see ARIAL
¹arean \er-ē-ən\ see ¹ARIAN
²arean \ar-ē-ən\ see ²ARIAN
ared \erd\ see AIRED
aredness \ar-əd-nəs\ see
　　ARIDNESS
arel \ar-əl\ see ²ARREL
¹arely \er-lē\ see AIRLY

²arely \är-lē\ see ARLIE
arem \er-əm\ see ²ARUM
¹arence \er-əns\ clarence,
    Clarence, Terence, Terrance,
    Terrence, forbearance,
    transparence
²arence \ar-ən(ts)\ see ARENTS
¹arent \er-ənt\ daren't, errant,
    parent, aberrant, afferent,
    apparent, declarant, deferent,
    efferent, godparent,
    grandparent, inapparent,
    inerrant, knight-errant,
    sederunt, stepparent,
    transparent, semitransparent
²arent \ar-ənt\ arrant, daren't,
    parent, apparent, declarant,
    godparent, grandparent,
    stepparent, transparent,
    inapparent, semitransparent
¹aren't \er-ənt\ see ¹ARENT
²aren't \ar-ənt\ see ²ARENT
arents \ar-ən(t)s\ Barents,
    Clarence—*also plurals of*
    nouns listed at ²ARENT
¹arer \er-ər\ see ¹EARER
²arer \ar-ər\ see ³EARER
¹ares \erz\ see AIRS
²ares \ar-ēz\ Ares, caries, nares,
    Antares, Buenos Aires,
    primus inter pares—*also*
    plurals and possessives of
    nouns and third singular
    presents of verbs listed at
    ³ARRY
³ares \är-əs\ see ¹ORRIS
aret \ar-ət\ see ARAT
areve \är-və\ see ARVA
¹arey \ar-ē\ see ³ARRY
²arey \er-ē\ see ¹ARY
arez \är-əs\ see ¹ORRIS
¹arf \ärf\ barf, scarf

²arf \örf\ see ORPH
arfarin \ör-fə-rən\ warfarin,
    hematoporphyrin
argain \är-gən\ bargain, jargon,
    plea-bargain
arge \ärj\ barge, charge, large,
    marge, Marge, parge, sarge,
    sparge, targe, discharge,
    enlarge, litharge, recharge,
    surcharge, take-charge,
    uncharge, by and large,
    hypercharge, overcharge,
    supercharge, undercharge
argent \är-jənt\ argent, margent,
    sargent, sergeant
arger \är-jər\ charger,
    discharger, enlarger,
    recharger, supercharger,
    turbocharger,
    turbosupercharger
arget \är-gət\ argot, garget,
    target, nontarget
argle \är-gəl\ gargle, argle-
    bargle
argo \är-gō\ Argo, argot, cargo,
    Fargo, largo, Margo, Margot,
    embargo, supercargo
argon \är-gən\ see ARGAIN
¹argot \är-gət\ see ARGET
²argot \är-gō\ see ARGO
arh \är\ see ³AR
¹ari \är-ē\ Bari, gharry, laari,
    sari, scarry, sorry, starry,
    Bihari, curare, Imari, safari,
    scalare, shikari, tamari,
    calamari, cheboksary,
    Kalahari, Stradivari,
    zamindari, certiorari
²ari \er-ē\ see ¹ARY
³ari \ar-ē\ see ³ARRY
aria \er-ē-ə\ area, Beria, feria,
    kerria, varia, Bavaria,

Bulgaria, hysteria, malaria,
planaria, Samaria, adularia,
Carpentaria, cineraria,
fritillaria, laminaria,
luminaria, militaria,
sanguinaria, calceolaria, opera
seria, acetabularia

arial \er-ē-əl\ aerial, areal,
Ariel, burial, gharial,
glossarial, notarial, subaerial,
vicarial, actuarial, adversarial,
estuarial, secretarial,
prothonotarial

¹**arian** \er-ē-ən\ Arian, Aryan,
Carian, Marian, Marion,
parian, Parian, agrarian,
Aquarian, barbarian,
Bavarian, Bulgarian,
Cancerian, cesarean,
Caesarian, cnidarian,
frutarian, grammarian,
Hungarian, Khymerian,
librarian, Maid Marian,
ovarian, Pierian, riparian,
rosarian, Rotarian, sectarian,
Sumerian, Tartarean,
Tartarian, Tocharian,
Tractarian, Vulgarian,
Wagnerian, antiquarian,
apiarian, centenarian,
culinarian, Indo-Aryan,
jubilarian, lapidarian,
libertarian, millenarian,
nonsectarian, postlapsarian,
prelapsarian, Presbyterian,
proletarian, Rastafarian,
Ripuarian, Sabbatarian,
Sagittarian, sanitarian,
seminarian, trinitarian,
Trinitarian, unitarian,
Unitarian, vegetarian,
zoantharian, abecedarian,

Austro-Hungarian,
authoritarian, communitarian,
disciplinarian, documentarian,
egalitarian, equalitarian,
futilitarian, hereditarian,
humanitarian, majoritarian,
necessitarian, nonagenarian,
octogenarian, parliamentarian,
postmillinarian,
premillinarian, predestinarian,
radiolarian, Sacramentarian,
sexagenarian, totalitarian,
utilitarian, veterinarian,
establishmentarian,
inegalitarian, latitudinarian,
platitudinarian,
septuagenarian, solitudinarian,
uniformitarian, valetudinarian,
disestablishmentarian

²**arian** \ar-ē-ən\ Arian, Aryan,
carrion, clarion, Marian,
Marion, parian, Parian,
agrarian, Aquarian, barbarian,
Bavarian, Bulgarian,
caesarean, Caesarian,
cesarean, contrarian,
Hungarian, Megarian,
ovarian, rosarian, Tartarean,
Tartarian, Tocharian,
vulgarian, Indo-Aryan,
Rastafarian, Austro-Hungarian

ariance \ar-ē-əns\ tarriance,
variance, covariance,
vicariance

ariant \ar-ē-ənt\ variant,
vicariant

¹**ariat** \er-ē-ət\ heriot, lariat,
variate, bivariate, salariat,
vicariate, commissariat,
multivariate, proletariat,
secretariat, undersecretariat

²**ariat** \är-ē-ət\ see ¹AUREATE

³**ariat** \ar-ē-ət\ chariot, lariat,
  bivariate, salariat,
  commissariat, proletariat,
  Judas Iscariot
ariate \er-ē-ət\ see ¹ARIAT
arib \ar-əb\ see ARAB
aric \ar-ik\ barrack, carrack,
  Amharic, barbaric, Dinaric,
  Megaric, Pindaric, isobaric,
  Balearic
arice \ar-əs\ see ²ARIS
aricide \ar-ə-sīd\ see ARRICIDE
arid \ar-əd\ arid, farad,
  semiarid
aridin \ar-ə-dⁿn\ see ARRIDAN
aridness \ar-əd-nəs\ aridness,
  preparedness
¹**aried** \er-ēd\ see ERRIED
²**aried** \ar-ēd\ see ARRIED
ariel \er-ē-əl\ see ARIAL
¹**arier** \er-ē-ər\ see ERRIER
²**arier** \ar-ē-ər\ see ²ARRIER
aries \ar-ēz\ see ²ARES
ariff \ar-əf\ paraph, tariff
aril \ar-əl\ see ²ARREL
¹**arilee** \ar-ə-lē\ see ARALEE
²**arilee** \er-ə-lē\ see ARILY
arily \er-ə-lē\ Marilee, merrily,
  Merrily, Saralee, scarily,
  sterily, verily, contrarily,
  primarily, arbitrarily,
  customarily, dietarily,
  exemplarily, fragmentarily,
  honorarily, literarily,
  mercenarily, militarily,
  momentarily, necessarily,
  salutarily, sanguinarily,
  sanitarily, secondarily,
  temporarily, unitarily,
  voluntarily, contemporarily,
  elementarily, extemporarily,
  extraordinarily, hereditarily,

imaginarily, involuntarily,
preliminarily, rudimentarily,
subsidiarily, unnecessarily,
documentarily, evolutionarily,
revolutionarily
arin \är-ən\ see ¹ORIN
arinate \ar-ə-nət\ see ARONET
arinet \ar-ə-nət\ see ARONET
¹**aring** \ar-iŋ\ airing, Bering,
  fairing, flaring, glaring,
  herring, paring, raring,
  sparing, tearing, wearing,
  cheeseparing, childbearing,
  seafaring, time-sharing,
  unerring, unsparing,
  wayfaring
²**aring** \er-ən\ see ¹ARON
ario \er-ē-ō\ stereo, Ontario
¹**arion** \ar-ē-ən\ see ²ARIAN
²**arion** \er-ē-ən\ see ¹ARIAN
ariot \ar-ē-ət\ see ³ARIAT
arious \ar-ē-əs\ Arius, carious,
  Darious, scarious, various,
  Aquarius, burglarious,
  calcareous, contrarious,
  denarius, gregarious,
  guarnerius, hilarious,
  nefarious, precarious,
  senarius, vagarious, vicarious,
  multifarious, omnifarious,
  septenarius, Stradivarius,
  Sagittarius, temerarious
¹**aris** \är-əs\ see ¹ORRIS
²**aris** \ar-əs\ arras, arris, Clarice,
  harass, Harris, heiress, Paris,
  parous, varus, coheiress,
  embarrass, Polaris,
  disembarrass, millionairess,
  Lewis with Harris, plaster of
  paris
¹**arish** \er-ish\ bearish, cherish,

fairish, garish, perish,
squarish, nightmarish
²**arish** \ar-ish\ garish, marish,
parish
arison \ar-ə-sən\ characin,
garrison, Garrison, Harrison,
Saracen, warison, caparison,
comparison
arist \er-əst\ Marist, querist,
aquarist, pleinairist, scenarist,
apiarist—*also superlatives of
adjectives listed at* ⁴ARE
aritan \er-ət-ᵊn\ see ERATIN
aritor \ar-ət-ər\ see ARATOR
¹**arity** \er-ət-ē\ see ERITY
²**arity** \ar-ət-ē\ carroty, charity,
clarity, parity, rarity,
barbarity, disparity, hilarity,
imparity, polarity, unclarity,
vulgarity, angularity,
familiarity, insularity,
peculiarity, popularity,
regularity, similarity,
singularity, solidarity,
complementarity,
dissimilarity, irregularity,
particularity, unfamiliarity,
unpopularity
arium \er-ē-əm\ barium,
aquarium, herbarium,
sacrarium, samarium,
solarium, terrarium, velarium,
vivarium, cinerarium,
columbarium, honorarium,
leprosarium, oceanarium,
planetarium, sanitarium,
syllabarium, termitarium,
armamentarium
arius \er-ē-əs\ see ARIOUS
¹**ark** \ärk\ arc, ark, bark, Clark,
Clarke, dark, hark, lark, marc,
Marc, mark, Mark, marque,

narc, nark, park, Park, quark,
sark, shark, spark, stark,
aardvark, airpark, anarch,
ballpark, birchbark,
birthmark, Bismarck,
bookmark, debark, demark,
Denmark, earmark, embark,
endarch, exarch, footmark,
futhark, Graustark, hallmark,
ironbark, landmark, Lake
Clark, Lamarck, monarch,
ostmark, Ozark, Petrarch,
pitch-dark, Plutarch,
pockmark, postmark,
pressmark, pugmark,
reichsmark, remark, remarque,
Remarque, ringbark, seamark,
shagbark, sitzmark, skylark,
soapbark, tanbark, tetrarch,
tidemark, titlark, touchmark,
trademark, acritarch, cutty
sark, deutsche mark,
disembark, double-park,
hierarch, Joan of Arc,
matriarch, meadowlark,
metalmark, minipark,
oligarch, patriarch,
stringybark, telemark,
trierarch, watermark,
heresiarch, symposiarch
²**ark** \ȯrk\ see ²ORK
³**ark** \ərk\ see ¹ORK
¹**arka** \är-kə\ charka, parka,
anasarca, Hamilcar Barca
²**arka** \ər-kə\ see ¹URKA
arke \ärk\ see ¹ARK
arked \ärkt\ marked, chop-
marked, infarct, ripple-
marked, unremarked—*also
pasts of verbs listed at* ¹ARK
arken \är-kən\ darken, hearken
arker \är-kər\ barker, larker,

marker, parker, Parker,
sparker, bookmarker,
skylarker, nosey parker—*also
comparatives of adjectives
listed at* ¹ARK
arket \är-kət\ market, down-
market, mass-market,
newmarket, test-market,
upmarket, aftermarket,
hypermarket, matriarchate,
patriarchate, supermarket
arkey \är-kē\ see ARCHY
arkian \är-kē-ən\ Graustarkian,
Lamarckian, Monarchian
arkic \är-kik\ see ARCHIC
arking \är-kiŋ\ barking,
Barking, carking, parking,
loan-sharking
arkle \är-kəl\ see ARCHAL
arks \ärks\ Marks, parks—*also
plurals of nouns and third
person singular presents of
verbs listed at* ARK
arky \är-kē\ see ARCHY
arl \ärl\ carl, Carl, farl, gnarl,
jarl, Karl, marl, parle, quarrel,
snarl, ensnarl, housecarl,
unsnarl, Albemarle
arla \är-lə\ Carla, Darla, Karla,
Marla
arlan \ä-lən\ see ARLINE
arland \är-lənd\ garland,
Garland, Harland
arlatan \är-lət-ᵊn\ charlatan,
tarlatan
arlay \är-lē\ see ARLIE
arle \ärl\ see ARL
arlen \är-lən\ see ARLINE
arler \är-lər\ see ARLOR
arless \är-ləs\ Carlos, parlous,
scarless, starless
arlet \är-lət\ charlotte,

Charlotte, harlot, scarlet,
starlet, varlet
arley \är-lē\ see ARLIE
arlic \är-lik\ garlic, pilgarlic
arlie \är-lē\ barley, charlie,
Charlie, gnarly, Harley,
marly, parlay, parley, snarly,
yarely, bizarrely, Mr. Charlie
arlin \är-lən\ see ARLINE
arline \är-lən\ Arlen, carline,
Harlan, marlin, Marlin,
marline, Marlyn
arling \är-liŋ\ carling, darling,
Darling, starling
arlor \är-lər\ parlor, quarreler,
snarler
arlos \är-ləs\ see ARLESS
arlot \är-lət\ see ARLET
arlotte \är-lət\ see ARLET
arlous \är-ləs\ see ARLESS
arlow \är-lō\ Barlow, Harlow
arly \är-lē\ see ARLIE
arlyn \ä-lən\ see ARLINE
¹arm \ärm\ arm, barm, charm,
farm, harm, smarm, alarm,
disarm, firearm, forearm,
gendarme, gisarme, poor
farm, rearm, sidearm, stiff-
arm, straight-arm, strong-arm,
tonearm, unarm, yardarm,
overarm, underarm
²arm \äm\ see ¹OM
³arm \òrm\ see ²ORM
¹arma \är-mə\ dharma, karma,
Parma
²arma \ər-mə\ see ERMA
arman \är-mən\ barman,
Carmen, carmine, Harmon
armed \ärmd\ armed, charmed,
unarmed—*also pasts of verbs
listed at* ¹ARM
armen \är-mən\ see ARMAN

arment \är-mənt\ garment,
varmint, debarment,
disbarment, undergarment,
overgarment

¹**armer** \är-mər\ armor,
charmer, farmer, harmer,
disarmer

²**armer** \or-mər\ see ¹ORMER

armic \ər-mik\ see ERMIC

armine \är-mən\ see ARMAN

¹**arming** \är-miŋ\ charming,
farming, alarming, disarming

²**arming** \or-miŋ\ see ORMING

armint \är-mənt\ see ARMENT

armless \ärm-ləs\ armless,
charmless, harmless

armoir \är-mər\ see ¹ARMER

armon \är-mən\ see ARMAN

army \är-mē\ army, barmy,
smarmy

¹**arn** \ärn\ Arne, barn, darn,
Marne, tarn, yarn, carbarn,
lucarne

²**arn** \orn\ see ²ORN

arna \ər-nə\ see ERNA

arnal \ärn-ᵊl\ see ARNEL

arnate \är-nət\ Barnet, garnet,
discarnate, incarnate

¹**arne** \ärn\ see ¹ARN

²**arne** \är-nē\ see ARNY

arnel \ärn-ᵊl\ carnal, charnel,
darnel

¹**arner** \är-nər\ darner, garner,
yarner

²**arner** \or-nər\ see ORNER

arness \är-nəs\ harness,
bizarreness

arnet \är-nət\ see ARNATE

arney \är-nē\ see ARNY

arnhem \är-nəm\ see ARNUM

arning \or-niŋ\ see ORNING

arnish \är-nish\ garnish, tarnish,
varnish

arnum \är-nəm\ Arnhem,
Barnum

arny \är-nē\ Barney, barny,
blarney, carny, Killarney,
chili con carne

¹**aro** \er-ō\ see ²ERO

²**aro** \ar-ō\ see ²ARROW

³**aro** \är-ə\ see ¹ARA

⁴**aro** \är-ō\ see ¹ORROW

arob \ar-əb\ see ARAB

arody \ar-əd-ē\ see ARADAY

¹**aroe** \ar-ō\ see ²ARROW

²**aroe** \er-ō\ see ²ERO

arol \ar-əl\ see ²ARREL

¹**arold** \ar-əld\ Darold, Harold

²**arold** \er-əld\ see ERALD

arole \ar-əl\ see ²ARREL

arom \er-əm\ see ²ARUM

¹**aron** \er-ən\ Aaron, Charon,
Erin, garron, heron, perron,
raring, Sharon, Sharron,
sierran, rose of Sharon, sub-
Saharan

²**aron** \ar-ən\ Aaron, baron,
barren, Charon, garron,
Sharon, Sharron, rose of
Sharon, sub-Saharan

aronet \ar-ə-nət\ baronet,
carinate, clarinet

¹**arous** \er-əs\ see ERROUS

²**arous** \ar-əs\ see ²ARIS

¹**arp** \ärp\ carp, harp, scarp,
sharp, tarp, cardsharp, escarp,
Jews harp, Autoharp,
vibraharp

²**arp** \orp\ see ORP

arpen \är-pən\ sharpen, tarpon

arper \är-pər\ carper, harper,
scarper, sharper, cardsharper

arpie \är-pē\ see ARPY

arpon \är-pən\ see ARPEN
arpy \är-pē\ harpy, sharpie
arque \ärk\ see ¹ARK
arquetry \är-kə-trē\ marquetry,
　parquetry
arqui \är-kē\ see ARCHY
arrable \ar-ə-bəl\ see ARABLE
¹arrack \ar-ik\ see ARIC
²arrack \ar-ək\ arrack, barrack,
　carrack
arragon \ar-ə-gən\ see ARAGON
arral \ar-əl\ see ²ARREL
arram \ar-əm\ see ²ARUM
¹arrant \ar-ənt\ see ²ARENT
²arrant \òr-ənt\ see ORRENT
arras \ar-əs\ see ²ARIS
arrass \ar-əs\ see ²ARIS
arrative \ar-ət-iv\ see ²ARATIVE
arrator \ar-ət-ər\ see ARATOR
arre \är\ see ³AR
arred \ärd\ see ¹ARD
¹arrel \òrl\ see ³ORAL
²arrel \ar-əl\ Aral, aril, barrel,
　Beryl, carol, Carol, Carole,
　Caryl, carrel, Carroll, Darrel,
　Darrell, Darryl, Daryl, Errol,
　Karol, parol, parral, parrel,
　apparel, cracker-barrel,
　double-barrel
arreler \är-lər\ see ARLOR
arrell \ar-əl\ see ²ARREL
arrely \är-lē\ see ARLIE
¹arren \ar-ən\ see ²ARON
²arren \òr-ən\ see ²ORIN
³arren \är-ən\ see ¹ORIN
arrener \òr-ə-nər\ see ORONER
arreness \är-nəs\ see ARNESS
arret \ar-ət\ see ARAT
arrett \ar-ət\ see ARAT
arrh \är\ see ³AR
arriage \ar-ij\ carriage,
　marriage, disparage,
miscarriage, intermarriage,
undercarriage
arriance \ar-ē-əns\ see ARIANCE
arricide \ar-ə-sīd\ parricide,
　acaricide
arridan \ar-ə-dᵊn\ harridan,
　cantharidin
arrie \ar-ē\ see ³ARRY
arried \ar-ēd\ harried, married,
　varied, unmarried
¹arrier \òr-ē-ər\ see ARRIOR
²arrier \ar-ē-ər\ barrier, carrier,
　farrier, harrier, varier,
　ballcarrier, spear-carrier
arrion \ar-ē-ən\ see ²ARIAN
arrior \òr-ē-ər\ quarrier, sorrier,
　warrior
arris \ar-əs\ see ²ARIS
arrison \ar-ə-sən\ see ARISON
arro \är-ō\ see ¹ORROW
arroll \ar-əl\ see ²ARREL
arron \ar-ən\ see ²ARON
arrot \ar-ət\ see ARAT
arroty \ar-ət-ē\ see ²ARITY
arrow \ar-ō\ aero, arrow,
　barrow, Darrow, Faeroe, faro,
　Faroe, farrow, harrow,
　Harrow, marrow, narrow,
　pharaoh, sparrow, taro, tarot,
　yarrow, handbarrow, Point
　Barrow, wheelbarrow
arrowy \ar-ə-wē\ arrowy,
　marrowy
¹arry \är-ē\ see ¹ARI
²arry \òr-ē\ see ORY
³arry \ar-ē\ Barrie, Barry,
　Carey, Carrie, carry, Cary,
　chary, Gary, Garry, gharry,
　harry, Harry, Larry, marry,
　nary, parry, Shari, tarry,
　glengarry, miscarry, safari,
　shikari, cash-and-carry, hari-

kari, intermarry, Stradivari;
Tom, Dick, and Harry

arryl \ar-əl\ see ²ARREL

ars \ärz\ Lars, Mars, ours—*also
plurals and possessives of
nouns and third person
singular presents of verbs
listed at* ³AR

arsal \är-səl\ parcel, versal,
tarsal, metatarsal

¹arse \ärs\ arse, farce, marse,
parse, sparse

²arse \ärz\ see ARS

arsh \ärsh\ harsh, marsh,
demarche

arshal \är-shəl\ see ARTIAL

arshall \är-shəl\ see ARTIAL

arshen \är-shən\ harshen,
martian

arsi \är-sē\ see ARCY

arsis \är-səs\ see ARSUS

arsle \äs-əl\ see OSSAL

arson \ärs-ᵊn\ arson, Carson,
parson

arsus \är-səs\ arsis, tarsus,
Tarsus, catharsis, metatarsus

¹art \ärt\ art, Art, Bart, cart,
chart, Chartres, dart, hart,
Harte, heart, kart, mart, part,
Sartre, scart, smart, start, tart,
apart, blackheart, compart,
depart, Descartes, dispart,
dogcart, Earhart, flowchart,
forepart, go-cart, greenheart,
handcart, Hobart, impart,
jump-start, Mozart,
mouthpart, outsmart, oxcart,
oxheart, pushcart, rampart,
redstart, restart, street-smart,
Stuttgart, sweetheart, tipcart,
upstart, à la carte, anti-art,
applecart, Bonaparte,

counterpart, heart-to-heart,
purpleheart, underpart,
upperpart

²art \ȯrt\ see ¹ORT

arta \är-tə\ Marta, Sparta,
Djarkarta, Magna Carta, Santa
Marta, Surakarta, yogyakarta

artable \ärt-ə-bəl\ see ARTIBLE

¹artan \ärt-ᵊn\ see ARTEN

²artan \ȯrt-ᵊn\ see ORTEN

artar \ärt-ər\ see ¹ARTER

¹arte \ärt-ē\ see ¹ARTY

²arte \ärt\ see ¹ART

¹arted \ärt-əd\ see EARTED

²arted \ȯrt-əd\ see ORTED

arten \ärt-ᵊn\ Barton, carton,
hearten, marten, martin,
Martin, smarten, Spartan,
tartan, baum marten,
dishearten, Dumbarton,
freemartin, Saint Martin, Sint
Maarten, kindergarten

¹arter \ärt-ər\ barter, carter,
Carter, charter, darter, garter,
martyr, starter, tartar,
nonstarter, self-starter,
protomartyr—*also
comparatives of adjectives
listed at* ¹ART

²arter \ȯt-ər\ see ¹ATER

³arter \ȯrt-ər\ see ORTER

artern \ȯt-ərn\ see AUTERNE

artery \ärt-ə-rē\ artery, martyry

artes \ärt\ see ¹ART

artford \ärt-fərd\ Hartford,
Hertford

arth \ärth\ garth, Garth, hearth,
Hogarth

arti \ärt-ē\ see ¹ARTY

artial \är-shəl\ marshal,
Marshal, Marshall, martial,

Martial, partial, court-martial, impartial

artian \är-shən\ see ARSHEN

artible \ärt-ə-bəl\ partible, startable, impartible, restartable

¹**artic** \ärt-ik\ arctic, Arctic, antarctic, Antarctic, cathartic, Nearctic, Palearctic

²**artic** \ort-ik\ quartic, aortic

article \ärt-i-kəl\ article, particle, microparticle

artile \ort-ᵊl\ see ORTAL

artily \ärt-ᵊl-ē\ artily, heartily

artin \ärt-ᵊn\ see ARTEN

arting \ärt-iŋ\ carting, charting, karting, parting, starting, flowcharting, self-starting

artisan \ärt-ə-zən\ artisan, bartizan, partisan, bipartisan, nonpartisan

artist \ärt-əst\ artist, chartist, Chartist, Bonapartist

artizan \ärt-ə-zən\ see ARTISAN

artless \ärt-ləs\ artless, heartless

artlet \ärt-lət\ martlet, partlet, tartlet

¹**artly** \ärt-lē\ partly, smartly, tartly

²**artly** \ort-lē\ see ²ORTLY

artment \ärt-mənt\ apartment, compartment, department

artner \ärt-nər\ partner, kindergartner

¹**arton** \ort-ᵊn\ see ORTON

²**arton** \ärt-ᵊn\ see ARTEN

artre \ärt\ see ¹ART

artres \ärt\ see ¹ART

artridge \är-trij\ cartridge, partridge

¹**arts** \är\ see ³AR

²**arts** \ärts\ Hartz—*also plurals*

and possessives of nouns and third person singular presents of verbs listed at ¹ART

arture \är-chər\ see ARCHER

¹**arty** \ärt-ē\ arty, hearty, party, smarty, tarty, Astarte, ex parte, Havarti, Buonaparte, commedia del l'arte

²**arty** \ort-ē\ see ORTY

artyr \ärt-ər\ see ¹ARTER

artyry \ärt-ə-rē\ see ARTERY

¹**artz** \orts\ see ORTS

²**artz** \ärts\ see ²ARTS

aru \ä-rü\ Bukaru, Johore Bahru, Pakan Baru

¹**arum** \är-əm\ larum, alarum

²**arum** \er-əm\ arum, carom, harem, Sarum, Muharram, harum-scarum, arbiter elegantiarum

arus \ar-əs\ see ²ARIS

arva \är-və\ larva, Marva, parve, pareve

arval \är-vəl\ see ARVEL

¹**arve** \ärv\ carve, starve, varve

²**arve** \är-və\ see ARVA

arvel \är-vəl\ carvel, larval, marvel

arven \är-vən\ carven, Marvin, Caernarvon

arvin \är-vən\ see ARVEN

arvon \är-vən\ see ARVEN

¹**ary** \er-ē\ aerie, aery, airy, berry, bury, Carey, Cary, Cherie, cherry, Cherry, chary, clary, dairy, Derry, faerie, fairy, ferry, Gary, Garry, Gerry, glairy, glary, hairy, Jere, Jeri, Jerrie, Jerry, kerry, Kerry, Mary, marry, merry, Merry, nary, perry, Perry, prairie, quaere, query, scary,

serry, Shari, Sheri, Sherrie,
sherry, Sherry, skerry, terry,
Terry, vary, very, wary,
wherry, baneberry, barberry,
bayberry, bearberry, bilberry,
blackberry, blaeberry,
blueberry, Bradbury,
bunchberry, Burberry, canary,
Canary, chokeberry,
chokecherry, cloudberry,
contrary, coralberry,
costmary, cowberry,
cranberry, crowberry,
deerberry, dewberry, equerry,
gooseberry, ground-cherry,
hackberry, hegari, inkberry,
Juneberry, knobkerrie, library,
mulberry, nondairy,
pokeberry, primary, raspberry,
rosemary, Rosemary, scalare,
shadberry, sheepberry,
snowberry, soapberry,
strawberry, summary,
teaberry, tilbury, twinberry,
unwary, vagary, wolfberry,
youngberry, actuary,
adversary, airy-fairy,
ancillary, antiquary, apiary,
arbitrary, aviary, axillary,
beriberi, bestiary, biliary,
boysenberry, breviary,
budgetary, calamari,
calamary, candleberry,
Canterbury, capillary,
cartulary, cassowary,
catenary, cautionary, cavitary,
cemetery, centenary,
certiorari, chartulary,
checkerberry, chinaberry,
ciliary, cinerary, cometary,
commentary, commissary,
condottiere, corollary,

coronary, culinary, customary,
dictionary, dietary, dignitary,
dingleberry, dromedary,
dysentery, elderberry,
emissary, estuary, farkleberry,
February, formicary,
formulary, fragmentary,
fritillary, functionary,
funerary, honorary,
huckleberry, intermarry,
janissary, January, lamasery,
lapidary, lectionary,
legendary, legionary, limitary,
lingonberry, literary,
loganberry, luminary,
mammillary, mandatary,
maxillary, medullary,
mercenary, miliary, military,
millenary, milliary, millinery,
miserere, missionary,
momentary, monastery,
monetary, mortuary,
necessary, ordinary, ossuary,
papillary, parcenary,
partridgeberry, pensionary,
phalanstery, pigmentary,
plagiary, planetary,
Pondicherry, prebendary,
presbytery, pulmonary,
pupillary, quaternary,
questionary, reliquary,
rowanberry, salivary,
salmonberry, salutary,
sanctuary, sanguinary,
sanitary, secondary, secretary,
sedentary, seminary,
serviceberry, silverberry,
solitary, stationary, stationery,
statuary, Stradivari,
subcontrary, sublunary,
sugarberry, sumptuary,
syllabary, temporary,

termitary, tertiary, textuary,
thimbleberry, Tipperary, Tom
and Jerry, topiary, tributary,
tutelary, unitary, urinary,
vestiary, visionary, voluntary,
vulnerary, Waterbury,
whortleberry, winterberry,
ablutionary, accretionary,
antiphonary, apothecary,
bicentenary, bilmillenary,
concessionary, conclusionary,
concretionary, confectionary,
confectionery, consigliere,
constabulary, contemporary,
convulsionary, coparcenary,
depository, delusionary,
digressionary, disciplinary,
discretionary, distributary,
diversionary, electuary,
epistolary, exclusionary,
expansionary, expeditionary,
extemporary, extortionary,
extraordinary, fiduciary,
hereditary, illusionary,
imaginary, incendiary,
inflationary, insanitary,
intercalary, involuntary,
itinerary, judiciary,
libationary, obituary,
officiary, pecuniary,
petitionary, precautionary,
preliminary, presidiary,
previsionary, probationary,
proprietary, provisionary,
reactionary, recessionary,
reflationary, residuary,
reversionary, revisionary,
stagflationary, stipendiary,
subliterary, subsidiary,
subversionary, tercentenary,
traditionary, tumultuary,
unnecessary, veterinary,

vocabulary, voluptuary,
abolitionary, beneficiary,
consuetudinary, deflationary,
devolutionary, disinflationary,
domiciliary, eleemosynary,
elocutionary, evidentiary,
evolutionary, extraliterary,
intermediary, paramilitary,
penitentiary, quatercentenary,
revolutionary, semicentenary,
semilegendary,
sesquicentenary, superciliary,
supernumerary,
tintinnabulary,
transdisciplinary,
usufructuary, valetudinary,
interdisciplinary,
plenipotentiary,
counterrevolutionary

²ary \ar-ē\ see ³ARRY

³ary \är-ē\ see ¹ARI

¹aryan \er-ē-ən\ see ¹ARIAN

²aryan \ar-ē-ən\ see ²ARIAN

aryl \ar-əl\ see ²ARREL

¹as \ash\ see ³ASH

²as \as\ see ³ASS

³as \az\ see AZZ

⁴as \ä\ see ¹A

⁵as \äsh\ see ¹ASH

⁶as \äz\ see ¹OISE

⁷as \əz\ see ¹EUSE

⁸as \äs\ see ¹OS

⁹as \ȯ\ see ¹AW

¹asa \äs-ə\ casa, fossa, glossa,
Lhasa, Ossa, kielbasa,
Kinshasa, Landrace,
Mombasa, tabula rasa

²asa \äz-ə\ see ¹AZA

³asa \as-ə\ see ASSA

¹asable \ā-zə-bəl\ grazeable,
persuasible, paraphrasable

²asable \ā-sə-bəl\ see ACEABLE

¹asal \ā-səl\ basal, Basil, stay
    sail, forestay sail
²asal \ā-zəl\ basal, Basil, hazel,
    Hazel, nasal, phrasal,
    appraisal, Azazel
asally \āz-lē\ see AISLEY
asca \as-kə\ see ASKA
ascal \as-kəl\ paschal, rascal
ascan \as-kən\ see ASKIN
ascar \as-kər\ see ASKER
¹ascence \ās-ᵊns\ nascence,
    complacence, complaisance,
    renascence
²ascence \as-ᵊns\ nascence,
    renascence
¹ascent \as-ᵊnt\ nascent, passant,
    renascent
²ascent \ās-ᵊnt\ see ACENT
¹asch \ask\ see ASK
²asch \äsh\ see ¹ASH
³asch \òsh\ see ²ASH
aschal \as-kəl\ see ASCAL
¹ascia \ā-shə\ see ACIA
²ascia \ash-ə\ see ²ASHA
ascible \as-ə-bəl\ see ASSABLE
ascicle \as-i-kəl\ see ASSICAL
¹asco \äs-kō\ see OSCOE
²asco \as-kō\ fiasco, Tabasco
ascon \as-kən\ see ASKIN
ascot \as-kət\ see ASKET
ascus \as-kəs\ Damascus,
    Velazquez
¹ase \ās\ see ¹ACE
²ase \āz\ see ¹AZE
³ase \äz\ see ¹OISE
asel \äz-əl\ see OZZLE
ased \āst\ see ACED
aseless \ā-sləs\ see ACELESS
aseman \ā-smən\ see ACEMAN
asement \ās-mənt\ basement,
    casement, debasement,
    bargain-basement

¹aser \ā-sər\ see ¹ACER
²aser \ā-zər\ see AZER
asey \ā-sē\ see ACY
¹ash \äsh\ bosh, cosh, Fosh,
    frosh, gosh, gouache, josh,
    Mâche, nosh, posh, quash,
    slosh, squash, swash, tosh,
    wash, awash, backwash,
    blackwash, cohosh, czardas,
    Dias, Diaz, downwash,
    eyewash, galosh, ganache,
    goulash, kibosh, midrash,
    mishmash, mouthwash,
    musquash, panache, rainwash,
    Siwash, whitewash, wish-
    wash, hamantasch,
    mackintosh, McIntosh
²ash \òsh\ Bosch, Foch, gosh,
    grosz, quash, slosh, squash,
    swash, wash, awash,
    backwash, Balkhash,
    blackwash, brainwash,
    brioche, Bydgoszcz,
    downwash, eyewash,
    hogwash, Iasi, mouthwash,
    outwash, rainwash, Siwash,
    whitewash, wish-wash,
    hamantasch
³ash \ash\ ash, bash, brash,
    cache, cash, clash, crash,
    dash, fash, flash, gash, gnash,
    hash, lash, mash, pash, plash,
    rash, sash, slash, smash,
    splash, stash, thrash, thresh,
    trash, abash, backlash,
    backsplash, Balkhash, calash,
    Chumash, czardas, encash,
    eyelash, goulash, mishmash,
    moustache, mustache,
    panache, potash, rehash,
    slapdash, soutache, stramash,
    tongue-lash, unlash, whiplash,

balderdash, calabash,
succotash

¹asha \äsh-ə\ kasha, pasha,
quassia, Falasha

²asha \ash-ə\ cassia, fascia,
pasha

ashan \ash-ən\ see ASSION

¹ashed \ósht\ sloshed,
stonewashed, unwashed—*also
pasts of verbs listed at* ²ASH

²ashed \asht\ dashed, Rasht,
smashed, unabashed—*also
pasts of verbs listed at* ³ASH

ashen \ash-ən\ see ASSION

¹asher \äsh-ər\ josher, nosher,
squasher, swasher, washer,
dishwasher

²asher \ósh-ər\ swasher,
washer, brainwasher,
dishwasher, whitewasher

³asher \ash-ər\ Asher, basher,
brasher, clasher, crasher,
dasher, flasher, masher,
rasher, slasher, smasher,
splasher, thrasher, gate-
crasher, haberdasher

ashew \a-shü\ cachou, cashew

¹ashi \äsh-ē\ see ¹ASHY

²ashi \ash-ē\ see ²ASHY

ashing \ash-iŋ\ crashing,
dashing, flashing, mashing,
slashing, smashing

ashion \ash-ən\ see ASSION

asht \asht\ see ²ASHED

¹ashy \äsh-ē\ dashi, Iasi, Kashi,
squashy, washy, Funabashi,
Lubumbashi, Toyohashi,
wishy-washy

²ashy \ash-ē\ ashy, flashy,
Kashi, splashy, trashy

¹asi \äs-ē\ see ¹OSSY

²asi \äz-ē\ see ¹AZI

³asi \ósh\ see ²ASH

⁴asi \ash-ē\ see ¹ASHY

asia \ā-zhə\ Asia, aphasia,
Eurasia, fantasia, Malaysia,
Anastasia, Australasia,
euthanasia, antonomasia

¹asian \ā-shən\ see ¹ATION

²asian \ā-zhən\ see ASION

asible \ā-zə-bəl\ see ¹ASABLE

asic \ā-zik\ basic, phasic,
biphasic, diphasic,
multiphasic, polyphasic

asid \as-əd\ see ACID

asie \ā-sē\ see ACY

¹asil \as-əl\ see ²ASSEL

²asil \az-əl\ see AZZLE

³asil \ās-əl\ see ¹ASAL

⁴asil \āz-əl\ see ²ASAL

⁵asil \äz-əl\ see OZZLE

asin \ās-ᵊn\ see ¹ASON

¹asing \ā-siŋ\ see ACING

²asing \ā-ziŋ\ see AISING

asion \ā-zhən\ Asian, suasion,
abrasion, Caucasian,
corrasion, dissuasion,
equation, Eurasian, evasion,
invasion, occasion,
persuasion, pervasion,
Amerasian, Athanasian,
dermabrasion, Rabelaisian,
overpersuasion

asional \āzh-nəl\ equational,
occasional

¹asis \ā-səs\ basis, stasis, oasis

²asis \as-əs\ see ²ASSIS

asium \ā-zē-əm\ dichasium,
gymnasium

asive \ā-siv\ suasive, abrasive,
assuasive, corrasive,
dissuasive, embracive,
evasive, invasive, persuasive,
pervasive, noninvasive

ask \ask\ ask, bask, Basque,
cask, casque, flask, mask,
masque, Pasch, task, unmask,
photomask
aska \as-kə\ Alaska, Itasca,
Nebraska, Athabaska
askan \as-kən\ see ASKIN
asked \ast\ see ²AST
asker \as-kər\ lascar, masker,
masquer, Madagascar
asket \as-kət\ ascot, basket,
casket, gasket, breadbasket,
handbasket, wastebasket,
workbasket
askin \as-kən\ gascon, gaskin,
Alaskan, Tarascan,
Athapaskan
asking \as-kiŋ\ multitasking—
*also present participles of
verbs listed at* ASK
asm \az-əm\ chasm, plasm,
spasm, chiasm, orgasm,
phantasm, sarcasm, chiliasm,
ectoplasm, pleonasm,
enthusiasm, blepharospasm,
iconoclasm
asma \az-mə\ asthma, plasma,
chiasma, miasma, phantasma
asman \az-mən\ see ASMINE
asmine \az-mən\ jasmine,
Tasman
asn't \əz-ᵊnt\ doesn't, wasn't
¹aso \as-ō\ see ¹ASSO
²aso \äs-ō\ see ²ASSO
¹ason \ās-ᵊn\ basin, caisson,
chasten, hasten, Jason, mason,
Mason, Foxe Basin,
Freemason, Great Basin,
stonemason, washbasin,
diapason, Donets Basin
²ason \āz-ᵊn\ see AZON
asp \asp\ asp, clasp, gasp,

grasp, hasp, rasp, enclasp,
handclasp, last-gasp, unclasp
asper \as-pər\ clasper, jasper,
Jasper
asperate \as-prət\ aspirate,
exasperate
aspirate \as-prət\ see ASPERATE
asque \ask\ see ASK
asquer \as-kər\ see ASKER
¹ass \ās\ see ¹ACE
²ass \äs\ see ¹OS
³ass \as\ as, bass, Bass, brass,
class, crass, frass, gas, glass,
grass, has, lass, mass, pass,
sass, sauce, strass, tace, tasse,
trass, vas, wrasse, admass,
alas, Alsace, amass, avgas,
bagasse, band-pass, bluegrass,
bromegrass, bunchgrass,
bypass, cordgrass, crabgrass,
crevasse, cuirass, cut-grass,
declass, degas, Donbas,
Drygas, eelgrass, en masse,
eyeglass, first-class,
groundmass, harass, high-
class, hourglass, impasse,
knotgrass, Kuzbass, landmass,
Madras, morass, outclass,
outgas, palliasse, Petras,
plateglass, repass, ribgrass,
rubasse, ryegrass, sandglass,
shortgrass, spyglass, subclass,
sunglass, surpass, switchgrass,
tallgrass, teargas, trespass,
Troas, wineglass, wiseass,
witchgrass, biogas, biomass,
demiglace, demitasse,
fiberglass, gallowglass,
gravitas, Hallowmas,
hardinggrass, hippocras,
isinglass, Kiribati,
lemongrass, lower-class,

middle-class, overpass,
pampas grass, peppergrass,
Plexiglas, sassafras,
superclass, underclass,
underpass, upper-class,
weatherglass

assa \as-ə\ massa, Lake Nyasa,
Manasseh

assable \as-ə-bəl\ chasuble,
passable, passible,
impassable, impassible,
irascible

assail \äs-əl\ see OSSAL

assailer \äs-ə-lər\ see OSSULAR

assal \as-əl\ see ²ASSEL

assant \as-ᵊnt\ see ¹ASCENT

assar \as-ər\ see ASSER

¹asse \as\ see ³ASS

²asse \äs\ see ¹OS

assed \ast\ see ²AST

assee \as-ē\ see ASSY

asseh \as-ə\ see ASSA

¹assel \äs-əl\ see OSSAL

²assel \as-əl\ acyl, basil, castle,
facile, gracile, hassle, Kassel,
passel, tassel, vassal, wrestle,
forecastle, Newcastle

asser \as-ər\ crasser, gasser,
Nasser, placer, harasser,
antimacassar

asset \as-ət\ see ²ACET

¹assia \ash-ə\ see ²ASHA

²assia \äsh-ə\ see ¹ASHA

assian \ash-ən\ see ASSION

assible \as-ə-bəl\ see ASSABLE

assic \as-ik\ classic, Jurassic,
Liassic, thalassic, Triassic,
neoclassic, pseudoclassic,
semiclassic

assical \as-i-kəl\ classical,
fascicle, postclassical,
unclassical, semiclassical

assid \as-əd\ see ACID

¹assie \as-ē\ see ASSY

²assie \äs-ē\ see ¹OSSY

¹assim \äs-əm\ see OSSUM

²assim \as-əm\ passim,
sargassum

assin \as-ᵊn\ see ²ASTEN

assion \ash-ən\ ashen, fashion,
passion, ration, Circassian,
compassion, dispassion,
impassion, refashion,
Wakashan

assional \ash-nəl\ see ³ATIONAL

¹assis \as-ē\ see ASSY

²assis \as-əs\ classis, stasis,
Parnassus, Halicarnassus

assist \ā-səst\ bassist, racist,
contrabassist

assive \as-iv\ massive, passive,
impassive

assle \as-əl\ see ²ASSEL

assless \as-ləs\ classless,
glassless, massless

assment \as-mənt\ blastment,
amassment, harassment

assness \as-nəs\ see ASTNESS

¹asso \as-ō\ basso, lasso, El
Paso, Picasso, sargasso,
Sargasso, Bobo-Dioulasso

²asso \äs-ō\ Campo Basso,
Burkina Faso

assock \as-ək\ cassock, hassock

assum \as-əm\ see ²ASSIM

assus \as-əs\ see ASSIS

assy \as-ē\ brassy, chassis,
classy, gassy, glacis, glassie,
glassy, grassy, lassie, massy,
sassy, saucy, Malagasy,
Tallahassee, Haile Salassie

¹ast \əst\ see ¹UST

²ast \ast\ bast, blast, cast, caste,
clast, fast, gast, ghast, hast,

last, mast, past, vast, aghast,
avast, bedfast, Belfast,
bombast, broadcast, bypast,
contrast, dicast, dismast,
downcast, dynast, fantast,
flypast, forecast, foremast,
forepassed, gymnast, half-
caste, half-mast, handfast,
holdfast, lightfast, mainmast,
makefast, march-past,
miscast, newscast, oblast,
offcast, outcast, outcaste,
precast, recast, repast,
roughcast, sandblast, sand-
cast, shamefast, soothfast,
sportscast, steadfast, sunfast,
topmast, trade-last, typecast,
unasked, upcast, windblast,
acid-fast, chiliast, cineast,
colorcast, colorfast,
flabbergast, fore-topmast,
hard-and-fast, main-topmast,
mizzenmast, narrowcast,
opencast, overcast, pederast,
rebroadcast, scholiast,
simulcast, telecast,
weathercast, ecdysiast,
encomiast, enthusiast,
iconoclast, radiocast,
symposiast, radiobroadcast—
also pasts of verbs listed at
³ASS

¹asta \äs-tə\ see OSTA
²asta \as-tə\ Rasta, canasta,
Jocasta, Mount Shasta
astable \at-ə-bəl\ see ATIBLE
astard \as-tərd\ bastard,
dastard, mastered, plastered
¹aste \āst\ see ACED
²aste \ast\ see ²AST
asted \as-təd\ blasted, masted,

plastid—*also pasts of verbs
listed at* ²AST
asteful \āst-fəl\ tasteful,
wasteful, distasteful
¹asten \ās-ᵊn\ see ¹ASON
²asten \as-ᵊn\ fasten, assassin,
unfasten
¹aster \ā-stər\ taster, waster
²aster \as-tər\ aster, Astor,
caster, castor, Castor, faster,
gaster, master, pastor, plaster,
raster, bandmaster,
bushmaster, cadastre,
choirmaster, disaster,
drillmaster, headmaster,
linecaster, loadmaster,
paymaster, piaster, pilaster,
postmaster, quizmaster,
remaster, ringmaster,
schoolmaster, scoutmaster,
shinplaster, shipmaster,
spymaster, taskmaster, three-
master, toastmaster,
truckmaster, wharfmaster,
whoremaster, yardmaster,
alabaster, burgomaster,
concertmaster, criticaster,
ironmaster, oleaster,
overmaster, poetaster,
quartermaster, rallymaster,
stationmaster, weathercaster,
Zoroaster, cotoneaster
astered \as-tərd\ see ASTARD
astering \as-tə-riŋ\
overmastering—*also present
participles of verbs listed at*
ASTER
astes \as-tēz\ cerastes,
Ecclesiastes—*also plurals
and possessives of nouns
listed at* ²ASTY
asthma \az-mə\ see ASMA

astian \as-chən\ see ASTION
astic \as-tik\ drastic, mastic,
  plastic, spastic, bombastic,
  dynastic, elastic, fantastic,
  gymnastic, monastic,
  sarcastic, scholastic,
  stochastic, anelastic,
  Hudibrastic, inelastic,
  onomastic, orgiastic,
  paraphrastic, pederastic,
  periphrastic, superplastic,
  ecclesiastic, enthusiastic,
  iconoclastic, interscholastic,
  semimonastic
astics \as-tiks\ gymnastics,
  slimnastics
astid \as-təd\ see ASTED
astie \as-tē\ see ²ASTY
astiness \ā-stē-nəs\ hastiness,
  pastiness
¹asting \ā-stiŋ\ basting,
  wasting—*also present
  participles of verbs listed at*
  ACED
²asting \as-tiŋ\ typecasting,
  everlasting, narrowcasting,
  overcasting
astion \as-chən\ bastion,
  Erastian
astle \as-əl\ see ²ASSEL
astly \ast-lē\ ghastly, lastly
astment \as-mənt\ see ASSMENT
astness \as-nəs\ crassness,
  fastness, gastness, pastness
asto \as-tō\ impasto, antipasto
astor \as-tər\ see ²ASTER
astoral \as-trəl\ see ASTRAL
astral \as-trəl\ astral, gastral,
  pastoral, plastral, cadastral
astre \as-tər\ see ²ASTER
astric \as-trik\ gastric,
  nasogastric

astrophe \as-trə-fē\ anastrophe,
  catastrophe
¹asty \ā-stē\ hasty, pasty, tasty
²asty \as-tē\ blastie, nasty,
  pasty, vasty, capacity,
  contrasty, pederasty,
  angioplasty, bepharoplasty,
  osteoplasty, overcapacity
asuble \as-ə-bəl\ see ASSABLE
¹asure \ā-shər\ glacier, Glacier,
  rasure, erasure
²asure \ā-zhər\ see AZIER
asy \as-ē\ see ASSY
¹at \ä\ see ¹A
²at \ät\ see ¹OT
³at \ət\ see ¹UT
⁴at \ȯt\ see ¹OUGHT
⁵at \at\ bat, batt, blat, brat, cat,
  Cat, chat, chert, drat, fat, flat,
  frat, gat, gnat, hat, mat, matt,
  Matt, matte, pat, Pat, plait,
  plat, rat, Rat, sat, scat, scatt,
  skat, slat, spat, splat, sprat,
  stat, tat, that, vat, all that, at
  bat, backchat, begat, bobcat,
  brickbat, bullbat, Cassatt,
  chitchat, combat, comsat,
  cowpat, cravat, Croat, defat,
  dingbat, doormat, expat, fiat,
  firebrat, format, Hallstatt,
  hellcat, hepcat, high-hat, jurat,
  meerkat, muscat, Muscat,
  muskrat, nonfat, polecat,
  Sadat, savate, Sno-Cat, stand
  pat, standpat, stonechat,
  strawhat, Surat, thereat, tipcat,
  tomcat, whereat, whinchat,
  wildcat, wombat, acrobat,
  apparat, Ararat, assignat,
  autocrat, Automat, bureaucrat,
  butterfat, caveat, cervelat,
  concordat, copycat, democrat,

diplomat, Dixiecrat, Eurocrat, habitat, Kattegat, Laundromat, marrowfat, mobocrat, monocrat, Montserrat, ochlocrat, pas de quatre, photostat, pit-a-pat, plutocrat, pussycat, rat-a-tat, scaredy-cat, semimatte, technocrat, theocrat, thermostat, tit for tat, Uniate, ziggurat, aristocrat, gerontocrat, heliostat, Jehoshaphat, magnificat, meritocrat, Physiocrat, requiescat, thalassocrat, proletoriat, professoriat, secretariat

⁶**at** \a\ see ³AH

¹**ata** \ät-ə\ cotta, kata, balata, cantata, Carlotta, data, errata, fermata, frittata, La Plata, Maratha, Niigata, non grata, pinata, pro rata, reata, riata, regatta, sonata, Sorata, toccata, caponata, Hirakata, Mar del Plata, serenata, terracotta, Uspallata, Basilicata, desiderata, inamorata, medulla oblongata, missa cantata, persona grata, res judicata, persona non grata, res adjudicata, Rio de la Plata

²**ata** \āt-ə\ beta, data, eta, strata, theta, zeta, muleta, peseta, potato, pro rata, substrata, tomato, viewdata, corona radiata

³**ata** \at-ə\ data, errata, mulatto, non grata, pro rata, reata, regatta, riata, viewdata, paramatta, Paramatta, persona grata, persona non grata

¹**atable** \āt-ə-bəl\ datable, ratable, statable, debatable, dilatable, inflatable, locatable, rotatable, translatable, allocatable, circulatable, confiscatable, correlatable, detonatable, undebatable

²**atable** \at-ə-bəl\ see ATIBLE

atal \āt-ᵊl\ fatal, natal, ratel, shtetl, hiatal, postnatal, prenatal, antenatal, neonatal, perinatal

atalie \at-ᵊl-ē\ see ATTILY

atally \āt-ᵊl-ē\ fatally, natally, postnatally, prenatally, antenatally, neonatally, perinatally

atalyst \at-ᵊl-əst\ catalyst, philatelist

¹**atan** \āt-ən\ see ¹ATEN

²**atan** \at-ᵊn\ see ²ATIN

atancy \āt-ᵊn-sē\ blatancy, latency, dilatancy

¹**atant** \āt-ᵊnt\ blatant, latent, natant, patent, statant

²**atant** \at-ᵊnt\ patent, combatant, noncombatant

atany \at-ᵊn-ē\ atony, rhatany

atar \ät-ər\ see OTTER

atary \ät-ə-rē\ see OTTERY

¹**atch** \ech\ see ETCH

²**atch** \äch\ see OTCH

³**atch** \óch\ see ¹AUCH

⁴**atch** \ach\ bach, batch, catch, cratch, hatch, klatch, latch, match, natch, patch, ratch, scratch, snatch, thatch, attach, book-match, crosshatch, crosspatch, despatch, detach, dispatch, nuthatch, outmatch, potlatch, rematch, Sasquatch, throatlatch, unlatch, Wasatch,

coffee klatch, kaffeeklatsch, overmatch

¹atcher \äch-ər\ botcher, watcher, bird-watcher, clock-watcher, debaucher, topnotcher

²atcher \ach-ər\ batcher, catcher, hatcher, matcher, scratcher, stature, thatcher, cowcatcher, dispatcher, dogcatcher, eye-catcher, flycatcher, gnatcatcher, oyster catcher

atchet \ach-ət\ hatchet, latchet, rachet, ratchet

atchily \ach-ə-lē\ patchily, patchouli

atching \ach-iŋ\ back-scratching, cross-hatching, eye-catching, nonmatching

atchman \äch-mən\ see OTCHMAN

atchment \ach-mənt\ catchment, hatchment, attachment, detachment

atchouli \ach-ə-lē\ see ATCHILY

atchy \ach-ē\ catchy, patchy, scratchy, Apache

¹ate \āt\ ait, ate, bait, bate, blate, cate, Cate, crate, date, eight, fate, fete, freight, gait, gate, grate, great, haet, hate, Kate, late, mate, pate, plait, plate, prate, quoit, rate, sate, skate, slate, spate, state, straight, strait, teth, trait, wait, weight, abate, ablate, adnate, aerate, age-mate, agnate, airdate, airfreight, alate, arête, await, backdate, baldpate, bedmate, bedplate, berate, birthrate, bistate, bookplate,

breastplate, casemate, castrate, caudate, cerate, cheapskate, checkmate, chordate, classmate, clavate, cognate, collate, comate, conflate, connate, cordate, create, cremate, crenate, curate, cut-rate, deadweight, debate, deflate, delate, dentate, derate, dictate, dilate, disrate, donate, doorplate, downstate, drawplate, elate, equate, estate, faceplate, falcate, fellate, filtrate, first-rate, fishplate, fixate, flatmate, floodgate, flyweight, formate, frustrate, gelate, gestate, gyrate, hamate, hastate, headgate, helpmate, housemate, hydrate, ice-skate, inflate, ingrate, inmate, innate, instate, irate, jailbait, jugate, khanate, Kuwait, lactate, legate, liftgate, ligate, lightweight, liquate, lobate, locate, lunate, lustrate, lych-gate, lyrate, magnate, makebate, makeweight, mandate, messmate, migrate, misstate, mutate, nameplate, narrate, negate, Newgate, nitrate, notate, nutate, oblate, orate, ornate, ovate, palmate, palpate, peltate, phonate, pinnate, placate, playmate, plicate, portrait, postdate, predate, primate, probate, prolate, prorate, prostate, prostrate, pulsate, punctate, pupate, quadrate, ramate, rebate, red-bait, relate, restate, roommate, rostrate, rotate, saccate, schoolmate, seatmate, sedate, sensate, septate, serrate, shipmate, short weight, soleplate, spectate, spicate, squamate, stagnate, stalemate, stellate, striate, sublate, substrate, sulcate, summate, tailgate, teammate, Tebet, tenth-rate, ternate, terneplate, testate, third-rate, tinplate, toeplate, tollgate, tractate, translate, tristate, truncate, unweight, update, uprate, upstate, V-8, vacate, vallate, valvate, vibrate, virgate, vulgate, whitebait, workmate, zonate, abdicate, abnegate, abrogate, absorbate, acclimate, acerbate, acetate, activate, actuate, acylate, adsorbate, advocate, adulate, adumbrate, aggravate, aggregate, agitate, allocate, altercate, alternate, ambulate, amputate, animate, annotate, annulate, antedate, antiquate, apartheid, apostate, approbate, approximate, arbitrate, arcuate, arrogate, aspirate, automate, aviate, bantamweight, bifurcate, billingsgate, bipinnate, boilerplate, bombinate, brachiate, cachinnate, calculate, calibrate, caliphate, candidate, cantillate, capitate, captivate, carbonate, carbon-date, carinate, castigate, catenate, cavitate, celebrate, cerebrate, circinate, circulate, city-state, cogitate, collimate, collocate, commentate,

commutate, compensate, complicate, concentrate, condensate, confiscate, conglobate, conjugate, consecrate, constellate, consternate, constipate, consummate, contemplate, copperplate, copulate, coronate, correlate, corrugate, coruscate, counterweight, crenulate, crepitate, criminate, cruciate, cucullate, culminate, cultivate, cumulate, cuneate, cupulate, cuspidate, cyclamate, decimate, decollate, decorate, decussate, dedicate, defalcate, defecate, delegate, demarcate, demonstrate, denigrate, deviate, deprecate, depredate, derivate, derogate, desecrate, desiccate, designate, desolate, detonate, devastate, deviate, digitate, diplomate, discarnate, dislocate, dissertate, dissipate, distillate, divagate, dominate, duplicate, edentate, educate, elevate, elongate, eluate, emanate, emigrate, emirate, emulate, enervate, ephorate, escalate, estimate, estivate, excavate, exculpate, execrate, expiate, explicate, expurgate, exsiccate, extirpate, extricate, exudate, fabricate, fascinate, featherweight, fecundate, federate, fenestrate, festinate, fibrillate, flabellate, flagellate, flocculate, fluctuate, fluoridate, foliate, formulate, fornicate, fractionate, fragmentate, fulminate, fumigate, fustigate, geminate, generate, germinate, glaciate, Golden Gate, graduate, granulate, gratulate, gravitate, heavyweight, hebetate, herniate, hesitate, hibernate, hundredweight, hyphenate, ideate, illustrate, imamate, imbricate, imitate, immigrate, immolate, impetrate, implicate, imprecate, impregnate, incarnate, increate, incubate, inculcate, inculpate, incurvate, indagate, indicate, indurate, infiltrate, innervate, innovate, insensate, insolate, inspissate, instigate, insulate, interstate, intestate, intimate, intonate, intraplate, inundate, invocate, iodate, irrigate, irritate, isolate, iterate, jubilate, juniorate, lacerate, laminate, Latinate, laureate, legislate, levigate, levitate, liberate, liquidate, litigate, littermate, lubricate, macerate, machinate, magistrate, marginate, margravate, marinate, masticate, masturbate, maturate, mediate, medicate, meditate, meliorate, menstruate, microstate, micturate, middleweight, militate, ministrate, miscreate, mithridate, mitigate, moderate, modulate, motivate, multistate, mutilate, nation-state, nauseate, navigate, neonate, nictitate, niobate, nominate, numerate,

obfuscate, objurgate, obligate, obovate, obviate, operate, opiate, orchestrate, ordinate, oscillate, osculate, out-of-date, overstate, overweight, ovulate, paginate, palliate, palpitate, paperweight, patinate, peculate, penetrate, pennyweight, percolate, perennate, perforate, permeate, perorate, perpetrate, personate, pollinate, populate, postulate, potentate, predicate, procreate, profligate, promulgate, propagate, prorogate, pullulate, pulmonate, punctuate, quantitate, rabbinate, radiate, re-create, reclinate, recreate, regulate, reinstate, relegate, relocate, reluctate, remonstrate, renovate, replicate, reprobate, resonate, retardate, retranslate, roseate, rubricate, ruminate, runagate, rusticate, sagittate, salivate, sanitate, satiate, saturate, scintillate, second-rate, segregate, separate, sequestrate, seriate, sibilate, simulate, sinuate, situate, speculate, spoliate, stablemate, stimulate, stipulate, strangulate, stridulate, stylobate, subjugate, sublimate, subrogate, subulate, suffocate, sultanate, supplicate, surrogate, syncopate, syndicate, tablemate, tabulate, terminate, tessellate, tête-à-tête, thirty-eight, titillate,

titivate, tolerate, transmigrate,
transudate, tribulate, tribunate,
trifurcate, trilobate, tripinnate,
triplicate, tunicate, turbinate,
ulcerate, ululate, umbellate,
uncinate, underrate,
understate, underweight,
undulate, ungulate, urinate,
vaccinate, vacillate, validate,
valuate, variate, vaticinate,
vegetate, venerate, ventilate,
vertebrate, vicarate, vindicate,
violate, vitiate, Watergate,
welterweight, abbreviate,
abominate, accelerate,
accentuate, accommodate,
acculturate, accumulate,
acidulate, adjudicate,
administrate, adulterate,
affiliate, agglomerate,
agglutinate, alienate, alleviate,
alliterate, amalgamate,
ameliorate, annihilate,
annunciate, anticipate,
apostolate, appreciate,
appropriate, articulate,
asphyxiate, assassinate,
asseverate, assimilate,
associate, attenuate,
authenticate, barbiturate,
bicarbonate, calumniate,
campanulate, capacitate,
capitulate, catholicate,
certificate, circumvallate,
coagulate, coelenterate,
collaborate, commemorate,
commiserate, communicate,
compassionate, concatenate,
concelebrate, conciliate,
confabulate, confederate,
conglomerate, congratulate,
consociate, consolidate,

contaminate, cooperate,
coordinate, corroborate, de-
escalate, deaerate, debilitate,
decapitate, decerebrate,
deconcentrate, deconsecrate,
decrepitate, defibrinate,
defribrillate, degenerate,
deliberate, delineate,
demodulate, denominate,
depopulate, depreciate,
deregulate, desegregate,
desiderate, devaluate,
diaconate, dilapidate,
discriminate, disintegrate,
disseminate, dissimilate,
dissimulate, dissociate,
divaricate, domesticate,
edulcorate, effectuate,
ejaculate, elaborate,
electroplate, eliminate,
elucidate, elucubrate, elutriate,
emaciate, emancipate,
emarginate, emasculate,
encapsulate, enumerate,
enunciate, episcopate,
equilibrate, equivocate,
eradicate, etiolate, evacuate,
evaluate, evaporate, eventuate,
eviscerate, exacerbate,
exaggerate, exasperate,
excogitate, excoriate,
excruciate, exfoliate,
exhilarate, exonerate,
expatiate, expatriate,
expectorate, expostulate,
expropriate, extenuate,
exterminate, extrapolate,
extravagate, exuberate,
facilitate, fantasticate,
felicitate, gesticulate,
habilitate, habituate,
hallucinate, homologate,

humiliate, hypothecate,
illuminate, impersonate,
inactivate, inaugurate,
incarcerate, incinerate,
incorporate, incriminate,
indoctrinate, inebriate,
infatuate, infuriate, ingratiate,
ingurgitate, initiate, inoculate,
inosculate, inseminate,
insinuate, instantiate,
intenerate, intercalate,
interpellate, interpolate,
interrelate, interrogate,
intimidate, intoxicate,
invaginate, invalidate,
investigate, invigilate,
invigorate, irradiate,
italianate, itinerate, lanceolate,
legitimate, luxuriate,
machicolate, mandarinate,
manipulate, matriarchate,
matriculate, Merthiolate,
necessitate, negotiate,
noncandidate, obliterate,
obnubilate, officiate, orientate,
originate, oxygenate,
participate, particulate,
patriarchate, patriciate,
penicillate, perambulate,
peregrinate, perpetuate,
pontificate, potentiate,
precipitate, predestinate,
predominate, prefabricate,
premeditate, prenominate,
preponderate, prevaricate,
procrastinate, prognosticate,
proliferate, propitiate,
proportionate, quadruplicate,
quintuplicate, reciprocate,
recriminate, recuperate,
redecorate, redintegrate,
reduplicate, reeducate,

refrigerate, regenerate,
regurgitate, reincarnate,
reintegrate, reiterate,
rejuvenate, remunerate,
renominate, repatriate,
repristinate, repudiate,
resupinate, resuscitate,
retaliate, reticulate, revaluate,
revegetate, reverberate,
scholasticate, self-portrait,
seventy-eight, sextuplicate,
somnambulate, sophisticate,
stereobate, subordinate,
substantiate, syllabicate,
tergiversate, transliterate,
transvaluate, triangulate,
variegate, vituperate,
vociferate, beneficiate,
circumambulate,
circumnavigate,
circumstantiate,
contraindicate, decontaminate,
deteriorate, differentiate,
disaffiliate, disambiguate,
disarticulate, disassociate,
discombobulate, disintoxicate,
disorientate, disproportionate,
domiciliate, excommunicate,
free-associate, hyperventilate,
incapacitate, individuate,
intermediate, interpenetrate,
lithium niobate,
superheavyweight,
microencapsulate,
misappropriate, multivariate,
ratiocinate, recapitulate,
rehabilitate, renegotiate,
superannuate, superelevate,
superordinate, supersaturate,
transilluminate,
transubstantiate,
underestimate,

intercommunicate,
diammonium phosphate,
phosphoenolpyruvate,
peroxyacetyl nitrate

²ate \at\ see ⁵AT

³ate \ät\ see ¹OT

⁴ate \ät-ē\ see ATI

⁵ate \ət\ see ¹UT

ated \āt-əd\ gaited, lated, pated,
stated, belated, ill-fated,
outdated, pustulated, related,
striated, three-gaited,
truncated, unbated, X-rated,
aberrated, addlepated,
animated, asteriated,
calculated, capsulated,
carbonated, carburated,
castellated, complicated,
crenellated, disrelated,
elevated, fenestrated,
fimbriated, floriated, foliated,
inspissated, intoxicated,
laminated, marginated,
mentholated, perforated,
pileated, pixilated, saturated,
tessellated, trabeated,
unabated, uncreated,
understated, variegated,
affiliated, configurated,
coordinated, decaffeinated,
domesticated, incorporated,
inebriated, interrelated,
intoxicated, opinionated,
sophisticated, uncalculated,
uncelebrated, uncomplicated,
underinflated, unmediated,
unmitigated, unsaturated,
unsegregated, unadulterated,
unanticipated, unarticulated,
unconsolidated,
undereducated,
underpopulated,

undissociated,
unsophisticated,
polyunsaturated,
underappreciated—*also pasts
of verbs listed at* ¹ATE

ateful \āt-fəl\ fateful, grateful,
hateful, ungrateful

¹atel \ət-ᵊl\ see OTTLE

²atel \āt-ᵊl\ see ATAL

ateless \āt-ləs\ dateless,
stateless, weightless

atelist \at-ᵊl-əst\ see ATALYST

¹ately \āt-lē\ greatly, lately,
stately, straightly, straitly,
innately, irately, ornately, up-
to-dately, Johnny-come-lately

²ately \at-ᵊl-ē\ see ATTILY

atem \ät-əm\ see ¹ATUM

atement \āt-mənt\ statement,
abatement, debatement,
misstatement, restatement,
overstatement, reinstatement,
understatement

¹aten \āt-ᵊn\ greaten, laten,
Satan, straighten, straiten,
Keewatin

²aten \at-ᵊn\ see ²ATIN

³aten \ät-ᵊn\ see OTTEN

¹atent \āt-ᵊnt\ see ¹ATANT

²atent \at-ᵊnt\ see ²ATANT

¹ater \ȯt-ər\ daughter, slaughter,
tauter, water, backwater,
bathwater, blackwater,
breakwater, cutwater, dewater,
deepwater, dishwater,
firewater, floodwater,
forequarter, freshwater,
goddaughter, granddaughter,
groundwater, headwater,
hindquarter, jerkwater,
limewater, manslaughter,
meltwater, rainwater,

rosewater, saltwater, seawater,
self-slaughter, shearwater,
springwater, stepdaughter,
tailwater, tidewater,
wastewater, milk-and-water,
polywater, underwater

²ater \āt-ər\ see ATOR

ateral \at-ə-rəl\ lateral,
bilateral, collateral, trilateral,
contralateral, dorsolateral,
equilateral, ipsilateral,
multilateral, quadrilateral,
unilateral, ventrolateral,
posterolateral

aterer \ȯt-ər-ər\ slaughterer,
waterer, dewaterer

ateress \āt-ə-rəs\ cateress,
traitorous

atering \ȯt-ə-riŋ\ mouth-
watering—*also present
participles of verbs listed at*
¹ATER

¹atery \ät-ə-rē\ see OTTERY

²atery \ȯt-ə-rē\ cautery, watery

¹ates \āts\ Yeats, Gulf States,
Papal States, Persian Gulf
States, United States,
Federated Malay States,
United Arab Emirates—*also
plurals and possessives of
nouns and third person
singular presents of verbs
listed at* ATE

²ates \āt-ēz\ Achates, nates,
Euphrates, Penates—*also
plurals and possessives of
nouns listed at* ATY

atest \āt-əst\ latest, statist—*also
superlatives of adjectives
listed at* ¹ATE

atey \āt-ē\ see ATY

¹ath \äth\ see ¹OTH

²ath \ȯth\ see ²OTH

³ath \ath\ bath, hath, lath, math,
path, rathe, snath, strath,
wrath, birdbath, bloodbath,
bypath, footbath, footpath,
sunbath, towpath, warpath,
aftermath, polymath,
psychopath, telepath,
naturopath, osteopath,
sociopath

atha \ät-ə\ see ¹ATA

¹athe \āth\ swathe, enswathe,
unswathe

²athe \āth\ bathe, lathe, rathe,
saithe, scathe, spathe, swathe,
sunbathe, unswathe

³athe \ath\ see ³ATH

atheless \āth-ləs\ see AITHLESS

¹ather \äth-ər\ bother, father,
pother, rather, forefather,
godfather, grandfather,
housefather, stepfather

²ather \əth-ər\ see ¹OTHER

³ather \ath-ər\ blather, Cather,
gather, lather, Mather, rather,
slather, forgather, ingather,
wool-gather

athering \ath-riŋ\ ingathering,
woolgathering

athi \ät-ē\ see ATI

athic \ath-ik\ empathic,
amphipathic, psychopathic,
telepathic, homeopathic,
idiopathic, sociopathic

athlon \ath-lən\ biathlon,
decathlon, pentathlon,
triathlon

athy \ath-ē\ Cathie, Cathy,
Kathie, Kathy, wrathy,
allelopathy

¹ati \ät-ē\ Ate, Dottie, dotty,
Dotty, grotty, knotty, naughty,

plotty, potty, Scottie, Scotty,
snotty, spotty, squatty, Amati,
basmati, chapati, coati,
flokati, karate, Marathi,
metate, Scarlatti, Tol'yati,
glitterati, Gujarati, Hakodate,
literati, manicotti, illuminati
²**ati** \atē\ see ATTY
³**ati** \äts\ see OTS
⁴**ati** \as\ see ³ASS
atia \ā-shə\ see ACIA
atial \ā-shəl\ see ACIAL
atian \ā-shən\ see ¹ATION
atians \ā-shənz\ see ATIONS
atible \at-ə-bəl\ compatible,
getatable, incompatible, self-
compatible, biocompatible,
self-incompatible
¹**atic** \ät-ik\ see ¹OTIC
²**atic** \at-ik\ attic, Attic, batik,
phatic, static, vatic, agnatic,
aquatic, astatic, asthmatic,
chromatic, climatic, comatic,
dalmatic, dogmatic, dramatic,
ecstatic, emphatic, erratic,
fanatic, hepatic, judgmatic,
komatik, lymphatic,
magmatic, neumatic,
phlegmatic, plasmatic,
pneumatic, pragmatic,
prismatic, protatic, quadratic,
rheumatic, schematic,
schismatic, sciatic, sematic,
Socratic, somatic, spermatic,
stigmatic, sylvatic, thematic,
traumatic, villatic, achromatic,
acrobatic, Adriatic, aerobatic,
anabatic, antistatic, aromatic,
Asiatic, astigmatic, autocratic,
automatic, bureaucratic,
charismatic, cinematic,
democratic, dilemmatic,
diplomatic, Dixiecratic,
Eleatic, emblematic,
enigmatic, enzymatic,
fungistatic, Hanseatic,
hieratic, Hippocratic,
kerygmatic, leviratic,
melismatic, miasmatic,
mobocratic, monocratic,
morganatic, numismatic,
ochlocratic, operatic,
phonematic, plutocratic, pre-
Socratic, problematic,
programmatic, symptomatic,
syntagmatic, systematic,
technocratic, theocratic,
timocratic, undogmatic,
undramatic, anagrammatic,
apothegmatic, aristocratic,
asymptomatic, axiomatic,
conglomeratic, diagrammatic,
diaphragmatic, epigrammatic,
gerontocratic, gynecocratic,
homeostatic, idiomatic,
logogrammatic, melodramatic,
meritocratic, monochromatic,
monodramatic,
monogrammatic,
pantisocratic, paradigmatic,
physiocratic, psychodramatic,
psychosomatic, semiaquatic,
theorematic, undemocratic,
undiplomatic, antidemocratic,
Austroasiatic, biosystematic,
ideogrammatic, semiautomatic
atica \at-i-kə\ Attica, hepatica,
sciatica, viatica
atical \at-i-kəl\ statical,
dogmatical, erratical,
fanatical, grammatical,
piratical, pragmatical,
sabbatical, schismatical,
autocratical, emblematical,

enigmatical, magistratical,
mathematical, ochlocratical,
problematical, systematical,
theocratical, timocratical,
ungrammatical,
anagrammatical,
diagrammatical,
epigrammatical,
pantisocratical

atics \at-iks\ statics, chromatics,
dogmatics, dramatics,
pneumatics, pragmatics,
acrobatics, informatics,
mathematics, numismatics,
systematics, melodramatics,
psychosomatics—*also plurals
and possessives of nouns
listed at* ²ATIC

atie \āt-ē\ see ATY

atiens \ā-shənz\ see ATIONS

atient \ā-shənt\ patient,
impatient, inpatient,
outpatient, rubefacient,
somnifacient, abortifacient

atik \at-ik\ see ²ATIC

atile \at-ᵊl-ē\ see ATTILY

atim \āt-əm\ see ²ATUM

¹atin \ät-ᵊn\ see OTTEN

²atin \at-ᵊn\ batten, fatten,
flatten, gratin, Latin, latten,
matin, paten, patten, Patton,
platan, platen, ratton, satin,
cisplatin, manhattan,
Manhattan, Powhatan,
lovastatin, Neo-Latin

³atin \āt-ᵊn\ see ¹ATEN

atinate \at-ᵊn-ət\ concatenate,
Palatinate, Rhineland-
Palatinate

ating \āt-iŋ\ bating, grating,
plating, rating, skating,
slating, abating, bearbaiting,

bullbaiting, frustrating, self-
rating, calculating,
lancinating, maid-in-waiting,
nauseating, operating,
titillating, humiliating, lady-
in-waiting, nonterminating,
self-liquidating, self-
regulating, self-replicating,
subordinating, uncalculating,
undeviating, unhesitating,
indiscriminating, self-
incriminating

atinous \at-nəs\ see ATNESS

¹ation \ā-shən\ Asian, Haitian,
nation, Nation, ration, station,
Thracian, ablation, agnation,
Alsatian, carnation, castration,
causation, cessation, cetacean,
chrismation, citation,
cognation, collation, conation,
conflation, creation,
cremation, crenation,
Croatian, crustacean,
cunctation, dalmatian,
damnation, deflation,
dictation, dilation, donation,
duration, elation, enation,
equation, Eurasian, filtration,
fixation, flotation, formation,
foundation, frustration,
furcation, gestation, gradation,
gustation, gyration, hydration,
illation, inflation, lactation,
laudation, lavation, legation,
libation, libration, ligation,
location, lustration, mentation,
migration, mutation,
narration, natation, negation,
nitration, notation, novation,
nutation, oblation, oration,
outstation, ovation, phonation,
planation, plantation,

plication, potation, predation,
privation, probation,
pronation, proration,
prostration, pulsation,
purgation, quotation, reflation,
relation, rogation, rotation,
saltation, salvation, sedation,
sensation, serration,
slumpflation, squamation,
stagflation, stagnation,
starvation, striation,
stylization, sublation,
substation, summation,
tarnation, taxation,
temptation, translation,
truncation, vacation, venation,
vexation, vibration, vocation,
workstation, zonation,
abdication, aberration,
abjuration, abnegation,
acceptation, acclamation,
acclimation, accusation,
activation, actuation,
adaptation, adjuration,
admiration, adoration,
adulation, adumbration,
advocation, affectation,
affirmation, aggravation,
aggregation, allegation,
allocation, amputation,
alteration, altercation,
alternation, Amerasian,
angulation, animation,
annexation, annotation,
annulation, antiquation,
Appalachian, appellation,
application, approbation,
arbitration, aspiration,
assentation, assignation,
attestation, augmentation,
Aurignacian, automation,
aviation, avocation,

blaxploitation, botheration,
brachiation, cachinnation,
calculation, calibration,
cancellation, capitation,
captivation, carbonation,
carburation, castigation,
celebration, cementation,
cerebration, circulation,
claudication, cogitation,
collocation, coloration,
combination, commendation,
commination, commutation,
compellation, compensation,
compilation, complication,
compurgation, computation,
concentration, condemnation,
condensation, condonation,
confirmation, confiscation,
conflagration, conformation,
confrontation, confutation,
congelation, congregation,
conjugation, conjuration,
connotation, consecration,
conservation, consolation,
conspiration, constellation,
consternation, constipation,
consultation, consummation,
contemplation, contestation,
conurbation, conversation,
convocation, copulation,
coronation, corporation,
correlation, corrugation,
coruscation, crenellation,
culmination, cupellation,
cuspidation, cybernation,
decimation, declamation,
declaration, declination,
decoration, dedication,
defalcation, defamation,
defecation, defloration,
deformation, degradation,
degustation, dehydration,

delectation, delegation,
demarcation, demonstration,
denegation, denigration,
denotation, depilation,
deportation, depravation,
depredation, deprivation,
deputation, derivation,
derogation, desecration,
desiccation, designation,
desolation, desperation,
destination, detestation,
detonation, devastation,
deviation, dilatation,
disclamation, disinflation,
dislocation, dispensation,
disputation, disrelation,
dissertation, dissipation,
distillation, divination,
domination, dubitation,
duplication, education,
elevation, elongation,
emanation, embarkation,
embrocation, emendation,
emigration, emulation,
encrustation, enervation,
epilation, equitation,
eructation, escalation,
estimation, estivation,
evocation, exaltation,
excavation, excitation,
exclamation, exculpation,
execration, exhalation,
exhortation, expectation,
expiation, expiration,
explanation, explication,
exploitation, exploration,
exportation, expurgation,
extirpation, extrication,
exudation, exultation,
fabrication, fascination,
federation, fenestration,
fermentation, fibrillation,
figuration, filiation,
flagellation, fluoridation,
fluctuation, foliation,
fomentation, formulation,
fornication, fragmentation,
fulguration, fulmination,
fumigation, gemination,
generation, germination,
glaciation, graduation,
granulation, gravitation,
habitation, hesitation,
hibernation, hyphenation,
ideation, illustration,
imbrication, imitation,
immigration, immolation,
implantation, implication,
importation, imprecation,
imputation, incantation,
incarnation, incitation,
inclination, incrustation,
incubation, inculcation,
indentation, indexation,
indication, indignation,
induration, infestation,
infiltration, inflammation,
information, inhalation,
innovation, insolation,
inspiration, installation,
instauration, insufflation,
insulation, intonation,
inundation, invitation,
invocation, irrigation,
irritation, isolation, iteration,
jactitation, jubilation,
laceration, lacrimation,
lamentation, lamination,
legislation, levitation,
liberation, limitation,
lineation, liquidation,
literation, litigation,
lubrication, lucubration,
maceration, machination,

maculation, malformation,
malversation, margination,
mastication, masturbation,
maturation, mediation,
medication, meditation,
melioration, menstruation,
mensuration, metrication,
ministration, moderation,
modulation, molestation,
motivation, navigation,
nomination, numeration,
obfuscation, objurgation,
obligation, observation,
obturation, occultation,
occupation, operation,
orchestration, ordination,
oscillation, osculation,
ostentation, ovulation,
oxidation, ozonation,
pagination, palliation,
palpitation, patination,
penetration, perforation,
permeation, permutation,
peroration, perpetration,
perspiration, perturbation,
pigmentation, pixilation,
pollination, population,
postulation, predication,
preformation, prelibation,
preparation, presentation,
proclamation, procreation,
procuration, profanation,
prolongation, propagation,
prorogation, protestation,
provocation, publication,
punctuation, radiation,
recitation, reclamation,
recordation, re-creation,
recreation, reformation,
refutation, registration,
regulation, relaxation,
relocation, reparation,

replantation, replication,
reprobation, reputation,
reservation, resignation,
respiration, restoration,
retardation, revelation,
revocation, ruination,
salivation, salutation,
sanitation, satiation,
saturation, scatteration,
scintillation, segmentation,
segregation, separation,
sequestration, sexploitation,
simulation, situation,
solmization, speciation,
speculation, spoliation,
sternutation, stimulation,
stipulation, strangulation,
structuration, subjugation,
sublimation, subrogation,
suffocation, suspiration,
susurration, sustentation,
syncopation, syndication,
tabulation, termination,
tessellation, titillation,
titivation, toleration,
transformation, translocation,
transmigration, transmutation,
transpiration, transplantation,
transportation, trepidation,
tribulation, trituration,
ulceration, ululation,
undulation, urination,
usurpation, vaccination,
vacillation, validation,
valuation, variation,
vegetation, veneration,
ventilation, vindication,
violation, visitation,
abbreviation, abomination,
acceleration, accentuation,
accommodation, accreditation,
acculturation, accumulation,

actualization, adjudication, administration, adulteration, affiliation, afforestation, agglomeration, agglutination, alienation, alleviation, alliteration, amalgamation, amelioration, amortization, amplification, analyzation, anglicization, annihilation, annunciation, anticipation, appreciation, appropriation, approximation, argumentation, articulation, asphyxiation, assassination, asseveration, assimilation, association, attenuation, authorization, autoxidation, barbarization, bastardization, beautification, bowdlerization, brutalization, canalization, canonization, capacitation, capitulation, carbonylation, centralization, certification, cicatrization, civilization, clarification, classification, coagulation, coeducation, cohabitation, colonization, collaboration, columniation, commemoration, commiseration, communication, communization, compartmentation, complementation, concatenation, conciliation, confabulation, confederation, configuration, conglomeration, congratulation, consideration, consociation, consolidation, contamination, continuation, cooperation, coordination, corroboration, crustification, crystallization, deactivation, debilitation, decapitation, decompensation, defenestration, deforestation, degeneration, deglaciation, deification, deliberation, delineation, denomination, denunciation, depopulation, depreciation, deregulation, desegregation, despoliation, determination, devaluation, dilapidation, diphthongization, disapprobation, discoloration, discrimination, disembarkation, disinclination, disinformation, disintegration, dissemination, dissimilation, dissimulation, dissociation, divarication, documentation, domestication, dramatization, echolocation, edification, ejaculation, elaboration, elicitation, elimination, elucidation, emaciation, emancipation, emasculation, enumeration, enunciation, epoxidation, equalization, equivocation, eradication, evacuation, evagination, evaluation, evaporation, evisceration, exacerbation, exaggeration, examination, exasperation, excoriation, excruciation, exercitation, exhilaration, exoneration, expostulation, expropriation, extenuation, extermination, extrapolation, facilitation, factorization, falsification, fantastication, feminization, fertilization,

Finlandization, formalization, formulization, fortification, fossilization, fructification, gasification, gentrification, gesticulation, glamorization, globalization, glorification, glycosylation, gratification, habituation, hallucination, harmonization, haruspication, hellenization, humanization, hyperinflation, idolization, illumination, imagination, immunization, impersonation, implementation, improvisation, inauguration, incarceration, incardination, incineration, incorporation, incrimination, indoctrination, inebriation, infatuation, ingratiation, inhabitation, initiation, inoculation, insemination, insinuation, instrumentation, internalization, interpretation, interrelation, intimidation, intoxication, invagination, investigation, invigoration, irradiation, itemization, jollification, justification, labanotation, laicization, latinization, legalization, lionization, localization, machicolation, magnetization, magnification, maladaptation, manifestation, masculinization, matriculation, maximization, mechanization, miscegenation, mobilization, modernization, modification, mollification, mongrelization, monopolization, moralization,

mortification, multiplication, mystification, nationalization, naturalization, necessitation, negotiation, neutralization, normalization, notarization, notification, novelization, nullification, optimization, organization, orientation, ornamentation, ossification, pacification, paralyzation, participation, pasteurization, patronization, penalization, perambulation, perpetuation, perseveration, personalization, plasticization, pluralization, petrification, polarization, pontification, preadaptation, precipitation, predestination, prefiguration, premeditation, preoccupation, preregistration, prettification, procrastination, prognostication, proliferation, pronunciation, propitiation, pulverization, purification, qualification, quantification, ramification, randomization, ratification, ratiocination, realization, reciprocation, recombination, recommendation, recrimination, recuperation, redecoration, reduplication, reforestation, refrigeration, regeneration, regimentation, regurgitation, reification, reincarnation, reintegration, remediation, remuneration, renunciation, representation, republication, repudiation, reticulation, retrogradation, reverberation, robotization, romanization, sanctification, sanitization, scarification, secularization, sedimentation, sensitization, Serbo-Croatian, signification, simplification, socialization, solemnization, solicitation, solidification, sophistication, specialization, specification, stabilization, standardization, sterilization, stratification, stultification, subalternation, subinfeudation, subordination, subpopulation, subsidization, summarization, supplementation, syllabication, symbolization, synchronization, systemization, teleportation, tergiversation, terrorization, theorization, transfiguration, transliteration, transvaluation, traumatization, triangulation, trivialization, uglification, unification, unionization, urbanization, vandalization, vaporization, variegation, vaticination, velarization, verbalization, verification, versification, victimization, vilification, vinification, vitalization, vituperation, vocalization, vociferation, vulgarization, westernization, x-radiation, acclimatization, allegorization, alphabetization, autocorrelation, automatization, beneficiation, capitalization, characterization, circumnavigation, codetermination,

commercialization, conceptualization, consubstantiation, containerization, counterreformation, criminalization, cross-examination, cryopreservation, decarboxylation, decimilization, de-Stalinization, decasualization, decentralization, declassification, decontamination, dehumanization, dehydrogenation, delegitimation, demystification, derealization, derivitization, desulfurization, deterioration, differentiation, disassociation, discombobulation, disorientation, disorganization, disproportionation, disqualification, diversification, dolomitization, electrification, excommunication, exemplification, experimentation, extemporization, externalization, familiarization, federalization, generalization, homogenization, hospitalization, hyperventilation, idealization, identification, immobilization, immortalization, incapacitation, inconsideration,

incoordination,
indemnification,
indetermination,
indiscrimination,
individuation,
institutionalization,
insubordination,
intensification, intermediation,
intermodulation,
intrapopulation, italicization,
legitimization, lexicalization,
maladministration,
mathematization,
megacorporation,
militarization, miniaturization,
misappropriation,
miscommunication,
misinterpretation,
mispronunciation,
misrepresentation,
noncooperation,
nonproliferation,
overcompensation,
overpopulation, palatalization,
periodization, personification,
photoduplication,
photoexcitation,
popularization,
predetermination,
prestidigitation,
proselytization, radicalization,
ratiocination, rationalization,
reafforestation, recapitulation,
reconciliation,
reconsideration, rehabilitation,
reinterpretation, renegotiation,
reorganization, revitalization,
ritualization, Schrödinger
equation, subvocalization,
supererogation,
syllabification,
tintinnabulation,
transubstantiation,
unappreciation,
underestimation,
undervaluation,
unsophistication,
visualization,
Americanization,
automanipulation,
decriminalization,
depersonalization,
electrodesiccation,
intercommunication,
industrialization,
materialization,
oversimplification,
particularization,
pictorialization,
photointerpretation,
pseudosophistication,
recapitalization,
spiritualization,
telecommunication,
universalization,
biodeterioration,
deindustrialization,
intellectualization,
reindustrialization,
internationalization,
deinstitutionalization
²ation \ā-zhən\ see ASION
³ation \ash-ən\ see ASSION
¹ational \ā-shnəl\ stational,
citational, formational,
gestational, gradational,
migrational, narrational,
notational, relational,
sensational, vocational,
aberrational, adaptational,
avocational, compensational,
computational,
conformational,
confrontational,

congregational, conjugational,
connotational, conservational,
conversational, convocational,
derivational, educational,
fluctuational, generational,
gravitational, ideational,
informational, innovational,
inspirational, invitational,
irrotational, limitational,
navigational, observational,
operational, orchestrational,
postranslational,
prevocational, progestational,
recreational, reformational,
situational, transformational,
communicational,
coeducational,
denominational,
improvisational,
interpretational,
investigational,
organizational,
representational,
nonrepresentational,
reorganizational,
interdenominational

²ational \āzh-nəl\ see ASIONAL

³ational \ash-nəl\ national,
passional, rational, binational,
cross-national, irrational,
transnational, international,
multinational, supranational,
suprarational

ationist \ā-shnəst\ salvationist,
vacationist, annexationist,
confrontationist,
conservationist, educationist,
integrationist, isolationist,
liberationist, operationist,
preservationist, recreationist,
segregationist, separationist,
preservationist,
accomodationist,
administrationist,
assimilationist, associationist,
collaborationist,
emancipationist

ations \ā-shənz\ Galatians,
impatiens, relations,
Lamentations, Revelations,
United Nations, Rhode Island
and Providence Plantations

atious \ā-shəs\ see ACIOUS

¹atis \at-əs\ see ³ATUS

²atis \ät-əs\ see OTTIS

atist \āt-əst\ see ATEST

atitude \at-ə-tüd\ see ATTITUDE

atium \ā-shē-əm\ Latium,
pancratium, solatium

atius \ā-shəs\ see ACIOUS

ative \āt-iv\ dative, native,
stative, ablative, constative,
creative, dilative, mutative,
rotative, summative,
translative, aggregative,
agitative, alterative,
applicative, carminative,
cogitative, combinative,
commutative, connotative,
consecrative, consultative,
contemplative, copulative,
corporative, cumulative,
decorative, denotative,
dissipative, educative,
explicative, facultative,
federative, generative,
germinative, imitative,
implicative, innovative,
integrative, irritative, iterative,
legislative, limitative,
meditative, meliorative,
motivative, nominative,
nuncupative, operative,
palliative, pejorative,

penetrative, procreative,
propagative, qualitative,
quantitative, recreative,
regulative, replicative,
separative, speculative,
terminative, vegetative,
accelerative, accumulative,
administrative, agglutinative,
alliterative, appreciative,
assimilative, associative,
authoritative, collaborative,
commemorative,
commiserative,
communicative,
contaminative, continuative,
cooperative, corroborative,
degenerative, deliberative,
delineative, determinative,
discriminative, evaporative,
exhilarative, exonerative,
illuminative, interpretative,
investigative, justificative,
multiplicative, obliterative,
opinionative, originative,
postoperative, premeditative,
preoperative, proliferative,
reciprocative, recuperative,
regenerative, remunerative,
reverberative, significative,
vituperative,
excommunicative,
incommunicative,
noncooperative, quasi-
legislative, semiquantitative,
uncommunicative
atl \ät-ᵊl\ see OTTLE
atlas \at-ləs\ atlas, Atlas, hatless
atless \at-ləs\ see ATLAS
atli \ät-lē\ see OTLY
atling \at-liŋ\ fatling, flatling,
rattling
atly \at-lē\ flatly, rattly

atnam \ət-nəm\ Machilipatnam,
Vishakhapatnam
atness \at-nəs\ fatness, flatness,
platinous, gelatinous
¹ato \ät-ō\ auto, blotto, grotto,
lotto, motto, otto, Otto, potto,
annatto, castrato, legato,
marcato, mulatto, rabato,
rebato, ridotto, rubato,
sfumato, spiccato, staccato,
agitato, animato, ben trovato,
Guanajuato, moderato,
obbligato, ostinato, pizzicato
²ato \āt-ō\ Cato, Plato, Orvieto,
potato, tomato, Barquisimeto
atomist \at-ə-məst\ atomist,
anatomist
atomy \at-ə-mē\ atomy,
anatomy
aton \at-ᵊn\ see ²ATIN
atony \at-ᵊn-ē\ see ATANY
ator \āt-ər\ baiter, cater, crater,
Crater, dater, faitour,
freighter, gaiter, gator, grater,
hater, krater, later, mater,
plater, rater, satyr, skater,
slater, stater, stator, tater,
traitor, waiter, aerator,
collator, Bay Stater, creator,
curator, debater, Decatur,
dictator, donator, dumbwaiter,
equator, first-rater, glossator,
headwaiter, levator, locator,
mandator, Mercator, narrator,
pronator, pulsator, rotator,
spectator, tailgater, testator,
theater, third-rater, translator,
upstater, vibrator, actuator,
abdicator, activator, adulator,
advocator, agitator, alligator,
allocator, alternator, animator,
annotator, applicator,

arbitrator, aspirator, aviator,
buccinator, calculator,
captivator, carburetor,
celebrator, circulator,
commentator, commutator,
compensator, compurgator,
concentrator, confiscator,
congregator, consecrator,
consummator, contemplator,
corporator, correlator,
depredator, desecrater,
desecrator, designator,
cultivator, decorator,
delegator, demonstrator,
detonator, deviator, dissipater,
dominator, duplicator, dura
mater, educator, elevator,
emulator, escalator, estimator,
excavator, explicator,
expurgator, extirpator,
fascinator, formulator,
fornicator, generator,
gladiator, hibernator,
illustrator, incubator,
indicator, infiltrator,
innovator, inhalator,
inspirator, insulator,
integrator, lacrimator,
liquidator, literator, mediator,
moderator, motivator,
navigator, nomenclator,
nominator, numerator,
obturator, operator,
orchestrator, oscillator,
percolator, perpetrator, pia
mater, pollinator, postulator,
procreator, procurator,
propagator, radiator,
regulator, resonator,
respirator, revelator, second-
rater, selling-plater, separator,
simulator, subjugator,
syndicator, tabulator,
terminator, valuator,
ventilator, violator,
accelerator, accommodator,
accumulator, administrator,
adulterator, alienator,
alleviator, annihilator,
annunciator, anticipator,
appreciator, appropriator,
assassinator, attenuator,
continuator, calumniator,
collaborator, commemorator,
communicator, conciliator,
congratulator, consolidator,
contaminator, cooperator,
coordinator, corroborator,
defibrillator, delineator,
denominator, depreciator,
determinator, discriminator,
disseminator, dissimulator,
ejaculator, eliminator,
emancipator, enumerator,
equivocator, eradicator,
evaluator, evaporator,
exterminator, extrapolator,
impersonator, improvisator,
incinerator, inseminator,
interrogator, intimidator,
investigator, negotiator,
oxygenator, pacificator,
perambulator, predestinator,
procrastinator, purificator,
redecorator, refrigerator,
regenerator, resuscitator,
totalizator, subordinator,
excommunicator,
rehabilitator, turbogenerator,
immunomodulator—*also
comparatives of adjectives
listed at* ¹ATE

atra \ä-trə\ Tatra, Sumatra

¹atre \ätrᵊ\ coup de theatre, pas de quatre

²atre \at\ see ⁵AT

atric \a-trik\ Patrick, sympatric, theatric, allopatric, geriatric, pediatric, podiatric, psychiatric

atrick \a-trik\ see ATRIC

atrics \a-triks\ theatrics, pediatrics

atrist \a-trəst\ geriatrist, physiatrist

atrix \ā-triks\ matrix, cicatrix, testatrix, aviatrix, dominatrix, executrix, mediatrix, administratrix

atron \ā-trən\ matron, natron, patron

¹ats \äts\ see OTS

²ats \ats\ bats, rats, ersatz—*also plurals and possessives of nouns and third singular presents of verbs listed at ⁵AT*

atsa \ät-sə\ see ¹ATZO

atsch \ach\ see ⁴ATCH

atsk \ätsk\ Bratsk, Okhotsk, Petrozavodsk

atsu \ät-sü\ Hamamatsu, shiatsu, shiatzu, Takamatsu

atsy \at-sē\ see ³AZI

¹att \at\ see ⁵AT

²att \ät\ see ¹OT

atta \ät-ə\ see ¹ATA

attage \ät-ij\ see OTTAGE

attan \at-ᵊn\ see ²ATIN

atte \at\ see ⁵AT

atted \a-təd\ superfatted—*also pasts of verbs listed at ⁵AT*

attel \at-ᵊl\ see ATTLE

atten \at-ᵊn\ see ²ATIN

atter \at-ər\ attar, batter, blatter, chatter, clatter, fatter, flatter, hatter, latter, matter, natter, patter, platter, ratter, satyr, scatter, shatter, smatter, spatter, splatter, tatter, backscatter, bespatter, flathatter, standpatter, wildcatter, antimatter, pitter-patter

attering \at-ə-riŋ\ nattering, smattering, backscattering, earth-shattering, self-flattering, unflattering, Rayleigh scattering

attern \at-ərn\ pattern, Saturn, slattern

attery \at-ə-rē\ battery, cattery, clattery, flattery, mattery, Cape Flattery, self-flattery

¹atti \ät-ē\ see ¹ATI

²atti \at-ē\ see ATTY

attic \at-ik\ see ²ATIC

attica \at-i-kə\ see ATICA

¹attice \at-əs\ see ³ATUS

²attice \at-ish\ see ATTISH

attie \at-ē\ see ATTY

attily \at-ᵊl-ē\ cattily, chattily, Natalie, Nathalie, nattily, rattly, philately, sal volatile

atting \at-iŋ\ batting, matting, tatting

attish \at-ish\ brattish, fattish, flattish

attitude \at-ə-tüd\ attitude, latitude

attle \at-ᵊl\ battle, brattle, cattle, chattel, prattle, rattle, tattle, embattle, Seattle, tittle-tattle

attler \at-lər\ battler, prattler, rattler, tattler

attling \at-liŋ\ see ATLING

¹attly \at-ᵊl-ē\ see ATTILY

²attly \at-lē\ see ATLY

¹atto \at-ə\ see ³ATA

²**atto** \ät-ō\ see ¹ATO

atton \at-ᵊn\ see ²ATIN

atty \at-ē\ batty, catty, bratty, chatty, fatty, Hattie, natty, Patti, Pattie, patty, Patty, platy, ratty, scatty, tattie, tatty, Cincinnati

¹**atum** \ät-əm\ bottom, datum, satem, erratum, pomatum, desideratum

²**atum** \āt-əm\ datum, pomatum, substratum, verbatim, ageratum, literatim, seriatim, ultimatum, corpus allatum, corpus striatum, desideratum

³**atum** \at-əm\ atom, datum, erratum, substratum, seriatim

atuous \ach-wəs\ fatuous, ignis fatuus

atur \āt-ər\ see ATOR

atural \ach-rəl\ natural, connatural, transnatural, unnatural, preternatural, seminatural, supernatural

¹**ature** \ā-chər\ nature, denature, 4-H'er, magistrature, nomenclature, supernature

²**ature** \ach-ər\ see ²ATCHER

aturn \at-ərn\ see ATTERN

¹**atus** \āt-əs\ flatus, gratis, status, stratus, afflatus, hiatus, meatus, apparatus, coitus reservatus

²**atus** \ät-əs\ see OTTIS

³**atus** \at-əs\ brattice, gratis, lattice, status, stratus, clematis, altostratus, apparatus, cirrostratus, nimbostratus

atute \ach-ət\ see ATCHET

atuus \ach-wəs\ see ATUOUS

aty \āt-ē\ eighty, Haiti, Katie, Katy, Leyte, matey, platy, slaty, weighty, yeti, 1080, Papeete

atyr \āt-ər\ see ATOR

¹**atz** \ats\ see ²ATS

²**atz** \äts\ see OTS

¹**atzo** \ät-sə\ matzo, tazza, Hidatsa, piazza

²**atzo** \ät-sō\ see ¹AZZO

atzu \ät-sü\ see ATSU

¹**au** \ō\ see ¹OW

²**au** \ü\ see ¹EW

³**au** \aủ\ see ²OW

⁴**au** \ò\ see ¹AW

aub \äb\ see ¹OB

auba \ò-bə\ carnauba, Catawba

aube \ōb\ see ¹OBE

auber \òb-ər\ dauber, Micawber

auble \äb-əl\ see ¹ABBLE

¹**auce** \as\ see ³ASS

²**auce** \òs\ see ¹OSS

aucer \ò-sər\ see OSSER

aucet \äs-ət\ see OSSET

¹**auch** \òch\ nautch, watch, debauch

²**auch** \äch\ see OTCH

auche \ōsh\ see ²OCHE

auchely \ōsh-lē\ see OCIALLY

auckland \òk-lənd\ Auckland, Falkland

aucous \ò-kəs\ caucus, glaucous, raucous

aucus \ò-kəs\ see AUCOUS

aucy \as-ē\ see ASSY

¹**aud** \òd\ awed, baud, bawd, broad, Claud, Claude, clawed, fraud, gaud, god, jawed, laud, Maud, Maude, yod, abroad, applaud, belaud, defraud, dewclawed, maraud, whipsawed, eisteddfod, lantern-jawed, quartersawed—

also pasts of verbs listed at ¹AW

²**aud** \äd\ see ¹OD

audable \ȯd-ə-bəl\ audible, laudable, applaudable, illaudable, inaudible

audal \ȯd-ᵊl\ caudal, caudle, dawdle

audative \ȯd-ət-iv\ see AUDITIVE

¹**aude** \au̇d-ē\ see OWDY

²**aude** \ȯd-ē\ see AWDY

³**aude** \au̇d-ə\ howdah, cum laude, magna cum laude, summa cum laude

⁴**aude** \ȯd\ see ¹AUD

audible \ȯd-ə-bəl\ see AUDABLE

auding \ȯd-iŋ\ auding, applauding, self-applauding

audit \ȯd-ət\ audit, plaudit

auditive \ȯd-ət-iv\ auditive, laudative

audle \ȯd-ᵊl\ see AUDAL

¹**audy** \äd-ē\ see ¹ODY

²**audy** \ȯd-ē\ see AWDY

auer \au̇r\ see ²OWER

auf \au̇f\ see OWFF

auffeur \ō-fər\ see OFER

auga \ȯ-gə\ massasauga, Mississauga, Onondaga

auge \āj\ see ³AGE

augeable \ā-jə-bəl\ see AGEABLE

auged \ājd\ see AGED

¹**auger** \ȯ-gər\ see ²OGGER

²**auger** \ā-jər\ see ¹AGER

¹**augh** \af\ see APH

²**augh** \ä\ see ¹A

³**augh** \äk\ see ¹ACH

⁴**augh** \ȯ\ see ¹AW

aughable \af-ə-bəl\ see AFFABLE

augham \ȯm\ see ¹AUM

¹**aughn** \än\ see ¹ON

²**aughn** \ȯn\ see ³ON

¹**aught** \ät\ see ¹OT

²**aught** \ȯt\ see ¹OUGHT

¹**aughter** \af-tər\ see AFTER

²**aughter** \ȯt-ər\ see ¹ATER

aughterer \ȯt-ər-ər\ see ATERER

¹**aughty** \ȯt-ē\ haughty, naughty, zloty, Michelangelo Buonarroti

²**aughty** \ät-ē\ see ATI

augre \ȯg-ər\ see ²OGGER

augur \ȯg-ər\ see ²OGGER

augury \ȯ-gə-rē\ see ²OGGERY

aui \au̇-ē\ see OWIE

auk \ȯk\ see ALK

aukee \ȯ-kē\ see ALKIE

aul \ȯl\ see ALL

aulay \ȯ-lē\ see AWLY

¹**auld** \ȯl\ see ALL

²**auld** \ō\ see ¹OW

auldron \ȯl-drən\ see ALDRON

auled \ȯld\ see ALD

auler \ȯ-lər\ see ¹ALLER

aulin \ȯ-lən\ see ALLEN

auling \ȯ-liŋ\ see ALLING

aulish \ȯ-lish\ see ALLISH

aulk \ȯk\ see ALK

aulker \ȯ-kər\ see ALKER

aulking \ȯ-kiŋ\ see ALKING

aulle \ȯl\ see ¹ALL

aulm \ȯm\ see ¹AUM

¹**ault** \ȯlt\ see ALT

²**ault** \ō\ see ¹OW

aulter \ȯl-tər\ see ALTER

aulting \ȯl-tiŋ\ see ALTING

aultless \ȯlt-ləs\ see ALTLESS

aulty \ȯl-tē\ see ALTY

¹**aum** \ȯm\ gaum, haulm, Maugham, poem, qualm, shawm, meerschaum, Radom

²**aum** \äm\ see ¹OM

¹**aun** \än\ see ¹ON

²**aun** \ən\ see UN

³**aun** \ȯn\ see ³ON

⁴**aun** \au̇n\ see ²OWN

¹**auna** \än-ə\ see ¹ANA

²**auna** \ȯn-ə\ see ¹ONNA

aunce \ȯns\ jaunce, launce

¹**aunch** \änch\ conch, cranch, craunch, paunch, raunch, stanch, Romansh

²**aunch** \ȯnch\ craunch, haunch, launch, paunch, raunch, stanch, staunch

auncher \ȯn-chər\ launcher, stancher, stauncher

aunchy \ȯn-chē\ paunchy, raunchy

aund \ȯnd\ awned, maund— *also pasts of verbs listed at* ³ON

¹**aunder** \ȯn-dər\ launder, maunder

²**aunder** \än-dər\ see ¹ONDER

aunish \än-ish\ see ONISH

¹**aunt** \ȯnt\ daunt, flaunt, gaunt, haunt, jaunt, taunt, vaunt, want, wont, avant, avaunt, keeshond, romaunt, John of Gaunt

²**aunt** \ant\ see ⁵ANT

³**aunt** \änt\ see ²ANT

aunted \ȯnt-əd\ see ONTED

¹**aunter** \änt-ər\ saunter, mishanter, rencontre

²**aunter** \ȯnt-ər\ gaunter, haunter, saunter

¹**aunty** \ȯnt-ē\ flaunty, jaunty, vaunty

²**aunty** \änt-ē\ see ¹ANTI

aunus \än-əs\ see ¹ONUS

aup \ȯp\ gawp, scaup, whaup, yawp

aupe \ōp\ see OPE

auphin \ȯ-fən\ see OFFIN

¹**aur** \au̇r\ see ²OWER

²**aur** \ȯr\ see ¹OR

¹**aura** \ȯr-ə\ see ²ORA

²**aura** \är-ə\ see ¹ARA

aural \ȯr-əl\ see ²ORAL

¹**aure** \ōr\ see ¹ORE

²**aure** \ȯr\ see ¹OR

aurea \ȯr-ē-ə\ see ORIA

aurean \ȯr-ē-ən\ see ORIAN

¹**aureate** \är-ē-ət\ baccalaureate, commisariat

²**aureate** \ȯr-ē-ət\ aureate, laureate, baccalaureate, professoriat

aurel \ȯr-əl\ see ²ORAL

¹**auren** \är-ən\ see ¹ORIN

²**auren** \ȯr-ən\ see ²ORIN

aurence \ȯr-ən(t)s\ see AWRENCE

aureus \ȯr-ē-əs\ see ORIOUS

auri \au̇r-ē\ see OWERY

aurian \ȯr-ē-ən\ see ORIAN

auric \ȯr-ik\ see ORIC

¹**aurice** \är-əs\ see ¹ORRIS

²**aurice** \ȯr-əs\ see AURUS

auricle \ȯr-i-kəl\ see ORICAL

¹**aurie** \ȯr-ē\ see ORY

²**aurie** \är-ē\ see ARI

aurous \ȯr-əs\ see AURUS

aurus \ȯr-əs\ aurous, Boris, chorus, Doris, Flores, Horace, Maurice, morris, Morris, Norris, orris, porous, sorus, Taurus, Torres, torus, canorous, Centaurus, clitoris, decorous, Delores, Dolores, pelorus, phosphorous, sonorous, thesaurus,

allosaurus, brontosaurus,
stegosaurus, apatosaurus,
tyrannosaurus
aury \ȯr-ē\ see ORY
¹aus \ā-əs\ see ¹AIS
²aus \au̇s\ see ²OUSE
³aus \ȯz\ see ¹AUSE
ausal \ȯ-zəl\ causal, clausal,
menopausal, postmenopausal
¹ause \ȯz\ Broz, cause, clause,
gauze, hawse, pause, tawse,
yaws, applause, because,
kolkhoz, sovkhoz, aeropause,
diapause, menopause, Santa
Claus—*also plurals and
possessives of nouns and
third person singular presents
of verbs listed at* ¹AW
²ause \əz\ see ¹EUSE
auseous \ȯ-shəs\ see AUTIOUS
auser \ȯ-zər\ causer, hawser
ausey \ȯ-zē\ causey, gauzy
auss \au̇s\ see ¹OUSE
¹aussie \äs-ē\ see ¹OSSY
²aussie \ȯ-sē\ see ²OSSY
¹aust \au̇st\ see OUST
²aust \ȯst\ see ³OST
austen \ȯs-tən\ see OSTON
austin \ȯs-tən\ see OSTON
austless \ȯst-ləs\ costless,
exhaustless
¹austral \äs-trəl\ see OSTREL
²austral \ȯs-trəl\ see ¹OSTRAL
¹aut \ō\ see ¹OW
²aut \au̇t\ see ³OUT
³aut \ät\ see ¹OT
⁴aut \ȯt\ see ¹OUGHT
autch \ȯch\ see ¹AUCH
aute \ōt\ see OAT
auten \ȯt-ᵊn\ boughten, tauten
auterne \ȯt-ərn\ quartern,
sauterne, sauternes

auternes \ȯt-ərn\ see AUTERNE
autery \ȯt-ə-rē\ see ATERY
autic \ȯt-ik\ orthotic,
aeronautic, astronautic
autical \ȯt-i-kəl\ nautical,
aeronautical, astronautical
autics \ät-iks\ see OTICS
aution \ȯ-shən\ caution,
groschen, incaution,
precaution
autious \ȯ-shəs\ cautious,
nauseous, incautious
¹auto \ȯt-ō\ auto, Giotto, risotto
²auto \ät-ō\ see ¹ATO
auve \ōv\ see ²OVE
auze \ȯz\ see ¹AUSE
auzer \au̇-zər\ see OUSER
auzy \ȯ-zē\ see AUSEY
¹av \äv\ see ²OLVE
²av \av\ see ²ALVE
¹ava \äv-ə\ brava, fava, guava,
java, Java, kava, lava,
baklava, cassava, ottava,
balaclava, Bratislava, Costa
Brava, lavalava, piassava,
Warszawa
²ava \av-ə\ java, Ungava,
balaclava
avage \av-ij\ ravage, savage
avan \ā-vən\ see ¹AVEN
avant \av-ənt\ haven't, savant
avarice \av-rəs\ see AVEROUS
¹ave \äv-ā\ ave, clave, grave,
Jahveh, soave
²ave \āv\ brave, clave, cave,
crave, Dave, fave, gave,
glaive, grave, knave, lave,
nave, pave, rave, save, shave,
slave, stave, they've, trave,
waive, wave, Wave, airwave,
behave, concave, conclave,
deprave, dissave, drawshave,

enclave, engrave, enslave, exclave, forgave, Great Slave, margrave, octave, outbrave, p-wave, palsgrave, shortwave, spokeshave, after-shave, architrave, biconcave, microwave, contraoctave, photoengrave

³ave \av\ see ³ALVE

⁴ave \äv\ see ²OLVE

aved \āvd\ waved, depraved, unsaved—*also pasts of verbs listed at* ²AVE

avel \av-əl\ cavil, gavel, gravel, ravel, travel, unravel

aveless \āv-ləs\ graveless, waveless

aveling \av-liŋ\ raveling, traveling

avement \āv-mənt\ pavement, depravement, enslavement

¹aven \ā-vən\ Avon, Cavan, craven, graven, haven, maven, raven, shaven, New Haven, riboflavin, Stratford-upon-Avon

²aven \av-ən\ see AVIN

aven't \av-ənt\ see AVANT

¹aver \äv-ər\ slaver, palaver, windhover

²aver \ā-vər\ caver, claver, favor, flavor, graver, haver, laver, quaver, raver, saver, savor, shaver, slaver, waiver, waver, disfavor, enslaver, face-saver, flag-waver, lifesaver, semiquaver, demisemiquaver, hemidemisemiquaver—*also comparatives of adjectives listed at* ²AVE

³aver \av-ər\ slaver, cadaver, palaver

avern \av-ərn\ cavern, klavern, tavern

averous \av-rəs\ avarice, cadaverous

avery \āv-rē\ bravery, knavery, quavery, savory, slavery, wavery, unsavory

avey \ā-vē\ see AVY

avia \ā-vē-ə\ Moldavia, Moravia, Scandinavia

avial \ā-vē-əl\ gavial, margravial

avian \ā-vē-ən\ avian, Shavian, Moravian, Scandinavian

avid \av-əd\ avid, gravid, pavid

avie \ā-vē\ see AVY

avil \av-əl\ see AVEL

avin \av-ən\ Avon, raven, ravin, savin, spavin

aving \ā-viŋ\ caving, craving, paving, raving, saving, shaving, flagwaving, lifesaving, timesaving, laborsaving

avis \ā-vəs\ Davis, favus, mavis, Mavis, rara avis

¹avish \ā-vish\ knavish, slavish

²avish \av-ish\ lavish, ravish

avist \äv-əst\ Slavist, suavest, Pan-Slavist

avity \av-ət-ē\ cavity, gravity, concavity, depravity, antigravity, microgravity, supergravity

avl \äv-əl\ see ¹OVEL

¹avo \äv-ō\ bravo, Bravo, centavo, octavo

²avo \ā-vō\ octavo, relievo, mezzo relievo

¹avon \ā-vən\ see ¹AVEN

²**avon** \a-vən\ see AVIN

avor \ā-vər\ see ²AVER

avored \ā-vərd\ favored,
flavored, ill-favored, well-
favored—*also pasts of verbs
listed at* ²AVER

avory \āv-rē\ see AVERY

avus \ā-vəs\ see AVIS

avvy \av-ē\ navvy, savvy

avy \ā-vē\ cavy, Davey, Davy,
gravy, navy, shavie, slavey,
wavy

¹**aw** \ȯ\ aw, awe, blaw, braw,
ca, caw, chaw, claw, craw,
daw, draw, faugh, flaw, gnaw,
haugh, haw, jaw, la, law,
maw, pa, paw, pshaw, Ra,
rah, raw, saw, shah, shaw,
Shaw, slaw, spa, squaw,
straw, tau, taw, thaw, yaw,
backsaw, bashaw, bedstraw,
bucksaw, bylaw, catclaw,
cat's-paw, coleslaw,
cumshaw, cushaw, Danelaw,
declaw, dewclaw, Esau,
forepaw, fretsaw, grandma,
grandpa, guffaw, hacksaw,
handsaw, hawkshaw, hee-
haw, hurrah, in-law, jackdaw,
jackstraw, jigsaw, kickshaw,
lockjaw, macaw, Nassau, old-
squaw, outdraw, outlaw,
pasha, pooh-bah, ricksha,
rickshaw, ringtaw, ripsaw,
scofflaw, scrimshaw, seesaw,
southpaw, trishaw, tussah,
undraw, Utah, vizsla,
Warsaw, whipsaw, windflaw,
wiredraw, withdraw,
Arkansas, Chickasaw,
Chippewa, clapperclaw,
decree-law, foofaraw,

jinrikisha, Kiowa, Mackinac,
mackinaw, Omaha, Ottawa,
overawe, overdraw, oversaw,
overslaugh, padishah,
panama, son-in-law,
usquebaugh, Wichita,
williwaw, windlestraw,
Yakima, brother-in-law,
daughter-in-law, father-in-law,
mother-in-law, pipsissewa,
serjeant-at-law, sister-in-law,
Straits of Mackinac

²**aw** \äv\ see ²OLVE

³**aw** \ȯf\ see ²OFF

⁴**aw** \äf\ see ¹OFF

¹**awa** \ä-wə\ Chihuahua,
Tarawa, Urawa, Fujisawa,
Ichikawa, Kanzawa, Okinawa,
Ahashikawa

²**awa** \ä-və\ see ¹AVA

awain \au̇-ən\ see ²OWAN

awan \au̇-ən\ see ²OWAN

awar \au̇r\ see ²OWER

awba \ȯ-bə\ see AUBA

¹**awber** \äb-ər\ see OBBER

²**awber** \ȯb-ər\ see AUBER

awd \ȯd\ see ¹AUD

awddle \äd-ᵊl\ see ODDLE

awdle \ȯd-ᵊl\ see AUDAL

awdry \ȯ-drē\ Audrey, tawdry

awdust \ȯd-əst\ see ¹ADIST

awdy \ȯd-ē\ bawdy, gaudy,
summa cum laude

awe \ȯ\ see ¹AW

awed \ȯd\ see ¹AUD

aweless \ȯ-ləs\ see AWLESS

awer \ȯr\ see ¹OR

awers \ōrz\ see OORS

awful \ȯ-fəl\ awful, coffle,
lawful, offal, god-awful,
unlawful

awfully \òf-ə-lē\ awfully,
lawfully, offaly, unlawfully
awing \óiŋ\ cloying, drawing,
wappenschawing
awk \ók\ see ALK
awker \ò-kər\ see ALKER
awkes \óks\ Fawkes—*also*
possessives and plurals of
nouns, third person singular
presents of verbs listed at ALK
awkish \ò-kish\ gawkish,
hawkish, mawkish
awky \ò-kē\ see ALKIE
awl \ól\ see ALL
awler \ò-lər\ see ¹ALLER
awless \ò-ləs\ aweless, flawless,
lawless
awling \ò-liŋ\ see ALLING
awly \ò-lē\ brawly, crawly,
dolly, drawly, Raleigh,
scrawly, squally, Bengali,
Macaulay
awm \óm\ see ¹AUM
¹awn \än\ see ¹ON
²awn \ón\ see ³ON
awned \ónd\ see AUND
¹awner \ón-ər\ fawner, goner,
pawner, prawner, spawner
²awner \än-ər\ see ¹ONOR
awney \ò-nē\ see ¹AWNY
awning \än-iŋ\ see ¹ONING
awnly \än-lē\ see ¹ANLY
¹awny \ò-nē\ brawny, fawny,
lawny, sawney, scrawny,
Taney, tawny, mulligatawny
²awny \än-ē\ see ¹ANI
awp \óp\ see AUP
awrence \ór-ən(t)s\ Florence,
Laurence, Lawrence,
Torrence, abhorrence, Saint
Lawrence—*also possessives*

and plurals of nouns listed at
ORRENT
awry \òr-ē\ see ORY
aws \óz\ see ¹AUSE
awse \óz\ see ¹AUSE
awser \ó-zər\ see AUSER
awsi \aù-sē\ see ²OUSY
awy \ói\ see OY
awyer \ò-yər\ lawyer, sawyer
¹ax \äks\ see OX
²ax \aks\ ax, fax, flax, lax, max,
Max, pax, rax, sax, tax, wax,
addax, Ajax, anthrax, banjax,
beeswax, borax, broadax,
climax, coax, earwax, galax,
gravlax, hyrax, meat-ax,
panchax, pickax, poleax,
pretax, relax, smilax, storax,
styrax, surtax, syntax, thorax,
toadflax, aftertax, battle-ax,
Halifax, minimax, overtax,
parallax, supertax, anticlimax,
Astyanax—*also plurals and*
possessives of nouns and
third person singular presents
of verbs listed at ²ACK
axant \ak-sənt\ see ACCENT
axen \ak-sən\ see AXON
axi \ak-sē\ see AXY
axic \ak-sik\ ataraxic,
stereotaxic
axis \ak-səs\ axis, Naxos, praxis
axman \ak-smən\ axman,
cracksman
axon \ak-sən\ flaxen, Jackson,
Klaxon, Saxon, waxen, Port
Jackson, Anglo-Saxon
axos \ak-səs\ see AXIS
axy \ak-sē\ flaxy, maxi, taxi,
waxy
¹ay \ā\ a , ae, aye, bay, bey,
blae, brae, bray, chez, clay,

Clay, day, dey, dray, eh, fay,
Fay, Faye, fey, flay, fley, frae,
fray, Frey, gay, Gay, gey,
gley, gray, Gray, greige,
Grey, hae, hay, he, hey, Hue,
j, jay, Jay, Jaye, k, kay, Kay,
Kaye, lay, lei, may, May, nay,
né, née, neigh, pay, pe, play,
pray, prey, qua, quai, quay,
Rae, ray, Ray, re, say, sei,
shay, slay, sleigh, spae, spay,
splay, spray, stay, stray, sway,
they, tray, trey, way, weigh,
whey, yea, abbé, affray,
agley, airplay, airway, all-day,
allay, allée, Angers, Anhui,
Anhwei, archway, array,
ashtray, assay, astray, Augier,
away, aweigh, backstay,
ballet, beignet, belay,
beltway, benday, Benet, beret,
betray, bewray, bidet,
bikeway, birthday, Biscay,
Bizet, blasé, bobstay,
Bombay, bombe, bouchée,
bouclé, boule, bouquet,
bourrée, breezeway,
Broadway, buffet, byplay,
byway, cachet, café, cahier,
Cambay, Cape May, Cartier,
Cathay, causeway, chaîné,
chalet, chambray, chassé, ciré,
cliché, cloqué, congé, convey,
corvée, coudé, coupé,
crawlway, crochet, croquet,
crossway, cube, curé, cy pres,
DA, daresay, decay, deejay,
defray, delay, dengue,
dismay, display, distrait, DJ,
donnée, doomsday, doorway,
dossier, downplay, dragée,
driveway, duvet, embay,
entrée, épée, essay, estray,
Ewe, fairway, filé, filet, fillet,
fireclay, fishway, flambé,
floodway, flyway, folkway,
footway, foray, forebay,
foreplay, forestay, formée,
forte, fouetté, four-way,
fourchée, foyer, franglais,
frappé, freeway, frieze, frisé,
fumet, gainsay, Galway,
gamay, gangway, Gaspé,
gateway, gelée, glacé, godet,
gourmet, Green Bay,
greenway, guideway, gunplay,
halfway, hallway, hatchway,
headway, hearsay, Hebei,
Hefei, heyday, highway,
homestay, hooray, horseplay,
Hubei, in re, inlay, inveigh,
issei, jackstay, jeté, keyway,
Kobe, koine, kouprey, lamé,
laneway, leeway, lifeway,
Lomé, Lough Neagh, lwei,
lycée, M-day, maguey,
mainstay, Malay, malgré,
man-day, Mande, Manet,
manqué, margay, Marseilles,
massé, maté, May Day,
Mayday, melee, metier, meze,
midday, Midway, Millay,
Millet, mislay, misplay,
moiré, Monet, moray, nevé,
Niamey, nisei, noonday,
Norway, nosegay, obey, ofay,
OK, olé, ombré, osprey,
outlay, outré, outstay,
outweigh, oyez, PA, parfait,
parkway, parlay, parquet,
partway, passé, pâté, pathway,
pavé, payday, per se, pince-
nez, piqué, piquet, PK, plié,
plissé, pommée, Pompeii,

portray, prepay, projet,
pulque, puree, purvey, quale,
raceway, railway, rappee,
relay, Rene, Renee, repay,
replay, risqué, roadway, role-
play, ropeway, rosé, rosebay,
Roubaix, roué, routeway,
runway, sachet, Salé, sansei,
sashay, sauté, screenplay,
seaway, semé, shar-pei,
shipway, short-day, sideway,
Skopje, skyway, slideway,
slipway, sluiceway, soigné,
soiree, someday, someway,
soothsay, soufflé, speedway,
spillway, stairway, sternway,
stingray, straightway,
strathspey, subway, survey,
swordplay, Taipei, tempeh,
thoughtway, three-way,
thruway, tideway, Tigré,
today, Tokay, tollway,
Torbay, touché, toupee,
trackway, tramway, unlay,
unsay, valet, V-day, veejay,
vide, visé, Vouvray, walkway,
waylay, weekday, windway,
wireway, wordplay, workday,
X ray, x-ray, Yaoundé, Adige,
A-OK, alleyway, anyway,
appliqué, arrivé, atelier,
attaché, ballonet, Beaujolais,
beurre manié, BHA, botonée,
braciole, breakaway, bustier,
cabaret, cableway, Camagüey,
canapé, cap-a-pie, caraway,
carriageway, Cartier,
cassoulet, castaway,
champlevé, chansonnier,
chardonnay, Charolais,
chevalier, Chippewa,
cloisonné, consommé,

coryphée, croupier, crudités,
cutaway, day-to-day,
debauchee, déclassé, dégagé,
degree-day, démodé, devotee,
disarray, disobey, distingué,
divorcé, divorcée, DNA,
émigré, engagé, entranceway,
entremets, entryway, espalier,
etoufée, everyday, exposé,
expressway, fadeaway,
fallaway, faraday, Faraday,
faraway, fiancé, fiancée,
flageolet, flyaway, foldaway,
Galloway, Georgian Bay,
getaway, giveaway, gratiné,
gratinée, guillemet, Harare,
haulageway, Hemingway,
hereaway, hideaway, HLA,
Hogmanay, holiday, Hugh
Capet, IgA, inter se, interplay,
intraday, IPA, IRA, Joliet,
Kootenay, Kutenai, kyrie,
lackaday, latter-day, layaway,
lingerie, macramé, Mandalay,
Massenet, matinee, MIA,
Molise, Monterrey,
motorway, muscadet,
negligee, overlay, overplay,
overstay, overweigh,
Paraguay, passageway,
patissier, Petare, photoplay,
pikake, piolet, pis aller, play-
by-play, poly (A), Ponape,
popinjay, pourparler, pousse-
café, present-day, protégé,
protégée, Rabelais,
rambouillet, ratiné, recamier,
rechauffé, recherché,
reconvey, repartee, repoussé,
résumé, retroussé, ricochet,
right-of-way, rockaway,
rondelet, roundelay, RNA,

runaway, Saguenay, San Jose,
San José, Santa Fe, São
Tomé, semplice, sobriquet,
sommelier, steerageway,
standaway, stowaway,
straightaway, Table Bay,
taboret, take-away, tarsier,
taxiway, tearaway, teleplay,
Tempere, Tenebrae, thataway,
throwaway, Thunder Bay,
Udine, underlay, underpay,
underplay, underway,
Uruguay, velouté, Venite,
vérité, vertebra, virelay,
walkaway, waterway,
wellaway, Whitsunday,
workaday, Yenisey, Zuider
Zee, Agnus Dei, areaway,
auto-da-fé, bichon frisé,
boulevardier, cabriolet, café
au lait, cantabile, cDNA,
communiqué, costumier,
couturier, décolleté, diamanté,
Dies Irae, eglomisé, felo-de-
se, Fiesole, garde-manger,
habitué, Jubilate, laissez-
passer, Lavoisier, marrons
glacé, mezzo forte, Morgan le
Fay, objet trouvé, out-of-the-
way, papier collé, papier-
mâché, pas de bourrée, photo-
essay, Port Philip Bay,
pouilly-fuissé, Pouilly-Fumé,
prêt-à-porter, roche
moutonnée, roman à clef,
roturier, sine die, sub judice,
superhighway, ukiyo-e, Ulan-
Ude, yerba maté, Alto Adige,
arrière pensée, Guanabara
Bay, lettre de cachet,
catalogue raisonné, cinema
verite, Dumfries and

Galloway, vers de société,
video verité, sinfonia
concertante, Trentino-Alto
Adige
²**ay** \ē\ see ¹EE
³**ay** \ī\ see ¹Y
¹**aya** \ä-yə\ ayah, maya, taille,
Malaya, Koshigaya
²**aya** \ī-ə\ see ¹IAH
³**aya** \ā-ə\ see ¹AIA
ayable \ā-ə-bəl\ payable,
playable, sayable, defrayable,
displayable, unsayable
ayah \ī-ə\ see ¹IAH
ayal \āl\ see AIL
¹**ayan** \ā-ən\ crayon, Chilean,
Malayan, ouabain, papain,
Pompeian, Pompeiian,
Galilean, Himalayan
²**ayan** \ī-ən\ see ¹ION
¹**aybe** \ā-bē\ see ABY
²**aybe** \eb-ē\ see EBBY
ayday \ā-dā\ Ede, Mayday,
May Day
ayden \ī-dᵊn\ see IDEN
¹**aye** \ā\ see ¹AY
²**aye** \ī\ see ¹Y
ayed \ād\ see ¹ADE
¹**ayer** \ā-ər\ brayer, layer,
mayor, payer, player, prayer,
preyer, sayer, sprayer, stayer,
strayer, ballplayer, betrayer,
bilayer, bricklayer, cardplayer,
conveyer, crocheter, decayer,
delayer, doomsayer,
doomsdayer, gainsayer,
horseplayer, inlayer, essayer,
forayer, inveigher, obeyer,
manslayer, minelayer,
portrayer, purveyor, ratepayer,
soothsayer, swordplayer,
surveyor, taxpayer, tracklayer,

yea-sayer, disobeyer,
holidayer—*also comparatives
of adjectives listed at* ¹AY
²**ayer** \er\ see ⁴ARE
ayered \erd\ see AIRED
ayest \ā-əst\ mayest, sayest,
épéeist, essayist, fideist,
Hebraist, Mithraist—*also
superlatives of adjectives
listed at* ¹AY
¹**ayin** \ī-ən\ see ¹ION
²**ayin** \īn\ see ¹INE
³**ayin** \ä-yən\ see AIIAN
aying \ā-iŋ\ gleying, maying,
playing, saying, bricklaying,
delaying, long-playing,
soothsaying, surveying,
taxpaying, tracklaying
ayish \ā-ish\ clayish, grayish
ayist \ā-əst\ see AYEST
ayle \āl\ see AIL
ayless \ā-ləs\ rayless, talus,
wayless, Morelos, aurora
australis, Corona Australis
ayling \ā-liŋ\ see AILING
aylor \ā-lər\ see AILER
ayly \ā-lē\ see AILY
ayman \ā-mən\ see ¹AMEN
ayment \ā-mənt\ ament,
claimant, clamant, payment,
raiment, co-payment,
embayment, prepayment,
underlayment, underpayment
ayne \ān\ see ¹ANE
ayness \ā-nəs\ anus, feyness,
gayness, grayness, heinous,
Janus, manus, awayness,
uranous, Uranus,
everydayness
aynim \ā-nəm\ see ¹ANUM
ayn't \ā-ənt\ see EYANT
¹**ayo** \ā-ō\ see ¹EO

²**ayo** \ī-ō\ see ¹IO
¹**ayon** \an\ see ⁵AN
²**ayon** \ā-ən\ see ¹AYAN
ayor \ā-ər\ see ¹AYER
¹**ayou** \ī-ə\ see ¹IAH
²**ayou** \ī-ō\ see ¹IO
ayr \er\ see ⁴ARE
¹**ays** \ez\ fez, Fez, Geez, prez,
says, Cortez, gainsays, Inez,
Suez, unsays, crème anglaise,
Louis Seize, Louis Treize,
Isthmus of Suez, Vincente
López
²**ays** \āz\ see ¹AZE
aysia \ā-zhə\ see ASIA
ay-so \ā-sō\ see ¹ESO
ayton \āt-ᵊn\ Clayton, Dayton,
Layton
¹**ayyid** \ī-əd\ see YAD
²**ayyid** \ēd-ē\ see EEDY
¹**az** \az\ see AZZ
²**az** \äz\ see ¹OISE
³**az** \äts\ see OTS
¹**aza** \äz-ə\ Gaza, plaza, piazza,
tabula rasa
²**aza** \az-ə\ plaza, piazza
¹**azar** \äz-ər\ see OZZER
²**azar** \az-ər\ lazar, alcazar,
Belshazzar
azard \az-ərd\ hazard, mazard,
mazzard, haphazard
¹**aze** \āz\ baize, blaze, braise,
braze, chaise, craze, days,
daze, Draize, faze, feaze,
fraise, gaze, glaze, graze,
Hays, haze, lase, laze, maize,
maze, phase, phrase, praise,
raise, rase, raze, smaze, vase,
ways, ablaze, agaze, amaze,
appraise, breadthways,
catchphrase, crossways,
deglaze, dispraise, edgeways,

emblaze, endways, flatways,
foodways, gainsays,
hereways, leastways,
lengthways, liaise, malaise,
mores, pj's, sideways,
slantways, stargaze, ukase,
upraise, weekdays, anyways,
chrysoprase, cornerways,
crème anglaise, holidays,
Louis Seize, Louis Treize,
lyonnaise, mayonnaise,
metaphrase, multiphase,
nowadays, overglaze,
overgraze, paraphrase,
polonaise, polyphase, single-
phase, underglaze—*also
plurals and possessives of
nouns and third person
singular presents of verbs
listed at* ¹AY

²aze \äz\ see ¹OISE

³aze \äz-ē\ see ¹AZI

azeable \ā-zə-bəl\ see ¹ASABLE

azed \āzd\ unfazed—*pasts of
verbs listed at* ¹AZE

azel \ā-zəl\ see ²ASAL

azement \āz-mənt\ amazement,
appraisement

azen \āz-ᵊn\ see AZON

azer \ā-zər\ blazer, brazer,
Fraser, gazer, glazer, grazer,
hazer, laser, maser, mazer,
praiser, razer, razor, appraiser,
fund-raiser, hair-raiser, hell-
raiser, stargazer, trailblazer,
paraphraser, free-electron
laser

¹azi \äz-ē\ quasi, Swazi,
Benghazi, Anasazi, kamikaze

²azi \az-ē\ see AZZY

³azi \at-sē\ Nazi, patsy, Patsy,
neo-Nazi

⁴azi \ät-sē\ Nazi, neo-Nazi

azier \ā-zhər\ brazier, Frasier,
glacier, glazier, grazier,
leisure, measure, pleasure,
rasure, treasure, admeasure,
embrasure, erasure

azing \ā-ziŋ\ see AISING

azo \az-ō\ diazo, terrazzo

azon \āz-ᵊn\ blazon, brazen,
raisin, emblazon, Marquesan,
diapason, hexenbesen

azor \ā-zər\ see AZER

azquez \as-kəs\ see ASCUS

azy \ā-zē\ crazy, daisy, Daisy,
hazy, lazy, mazy, stir-crazy,
witch of Agnesi

azz \az\ as, has, jazz, razz, spaz,
Hejaz, La Paz, pizzazz, topaz,
whenas, whereas, razzmatazz

¹azza \az-ə\ see ²AZA

²azza \äz-ə\ see ¹AZA

³azza \ät-sə\ see ¹ATZO

azzar \az-ər\ see ²AZAR

azzard \az-ərd\ see AZARD

azzle \az-əl\ basil, Basil, dazzle,
frazzle, bedazzle, razzle-
dazzle

¹azzo \ät-sō\ matzo, palazzo,
terrazzo, paparazzo

²azzo \az-ō\ see AZO

azzy \az-ē\ jazzy, snazzy,
Ashkenazi

e

¹e \ā\ see ¹AY

²e \ē\ see ¹EE

³e \ə\ see ³U

é \ā\ see ¹AY

¹ea \ā\ see ¹AY

²ea \ā-ə\ see ¹AIA

³ea \ē\ see ¹EE

⁴ea \ē-ə\ see ¹IA

eabee \ē-bē\ see ¹EBE

eace \ēs\ see IECE

eaceable \ē-sə-bəl\ see
¹EASABLE

each \ēch\ beach, beech, bleach,
breach, breech, each, fleech,
leach, leech, peach, pleach,
preach, reach, screech,
speech, teach, beseech,
forereach, impeach, Long
Beach, outreach, unteach,
overreach, practice-teach,
Huntington Beach

eachable \ē-chə-bəl\
bleachable, leachable,
reachable, teachable,
impeachable, unimpeachable

eacher \ē-chər\ bleacher,
creature, feature, leacher,
preacher, reacher, screecher,
teacher, defeature, disfeature,
schoolteacher

eacherous \ech-rəs\ see
ECHEROUS

eachery \ech-rē\ see ECHERY

eaching \ē-chiŋ\ see EECHING

eachment \ēch-mənt\
preachment, impeachment

eachy \ē-chē\ beachy, chichi,
Nietzsche, peachy, preachy,
screechy, caliche, Campeche

eacle \ē-kəl\ see ¹ECAL

eacly \ē-klē\ see EEKLY

eacon \ē-kən\ beacon, deacon,
sleeken, weaken, archdeacon,
Mohican, subdeacon,
Neorican

¹ead \ed\ bed, bled, bread, bred,
dead, dread, ed, Ed, fed, fled,
Fred, head, Jed, lead, led,
med, Ned, ped, pled, read,
red, Red, redd, said, shed,
shred, sled, sped, spread,
stead, ted, Ted, thread, tread,
wed, zed, abed, afraid, ahead,
airhead, baldhead, beachhead,
bedspread, bedstead,
beebread, behead, bestead,
bighead, biped, blackhead,
blockhead, bloodred,
bloodshed, bobsled,
bonehead, bridgehead, brown
bread, bulkhead, bullhead,
cathead, childbed, coed,
cokehead, corn-fed, cowshed,
crispbread, crossbred,
crosshead, daybed, deadhead,
death's-head, deathbed,
dispread, dogsled, dopehead,
drophead, drumhead,
dumbhead, egghead, embed,
far-red, farmstead, fathead,
flatbed, forehead, foresaid,
gainsaid, Gateshead, godhead,

green-head, half-bred,
hardhead, highbred, hogshead,
homebred, homestead,
hophead, hotbed, hothead, ill-
bred, inbred, instead, jarhead,
juicehead, lamed, light bread,
longhead, lowbred, lunkhead,
masthead, meathead, misled,
misread, moped, naled,
nonsked, outsped, outspread,
packthread, phys ed, pinhead,
pithead, pothead, premed,
printhead, purebred, railhead,
re-tread, redhead, retread,
riverbed, roadbed, roadstead,
Roundhead, saphead,
scarehead, seabed, seedbed,
sheep ked, sheepshead,
sheetfed, shewbread,
shortbread, sickbed, skinhead,
snowshed, softhead, sorehead,
spearhead, springhead,
steelhead, straightbred,
streambed, subhead,
sweetbread, swellhead,
thickhead, thunderhead,
toolhead, toolshed, towhead,
trailhead, unbred, undead,
unread, unsaid, unthread,
untread, warhead, webfed,
well-bred, well-read,
wellhead, white-bread,
whitehead, widespread,
wingspread, woodshed,
woolshed, acidhead,
aforesaid, arrowhead,
barrelhead, Birkenhead,
bubblehead, bufflehead,
chowderhead, chucklehead,
colorbred, copperhead,
dragonhead, dunderhead,
featherbed, featherhead,
fiddlehead, figurehead, fire-
engine red, fountainhead,
gingerbread, go-ahead,
hammerhead, infrared,
interbred, knucklehead,
letterhead, loggerhead,
lowlihead, maidenhead,
newlywed, overhead,
overspread, pinniped, pointy-
head, poppyhead, quadruped,
saddlebred, Saint John's
bread, Samoyed, showerhead,
sleepyhead, slugabed,
standardbred, straight-ahead,
timberhead, thoroughbred,
underbred, underfed,
watershed, woodenhead, far-
infrared, near-infrared, West
Quoddy Head, parallelepiped
²ead \ēd\ see EED
³ead \əd\ see ¹UD
¹eadable \ēd-ə-bəl\ kneadable,
pleadable, readable
²eadable \ed-ə-bəl\ see EDIBLE
¹eaded \ed-əd\ bedded, headed,
bareheaded, bigheaded,
bullheaded, clearheaded,
coolheaded, eggheaded,
embedded, fatheaded,
hardheaded, hotheaded, light-
headed, longheaded,
lunkheaded, pigheaded,
pinheaded, roundheaded,
sapheaded, softheaded,
soreheaded, swelled-headed,
swellheaded, thickheaded,
towheaded, bubbleheaded,
chowderheaded,
chuckleheaded, dunderheaded,
featherheaded, unleaded,
white-headed, empty-headed,
hydra-headed, knuckleheaded,

levelheaded, muddleheaded,
pointy-headed, puzzleheaded,
woodenheaded, woolly-
headed

²**eaded** \ē-dəd\ see EEDED

eaden \ed-ᵊn\ deaden, leaden,
redden, steading, Armageddon

¹**eader** \ēd-ər\ cedar, ceder,
feeder, kneader, leader,
pleader, reader, seeder,
speeder, weeder, bandleader,
cheerleader, conceder, lip-
reader, newsreader, nonreader,
proofreader, repleader,
ringleader, seceder,
stampeder, stockbreeder,
succeeder, copyreader,
interpleader

²**eader** \ed-ər\ bedder, cheddar,
chedar, header, shedder,
shredder, sledder, spreader,
tedder, threader, wedder,
homesteader, doubleheader,
triple-header

eadily \ed-ᵊl-ē\ headily, readily,
unsteadily

¹**eading** \ed-iŋ\ bedding,
heading, Reading, steading,
wedding, bobsledding,
farmsteading, subheading,
wide-spreading

²**eading** \ed-ᵊn\ see EADEN

³**eading** \ēd-ᵊn\ see EDON

⁴**eading** \ēd-iŋ\ see ¹EEDING

¹**eadle** \ed-ᵊl\ see ¹EDAL

²**eadle** \ēd-ᵊl\ see EEDLE

eadly \ed-lē\ see EDLEY

eadow \ed-ə\ see EDDA

¹**eadsman** \edz-mən\ headsman,
leadsman

²**eadsman** \ēdz-mən\ see
EEDSMAN

¹**eady** \ed-ē\ Eddie, eddy, Eddy,
Freddie, heady, leady, ready,
steady, Teddie, teddy, Teddy,
thready, already, makeready,
unsteady, gingerbready,
rough-and-ready

²**eady** \ēd-ē\ see EEDY

¹**eaf** \ef\ see ¹EF

²**eaf** \ēf\ see ¹IEF

eafless \ē-fləs\ see IEFLESS

eafy \ē-fē\ see EEFY

eag \ēg\ see IGUE

eagan \ā-gən\ see AGIN

eager \ē-gər\ eager, leaguer,
meager, beleaguer, intriguer,
Xinjiang Uygur

eagh \ā\ see ¹AY

eagle \ē-gəl\ see EGAL

eague \ēg\ see IGUE

eaguer \ē-gər\ see EAGER

eah \ē-ə\ see ¹IA

¹**eak** \ēk\ beak, bleak, cheek,
chic, cleek, clique, creak,
creek, Creek, eke, flic, freak,
geek, gleek, Greek, keek,
leak, leek, meek, peak, peek,
peke, pic, pique, reek, screak,
seek, sheik, sheikh, shriek,
sic, Sikh, sleek, sneak, speak,
squeak, steek, streak, streek,
teak, tweak, weak, week,
wreak, antique, apeak, batik,
Belgique, Belleek, bespeak,
bezique, boutique, cacique,
caique, critique, debeak,
forepeak, forespeak, grosbeak,
hairstreak, halfbeak,
houseleek, misspeak, muzhik,
mystique, newspeak, nonpeak,
oblique, off-peak, outspeak,
perique, physique, Pikes Peak,
pip-squeak, pratique, relique,

technic, technique, Tajik,
unique, unspeak, workweek,
biunique, Bolshevik,
Chesapeake, dominique,
doublespeak, ecofreak,
fenugreek, hide-and-seek,
Lassen Peak, Martinique,
Menshevik, Mozambique,
semi-antique, verd antique,
Veronique, electroweak, opéra
comique, realpolitik

²**eak** \āk\ see ¹AKE

³**eak** \ek\ see ECK

eakable \ā-kə-bəl\ see AKABLE

eake \ēk\ see ¹EAK

¹**eaked** \ē-kəd\ peaked, streaked

²**eaked** \ēkt\ beaked, freaked,
peaked, streaked, apple-
cheeked—*also pasts of verbs
listed at* ¹EAK

³**eaked** \ik-əd\ see ¹ICKED

eaken \ē-kən\ see EACON

¹**eaker** \ē-kər\ beaker, leaker,
reeker, seeker, sneaker,
speaker, squeaker,
loudspeaker, self-seeker,
sunseeker, doublespeaker—
*also comparatives of
adjectives listed at* ¹EAK

²**eaker** \ā-kər\ see ¹AKER

¹**eaking** \ē-kiŋ\ freaking,
sneaking, speaking, streaking,
heat-seeking, self-seeking

²**eaking** \ā-kiŋ\ see ¹AKING

eakish \ē-kish\ bleakish,
cliquish, freakish, weakish

eakly \ē-klē\ see EEKLY

eaky \ē-kē\ cheeky, cliquey,
creaky, freaky, leaky, piki,
reeky, sneaky, screaky,
squeaky, streaky, tiki,

daishiki, dashiki, Tajiki, cock-
a-leekie, Kurashiki, Manihiki

¹**eal** \ē-əl\ empyreal, hymeneal,
laryngeal, apophyseal,
pharmacopeial

²**eal** \ēl\ ceil, chiel, creel, deal,
deil, eel, feel, heal, heel, he'll,
keel, Kiel, kneel, leal, meal,
Neal, Neil, peal, peel, real,
reel, seal, seel, she'll, shiel,
speel, spiel, squeal, steal,
steel, Steele, Streel, teal,
tuille, veal, weal, we'll,
wheal, wheel, zeal, aiguille,
allheal, anneal, appeal, Arbil,
bastille, Bastille, bonemeal,
bonspiel, Camille, Castile,
cartwheel, Cecile, chainwheel,
chenille, cogwheel, conceal,
congeal, cornmeal, enwheel,
Erbil, flywheel, forefeel, four-
wheel, freewheel, genteel,
handwheel, ideal, inchmeal,
Irbil, irreal, Kuril, Lucille,
misdeal, mobile, Mobile,
newsreel, nosewheel, oatmeal,
O'Neill, ordeal, pastille,
piecemeal, pinwheel, repeal,
reveal, schlemiel, self-heal,
side-wheel, singspiel,
somedeal, stabile, surreal,
tahsil, Tarheel, thumbwheel,
unreal, unreel, unseal, acetyl,
airmobile, Ardabil, bidonville,
beau ideal, blastocoel,
bloodmobile, Bogomil,
bookmobile, campanile,
chamomile, cochineal,
cockatiel, commonweal,
difficile, dishabille, down-at-
heel, glockenspiel, goldenseal,
Guayaquil, manchineel,

megadeal, mercantile,
pimpmobile, skimobile,
snowmobile, thunderpeal,
waterwheel, automobile,
Solomon's seal, varicocele

³eal \āl\ see AIL

⁴eal \il\ see ILL

ealable \ē-lə-bəl\ peelable,
reelable, stealable, appealable,
concealable, revealable,
repealable, irrepealable,
unappealable

ealand \ē-lənd\ see ELAND

eald \ēld\ see IELD

ealed \ēld\ see IELD

ealer \ē-lər\ dealer, feeler,
healer, heeler, kneeler, peeler,
reeler, sealer, spieler,
squealer, stealer, stelar,
vealer, velar, wheeler,
appealer, concealer, four-
wheeler, freewheeler,
newsdealer, repealer, revealer,
scene-stealer, side-wheeler,
stern-wheeler, three-wheeler,
two-wheeler, double-dealer,
eighteen-wheeler, 18-wheeler,
snowmobiler, wheeler-dealer

ealie \ē-lē\ see EELY

ealing \ē-liŋ\ see EELING

¹eally \ē-ə-lē\ leally, ideally,
hymeneally, industrially

²eally \il-ē\ see ¹ILLY

³eally \ē-lē\ see EELY

ealm \elm\ see ELM

ealment \ēl-mənt\ concealment,
congealment, revealment

ealot \el-ət\ see ELLATE

ealotry \el-ə-trē\ see ELOTRY

ealous \el-əs\ Ellis, Hellas,
jealous, trellis, zealous,
cancellous, ocellus

ealousy \el-ə-sē\ see ELACY

ealth \elth\ health, stealth,
wealth, commonwealth

ealthy \el-thē\ healthy, stealthy,
wealthy, unhealthy

ealty \ēl-tē\ fealty, realty

¹eam \ēm\ beam, bream, cream,
deem, deme, dream, gleam,
mime, neem, Nîmes, ream,
scheme, scream, seam, seem,
seme, steam, stream, team,
teem, theme, abeam, agleam,
airstream, berseem, beseem,
bireme, blaspheme,
bloodstream, centime,
daydream, downstream,
esteem, extreme, grapheme,
Gulf Stream, hakim,
headstream, hornbeam, ice
cream, inseam, kilim, lexeme,
mainstream, midstream,
millime, millstream,
moonbeam, morpheme, redeem,
regime, sememe, sidestream,
slipstream, sunbeam,
supreme, Tarim, taxeme,
toneme, trireme, unseam,
upstream, academe,
disesteem, double-team,
enthymeme, misesteem,
monotreme, self-esteem,
succès d'estime, treponeme

²eam \im\ see ¹IM

eaman \ē-mən\ see ¹EMON

¹eamed \emt\ see EMPT

²eamed \emd\ beamed, steamed,
teamed—*also pasts of verbs
listed at* ¹EAM

eamer \ē-mər\ creamer,
dreamer, femur, lemur,
reamer, schemer, screamer,

seamer, steamer, streamer,
blasphemer, daydreamer,
redeemer
eaming \ē-miŋ\ see EEMING
eamish \ē-mish\ beamish,
squeamish
eamless \ēm-ləs\ dreamless,
seamless
eamon \ē-mən\ see ¹EMON
eamster \ēm-stər\ seamster,
teamster
eamy \ē-mē\ beamy, creamy,
dreamy, gleamy, preemie,
seamy, steamy, polysemy
¹ean \ē-ən\ aeon, eon, Ian,
Leon, paean, peon, paeon,
zein, Achaean, Actaeon,
Aegean, Antaean, Archean,
Augean, Chaldean, Chilean,
Fijian, Korean, Kuchean,
Linnaean, Mandaean,
Matthean, pampean, plebeian,
protean, pygmaean, Tupi-
Guaranian, Tupian, apogean,
Aramaean, Atlantean,
Caribbean, Cerberean,
circadian, cyclopean,
Clytherean, Damoclean,
empyrean, epigean, European,
Galilean, Hasmonaean,
Herculean, Jacobean,
kallikrein, Maccabean,
Manichaean, Mycenaean,
Odyssean, panacean,
perigean, Sadducean,
Sisyphean, Typhoean,
Tyrolean, antipodean,
epicurean, Laodicean, Ponce
de Leon, proboscidean,
Pythagorean, terpsichorean,
un-European, epithalamion,
Indo-European

²ean \ēn\ see ³INE
³ean \ȯn\ see ³ON
⁴ean \ā-ən\ see ¹AYAN
eane \ēn\ see ³INE
eaner \ē-nər\ cleaner, gleaner,
keener, meaner, preener,
teener, weaner, weiner,
wiener, congener, demeanor,
fourteener, carabiner,
intervenor, misdemeanor,
submariner, trampoliner
eanery \ēn-rē\ beanery,
deanery, greenery, scenery,
machinery, turbomachinery
eanid \ē-ə-nəd\ Leonid,
Oceanid
eanie \ē-nē\ see ¹INI
eaning \ē-niŋ\ greening,
leaning, meaning, screening,
housecleaning, spring-
cleaning, sunscreening,
unmeaning, well-meaning,
overweening—*also present
participles of verbs listed at*
³INE
¹eanist \ē-nəst\ see ²INIST
²eanist \ē-ə-nist\ see IANIST
eanliness \en-lē-nəs\ see
ENDLINESS
eanling \ēn-liŋ\ greenling,
weanling, yeanling
¹eanly \ēn-lē\ cleanly, greenly,
leanly, meanly, queenly,
pristinely, routinely,
serpentinely, uncleanly
²eanly \en-lē\ see ENDLY
eanne \ēn\ see ³INE
eanness \ēn-nəs\ cleanness,
greenness, meanness,
betweenness, uncleanness
eannie \ē-nē\ see ¹INI
eano \ē-nō\ see ²INO

eanor \ē-nər\ see EANER
eanse \enz\ see [1]ENS
eant \ent\ see [1]ENT
eany \ē-nē\ see [1]INI
eap \ēp\ see EEP
eapen \ē-pən\ see EEPEN
eaper \ē-pər\ see EEPER
eapie \ē-pē\ see EEPY
eapish \ē-pish\ see EEPISH
eapo \ē-pō\ see EPOT
[1]**ear** \er\ see [4]ARE
[2]**ear** \ir\ see [2]EER
[1]**earable** \er-ə-bəl\ bearable, shareable, terrible, wearable, unbearable, unwearable
[2]**earable** \ar-ə-bəl\ see ARABLE
earage \ir-ij\ see EERAGE
[1]**earance** \ir-əns\ see [1]ERENCE
[2]**earance** \er-əns\ see ARENCE
earch \ərch\ see URCH
[1]**eard** \ird\ beard, eared, tiered, weird, afeard, bat-eared, bluebeard, crop-eared, dog-eared, graybeard, lop-eared, misleared, whitebeard, chandeliered, engineered, pre-engineered—*also pasts of verbs listed at* [2]EER
[2]**eard** \ərd\ see IRD
eare \ir\ see [2]EER
earean \ir-ē-ən\ see [1]ERIAN
[1]**eared** \erd\ see AIRED
[2]**eared** \ird\ see [1]EARD
[1]**earer** \er-ər\ airer, bearer, carer, error, sharer, terror, casebearer, crossbearer, cupbearer, declarer, furbearer, pallbearer, seafarer, talebearer, torchbearer, trainbearer, wayfarer, color-bearer, standard-bearer, stretcher-bearer—*also*

comparatives of adjectives listed at [4]ARE
[2]**earer** \ir-ər\ cheerer, clearer, fearer, hearer, mirror, shearer, smearer, coherer, sheepshearer, veneerer, electioneerer—*also comparatives of adjectives listed at* [2]EER
[3]**earer** \ar-ər\ airer, bearer, casebearer, crossbearer, cupbearer, declarer, furbearer, live-bearer, pallbearer, seafarer, talebearer, torchbearer, trainbearer, wayfarer, color-bearer, standard-bearer, stretcher-bearer
earful \ir-fəl\ cheerful, earful, fearful, tearful
earies \ir-ēz\ see ERIES
[1]**earing** \ir-iŋ\ clearing, earing, earring, gearing, God-fearing, sheepshearing, fictioneering, hard-of-hearing, orienteering—*also present participles of verbs listed at* [2]EER
[2]**earing** \er-iŋ\ see [1]ARING
earish \er-ish\ see [1]ARISH
earl \ərl\ see [1]IRL
earle \irl\ see [1]IRL
earler \ər-lər\ see IRLER
earless \ir-ləs\ cheerless, fearless, gearless, peerless, tearless
[1]**earling** \ir-liŋ\ shearling, yearling
[2]**earling** \ər-lən\ see ERLIN
[1]**early** \ir-lē\ clearly, dearly, merely, nearly, queerly, yearly, austerely, biyearly,

severely, sincerely, cavalierly,
semiyearly, insincerely

²**early** \ər-lē\ see URLY

earn \ərn\ see URN

earned \ərnd\ see URNED

earner \ər-nər\ see URNER

earnist \ər-nəst\ see ERNIST

earnt \ərnt\ burnt, learnt,
weren't

earring \ir-iŋ\ see ¹EARING

earsal \ər-səl\ see ¹ERSAL

earse \ərs\ see ERSE

earser \ər-sər\ see URSOR

earst \ərst\ see URST

eart \ärt\ see ¹ART

earted \ärt-əd\ hearted, parted,
bighearted, coldhearted,
downhearted, fainthearted,
freehearted, good-hearted,
greathearted, halfhearted,
hard-hearted, kindhearted,
largehearted, lighthearted,
proudhearted, softhearted,
stouthearted, truehearted,
uncharted, warmhearted,
weakhearted, wholehearted,
brokenhearted,
chickenhearted, heavyhearted,
ironhearted, lionhearted,
openhearted, single-hearted,
stonyhearted, tenderhearted—
also pasts of verbs listed at
¹ART

¹**earth** \ärth\ see ARTH

²**earth** \ərth\ see IRTH

eartha \ər-thə\ see ERTHA

earthen \ər-thən\ see URTHEN

earthy \ər-thē\ see ORTHY

eartily \ärt-ᵊl-ē\ see ARTILY

eartless \ärt-ləs\ see ARTLESS

earty \ärt-ē\ see ¹ARTY

eary \ir-ē\ aerie, beery, bleary,
cheery, dreary, eerie, Erie,
leery, Peary, peri, quaere,
query, smeary, sphery, teary,
veery, weary, aweary,
Kashmiri, Lake Erie,
Valkyrie, world-weary, hara-
kiri, miserere, overweary,
whigmaleerie, Mount
Dhaulagiri

eas \ē-əs\ see ¹EUS

¹**easable** \ē-sə-bəl\ peaceable,
increasable

²**easable** \ē-zə-bəl\ see EASIBLE

¹**easand** \iz-ᵊn\ see ²ISON

²**easand** \ēz-ᵊnd\ see EASONED

¹**ease** \ēs\ see IECE

²**ease** \ēz\ see EZE

¹**eased** \ēzd\ pleased, diseased—
also pasts of verbs listed at
EZE

²**eased** \ēst\ see ¹EAST

easel \ē-zəl\ bezel, deasil,
diesel, easel, measle, teasel,
weasel

easeless \ē-sləs\ ceaseless,
creaseless, greaseless

easelly \ē-zlē\ see EASLY

easement \ēz-mənt\ easement,
appeasement

¹**easer** \ē-sər\ creaser, greaser,
piecer, increaser, one-piecer,
releaser, two-piecer

²**easer** \ē-zər\ Caesar, freezer,
geezer, greaser, pleaser,
sneezer, squeezer, teaser,
tweezer, appeaser, brainteaser,
crowd-pleaser, misfeasor,
stripteaser, timepleaser

eash \ēsh\ see ²ICHE

easible \ē-zə-bəl\ feasible,
squeezable, appeasable,
defeasible, infeasible,

inappeasable, indefeasible, unappeasable

easil \ē-zəl\ see EASEL

easily \ēz-lē\ see EASLY

¹easing \ē-siŋ\ leasing, unceasing—*also present participles of verbs listed at* IECE

²easing \ē-ziŋ\ pleasing, subfreezing—*also present participles of verbs listed at* EZE

easingly \ē-siŋ-lē\ decreasingly, increasingly, unceasingly

easle \ē-zəl\ see EASEL

easly \ēz-ə-lē\ easily, measly, weaselly

eason \ēz-ᵊn\ reason, season, seisin, treason, disseisin, off-season, unreason, diocesan

easonable \ēz-nə-bəl\ reasonable, seasonable, treasonable, unreasonable, unseasonable

easoned \ēz-ᵊnd\ weasand, unreasoned—*also pasts of verbs listed at* EASON

easoning \ēz-niŋ\ seasoning, unreasoning

easonless \ēz-ᵊn-ləs\ reasonless, seasonless

easor \ē-zər\ see ²EASER

¹east \ēst\ beast, east, East, feast, fleeced, geest, least, piste, priest, reest, triste, yeast, archpriest, artiste, batiste, deceased, Far East, hartebeest, modiste, Near East, northeast, southeast, tachiste, arriviste, dirigiste, hartebeest, Middle East, north-northeast, pointillist,

wildebeest—*also pasts of verbs listed at* IECE

²east \est\ see EST

easted \es-təd\ see ESTED

easter \ē-stər\ Dniester, Easter, keister, leister, quaestor, down-easter, northeaster, southeaster

eastie \ē-stē\ see EASTY

eastly \ēst-lē\ beastly, Priestley, priestly

easty \ē-stē\ beastie, yeasty

easurable \ezh-rə-bəl\ pleasurable, treasurable, immeasurable

¹easure \ezh-ər\ leisure, measure, pleasure, treasure, admeasure, displeasure, countermeasure

²easure \ā-zhər\ see AZIER

easurer \ezh-ər-ər\ measurer, treasurer

¹easy \ē-zē\ breezy, cheesy, easy, greasy, queasy, sleazy, sneezy, wheezy, pachisi, Parcheesi, speakeasy, uneasy, Zambezi

²easy \ē-sē\ see EECY

¹eat \ēt\ beat, beet, bleat, cheat, cleat, Crete, deet, eat, feat, fleet, Geat, gleet, greet, heat, keet, lied, meat, meet, mete, neat, peat, Pete, pleat, seat, sheet, skeet, sleet, street, suite, sweet, teat, treat, tweet, weet, wheat, accrete, aesthete, afreet, athlete, backbeat, backseat, backstreet, bedsheet, bolete, Bradstreet, broadsheet, browbeat, buckwheat, bystreet, clipsheet, compete, compleat, complete, conceit,

concrete, crabmeat, deadbeat,
deceit, defeat, delete, deplete,
discreet, discrete, disseat,
downbeat, drumbeat, effete,
elite, en suite, entreat,
escheat, esthete, excrete,
facete, forcemeat, foresheet,
groundsheet, heartbeat, heat-
treat, helpmeet, hoofbeat, ill-
treat, mainsheet, maltreat,
mesquite, mincemeat,
mistreat, offbeat, petite,
preheat, receipt, recheat,
regreet, repeat, replete, retreat,
secrete, slip-sheet, sweetmeat,
terete, unmeet, unseat, upbeat,
vegete, volkslied, zizith,
aquavit, biathlete, bittersweet,
cellulite, corps d'elite,
countryseat, decathlete,
exegete, incomplete,
indiscreet, indiscrete, lorikeet,
marguerite, Marguerite,
Masorete, meadowsweet,
Nayarit, obsolete, overeat,
overheat, Paraclete, parakeet,
pentathlete, plebiscite,
polychaete, progamete, self-
conceit, semisweet, tête-à-tête,
superheat, triathlete, winding-
sheet
²**eat** \āt\ see ¹ATE
³**eat** \et\ see ¹ET
⁴**eat** \it\ see ¹IT
eatable \ēt-ə-bəl\ eatable,
heatable, treatable, depletable,
escheatable, repeatable,
unbeatable
¹**eated** \ēt-əd\ heated, pleated,
conceited, deep-seated,
repeated, overheated,

superheated—*also pasts of
verbs listed at* ¹EAT
²**eated** \et-əd\ see ETID
³**eated** \it-əd\ see ITTED
¹**eaten** \ēt-ᵊn\ eaten, beaten,
Cretan, cretin, Eaton, Eton,
neaten, sweeten, wheaten,
browbeaten, moth-eaten,
secretin, unbeaten, worm-
eaten, overeaten, weather-
beaten
²**eaten** \āt-ᵊn\ see ¹ATEN
¹**eater** \ēt-ər\ beater, bleater,
cheater, eater, fetor, greeter,
heater, liter, meter, peter,
Peter, pleater, praetor, rhetor,
seater, sheeter, skeeter, teeter,
treater, tweeter, anteater,
beefeater, blue peter,
Demeter, drumbeater,
eggbeater, excreter, fire-eater,
flowmeter, man-eater, Main
Streeter, maltreater, preheater,
propraetor, repeater, saltpeter,
secretor, seedeater, toadeater,
Wall Streeter, windcheater,
world-beater, altimeter,
centiliter, centimeter, deciliter,
decimeter, drunkometer,
lotus-eater, milliliter,
millimeter, overeater,
taximeter—*also comparatives
of adjectives listed at* ¹EAT
²**eater** \et-ər\ see ETTER
eatery \ēt-ə-rē\ see ETORY
¹**eath** \ēth\ eath, heath, Keith,
Meath, neath, sheath, wreath,
beneath, bequeath, hadith,
monteith, underneath
²**eath** \ēth\ see EATHE
eathe \ēth\ breathe, Meath,
seethe, sheathe, teethe,

wreathe, bequeath, ensheathe, enwreathe, inbreathe, unsheathe, unwreathe, Westmeath

eathean \ē-thē-ən\ lethean, Promethean

¹eather \eth-ər\ see ¹ETHER

²eather \ē-thər\ see EITHER

eathern \eth-ərn\ see ETHERN

eathery \eth-rē\ feathery, heathery, leathery

eathing \ē-thiŋ\ breathing, sheathing, teething, firebreathing

eathless \eth-ləs\ breathless, deathless

eathy \ē-thē\ heathy, lethe, wreathy

eating \ēt-iŋ\ beating, eating, meeting, seating, sheeting, sweeting, breast-beating, drumbeating, fire-eating, man-eating, unweeting, Sunday-go-to-meeting

eatise \ēt-əs\ see ETUS

¹eatly \āt-lē\ see ¹ATELY

²eatly \ēt-lē\ see EETLY

eaton \ēt-ᵊn\ see ¹EATEN

¹eats \ēts\ Keats—*also possessives and plurals of nouns and third person singular presents of verbs listed at* EAT

²eats \āts\ see ¹ATES

eature \ē-chər\ see EACHER

eaty \ēt-ē\ meaty, peaty, sleety, sweetie, treaty, ziti, entreaty, Tahiti, Dolomiti, spermaceti

eau \ō\ see ¹OW

eaucracy \äk-rə-sē\ see OCRACY

eauteous \üt-ē-əs\ see UTEOUS

eautiful \üt-i-fəl\ see UTIFUL

eauty \üt-ē\ see ¹OOTY

eaux \ō\ see ¹OW

eavable \ē-və-bəl\ see EIVABLE

eaval \ē-vəl\ see IEVAL

¹eave \ēv\ breve, cleave, eve, Eve, greave, grieve, heave, leave, lief, peeve, reave, reeve, reive, scrieve, sheave, shrieve, sleave, sleeve, steeve, Steve, thieve, weave, weve, Abib, achieve, aggrieve, believe, bereave, conceive, deceive, inweave, khedive, Maldive, motive, naive, perceive, qui vive, receive, relieve, reprieve, retrieve, shirtsleeve, unreeve, unweave, upheave, apperceive, by-your-leave, disbelieve, Genevieve, interleave, interweave, Laccadive, make-believe, misbelieve, misconceive, preconceive, semibreve, Tel Aviv, undeceive, adam-and-eve, recitative, ticket-of-leave, underachieve, Saint Agnes' Eve

²eave \iv\ see ²IVE

eaved \ēvd\ leaved, sleeved, aggrieved, bereaved, relieved—*also pasts of verbs listed at* ¹EAVE

eavement \ēv-mənt\ see EVEMENT

eaven \ev-ən\ devon, Devon, Evan, heaven, Kevin, leaven, levin, Nevin, seven, Sevin, sweven, eleven, replevin, South Devon

eaver \ē-vər\ see IEVER

eavers \ē-vərz\ cleavers, vivers

eaves \ēvz\ eaves, Treves, shirtsleeves

eavey \ē-vē\ peavey, divi-divi

eaward \ē-wərd\ see EEWARD

¹eaze \ēz\ see EZE

²eaze \āz\ see ¹AZE

eazo \ē-zō\ see ¹IZO

eazy \ē-zē\ see ¹EASY

eb \eb\ bleb, deb, ebb, neb, pleb, reb, Reb, web, ardeb, celeb, cobweb, cubeb, Deneb, Horeb, subdeb, Zagreb, zineb, cause célèbre, Johnny Reb, spiderweb

eba \ē-bə\ Chiba, Reba, Sheba, amoeba, zareba, copaiba, Curitiba

ebate \ab-ət\ see ABIT

ebb \eb\ see EB

ebbie \eb-ē\ see EBBY

ebble \eb-əl\ pebble, rebel, treble

ebbuck \eb-ək\ kebbuck, rebec

ebby \eb-ē\ blebby, Debbie, Debby, maybe, webby, cobwebby

¹ebe \ē-bē\ BB, freebie, Hebe, phoebe, Phoebe, Seabee, caribe, Galibi

²ebe \ēb\ glebe, grebe, hebe, plebe, ephebe, sahib

ebec \eb-ək\ see EBBUCK

ebel \eb-əl\ see EBBLE

eber \ā-bər\ see ABOR

ebes \ēbz\ Thebes—*also possessives and plurals of nouns listed at* EBE

eble \eb-əl\ see EBBLE

ebo \ē-bō\ see IBO

ebral \ē-brəl\ cerebral, palpebral, vertebral

ebrity \eb-rət-ē\ celebrity, muliebrity

¹ebs \eps\ see EPS

²ebs \ebz\ Debs—*also possessives and plurals of nouns, third person singular presents of verbs listed at* EB

ebt \et\ see ¹ET

ebted \et-əd\ see ETID

ebtor \et-ər\ see ETTER

ebus \ē-bəs\ Phoebus, rebus, ephebus

¹ec \ek\ see ECK

²ec \ets\ see ETS

eca \ē-kə\ see ¹IKA

ecal \ē-kəl\ cecal, fecal, meikle, treacle, intrathecal, bibliothecal

ecan \ek-ən\ see ECKON

ecant \ē-kənt\ piquant, secant

ecas \ā-kəs\ Turksand Caicos, Zacatecas

ecca \ek-ə\ Decca, mecca, Mecca, weka, Rebecca, Rebekah, Rijeka

eccable \ek-ə-bəl\ see ECKABLE

eccan \ek-ən\ see ECKON

ecce \ek-ē\ see ECKY

ecco \ek-ō\ see ECHO

ecency \ēs-ᵊn-sē\ decency, recency, indecency

ecent \ēs-ᵊnt\ decent, recent, indecent, obeisant

eces \ē-sēz\ see ECIES

¹ech \ek\ see ECK

²ech \ək\ see UCK

³ech \esh\ see ¹ESH

¹eche \āsh\ crèche, flèche, Laoighis, Leix, resh, seiche, bobeche, Bangladesh, tête-bêche, Andhra Pradesh, Madhya Pradesh, Uttar

Pradesh, Himadral Pradesh,
Arunachal Pradesh
²**eche** \esh\ see ¹ESH
eche \ē-chē\ see EACHY
êche \esh\ see ¹ESH
èche \esh\ see ¹ESH
eched \echt\ see ETCHED
echerous \ech-rəs\ lecherous,
treacherous
echery \ech-rē\ lechery,
treachery
echie \ek-ē\ see ECKY
echin \ek-ən\ see ECKON
echo \ek-ō\ deco, echo, gecko,
secco, el Greco, reecho
echnical \ek-ni-kəl\ technical,
biotechnical, geotechnical
echt \ekt\ see ECT
ecia \ē-shə\ see ¹ESIA
ecially \esh-lē\ see ESHLY
ecian \ē-shən\ see ¹ETION
ecibel \es-ə-bəl\ see ESSIBLE
¹**ecie** \ē-sē\ see EECY
²**ecie** \ē-shē\ see ISHI
ecies \ē-sēz\ feces, species,
theses, prostheses, subspecies,
exegeses
¹**ecil** \ē-səl\ Cecil, diesel
²**ecil** \es-əl\ see ¹ESTLE
ecile \es-əl\ see ¹ESTLE
ecily \es-ə-lē\ see ESSALY
ecimal \es-ə-məl\ see ESIMAL
eciman \es-mən\ see ESSMAN
ecious \ē-shəs\ specious,
capricious, facetious,
Lucretius
ecium \ē-shē-əm\ aecium,
lutecium, technetium,
zoecium, androecium,
apothecium, gynoecium,
paramecium, perithecium
eck \ek\ beck, check, cheque,

Czech, deck, dreck, fleck,
heck, lek, neck, pec, peck,
reck, sec, sneck, spec, speck,
trek, wreak, wreck, Aztec,
Baalbek, backcheck, bedeck,
breakneck, Capek, cromlech,
crookneck, cross-check,
cusec, ewe-neck, exec,
flyspeck, fore-check,
foredeck, gooseneck, haček,
hatcheck, henpeck, high tech,
kopeck, limbeck, low-tech,
Lubeck, Mixtec, paycheck,
pinchbeck, Quebec, rebec,
redneck, ringneck, roll-neck,
roughneck, samekh,
shipwreck, spot-check,
Steinbeck, tenrec, Toltec,
Uzbek, wryneck, xebec,
afterdeck, à la grecque,
Aquidneck, biotech,
bodycheck, bottleneck,
Chiang Kai-shek,
countercheck, demi-sec,
discotheque, double-check,
double-deck, hunt-and-peck,
leatherneck, littleneck, Pont
l'évêque, quarterdeck,
rubberneck, triple sec,
turtleneck, Yucatec, Zapotec,
cinematheque, Melchizedek,
de Toulouse-Lautrec
eckable \ek-ə-bəl\ checkable,
impeccable
ecked \ekt\ see ECT
ecker \ek-ər\ checker, chequer,
decker, pecker, trekker,
wrecker, exchequer, three-
decker, woodpecker,
dominicker, double-decker,
rubbernecker, triple-decker
ecking \ek-iŋ\ decking, necking

ecklace \ek-ləs\ see ECKLESS

eckle \ek-əl\ deckle, freckle,
heckle, shekel, speckle,
kenspeckle

eckless \ek-ləs\ feckless,
checkless, necklace, reckless,
affectless

ecko \ek-ō\ see ECHO

eckon \ek-ən\ beckon, Brecon,
Deccan, reckon, zechin,
Aztecan, misreckon, Toltecan,
Yucatecan

ecks \ecks\ eks\ see EX

ecky \ek-ē\ Becky, recce,
techie, shimonoseki

econ \ek-ən\ see ECKON

¹econd \ek-ənd\ see ECUND

²econd \ek-ənt\ see ECCANT

ecque \ek\ see ECK

ecs \eks\ see EX

ect \ekt\ necked, sect, specked,
abject, affect, aspect, bisect,
cathect, collect, confect,
connect, convect, correct,
defect, deflect, deject, detect,
direct, dissect, effect, eject,
elect, erect, ewe-necked,
expect, goosenecked, infect,
inflect, inject, insect, inspect,
neglect, object, pandect,
perfect, porrect, prefect,
prelect, project, prospect,
protect, rednecked, refect,
reflect, reject, resect, respect,
ring-necked, select, stiff-
necked, subject, suspect,
traject, transect, trisect,
Utrecht, V-necked, acrolect,
architect, circumspect,
deselect, dialect, disaffect,
disconnect, disinfect,
disrespect, double-decked,

genuflect, grapholect,
incorrect, indirect, intellect,
interject, intersect, introject,
introspect, misdirect,
preselect, re-collect, recollect,
redirect, reelect, resurrect,
retrospect, self-respect,
turtlenecked, vivisect,
aftereffect, hypercorrect,
idiolect, interconnect,
megaproject, semierect, semi-
indirect—*also pasts of verbs
listed at* ECK

ecta \ek-tə\ dejecta, ejecta,
perfecta, trifecta

ectable \ek-tə-bəl\ affectable,
collectible, correctable,
deflectable, delectable,
detectable, ejectable,
erectable, expectable,
inflectable, injectable,
electable, indefectible,
perfectible, projectable,
respectable, disrespectable,
indefectible

ectacle \ek-ti-kəl\ see ECTICAL

ectal \ek-tᵊl\ see ECTILE

ectance \ek-təns\ expectance,
reflectance

ectant \ek-tənt\ expectant,
humectant, injectant,
protectant, disinfectant

ectar \ek-tər\ see ECTOR

ectarous \ek-trəs\ see ECTRESS

ectary \ek-tə-rē\ sectary,
insectary

ected \ek-təd\ affected,
collected, complected,
dejected, recollected, self-
affected, self-collected, self-
elected, self-selected,
unaffected, undirected,

unexpected, unselected, inner-
directed, other-directed—*also
pasts of verbs listed at* ECT
ecten \ek-tən\ nekton, pecten,
  pectin, fibronectin, ivermectin
ecter \ek-tər\ see ECTOR
ectible \ek-tə-bəl\ see ECTABLE
ectic \ek-tik\ hectic, pectic,
  cathectic, eclectic, synectic,
  anorectic, apoplectic,
  catalectic, dialectic
ectical \ek-ti-kəl\ spectacle,
  dialectical
ectile \ek-tᵊl\ sectile, erectile,
  insectile, projectile,
  colorectal, dialectal
ectin \ek-tən\ see ECTEN
ecting \ek-tiŋ\ affecting, self-
  respecting, self-correcting
ection \ek-shən\ flexion,
  lection, section, abjection,
  advection, affection,
  bisection, collection,
  complexion, confection,
  connection, connexion,
  convection, correction, C-
  section, defection, deflection,
  dejection, detection, direction,
  dissection, ejection, election,
  erection, evection, infection,
  inflection, injection,
  inspection, midsection,
  objection, perfection,
  prelection, projection,
  protection, refection,
  reflection, rejection, resection,
  selection, subjection,
  subsection, trajection,
  transection, trisection, by-
  election, circumspection,
  disaffection, disconnection,
  disinfection, genuflection,

imperfection, indirection,
  introjection, introspection,
  insurrection, intellection,
  interjection, intersection,
  misdirection, predilection,
  preselection, recollection,
  redirection, reelection,
  reinfection, resurrection,
  retroflexion, retrospection,
  vivisection, antirejection,
  hypercorrection,
  interconnection, Cesarean
  section
ectional \ek-shnəl\ sectional,
  affectional, bisectional,
  complexional, connectional,
  convectional, correctional,
  cross-sectional, directional,
  inflectional, projectional,
  reflectional, bidirectional,
  introspectional, interjectional,
  resurrectional, vivisectional,
  omnidirectional,
  unidirectional
ectionist \ek-shə-nəst\
  perfectionist, projectionist,
  protectionist, selectionist,
  introspectionist,
  resurrectionist, vivisectionist
ective \ek-tiv\ advective,
  affective, adjective, bijective,
  collective, connective,
  convective, corrective,
  defective, deflective,
  detective, directive, effective,
  elective, ejective, infective,
  inflective, injective, invective,
  objective, perfective,
  perspective, projective,
  prospective, reflective,
  respective, selective,
  subjective, cost-effective,

imperfective, ineffective,
intellective, introspective,
nondirective, nonobjective,
retrospective, cryoprotective,
intersubjective

ectless \ek-ləs\ see ECKLESS

ectly \ekt-lē\ abjectly, correctly,
directly, erectly, incorrectly,
indirectly

ectness \ekt-nəs\ abjectness,
correctness, directness,
erectness, selectness,
incorrectness, indirectness,
hypercorrectness

ecto \ek-tō\ recto, perfecto

ectomy \ek-tə-mē\ mastectomy,
vasectomy, appendectomy,
hysterectomy, tonsillectomy,
clitoridectomy

ector \ek-tər\ hector, Hector,
lector, nectar, rector, sector,
specter, vector, bisector,
collector, convector, corrector,
defector, deflector, detector,
director, dissector, effector,
ejector, elector, erector,
infector, injector, inspector,
neglecter, objector, perfecter,
projector, prospector,
protector, reflector, selector,
trisector, vivisector

ectoral \ek-trəl\ spectral,
pectoral, electoral, protectoral,
multispectral

ectorate \ek-tə-rət\ rectorate,
directorate, electorate,
inspectorate, protectorate

ectory \ek-tə-rē\ rectory,
directory, protectory,
refectory, trajectory,
ex-directory

ectral \ek-trəl\ see ECTORAL

ectress \ek-trəs\ nectarous,
directress, electress,
protectress

ectrix \ek-triks\ rectrix,
directrix

ectrum \ek-trəm\ plectrum,
spectrum, electrum

¹ectual \ek-chə-wəl\ effectual,
ineffectual, intellectual, anti-
intellectual

²ectual \eksh-wəl\ see EXUAL

ectually \ek-chə-lē\ effectually,
ineffectually, intellectually

¹ectural \ek-chə-rəl\
conjectural, prefectural,
architectural

²ectural \ek-shrəl\ flexural,
conjectural, architectural

ecture \ek-chər\ lecture,
conjecture, prefecture,
architecture

ectus \ek-təs\ conspectus,
prospectus

ecular \ek-yə-lər\ secular,
specular, molecular

ecum \ē-kəm\ vade mecum,
subpoena duces tecum

ecund \ek-ənd\ fecund, second,
femtosecond, microsecond,
millisecond, nanosecond—
also pasts of verbs listed at
ECKON

ecutive \ek-ət-iv\ consecutive,
executive, inconsecutive

ed \ed\ see ¹EAD

e'd \ēd\ see EED

¹eda \ēd-ə\ Freda, Frieda, Leda,
Vida, Machida, alameda, olla
podrida

²eda \ād-ə\ see ³ADA

¹edal \ed-ᵊl\ heddle, medal,
meddle, pedal, peddle,

treadle, backpedal, bipedal, soft-pedal, intermeddle

²edal \ēd-ᵊl\ see EEDLE

edance \ēd-ᵊns\ see EDENCE

¹edar \ed-ər\ see ²EADER

²edar \ēd-ər\ see ¹EADER

edator \ed-ət-ər\ see EDITOR

edd \ed\ see ¹EAD

edda \ed-ə\ Jedda, Vedda

eddar \ed-ər\ see ²EADER

edded \ed-əd\ see EADED

edden \ed-ᵊn\ see EADEN

edder \ed-ər\ see ²EADER

eddie \ed-ē\ see ¹EADY

edding \ed-iŋ\ see ¹EADING

eddle \ed-ᵊl\ see ¹EDAL

eddler \ed-lər\ meddler, medlar, peddler

eddon \ed-ᵊn\ see EADEN

eddy \ed-ē\ see ¹EADY

¹ede \ād\ see ¹ADE

²ede \ēd\ see EED

³ede \ā-dā\ see AYDAY

edeas \ēd-ē-əs\ see ¹EDIOUS

eded \ē-dəd\ see EEDED

edel \ād-ᵊl\ see ADLE

eden \ēd-ᵊn\ Eden, Sweden, Dunedin

edence \ēd-ᵊns\ credence, impedance, precedence, antecedence

edent \ēd-ᵊnt\ credent, needn't, decedent, precedent, succedent, antecedent

¹eder \ād-ər\ see ADER

²eder \ ēd-ər\ see ¹EADER

edes \ē-dēz\ Diomedes, Archimedes

edge \ej\ dredge, edge, fledge, hedge, kedge, ledge, pledge, sedge, sledge, veg, wedge, allege, frankpledge, gilt-edge,

two-edged, hard-edge, knife-edge, nutsedge, straightedge, featheredge, sortilege

edged \ejd\ edged, wedged, alleged, full-fledged, gilt-edged, two-edged, unfledged, deckle-edged, double-edged— *also pasts of verbs listed at* EDGE

edger \ej-ər\ dredger, edger, hedger, ledger, leger, pledger

edgie \ej-ē\ see EDGY

edgy \ej-ē\ edgy, ledgy, Reggie, sedgy, veggie, wedgie, wedgy, Himeji

edi \ād-ē\ see ADY

edia \ēd-ē-ə\ media, Media, acedia, cyclopedia, via media, encyclopedia

edial \ēd-ē-əl\ medial, predial, remedial

edian \ēd-ē-ən\ median, comedian, tragedian

ediant \ēd-ē-ənt\ see EDIENT

edible \ed-ə-bəl\ credible, edible, spreadable, incredible, inedible

¹edic \ēd-ik\ comedic, cyclopedic, logaoedic, orthopedic, encyclopedic

²edic \ed-ik\ Eddic, medic, comedic, paramedic, samoyedic

³edic \ād-ik\ see ¹ADIC

edicable \ed-i-kə-bəl\ medicable, predicable, immedicable

edical \ed-i-kəl\ medical, pedicle, premedical, biomedical, paramedical

edicate \ed-i-kət\ dedicate, predicate

edicle \ed-i-kəl\ see EDICAL

edience \ēd-ē-əns\ expedience, obedience, disobedience, inexpedience

edient \ēd-ē-ənt\ mediant, expedient, ingredient, obedient, submediant, disobedient, inexpedient

ediment \ed-ə-mənt\ pediment, sediment, impediment

edin \ēd-ᵊn\ see EDEN

eding \ēd-iŋ\ see ¹EEDING

¹edious \ēd-ē-əs\ tedious, supersedeas

²edious \ē-jəs\ see EGIS

edist \ēd-əst\ orthopedist, encyclopedist

edit \ed-ət\ credit, edit, accredit, coedit, discredit, noncredit, reedit, subedit, copyedit

editor \ed-ət-ər\ creditor, editor, predator, coeditor, subeditor

edium \ēd-ē-əm\ medium, tedium, cypripedium

edlar \ed-lər\ see EDDLER

edley \ed-lē\ deadly, medley, redly, chance-medley

edly \ed-lē\ see EDLEY

¹edo \ēd-ō\ credo, lido, Lido, speedo, aikido, libido, Toledo, torpedo, tuxedo

²edo \ād-ō\ see ²ADO

³edo \ēd-ə\ see ¹EDA

⁴edo \e-dō\ Edo, meadow, Yedo

edom \ēd-əm\ see EDUM

edon \ēd-ᵊn\ bleeding, Eden, steading, Sarpedon, boustrophedon

edouin \ed-wən\ see EDWIN

edra \ē-drə\ Phaedra, cathedra

edral \ē-drəl\ cathedral, dihedral, trihedral, hemihedral, holohedral, octahedral, pentahedral, polyhedral, procathedral, tetrahedral, dodecahedral, icosahedral, tetartohedral

edro \ā-drō\ Pedro, Murviedro

edulous \ej-ə-ləs\ credulous, sedulous, incredulous

edum \ēd-əm\ Edam, Edom, freedom, sedum

edure \ē-jər\ besieger, procedure, supersedure

edwin \ed-wən\ Edwin, bedouin

¹ee \ē\ b, be, bee, Brie, c, cay, cee, Cree, d, dee, Dee, dree, e, fee, flea, flee, free, g, gee, ghee, gie, glee, gree, he, key, Key, Klee, knee, lea, lee, Lee, Leigh, li, me, mi, p, pea, plea, pree, quay, re, scree, sea, see, she, shri, si, ski, spree, sri, t, tea, tee, the, thee, three, ti, tree, Tshi, twee, Twi, v, vee, we, wee, whee, ye, z, zee, agley, aiguille, agree, alee, ani, Bacchae, bailee, Bangui, banshee, bargee, bawbee, Belgae, Black Sea, bohea, bootee, bougie, buckshee, bungee, burgee, Bt, Capri, carefree, Castries, CB, CD, Chablis, Chaldee, chick-pea, Chi-li, chili, confit, cowpea, croquis, curie, Curie, Dead Sea, debris, decree, deep-sea, degree, Denis, donee, DP, draftee, drawee, Dundee, emcee, ennui, esprit, etui, farci, feoffee, foresee, fusee, GB, germfree, glacis, goatee, grand prix, grandee, grantee, GT, heart-free, he/she, HIV,

Horae, IC, IV, Jaycee, jaygee, jayvee, knock-knee, KP, latchkey, lessee, look-see, low-key, LP, mame, maquis, Marie, marquee, MC, métis, Midi, mille-feuille, muggee, must-see, Nancy, ngwee, OD, off-key, ogee, Osee, Parcae, pardie, passkey, Pawnee, payee, PC, perdie, per se, PG, pledgee, pongee, post-free, précis, puree, puttee, qt, raki, rani, razee, rooftree, rupee, rushee, RV, sati, scotfree, settee, Shaanxi, Shanxi, Shawnee, s/he, sightsee, signee, sirree, spadille, spahi, spondee, squeegee, squilgee, standee, strophe, suttee, sycee, T_3, T-3, TB, testee, 3-D, titi, to-be, topee, towhee, townee, trainee, trustee, trusty, Tupi, turfski, turnkey, tutee, Tutsi, tutti, TV, unbe, vendee, vestee, Volsci, vouchee, whangee, whoopee, would-be, Yang-Tze, yen-shee, abatis, ABC, ABD, absentee, addressee, adoptee, advisee, alienee, allottee, ambergris, AMP, amputee, appellee, appointee, après-ski, arrestee, assignee, attendee, B.V.D., Bahai, barley-bree, batterie, billi-bi, bonhomie, booboisie, bourgeoisie, brasserie, brusquerie, bumblebee, camporee, cap-a-pie, causerie, CCD, chickaree, chimpanzee, coati, Coligny, committee, conferee, consignee, counselee, context-free, counterplea, Danae, DDD, Debussy, departee, DDT, debauchee, DDE, deportee, dernier cri, deshabille, designee, detainee, devisee, devotee, diploe, disagree, discharge, dishabille, divorce, divorcee, DME, DMT, dungaree, duty-free, eau-de-vie, employee, endorsee, enlistee, enrollee, epopee, escadrille, escapee, ESP, evictee, expellee, FAD, fancy-free, fantasie, fantasy, fedayee, filigree, fleur-de-lis, formulae, franchisee, fricassee, galilee, Galilee, garnishee, gaucherie, Gemini, GTP, guarani, guarantee, Hawaii, honeybee, honoree, humble-bee, hydro-ski, IgE, IgG, inductee, internee, invitee, IUD, jacquerie, jamboree, Jiangxi, jus soli, Kayseri, kidnappee, LCD, LED, legatee, libelee, licensee, LSD, maître d', manatee, Medici, millidegree, murderee, NAD, nominee, obligee, oversea, oversee, parolee, parti pris, patentee, pedigree, peppertree, picotee, piroshki, point d'appui, potpourri, praecipe, presentee, promisee, rapparee, referee, refugee, rejectee, renminbi, repartee, retiree, retrainee, returnee, Rosemarie, RPV, saddletree, Sadducee, San Luis, sangaree, Savaii, selectee, Semele, shivaree, snickersnee, SOB, SST, STD,

Tenebrae, Tennessee, thirty-
three, TNT, toile de Jouy,
torii, transferee, undersea,
Urümqi, vaccinee, value-free,
verdigris, VIP, vis-à-vis,
warrantee, Adar Sheni, Agri
Dagi, alienee, biographee,
bouquet garni, casus belli,
charcuterie, charivari,
chincherinchee, chinoiserie,
covenantee, DBCP, dedicatee,
de Medici, delegatee,
distributee, ESOP, evacuee,
examinee, exuviae, facetiae,
fait accompli, felo-de-se,
fortunately, Galilei, HTLV,
interrogee, interviewee,
jaborandi, Jiamusi, minutiae,
Omega-3, Pasiphae,
patisserie, prima facie,
reliquiae, relocatee, Sargasso
Sea, Simon Legree, Sault
Sainte Marie, Southend on
Sea, communicatee, HTLV-
III, taedium vitae, Tupi-
Guarani, ignoratio elenchi,
petitio principii
²**ee** \ā\ see ¹AY
ée \ā\ see ¹AY
eeable \ē-ə-bəl\ seeable,
skiable, agreeable,
foreseeable, disagreeable
eebie \ē-bē\ see ¹EBE
eece \ēs\ see IECE
eeced \ēst\ see ¹EAST
eech \ēch\ see EACH
eecher \ē-chər\ see EACHER
eeches \ich-əz\ see ITCHES
eeching \ē-chiŋ\ breeching, far-
reaching—*also present
participles of verbs listed at*
EACH

eechy \ē-chē\ see EACHY
eecy \ē-sē\ fleecy, greasy,
specie, Tbilisi, AC/DC
eed \ēd\ bead, Bede, bleed,
brede, breed, cede, creed,
deed, feed, Gide, glede, gleed,
greed, he'd, heed, keyed,
knead, kneed, lead, mead,
Mead, Mede, meed, need,
plead, read, rede, reed, Reed,
Reid, screed, seed, she'd,
speed, steed, swede, Swede,
treed, tweed, Tweed, we'd,
weed, accede, airspeed,
allseed, bindweed, birdseed,
blueweed, bourride, breast-
feed, bugseed, burweed,
cheerlead, chickweed,
concede, crossbreed,
cudweed, debride, degreed,
duckweed, exceed, fairlead,
fireweed, flaxseed, Godspeed,
gulfweed, half-breed, hand-
feed, hawkweed, hayseed,
high-speed, horseweed,
impede, implead, inbreed,
indeed, ironweed, Jamshid,
jetbead, knapweed, knotweed,
Lake Mead, linseed, lip-read,
milkweed, misdeed, mislead,
misread, moonseed,
nosebleed, off-speed, oilseed,
pigweed, pinweed, pokeweed,
pondweed, Port Said, precede,
proceed, proofread, ragweed,
rapeseed, recede, reseed,
rockweed, seaweed, secede,
self-feed, Siegfried, sight-
read, silkweed, smartweed,
snakeweed, sneezeweed,
speed-read, spoon-feed, stall-
feed, stampede, stickseed,

stickweed, stinkweed,
succeed, ten-speed, tickseed,
weak-kneed, witchweed,
wormseed, aniseed, antecede,
beggarweed, bitterweed,
bottle-feed, bugleweed,
butterweed, carpetweed,
centipede, copyread,
cottonseed, cottonweed,
crazyweed, Ganymede,
interbreed, intercede,
interplead, jewelweed,
jimsonweed, locoweed,
millipede, overfeed,
pedigreed, pickerelweed,
pumpkinseed, retrocede,
riverweed, rosinweed,
Runnymede, silverweed,
supersede, thimbleweed,
tumbleweed, underfeed,
waterweed, velocipede

eedal \ēd-ᵊl\ see EEDLE

eeded \ē-dəd\ beaded, deeded,
kneaded, receded—*also pasts
of verbs listed at* EED

eeder \ēd-ər\ see ¹EADER

eedful \ēd-fəl\ heedful, needful

¹eeding \ēd-iŋ\ bleeding,
breeding, leading, reading,
reeding, inbreeding,
linebreeding, lipreading,
outbreeding, preceding,
speed-reading

²eeding \ēd-ᵊn\ see EDON

eedle \ēd-ᵊl\ aedile, beadle,
credal, creedal, daedal,
needle, wheedle

eedless \ēd-ləs\ deedless,
heedless, needless, seedless

eedn't \ēd-ᵊnt\ see EDENT

eedo \ēd-ō\ see ¹EDO

eedom \ēd-əm\ see EDUM

eeds \ēdz\ Leeds, needs,
Beskids, proceeds—*also
plurals and possessives of
nouns and third person
singular presents of verbs
listed at* EED

eedsman \ēdz-mən\ beadsman,
seedsman

eedy \ēd-ē\ beady, deedy,
greedy, needy, reedy, seedy,
speedy, tweedy, weedy

eef \ēf\ see ¹IEF

eefe \ēf\ see ¹IEF

eefy \ē-fē\ beefy, leafy, reefy

eegee \ē-jē\ see IJI

eeing \ē-iŋ\ seeing, skiing,
farseeing, ill-being, sight-
seeing, turfskiing, well-being,
heli-skiing, waterskiing

¹eek \ik\ see ICK

²eek \ēk\ see ¹EAK

eeked \ēkt\ see ²EAKED

eeken \ē-kən\ see EACON

eeker \ē-kər\ see ¹EAKER

eekie \ē-kē\ see EAKY

eeking \ē-kiŋ\ see ¹EAKING

eekly \ē-klē\ bleakly, chicly,
sleekly, weakly, weekly,
treacly, biweekly, midweekly,
newsweekly, triweekly,
semiweekly

eeks \ēks\ see ¹IXE

eeky \ē-kē\ see EAKY

eel \ēl\ see ²EAL

eelable \ē-lə-bəl\ see EALABLE

eele \ēl\ see ²EAL

eeled \ēld\ see IELD

eeler \ē-lər\ see EALER

eeley \ē-lē\ see EELY

eelie \ē-lē\ see EELY

eelin \ē-lən\ see ELIN

eeling \ē-liŋ\ ceiling, dealing,

Ealing, feeling, peeling, shieling, wheeling, appealing, Darjeeling, freewheeling, self-dealing, self-feeling, self-sealing, unfeeling, double-dealing, self-revealing, snowmobiling, unappealing—*also present participles of verbs listed at* ²EAL

eelson \el-sən\ see ELSON

eely \ē-lē\ Chi-li, dele, eely, Ely, freely, Greeley, mealie, mealy, really, seely, steelie, steely, stele, surreally, syli, vealy, wheelie, scungilli, Swahili, campanile, contumely, Isle of Ely, monostele, touchy-feely

eem \ēm\ see ¹EAM

eeman \ē-mən\ see ¹EMON

eemer \ē-mər\ see EAMER

eemie \ē-mē\ see EAMY

eeming \ē-miŋ\ seeming, streaming, redeeming, unbeseeming—*also present participles of verbs listed at* ¹EAM

eemly \ēm-lē\ seemly, supremely, unseemly

¹een \in\ see ¹IN

²een \ēn\ see ³INE

e'en \ēn\ see ³INE

eena \ē-nə\ see ²INA

eene \ēn\ see ³INE

eener \ē-nər\ see EANER

eenery \ēn-rē\ see EANERY

eening \ē-niŋ\ see EANING

eenling \ēn-liŋ\ see EANLING

eenly \ēn-lē\ see ¹EANLY

eenness \ēn-nəs\ see EANNESS

eens \ēnz\ Queens, teens, Grenadines, Philippines, smithereens

eenwich \in-ich\ see INACH

eeny \ē-nē\ see ¹INI

eep \ēp\ beep, bleep, cheap, cheep, clepe, creep, deep, heap, jeep, Jeep, keep, leap, neap, neep, peep, reap, seep, sheep, sleep, sneap, steep, sweep, threap, veep, weep, asleep, barkeep, bopeep, dustheap, housekeep, knee-deep, skin-deep, upkeep, upsweep, overleap, oversleep, Lakshadweep, Louis Philippe

eepage \ē-pij\ creepage, seepage

eepen \ē-pən\ cheapen, deepen, steepen

eepence \əp-əns\ see UPPANCE

eepenny \əp-nē\ see OPENNY

eeper \ē-pər\ beeper, creeper, keeper, leaper, Dnieper, peeper, reaper, sleeper, sweeper, weeper, barkeeper, beekeeper, bookkeeper, crowkeeper, doorkeeper, gamekeeper, gatekeeper, goalkeeper, greenkeeper, groundskeeper, housekeeper, innkeeper, lockkeeper, minesweeper, peacekeeper, scorekeeper, shopkeeper, stockkeeper, storekeeper, timekeeper, zookeeper, honeycreeper—*also comparatives of adjectives listed at* EEP

eepie \ē-pē\ see EEPY

eeping \ē-piŋ\ creeping, keeping, weeping, beekeeping, bookkeeping, gatekeeping, housekeeping,

minesweeping, peacekeeping,
safekeeping, timekeeping

eepish \ē-pish\ cheapish,
sheepish

eeple \ē-pəl\ see EOPLE

eepy \ē-pē\ cheapie, creepy,
seepy, sleepy, sweepy, tepee,
tipi, weepie, weepy

¹eer \ē-ər\ freer, seer, skier,
we're, CBer, decreer,
foreseer, sightseer, overseer,
water-skier

²eer \ir\ beer, bier, blear, cere,
cheer, clear, dear, deer, drear,
ear, fear, fere, fleer, gear,
hear, here, jeer, Lear, leer,
mere, mir, near, peer, pier,
Pierre, queer, rear, schmear,
sear, seer, sere, shear, sheer,
skirr, smear, sneer, spear,
speer, sphere, spier, steer,
tear, tier, Trier, Tyr, veer,
were, year, adhere, Aesir,
Ajmer, ambeer, appear, arrear,
Asir, austere, Ayrshire,
Berkshire, besmear, brassiere,
Cape Fear, career, cashier,
cashmere, Cheshire, chimere,
clavier, cohere, compeer,
destrier, dog-ear, Ellesmere,
emir, Empire, endear,
ensphere, eyrir, Fafnir,
Fifeshire, Flintshire, footgear,
frontier, gambier, Goodyear,
haltere, Hampshire, headgear,
inhere, Izmir, Kashmir, kefir,
killdeer, laveer, light-year,
man-year, menhir, mishear,
monsieur, mouse-ear, nadir,
Nairnshire, out-year, Pamir,
Perthshire, pickeer, portiere,
premier, premiere, redear,

rehear, reindeer, revere,
Revere, Robespierre, revers,
Saint Pierre, santir, severe,
Shakespeare, Shropshire,
sincere, slick-ear, tapir,
uprear, Vanir, veneer, vizier,
voir dire, wheatear, Wiltshire,
Ymir, Yorkshire, zaire, Zaire,
atmosphere, auctioneer,
balladeer, bandolier, bayadere,
Bedfordshire, Bedivere,
belvedere, biosphere, black-
tailed deer, bombardier,
boutonniere, brigadier,
buccaneer, budgeteer,
Cambridgeshire, cameleer,
cannoneer, cassimere,
cavalier, chandelier,
chanticleer, chevalier,
chiffonier, chocolatier,
commandeer, corsetiere,
cuirassier, Denbighshire,
Derbyshire, diapir, disappear,
domineer, Dumfriesshire,
ecosphere, Elzevir, engineer,
fictioneer, financier,
fourdrinier, fusilier, gadgeteer,
gasolier, gazetteer,
Gloucestershire, gondolier,
grenadier, Guinevere,
halberdier, hemisphere,
Herefordshire, Hertfordshire,
IJsselmere, insincere,
interfere, jardiniere, junketeer,
kerseymere, Lanarkshire,
Lancashire, lavaliere,
leafleteer, marketeer,
Meyerbeer, missileer,
Monmouthshire, Morayshire,
mountaineer, Mount Ranier,
muleteer, musketeer,
mutineer, Oxfordshire,

overhear, overseer, oversteer, pamphleteer, Pembrokeshire, persevere, pioneer, pistoleer, pontonier, privateer, profiteer, puppeteer, racketeer, Radnorshire, rocketeer, Rutlandshire, scrutineer, Selkirkshire, sloganeer, sonneteer, souvenir, Staffordshire, stratosphere, summiteer, Tyne and Wear, understeer, volunteer, Warwickshire, white-tailed deer, Windermere, Worcestershire, yesteryear, acyclovir, animalier, black marketeer, Buckinghamshire, Clackmannanshire, carabineer, Caernarvonshire, Cardiganshire, Carmarthenshire, charioteer, conventioneer, Dunbartonshire, electioneer, Eskisehir, Glamorganshire, free-marketeer, harquebusier, Huntingdonshire, Invernessshire, Kincardineshire, Montgomeryshire, Northamptonshire, Nottinghamshire, Merionethshire

e'er \er\ see [4]ARE

eerage \ir-ij\ peerage, steerage, arrearage

eered \ird\ see [1]EARD

eerer \ir-ər\ see [2]EARER

eeress \ir-əs\ see EROUS

eerful \ir-fəl\ see EARFUL

[1]eerie \ir-ē\ see EARY

[2]eerie \ē-rē\ see EIRIE

eering \ir-iŋ\ see [1]EARING

eerist \ir-əst\ see [1]ERIST

eerless \ir-ləs\ see EARLESS

eerly \ir-lē\ see [1]EARLY

eersman \irz-mən\ steersman, frontiersman

eerut \ir-ət\ see IRIT

eery \ir-ē\ see EARY

ees \ēz\ see EZE

eese \ēz\ see EZE

eesh \ēsh\ see [2]ICHE

eesi \ē-zē\ see [1]EASY

eesia \ē-zhə\ see [2]ESIA

eesome \ē-səm\ gleesome, threesome

[1]eest \āst\ see ACED

[2]eest \ēst\ see [1]EAST

eesy \ē-zē\ see [1]EASY

eet \ēt\ see [1]EAT

eetah \ēt-ə\ see [2]ITA

eete \āt-ē\ see ATY

eeten \ēt-°n\ see [1]EATEN

eeter \ēt-ər\ see [1]EATER

eethe \ēth\ see EATHE

eether \ē-thər\ see EITHER

eething \ē-thiŋ\ see EATHING

eetie \ēt-ē\ see EATY

eeting \ēt-iŋ\ see EATING

eetle \ēt-°l\ see ETAL

eetly \ēt-lē\ featly, fleetly, neatly, sweetly, completely, concretely, discreetly, discretely, effetely, bittersweetly, incompletely, indiscreetly

eety \ēt-ē\ see EATY

ee-um \ē-əm\ see [1]EUM

eeve \ēv\ see [1]EAVE

eeved \ēvd\ see EAVED

eeves \ēvz\ see EAVES

eevil \ē-vəl\ see IEVAL

eevish \ē-vish\ peevish, thievish

eeward \ē-wərd\ leeward,
   Leeward, seaward
eewee \ē-wē\ kiwi, peewee,
   pewee
eewit \ü-ət\ see UET
eez \ēz\ see EZE
eezable \ē-zə-bəl\ see EASIBLE
eeze \ēz\ see EZE
eezer \ē-zər\ see ²EASER
eezing \ē-ziŋ\ see ²EASING
eezy \ē-zē\ see ¹EASY
¹ef \ef\ chef, clef, deaf, ef, f,
   lev, ref, teff, aleph, Brezhnev,
   enfeoff, H-F, Kiev, Lwiw,
   stone-deaf, tone-deaf, emf,
   Kishinev
²ef \ā\ see ¹AY
³ef \ēf\ see ¹IEF
efanie \ef-ə-nē\ see EPHONY
efany \ef-ə-nē\ see EPHONY
efe \ef-ē\ see EFFIE
eferable \ef-rə-bəl\ preferable,
   referable
eference \ef-rəns\ deference,
   preference, reference, cross-
   reference
eferent \ef-rənt\ deferent,
   referent
eff \ef\ see ¹EF
effer \ef-ər\ see EPHOR
efic \ef-ik\ Efik, benefic, malefic
eficence \ef-ə-səns\ beneficence,
   maleficence
efik \e-fik\ see EFIC
efsk \efsk\ Izhefsk, Profopyevsk
eft \eft\ cleft, deft, eft, heft,
   klepht, left, theft, weft, bereft
efty \ef-tē\ hefty, lefty
¹eg \āg\ Craig, plague, vague,
   stravage, The Hague
²eg \eg\ beg, Craig, dreg, egg,
   gleg, Greg, Gregg, keg, leg,

peg, reg, skeg, squeg, yegg,
blackleg, bootleg, bowleg,
dogleg, foreleg, jackleg, jake
leg, muskeg, nutmeg, redleg,
renege, roughleg, Tuareg,
unpeg, Winnipeg, mumblety-
peg
³eg \ej\ see EDGE
¹ega \eg-ə\ omega, rutabaga
²ega \ā-gə\ see ²AGA
³ega \ē-gə\ see ¹IGA
egal \ē-gəl\ beagle, eagle, egal,
   legal, regal, illegal, porbeagle,
   spread-eagle, viceregal,
   extralegal, paralegal,
   medicolegal
egan \ē-gən\ Megan, vegan,
   Mohegan
egas \ā-gəs\ see AGUS
¹ege \ezh\ barege, cortege,
   Liège, manege, solfege
²ege \eg\ see ²EG
³ege \ej\ see EDGE
⁴ege \ēg\ see IGUE
⁵ege \ig\ see IG
eged \ejd\ see EDGED
egel \āgəl\ see AGEL
egent \ē-jənt\ regent, sejant,
   allegiant, vice-regent
eger \ej-ər\ see EDGER
egg \eg\ see ²EG
eggar \eg-ər\ see EGGER
eggary \eg-ə-rē\ beggary,
   Gregory
egger \eg-ər\ beggar,
   bootlegger, Heidegger,
   thousand-legger
eggie \ej-ē\ see EDGY
eggio \ej-ē-ō\ Reggio, arpeggio,
   solfeggio
eggs \egz\ see EGS

eggy \eg-ē\ dreggy, eggy, leggy, Peggy, plaguey, Carnegie

egia \ē-jə\ Ouija, aqua regia, aquilegia, paraplegia, quadriplegia

egian \ē-jən\ see EGION

egiant \ē-jənt\ see EGENT

egiate \ē-jət\ collegiate, elegit, intercollegiate

egic \ē-jik\ strategic, paraplegic, quadriplegic

egie \eg-ē\ see EGGY

egion \ē-jən\ legion, region, Norwegian, subregion, collegian

egious \ē-jəs\ see EGIS

egis \ē-jəs\ aegis, egis, Regis, tedious, egregious

egit \ē-jət\ see EGIATE

egm \em\ see ¹EM

egn \ān\ see ¹ANE

egnant \eg-nənt\ pregnant, regnant, impregnant, unpregnant

egnly \ān-lē\ see AINLY

egno \ān-yō\ see ¹ENO

¹ego \ē-gō\ chigoe, ego, Vigo, amigo, alter ego, impetigo, superego

²ego \ā-gō\ see ²AGO

egory \eg-ə-rē\ see EGGARY

egro \ē-grō\ Negro, Montenegro

egs \egz\ sheerlegs, yellowlegs, butter-and-eggs, daddy longlegs—*also plurals and possessives of nouns and third person singular presents of verbs listed at* ²EG

egular \eg-lər\ see EGLER

¹eh \ā\ see ¹AY

²eh \a\ see ³AH

ehen \ān\ see ¹ANE

ehner \ā-nər\ see AINER

¹ei \ēk\ dreich, skeigh

²ei \ā\ see ¹AY

³ei \ī\ see ¹Y

¹eia \ē-ə\ see ¹IA

²eia \ī-ə\ see ¹IAH

eial \ē-əl\ see ¹EAL

¹eian \ē-ən\ see ¹EAN

²eian \ā-ən\ see ¹AYAN

eic \ē-ik\ oleic, epigeic, logorrheic, mythopoeic, onomatopoeic

eich \ēk\ see ¹EI

eiche \āsh\ see ¹ECHE

eickel \ī-kəl\ see YCLE

¹eid \āt\ see ¹ATE

²eid \īt\ see ¹ITE

³eid \ēd\ see EED

¹eidel \ād-əl\ see ADLE

²eidel \īd-ᵊl\ see IDAL

eidi \īd-ē\ see IDAY

eidon \īd-ᵊn\ see IDEN

eier \īr\ see ¹IRE

eifer \ef-ər\ see EPHOR

¹eige \āzh\ beige, assuage

²eige \ā\ see ¹AY

eiger \ī-gər\ see IGER

¹eigh \ā\ see ¹AY

²eigh \ē\ see ¹EE

eighbor \ā-bər\ see ABOR

¹eight \āt\ see ¹ATE

²eight \īt\ see ¹ITE

eighter \āt-ər\ see ATOR

eightless \āt-ləs\ see ATELESS

eights \īts\ see IGHTS

eighty \āt-ē\ see ATY

eign \ān\ see ¹ANE

eigner \ā-nər\ see AINER

eii \ā\ see ¹AY

eiian \ā-ən\ see ¹AYAN

eiji \ā-jē\ see AGY

eik \ēk\ see ¹EAK

eikh \ēk\ see ¹EAK
eikle \ē-kəl\ see ECAL
¹eil \āl\ see AIL
²eil \el\ see ¹EL
³eil \ēl\ see ²EAL
⁴eil \īl\ see ¹ILE
eila \ē-lə\ see ¹ELA
eiled \āld\ see AILED
eiler \ī-lər\ see ILAR
¹eiling \ā-liŋ\ see AILING
²eiling \ē-liŋ\ see EELING
eill \ēl\ see ²EAL
eillance \ā-ləns\ see ALENCE
eillant \ā-lənt\ see ALANT
¹eilles \ā\ see ¹AY
²eilles \ālz\ see ALES
eilly \ā-lē\ see AILY
¹eim \ām\ see ¹AME
²eim \īm\ see ¹IME
eimer \ī-mər\ see ¹IMER
¹eims \äⁿs\ see ¹ANCE
²eims \ēmz\ Reims, Rheims—
  also possessives and plurals
  of nouns and third person
  singular presents of verbs
  listed at ¹EAM
¹ein \ān\ see ¹ANE
²ein \ē-ən\ see ¹EAN
³ein \ēn\ see ³INE
⁴ein \īn\ see ¹INE
¹eine \ān\ see ¹ANE
²eine \ēn\ see ³INE
³eine \ī-nə\ see ¹INA
⁴eine \en\ see ¹EN
eined \ānd\ see AINED
¹einer \ā-nər\ see AINER
²einer \ē-nər\ see EANER
eing \ē-iŋ\ see EEING
einie \ī-nē\ see ¹INY
eining \ā-niŋ\ see AINING
einous \ā-nəs\ see AYNESS
eins \ānz\ see AINS

einsman \ānz-mən\ see
  AINSMAN
eint \ānt\ see AINT
einte \ant\ see ⁵ANT
einture \an-chər\ see ²ANCHER
einy \ā-nē\ see AINY
eipt \ēt\ see ¹EAT
eir \er\ see ⁴ARE
eira \ir-ə\ see ²ERA
eird \ird\ see ¹EARD
eiress \ar-əs\ see ²ARIS
eiric \ī-rik\ see YRIC
eiro \er-ō\ see ²ERO
eirs \erz\ see AIRS
¹eis \ās\ see ¹ACE
²eis \ē-əs\ see ¹EUS
³eis \īs\ see ¹ICE
eisant \ēs-ᵊnt\ see ECENT
eise \ēz\ see EZE
eisel \ī-zəl\ see ²ISAL
eisen \īz-ᵊn\ see ¹IZEN
¹eiser \ī-sər\ see ICER
²eiser \ī-zər\ see IZER
¹eisha \ā-shə\ see ACIA
²eisha \ē-shə\ see ¹ESIA
eisin \ēz-ᵊn\ see EASON
eiss \īs\ see ¹ICE
eissen \īs-ᵊn\ see ¹ISON
¹eist \ā-əst\ see AYEST
²eist \īst\ see ¹IST
¹eister \ī-stər\ shyster,
  concertmeister, kapellmeister
²eister \ē-stər\ see EASTER
eisure \ē-zhər\ see EIZURE
¹eit \ē-ət\ fiat, albeit, howbeit
²eit \it\ see ¹IT
³eit \ēt\ see ¹EAT
⁴eit \īt\ see ¹ITE
eited \ēt-əd\ see ¹EATED
¹eiter \it-ər\ see ITTER
²eiter \ī-tər\ see ¹ITER
eith \ēth\ see ¹EATH

either \ē-thər\ breather, either,
neither, teether

eitus \īt-əs\ see ITIS

eity \ē-ət-ē\ deity, velleity,
corporeity, spontaneity,
synchroneity, diaphaneity,
homogeneity, incorporeity,
instantaneity,
contemporaneity,
extemporaneity,
heterogeneity, inhomogeneity

eivable \ē-və-bəl\ cleavable,
achievable, believable,
conceivable, deceivable,
perceivable, receivable,
relievable, retrievable,
imperceivable, inconceivable,
irretrievable, unbelievable,
unconceivable

eive \ēv\ see ¹EAVE

eiver \ē-vər\ see IEVER

eix \āsh\ see ¹ECHE

¹eize \āz\ see ¹AZE

²eize \ēz\ see EZE

eizure \ē-zhər\ leisure, seizure

ejant \ē-jənt\ see EGENT

eji \ej-ē\ see EDGY

ejo \ā-ō\ see ¹EO

ek \ek\ see ECK

¹eka \ek-ə\ see ECCA

²eka \ē-kə\ see ¹IKA

ekah \ek-ə\ see ECCA

eke \ēk\ see ¹EAK

ekel \ek-əl\ see ECKLE

ekh \ek\ see ECK

eki \ek-ē\ see ECKY

ekker \ek-ər\ see ECKER

ekoe \ē-kō\ see ICOT

ekton \ek-tən\ see ECTEN

¹el \el\ bel, bell, Bell, belle, cel,
cell, dell, dwell, el, ell, fell,
gel, Hel, hell, jell, knell, l,
mell, quell, sel, sell, shell,
smell, snell, spell, swell, tell,
they'll, well, yell, Adele,
Ardell, artel, barbell, befell,
Blackwell, bluebell, boatel,
bombshell, Boswell, botel,
bridewell, cadelle, cartel,
carvel, chandelle, clamshell,
compel, cormel, cornel,
corral, cowbell, Cromwell,
cupel, Danielle, diel, dispel,
doorbell, dumbbell, duxelles,
echelle, eggshell, Estelle,
excel, expel, farewell, fjeld,
foretell, gabelle, gazelle,
Giselle, gromwell, handbell,
hard-shell, harebell, hotel,
impel, indwell, inkwell, jurel,
lampshell, lapel, marcel,
maxwell, Maxwell, micelle,
Michele, Michelle, misspell,
morel, Moselle, motel,
nacelle, Nobel, noel, nouvelle,
nutshell, oat-cell, Orel,
Orwell, outsell, pall-mall,
Parnell, pastel, pell-mell,
pixel, pointelle, presell,
propel, quenelle, rakehell,
rappel, Ravel, rebel, refel,
repel, respell, retell, riel,
Rochelle, rondel, saurel,
scalpel, seashell, sequel,
Seychelles, soft-shell, solgel,
speedwell, spinel, stairwell,
unsell, unwell, upwell,
Weddell, wind-bell,
Annabelle, APL, aquarelle,
asphodel, Azazel, bagatelle,
BAL, barbicel, bechamel,
brocatelle, Camberwell,
caramel, caravel, carousel,
cascabel, chanterelle,

chaparral, Charles Martel,
citadel, clientele, cockleshell,
Cozumel, damozel, decibel,
demoiselle, fare-thee-well,
fontanel, immortelle, Isabel,
Isabelle, Jezebel, kiss-and-tell,
lenticel, mangonel, muscatel,
ne'er-do-well, Neufchatel,
nonpareil, organelle, oversell,
parallel, pedicel, pennoncel,
personnel, petronel, Philomel,
pimpernel, show-and-tell,
tortoiseshell, undersell, T4
cell, villanelle, William Tell,
zinfandel, Aix-la-Chapelle, au
naturel, crème caramel,
mademoiselle, maître d'hôtel,
matériel, Mont-Saint-Michel,
spirituel, T-helper cell,
Thompson's gazelle, VLDL,
antiparallel, antipersonnel,
AWOL
²**el** \āl\ see AIL
¹**ela** \ē-lə\ Gila, Leila, Lela,
selah, sheila, Sheila, stela,
Vila, Braila, candela, tequila,
weigela, sheila, Coahuila,
Philomela, sinsemilla, Tutuila
²**ela** \ā-lə\ see ³ALA
³**ela** \el-ə\ see ELLA
elable \el-ə-bəl\ see ELLABLE
elacy \el-ə-sē\ jealousy, prelacy
elagh \ā-lē\ see AILY
elah \ē-lə\ see ¹ELA
eland \ē-lənd\ eland, Leland,
Zealand, New Zealand
elanie \el-ə-nē\ see ELONY
elar \ē-lər\ see EALER
elate \el-ət\ see ELLATE
elatin \el-ət-°n\ see ELETON
elative \el-ət-iv\ relative,

appellative, correlative,
irrelative
elba \el-bə\ Elba, Elbe, Melba
elbe \el-bə\ see ELBA
elbert \el-bərt\ Delbert, Elbert,
Mount Elbert
elch \elch\ belch, squelch,
welch, Welch, Welsh
¹**eld** \eld\ eld, geld, held, meld,
shelled, weld, beheld,
danegeld, handheld, hard-
shelled, upheld, withheld, jet-
propelled, self-propelled,
unparalleled—*also pasts of
verbs listed at* ¹EL
²**eld** \el\ see ¹EL
³**eld** \elt\ see ELT
elda \el-də\ Zelda, Dar el Belda
eldam \el-dəm\ see ELDOM
elder \el-dər\ elder, welder
eldom \el-dəm\ beldam,
seldom, hoteldom
eldon \el-dən\ Sheldon, Weldon
eldt \elt\ see ELT
¹**ele** \ā-lē\ see AILY
²**ele** \el\ see ¹EL
³**ele** \el-ē\ see ELLY
⁴**ele** \ē-lē\ see EELY
¹**eled** \eld\ see ¹ELD
²**eled** \ēld\ see IELD
elen \el-ən\ see ELON
elena \el-ə-nə\ Elena, Helena
elens \el-ənz\ Saint Helens,
Mount Saint Helens—*also
plurals and possessives of
nouns at* ELON
eleon \ēl-yən\ see ²ELIAN
eletal \el-ət-°l\ pelletal, skeletal
eleton \el-ət-°n\ gelatin,
skeleton
eleus \ē-lē-əs\ see ELIOUS
elf \elf\ elf, Guelf, pelf, self,

shelf, bookshelf, herself,
hisself, himself, itself, meself,
myself, nonself, oneself,
ourself, top-shelf, thyself,
yourself, mantelshelf, do-it-
yourself

elfer \el-fər\ telpher, do-it-
yourselfer

elfish \el-fish\ elfish, selfish,
unselfish

elhi \el-ē\ see ELLY

eli \el-ē\ see ELLY

¹elia \ēl-yə\ Delia, Lelia, Shelia,
Amelia, camellia, Camellia,
Cecilia, Cornelia, Karelia,
lobelia, obelia, Ophelia,
Rumelia, sedilia, stapelia,
psychedelia, seguidilla

²elia \il-ē-ə\ see ¹ILIA

elial \ē-lē-əl\ Belial, epithelial

¹elian \ē-lē-ən\ Melian, Pelion,
abelian, Karelian, Mendelian

²elian \ēl-yən\ anthelion,
aphelion, carnelian,
chameleon, cornelian,
Mendelian, parhelion,
perihelion, Aristotelian,
Mephistophelian

³elian \el-ē-ən\ see ELLIAN

elible \el-ə-bəl\ see ELLABLE

¹elic \ē-lik\ parhelic, autotelic

²elic \el-ik\ melic, relic, telic,
angelic, Goidelic, smart aleck,
archangelic, autotelic,
philatelic, psychedelic

elical \el-i-kəl\ helical, pellicle,
angelical, double-helical,
evangelical

elier \el-yer\ see ELURE

elin \ē-lən\ shieling, theelin

¹elion \el-ē-ən\ see ELLIAN

²elion \ēl-yən\ see ²ELIAN

³elion \ēl-ē-ən\ see ¹ELIAN

elios \ē-lē-əs\ see ELIOUS

elious \ē-lē-əs\ Helios, Peleus,
Cornelius, contumelious

elish \el-ish\ see ELLISH

elist \el-əst\ trellised, cellist,
Nobelist, pastelist

¹elius \ā-lē-əs\ see ALIUS

²elius \ē-lē-əs\ see ELIOUS

elix \ē-liks\ Felix, helix, double
helix

¹elk \elk\ elk, whelk

²elk \ilk\ see ILK

ell \el\ see ¹EL

e'll \ēl\ see ²EAL

ella \el-ə\ Celle, Della, Ella,
fella, fellah, stella, Stella,
Benguela, candela, Capella,
Estella, favela, Gisela,
glabella, lamella, Luella,
Marcella, Mandela, novella,
paella, patella, prunella,
quiniela, rubella, sequela,
umbrella, vanilla, a cappella,
Cinderella, citronella,
columella, fraxinella, Isabella,
mortadella, mozzarella,
panatela, salmonella,
sarsaparilla, subumbrella,
tarantella, villanella,
valpolicella

ellable \el-ə-bəl\ fellable,
gelable, compellable,
expellable, indelible

ellah \el-ə\ see ELLA

ellan \el-ən\ see ELON

ellant \el-ənt\ gellant, appellant,
flagellant, propellant,
repellent, water-repellent

ellar \el-ər\ see ELLER

ellas \el-əs\ see EALOUS

ellate \el-ət\ helot, pellet,

prelate, zealot, appellate,
flagellate, haustellate,
lamellate, scutellate
ellative \el-ət-iv\ see ELATIVE
¹**elle** \el\ see ¹EL
²**elle** \el-ə\ see ELLA
ellean \el-ē-ən\ see ELLIAN
elled \eld\ see ¹ELD
ellen \el-ən\ see ELON
ellent \el-ənt\ see ELLANT
eller \el-ər\ cellar, dweller,
feller, heller, Keller, seller,
sheller, smeller, speller,
stellar, teller, yeller, best-
seller, bookseller, compeller,
expeller, foreteller, glabellar,
impeller, indweller, lamellar,
ocellar, patellar, propeller,
rathskeller, repeller, rostellar,
saltcellar, tale-teller,
cereballar, circumstellar,
columellar, fortune-teller,
interstellar, Rockefeller,
storyteller
¹**elles** \el\ see ¹EL
²**elles** \elz\ see ELLS
ellet \el-ət\ see ELLATE
elletal \el-ət-ᵊl\ see ELETAL
elley \el-ē\ see ELLY
elli \el-ē\ see ELLY
ellia \ēl-yə\ see ELIA
ellian \el-ē-ən\ Chellean,
Boswellian, pre-Chellean,
Sabellian, triskelion,
Pantagruelian, Machiavellian
ellicle \el-i-kəl\ see ELICAL
ellie \el-ē\ see ELLY
elline \el-ən\ see ELON
elling \el-iŋ\ belling, selling,
spelling, swelling, telling,
bookselling, compelling,
indwelling, misspelling, tale-

telling, upwelling, fortune-
telling, self-propelling—*also
present participles of verbs
listed at* ¹EL
ellington \el-iŋ-tən\ Ellington,
Wellington, beef Wellington
ellion \el-yən\ hellion, rebellion
ellis \el-əs\ see EALOUS
ellised \el-əst\ see ELIST
ellish \el-ish\ hellish, relish,
disrelish, embellish
ellist \el-əst\ see ELIST
ello \el-ō\ bellow, Bellow, cello,
fellow, Jell-O, mellow,
yellow, Yellow, bargello,
bedfellow, bordello, duello,
hail-fellow, Longfellow,
marshmallow, morello, niello,
Othello, playfellow,
schoolfellow, yokefellow,
Pirandello, punchinello,
ritornello, saltarello, Robin
Goodfellow, violoncello
ell-o \el-ō\ see ELLO
ellous \el-əs\ see EALOUS
¹**ellow** \el-ə\ see ELLA
²**ellow** \el-ō\ see ELLO
ells \elz\ Welles, Dardanelles—
*also plurals and possessives
of nouns and third person
singular presents of verbs
listed at* ¹EL
ellum \el-əm\ blellum, skellum,
vellum, postbellum, rostellum,
antebellum, cerebellum
ellus \el-əs\ see EALOUS
elly \el-ē\ belly, Delhi, deli,
felly, jelly, Kellie, Kelly,
Nellie, shelly, Shelley, Shelly,
smelly, tele, telly, wellie,
New Delhi, nice-nelly,
potbelly, rakehelly, sowbelly,

Boticelli, nervous Nellie,
underbelly, vermicelli,
Machiavelli, Dadra and Nagar
Haveli

ellyn \el-ən\ see ELON

elm \elm\ elm, helm, realm,
whelm, overwhelm,
underwhelm

elma \el-mə\ Selma, Velma

elmar \el-mər\ see ELMER

elmer \el-mər\ Delmar, Delmer,
Elmer

elmet \el-mət\ helmet, Helmut,
pelmet

elmut \el-mət\ see ELMET

elo \ē-lō\ see ²ILO

elon \el-ən\ Ellen, Ellyn, felon,
Helen, melon, avellan,
Magellan, McClellan,
muskmelon, Snellen, vitelline,
Mary Ellen, watermelon,
Strait of Magellan

elony \el-ə-nē\ felony, Melanie

elop \el-əp\ develop, envelop,
redevelop, overdevelop

elopment \el-əp-mənt\
development, envelopment,
redevelopment,
overdevelopment

elos \ā-ləs\ see AYLESS

elot \el-ət\ see ELLATE

elotry \el-ə-trē\ helotry,
zealotry

elp \elp\ help, kelp, skelp,
whelp, yelp

elpher \el-fər\ see ELFER

elsea \el-sē\ see ELSIE

elsh \elch\ see ELCH

elsie \el-sē\ Chelsea, Elsie,
Kensington and Chelsea

elson \el-sən\ keelson, nelson,
Nelson

elt \elt\ belt, celt, Celt, dealt,
delt, dwelt, felt, gelt, melt,
pelt, Scheldt, smelt, spelt,
svelte, veld, welt, black belt,
flybelt, forefelt, greenbelt,
heartfelt, hot-melt, jacksmelt,
Krefeld, self-belt, snowbelt,
snowmelt, Sunbelt, Bielefeld,
Roosevelt, shelterbelt

elte \elt\ see ELT

elted \el-təd\ bias-belted—*also
pasts of verbs listed at* ELT

elter \el-tər\ melter, pelter,
shelter, skelter, smelter,
spelter, swelter, welter, helter-
skelter

eltered \el-tərd\ earth-
sheltered—*also pasts of verbs
listed at* ELTER

elting \el-tiŋ\ belting, felting,
melting, pelting

elure \el-yər\ velure, hotelier

elve \elv\ delve, helve, shelve,
twelve

elves \elvz\ elves, ourselves,
theirselves, themselves,
yourselves—*also plurals and
possessives of nouns and
third person singular present
of verbs at* ELVE

elvin \el-vən\ Elvin, Kelvin,
Melvin, Melvyn

elvyn \el-vən\ see ELVIN

ely \ē-lē\ see EELY

¹em \em\ Clem, crème, em,
femme, gem, hem, m, mem,
phlegm, REM, Shem, stem,
them, ad rem, ahem, AM,
Arnhem, Belem, bluestem,
condemn, contemn, FM,
idem, in rem, item, mayhem,
millieme, modem, poem,

problem, pro tem, proem,
Shechem, ABM, anadem,
apothegm, apothem,
Bethlehem, diadem,
exanthem, ibidem, IgM,
meristem, OEM, SAM,
stratagem, ad hominem, carpe
diem, crème de la crème,
ICBM, post meridiem, star-
of-Bethlehem, terminus ad
quem

²**em** \əm\ see ¹UM

ema \ē-mə\ bema, Lima, Pima,
schema, Colima, eczema,
edema, diastema, emphysema,
Hiroshima, Iwo Jima,
Kagoshima, Matsushima,
terza rima, Tokushima, ottava
rima

emacist \em-ə-səst\ see EMICIST

¹**eman** \em-ən\ see ²EMON

²**eman** \ē-mən\ see ¹EMON

emane \em-ə-nē\ see EMONY

emanence \em-ə-nəns\ see
EMINENCE

emanent \em-ə-nənt\ see
EMINENT

ematis \em-ət-əs\ see EMITUS

ematist \em-ət-əst\ see EMITIST

ematous \em-ət-əs\ see EMITUS

ember \em-bər\ ember,
member, December,
dismember, November,
remember, September,
disremember

¹**emble** \äm-bəl\ wamble,
ensemble

²**emble** \em-bəl\ tremble,
assemble, atremble,
dissemble, resemble,
disassemble

embler \em-blər\ temblor,

trembler, assembler,
dissembler

emblor \em-blər\ see EMBLER

embly \em-blē\ trembly,
assembly, disassembly, self-
assembly, subassembly

¹**eme** \em\ see ¹EM

²**eme** \ēm\ see ¹EAM

emel \ā-məl\ see EMILE

emely \ēm-lē\ see EEMLY

¹**emen** \ē-mən\ see ¹EMON

²**emen** \em-ən\ see ²EMON

³**emen** \ā-mən\ see ¹AMEN

emer \ē-mər\ see EAMER

emeral \em-rəl\ femoral,
ephemeral

emery \em-rē\ emery, Emery,
Emory, memory

emesis \em-ə-səs\ emesis,
nemesis

emi \em-ē\ see EMMY

emia \ē-mē-ə\ anemia,
bohemia, Bohemia, leukemia,
toxemia, academia,
septicemia, thalassemia,
hypoglycemia, hypokalemia,
beta-thalassemia

emian \ē-mē-ən\ anthemion,
Bohemian

¹**emic** \ē-mik\ emic, anemic,
graphemic, morphemic,
lexemic, phonemic, taxemic,
tonemic, epistemic

²**emic** \em-ik\ chemic, alchemic,
endemic, pandemic, polemic,
sachemic, systemic, totemic,
academic, epidemic, epistemic

emical \em-i-kəl\ chemical,
alchemical, polemical,
academical, biochemical,
epidemical, petrochemical,
biogeochemical

emicist \em-ə-səst\ polemicist,
supremacist

emics \ē-miks\ graphemics,
morphemics, phonemics,
proxemics

emile \ā-məl\ Emile, Memel

eminal \em-ən-ᵊl\ geminal,
seminal

eminate \em-ə-nət\ geminate,
effeminate

eminence \em-ə-nəns\
eminence, remanence,
preeminence

eminent \em-ə-nənt\ eminent,
remanent, preeminent

eming \em-iŋ\ Fleming,
Heminge, lemming

eminge \em-iŋ\ see EMING

emini \em-ə-nē\ see EMONY

eminy \em-ə-nē\ see EMONY

emion \ē-mē-ən\ see EMIAN

emis \ē-məs\ see EMUS

emish \em-ish\ blemish,
Flemish

emist \em-əst\ chemist,
polemist, biochemist

emitist \em-ət-əst\ Semitist,
systematist

emitus \em-ət-əs\ clematis,
fremitus, edematous

emlin \em-lən\ gremlin, kremlin

emma \em-ə\ Emma, gemma,
lemma, stemma, dilemma

emme \em\ see ¹EM

emmer \em-ər\ emmer,
hemmer, stemmer, tremor,
condemner, contemner

emming \em-iŋ\ see EMING

emmy \em-ē\ Emmy, gemmy,
jemmy, phlegmy, semi,
stemmy

emn \em\ see ¹EM

emner \em-ər\ see EMMER

emnity \em-nət-ē\ indemnity,
solemnity

emo \em-ō\ demo, memo

¹emon \ē-mən\ demon, freeman,
Freeman, gleeman, Piman,
seaman, semen, Lake Leman,
pentstemon, Philemon,
cacodemon, Lacedaemon

²emon \em-ən\ Bremen, leman,
lemon, Yemen

emone \em-ə-nē\ see EMONY

emony \em-ə-nē\ Gemini,
lemony, anemone, bigeminy,
Gethsemane, hegemony

emor \em-ər\ see EMMER

emoral \em-rəl\ see EMERAL

emory \em-rē\ see EMERY

emous \ē-məs\ see EMUS

emp \emp\ hemp, kemp, temp

emperer \em-pər-ər\ emperor,
temperer

emperor \em-pər-ər\ see
EMPERER

emplar \em-plər\ Templar,
exemplar

emple \em-pəl\ semple, temple

emps \äⁿ\ see ¹ANT

empt \emt\ dreamt, kempt,
tempt, attempt, contempt,
exempt, preempt, undreamed,
unkempt, tax-exempt

emptable \em-tə-bəl\
attemptable, contemptible

emptible \em-tə-bəl\ see
EMPTABLE

emption \em-shən\ exemption,
preemption, redemption

emptive \em-tiv\ preemptive,
redemptive

emptor \em-tər\ tempter,
preemptor, caveat emptor

emptory \em-trē\ peremptory, redemptory

emulous \em-yə-ləs\ emulous, tremulous

emur \ē-mər\ see EAMER

emus \ē-məs\ Remus, in extremis, Polyphemus, polysemous

emy \ē-mē\ see EAMY

¹en \en\ ben, Ben, den, en, fen, gen, glen, Glen, Glenn, Gwen, hen, ken, Ken, Len, men, n, pen, Penn, Rennes, Seine, sen, Sten, ten, then, wen, when, wren, Wren, yen, Zen, again, amen, Ardennes, Big Ben, Cayenne, Cevennes, Cheyenne, Chosen, Dairen, doyen, doyenne, Duchenne, Fulcien, hapten, hymen, Karen, La Tène, moorhen, peahen, pigpen, Phnom Penh, playpen, RN, Touraine, Tynmen, somewhen, Adrienne, Debrecen, DPN, five-and-ten, FMN, julienne, Kerguelen, La Fontaine, LPN, madrilene, mise-en-scène, samisen, Sun Yat-sen, TPN, carcinogen, comedienne, equestrienne, tamoxifen, tragedienne, Valenciennes

²en \ēn\ see ³INE

³en \aⁿ\ see ⁴IN

⁴en \ən\ see UN

⁵en \äⁿ\ see ¹ANT

¹ena \ā-nä\ see ¹AENA

²ena \ā-nə\ see ²ANA

³ena \än-yə\ see ³ANIA

⁴ena \ē-nə\ see ²INA

enable \en-ə-bəl\ tenable, amenable, untenable

enace \en-əs\ see ¹ENIS

enacle \en-i-kəl\ see ENICAL

enae \e-nē\ see ¹INI

enal \ēn-ᵊl\ penal, renal, venal, adrenal, vaccinal, duodenal

enancy \en-ən-sē\ tenancy, lieutenancy, subtenancy

enant \en-ənt\ pennant, tenant, lieutenant, se tenant, subtenant, sublieutenant, undertenant

enary \en-ə-rē\ hennery, plenary, senary, venery, centenary, millenary, bicentenary, bimillenary, quincentenary, tercentenary, quatercentenary, semicentenary, sesquicentenary

enas \ē-nəs\ see ¹ENUS

enate \en-ət\ see ENNET

enator \en-ət-ər\ see ENITOR

ençal \en-səl\ see ENCIL

¹ence \ens\ see ENSE

²ence \äⁿs\ see ¹ANCE

³ence \äns\ see ²ANCE

encel \en-səl\ see ENCIL

enceless \en-sləs\ see ENSELESS

encer \en-sər\ see ENSOR

ench \ench\ bench, blench, clench, drench, french, French, mensch, quench, stench, tench, trench, wench, wrench, entrench, luftmensch, retrench, unclench, workbench, Anglo-French, Mariana Trench

enchant \en-chənt\ see ENTIENT

enched \encht\ trenched, unblenched—*also pasts of verbs listed at* ENCH

encher \en-chər\ see ENTURE

enchman \ench-mən\
Frenchman, henchman
encia \en-chə\ see ENTIA
encil \en-səl\ mensal, pencel,
pencil, stencil, tensile, blue-
pencil, commensal, extensile,
Provençal, prehensile, red-
pencil, utensil, intercensal
ençon \en-sən\ see ENSIGN
ency \en-sē\ Montmorency,
residency, nonresidency
end \end\ bend, blend, blende,
end, fend, friend, lend, mend,
rend, scend, send, shend,
spend, tend, trend, vend,
wend, Wend, addend, amend,
append, ascend, attend,
augend, befriend, Big Bend,
bookend, boyfriend, closed-
end, commend, compend,
contend, dead end, dead-end,
defend, depend, descend,
distend, downtrend, emend,
expend, extend, forfend,
girlfriend, godsend,
hornblende, impend, intend,
Land's End, low-end,
missend, misspend, offend,
outspend, perpend,
pitchblende, portend, pretend,
propend, protend, rear-end,
resend, South Bend, stipend,
subtend, suspend, transcend,
unbend, unkenned, upend,
uptrend, weekend, year-end,
adherend, apprehend, bitter
end, comprehend,
condescend, Damavend,
discommend, dividend,
minuend, overspend,
recommend, repetend,
reprehend, subtrahend,
vilipend, hyperextend,
misapprehend, overextend,
superintend—*also pasts of
verbs listed at* ¹EN
enda \en-də\ Brenda, Glenda,
Venda, agenda, hacienda—
also plurals of nouns listed at
ENDUM
endable \en-də-bəl\ lendable,
mendable, spendable,
vendible, amendable,
ascendable, commendable,
defendable, dependable,
descendible, expendable,
extendable, unbendable,
comprehendable,
recommendable
endal \en-dᵊl\ Grendel, Kendall,
Mendel, Wendell, prebendal,
pudendal
endall \en-dᵊl\ see ENDAL
endance \en-dəns\ see ENDENCE
endancy \en-dən-sē\ see
ENDENCY
endant \en-dənt\ see ENDENT
¹ende \end\ see END
²ende \en-dē\ see ENDI
ended \en-dəd\ ended, splendid,
befriended, unfriended,
double-ended, open-ended,
undescended—*also pasts of
verbs listed at* END
endel \en-dᵊl\ see ENDAL
endell \en-dᵊl\ see ENDAL
endence \en-dəns\ tendance,
ascendance, attendance,
intendance, resplendence,
transcendence,
condescendence,
independence, Independence,
superintendence
endency \en-dən-sē\ pendency,

tendency, ascendancy, dependency, resplendency, transcendency, superintendency, independency

endent \en-dənt\ pendant, pendent, splendent, appendant, ascendant, attendant, defendant, dependent, descendant, impendent, intendant, respendent, transcendent, independent, superintendant, semi-independent

ender \en-dər\ bender, blender, fender, gender, lender, render, mender, slender, spender, sender, splendor, tender, vendor, amender, ascender, attender, auslander, bartender, commender, contender, defender, descender, emender, engender, expender, extender, fork-tender, goaltender, hellbender, intender, offender, pretender, surrender, suspender, tailender, weekender, double-ender, moneylender, over-spender, self-surrender

endi \en-dē\ bendy, Mende, trendy, Wendy, effendi, modus vivendi

endible \en-də-bəl\ see ENDABLE

endid \en-dəd\ see ENDED

ending \en-diŋ\ bending, ending, pending, sending, ascending, attending, fence-mending, goaltending, heartrending, mind-bending, unbending, unending,

uncomprehending, unpretending, uncomprehending—*also present participles of verbs listed at* END

endium \en-dē-əm\ compendium, antependium

endless \end-ləs\ endless, friendless

endliness \en-lē-nəs\ cleanliness, friendliness, uncleanliness, unfriendliness

endly \en-lē\ cleanly, friendly, loop of Henle, uncleanly, unfriendly

endment \en-mənt\ amendment, intendment

endo \en-dō\ kendo, crescendo, stringendo, decrescendo, innuendo, diminuendo

endor \en-dər\ see ENDER

endous \en-dəs\ horrendous, stupendous, tremendous

endron \en-drən\ philodendron, rhododendron

ends \enz\ see ¹ENS

endum \en-dəm\ addendum, agendum, pudendum, corrigendum, referendum, definiendum

endy \en-dē\ see ENDI

¹ene \ā-nā\ nene, sene

²ene \en\ see ¹EN

³ene \en-ē\ see ENNY

⁴ene \ē-nē\ see ¹INI

⁵ene \ēn\ see ³INE

⁶ene \ān\ see ¹ANE

enel \en-ᵊl\ see ENNEL

eneous \ē-nē-əs\ genius, homogeneous, heterogeneous

ener \ē-nər\ see EANER

enerable \en-rə-bəl\ generable, venerable, regenerable

eneracy \en-rə-sē\ degeneracy, regeneracy

enerate \en-rət\ degenerate, regenerate, unregenerate

enerative \en-rət-iv\ generative, degenerative, regenerative, neurodegenerative

eneris \en-ə-rəs\ mons veneris, sui generis

¹**enery** \en-ə-rē\ see ²ENARY

²**enery** \ēn-rē\ see EANERY

¹**enet** \en-ət\ see ENNET

²**enet** \ē-nət\ see EANUT

¹**eng** \aŋ\ see ²ANG

²**eng** \əŋ\ see ¹UNG

enge \enj\ venge, avenge, revenge, Stonehenge

engi \eŋ-gē\ dengue, sengi

english \iŋ-glish\ English, Yinglish

engo \eŋ-gō\ marengo, camerlengo

¹**ength** \eŋth\ length, strength, full-length, half-length, wavelength, understrength, industrial-strength

²**ength** \enth\ see ENTH

engthen \eŋ-thən\ lengthen, strengthen

engue \eŋ-gē\ see ENGI

enh \en\ see ¹EN

¹**enia** \ē-nē-ə\ taenia, Slovenia, sarracenia, schizophrenia

²**enia** \ē-nyə\ Armenia, Encaenia, Eugenia, gardenia, Ruthenia, Tigrinya

enial \ē-nē-əl\ genial, menial, venial, congenial

enian \ē-nē-ən\ Fenian, Armenian, Essenian, Icenian, sirenian, Slovenian, Tyrrhenian, Achaemenian, Magdalenian

¹**enic** \ēn-ik\ genic, scenic

²**enic** \en-ik\ fennec, pfennig, phrenic, splenic, sthenic, arsenic, asthenic, Edenic, Essenic, eugenic, Hellenic, hygienic, irenic, transgenic, allergenic, androgenic, autogenic, calisthenic, chromogenic, cryogenic, cryptogenic, hygienic, mutagenic, Panhellenic, pathogenic, photogenic, Saracenic, schizophrenic, telegenic, carcinogenic, cariogenic, hallucinogenic, hypoallergenic

enical \en-i-kəl\ cenacle, arsenical, galenical, ecumenical

enice \en-əs\ see ¹ENIS

enicist \en-ə-səst\ eugenicist, ecumenicist

enics \en-iks\ eugenics, euphenics, euthenics, hygienics, calisthenics, cryogenics—*also plurals and possessives of nouns listed at* ²ENIC

¹**enie** \en-ē\ see ENNY

²**enie** \ē-nē\ see ¹INI

enience \ē-nyəns\ lenience, convenience, provenience, inconvenience

enient \ēn-yənt\ convenient, prevenient

enim \en-əm\ see ENOM

enin \en-ən\ see ENNON

enior \ē-nyər\ senior, monsignor

¹enis \en-əs\ Denis, Dennis,
Denys, genus, menace,
tenace, tennis, Venice,
frontenis, summum genus
²enis \ē-nəs\ see ¹ENUS
¹enison \en-ə-sən\ benison,
Tennyson, venison
²enison \en-ə-zən\ benison,
denizen, venison
enist \en-əst\ tennist, euthenist
enitive \en-ət-iv\ genitive,
lenitive, philoprogenitive,
polyphiloprogenitive
enitor \en-ət-ər\ senator,
progenitor, primogenitor
enity \en-ət-ē\ see ENTITY
enium \ē-nē-əm\ hymenium,
proscenium
enius \ē-nē-əs\ see ENEOUS
enizen \en-ə-zən\ see ²ENISON
enn \en\ see ¹EN
enna \en-ə\ Glenna, henna,
senna, antenna, duenna,
Gehenna, sienna, Vienna
ennae \en-ē\ see ENNY
ennant \en-ənt\ see ENANT
¹enne \en\ see ¹EN
²enne \en-ē\ see ENNY
³enne \an\ see ⁵AN
ennec \en-ik\ see ²ENIC
enned \end\ see END
ennel \en-ᵊl\ crenel, fennel,
kennel, unkennel
enner \en-ər\ see ¹ENOR
ennery \en-ə-rē\ see ²ENARY
ennes \en\ see ¹EN
ennet \en-ət\ Bennett, genet,
jennet, rennet, senate, sennet,
sennit, tenet
ennett \en-ət\ see ENNET
enney \en-ē\ see ENNY
enni \en-ē\ see ENNY

ennial \en-ē-əl\ biennial,
centennial, decennial,
millennial, perennial,
quadrennial, quinquennial,
septennial, triennial,
vicennial, bicentennial,
bimillennial, postmillennial,
premillennial, quincentennial,
tercentennial, semicentennial,
sesquicentennial,
quadricentennial
ennies \en-ēz\ tennies—*also
possessives and plurals of
nouns listed at* ENNY
ennig \en-ik\ see ²ENIC
ennin \en-ən\ see ENNON
ennis \en-əs\ see ¹ENIS
ennist \en-əst\ see ENIST
ennit \en-ət\ see ENNET
ennium \en-ē-əm\ biennium,
decennium, millennium,
quadrennium, quinquennium,
triennium
ennon \en-ən\ Lenin, pennon,
rennin, tenon, antivenin
enny \en-ē\ any, benne, benny,
Benny, blenney, Dene,
Denny, fenny, genie, Jennie,
jenny, Jenny, many, penni,
penny, Penny, antennae,
catchpenny, halfpenny,
Kilkenny, Na-dene,
pinchpenny, sixpenny,
tenpenny, threepenny,
truepenny, twopenny,
lilangeni, spinning jenny
ennyson \en-ə-sən\ see ¹ENISON
¹eno \ān-yō\ segno, dal segno,
jalapeño
²eno \en-ō\ steno, ripieno
³eno \ā-nō\ see ²ANO
enoch \ē-nik\ see ¹INIC

enom \en-əm\ denim, plenum, venom, envenom

enon \en-ən\ see ENNON

¹enor \en-ər\ Brenner, Jenner, tenner, tenor, tenour, countertenor, heldentenor

²enor \ē-nər\ see EANER

enour \en-ər\ see ¹ENOR

enous \ē-nəs\ see ¹ENUS

¹ens \enz\ cleanse, gens, lens, amends, beam-ends, weekends, sapiens, definiens, locum tenens—*also plurals and possessives of nouns and third person singular presents of verbs listed at* ¹EN

²ens \ens\ see ENSE

ensable \en-sə-bəl\ see ENSIBLE

ensal \en-səl\ see ENCIL

ensary \ens-rē\ see ENSORY

ensch \ench\ see ENCH

ense \ens\ cense, dense, fence, flense, gens, hence, mense, pence, sense, spence, tense, thence, whence, commence, condense, defense, dispense, expense, immense, incense, intense, missense, nonsense, offense, prepense, pretense, propense, sequence, sixpence, subsequence, suspense, twopence, accidence, antisense, commonsense, confidence, consequence, diffidence, evidence, frankincense, multisense, nondefense, providence, Providence, recompense, residence, self-defense, subsequence, coincidence, ego-defense, inconsequence, New Providence, nonresidence, self-confidence, self-evidence

enseful \ens-fəl\ menseful, senseful, suspenseful

enseless \en-sləs\ fenceless, senseless, defenseless, offenseless

ensem \en-səm\ see ENSUM

enser \en-sər\ see ENSOR

ensian \en-chən\ see ENSION

ensible \en-sə-bəl\ sensible, compensable, condensable, defensible, dispensable, distensible, extensible, insensible, ostensible, apprehensible, commonsensible, comprehensible, incondensable, indefensible, indispensable, reprehensible, supersensible, incomprehensible

ensign \en-sən\ ensign, alençon

ensil \en-səl\ see ENCIL

ensile \en-səl\ see ENCIL

ension \en-chən\ gentian, mention, pension, tension, abstention, ascension, attention, contention, convention, declension, descension, detention, dimension, dissension, distension, extension, indention, intension, intention, invention, Laurentian, low-tension, posttension, prehension, pretension, prevention, recension, retention, subvention, suspension, sustention, Vincentian, Waldensian, Albigensian, apprehension,

circumvention,
comprehension,
condescension, contravention,
hypertension, hypotension,
inattention, reinvention,
reprehension, salientian,
incomprehension,
misapprehension,
nonintervention,
overextension,
Premonstratensian

ensional \ench-nəl\ tensional,
ascensional, attentional,
conventional, declensional,
dimensional, extensional,
intensional, intentional,
unconventional,
tridimensional,
unidimensional

ensioner \ench-nər\ see
ENTIONER

ensis \en-səs\ see ENSUS

ensitive \en-sət-iv\ sensitive,
insensitive, photosensitive,
hypersensitive, oversensitive,
photosensitive, supersensitive

ensity \en-sət-ē\ density,
tensity, extensity, immensity,
intensity, propensity

ensive \en-siv\ pensive, tensive,
ascensive, defensive,
expensive, extensive,
intensive, offensive,
ostensive, protensive,
suspensive, apprehensive,
coextensive, comprehensive,
hypertensive, hypotensive,
inexpensive, inoffensive,
reprehensive, self-defensive,
counteroffensive, labor-
intensive

ensor \en-sər\ censer, censor,

fencer, sensor, spencer,
Spencer, Spenser, tensor,
commencer, condenser,
dispenser, extensor,
precensor, sequencer,
suspensor, biosensor—*also
comparatives of adjectives
listed at* ENSE

ensory \ens-rē\ sensory,
dispensary, suspensory,
extrasensory, multisensory,
supersensory

¹**ensual** \en-chəl\ see ENTIAL

²**ensual** \ench-wəl\ see ¹ENTUAL

ensum \en-səm\ sensum, per
mensem

ensurable \ens-rə-bəl\
censurable, mensurable,
commensurable,
immensurable,
incommensurable

ensure \en-chər\ see ENTURE

ensus \en-səs\ census,
consensus, dissensus,
amanuensis

¹**ent** \ent\ bent, Brent, cent,
dent, gent, Ghent, Gwent,
hent, Kent, leant, lent, Lent,
meant, pent, rent, scent, sent,
sklent, spent, sprent, tent,
Trent, vent, went, absent,
accent, Advent, anent, ascent,
assent, augment, besprent,
cement, chimkent, comment,
concent, consent, content,
convent, descent, detent,
dissent, docent, event, extent,
ferment, foment, forewent,
forspent, fragment, frequent,
hell-bent, indent, intent,
invent, lament, loment, low-
rent, mordent, outspent,

outwent, percent, pigment,
portent, present, prevent,
quitrent, relent, repent, resent,
segment, Tashkent, torment,
unbent, well-meant, wisent,
accident, aliment, argument,
circumvent, compartment,
complement, compliment,
confident, devilment,
diffident, discontent,
document, evident, heaven-
sent, implement, instrument,
Jack-a-Lent, malcontent,
nonevent, Occident,
ornament, orient, president,
provident, regiment, reinvent,
represent, re-present, resident,
sediment, self-content, Stoke
on Trent, subsequent,
underwent, supplement,
coincident, disorient,
experiment, ferro-cement,
inconsequent, misrepresent,
nonresident, privatdocent,
self-evident

²ent \änt\ see ²ANT

³ent \äⁿ\ see ¹ANT

enta \ent-ə\ menta, yenta,
magenta, momenta, placenta,
polenta, tegmenta, tomenta,
irredenta, impedimenta

entable \ent-ə-bəl\ presentable,
documentable, fermentable,
preventable, representable,
sedimentable

entacle \ent-i-kəl\ see ENTICAL

entage \ent-ij\ tentage, ventage,
percentage

ental \ent-°l\ cental, dental,
dentil, gentle, lentil, mental,
rental, cliental, fragmental,
judgmental, parental,
placental, segmental,
accidental, adjustmental,
apartmental, biparental,
compartmental,
complemental, condimental,
continental, departmental,
deterimental, developmental,
documental, excremental,
elemental, environmental,
firmamental, fundamental,
governmental, grandparental,
incidental, incremental,
instrumental, managemental,
monumental, nonjudgmental,
occidental, oriental,
ornamental, regimental,
rudimental, sacramental,
sentimental, supplemental,
temperamental,
transcendental, vestamental,
coincidental, developmental,
experimental, presentimental,
subcontinental,
transcontinental, uniparental,
intercontinental,
interdepartmental,
intergovernmental,
semigovernmental

entalist \ent-°l-əst\ gentlest,
mentalist, documentalist,
fundamentalist,
governmentalist,
incrementalist,
instrumentalist, orientalist,
sacramentalist, sentimentalist,
transcendentalist,
environmentalist,
experimentalist

entalness \ent-°l-nəs\ see
ENTLENESS

entance \ent-°ns\ see ENTENCE

entary \en-trē\ gentry, sentry,

passementerie, reentry,
subentry, alimentary,
complementary,
complimentary, documentary,
elementary, filamentary,
integumentary, parliamentary,
rudimentary, sedimentary,
supplementary, tenementary,
testamentary,
uncomplimentary,
unparliamentary,
semidocumentary

entative \ent-ət-iv\ tentative,
augmentative, fermentative,
frequentative, presentative,
preventative, argumentative,
representative,
misrepresentative

¹ente \en-tā\ al dente,
lentamente

²ente \ent-ē\ see ENTY

³ente \änt\ see ²ANT

ented \ent-əd\ tented,
augmented, contented,
demented, lamented,
segmented, untented,
battlemented, malcontented,
oriented, self-contented,
unfrequented, unprecedented,
overrepresented,
underrepresented—*also pasts
of verbs listed at* ¹ENT

enten \ent-ᵊn\ Benton, dentin,
Denton, Kenton, Lenten,
Quentin, Trenton

entence \ent-ᵊns\ sentence,
repentance

enter \ent-ər\ center, enter,
mentor, renter, stentor, tenter,
venter, assenter, augmentor,
cementer, concenter,
consentor, dissenter, incenter,

indenter, fermenter,
frequenter, inventor,
precentor, preventer, rack-
renter, reenter, repenter,
subcenter, tormentor,
documenter, epicenter,
representer, supplementer,
hypocenter, metacenter,
experimenter, hundred-
percenter

entered \en-tərd\ centered, face-
centered, self-centered, body-
centered—*also pasts of verbs
listed at* ENTER

enterie \en-trē\ see ENTARY

entful \ent-fəl\ eventful,
resentful, uneventful

enth \enth\ nth, strength, tenth,
crème de menthe

enthe \enth\ see ENTH

enthesis \en-thə-səs\ epenthesis,
parenthesis

enti \ent-ē\ see ENTY

entia \en-chə\ dementia,
Florentia, sententia, Valencia,
differentia, in absentia

ential \en-chəl\ cadential,
consensual, credential,
demential, essential, eventual,
potential, prudential, sciential,
sentential, sequential,
tangential, torrential,
componential, conferential,
confidential, consequential,
deferential, differential,
evidential, existential,
expedential, exponential,
inessential, inferential,
influential, nonessential,
penitential, pestilential,
preferential, presidential,
providential, referential,

residential, reverential,
transferential, unessential,
circumferential, equipotential,
experiential, inconsequential,
intelligential, interferential,
jurisprudential, multipotential,
reminiscential

entialist \en-chə-ləst\
essentialist, existentialist

entian \en-chən\ see ENSION

entiary \ench-rē\ century,
penitentiary, plenipotentiary

entic \ent-ik\ lentic, argentic,
authentic, crescentic, identic,
inauthentic

entical \ent-i-kəl\ denticle,
pentacle, tentacle,
conventicle, identical,
nonidentical, self-identical

entice \ent-əs\ see ENTOUS

enticle \ent-i-kəl\ see ENTICAL

entient \en-chənt\ penchant,
sentient, trenchant,
dissentient, insentient,
presentient

entil \ent-°l\ see ENTAL

entin \ent-°n\ see ENTEN

enting \ent-iŋ\ dissenting,
unrelenting

ention \en-chən\ see ENSION

entionable \ench-nə-bəl\
mentionable, pensionable,
unmentionable

entional \ench- nəl\ see
ENSIONAL

entioned \en-chənd\
aforementioned, well-
intentioned—*also pasts of
verbs listed at* ENSION

entioner \ench-nər\ mentioner,
pensioner, tensioner

entious \en-chəs\ abstentious,
contentious, dissentious,
licentious, pretentious,
sententious, tendentious,
conscientious, unpretentious

entis \ent-əs\ see ENTOUS

entist \ent-əst\ dentist,
cinquecentist, irredentist

entity \en-ət-ē\ entity, lenity,
amenity, identity, nonentity,
obscenity, serenity, coidentity,
self-identity

entium \ent-ē-əm\ jus gentium,
unnilpentium

entive \ent-iv\ adventive,
attentive, incentive, inventive,
pendentive, preventive,
retentive, argumentive,
disincentive, inattentive

entle \ent-°l\ see ENTAL

entleness \ent-°l-nəs\
gentleness, accidentalness

entment \ent-mənt\
contentment, presentment,
resentment, discontentment,
self-contentment

ento \en-tō\ cento, lento,
Trento, memento, pimento,
pimiento, seicento, trecento,
cinquecento, papiamento,
portamento, quatrocento,
Sacramento, aggiornamento,
divertimento,
pronunciamento, risorgimento

enton \ent-°n\ see ENTEN

entor \ent-ər\ see ENTER

entous \ent-əs\ prentice,
apprentice, argentous,
momentous, portentous,
compos mentis, filamentous,
ligamentous, non compos
mentis, in loco parentis

entral \en-trəl\ central, ventral, subcentral, dorsiventral

entress \en-trəs\ gentrice, inventress

entric \en-trik\ centric, acentric, concentric, dicentric, eccentric, acrocentric, androcentric, Christocentric, egocentric, ethnocentric, Eurocentric, geocentric, phallocentric, polycentric, theocentric, topocentric, anthropocentric, areocentric, Europocentric, heliocentric, selenocentric

entrice \en-trəs\ see ENTRESS

entry \en-trē\ see ENTARY

ents \ents\ gents, events, dollars-and-cents—*also plurals of nouns listed at* ¹ENT

¹entual \en-chə-wəl\ sensual, accentual, consensual, conventual, eventual

²entual \en-chəl\ see ENTIAL

entum \ent-əm\ centum, mentum, cementum, momentum, per centum, tegmentum, tomentum, argumentum

enture \en-chər\ bencher, censure, denture, drencher, trencher, venture, wencher, adventure, backbencher, debenture, front-bencher, indenture, misventure, misadventure, peradventure

enturer \ench-rər\ venturer, adventurer

enturess \ench-rəs\ see ENTUROUS

enturous \ench-rəs\ venturous, adventuress, adventurous

entury \ench-rē\ see ENTIARY

enty \ent-ē\ plenty, sente, senti, tenty, twenty, aplenty, licente, cognoscente, twenty-twenty, Deo volente, dolce far niente

enuis \en-yə-wəs\ see ENUOUS

enum \en-əm\ see ENOM

enuous \en-yə-wəs\ strenuous, tenuis, tenuous, ingenuous, disingenuous

¹enus \ē-nəs\ genus, lenis, penis, venous, Venus, Campinas, Delphinus, Maecenas, Quirinus, silenus, intravenous

²enus \en-əs\ see ¹ENIS

eny \ā-nē\ see AINY

enys \en-əs\ see ¹ENIS

¹enza \en-zə\ Penza, cadenza, credenza, influenza

²enza \en-sə\ Polenza, Vicenza, Piacenza

¹eo \ā-ō\ mayo, Mayo, cacao, paseo, rodeo, aparejo, Bulawayo, cicisbeo, zapateo, Montevideo

²eo \ē-ō\ see ²IO

¹eoff \ef\ see ¹EF

²eoff \ēf\ see ¹IEF

eoffor \ef-ər\ see EPHOR

eolate \ē-ə-lət\ triolet, alveolate, areolate, urceolate

eoman \ō-mən\ see OMAN

¹eon \ē-ən\ see ¹EAN

²eon \ē-än\ eon, freon, neon, prion

eonid \ē-ə-nəd\ see EANID

eopard \ep-ərd\ jeopard, leopard, peppered, shepard, shepherd

eopardess \ep-ərd-əs\ shepherdess, leopardess

eople \ē-pəl\ people, pipal,
  steeple, craftspeople,
  dispeople, laypeople,
  newspeople, salespeople,
  spokespeople, townspeople,
  tradespeople, tribespeople,
  unpeople, workpeople,
  anchorpeople, businesspeople,
  congresspeople

eopled \ē-pəld\ unpeopled—
  also pasts of verbs listed at
  EOPLE

eordie \òrd-ē\ see ¹ORDY

eorem \ir-əm\ see ERUM

eorge \òrj\ see ORGE

eorgian \òr-jən\ see ORGIAN

eorist \ir-əst\ see ¹ERIST

eoul \ōl\ see ¹OLE

eous \ē-əs\ see ¹EUS

ep \ep\ hep, pep, prep, rep,
  schlepp, skep, step, steppe,
  strep, yep, Alep, crowstep,
  doorstep, footstep, goose-step,
  instep, lockstep, misstep, one-
  step, quickstep, salep,
  sidestep, two-step, unstep,
  corbiestep, demirep, overstep,
  step-by-step, Gaziantep

eparable \ep-rə-bəl\ reparable,
  separable, inseparable,
  irreparable

epard \ep-ərd\ see EOPARD

epe \āp\ see ¹APE

epee \ē-pē\ see EEPY

eper \ep-ər\ see EPPER

eperous \ep-rəs\ leprous,
  obstreperous

epey \ā-pē\ see APEY

eph \ef\ see ¹EF

epha \ē-fə\ ephah, Recife,
  synalepha, synaloepha

ephalin \ef-ə-lən\ cephalin,

encephalon, enkephalin,
  acanthocephalan

ephaly \ef-ə-lē\ anencephaly,
  brachycephaly, microcephaly

ephen \ē-vən\ see EVEN

epherd \ep-ərd\ see EOPARD

epherdess \ep-ərd-əs\ see
  EOPARDESS

ephone \ef-ə-nē\ see EPHONY

ephony \ef-ə-nē\ Stefanie,
  Stefany, Persephone,
  telephony

ephor \ef-ər\ deafer, ephor,
  feoffor, heifer, zephyr,
  hasenpfeffer

ephrine \ef-rən\ epinephrine,
  norepinephrine

epht \eft\ see EFT

ephyr \ef-ər\ see EPHOR

epi \ā-pē\ see APEY

epid \ep-əd\ tepid, trepid,
  intrepid

epo \ēp-ō\ see EPOT

epot \ēp-ō\ depot, Ipo, pepo, el
  cheapo

epp \ep\ see EP

eppe \ep\ see EP

epped \ept\ see EPT

epper \ep-ər\ hepper, leper,
  pepper, stepper, Colepeper,
  Culpeper, sidestepper

eppy \ep-ē\ peppy, preppy,
  orthoepy

eprous \ep-rəs\ see EPEROUS

eps \eps\ biceps, forceps,
  triceps, quadriceps, editio
  princeps—*also plurals and
  possessives of nouns and
  third person singular presents
  of verbs listed at* EP

epsis \ep-səs\ skepsis, prolepsis,
  syllepsis, omphaloskepsis

epsy \ep-sē\ catalepsy, epilepsy, narcolepsy, nympholepsy

ept \ept\ crept, kept, sept, slept, stepped, swept, wept, accept, adept, backswept, concept, except, incept, inept, percept, precept, transept, upswept, windswept, yclept, high-concept, intercept, nympholept, overslept, self-concept—*also pasts of verbs listed at* EP

eptable \ep-tə-bəl\ see EPTIBLE

eptacle \ep-ti-kəl\ skeptical, conceptacle, receptacle

epter \ep-tər\ see EPTOR

eptible \ep-tə-bəl\ acceptable, perceptible, susceptible, imperceptible, insusceptible, unacceptable

eptic \ep-tik\ peptic, septic, skeptic, aseptic, dyspeptic, eupeptic, proleptic, sylleptic, antiseptic, cataleptic, epileptic, narcoleptic, nympholeptic

eptical \ep-ti-kəl\ see EPTACLE

eptile \ep-t°l\ see EPTAL

eption \ep-shən\ conception, deception, exception, inception, perception, reception, subreption, apperception, contraception, interception, misconception, preconception, self-conception, self-perception

eptional \ep-shnəl\ conceptional, deceptional, exceptional, unexceptional

eptive \ep-tiv\ acceptive, conceptive, deceptive, exceptive, inceptive, perceptive, preceptive, receptive, susceptive, apperceptive, contraceptive, imperceptive

eptor \ep-tər\ scepter, accepter, acceptor, inceptor, preceptor, receptor, intercepter, interceptor

eptual \ep-chəl\ conceptual, perceptual

eptus \ep-təs\ conceptus, textus receptus

epy \ep-ē\ see EPPY

epys \ēps\ Pepys—*also possessives and plurals of nouns and third person singular presents of verbs listed at* EEP

equal \ē-kwəl\ equal, prequel, sequel, coequal, unequal

eque \ek\ see ECK

equel \ē-kwəl\ see EQUAL

equence \ē-kwəns\ frequence, sequence, infrequence, subsequence

equency \ē-kwən-sē\ frequency, sequency, infrequency

equent \ē-kwənt\ frequent, sequent, infrequent

equer \ek-ər\ see ECKER

¹er \ā\ see ¹AY

²er \er\ see ⁴ARE

³er \ər\ see ¹EUR

⁴er \ir\ see ²EER

¹era \er-ə\ era, Sara, Sarah, sclera, terra, caldera, Rivera, sierra, tiara, aloe vera, ciguatera, cordillera, guayabera, habanera, Halmahera, riviera, Riviera, Santa Clara

²era \ir-ə\ era, gerah, Hera, lira,

Pyrrha, sera, sirrah, Vera,
wirra, chimaera, chimera,
hetaera, lempira, Madeira,
mbira, Altamira

erable \ər-ə-bəl\ thurible,
conferrable, deferrable,
deterrable, inferable,
preferable, transferable

erah \ir-ə\ see ²ERA

¹eral \ir-əl\ Cyril, feral, seral,
spheral, virile

²eral \er-əl\ see ERIL

³eral \ər-əl\ see ERRAL

erald \er-əld\ Gerald, Harold,
herald, Jerald, Jerold, Jerrold,
Fitzgerald, FitzGerald

eraph \er-əf\ see ERIF

erapy \er-əld\ therapy,
chemotherapy, chronotherapy,
aromatherapy

eratin \er-ət-ᵊn\ keratin,
Sheraton, Samaritan

erative \er-ət-iv\ see ¹ARATIVE

eraton \er-ət-ᵊn\ see ERATIN

erb \ərb\ blurb, curb, herb,
kerb, Serb, verb, acerb,
adverb, disturb, exurb,
perturb, potherb, pro-verb,
proverb, reverb, suburb,
superb

erbal \ər-bəl\ burble, gerbil,
herbal, verbal, deverbal,
nonverbal, preverbal

erbalist \ər-bə-ləst\ herbalist,
verbalist, hyperbolist

erbally \ər-bə-lē\ verbally,
hyperbole, nonverbally

erber \ər-bər\ see URBER

erberis \ər-bər-əs\ berberis,
Cerberus

erberus \ər-bər-əs\ see
ERBERIS

erbet \ər-bət\ see URBIT

erbia \ər-bē-ə\ see URBIA

erbial \ər-bē-əl\ adverbial,
proverbial

erbid \ər-bəd\ see URBID

erbil \ər-bəl\ see ERBAL

erbium \ər-bē-əm\ erbium,
terbium, ytterbium

erbole \ər-bə-lē\ see ERBALLY

erbolist \ər-bə-ləst\ see
ERBALIST

erby \ər-bē\ derby, Derby,
herby, Kirby

ercal \ər-kəl\ see IRCLE

erce \ərs\ see ERSE

ercé \ers\ see ¹ARCE

ercel \ər-səl\ see ¹ERSAL

ercement \ər-smənt\
amercement, disbursement,
reimbursement

ercer \ər-sər\ see URSOR

ercery \ərs-rē\ see URSARY

erch \ərch\ see URCH

ercia \ər-shə\ see ERTIA

ercial \ər-shəl\ Herschel,
Hershel, commercial, inertial,
controversial, uncommercial,
semicommercial

ercian \ər-shən\ see ERTIAN

ercible \ər-sə-bəl\ see ERSIBLE

ercion \ər-zhən\ see ¹ERSION

ercis \ər-səs\ see ERSUS

ercive \ər-siv\ see ERSIVE

ercular \ər-kyə-lər\ see
IRCULAR

ercy \ər-sē\ Circe, mercy,
Percy, pursy, gramercy,
controversy

erd \ərd\ see IRD

¹erde \erd\ see AIRED

²erde \ərd\ see IRD

³erde \ərd-ē\ see URDY

erder \ərd-ər\ birder, girder,
   herder, murder, self-murder,
   sheepherder
erderer \ərd-ər-ər\ see
   URDERER
¹erdi \ər-dē\ see URDY
²erdi \er-dē\ Verdi, Monteverdi
erdin \ərd-ᵊn\ see URDEN
erding \ərd-iŋ\ wording,
   sheepherding
erdu \ər-dü\ perdu, perdue,
   Urdu
erdue \ər-dü\ see ERDU
erdure \ər-jər\ see ERGER
¹ere \er\ see ⁴ARE
²ere \er-ē\ see ¹ARY
³ere \ir\ see ²EER
⁴ere \ir-ē\ see EARY
⁵ere \ər\ see ¹EUR
e're \ē-ər\ see ¹EER
ère \er\ see ⁴ARE
ereal \ir-ē-əl\ see ERIAL
ereid \ir-ē-əd\ see ERIOD
erek \erik\ see ¹ERIC
erely \ir-lē\ see ¹EARLY
erement \er-ə-mənt\ see
   ERIMENT
¹erence \ir-əns\ clearance,
   adherence, appearance,
   coherence, inherence,
   incoherence, interference,
   perseverance
²erence \ər-əns\ see URRENCE
³erence \er-ᵊns\ see ARENCE
¹erency \ir-ən-sē\ coherency,
   vicegerency
²erency \er-ən-sē\ see ERRANCY
¹erent \ir-ənt\ gerent, adherent,
   coherent, inherent, sederunt,
   vicegerent, incoherent
²erent \er-ənt\ see ¹ARENT
¹eren't \ərnt\ see EARNT

²eren't \ər-ənt\ see URRENT
ereo \er-ē-ō\ see ARIO
ereous \ir-ē-əs\ see ERIOUS
erer \ir-ər\ see ²EARER
¹eres \erz\ see AIRS
²eres \ir-ēz\ see ERIES
³eres \ərs\ see ERS
eresy \er-ə-sē\ clerisy, heresy
ereth \er-ət\ see ERIT
ereus \ir-ē-əs\ see ERIOUS
erf \ərf\ see URF
erg \ərg\ berg, burg, erg,
   Augsburg, Boksburg, exergue,
   hamburg, Hamburg,
   Hapsburg, homburg, iceberg,
   Lemberg, Limburg,
   Lindbergh, Newburg,
   Pittsburgh, Salzburg,
   Sandburg, Strasbourg,
   svedberg, Tilburg,
   Drakensberg, Gutenberg,
   Harrisburg, Inselberg,
   Königsberg, Luxembourg,
   Magdeburg, Nuremberg,
   Toggenburg, Venusberg,
   Wallenberg, Würtemberg,
   Rube Goldberg,
   Johannesburg, St. Petersburg,
   von Hindenberg, Baden-
   Wurtenberg, Pietermaritzburg,
   Yekaterinburg, Roodepoort-
   Maraisburg
ergative \ər-gə-tir\ ergative,
   purgative
erge \ərj\ see URGE
ergeant \är-jənt\ see ARGENT
ergen \ər-gən\ Bergen,
   Spitzbergen
ergence \ər-jəns\ convergence,
   divergence, emergence,
   immergence, insurgence,
   resurgence, submergence

ergency \ər-jən-sē\ urgency,
convergency, detergency,
divergency, emergency,
insurgency, counterinsurgency

ergent \ər-jənt\ see URGENT

ergeon \ər-jin\ see URGEON

erger \ər-jər\ merger, perjure,
purger, scourger, urger,
verdure, verger, deterger

ergh \ərg\ see ERG

ergic \ər-jik\ allergic, synergic,
theurgic, demiurgic,
dramaturgic, thaumaturgic,
alpha-adrenergic, beta-
adrenergic

ergid \ər-jid\ see URGID

¹ergne \ərn\ see URN

²ergne \ern\ see ¹ERN

ergo \ər-gō\ ergo, Virgo

ergue \ərg\ see ERG

ergy \ər-jē\ see URGY

¹eri \er-ē\ see ¹ARY

²eri \ir-ē\ see EARY

¹eria \ir-ē-ə\ feria, Styria, Syria,
Algeria, Assyria, asteria,
bacteria, collyria, criteria,
diphtheria, Egeria, franseria,
Illyria, Liberia, Nigeria,
plumeria, porphyria, Siberia,
wisteria, cafeteria,
cryptomeria, latimeria,
sansevieria, washateria, opera
seria

²eria \er-ē-ə\ see ARIA

erial \ir-ē-əl\ aerial, cereal,
ferial, serial, arterial,
bacterial, empyreal, ethereal,
funereal, imperial, material,
sidereal, venereal, vizierial,
immaterial, magisterial,
managerial, ministerial,
presbyterial

¹erian \ir-ē-ən\ Adlerian,
Assyrian, Aterian,
Cimmerian, criterion,
Hesperian, Hutterian,
Hyperion, Iberian, Illyrian,
Mousterian, Mullerian,
Pierian, Shakespearean,
Spencerian, Spenglerian,
Sumerian, valerian, Valerian,
Wagnerian, Hanoverian,
Presbyterian, Thraco-Illyrian

²erian \er-ē-ən\ see ¹ARIAN

¹eric \er-ik\ Berwick, cleric,
Derek, derrick, Eric, Erich,
Erik, ferric, Herrick, xeric,
aspheric, chimeric, choleric,
cholesteric, entheric, generic,
Homeric, mesmeric, numeric,
alphanumeric, atmospheric,
climacteric, congeneric,
dysenteric, esoteric

²eric \ir-ik\ lyric, pyric, pyrrhic,
spheric, xeric, aspheric,
chimeric, empiric, satiric,
satyric, atmospheric,
hemispheric, stratospheric,
panegyric

erica \er-i-kə\ erica, Erica,
Erika, America, esoterica,
North America, South
America, Latin America

¹erical \er-i-kəl\ clerical,
chimerical, numerical,
anticlerical

²erical \ir-i-kəl\ lyrical, miracle,
spherical, spiracle, empirical,
hemispherical

erich \erik\ see ¹ERIC

erics \er-iks\ sferics, hysterics—
*also plurals and possessives
of nouns listed at* ¹ERIC

eried \ir-ē-əd\ see ERIOD

eries \ir-ēz\ Ceres, series, dundrearies, miniseries—*also plurals and possessives of nouns and third person singular presents of verbs listed at* EARY

erif \er-əf\ seraph, serif, sheriff, teraph, sans serif

eriff \er-əf\ see ERIF

erik \erik\ see ¹ERIC

erika \er-i-kə\ see ERICA

eril \er-əl\ beryl, Beryl, Cheryl, Errol, feral, ferrule, ferule, Merrill, peril, Sherrill, Sheryl, sterile, Terrell, Terrill, imperil, chrysoberyl

erilant \er-ə-lənt\ see ERULENT

erile \er-əl\ see ERIL

erilous \er-ə-ləs\ perilous, querulous, glomerulus

eriment \er-ə-mənt\ cerement, experiment, gedankenexperiment

erin \er-ən\ see ¹ARON

ering \ar-iŋ\ see ¹ARING

eriod \ir-ē-əd\ myriad, nereid, Nereid, period, photoperiod

erion \ir-ē-ən\ see ¹ERIAN

erior \ir-ē-ər\ anterior, exterior, inferior, interior, posterior, superior, ulterior, Lake Superior—*also comparatives of adjectives listed at* EARY

eriot \er-ē-ət\ see ¹ARIAT

erious \ir-ē-əs\ cereus, Nereus, serious, Sirius, cinereous, delirious, Guarnerius, imperious, mysterious, Tiberius, deleterious

¹eris \ir-əs\ see EROUS

²eris \er-əs\ see ERROUS

¹erist \ir-əst\ querist, theorist, verist, careerist, panegyrist— *also superlatives of adjectives listed at* ²EER

²erist \er-əst\ see ARIST

erisy \er-ə-sē\ see ERESY

erit \er-ət\ ferret, merit, terret, demerit, inherit, disinherit, Shemini Atzereth

eritable \er-ət-ə-bəl\ heritable, veritable, inheritable

eritor \er-ət-ər\ ferreter, heritor, inheritor

erity \er-ət-ē\ ferity, ferrety, rarity, verity, asperity, celerity, dexterity, legerity, posterity, prosperity, severity, sincerity, temerity, insincerity, ambidexterity, subsidiarity

erium \ir-ē-əm\ Miriam, criterium, bacterium, collyrium, delirium, imperium, psalterium, atmospherium, magisterium, archaeobacterium

¹erius \er-ē-əs\ see ARIOUS

²erius \ir-ē-əs\ see ERIOUS

erjure \ər-jər\ see ERGER

erjury \ərj-rē\ perjury, surgery, microsurgery, neurosurgery

erk \ərk\ see ¹ORK

erker \ər-kər\ see ¹ORKER

erkin \ər-kən\ see IRKIN

erking \ər-kiŋ\ see ORKING

erkly \ər-klē\ clerkly, berserkly

erky \ər-kē\ birkie, jerky, murky, perky, smirky, turkey, Turkey, Turki, Albuquerque, herky-jerky

erle \ərl\ see ¹IRL

erlie \er-lē\ see AIRLY

erlin \ər-lən\ merlin, Merlin,

merlon, Merlyn, purlin,
yearling

erling \ər-liŋ\ see URLING

erlon \ər-lən\ see ERLIN

erlyn \ər-lən\ see ERLIN

erm \ərm\ see ¹ORM

erma \ər-mə\ dharma, Erma,
herma, Irma, scleroderma,
terra firma

ermal \ər-məl\ dermal, thermal,
nonthermal, subdermal,
transdermal, ectodermal,
endothermal, epidermal,
exothermal, hydrothermal,
hypodermal, hypothermal

erman \ər-mən\ ermine,
german, German, germen,
Herman, Hermann, merman,
sermon, Sherman, Thurman,
vermin, determine, extermine,
Mount Hermon, predetermine,
cousin-german, Tibeto-
Burman

ermanent \ər-mə-nənt\
permanent, determinant,
impermanent, semipermanent

ermann \ər-mən\ see ERMAN

ermary \ərm-rē\ see IRMARY

erment \ər-mənt\ averment,
conferment, deferment,
determent, interment,
preferment, disinterment

ermer \ər-mər\ see URMUR

ermes \ər-mēz\ Hermes, kermes

ermi \ər-mē\ see ERMY

ermic \ər-mik\ dharmic,
thermic, geothermic,
hypodermic, taxidermic,
electrothermic

ermin \ər-mən\ see ERMAN

erminable \ərm-nə-bəl\

terminable, determinable,
interminable, indeterminable

erminal \ərm-nəl\ germinal,
terminal, preterminal,
subterminal

erminant \ər-mə-nənt\ see
ERMANENT

ermine \ər-mən\ see ERMAN

ermined \ər-mənd\ ermined,
determined, self-determined,
overdetermined

erminous \ər-mə-nəs\ terminus,
verminous, conterminous,
coterminous

erminus \ər-mə-nəs\ see
ERMINOUS

ermis \ər-məs\ dermis, kermis,
kirmess, thermos, endodermis,
epidermis, exodermis

ermit \ər-mət\ hermit, Kermit,
Thermit

ermon \ər-mən\ see ERMAN

ermos \ər-məs\ see ERMIS

ermy \ər-mē\ fermi, germy,
squirmy, wormy, diathermy,
endothermy, taxidermy

¹ern \ern\ bairn, Bern, cairn,
hern, Nairn, Auvergne,
moderne, Pitcairn, Sauternes,
Ygerne, art moderne

²ern \ərn\ see URN

erna \ər-nə\ dharna, Myrna,
sterna, Verna, cisterna

ernal \ərn-ᵊl\ colonel, journal,
kernel, sternal, vernal,
diurnal, eternal, external,
fraternal, hibernal, infernal,
internal, maternal, nocturnal,
paternal, supernal, coeternal,
sempiternal, semidiurnal

ernary \ər-nə-rē\ fernery,
ternary, turnery, quaternary

¹**erne** \ern\ see ¹ERN
²**erne** \ərn\ see URN
erned \ərnd\ see URNED
ernel \ərn-ºl\ see ERNAL
erner \ər-nər\ see URNER
¹**ernes** \ern\ see ¹ERN
²**ernes** \ərn\ see URN
ernest \ər-nəst\ see ERNIST
ernia \ər-ne-ə\ hernia, Ibernia
ernian \ər-ne-ən\ Hibernian,
  quaternion, Saturnian
ernible \ər-nə-bəl\ see
  URNABLE
ernie \ər-ne\ see ¹OURNEY
ernier \ər-ne-ər\ see OURNEYER
ernion \ər-ne-ən\ see ERNIAN
ernist \ər-nəst\ earnest, Earnest,
  Ernest, internist
ernity \ər-nət-e\ eternity,
  fraternity, maternity,
  modernity, paternity,
  quaternity, coeternity,
  confraternity, sempiternity
ernment \ərn-mənt\
  adjournment, attornment,
  concernment, discernment,
  internment
ernum \ər-nəm\ see URNUM
erny \ər-ne\ see ¹OURNEY
¹**ero** \e-ro\ giro, gyro, hero,
  Hero, Nero, zero, subzero,
  antihero, superhero
²**ero** \er-o\ aero, cero, Duero,
  Faeroe, faro, Faroe, pharaoh,
  taro, tarot, bolero, bracero,
  cruzeiro, Guerrero, Herero,
  Madero, montero, pampero,
  primero, ranchero, sombrero,
  torero, vaquero, burladero,
  caballero, Mescalero,
  novillero, banderillero,
  carabinero, embarcadero, Rio
  de Janeiro
³**ero** \ir-o\ giro, guiro, gyro,
  hero, zero, primero
erod \er-əd\ Herod, out-Herod,
  viverrid
erold \er-əld\ see ERALD
eron \er-ən\ see ¹ARON
erous \ir-əs\ cerous, cirrous,
  cirrus, Eris, peeress, Pyrrhus,
  scirrhous, scirrhus, seeress,
  serous
erp \ərp\ see URP
erpe \ər-pe\ see IRPY
erque \ər-ke\ see ERKY
¹**err** \er\ see ⁴ARE
²**err** \ər\ see ¹EUR
erra \er-ə\ see ¹ERA
errable \ər-ə-bəl\ see ERABLE
errace \er-əs\ see ERROUS
erral \ər-əl\ bharal, scurrile,
  squirrel, conferral, deferral,
  demurral, referral, transferal
errance \er-əns\ see ARENCE
errancy \er-ən-se\ errancy,
  aberrancy, coherency,
  inerrancy
errand \er-ənd\ errand, gerund
errant \er-ənt\ see ¹ARENT
erre \er\ see ⁴ARE
errell \er-əl\ see ERIL
¹**errence** \ər-əns\ see URRENCE
²**errence** \er-əns\ see ARENCE
errent \ər-ənt\ see URRENT
errer \ər-ər\ burrer, stirrer,
  conferrer, deferrer, demurer,
  demurrer, deterrer, inferrer,
  preferrer, referrer, transferrer
erret \er-ət\ see ERIT
erreter \er-ət-ər\ see ERITOR
erria \er-e-ə\ see ARIA
errible \er-ə-bəl\ see ¹EARABLE

erric \er-ik\ see ¹ERIC

errick \er-ik\ see ¹ERIC

errid \er-əd\ see EROD

errie \er-ē\ see ¹ARY

erried \er-ēd\ berried, serried, varied—*also pasts of verbs listed at* ¹ARY

errier \er-ē-ər\ burier, terrier, varier, bullterrier—*also comparatives of adjectives listed at* ¹ARY

errill \er-əl\ see ERIL

errily \er-ə-lē\ see ARILY

¹erring \ar-iŋ\ see ¹ARING

²erring \ər-iŋ\ see URRING

erris \er-əs\ see ERROUS

errol \er-əl\ see ERIL

errold \er-əld\ see ERALD

erron \er-ən\ see ¹ARON

error \er-ər\ see ¹EARER

errous \er-əs\ derris, Eris, ferrous, parous, terrace, nonferrous, millionairess

errule \er-əl\ see ERIL

erry \er-ē\ see ¹ARY

¹ers \ərz\ furze, hers, somewheres, Voyageurs—*also plurals and possessives of nouns and third person singular presents of verbs listed at* ¹EUR

²ers \ā\ see ¹AY

ersa \ər-sə\ bursa, Bursa, vice versa

ersable \ər-sə-bəl\ see ERSIBLE

¹ersal \ər-səl\ bursal, tercel, versal, dispersal, rehearsal, reversal, transversal, traversal, universal

²ersal \är-səl\ see ARSAL

ersant \ərs-ᵊnt\ versant, conversant

ersary \ərs-rē\ see URSARY

erse \ərs\ birse, burse, curse, Erse, hearse, nurse, perse, purse, terce, terse, thyrse, verse, worse, adverse, amerce, asperse, averse, coerce, commerce, converse, cutpurse, disburse, disperse, diverse, immerse, inverse, Nez Perce, obverse, perverse, rehearse, reverse, sesterce, stress-verse, submerse, transverse, traverse, intersperse, reimburse, universe

ersed \ərst\ see URST

erser \ər-sər\ see URSOR

ersey \ər-zē\ furzy, jersey, Jersey, kersey, Mersey, New Jersey

erschel \ər-shəl\ see ERCIAL

ershel \ər-shəl\ see ERCIAL

ersial \ər-shəl\ see ERCIAL

ersian \ər-zhən\ see ¹ERSION

ersible \ər-sə-bəl\ coercible, conversable, dispersible, eversible, immersible, reversible, submersible, traversable, incoercible, irreversible, semisubmersible

¹ersion \ər-zhən\ Persian, version, aspersion, aversion, coercion, conversion, dispersion, diversion, emersion, eversion, excursion, immersion, incursion, inversion, perversion, recursion, reversion, submersion, subversion, ambiversion, extroversion, interspersion, introversion, reconversion, retroversion,

animadversion,
seroconversion
²**ersion** \ər-shən\ see ERTIAN
ersional \ər-zhə-nəl\ versional,
conversional, reversional
ersionist \ər-zhə-nəst\
diversionist, excursionist
¹**ersity** \ər-sət-ē\ adversity,
diversity, multiversity,
university, biodiversity
²**ersity** \ər-stē\ see IRSTY
ersive \ər-siv\ cursive,
ambersive, aversive, coercive,
detersive, discursive,
dispersive, excursive,
inversive, perversive,
recursive, subversive,
extroversive, introversive
erson \ərs-ᵊn\ person, worsen,
chairperson, craftsperson,
draftsperson, houseperson,
MacPherson, newsperson,
nonperson, salesperson,
spokesperson, unperson,
anchorperson, businessperson,
gentleperson, weatherperson
erst \ərst\ see URST
ersted \ər-stəd\ oersted,
worsted, kilooersted
ersus \ər-səs\ cercis, thyrsus,
versus, excursus
ersy \ər-sē\ see ERCY
¹**ert** \ərt\ Bert, blurt, Burt, chert,
curt, dirt, flirt, girt, hurt, Kurt,
pert, quirt, shirt, skirt, spurt,
squirt, sturt, vert, wert, wort,
advert, alert, assert, avert,
bellwort, birthwort,
Blackshirt, brownshirt, Cape
Vert, colewort, concert,
convert, covert, desert,
dessert, dissert, divert, evert,

exert, expert, exsert, figwort,
fleawort, frankfurt, glasswort,
hoopskirt, hornwort, inert,
insert, invert, lousewort,
lungwort, madwort, milkwort,
nightshirt, outskirt, overt,
pervert, pilewort, ragwort,
redshirt, revert, ribwort,
saltwort, sandwort, seagirt,
Shubert, soapwort, spearwort,
spleenwort, stitchwort,
stonewort, subvert, sweatshirt,
toothwort, T-shirt, ungirt,
ambivert, bladderwort,
butterwort, controvert,
disconcert, extrovert,
feverwort, inexpert, introvert,
liverwort, malapert, miniskirt,
mitrewort, moneywort,
overshirt, overskirt,
pennywort, pettiskirt,
preconcert, reconvert, Saint-
John's-wort, spiderwort,
swallowwort, thoroughwort,
undershirt, underskirt,
animadvert, interconvert
²**ert** \er\ see ⁴ARE
³**ert** \at\ see ⁵AT
erta \ərt-ə\ Gerta, Alberta,
Roberta
ertain \ərt-ᵊn\ burton, Burton,
certain, curtain, Merton,
uncertain
ertant \ərt-ᵊnt\ see ERTENT
erted \ərt-əd\ skirted,
concerted, perverted,
T-shirted, extroverted,
miniskirted, undershirted—
also pasts of verbs listed at
¹ERT
ertedly \ərt-əd-lē\ assertedly,
concertedly, pervertedly

ertence \ərt-ᵊns\ advertence, inadvertence

ertent \ərt-ᵊnt\ advertent, revertant, inadvertent

erter \ərt-ər\ blurter, skirter, squirter, stertor, converter, inverter, subverter, controverter—*also comparatives of adjectives listed at* ¹ERT

¹ertes \ərt-ēz\ certes, Laertes

²ertes \ərts\ see ERTS

ertford \ärt-fərd\ see ARTFORD

erth \ərth\ see IRTH

ertha \ər-thə\ Bertha, Eartha

ertia \ər-shə\ Mercia, Murcia, inertia

ertial \ər-shəl\ see ERCIAL

ertian \ər-shən\ tertian, assertion, Cistercian, desertion, exertion, insertion, Mercian, self-assertion

ertible \ərt-ə-bəl\ convertible, invertible, controvertible, inconvertible, incontrovertible, interconvertible

ertile \ərt-ᵊl\ curtal, fertile, hurtle, kirtle, myrtle, Myrtle, spurtle, turtle, cross-fertile, exsertile, infertile, interfertile

ertinence \ərt-ᵊn-əns\ pertinence, purtenance, appurtenance, impertinence

¹ertinent \ərt-ᵊn-ənt\ pertinent, appurtenant, impertinent

²ertinent \ərt-nənt\ see IRTINENT

erting \ərt-iŋ\ shirting, skirting, disconcerting, self-asserting—*also present participles of verbs listed at* ¹ERT

ertion \ər-shən\ see ERTIAN

ertisement \ərt-əs-mənt\ advertisement, divertissement

ertium \ər-shəm\ see URTIUM

ertive \ərt-iv\ furtive, assertive, self-assertive, unassertive

erton \ərt-n\ see ERTAIN

ertor \ərt-ər\ see ERTER

erts \ərts\ certes, hertz, nerts, weltschmerz, gigahertz, kilohertz, megahertz—*also plurals and possessives of nouns and third person singular presents of verbs listed at* ¹ERT

erty \ər-tē\ see IRTY

ertz \ərts\ see ERTS

erule \er-əl\ see ERIL

erulent \er-ə-lənt\ sterilant, puberulent, pulverulent

erulous \er-ə-ləs\ see ERILOUS

erum \ir-əm\ theorem, serum

erund \er-ənd\ see ERRAND

erunt \er-ənt\ see ¹ARENT

erval \ər-vəl\ see ERVIL

ervancy \ər-vən-sē\ see ERVENCY

ervant \ər-vənt\ fervent, servant, maidservant, manservant, observant

ervative \ər-vət-iv\ conservative, preservative, archconservative, neoconservative, semiconservative

ervator \ər-vət-ər\ see ERVITOR

erve \ərv\ curve, MIRV, nerve, serve, swerve, verve, conserve, deserve, disserve, hors d'oeuvre, incurve, innerve, observe, preserve,

reserve, self-serve, subserve,
unnerve, unreserve

erved \ərvd\ nerved, decurved,
deserved, recurved, reserved,
underserved, unreserved—
also pasts of verbs listed at
ERVE

ervency \ər-vən-sē\ fervency,
conservancy

ervent \ər-vənt\ see ERVANT

erver \ər-vər\ fervor, server,
deserver, observer, timeserver

ervice \ər-vəs\ nervous, service,
disservice, full-service, in-
service, self-service,
interservice

ervil \ər-vəl\ chervil, serval,
servile

ervile \ər-vəl\ see ERVIL

erviness \ər-vē-nəs\ nerviness,
topsy-turviness

erving \ər-viŋ\ Irving, serving,
deserving, self-serving,
timeserving, unswerving

ervitor \ər-vət-ər\ servitor,
conservator

ervor \ər-vər\ see ERVER

ervous \ər-vəs\ see ERVICE

ervy \ər-vē\ see URVY

erwick \er-ik\ see ¹ERIC

erwin \ər-wən\ Irwin, Sherwin

¹ery \er-ē\ see ¹ARY

²ery \ir-ē\ see EARY

eryl \er-əl\ see ERIL

erz \erts\ see ¹ERTZ

¹es \ā\ see ¹AY

²es \ās\ see ¹ACE

³es \āz\ see ¹AZE

⁴es \es\ see ESS

⁵es \ēz\ see EZE

e's \ēz\ see EZE

¹esa \ā-sə\ mesa, Mesa, presa,
omasa, Teresa, Theresa

²esa \ā-zə\ presa, impresa,
marchesa, Bel Paese, Maria
Theresa

esage \es-ij\ see ESSAGE

¹esan \āz-ᵊn\ see AZON

²esan \ēz-ᵊn\ see EASON

esant \ez-ᵊnt\ bezant, peasant,
pheasant, pleasant, present,
unpleasant, omnipresent

esas \ā-zəs\ Marquesas—*also
plurals and possessives of
nouns listed at* ²ESA

esce \es\ see ESS

escence \es-ᵊns\ essence,
candescence, concrescence,
excrescence, florescence,
fluorescence, pearlescence,
pubescence, putrescence,
quiescence, quintessence,
senescence, tumescence,
turgescence, virescence,
acquiescence, adolescence,
arborescence, coalescence,
convalescence, decalescence,
defervescence, deliquescence,
detumescence, effervescence,
efflorescence, evanescence,
incandescence, inflorescence,
iridescence, juvenescence,
luminescence, obsolescence,
opalescence, prepubescence,
preadolescence

escency \es-ᵊn-sē\ excrescency,
incessancy

escent \es-ᵊnt\ crescent,
Crescent, candescent,
canescent, concrescent,
decrescent, depressant,
excrescent, fluorescent,
frutescent, incessant,

increscent, liquescent,
pearlescent, pubescent,
putrescent, quiescent,
rufescent, senescent,
suppressant, tumescent,
turgescent, virescent,
acaulescent, acquiescent,
adolescent, coalescent,
convalescent, detumescent,
effervescent, efflorescent,
arborescent, evanescent,
incandescent, inflorescent,
intumescent, irridescent,
juvenescent, luminescent,
opalescent, phosphorescent,
prepubescent, recrudescent,
viridescent, antidepressant,
preadolescent

escible \es-ə-bəl\ see ESSIBLE
escience \ēsh-əns\ nescience,
prescience
escive \es-iv\ see ESSIVE
esco \es-kō\ alfresco, barbaresco
escue \es-kyü\ fescue, rescue
¹ese \ēs\ see IECE
²ese \ēz\ see EZE
³ese \ā-sē\ see ACY
esence \ez-ᵊns\ pleasance,
presence, omnipresence
eseus \ē-sē-əs\ Theseus,
Tiresias
¹esh \esh\ crèche, flèche, flesh,
fresh, mesh, thresh, afresh,
bobeche, calèche, crème
fraîche, enmesh, gooseflesh,
horseflesh, immesh, parfleche,
refresh, tête-bêche,
Bangladesh, Gilgamesh,
intermesh, Marrakech, Andhra
Pradesh, Madhya Pradesh,
Uttar Pradesh, Himachral
Pradesh, Arunachal Pradesh

²esh \āsh\ see ¹ECHE
³esh \ash\ see ³ASH
eshed \esht\ fleshed, meshed—
also pasts of verbs listed at
¹ESH
eshen \esh-ən\ see ESSION
eshener \esh-ə-nər\ see
ESSIONER
esher \esh-ər\ see ESSURE
eshly \esh-lē\ fleshly, freshly,
specially, especially
eshment \esh-mənt\ fleshment,
enmeshment, refreshment
¹esi \ā-zē\ see AZY
²esi \ā-sē\ see ACY
¹esia \ē-shə\ geisha, Moesia,
Letitia, Lucretia, Magnesia,
Phoenicia, alpoecia
²esia \ē-zhə\ freesia, amnesia,
esthesia, frambesia, magnesia,
rafflesia, Silesia, Tunisia,
analgesia, anesthesia,
Austronesia, Indonesia,
Melanesia, Micronesia,
Polynesia, synesthesia
esial \ē-zē-əl\ mesial, ecclesial
¹esian \ē-zhən\ Friesian,
Frisian, lesion, adhesion,
Cartesian, cohesion, etesian,
Salesian, Austronesian,
holstein-friesian, Indonesian,
Melanesian, Micronesian,
Polynesian
²esian \ē-shən\ see ¹ETION
esias \ē-sē-əs\ see ESEUS
esicant \es-i-kənt\ see ESICCANT
esiccant \es-i-kənt\ desiccant,
vesicant
esidency \ez-əd-ən-sē\
presidency, residency,
nonresidency, vice-presidency
esident \ez-əd-ənt\ president,

resident, nonresident, vice-
president

esima \es-ə-mə\
Quinquagesima, Sexagesima,
Septuagesima

esimal \es-ə-məl\ centesimal,
millesimal, vigesimal,
duodecimal, planetesimal,
sexagesimal, infinitesimal

esin \ez-ᵊn\ resin, muezzin,
oleoresin

esion \ē-zhən\ see ¹ESIAN

esis \ē-səs\ Croesus, thesis,
tmesis, ascesis, askesis,
esthesis, mimesis, prosthesis,
anamnesis, catachresis,
catechesis, Dionysus,
exegesis, hyperkinesis,
Peloponnesus, psychokinesis,
telekinesis, amniocentesis

esium \ē-zē-əm\ see EZIUM

esive \ē-siv\ adhesive, cohesive,
self-adhesive

esk \esk\ see ESQUE

esley \es-lē\ see ESSLY

eslie \es-lē\ see ESSLY

esne \ēn\ see ³INE

¹eso \ā-sō\ peso, say-so

²eso \es-ō\ see ESSO

espass \es-pəs\ Thespis,
trespass

espis \es-pəs\ see ESPASS

espite \es-pət\ see ESPOT

espot \es-pət\ despot, respite

esque \esk\ desk, burlesque,
grotesque, moresque,
arabesque, Bunyanesque,
copydesk, gigantesque,
humoresque, Junoesque,
Kafkaesque, picaresque,
picturesque, plateresque,
Rubenesque, Romanesque,
sculpturesque, statuesque,
churrigueresque

ess \es\ bless, cess, chess, cress,
dress, ess, fess, guess, Hesse,
jess, less, loess, mess, ness,
press, s, stress, tress, yes,
abscess, access, address,
aggress, assess, caress,
clothespress, coatdress,
compress, confess, CS,
depress, digress, distress,
duress, egress, excess,
express, finesse, handpress,
headdress, housedress,
impress, ingress, largess,
Meknes, nightdress, noblesse,
obsess, oppress, outguess,
pantdress, possess, precess,
prestress, princess, process,
profess, progress, re-press,
recess, redress, regress,
repress, shirtdress, sidedress,
SS, success, sundress,
suppress, top-dress,
transgress, undress, unless,
winepress, ABS, acquiesce,
baroness, coalesce,
convalesce, DES, decompress,
deliquesce, derepress,
dispossess, effervesce,
effloresce, evanesce,
gentilesse, GR-S, IHS, in-
process, incandesce,
intumesce, inverness,
Inverness, letterpress,
luminesce, Lyonnesse,
minidress, nonetheless,
obsolesce, otherguess,
overdress, pennycress,
phosphoresce, politesse,
prepossess, preprocess,
recrudesce, repossess,

reprocess, retrogress, second-guess, SOS, sweaterdress, unsuccess, watercress, window-dress, another-guess, nevertheless

essa \es-ə\ see ³ESSE

essable \es-ə-bəl\ see ESSIBLE

essage \es-ij\ message, presage, expressage

essaly \es-ə-lē\ Cecily, Thessaly

essamine \es-mən\ see ESSMAN

essan \es-ᵊn\ see ESSEN

essancy \es-ᵊn-sē\ see ESCENCY

essant \es-ᵊnt\ see ESCENT

¹esse \es\ see ESS

²esse \es-ē\ see ESSY

³esse \es-ə\ Hesse, Odessa, Vanessa

essed \est\ see EST

essedly \es-əd-lē\ blessedly, confessedly, professedly, possessedly, self-possessedly

essel \es-əl\ see ¹ESTLE

essen \es-ᵊn\ Essen, lessen, lesson, messan, delicatessen

essence \es-ᵊns\ see ESCENCE

esser \es-ər\ see ESSOR

essex \es-iks\ Essex, Wessex

essful \es-fəl\ stressful, distressful, successful, unsuccessful

essian \esh-ən\ see ESSION

essible \es-ə-bəl\ decibel, accessible, addressable, compressible, confessable, depressible, expressible, impressible, processible, putrescible, suppressible, inaccessible, incompressible, inexpressible, insuppressible, irrepressible

essie \es-ē\ see ESSY

essile \es-əl\ see ¹ESTLE

ession \esh-ən\ cession, freshen, hessian, session, accession, aggression, compression, concession, confession, depression, digression, discretion, egression, expression, impression, ingression, obsession, oppression, possession, precession, procession, profession, progression, recession, refreshen, regression, repression, secession, succession, suppression, transgression, decompression, dispossession, indiscretion, intercession, intersession, introgression, misimpression, prepossession, reimpression, repossession, retrogression, self-confession, self-expression, self-possession, supersession

essional \esh-ə-nəl\ sessional, acessional, concessional, congressional, diagressional, expressional, obsessional, possessional, precessional, processional, professional, progressional, recessional, successional, paraprofessional, preprofessional, subprofessional, paraprofessional, semiprofessional

essioner \esh-ə-nər\ freshener, concessioner

essionist \esh-ə-nəst\ expressionist, repressionist, impressionist, secessionist

essity \es-tē\ see ESTY
essive \es-iv\ crescive,
   aggressive, caressive,
   compressive, concessive,
   degressive, depressive,
   digressive, excessive,
   expressive, impressive,
   ingressive, obsessive,
   oppressive, possessive,
   progressive, recessive,
   regressive, successive,
   suppressive, transgressive,
   inexpressive, retrogressive,
   unexpressive, manic-
   depressive
essly \es-lē\ Leslie, Lesley,
   Wesley, expressly
essman \es-mən\ chessman,
   pressman, expressman,
   jessamine, specimen
essment \es-mənt\ see ESTMENT
esso \es-ō\ gesso, espresso
esson \es-ᵊn\ see ESSEN
essor \es-ər\ dresser, guesser,
   lesser, pressor, stressor,
   addresser, aggressor, assessor,
   caresser, compressor,
   confessor, depressor,
   expressor, hairdresser,
   oppressor, processor,
   professor, regressor, repressor,
   successor, suppresssor,
   transgressor, vinedresser,
   antecessor, dispossessor,
   intercessor, predecessor,
   repossessor, second-guesser,
   microprocessor,
   multiprocessor
essory \es-ə-rē\ pessary,
   accessory, possessory,
   intercessory
essure \esh-ər\ pressure,

impressure, low-pressure,
   refresher, acupressure,
   overpressure
essy \es-ē\ Bessie, dressy, Jesse,
   Jessie, messy
est \est\ best, breast, Brest,
   chest, crest, gest, geste, guest,
   hest, jessed, jest, lest, nest,
   pest, prest, quest, rest, test,
   tressed, vest, west, West,
   wrest, zest, abreast, appressed,
   armrest, arrest, attest,
   backrest, beau geste, behest,
   bequest, bird's-nest, celeste,
   Celeste, compressed, congest,
   conquest, contest, detest,
   devest, digest, divest, egest,
   field-test, flight-test, footrest,
   gabfest, hard-pressed,
   headrest, hillcrest, houseguest,
   imprest, incest, infest, ingest,
   inquest, interest, invest, low-
   test, Mae West, Midwest,
   molest, northwest, posttest,
   pretest, professed, protest,
   redbreast, repressed, request,
   retest, revest, slugfest,
   southwest, suggest, trapnest,
   Trieste, t-test, unblessed,
   undressed, unrest, unstressed,
   almagest, anapest, Bucharest,
   Budapest, decongest,
   disinfest, disinvest, empty-
   nest, galley-west, manifest,
   north-northwest, palimpsest,
   predigest, reinvest, rinderpest,
   second-best, self-addressed,
   self-confessed, self-interest,
   self-possessed, supraprotest,
   sweatervest, uninterest,
   unprofessed, autosuggest,
   disinterest, robin redbreast,

underinvest, thirty-second
rest—*also pasts of verbs
listed at* ESS

esta \es-tə\ cesta, cuesta, testa,
vesta, Vesta, Avesta, celesta,
egesta, fiesta, ingesta, siesta,
Zend-Avesta

estable \es-tə-bəl\ see ESTIBLE

estae \es-tē\ see ESTY

estal \es-t°l\ crestal, pestle,
vestal

estan \es-tən\ see ESTINE

estant \es-tənt\ arrestant,
contestant, infestant,
protestant, Protestant,
decongestant, disinfestant,
manifestant

este \est\ see EST

ested \es-təd\ bested, crested,
nested, tested, vested, time-
tested, barrel-chested, double-
breasted, hairy-chested,
indigested, single-breasted—
also pasts of verbs listed at
EST

ester \es-tər\ Chester, ester,
Esther, fester, Hester, jester,
Leicester, Lester, nester,
Nestor, pester, quaestor,
quester, questor, nester, tester,
wester, yester, zester,
ancestor, arrester, contester,
detester, digester, infester,
investor, Manchester,
molester, northwester,
Rochester, semester,
sequester, southwester,
sou'wester, suggester,
Sylvester, trimester,
Winchester, arbalester, empty-
nester, monoester, polyester

esti \es-tē\ see ESTY

estial \es-tē-əl\ celestial,
forestial

estible \es-tə-bəl\ testable,
comestible, detestable,
digestible, ingestible,
investable, suggestible,
incontestable, indigestible

estic \es-tik\ gestic, domestic,
majestic, anapestic,
catachrestic

estical \es-ti-kəl\ see ESTICLE

esticle \es-ti-kəl\ testicle,
catachrestical

estimate \es-tə-mət\ estimate,
guesstimate

estinate \es-tə-nət\ festinate,
predestinate

estine \es-tən\ destine, Preston,
Avestan, clandestine,
intestine, predestine

esting \es-tiŋ\ cresting, vesting,
westing, arresting

estion \es-chən\ question,
congestion, cross-question,
digestion, egestion, ingestion,
self-question, suggestion,
decongestion, indigestion,
self-suggestion,
autosuggestion

estis \es-təs\ cestus, testis,
Alcestis, asbestos, Hephaestus

estival \es-tə-vəl\ estival,
festival

estive \es-tiv\ festive, restive,
congestive, digestive,
egestive, ingestive,
suggestive, decongestive

¹estle \es-əl\ Bessel, Cecil,
decile, nestle, pestle, sessile,
trestle, vessel, wrestle, Indian-
wrestle

²estle \as-əl\ see ²ASSEL

³**estle** \əs-əl\ see USTLE

estless \est-ləs\ crestless,
   restless

estment \es-mənt\ vestment,
   arrestment, assessment,
   divestment, impressment,
   investment, disinvestment,
   reinvestment

esto \es-tō\ pesto, presto,
   manifesto

eston \es-tən\ see ESTINE

estor \es-tər\ see ESTER

estos \es-təs\ see ESTIS

estra \es-trə\ fenestra, orchestra,
   palaestra, Clytemnestra

estral \es-trəl\ estral, kestrel,
   ancestral, campestral,
   fenestral, semestral, orchestral

estrel \es-trəl\ see ESTRAL

estress \es-trəs\ see ESTRUS

estrial \es-trē-əl\ semestrial,
   terrestrial, extraterrestrial

estrian \es-trē-ən\ equestrian,
   pedestrian

estrous \es-trəs\ see ESTRUS

estrum \es-trəm\ estrum,
   sequestrum

estrus \es-trəs\ estrous, estrus,
   ancestress

estry \es-trē\ vestry, ancestry

estuous \es-chə-wəs\
   incestuous, tempestuous

esture \es-chər\ gesture, vesture

estus \es-təs\ see ESTIS

esty \es-tē\ chesty, testae, testy,
   pesty, zesty, res gestae,
   necessity, Tibesti

esus \ē-səs\ see ESIS

¹**et** \et\ bet, Bret, Brett, debt, et,
   fret, get, jet, let, Lett, met,
   net, pet, ret, set, stet, sweat,
   Tet, threat, vet, wet, whet,

yet, abet, aigrette, Annette,
asset, Babette, backset,
baguette, banquette, barbette,
Barnet, Barnett, barquette,
barrette, beget, beset,
blanquette, boneset, brevet,
briquette, brochette, brunet,
burette, burnet, cadet,
cassette, cermet, Claudette,
Colette, coquet, coquette,
cornet, corselet, corvette,
coset, courgette, croquette,
curette, curvet, cuvette,
daleth, dinette, diskette,
dragnet, duet, egret, fan-jet,
fishnet, flechette, forget,
frisette, gazette, georgette,
Georgette, gillnet, godet,
grisette, handset, hard-set,
headset, ink-jet, inlet, inset,
Janette, Jeanette, Jeannette,
Juliet, kismet, layette,
lorgnette, lunette, Lynette,
maquette, Marquette, mind-
set, moonset, moquette,
motet, musette, Nanette,
Nannette, noisette, nonet,
nymphet, octet, offset, onset,
Osset, outlet, outset, paillette,
palet, pallette, palmette,
Paulette, pipette, piquet,
planchette, poussette, preset,
quartet, quickset, quintet,
raclette, ramet, regret, reset,
revet, rocket, roomette,
rosette, roulette, saw-whet,
septet, sestet, sextet, sharp-
set, soubrette, spinet, stylet,
sublet, subset, sunset, Syrette,
tacet, thickset, Tibet, toilette,
tonette, trijet, twinset, typeset,
unset, upset, vedette, vignette,

well-set, Yvette, aiguillette,
alphabet, anchoret,
andouilette, anisette,
Antoinette, avocet, banneret,
basinet, bassinet, bayonet,
Bernadette, bobbinet,
briolette, burgonet, calumet,
canzonet, castanet, cellarette,
chemisette, cigarette, clarinet,
consolette, coronet, corselet,
crepe suzette, dragonet,
electret, en brochette, epaulet,
epithet, etiquette, falconet,
farmerette, featurette,
flageolet, flannelette,
guillemet, heavyset, jaconet,
Juliett, kitchenette, Lafayette,
landaulet, lanneret,
launderette, Leatherette,
luncheonette, maisonette,
majorette, marmoset,
marquisette, martinet,
mignonette, minaret, minuet,
miquelet, novelette, Olivet,
oubliette, parapet, paupiette,
photoset, pirouette, quodlibet,
rondelet, Samoset, satinet,
scilicet, sermonette, serviette,
silhouette, sobriquet, solleret,
somerset, Somerset, soviet,
spinneret, statuette,
stockinette, suffragette,
superjet, swimmeret, taboret,
thermoset, towelette,
trebuchet, tricolette, underlet,
usherette, vinaigrette,
wagonette, analphabet,
bachelorette, drum majorette,
electrojet, Hospitalet,
marionette, microcassette,
micropipette, musique
concrète, photo-offset,
videlicet, audiocassette,
caulifloweret, hail-fellow-
well-met, Marie Antoinette,
videocassette

²**et** \ā\ see ¹AY

³**et** \āt\ see ¹ATE

⁴**et** \es\ see ESS

¹**eta** \āt-ə\ see ²ATA

²**eta** \et-ə\ see ETTA

³**eta** \ēt-ə\ see ²ITA

¹**etable** \et-ə-bəl\ see ETTABLE

²**etable** \ēt-ə-bəl\ see EATABLE

¹**etal** \ēt-ᵊl\ beetle, betel, fetal,
decretal, excretal

²**etal** \et-ᵊl\ see ETTLE

¹**etan** \et-ᵊn\ Breton, threaten,
Cape Breton, Tibetan

²**etan** \ēt-ᵊn\ see ¹EATEN

etch \ech\ catch, etch, fetch,
fletch, ketch, kvetch, lech,
letch, retch, sketch, stretch,
vetch, wretch, backstretch,
homestretch, outstretch

etched \echt\ teched,
farfetched—*also pasts of
verbs listed at* ETCH

etcher \ech-ər\ etcher, catcher,
fetcher, fletcher, Fletcher,
lecher, sketcher, stretcher,
cowcatcher, dogcatcher, eye-
catcher, flycatcher,
gnatcatcher

etching \ech-iŋ\ etching,
fletching—*also present
participles of verbs listed at*
ETCH

etchy \ech-ē\ sketchy, stretchy,
tetchy

¹**ete** \āt\ see ¹ATE

²**ete** \et\ see ¹ET

³**ete** \ēt\ see ¹EAT

⁴**ete** \āt-ē\ see ATY

ête \āt\ see ¹ATE

eted \ād\ see ¹ADE

etel \ēt-ᵊl\ see ETAL

etely \ēt-lē\ see EETLY

eteor \ēt-ē-ər\ meteor, confiteor—*also comparatives of adjectives listed at* EATY

eter \ēt-ər\ see ¹EATER

etera \e-trə\ see ETRA

eterate \et-ə-rət\ see ETERIT

eterit \et-ə-rət\ preterit, inveterate

etes \ēt-əs\ see ETUS

¹eth \eth\ Beth, breath, breadth, death, saith, Seth, snath, daleth, handbreadth, hairbreadth, Macbeth, Ashtoreth, isopleth, megadeath, shibboleth, Elisabeth, Elizabeth

²eth \ās\ see ¹ACE

³eth \āt\ see ¹ATE

⁴eth \et\ see ¹ET

etha \ē-thə\ Aretha, Ibiza

ethane \e-thān\ ethane, methane, nitromethane, dichloroethane

ethe \ē-thē\ see EATHY

¹ether \eth̲-ər\ blether, feather, heather, Heather, leather, nether, tether, weather, wether, whether, aweather, bellwether, pinfeather, together, untether, altogether, get-together

²ether \əth̲-ər\ see ¹OTHER

ethic \eth-ik\ ethic, erethic

ethral \ē-thrəl\ urethral, bulbourethral

ethyl \eth-əl\ bethel, Ethel, ethyl, methyl, triethyl

¹eti \ēt-ē\ see EATY

²eti \āt-ē\ see ATY

etia \ē-shə\ see ¹ESIA

etian \ē-shən\ see ¹ETION

¹etic \ēt-ik\ thetic, acetic, docetic

etic \et-ik\ etic, thetic, aesthetic, ascetic, athletic, balletic, bathetic, cosmetic, docetic, eidetic, emetic, frenetic, gametic, genetic, hermetic, kinetic, limnetic, magnetic, mimetic, noetic, Ossetic, paretic, pathetic, phenetic, phonetic, phrenetic, phyletic, poetic, prophetic, prosthetic, pyretic, splenetic, syncretic, syndetic, synthetic, tonetic, Venetic, alphabetic, analgetic, anesthetic, antithetic, apathetic, asyndetic, copacetic, cybernetic, diabetic, dietetic, digenetic, diphyletic, diuretic, empathetic, energetic, epithetic, geodetic, homiletic, Masoretic, nomothetic, parenthetic, sympathetic, synergetic, synesthetic, aeromagnetic, antimagnetic, antipathetic, antipoetic, antipyretic, apologetic, epexigetic, epigenetic, ferrimagnetic, ferromagnetic, geomagnetic, gyromagnetic, homogametic, hydrokinetic, hydromagnetic, hyperkinetic, isomagnetic, monophyletic, morphogenetic, ontogenetic, optokinetic, palingenetic, paramagnetic, pathogenetic, peripatetic, phylogenetic, polyphyletic, psychokinetic, telekinetic, thermomagnetic, aposiopetic, cyanogenetic, electrokinetic, electromagnetic, heterogametic, parasympathetic, parthenogenetic, psychotomimetic, unapologetic, onomatopoetic

etical \et-i-kəl\ metical, reticle, aesthetical, genetical, heretical, phonetical, antithetical, arithmetical, catechetical, cybernetical, epithetical, exegetical, geodetical, hypothetical, parenthetical, theoretical, atheoretical, epexegetical

eticist \et-ə-səst\ geneticist, kineticist, cyberneticist

etics \et-iks\ aesthetics, athletics, genetics, homiletics, kinetics, phonetics, poetics, tonetics, cybernetics, dietetics, apologetics, cytogenetics, immunogenetics—*also plurals and possessives of nouns listed at* ETIC

etid \et-əd\ fetid, fretted, sweated, indebted, parapeted—*also pasts of verbs listed at* ¹ET

etin \ēt-ᵊn\ see ¹EATEN

¹etion \ē-shən\ Grecian, accretion, Capetian, completion, concretion, deletion, depletion, excretion, Ossetian, Phoenician, repletion, secretion, suppletion, Tahitian, Austronesian, Diocletian,

Melanesian, Polynesian, Taracahitian

²etion \esh-ən\ see ESSION

etious \ē-shəs\ see ECIOUS

¹etis \ēt-əs\ see ETUS

²etis \et-əs\ see ETTUCE

etist \et-əst\ cornetist, librettist, vignettist, clarinetist, exegetist, operettist—*also superlatives of adjectives listed at* ¹ET

etitive \et-ət-iv\ competitive, repetitive, uncompetitive, anticompetitive

etium \ē-shē-əm\ see ECIUM

etius \ē-shəs\ see ECIOUS

etive \ēt-iv\ accretive, completive, decretive, depletive, secretive, suppletive

¹etl \āt-ᵊl\ see ATAL

²etl \et-ᵊl\ see ETTLE

etland \et-lənd\ Shetland, wetland

etment \et-mənt\ abetment, besetment, curettement, revetment

¹eto \āt-ō\ see ²ATO

²eto \ēt-ō\ see ¹ITO

eton \ēt-ᵊn\ see ¹EATEN

¹etor \et-ər\ see ETTER

²etor \ēt-ər\ see ¹EATER

etory \ēt-ə-rē\ eatery, decretory, secretory, suppletory

etous \ēt-əs\ see ETUS

¹etra \e-trə\ Petra, tetra, etcetera

²etra \ē-trə\ Petra, Kenitra

¹etral \ē-trəl\ petrel, retral

²etral \e-trəl\ see ¹ETREL

être \etrᵊ\ fête champêtre, raison d'être

¹etrel \e-trəl\ petrel, petrol, retral

²etrel \ē-trəl\ see ¹ETRAL

etric \e-trik\ metric, obstetric, symmetric, asymmetric, barometric, decametric, dekametric, diametric, dissymmetric, geometric, hypsometric, isometric, optometric, psychometric, telemetric, volumetric, acidometric, amperometric, sociometric

etrical \e-tri-kəl\ metrical, obstetrical, symmetrical, asymmetrical, barometrical, diametrical, geometrical, unsymmetrical

etrics \e-triks\ obstetrics, geometrics, isometrics, sabermetrics

etrist \e-trəst\ metrist, belletrist

etrol \e-trəl\ see ¹ETREL

ets \ets\ let's, Donets, rillettes, Steinmetz, pantalets, solonetz, Sosnowiec—*also plurals and possessives of nouns and third person singular presents of verbs listed at* ¹ET

etsk \etsk\ Donetsk, Kuznetsk, Lipetsk, Novokuznetsk

ett \et\ see ¹ET

etta \et-ə\ betta, Etta, feta, geta, Greta, Quetta, biretta, cabretta, galleta, Loretta, mozzetta, pancetta, poinsettia, Rosetta, Valletta, vendetta, anchoveta, arietta, cabaletta, Henrietta, Marietta, operetta, sinfonietta

ettable \et-ə-bəl\ retable, wettable, forgettable, regrettable, unforgettable

ette \et\ see ¹ET

etter \et-ər\ better, bettor, debtor, fetter, getter, letter, netter, rhetor, setter, sweater, tetter, wetter, whetter, abettor, begetter, bonesetter, enfetter, gill-netter, go-getter, jet-setter, newsletter, pacesetter, pinsetter, red-letter, regretter, trendsetter, typesetter, unfetter, vignetter, carburetter—*also comparatives of adjectives listed at* ¹ET

ettered \et-ərd\ fettered, lettered, unfettered, unlettered

ettes \ets\ see ETS

ettia \et-ə\ see ETTA

ettie \et-ē\ see ¹ETTY

ettier \it-ē-ər\ see ITTIER

ettiness \it-ē-nəs\ see ITTINESS

etting \et-iŋ\ netting, setting, bed-wetting, bloodletting, go-getting, onsetting, typesetting, thermosetting, phototypesetting

ettish \et-ish\ fetish, Lettish, pettish, wettish, coquettish, novelettish

ettle \et-ᵊl\ fettle, kettle, metal, mettle, nettle, petal, settle, shtetl, bimetal, gunmetal, nonmetal, teakettle, unsettle, Citlaltepetl, Popocatepetl

ettlesome \et-ᵊl-səm\ mettlesome, nettlesome

ettling \et-liŋ\ fettling, settling, unsettling

etto \et-ō\ ghetto, stretto, cavetto, falsetto, in petto,

larghetto, libretto, palmetto,
stiletto, zucchetto, allegretto,
amaretto, amoretto, fianchetto,
Kazan Retto, lazaretto,
Tintoretto, vaporetto
ettor \et-ər\ see ETTER
ettuce \et-əs\ lettuce, Thetis,
Hymettus
ettus \et-əs\ see ETTUCE
¹etty \et-ē\ Betty, jetty, Nettie,
netty, petit, petty, sweaty,
yeti, brown Betty, cavetti,
confetti, libretti, machete,
Rossetti, spaghetti, amoretti,
Donizetti, Serengeti,
spermacetti, cappelletti,
cavalletti, vaporetti
²etty \it-ē\ see ITTY
etum \ēt-əm\ pinetum,
arboretum, equisetum
etus \ēt-əs\ Cetus, fetus, Thetis,
treatise, acetous, Admetus,
boletus, coitus, quietus,
diabetes
etzsche \ē-chē\ see EACHY
euben \ü-bən\ Cuban, Reuben,
Ruben, von Steuben
euce \üs\ see ¹USE
euced \ü-səd\ see UCID
eucey \ü-sē\ see UICY
euch \ük\ see UKE
euchre \ü-kər\ see UCRE
eucid \ü-səd\ see UCID
¹eud \üd\ see UDE
²eud \ȯid\ see ¹OID
eudal \üd-ᵊl\ see OODLE
eudist \üd-əst\ see ¹UDIST
eudo \üd-ō\ see UDO
eue \ü\ see ¹EW
euer \ü-ər\ see ¹EWER
euil \āl\ see AIL
euille \ē\ see ¹EE

euk \ük\ see UKE
eukin \ü-kən\ see UCAN
¹eul \əl\ see ¹ULL
²eul \ərl\ see ¹IRL
eulah \ü-lə\ see ULA
eulean \ü-lē-ən\ see ULEAN
¹eum \ē-əm\ geum, lyceum,
museum, no-see-um, odeum,
per diem, Te Deum,
athenaeum, coliseum,
colosseum, hypogeum,
mausoleum
²eum \ā-əm\ see AHUM
³eum \üm\ see ¹OOM
euma \ü-mə\ see UMA
eume \üm\ see ¹OOM
eumon \ü-mən\ see UMAN
eumy \ü-mē\ see OOMY
eunice \ü-nəs\ see EWNESS
eunt \u̇nt\ see ¹UNT
eunuch \ü-nik\ see UNIC
¹eur \ər\ birr, blur, buhr, burr,
Burr, chirr, churr, cur, curr,
err, fir, for, fur, her, knur,
murre, myrrh, per, purr, shirr,
sir, skirr, slur, spur, stir, thir,
'twere, were, whir, your,
you're, à deux, as per, astir,
auteur, aver, bestir, chasseur,
chauffeur, claqueur, coiffeur,
concur, confer, danseur, defer,
demur, deter, douceur, du
jour, farceur, flaneur, friseur,
frondeur, hauteur, him/her,
his/her, incur, infer, inter,
jongleur, larkspur, liqueur,
longspur, masseur, Malmö,
millefleur, occur, Pasteur,
poseur, prefer, recur, refer,
sandbur, sandspur, seigneur,
transfer, voyeur, accoucheur,
amateur, cocklebur,

colporteur, connoisseur, cri de
coeur, cross-refer, cubature,
curvature, de rigueur, disinter,
force majeure, franc-tireur,
monseigneur, nonconcur,
pasticheur, prosateur,
raconteur, rapporteur,
regisseur, saboteur, secateur,
underfur, voyageur,
arbitrageur, carillonneur,
conglomerateur, entrepreneur,
litterateur, provacateur,
restaurateur, agent
provocateur

²**eur** \ùr\ see ¹URE

eure \ər\ see ¹EUR

eurial \ùr-ē-əl\ see ¹URIAL

eurish \ər-ish\ see OURISH

eurs \ərz\ see ¹ERS

eury \ùr-ē\ see ¹URY

¹**eus** \ē-əs\ Aeneas, Aggeus,
Alpheus, Arius, Chryseis,
Linnaeus, Micheas, Piraeus,
uraeus, coryphaeus, epigeous,
scarabaeus, prelate nullius,
Duque de Caxias, Judas
Maccabaeus

²**eus** \üs\ see ¹USE

¹**euse** \əz\ buzz, 'cause, coz,
does, fuzz, 'twas, was, abuzz,
because, outdoes, undoes,
overdoes

²**euse** \üs\ see ¹USE

³**euse** \üz\ see ²USE

¹**eusel** \ü-səl\ see ¹USAL

²**eusel** \ü-zəl\ see ²USAL

eut \üt\ see UTE

euter \üt-ər\ see UTER

euth \üth\ see ²OOTH

eutian \ü-shən\ see UTION

eutic \üt-ik\ see UTIC

eutical \üt-i-kəl\ see UTICAL

eutics \üt-iks\ toreutics,
hermeneutics, therapeutics

eutist \üt-əst\ see UTIST

euton \üt-ᵊn\ see UTAN

eutonist \üt-ᵊn-əst\ see UTENIST

euve \əv\ see ¹OVE

euver \ü-vər\ see ³OVER

¹**eux** \ü\ see ¹EW

²**eux** \ər\ see ¹EUR

¹**ev** \ef\ see ¹EF

²**ev** \óf\ see ²OFF

eva \ē-və\ see ²IVA

eval \ē-vəl\ see IEVAL

evalent \ev-ə-lənt\ see EVOLENT

¹**evan** \ē-vən\ see EVEN

²**evan** \ev-ən\ see EAVEN

¹**eve** \ev\ breve, rev, Sevres,
Negev, alla breve

²**eve** \ēv\ see ¹EAVE

evel \ev-əl\ bevel, devil, level,
Neville, revel, baselevel,
bedevil, bi-level, daredevil,
dishevel, go-devil, split-level,
entry-level

eveler \ev-lər\ leveler, reveler

evelly \ev-ə-lē\ heavily, levelly,
reveille

evement \ēv-mənt\
achievement, aggrievement,
bereavement,
underachievement

even \ē-vən\ even, Stephen,
Steven, breakeven, break-
even, Genevan, Kesteven,
uneven

eventh \ev-ənth\ seventh,
eleventh

¹**ever** \ev-ər\ clever, ever, lever,
never, sever, Trevor, dissever,
endeavor, forever, however,
soever, whatever, whenever,
wherever, whichever,

whoever, whomever,
cantilever, howsoever, live-
forever, whatsoever,
whencesoever, whensoever,
wheresoever, whichsoever,
whomsoever, whosesoever,
whosoever, whithersoever

²**ever** \ē-vər\ see IEVER

everage \ev-rij\ beverage,
leverage

everence \ev-rəns\ reverence,
severance, disseverance,
irreverence

every \ev-rē\ every, reverie

eves \ēvz\ see EAVES

eviate \ē-vē-ət\ deviate, qiviut

evice \ev-əs\ clevis, crevice,
Ben Nevis

evil \ē-vəl\ see IEVAL

eville \ev-əl\ see EVEL

evilry \ev-əl-rē\ devilry, revelry

evin \ev-ən\ see EAVEN

evious \ē-vē-əs\ devious,
previous

¹**evis** \ev-əs\ see EVICE

²**evis** \ē-vəs\ see EVUS

evity \ev-ət-ē\ brevity, levity,
longevity

evo \ē-vō\ in vivo, relievo, ring-
a-lievo, alto-relievo, basso-
relievo, mezzo-relievo,
recitativo, Antananavivo

evocable \ev-ə-kə-bəl\
evocable, revocable,
irrevocable

evolence \ev-ə-ləns\ prevalence,
benevolence, malevolence

evolent \ev-ə-lənt\ prevalent,
benevolent, malevolent

evor \ev-ər\ see ¹EVER

evous \ē-vəs\ grievous, Nevis,

nevus, longevous, redivivus,
Saint Kitts and Nevis

evsk \efsk\ see EFSK

evus \ē-vəs\ see EVOUS

evy \ev-ē\ bevy, heavy, levee,
levy, replevy, top-heavy

¹**ew** \ü\ blue, boo, brew, chew,
clew, clue, coo, coup, crew,
cue, dew, do, doux, drew,
due, ewe, few, flew, flu, flue,
fou, glue, gnu, goo, hew, hue,
Hugh, Jew, knew, lieu, loo,
Lou, mew, moo, moue, mu,
new, nu, ooh, pew, phew, piu,
pooh, prau, q, queue, roux,
rue, screw, shoe, shoo, shrew,
Sioux, skew, slew, slough,
slue, smew, sou, sous, spew,
sprue, stew, strew, sue, Sue,
thew, threw, thro, through, to,
too, true, two, u, view, whew,
who, woo, Wu, xu, yew, you,
zoo, accrue, adieu, ado,
aircrew, airscrew, anew,
Anjou, askew, au jus, Baku,
bamboo, battu, battue, bedew,
beshrew, bestrew, bijou,
boubou, brand-new,
breakthrough, burgoo, cachou,
can-do, canoe, caoutchouc,
Cebu, Cheng-du, Chongju,
Chonju, construe, Corfu,
corkscrew, coypu, CQ, debut,
ecu, endue, ensue, eschew,
floor-through, fondue, fordo,
foreknew, Gansu, Gentoo,
Gifu, gansun, gumshoe, guru,
hairdo, hereto, Honshu,
horseshoe, how-to, HQ, Hutu,
imbrue, imbue, IQ, jackscrew,
K2, Kansu, karoo, Karoo,
kazoo, Khufu, kung fu,

Kwangju, leadscrew, lean-to,
make-do, Matthew, me-too,
mildew, milieu, miscue,
misdo, misknew, muumuu,
Nehru, non-U, old-shoe, one-
two, outdo, outgrew, perdu,
Peru, poilu, preview, pursue,
purview, ragout, redo, renew,
Ren Crew, review, revue,
rough-hew, run-through,
sandshoe, see-through, set-to,
setscrew, shampoo, Shih Tzu,
skiddoo, snafu, snowshoe,
soft-shoe, span-new, subdue,
surtout, taboo, Taegu, tattoo,
thank-you, thereto,
thumbscrew, to-do, too-too,
undo, undue, unglue,
unscrew, untrue, vatu,
vendue, venue, vertu, virtu,
wahoo, walk-through,
wherethrough, whereto, who's
who, withdrew, worldview,
aperçu, avenue, babassu,
ballyhoo, barbecue, barley-
broo, billet-doux, black-and-
blue, buckaroo, bugaboo,
callaloo, caribou, catechu,
clerihew, cockapoo, cockatoo,
Cotonou, counterview, déjà
vu, derring-do, detinue,
feverfew, follow-through,
gardyloo, hitherto, honeydew,
Ignaçu, ingenue, interview,
IOU, jabiru, Jiangsu,
kangaroo, Kathmandu,
kinkajou, loup-garou, Makalu,
manitou, marabou, Masaru,
Montague, Montesquieu,
ormolu, overdo, overdue,
overflew, overgrew, overshoe,
overstrew, overthrough,

overview, parvenu, parvenue,
pas de deux, passe-partout,
PDQ, peekaboo, Port Salut,
rendezvous, residue, retinue,
revenue, Richelieu, Ryukyu,
seppuku, Shikoku, succès fou,
switcheroo, talking-to,
teleview, Telugu, thereunto,
thirty-two, thitherto,
Timbuktu, tinamou, trou-de-
loup, twenty-two, view
halloo, vindaloo, wallaroo,
waterloo, well-to-do, whoop-
de-do, Xanadu, Aracaju,
Brian Boru, didgeridoo,
hullabaloo, Kota Bharu, Nova
Iguaçu, Ouagadougou,
pirarucu, Port du Salut, tu-
whit tu-whoo, Vanuatu,
Daman and Diu, Guangxi
Zhuangzu, Ningxia Huizu,
Havant and Waterloo

²ew \ō\ see ¹OW
¹ewable \ō-ə-bəl\ see ¹OWABLE
²ewable \ü-ə-bəl\ see UABLE
ewage \ü-ij\ brewage, sewage
ewal \ü-əl\ see ¹UEL
ewar \ü-ər\ see ¹EWER
¹eward \ùrd\ see ¹URED
²eward \ü-ərd\ Seward, steward
ewd \üd\ see UDE
ewdness \üd-nəs\ see UDINOUS
¹ewe \ō\ see ¹OW
²ewe \ü\ see ¹EW
ewed \üd\ see UDE
ewee \ē-wē\ see EEWEE
ewel \ü-əl\ see ¹UEL
eweled \üld\ see OOLED
ewell \ü-əl\ see ¹UEL
¹ewer \ü-ər\ brewer, chewer,
dewar, doer, ewer, fewer,
hewer, queuer, screwer,

sewer, skewer, spewer, suer,
viewer, wooer, you're,
horseshoer, me-tooer,
misdoer, previewer, renewer,
reviewer, shampooer,
snowshoer, tattooer, undoer,
wrongdoer, barbecuer,
evildoer, interviewer,
revenuer, televiewer—*also
comparatives of adjectives
listed at* ¹EW

²**ewer** \ur\ see ¹URE
³**ewer** \ō-ər\ see ⁴OER
ewerage \ur-ij\ see ¹OORAGE
ewery \ur-ē\ see ¹URY
ewess \ü-əs\ Jewess, lewis,
Lewis, Louis, Luis, Port
Louis, Saint Louis
ewey \ü-ē\ see EWY
ewie \ü-ē\ see EWY
¹**ewing** \ō-iŋ\ see ¹OING
²**ewing** \u-iŋ\ see ²OING
ewis \ü-əs\ see EWESS
ewish \ü-ish\ bluish, Jewish,
newish, shrewish, aguish
ewl \ül\ see ¹OOL
ewless \ü-ləs\ clueless,
crewless, dewless, shoeless,
viewless
ewly \ü-lē\ see ULY
ewman \ü-mən\ see UMAN
ewment \ü-mənt\ strewment,
accruement
ewn \ün\ see ¹OON
ewness \ü-nəs\ blueness,
dueness, Eunice, newness,
skewness, Tunis, askewness
ewpie \ü-pē\ see OOPY
ewry \ur-ē\ see ¹URY
ews \üz\ see ²USE
ewsman \üz-mən\ bluesman,
newsman

ewsy \ü-zē\ see OOZY
ewt \üt\ see UTE
ewter \üt-ər\ see UTER
ewterer \üt-ər-ər\ see UITERER
ewton \üt-ᵊn\ see UTAN
ewy \ü-ē\ bluey, buoy, chewy,
Dewey, dewy, flooey, gluey,
gooey, hooey, Louie, Louis,
newie, phooey, rouille,
screwy, sloughy, viewy, chop
suey, mildewy, Port Louis,
ratatouille, waterzooi
ex \eks\ dex, ex, flex, hex, lex,
rex, Rex, sex, specs, vex, x,
annex, apex, carex, codex,
complex, convex, cortex,
culex, desex, duplex, DX,
fourplex, ibex, ilex, index,
Kleenex, Lastex, latex, mirex,
murex, MX, narthex, perplex,
Perspex, pollex, Pyrex, reflex,
remex, Rx, scolex, silex,
silvex, simplex, spandex,
telex, Tex-Mex, triplex,
unsex, vertex, videotex,
vortex, analects, belowdecks,
biconvex, circumflex, cross-
index, googolplex, haruspex,
intersex, Malcolm X,
Middlesex, multiplex, PBX,
pontifex, retroflex, spinifex,
subindex, unisex—*also
plurals and possessives of
nouns and third person
singular presents of verbs
listed at* ECK
exas \ek-səs\ see EXUS
exed \ekst\ see EXT
exedly \ek-səd-lē\ vexedly,
perplexedly
exer \ek-sər\ flexor, hexer,

duplexer, indexer,
multiplexer, demultiplexer
exia \ek-sē-ə\ dyslexia, anorexia
exic \ek-sik\ dyslexic, anorexic
exical \ek-si-kəl\ lexical,
indexical, nonlexical
exion \ek-shən\ see ECTION
exis \ek-səs\ see EXUS
exity \ek-sət-ē\ complexity,
convexity, perplexity
exor \ek-sər\ see EXER
ext \ekst\ next, sexed, sext, text,
vexed, context, deflexed,
inflexed, perplexed, plaintext,
pretext, reflexed, subtext,
urtext, ciphertext, oversexed,
teletext, undersexed—*also
pasts of verbs listed at* EX
extant \ek-stənt\ extant, sextant
exterous \ek-strəs\ dexterous,
ambidextrous
extrous \ek-strəs\ see
EXTEROUS
extual \eks-chəl\ textual,
contextual, subtextual
exual \eksh-wəl\ sexual,
asexual, bisexual, effectual,
pansexual, transsexual,
ambisexual, homosexual,
hypersexual, intersexual,
parasexual, psychosexual,
unisexual, heterosexual,
sociosexual, anti-intellectual
exural \ek-shrəl\ see ²ECTURAL
exus \ek-səs\ lexis, nexus,
plexus, texas, Texas, Alexis
exy \ek-sē\ prexy, sexy,
apoplexy
¹ey \ā\ see ¹AY
²ey \ē\ see ¹EE
³ey \ī\ see ¹Y
¹eya \ā-ə\ see ¹AIA

²eya \ē-ə\ see ¹IA
eyance \ā-əns\ abeyance,
conveyance, purveyance,
surveillance, reconveyance
eyant \ā-ənt\ mayn't, abeyant,
surveillant
eyas \ī-əs\ see IAS
ey'd \ād\ see ¹ADE
eye \ī\ see ¹Y
¹eyed \ēd\ see EED
²eyed \īd\ see ¹IDE
eyedness \īd-nəs\ eyedness,
snideness, cockeyedness
eyeless \ī-ləs\ see ILUS
eyelet \ī-lət\ see ILOT
eyen \īn\ see ¹INE
¹eyer \ā-ər\ see ¹AYER
²eyer \īr\ see ¹IRE
eyes \īz\ see IZE
eying \ā-iŋ\ see AYING
¹ey'll \āl\ see AIL
²ey'll \el\ see ¹EL
eyn \in\ see ¹IN
eynes \ānz\ see AINS
eyness \ā-nəs\ see AYNESS
eyor \ā-ər\ see ¹AYER
ey're \er\ see ⁴ARE
eyre \er\ see ⁴ARE
eyrie \īr-ē\ see ¹IRY
eys \ēz\ see EZE
eyser \ī-zər\ see IZER
eyte \ā-tē\ see ATY
ey've \āv\ see ²AVE
¹ez \ez\ see ¹AYS
²ez \ā\ see ¹AY
³ez \ās\ see ¹ACE
eza \ē-zə\ Giza, Lisa, Pisa, visa,
mestiza, lespedeza
eze \ēz\ bise, breeze, cheese,
ease, feaze, feeze, freeze,
frieze, he's, jeez, lees, please,
res, seize, she's, sleaze,

sneeze, squeeze, tease,
tweeze, wheeze, Andes,
appease, Aries, Belize, betise,
Burmese, camise, Castries,
cerise, chemise, Chinese,
deep-freeze, Deep-freeze,
degrease, Denise, disease,
displease, disseise, d.t.'s,
Elise, fasces, fauces, Ganges,
headcheese, heartsease,
Hermes, Kirghiz, Louise,
Maltese, marquise, menses,
nates, Pisces, quick-freeze,
Ramses, reprise, sharp-freeze,
soubise, striptease, Tabriz,
Thales, trapeze, unease,
unfreeze, Xerxes, Amboinese,
Androcles, Annamese,
antifreeze, Assamese,
Balinese, Brooklynese,
Cantonese, Cervantes,
Chersonese, Congolese,
Cyclades. Damocles, diocese,
Eloise, Erinyes, expertise,
Faeroese, federalese,
genovese, gourmandise,
Hebrides, Heracles, Hercules,
Hunanese, Hyades, Japanese,
Javanese, Johnsonese,
journalese, Kanarese, Lake
Louise, legalese, litotes,
manganese, Nipponese,
overseas, Pekinese,
Pekingese, Pericles, Pleiades,
Portuguese, Pyrenees,
Siamese, Silures, Sinhalese,
Socrates, Sophocles,
Sporades, Albigenses,
antipodes, Aragonese,
archdiocese, Averroës, bona
fides, bureaucratese, cheval-
de-frise, computerese,
Diogenes, Dodecanese,
Eumenides, Euripides, Florida
Keys, Gaucher's disease,
governmentese, Great
Pyrenees, Hesperides,
Hippocrates, Hippomenes,
Hodgkin's disease, Indo-
Chinese, nephritides,
officialese, pentagonese,
Philoctetes, Sammarinese,
superficies, telegraphese,
Themistocles, Thucydides,
Vietnamese, Alcibiades,
Aristophanes, educationese,
ferromanganese, Lou Gehrig's
disease, Mephistopheles,
sociologese, sword of
Damocles, muscae volitantes,
Pillars of Hercules—*also
plurals and possessives of
nouns and third person
singular presents of verbs
listed at* ¹EE

ezel \ē-zəl\ see EASEL
ezi \ē-zē\ see ¹EASY
ezium \ē-zē-əm\ cesium,
  magnesium, trapezium
ezzle \ez-əl\ bezel, embezzle

i

¹**i** \ē\ see ¹EE

²**i** \ī\ see ¹Y

³**i** \ā\ see ¹AY

¹**ia** \ē-ə\ Gaea, kea, Leah, Mia, rhea, Rhea, rya, via, Achaea, Crimea, althaea, Apia, Bahia, buddleia, cabrilla, cattleya, Chaldea, Euboea, Hygeia, idea, Judea, Kaffiyeh, Korea, mantilla, Maria, Medea, mens rea, Morea, Nicaea, ohia, Omiya, Oriya, ouguiya, rupiah, sangria, Sofia, Sophia, spirea, tortilla, Baile Atha Cliath, Banranquilla, barathea, bougainvillea, camarilla, Caesarea, cascarilla, Cytherea, dulcinea, Eritrea, fantasia, Galatea, gonorrhea, granadilla, hamartia, Hialeah, Idumea, Ikaria, Jicarilla, Kampuchea, latakia, Latakia, logorrhea, Manzanilla, mausolea, mythopoeia, Nabatea, Nicosia, panacea, Parousia, pizzeria, ratafia, sabadilla, Santeria, sapodilla, seguidilla, sinfonia, Tanzania, trattoria, alfilaria, Andalucia, Andalusia, Ave Maria, Cassiopeia, Diego Garcia, echeveria, Ismailia, peripeteia, pharmacopoeia, prosopopoeia, onomatopoeia, Joseph of Arimathea

²**ia** \ī-ə\ see ¹IAH

³**ia** \ä\ see ¹A

¹**iable** \ī-ə-bəl\ dryable, dyeable, flyable, friable, liable, pliable, triable, viable, deniable, inviable, reliable, certifiable, classifiable, justifiable, liquefiable, notifiable, pacifiable, qualifiable, quantifiable, rectifiable, satisfiable, specifiable, undeniable, unifiable, verifiable, emulsifiable, identifiable, unfalsifiable

²**iable** \ē-ə-bəl\ see EEABLE

iacal \ī-ə-kəl\ dandiacal, heliacal, maniacal, theriacal, zodiacal, ammoniacal, elegiacal, simoniacal, dipsomaniacal, egomaniacal, hypochondriacal, monomaniacal, nympomaniacal, pyromaniacal, paradisiacal, bibliomaniacal, megalomaniacal

iad \ī-əd\ see YAD

¹**iah** \ī-ə\ ayah, maya, Maya, playa, Praia, stria, via, Aglaia, Mariah, messiah, papaya, pariah, Thalia, Hezekiah, jambalaya, Jeremiah, Nehemiah, Obadiah, Surabaja, Zechariah, Zephaniah, Atchafalaya, Iphigenia, peripeteia

²**iah** \ē-ə\ see ¹IA

¹**ial** \ī-əl\ dial, diel, pial, redial

²**ial** \īl\ see ¹ILE

ialer \ī-lər\ see ILAR

ially \ē-ə-lē\ see ¹EALLY

iam \ī-əm\ Priam, per diem

¹**ian** \ē-ən\ see ¹EAN

²**ian** \ī-ən\ see ¹ION

iance \ī-əns\ science, affiance, alliance, appliance, compliance, defiance, nonscience, reliance, mesalliance, misalliance

iancy \ī-ən-sē\ pliancy, compliancy

ianist \ē-t-nist\ pianist, Indo-Europeanist

iant \ī-ənt\ Bryant, client, giant, pliant, riant, affiant, compliant, defiant, reliant, incompliant, self-reliant, supergiant

iao \aú\ see ²OW

iaour \aúr\ see ²OWER

iaper \ī-pər\ see IPER

iar \īr\ see ¹IRE

¹**iary** \ī-ə-rē\ diary, fiery, miry, priory

²**iary** \īr-ē\ see ¹IRY

¹**ias** \ī-əs\ Aias, bias, dais, eyas, Laius, Lias, pious, Pius, Abdias, Elias, Messias, Nehemias, Tobias, Ananias, Jeremias, Malachias, Roncesvalles, Sophonias, Zacharias, Mount Saint Elias

²**ias** \ē-əs\ see ¹EUS

³**ias** \äsh\ see ¹ASH

iasis \ī-ə-səs\ diesis, diocese, archdiocese, psoriasis, acariasis, amebiasis, ascariasis, bilharziasis, helminthiasis, leishmaniasis, satyriasis, elephantiasis, hypochondriasis, schistosomiasis

¹**iat** \ē-ət\ see ¹EIT

²**iat** \ī-ət\ see IET

iate \ī-ət\ see IET

¹**iath** \ī-əth\ Wyeth, Goliath

²**iath** \ē-ə\ see ¹IA

iatry \ī-ə-trē\ podiatry, psychiatry

iaus \aús\ see ²OUSE

iaz \äsh\ see ¹ASH

¹**ib** \ib\ bib, bibb, crib, drib, fib, gib, glib, jib, lib, nib, rib, sib, squib, ad-lib, corncrib, midrib, sahib, memsahib

²**ib** \ēb\ see ²EBE

³**ib** \ēv\ see ¹EAVE

iba \ē-bə\ see EBA

ibable \ī-bə-bəl\ bribable, ascribable, describable, indescribable

ibal \ī-bəl\ bible, Bible, libel, scribal, tribal

ibb \ib\ see ¹IB

ibband \ib-ən\ see IBBON

ibbed \ibd\ bibbed, rock-ribbed—*also pasts of verbs listed at* ¹IB

ibber \ib-ər\ bibber, cribber, dibber, fibber, gibber, glibber, jibber, libber, ribber

ibbet \ib-ət\ gibbet, exhibit, inhibit, prohibit, flibbertigibbet

ibbing \ib-iŋ\ cribbing, ribbing

ibble \ib-əl\ dibble, dribble, fribble, gribble, kibble, nibble, quibble, scribble, sibyl, Sibyl

ibbler \ib-lər\ dribbler, nibbler, quibbler, scribbler

ibbly \ib-lē\ dribbly, ghibli, glibly

ibbon \ib-ən\ gibbon, Gibbon, ribbon, inhibin

ibby \ib-ē\ Libby, ribby

¹ibe \īb\ bribe, gibe, gybe, jibe, kibe, scribe, tribe, vibe, ascribe, conscribe, describe, imbibe, inscribe, prescribe, proscribe, subscribe, transcribe, circumscribe, diatribe, redescribe, superscribe, oversubscribe

²ibe \ē-bē\ see ¹EBE

ibel \ī-bəl\ see IBAL

iber \ī-bər\ briber, fiber, giber, Khyber, scriber, Tiber, describer, inscriber, prescriber, proscriber, subscriber, transcriber

ibi \ē-bē\ see ¹EBE

ibia \i-bē-ə\ Lybia, tibia, Namibia

ibin \ib-ən\ see IBBON

ibit \ib-ət\ see IBBET

ibitive \ib-ət-iv\ exhibitive, prohibitive

ibitor \ib-ət-ər\ exhibitor, inhibitor, ACE inhibitor

ible \ī-bəl\ see IBAL

iblet \ib-lət\ driblet, giblet, riblet

ibli \ib-lē\ see IBBLY

ibly \ib-lē\ see IBBLY

ibo \ē-bō\ Ibo, Kibo, gazebo

iboly \i-ə-lē\ see YBELE

ibrous \ī-brəs\ fibrous, hybris

ibs \ibz\ dibs, nibs, spareribs— *also plurals and possessives of nouns and third person singular presents of verbs listed at* ¹IB

ibular \ib-yə-lər\ fibular, mandibular, vestibular, infundibular

¹ibute \ib-yət\ tribute, attribute, contribute, distribute, redistribute

²ibute \ib-ət\ see IBBET

ibutive \ib-yət-iv\ attributive, contributive, distributive, retributive, redistributive

ibutor \ib-ət-ər\ see IBITOR

ibyl \ib-əl\ see IBBLE

¹ic \ik\ see ICK

²ic \ēk\ see ¹EAK

¹ica \ī-kə\ mica, Micah, pica, pika, plica, spica, Spica, Formica, lorica, balalaika

²ica \ē-kə\ see ¹IKA

icable \ik-ə-bəl\ despicable, explicable, extricable, inexplicable, inextricable

icah \ī-kə\ see ¹ICA

ical \ik-əl\ see ICKLE

icament \ik-ə-mənt\ medicament, predicament

ican \ē-kən\ see EACON

icar \ik-ər\ see ¹ICKER

icative \ik-ət-iv\ fricative, siccative, affricative, explicative, indicative, vindicative, multiplicative

iccative \ik-ət-iv\ see ICATIVE

iccio \ē-chō\ capriccio, pasticcio

¹ice \īs\ Bryce, dice, fice, fyce, gneiss, ice, lice, lyse, mice, nice, pice, price, rice, rise, slice, spice, splice, syce, thrice, trice, twice, vice, vise, advice, allspice, Brandeis, bride-price, concise, cut-price, deice, device, entice, excise, precise, suffice, beggars-lice, cockatrice, edelweiss,

imprecise, merchandise,
overprice, paradise, point-
device, sacrifice, underprice,
imparadise, self-sacrifice

²**ice** \ē-chā\ see ¹ICHE

³**ice** \ēs\ see IECE

⁴**ice** \ī-sē\ see ICY

⁵**ice** \īz\ see IZE

⁶**ice** \ēt-zə\ see ¹ITZA

iceless \ī-sləs\ iceless, priceless

icely \is-lē\ see ISTLY

iceous \ish-əs\ see ¹ICIOUS

icer \ī-sər\ dicer, Dreiser, nicer,
pricer, ricer, slicer, splicer,
deicer, sufficer, sacrificer,
self-sacrificer

ices \ī-sēz\ Pisces, Anchises,
Polynices, Coma Berenices

icety \ī-stē\ see EISTY

icey \ī-sē\ see ICY

¹**ich** \ich\ see ITCH

²**ich** \ik\ see ICK

ichael \ī-kəl\ see ¹YCLE

¹**iche** \ē-chā\ ceviche, seviche,
Beatrice, cantatrice

²**iche** \ēsh\ fiche, leash, quiche,
sneesh, baksheesh, corniche,
hashish, maxixe, pastiche,
schottische, unleash,
microfiche, nouveau riche

³**iche** \ish\ see ¹ISH

⁴**iche** \ich\ see ITCH

⁵**iche** \ē-chē\ see EACHY

¹**ichen** \ī-kən\ lichen, liken,
proteoglycan

²**ichen** \ich-ən\ see ITCHEN

ichener \ich-nər\ see ITCHENER

icher \ich-ər\ see ITCHER

iches \ich-əz\ see ITCHES

¹**ichi** \ē-chē\ see EACHY

²**ichi** \ē-shē\ see ISHI

ichment \ich-mənt\ see
ITCHMENT

ichore \ik-rē\ see ICKERY

ichu \ish-ü\ see ¹ISSUE

¹**icia** \ish-ə\ see ITIA

²**icia** \ēsh-ə\ see ¹ESIA

icial \ish-əl\ altricial, comitial,
initial, judicial, official,
simplicial, solstitial, surficial,
artificial, beneficial,
cicatricial, interstitial,
prejudicial, sacrificial,
superficial

ician \ē-shən\ see ¹ETION

icience \ish-əns\ omniscience,
insufficience

iciency \ish-ən-sē\ deficiency,
efficiency, proficiency,
sufficiency, inefficiency,
immunodeficiency

icient \ish-ənt\ deficient,
efficient, omniscient,
proficient, sufficient,
coefficient, cost-efficient,
inefficient, insufficient, self-
sufficient

icinable \is-nə-bəl\ see
ISTENABLE

icinal \is-ᵊn-əl\ vicinal,
medicinal, officinal, vaticinal

¹**icing** \ī-siŋ\ icing, splicing,
self-sufficing

²**icing** \ī-ziŋ\ see IZING

¹**icious** \ish-əs\ vicious,
ambitious, auspicious,
capricious, delicious,
factitious, fictitious, flagitious,
judicious, lubricious,
malicious, Mauritius,
nutritious, officious,
pernicious, propitious,
pumiceous, seditious,

sericeous, suspicious,
adscititious, adventitious,
avaricious, expeditious,
inauspicious, injudicious,
meretricious, prejudicious,
subreptitious, superstitious,
supposititious, surreptitious,
excrementitious, supposititious

²**icious** \ē-shəs\ see ECIOUS

icipal \is-ə-bəl\ see ISSIBLE

icipant \is-ə-pənt\ anticipant,
participant

icit \is-ət\ licit, complicit, elicit,
explicit, illicit, implicit,
solicit, inexplicit

¹**icitor** \is-ət-ər\ elicitor,
solicitor

²**icitor** \is-tər\ see ISTER

icitous \is-ət-əs\ complicitous,
duplicitous, felicitous,
solicitous, infelicitous

¹**icity** \is-ət-ē\ basicity,
causticity, centricity,
chronicity, complicity,
conicity, cyclicity, duplicity,
ethnicity, felicity, lubricity,
mendicity, plasticity,
publicity, rhythmicity,
seismicity, simplicity,
spasticity, sphericity, tonicity,
toxicity, triplicity, atomicity,
authenticity, canonicity,
catholicity, concentricity,
domesticity, eccentricity,
elasticity, electricity,
ellipticity, endemicity,
ergodicity, historicity,
iconicity, impudicity,
infelicity, multiplicity,
organicity, pneumaticity,
quadruplicity, specificity,
synchronicity, volcanicity,

aperiodicity, aromaticity,
automaticity, ecumenicity,
egocentricity, epidemicity,
ethnocentricity,
hydrophilicity,
hydrophobicity,
inauthenticity, inelasticity,
pathogenicity, periodicity,
theocentricity, aeroelasticity,
anthropocentricity,
carcinogenicity,
homoscedasticity,
quasiperiodicity

²**icity** \is-tē\ christie, Christie,
misty, twisty, wristy, Corpus
Christi, sacahuiste

ick \ik\ brick, chick, click,
crick, creek, Dick, flick, hick,
kick, KWIC, lick, mick, nick,
Nick, pic, pick, prick, quick,
rick, shtick, sic, sick, slick,
snick, spick, stick, strick,
thick, tic, tick, trick, wick,
airsick, alsike, bluetick,
bootlick, boychick, brainsick,
broomstick, carsick,
chopstick, cowlick, crabstick,
dabchick, dead-stick, detick,
dik-dik, dipstick, drop-kick,
drumstick, firebrick, flagstick,
goldbrick, greensick,
handpick, hayrick, heartsick,
homesick, joystick, lipstick,
lovesick, matchstick, moujik,
muzhik, nightstick, nitpick,
nonstick, nutpick, outslick,
peacenik, pigstick, pinprick,
placekick, redbrick, rubric,
seasick, self-stick, shashlik,
sidekick, slapstick, slipstick,
Tajik, toothpick, topkick,
unpick, unstick, uptick,

yardstick, bailiwick, biopic,
Bolshevik, candlestick,
candlewick, Dominic,
dominick, Dominick, double-
quick, EBCDIC, fiddlestick,
hemistich, heretic, lunatic,
Menshevik, meterstick,
overtrick, politic, politick,
polyptych, Reykjavik,
singlestick, taperstick,
undertrick, Watson-Crick,
arithmetic, carrot-and-stick,
computernik, impolitic,
kinnikinnick

icka \ē-kə\ see ¹IKA

¹**icked** \ik-əd\ picked, wicked

²**icked** \ikt\ see ¹ICT

ickel \ik-əl\ see ICKLE

icken \ik-ən\ chicken, quicken,
sicken, stricken, thicken,
awestricken, panic-stricken,
planet-stricken, poverty-
stricken

ickens \ik-ənz\ dickens,
Dickens, pickings—*also
plurals and possessives of
nouns and third person
singular presents of verbs
listed at* ICKEN

¹**icker** \ik-ər\ bicker, dicker,
flicker, icker, licker, liquor,
nicker, picker, pricker, sicker,
slicker, snicker, sticker, ticker,
tricker, vicar, whicker,
wicker, billsticker, bootlicker,
dropkicker, flea-flicker,
nitpicker, pigsticker,
placekicker, pot likker,
ragpicker, dominicker,
politicker—*also comparatives
of adjectives listed at* ICK

²**icker** \ek-ər\ see ECKER

ickery \ik-rē\ chicory, flickery,
hickory, snickery, trickery,
Terpsichore

icket \ik-ət\ cricket, picket,
Pickett, pricket, spigot,
stickit, thicket, ticket,
wicket, Big Thicket, big-
ticket

ickett \ik-ət\ see ICKET

ickety \ik-ət-ē\ rickety,
thickety, pernickety,
persnickety

ickey \ik-ē\ see ICKY

icki \ik-ē\ see ICKY

ickie \ik-ē\ see ICKY

icking \ik-iŋ\ ticking, wicking,
brain-picking, flat-picking,
high-sticking, nit-picking,
cotton-picking, finger-picking

ickings \ik-ənz\ see ICKENS

ickish \ik-ish\ hickish, sickish,
trickish

ickit \ik-ət\ see ICKET

ickle \ik-əl\ brickle, chicle,
fickle, mickle, nickel, pickle,
picul, prickle, sickle, stickle,
strickle, tical, tickle, trickle,
bicycle, icicle, obstacle,
Popsicle, spectacle, tricycle,
vehicle, pumpernickel

ickler \ik-lər\ stickler, tickler,
bicycler, particular

ickly \ik-lē\ fickly, prickly,
quickly, sickly, slickly,
impoliticly

ickness \ik-nəs\ lychnis,
quickness, sickness, slickness,
thickness, airsickness,
heartsickness, homesickness,
lovesickness, seasickness

icksy \ik-sē\ see IXIE

icky \ik-ē\ dickey, hickey, icky,

kicky, Mickey, picky, quickie,
rickey, sickie, sticky, tricky,
Vicki, Vickie, Vicky,
doohickey
icle \ik-əl\ see ICKLE
¹icly \ik-lē\ see ICKLY
²icly \ē-klē\ see EEKLY
ico \ē-kō\ see ICOT
icope \ik-ə-pē\ see ICOPY
icopy \ik-ə-pē\ wicopy,
  pericope
icory \ik-rē\ see ICKERY
icot \ē-kō\ fico, pekoe, picot,
  tricot, Tampico, Puerto Rico
ics \iks\ see ¹IX
¹ict \ikt\ picked, Pict, strict,
  ticked, addict, afflict, conflict,
  constrict, convict, delict,
  depict, edict, evict, inflict,
  lipsticked, predict, restrict,
  unlicked, benedict, Benedict,
  contradict, derelict, interdict,
  maledict, retrodict, eggs
  Benedict—*also pasts of verbs
  listed at* ICK
²ict \īt\ see ¹ITE
ictable \īt-ə-bəl\ see ¹ITABLE
ictal \ik-tᵊl\ fictile, rictal, edictal
icted \ik-təd\ conflicted,
  evicted, restricted—*also pasts
  of verbs listed at* ICT
icter \ik-tər\ see ICTOR
ictic \ik-tik\ deictic, panmictic,
  amphimictic, apodictic
ictile \ik-tᵊl\ see ICTAL
ictim \ik-təm\ see ICTUM
iction \ik-shən\ diction, fiction,
  friction, stiction, addiction,
  affliction, confliction,
  constriction, conviction,
  depiction, eviction,
  indiction, infliction,

nonfiction, prediction,
reliction, restriction,
transfixion, benediction,
contradiction, crucifixion,
dereliction, jurisdiction,
malediction, metafiction,
valediction
ictional \ik-shnəl\ fictional,
  frictional, nonfictional,
  jurisdictional
ictionist \ik-shnəst\ fictionist,
  restrictionist
ictive \ik-tiv\ fictive, addictive,
  afflictive, conflictive,
  constrictive, inflictive,
  restrictive, vindictive,
  nonrestrictive
ictment \īt-mənt\ see ITEMENT
ictor \ik-tər\ lictor, stricter,
  victor, constrictor, depicter,
  evictor, inflicter, contradictor,
  vasoconstrictor
ictory \ik-tə-rē\ victory,
  benedictory, contradictory,
  maledictory, valedictory
ictual \it-ᵊl\ see ITTLE
ictualler \it-ᵊl-ər\ see ITALER
ictum \ik-təm\ dictum, victim,
  obiter dictum
icture \ik-chər\ picture,
  stricture
icul \ik-əl\ see ICKLE
icula \ik-yə-lə\ auricula,
  Canicula
iculant \ik-yə-lənt\ gesticulant,
  matriculant
¹icular \ik-yə-lər\ spicular,
  acicular, articular, auricular,
  canicular, clavicular,
  curricular, cuticular,
  fascicular, follicular,
  funicular, lenticular,

navicular, orbicular, ossicular,
particular, radicular, reticular,
testicular, vehicular,
ventricular, vermicular,
versicular, vesicular,
appendicular, perpendicular,
extracurricular, extravehicular,
intra-articular,
supraventricular

²icular \ik-lər\ see ICKLER

icularly \ik-lē\ see ICKLY

iculate \ik-yə-lət\ articulate,
denticulate, geniculate,
particulate, reticulate,
straticulate, vermiculate,
inarticulate

iculous \ik-yə-ləs\ meticulous,
pediculous, ridiculous

iculum \ik-yə-ləm\ curriculum,
reticulum, diverticulum

icuous \ik-yə-wəs\ conspicuous,
perspicuous, transpicuous,
inconspicuous

icy \ī-sē\ dicey, icy, pricey,
spicy

¹id \id\ bid, chid, Cid, did, fid,
gid, grid, hid, id, kid, Kidd,
lid, mid, quid, rid, skid, slid,
squid, SQUID, whid, Yid,
amid, backslid, bifid, El Cid,
equid, eyelid, forbid,
grandkid, Madrid, nonskid,
outdid, resid, schoolkid, trifid,
undid, katydid, ootid, overbid,
overdid, pyramid, underbid,
tertium quid, Valadolid

²id \ēd\ see EED

I'd \īd\ see ¹IDE

¹ida \ēd-ə\ see ¹EDA

²ida \ī-də\ Haida, Ida, Vida

¹idable \īd-ə-bəl\ guidable,
decidable, dividable,
subdividable

²idable \id-ə-bəl\ see IDDABLE

idal \īd-ᵊl\ bridal, bridle, idle,
idol, idyll, seidel, sidle, tidal,
unbridle, Barmecidal,
fratricidal, fungicidal,
genocidal, germicidal,
herbicidal, homicidal,
intertidal, lunitidal, matricidal,
parricidal, patricidal,
septicidal, spermicidal,
suicidal, viricidal, virucidal,
bactericidal, infanticidal,
insecticidal

idance \īd-ᵊns\ guidance,
stridence, abidance,
misguidance

idas \īd-əs\ Midas, nidus

iday \īd-ē\ Friday, Heidi, tidy,
vide, alcaide, man Friday,
untidy, mala fide

idays \īd-ēz\ see ¹IDES

idd \id\ see ¹ID

iddable \id-ə-bəl\ biddable,
formidable

iddance \id-ᵊns\ riddance,
forbiddance

idden \id-ᵊn\ bidden, chiden,
hidden, midden, ridden,
stridden, swidden,
backslidden, bedridden,
bestridden, forbidden,
outbidden, unbidden,
overridden

idder \id-ər\ bidder, gridder,
kidder, siddur, skidder,
consider, forbidder,
reconsider, underbidder

iddie \id-ē\ see IDDY

iddish \id-ish\ kiddish, Yiddish

iddity \id-ət-ē\ see IDITY

iddle \id-ᵊl\ diddle, fiddle,
   griddle, middle, piddle, riddle,
   twiddle, unriddle, paradiddle,
   taradiddle
iddler \id-lər\ diddler, fiddler,
   middler, riddler, tiddler,
iddling \id-liŋ\ fiddling,
   middling, piddling, riddling
iddly \id-le\ diddly, ridley,
   tiddly
iddock \id-ik\ see IDIC
iddur \id-ər\ see IDDER
iddy \id-ē\ biddy, giddy, kiddie,
   middy, midi, skiddy, widdy
¹ide \īd\ bide, bride, chide,
   Clyde, eyed, fried, glide,
   guide, hide, I'd, pied, plied,
   pride, ride, side, slide, snide,
   stride, thighed, tide, tried,
   wide, abide, allied, applied,
   aside, astride, backside,
   backslide, bankside,
   beachside, bedside, beside,
   bestride, betide, blear-eyed,
   blindside, blowdried, blue-
   eyed, broadside, bromide,
   bug-eyed, Burnside, clear-
   eyed, cockeyed, cold-eyed,
   collide, confide, courtside,
   cowhide, cross-eyed,
   curbside, dayside, decide,
   deride, divide, dockside, doe-
   eyed, downside, dry-eyed,
   elide, fireside, foreside, four-
   eyed, freeze-dried, glass-eyed,
   graveside, green-eyed,
   hagride, hawkeyed, hayride,
   hillside, horsehide, inside,
   ironside, joyride, kingside,
   lakeside, landslide, lynx-eyed,
   misguide, moon-eyed,
   nearside, nightside, noontide,

offside, onside, outride,
   outside, pie-eyed, poolside,
   pop-eyed, preside, provide,
   quayside, queenside, rawhide,
   reside, ringside, riptide,
   roadside, seaside, sharp-eyed,
   shipside, shoreside,
   Shrovetide, sloe-eyed,
   snowslide, springtide, squint-
   eyed, stateside, statewide,
   storewide, Strathclyde,
   streamside, subside, tailslide,
   Tayside, tongue-tied, topside,
   trackside, trailside, untried,
   upside, vat-dyed, walleyed,
   waveguide, wayside, wide-
   eyed, wild-eyed, worldwide,
   yuletide, alkoxide, almond-
   eyed, alongside, Argus-eyed,
   Barmecide, bleary-eyed, bona
   fide, chicken-fried,
   Christmastide, citified,
   citywide, classified, coincide,
   countrified, countryside,
   countrywide, cut-and-dried,
   cyanide, deicide, demand-
   side, dewy-eyed, dignified,
   double-wide, downslide,
   Eastertide, eventide, feticide,
   fluoride, formamide,
   fratricide, fungicide,
   genocide, germicide, gimlet-
   eyed, glassy-eyed, goggle-
   eyed, googly-eyed, harbor-
   side, herbicide, homicide,
   Humberside, humified,
   matricide, Merseyside,
   misty-eyed, miticide,
   monoxide, mountainside,
   nationwide, Naugahyde,
   open-eyed, override,
   overstride, parricide,

Passiontide, patricide, pesticide, planetwide, qualified, rarefied, raticide, regicide, riverside, Riverside, set-aside, silverside, sissified, slickenside, spermicide, starry-eyed, subdivide, suicide, supply-side, trisulfide, underside, verbicide, vermicide, viricide, waterside, Whitsuntide, wintertide, acrylamide, antimonide, borohydride, dissatisfied, formaldehyde, infanticide, insecticide, interallied, Jekyll and Hyde, preoccupied, rodenticide, self-satisfied, thalidomide, Trinitytide, tyrannicide, uxoricide, monoglyceride, overqualified, parasiticide—*also pasts of verbs listed at* [1]Y

[2]**ide** \ēd\ *see* EED

idean \id-ē-ən\ *see* IDIAN

ided \īd-əd\ sided, lopsided, misguided, one-sided, slab-sided, two-sided, many-sided, sobersided—*also pasts of verbs listed at* [1]IDE

ideless \īd-ləs\ idlesse, tideless

iden \īd-ᵊn\ guidon, Hayden, widen, Poseidon

idence \īd-ᵊns\ *see* IDANCE

ideness \īd-nəs\ *see* EYEDNESS

ident \īd-ᵊnt\ strident, trident

ideon \id-ē-ən\ *see* IDIAN

ideous \id-ē-əs\ *see* IDIOUS

[1]**ider** \īd-ər\ bider, cider, eider, glider, guider, hider, rider, slider, spider, strider, stridor, abider, backslider, confider, decider, derider, divider, insider, joyrider, misguider, outrider, outsider, presider, provider, resider, rough rider, Top-Sider, subdivider, supply-sider, supercollider—*also comparatives of adjectives listed at* [1]IDE

[2]**ider** \id-ər\ *see* IDDER

[1]**ides** \īd-ēz\ Fridays, Aristides—*also plurals and possessives of nouns and third person singular presents of verbs listed at* IDAY

[2]**ides** \īdz\ ides, besides, burnsides, silversides, sobersides—*also plurals and possessives of nouns and third person singular presents of verbs listed at* [1]IDE

idge \ij\ bridge, fidge, fridge, midge, ridge, abridge, Blue Ridge, browridge, drawbridge, footbridge, Oxbridge, teethridge

idged \ijd\ ridged, unabridged—*also pasts of verbs listed at* IDGE

idgen \ij-ən\ *see* YGIAN

idget \ij-ət\ Brigitte, digit, fidget, midget, widget, double-digit

idgin \ij-ən\ *see* YGIAN

idi \id-ē\ *see* IDDY

idia \i-dē-ə\ Lydia, basidia, chlamydia, clostridia, coccidia, conidia, glochidia, nephridia, Numidia, oidia, peridia, Pisidia, presidia, pycnidia, pygidia, antheridia, enchiridia, hesperidia, miricidia, ommatidia

idian \id-ē-ən\ Gideon, Lydian,
Midian, ascidian, Dravidian,
euclidean, Floridian,
meridian, obsidian, ophidian,
quotidian, viridian,
enchiridion, non-euclidean

idic \id-ik\ piddock, acidic,
bromidic, Davidic, druidic,
fatidic, fluidic, Hasidic,
nuclidic

idical \id-i-kəl\ druidical,
fatidical, juridical, veridical,
pyramidical

idice \id-ə-sē\ Chalcidice,
Eurydice

idiem \id-ē-əm\ idiom, iridium,
presidium, rubidium, post
meridiem, ante meridiem

iding \īd-iŋ\ riding, Riding,
siding, tiding, abiding,
confiding, East Riding,
joyriding, West Riding, law-
abiding, nondividing

idiom \id-ē-əm\ see IDIEM

idious \id-ē-əs\ hideous,
fastidious, insidious,
invidious, perfidious

idity \id-ət-ē\ quiddity, acidity,
aridity, avidity, cupidity,
fluidity, flaccidity, floridity,
frigidity, gelidity, gravidity,
hispidity, humidity, hybridity,
limpidity, liquidity, lividity,
lucidity, morbidity, rabidity,
rapidity, rigidity, sapidity,
solidity, stupidity, tepidity,
timidity, torridity, turbidity,
turgidity, validity, vapidity,
viridity, viscidity, illiquidity,
insipidity, intrepidity,
invalidity

idium \id-ē-əm\ see IDIEM

idle \īd-ᵊl\ see IDAL

idlesse \īd-ləs\ see IDELESS

idley \id-lē\ see IDDLY

idney \id-nē\ kidney, Sidney,
Sydney

¹ido \īd-ō\ dido, Dido, fido,
Hokkaido

²ido \ēd-ō\ see ¹EDO

idol \īd-ᵊl\ see IDAL

¹idz \idz\ Beskids, rapids,
Grand Rapids—*also plurals
of nouns listed at* ¹ID

²ids \ēdz\ see EEDS

idst \idst\ didst, midst, amidst

¹idual \ij-wəl\ residual,
individual

²idual \ij-əl\ see IGIL

idulent \ij-ə-lənt\ see IGILANT

idulous \ij-ə-ləs\ stridulous,
acidulous

idus \īd-əs\ see IDAS

iduum \ij-ə-wəm\ triduum,
residuum

idy \īd-ē\ see IDAY

idyll \īd-ᵊl\ see IDAL

¹ie \ā\ see ¹AY

²ie \ē\ see ¹EE

³ie \ī\ see ¹Y

iece \ēs\ cease, crease, fleece,
grease, Greece, kris, lease,
Nice, niece, peace, piece,
apiece, Bernice, Burmese,
camise, caprice, cassis, cerise,
chemise, Chinese, Clarice,
Cochise, codpiece, coulisse,
crosspiece, decease, decrease,
degrease, Denise, Dumfries,
earpiece, Elise, eyepiece,
Felice, fieldpiece, grandniece,
hairpiece, headpiece,
heelpiece, increase, Janice,
lend-lease, Matisse, Maurice,

mouthpiece, nosepiece, obese, patsis, pelisse, police, release, release, seapiece, shankpiece, showpiece, sidepiece, stringpiece, sublease, surcease, tailpiece, Therese, timepiece, toepiece, two-piece, valise, workpiece, afterpiece, altarpiece, Amboinese, Annamese, Assamese, Balinese, Brooklynese, Cantonese, centerpiece, Chersonese, chimneypiece, diocese, directrice, ex libris, expertise, Faeroese, frontispiece, mantelpiece, masterpiece, Nipponese, Pekinese, Pekingese, Portugese, predecease, rerelease, São Luis, Siamese, Sinhalese, timed-release, verdigris, archdiocese, computerese, Dodecanese, officialese, telegraphese, Vietnamese, educationese

iecer \ē-sər\ see ¹EASER

¹ied \ēd\ see EED

²ied \ēt\ see ¹EAT

³ied \īd\ see ¹IDE

ieda \ēd-ə\ see ¹EDA

¹ief \ēf\ beef, brief, chief, fief, grief, kef, leaf, lief, reef, sheaf, thief, belief, debrief, endleaf, enfeoff, flyleaf, loose-leaf, massif, motif, naif, O'Keefe, relief, sharif, sherif, shinleaf, bas-relief, cloverleaf, disbelief, handkerchief, leatherleaf, neckerchief, leitmotiv, misbelief, overleaf, unbelief, waterleaf, aperitif,

Capitol Reef, Vinson Massif, Great Berrier Reef, Santa Cruz de Tenerife

²ief \ēv\ see ¹EAVE

iefless \ē-fləs\ briefless, leafless

iefly \ē-flē\ briefly, chiefly

¹ieg \ēg\ see IGUE

²ieg \ig\ see IG

¹iege \ēj\ liege, siege, besiege, prestige

²iege \ēzh\ see ¹IGE

ieger \ē-jər\ see EDURE

iek \ēk\ see ¹EAK

¹iel \ēl\ see ²EAL

²iel \ī-əl\ see ¹IAL

iela \el-ə\ see ELLA

ield \ēld\ bield, field, keeled, shield, weald, wheeled, wield, yield, afield, airfield, backfield, brickfield, coalfield, cornfield, downfield, Enfield, four-wheeled, Garfield, goldfield, grainfield, infield, Masefield, midfield, minefield, outfield, playfield, Sheffield, Smithfield, snowfield, Springfield, subfield, unsealed, upfield, well-heeled, windshield, Winfield, battlefield, broken-field, chesterfield, Chesterfield, color-field, Huddersfield, track-and-field, unaneled—*also pasts of verbs listed at* ²EAL

ielder \ēl-dər\ fielder, shielder, wielder, yielder, infielder, outfielder

ields \ēldz\ South Shields—*also possessives and plurals of nouns and third person*

singular presents of verbs
listed at IELD

ieler \ē-lər\ see EALER

ieless \ī-ləs\ see ILUS

¹**ieling** \ē-lən\ see ELIN

²**ieling** \ē-liŋ\ see EELING

¹**iem** \ē-əm\ see ¹EUM

²**iem** \ī-əm\ see IAM

ien \ēn\ see ³INE

ience \ī-əns\ see IANCE

iend \end\ see END

iendless \en-ləs\ see ENDLESS

iendliness \en-lē-nəs\ see
ENDLINESS

iendly \en-lē\ see ENDLY

iene \ēn\ see ³INE

¹**iener** \ē-nər\ see EANER

²**iener** \ē-nē\ see ¹INI

ienic \en-ik\ see ²ENIC

ienics \en-iks\ see ENICS

ienie \ē-nē\ see ¹INI

ienist \ē-nəst\ see ²INIST

iennes \en\ see ¹EN

ient \ī-ənt\ see IANT

ieper \ē-pər\ see EEPER

¹**ier** \ir\ see ²EER

²**ier** \ē-ər\ see ¹EER

³**ier** \īr\ see ¹IRE

ierate \ir-ət\ see IRIT

ierce \irs\ Bierce, birse, fierce,
pierce, Pierce, tierce,
transpierce

¹**iere** \er\ see ⁴ARE

²**iere** \ir\ see ²EER

iered \ird\ see ¹EARD

ieria \ir-ē-ə\ see ¹ERIA

ierial \ir-ē-əl\ see ERIAL

ierian \ir-ē-ən\ see ¹ERIAN

ierly \ir-lē\ see ¹EARLY

¹**ierre** \ir\ see ²EER

²**ierre** \er\ see ⁴ARE

iers \irz\ Algiers, Pamirs—*also*

plurals and possessives of
nouns and third person
singular presents of verbs
listed at EER

iersman \irz-mən\ see EERSMAN

iery \ī-rē\ see ¹IARY

¹**ies** \ēz\ see EZE

²**ies** \ē\ see ¹EE

³**ies** \ēs\ see IECE

¹**iesel** \ē-zəl\ see EASEL

²**iesel** \ē-sᵊl\ see ¹ECIL

ieseling \ēz-liŋ\ see ESLING

iesian \ē-zhən\ see ¹ESIAN

iesis \ī-ə-səs\ see IASIS

iesling \ēz-liŋ\ see ESLING

iest \ēst\ see ¹EAST

iester \ē-stər\ see EASTER

iestley \ēst-lē\ see EASTLY

iestly \ēst-lē\ see EASTLY

iet \ī-ət\ diet, fiat, quiet, riot,
striate, Wyatt, disquiet,
unquiet

ietal \ī-ət-ᵊl\ parietal, societal,
varietal

ieter \ī-ət-ər\ dieter, quieter,
rioter, proprietor

ietor \ī-ət-ər\ see IETER

ietzsche \ē-chē\ see EACHY

iety \ī-ət-ē\ piety, anxiety,
dubiety, impiety, nimiety,
propriety, satiety, sobriety,
society, Society, variety,
contrariety, impropriety,
inebriety, insobriety, notoriety

ieu \ü\ see ¹EW

ieur \ir\ see ²EER

iev \ef\ see ¹EF

ievable \ē-və-bəl\ see EIVABLE

ieval \ē-vəl\ evil, shrieval,
weevil, coeval, khedival,
medieval, primeval, reprieval,
retrieval, upheaval

¹ieve \iv\ see ²IVE
²ieve \ēv\ see ¹EAVE
ieved \ēvd\ see EAVED
ievement \ēv-mənt\ see
  EVEMENT
iever \ē-vər\ beaver, cleaver,
  fever, griever, leaver, reaver,
  reiver, weaver, achiever,
  believer, conceiver, deceiver,
  enfever, perceiver, receiver,
  reliever, retriever, upheaver,
  school-leaver, transceiver,
  cantilever, disbeliever,
  misbeliever, misconceiver,
  unbeliever, overachiever,
  underachiever
ievish \ē-vish\ see EEVISH
ievo \ē-vō\ see EVO
ievous \ē-vəs\ see EVOUS
ieze \ēz\ see EZE
¹if \if\ see IFF
²if \ēf\ see ¹IEF
¹ife \īf\ fife, Fife, knife, life,
  rife, strife, wife, alewife,
  drawknife, fishwife, flick-
  knife, goodwife, half-life,
  housewife, jackknife,
  loosestrife, lowlife, mid-life,
  nightlife, oldwife, penknife,
  pro-life, true-life, wakerife,
  whole-life, wildlife, afterlife,
  antilife, Duncan Phyfe, nurse-
  midwife, pocketknife,
  Yellowknife, right-to-life
²ife \ē-fə\ see EPHA
³ife \ēf\ see ¹IEF
ifeless \ī-fləs\ lifeless, strifeless,
  wifeless
ifer \ī-fər\ see IPHER
iferous \if-ər-əs\ coniferous,
  floriferous, lactiferous,
  luciferous, pestiferous,

somniferous, splendiferous,
  vociferous, carboniferous,
  luminiferous, odoriferous,
  salutiferous, seminiferous,
  soporiferous, sudoriferous
iff \if\ biff, cliff, glyph, if, iff,
  jiff, kif, miff, quiff, riff, Riff,
  skiff, sniff, spiff, spliff, stiff,
  syph, tiff, whiff, Er Rif,
  midriff, Plovdiv, triglyph,
  what-if, Wycliffe, anaglyph,
  bindle stiff, hieroglyph,
  hippogriff, logogriph,
  petroglyph
iffany \if-ə-nē\ see IPHONY
iffe \if\ see IFF
iffed \ift\ see IFT
iffen \if-ən\ see IFFIN
iffey \if-ē\ see IFFY
iffian \if-ē-ən\ Riffian,
  Pecksniffian
iffin \if-ən\ griffin, griffon,
  stiffen, tiffin
iffish \if-ish\ sniffish, stiffish
iffle \if-əl\ piffle, riffle, skiffle,
  sniffle, whiffle, Wiffle
iffler \if-lər\ riffler, sniffler,
  whiffler
iffness \if-nəs\ stiffness,
  swiftness
iffon \if-ən\ see IFFIN
iffy \if-ē\ iffy, cliffy, jiffy,
  Liffey, sniffy, spiffy
ific \if-ik\ glyphic, calcific,
  febrific, horrific, magnific,
  pacific, Pacific, prolific,
  salvific, specific, terrific,
  vivific, anaglyphic, beatific,
  calorific, colorific, felicific,
  frigorific, hieroglyphic,
  honorific, scientific, soporific,

sudorific, tenebrific,
prescientific
ifical \if-i-kəl\ magnifical,
pontifical
ificate \if-i-kət\ certificate,
pontificate
ificent \if-ə-sənt\ magnificent,
omnificent
ifle \ī-fəl\ rifle, stifle, trifle
ifling \ī-fliŋ\ rifling, stifling,
trifling
ift \ift\ drift, gift, grift, lift, rift,
shift, shrift, sift, squiffed,
swift, Swift, thrift, adrift,
airlift, blueshift, downshift,
face-lift, festschrift, forklift,
frameshift, gearshift, Great
Rift, makeshift, redshift,
shoplift, snowdrift,
spendthrift, spindrift,
spoondrift, unshift, uplift,
upshift—*also pasts of verbs
listed at* IFF
ifter \if-tər\ drifter, snifter,
swifter, sceneshifter, shape-
shifter, shoplifter
ifth \ith\ see ²ITH
iftness \if-nəs\ see IFFNESS
ifty \if-tē\ drifty, fifty, nifty,
shifty, thrifty, wifty, fifty-
fifty, LD50
ig \ig\ big, brig, dig, fig, frig,
gig, Grieg, grig, jig, pig, prig,
rig, sprig, swig, trig, twig,
vig, Whig, wig, zig, bagwig,
bigwig, bushpig, earwig,
hedgepig, lime-twig, renege,
shindig, unrig, caprifig, infra
dig, jury-rig, periwig,
thimblerig, whirligig,
WYSIWYG, Zagazig,
thingamajig

¹**iga** \ē-gə\ Riga, Vega, viga,
Antigua, omega, quadriga
²**iga** \ī-gə\ see AIGA
igamous \ig-ə-məs\ bigamous,
polygamous
igamy \ig-ə-mē\ bigamy,
digamy, polygamy
¹**igan** \ī-gən\ ligan, tigon
²**igan** \ig-ən\ see IGGIN
igand \ig-ənd\ brigand, ligand
igas \ī-gəs\ see YGOUS
igate \ig-ət\ see ¹IGOT
¹**ige** \ēzh\ siege, prestige,
noblesse oblige
²**ige** \ēj\ see ¹IEGE
igel \ij-əl\ see IGIL
igenous \ij-ə-nəs\ see IGINOUS
igeon \ij-ən\ see YGIAN
iger \ī-gər\ tiger,
braunschweiger
igerent \ij-rənt\ belligerent,
refrigerant, cobelligerent
iggan \ig-ən\ see IGGIN
iggard \ig-ərd\ niggard,
triggered—*also pasts of verbs
listed at* IGGER
igged \igd\ twigged, wigged,
bewigged, cat-rigged, square-
rigged, periwigged—*also
pasts of verbs listed at* IG
igger \ig-ər\ bigger, chigger,
digger, jigger, nigger, rigger,
rigor, snigger, swigger,
trigger, vigor, vigour,
ditchdigger, outrigger,
rejigger, reneger, square-
rigger, thimblerigger
iggered \ig-ərd\ see IGGARD
iggery \ig-ə-rē\ piggery,
priggery, Whiggery
iggie \ig-ē\ see IGGY

iggin \ig-ən\ biggin, piggin,
  wigan, balbriggan
iggish \ig-ish\ biggish, piggish,
  priggish, Whiggish
iggle \ig-əl\ giggle, higgle,
  jiggle, niggle, sniggle,
  squiggle, wiggle, wriggle
iggler \ig-lər\ giggler, higgler,
  niggler, wiggler, wriggler
iggy \ig-ē\ biggie, piggy,
  twiggy
igh \ī\ see ¹Y
ighed \īd\ see ¹IDE
ighland \ī-lənd\ highland,
  Highland, island, Thailand,
  Long Island, Rhode Island,
  Staten Island, Prince Edward
  Island
ighlander \ī-lən-dər\
  highlander, islander
ighlands \ī-lənz\ Highlands,
  Virgin Islands
ighly \ī-lē\ see YLY
ighness \ī-nəs\ see ¹INUS
ight \īt\ see ¹ITE
ightable \īt-ə-bəl\ see ¹ITABLE
ighted \īt-əd\ blighted, sighted,
  whited, attrited, benighted,
  clear-sighted, farsighted,
  foresighted, longsighted,
  nearsighted, sharp-sighted,
  shortsighted, skylighted,
  united, unrequited—*also pasts
  of verbs listed at* ¹ITE
ighten \īt-ᵊn\ brighten,
  Brighton, chitin, chiton,
  frighten, heighten, lighten,
  tighten, titan, Titan, triton,
  Triton, whiten, enlighten
ightener \īt-nər\ brightener,
  lightener, tightener, whitener
ightening \īt-niŋ\ see IGHTNING

ighter \īt-ər\ see ¹ITER
ightful \īt-fəl\ frightful, rightful,
  spiteful, sprightful, delightful,
  despiteful, foresightful,
  insightful
ightie \īt-ē\ see ²ITE
ightily \īt-ᵊl-ē\ flightily,
  mightily
ightiness \īt-ē-nəs\ flightiness,
  mightiness, almightiness
ighting \īt-iŋ\ see ITING
ightless \īt-ləs\ flightless,
  lightless, sightless
ightly \īt-lē\ knightly, lightly,
  nightly, rightly, sightly,
  sprightly, whitely, fortnightly,
  midnightly, unsightly—*also
  adverbs formed by adding* -ly
  to adjectives listed at ¹ITE
ightment \īt-mənt\ see ITEMENT
ightning \īt-niŋ\ lightning,
  tightening, belt-tightening
ightn't \īt-ᵊnt\ see ITANT
ighton \īt-ən\ see IGHTEN
ights \īts\ lights, nights, tights,
  footlights, houselights,
  weeknights, Dolomites, Golan
  Heights—*also plurals and
  possessives of nouns and
  third person singular presents
  of verbs listed at* ¹ITE
ightsome \īt-səm\ lightsome,
  delightsome
ighty \īt-ē\ see ²ITE
igian \ij-ən\ see YGIAN
igid \ij-əd\ Brigid, frigid, rigid
igil \ij-əl\ Rigel, sigil, strigil,
  vigil, residual
igilant \ij-ə-lənt\ vigilant,
  acidulent
igine \ij-ə-nē\ polygyny,
  aborigine

iginous \ij-ə-nəs\ caliginous, fuliginous, indigenous, polygynous, vertiginous

igion \ij-ən\ see YGIAN

igious \ij-əs\ litigious, prestigious, prodigious, religious, irreligious

igit \ij-ət\ see IDGET

igitte \ij-ət\ see IDGET

iglet \ig-lət\ piglet, wiglet

¹igm \im\ see ¹IM

²igm \īm\ see ¹IME

igma \ig-mə\ sigma, stigma, enigma, kerygma

igment \ig-mənt\ figment, pigment

ign \īn\ see ¹INE

ignable \ī-nə-bəl\ see INABLE

ignancy \ig-nən-sē\ benignancy, malignancy

ignant \ig-nənt\ benignant, indignant, malignant

igned \īnd\ see ¹IND

igneous \ig-nē-əs\ igneous, ligneous

igner \ī-nər\ see ¹INER

igness \ig-nəs\ bigness, Cygnus

ignet \ig-nət\ see YGNET

igning \ī-niŋ\ see INING

ignity \ig-nət-ē\ dignity, indignity, malignity

ignly \īn-lē\ see ¹INELY

ignment \īn-mənt\ alignment, assignment, confinement, consignment, enshrinement, refinement, nonalignment, realignment

ignon \in-yən\ see INION

ignor \ē-nyər\ see ENIOR

¹igo \ī-gō\ Sligo, prurigo, vitiligo

²igo \ē-gō\ see EGO

igoe \ē-gō\ see EGO

igon \ī-gən\ see ¹IGAN

igor \ig-ər\ see IGGER

igorous \ig-rəs\ rigorous, vigorous

¹igot \ig-ət\ bigot, frigate, gigot, spigot

²igot \ik-ət\ see ICKET

igour \ig-ər\ see IGGER

igrapher \ig-rə-fər\ calligrapher, epigrapher, polygrapher, serigrapher

igraphist \ig-rə-fəst\ calligraphist, epigraphist, polygraphist

igraphy \ig-rə-fē\ calligraphy, epigraphy, pseudepigraphy

igua \ē-gə\ see ¹IGA

igue \ēg\ gigue, Grieg, league, blitzkrieg, colleague, fatigue, garigue, intrigue, sitzkrieg, squeteague, wampumpeag

iguer \ē-gər\ see EAGER

iguous \ig-yə-wəs\ ambiguous, contiguous, exiguous, unambiguous

igured \ig-ərd\ see IGGARD

ii \ī\ see ¹Y

iing \ē-iŋ\ see EEING

ija \ē-jə\ see EGIA

ijah \ī-jə\ Elijah, steatopygia

iji \ē-jē\ Fiji, squeegee

ijl \īl\ see ¹ILE

ijn \īn\ see ¹INE

ijssel \ī-sə\ see ISAL

¹ik \ik\ see ICK

²ik \ēk\ see ¹EAK

¹ika \ē-kə\ pika, theca, areca, eureka, Frederica, Fredericka, paprika, Costa Rica, Dominica, oiticica, Topeka, Tanganyika, bibliotheca

²**ika** \ī-kə\ see ¹ICA
¹**ike** \ī-kē\ Nike, Psyche, crikey, spiky
²**ike** \īk\ bike, caique, dike, dyke, fyke, haik, hike, kike, like, mike, Mike, pike, psych, shrike, sike, spike, strike, trike, tyke, alike, belike, catlike, childlike, clocklike, dislike, fly-strike, garpike, godlike, handspike, hitchhike, homelike, Klondike, lifelike, mislike, pealike, prooflike, push-bike, rampike, restrike, scalelike, sheaflike, shunpike, suchlike, ten-strike, turnpike, unlike, Updike, Vandyke, warlike, wifelike, winglike, berrylike, businesslike, fatherlike, ladylike, look-alike, machinelike, marlinespike, marlinspike, minibike, motorbike, rubberlike, Scafell Pike, soundalike, thunderstrike, womanlike, workmanlike, unsportsmanlike
³**ike** \ik\ see ICK
¹**iked** \īkt\ liked, piked, spiked, vandyked—*also pasts of verbs listed at* ²IKE
²**iked** \ī-kəd\ see YCAD
iken \ī-kən\ see ¹ICHEN
iker \ī-kər\ biker, diker, duiker, hiker, piker, spiker, striker, disliker, hitchhiker, shunpiker, minibiker
ikes \īks\ yikes—*also possessives and plurals of nouns and third person singular presents of verbs listed at* IKE

ikey \ī-kē\ see ¹IKE
ikh \ēk\ see ¹EAK
¹**iki** \ik-ē\ see ICKY
²**iki** \ē-kē\ see EAKY
iking \ī-kiŋ\ liking, striking, Viking, shunpiking
ikker \ik-ər\ see ¹ICKER
iky \ī-kē\ see ¹IKE
¹**il** \il\ see ILL
²**il** \ēl\ see ²EAL
¹**ila** \il-ə\ see ²ILLA
²**ila** \ē-lə\ see ¹ELA
³**ila** \ī-lə\ Lila, Delilah
ilae \ī-le\ see YLY
ilage \ī-lij\ mileage, silage
ilah \ī-lə\ see ³ILA
ilament \il-ə-mənt\ filament, habiliment, monofilament
ilar \ī-lər\ dialer, filar, flier, hilar, miler, smiler, stylar, styler, tiler, Tyler, beguiler, bifilar, compiler, defiler, freestyler, profiler, rottweiler, stockpiler, unifilar
ilary \il-ə-rē\ see ILLARY
ilate \ī-lət\ see ILOT
ilbe \il-be\ see ILBY
ilbert \il-bərt\ filbert, gilbert, Gilbert
ilby \il-bē\ trilby, astilbe
¹**ilch** \ilk\ see ILK
²**ilch** \ilch\ filch, milch, zilch
¹**ild** \īld\ mild, piled, wild, Wilde, brainchild, godchild, grandchild, hog-wild, man-child, pantiled, Rothschild, schoolchild, self-styled, stepchild—*also pasts of verbs listed at* ¹ILE
²**ild** \il\ see ILL
³**ild** \ilt\ see ILT
⁴**ild** \ild\ see ILLED

ilda \il-də\ Hilda, tilde, Wilda

¹ilde \il-də\ see ILDA

²ilde \īld\ see ¹ILD

¹lder \il-dər\ builder, gilder, guilder, wilder, bewilder, boatbuilder, shipbuilder, upbuilder, bodybuilder, jerry-builder

²ilder \īl-dər\ milder, wilder, Wilder

ilding \il-diŋ\ building, gilding, hilding, abuilding, outbuilding, shipbuilding, bodybuilding—*also present participles of verbs listed at* ILLED

ildish \īl-dish\ childish, wildish

ildly \īld-lē\ childly, mildly, wildly

¹ile \īl\ aisle, bile, dial, faille, file, guile, I'll, isle, Kyle, lisle, Lyle, mile, Nile, phial, pile, rile, roil, smile, spile, stile, style, tile, trial, vial, vile, viol, while, wile, abseil, aedile, agile, anile, argyle, Argyll, audile, awhile, axile, beguile, Blue Nile, Carlyle, compile, condyle, cross-file, de Stijl, decile, defile, denial, docile, ductile, enisle, ensile, erewhile, erstwhile, espial, exile, febrile, fictile, fissile, flexile, fragile, freestyle, futile, genial, gentile, gracile, habile, hairstyle, Kabyle, labile, life-style, meanwhile, mistrial, mobile, motile, nubile, pantile, penile, pensile, profile, puerile, quartile, quintile, redial, reptile, resile, retrial, revile,

sandpile, scissile, sectile, senile, servile, sessile, stabile, stockpile, sundial, tactile, tensile, textile, turnstile, typestyle, unpile, utile, vagile, virile, woodpile, worthwhile, afebrile, airmobile, Anglophile, chamomile, contractile, crocodile, discophile, domicile, endostyle, epistyle, erectile, extensile, Francophile, Gallophile, halophile, homophile, hypostyle, infantile, interfile, juvenile, low-profile, mercantile, negrophile, oenophile, otherwhile, pedophile, percentile, peristyle, prehensile, projectile, protractile, pulsatile, reconcile, refractile, retractile, self-denial, Slavophile, spermophile, technopile, thermopile, turophile, urostyle, versatile, vibratile, xenophile, ailurophile, amphiprostyle, audiophile, bibliophile, electrophile, fluviatile, Germanophile, heterophile, Italophile, nucleophile

²ile \il\ see ILL

³ile \ē-lē\ see EELY

⁴ile \ēl\ see ²EAL

⁵ile \il-ē\ see ¹ILLY

ilead \il-ē-əd\ see ILIAD

ileage \ī-lij\ see ILAGE

ileal \il-ē-əl\ see ¹ILIAL

ileless \īl-ləs\ guileless, pileless, smileless

¹iler \ē-lər\ see EALER

²**iler** \ī-lər\ see ILAR
iles \īlz\ Giles, Miles, Niles, Wade-Giles, British Isles, Western Isles
ileum \il-ē-əm\ see ILIUM
iley \ī-lē\ see YLY
ilford \il-fərd\ Milford, Wilford
¹**ili** \il-ē\ see ¹ILLY
²**ili** \ē-lē\ see EELY
¹**ilia** \il-ē-ə\ Celia, cilia, Cecelia, Cecilia, Massilia, Anglophilia, basophilia, coprophilia, hemophilia, juvenilia, necrophilia, neophilia, pedophilia, sensibilia, memorabilia
²**ilia** \il-yə\ Brasilia, sedilia, bougainvillea, sensibilia, memorabilia
³**ilia** \ēl-yə\ see ELIA
iliad \il-ē-əd\ Gilead, Iliad, balm of Gilead
ilial \il-ē-əl\ filial, ileal, familial, unfilial
¹**ilian** \il-ē-ən\ Gillian, Ilian, Lillian, Basilian, reptilian, Abbevillian, crocodilian, preexilian, vespertilian
²**ilian** \il-yən\ see ILLION
ilias \il-ē-əs\ see ¹ILIOUS
iliate \il-ē-ət\ ciliate, affiliate
ilic \il-ik\ killick, acrylic, allylic, Cyrillic, dactylic, exilic, idyllic, sibylic, amphiphilic, Anglophilic, hemophilic, necrophilic, pedophilic, postexilic, zoophilic, bibliophilic
ilica \il-i-kə\ silica, basilica
ilican \il-i-kən\ see ILICON
ilicon \il-i-kən\ Millikan, silicon, spillikin, basilican, ferrosilicon
ilience \il-yəns\ see ILLIANCE
iliency \il-yən-sē\ see ILLIANCY
ilient \il-yənt\ brilliant, resilient
iliment \il-ə-mənt\ see ILAMENT
¹**iling** \ī-liŋ\ filing, piling, spiling, styling, tiling, hairstyling
²**iling** \ē-liŋ\ see EELING
¹**ilion** \il-yən\ see ILLION
²**ilion** \il-ē-ən\ see ¹ILIAN
¹**ilious** \il-ē-əs\ punctilious, supercilious, materfamilias, paterfamilias
²**ilious** \il-yəs\ bilious, atrabilious, supercilious
ilip \il-əp\ see ILLIP
ilitant \il-ə-tənt\ militant, rehabilitant
ility \il-ət-ē\ ability, agility, anility, civility, debility, docility, ductility, facility, fertility, fragility, futility, gentility, gracility, hostility, humility, lability, mobility, motility, nobility, nubility, scurrility, sectility, senility, stability, sterility, suability, tactility, tranquility, utility, vagility, virility, actability, affability, arability, audibility, bearability, biddability, breathability, brushability, capability, changeability, coilability, contractility, countability, credibility, crossability, culpability, curability, cutability, disability, disutility, drapability, drillability, drinkability, durability,

dyeability, edibility,
equability, erectility,
fallibility, feasibility,
fishability, flammability,
flexibility, forgeability,
formability, frangibility,
friability, gullibility,
imbecility, immobility,
inability, incivility, indocility,
infantility, infertility,
instability, inutility,
juvenility, laudability,
leachability, legibility,
liability, likability, livability,
mailability, meltability,
miscibility, movability,
mutability, notability,
packability, placability,
plausibility, playability,
portability, possibility,
potability, pregnability,
prehensility, printability,
probability, puerility,
readability, risibility,
roadability, salability,
sensibility, sewability,
shareability, sociability,
solubility, solvability,
spreadability, squeezability,
stainability, stretchability,
tenability, testability,
traceability, treatability,
tunability, usability,
vendability, versatility,
viability, visibility, volatility,
washability, wearability,
wettability, workability,
absorbability, acceptability,
accessibility, accountability,
adaptability, adjustability,
admirability, admissibility,
adoptability, adorability,

advisability, affectability,
agreeability, alterability,
amenability, amiability,
amicability, appealability,
applicability, approachability,
assumability, attainability,
automobility, availability,
believability, collapsibility,
combustability, comparability,
compatibility, compensability,
compressability,
computability, conceivability,
conductability, confirmability,
contemptibility,
contractibility, controllability,
convertibility, corrigibility,
corruptibility, cultivability,
damageability, decidability,
deductibility, defeasibility,
defensibility, delectability,
demonstrability, deniability,
dependability, desirability,
destructibility, detachability,
detectability, deterrability,
detonability, digestibility,
dilatability, dispensability,
disposability, dissociability,
dissolubility, distensibility,
distractibility, divisibility,
educability, electability,
eligibility, employability,
enforceability, equitability,
erasability, erodability,
exchangeability, excitability,
excludability, exhaustibility,
expansibility, expendability,
explosibility, exportability,
extensibility, extractibility,
extrudability, fashionability,
fatigability, filterability,
fissionability, formidability,
habitability, heritability,

illegibility, immiscibility, immovability, immutability, impalpability, impassability, impassibility, impeccability, implacability, implausibility, impossibility, impregnability, impressibility, improbability, improvability, inaudibility, incapability, incredibility, indelibility, inductibility, ineffability, infallibility, infeasibility, inflammability, inflexibility, infrangibility, infusibility, insensibility, insolubility, insurability, intangibility, invincibility, invisibility, irascibility, irritability, knowledgeability, machinability, maintainability, manageability, marketability, merchantability, measurability, modulability, navigability, negligibility, nonflammability, openability, operability, opposability, palatability, penetrability, perceptibility, perdurability, perfectibility, performability, perishability, permeability, permissibility, pleasurability, practicability, preferability, presentability, preservability, preventability, processibility, programmability, punishability, reasonability, refundability, reliability, renewability, repeatability, reputability, resistibility, respectability, responsibility, retrievability, reusability, reversability, salvageability, separability, severability,

serviceability, suggestability, supportability, suppressibility, survivability, susceptibility, sustainability, tolerability, trafficability, transferability, translatability, transmissibility, transplantability, transportability, unflappability, unthinkability, untouchability, variability, violability, vulnerability, weatherability, alienability, analyzability, assimilability, codifiability, commensurability, communicability, comprehensibility, decomposability, deliverability, discriminability, disrespectability, distinguishability, enumerability, exceptionability, hypnotizability, illimitability, impenetrability, imperishability, impermeability, impermissibility, imponderability, impracticability, impressionability, inaccessibility, inadmissibility, inadvisability, inalterability, inapplicability, incalculability, incombustibility, incomparability, incompatibility, incompressibility, inconceivability,

incontestability,
inconvertibility,
incorrigibility,
incorruptibility,
indefeasibility, indefensibility,
indefinability,
indestructibility,
indigestibility,
indispensability,
indissolubility, indivisibility,
indomitability, indubitability,
ineducability, ineffaceability,
ineligibility, ineluctability,
inevitability, inexhaustibility,
inexplicability,
inexpressibility,
inextricability, inheritability,
insatiability, inseparability,
insociability, insusceptibility,
intelligibility,
interchangeability,
intolerability, invariability,
invulnerability, irreducibility,
irreformability, irrefutability,
irremovability, irrepealability,
irreplaceability,
irrepressibility,
irreproachability,
irresistibility, irresponsibility,
irretrievability, irreversibility,
irrevocability,
maneuverability,
manipulability, negotiability,
polarizability, recognizability,
recoverability, rectifiability,
reprehensibility,
reproducibility,
substitutability,
unacceptability,
unaccountability,
understandability,
undesirability, verifiability,

biocompatability,
biodegradability,
differentiability, inalienability,
incommensurability,
incommunicability,
incomprehensibility,
indefatigability,
indistinguishability,
ineradicability,
incontrovertibility,
irreconcilability,
irreproducibility,
interoperability
ilium \il-ē-əm\ cilium, ileum,
ilium, Ilium, milium, trillium,
beryllium, penicillium
ilk \ilk\ bilk, ilk, milch, milk,
silk, buttermilk, liebfraumilch
ilker \il-kər\ bilker, milker
ilky \il-kē\ milky, silky
ill \il\ bill, Bill, brill, chill, dill,
drill, fill, frill, gill, grill,
grille, hill, ill, Jill, kill, krill,
mil, mill, mille, Milne, nil,
nill, Phil, pill, prill, quill, rill,
shill, shrill, sild, sill, skill,
spill, squill, still, swill, thill,
thrill, til, till, trill, twill, vill,
will, Will, anthill, backfill,
bluegill, Brazil, Catskill,
Churchill, cranesbill,
crossbill, de Mille, dentil,
deskill, distill, doorsill,
downhill, duckbill, dullsville,
dunghill, fiberfill, foothill,
freewill, fulfill, goodwill,
Granville, gristmill, handbill,
hawksbill, hornbill,
Huntsville, instill, Knoxville,
lambkill, landfill, limekiln,
manille, Melville, molehill,
mudsill, Nashville, no-till,

playbill, quadrille, refill,
roadkill, sawmill, self-will,
Seville, sheathbill, shoebill,
sidehill, sigil, spadille,
spoonbill, stabile, standstill,
stockstill, storksbill, T-bill,
treadmill, unreal, until, uphill,
vaudeville, waxbill, waybill,
windchill, windmill,
Brazzaville, chlorophyll,
daffodil, deshabille, de
Toqueville, dishabille,
escadrille, espadrille,
Evansville, Francophil,
Hooverville, Jacksonville,
Libreville, Louisville,
minimill, overfill, overkill,
overspill, razorbill, rototill,
tormentil, verticil, windowsill,
whippoorwill, winter-kill,
Yggdrasil, acidophil,
ivorybill, minoxydil, Nizhni
Togil, run-of-the-mill

I'll \īl\ see ¹ILE

¹**illa** \ē-yə\ barilla, cuadrilla,
banderilla, quesadilla

²**illa** \il-ə\ scilla, Scylla, squilla,
villa, Willa, ancilla, Aquila,
Attila, axilla, Camilla, cedilla,
chinchilla, flotilla, gorilla,
guerrilla, manila, Manila,
megillah, papilla, perilla,
Priscilla, scintilla, vanilla,
camarilla, cascarilla,
granadilla, potentilla,
sabadilla, sapodilla,
sarsaparilla

³**illa** \ē-ə\ see ¹IA

⁴**illa** \ēl-yə\ see ELIA

⁵**illa** \ē-lə\ see ¹ELA

illable \il-ə-bəl\ billable,
drillable, fillable, spillable,
syllable, tillable, disyllable,
refillable, trisyllable,
decasyllable, monosyllable,
octosyllable, polysyllable,
hendecasyllable

illage \il-ij\ grillage, millage,
pillage, spillage, tillage,
village, no-tillage, permillage,
Greenwich Village

illah \il-ə\ see ²ILLA

illain \il-ən\ see ILLON

illar \il-ər\ see ILLER

illary \il-ə-rē\ Hilary, Hillary,
phyllary, codicillary

illate \il-ət\ see ILLET

¹**ille** \il\ see ILL

²**ille** \ē\ see ¹EE

³**ille** \ēl\ see ²EAL

illea \il-yə\ see ²ILIA

illed \ild\ build, dilled, drilled,
gild, gilled, guild, skilled,
twilled, willed, Brynhild,
engild, gold-filled,
goodwilled, rebuild, self-
willed, spoonbilled, unbuild,
unskilled, upbuild, wergild,
jerry-build, overbuild,
semiskilled—*also pasts of
verbs listed at* ILL

illedness \il-nəs\ see ILLNESS

illein \il-ən\ see ILLON

iller \il-ər\ biller, chiller, driller,
filler, giller, griller, hiller,
killer, miller, Miller, pillar,
schiller, spiller, swiller,
thriller, tiller, triller, axillar,
distiller, fulfiller, painkiller,
pralltriller, von Schiller,
caterpillar, lady-killer,
Rototiller—*also comparatives
of adjectives listed at* ILL

illery \il-rē\ pillory, artillery, distillery

illes \il-ēz\ see ILLIES

illet \il-ət\ billet, fillet, millet, rillet, skillet, willet, distillate

illful \il-fəl\ skillful, willful, unskillful

¹illi \il-ē\ see ¹ILLY

²illi \ē-lē\ see EELY

¹illian \il-ē-ən\ see ¹ILIAN

²illian \il-yən\ see ILLION

illiance \il-yəns\ brilliance, resilience

illiancy \il-yən-sē\ brilliancy, resiliency

illiant \il-yənt\ see ILIENT

illick \il-ik\ see ILIC

illie \il-ē\ see ¹ILLY

illies \il-ēz\ willies, Achilles, Antilles, Greater Antilles, Lesser Antilles, Netherlands Antilles—*also plurals and possessives of nouns listed at* ¹ILLY

illikan \il-i-kən\ see ILICON

illikin \il-i-kən\ see ILICON

¹illin \il-əm\ see ILLUM

²illin \il-ən\ see ILLON

illing \il-iŋ\ billing, drilling, filling, killing, milling, schilling, shilling, skilling, twilling, willing, fulfilling, spine-chilling, unwilling

illion \il-yən\ billion, jillion, Lillian, million, pillion, trillion, zillion, caecilian, Castilian, centillion, civilian, cotillion, decillion, modillion, nonillion, octillion, pavilion, postilion, quadrillion, Quintilian, quintillion, reptilian, septillion, sextillion, toubillion, vaudevillian, vermilion, crocodilian, Maximilian, preexilian, quindecillion, sexdecillion, tredecillion, undecillion, vespertilian, vigintillion, duodecillion, novemdecillion, octodecillion, septendecillion, quattuordecillion

illip \il-əp\ fillip, Philip

illis \il-əs\ see ILLUS

illium \il-ē-əm\ see ILIUM

illness \il-nəs\ chillness, illness, shrillness, stillness

¹illo \il-ō\ billow, pillow, willow, Negrillo, tornillo, Amarillo, armadillo, cigarillo, coyotillo, peccadillo, tamarillo

²illo \ē-ō\ see ²IO

illon \il-ən\ billon, Dylan, Uilleann, villain, villein, tefillin, penicillin, amoxycillin

illory \il-rē\ see ILLERY

illous \il-əs\ see ILLUS

¹illow \il-ə\ see ²ILLA

²illow \il-ō\ see ¹ILLO

illowy \il-ə-wē\ billowy, pillowy, willowy

ills \ilz\ Black Hills, no-frills, Alban Hills—*also plurals and possessives of nouns, third person singular presents of verbs at* ILL

illum \il-əm\ chillum, vexillum

illus \il-əs\ Phyllis, villous, Willis, bacillus, lapillus, amaryllis, toga virilis

¹illy \il-ē\ Billie, billy, Chile, chili, chilly, dilly, filly, frilly, gillie, hilly, illy, Lillie, lily, Lily, Millie, really, Scilly,

silly, stilly, Willie, Willy,
bacilli, Caerphilly, daylily,
fusilli, guidwillie, hillbilly,
piccalilli, rockabilly, willy-
nilly

²**illy** \il-lē\ shrilly, stilly

¹**iln** \il\ see ILL

²**iln** \iln\ kiln, Milne

¹**ilne** \iln\ see ²ILN

²**ilne** \il\ see ILL

¹**ilo** \ī-lō\ milo, Milo, phyllo,
silo

²**ilo** \ē-lō\ helo, kilo, phyllo,
Iloilo

ilom \ī-ləm\ see ILUM

iloquence \il-ə-kwəns\
grandiloquence,
magniloquence

iloquent \il-ə-kwənt\
grandiloquent, magniloquent

iloquist \il-ə-kwəst\ soliloquist,
ventriloquist

iloquy \il-ə-kwē\ soliloquy,
ventriloquy

ilot \ī-lət\ eyelet, islet, Pilate,
pilot, stylet, copilot, autopilot,
Pontius Pilate

ils \ils\ fils, grilse, Nils

ilse \ils\ see ILS

ilt \ilt\ built, gilt, guilt, hilt, jilt,
kilt, lilt, milt, quilt, silt, stilt,
tilt, wilt, atilt, bloodguilt,
Brunhild, homebuilt, inbuilt,
rebuilt, unbuilt, uptilt, carvel-
built, clinker-built, custom-
built, purpose-built

ilter \il-tər\ filter, kilter, milter,
philter, off-kilter

ilth \ilth\ filth, spilth, tilth

iltie \il-tē\ see ILTY

ilton \ilt-ᵊn\ Hilton, Milton,
Stilton, Wilton

ilty \il-tē\ guilty, kiltie, milty,
silty, bloodguilty

ilum \ī-ləm\ filum, hilum,
phylum, whilom, xylem,
asylum

ilus \ī-ləs\ eyeless, pilus, stylus,
tieless

¹**ily** \ī-lē\ see YLY

²**ily** \il-ē\ see ¹ILLY

¹**im** \im\ bream, brim, dim,
glim, grim, Grimm, gym,
him, hymn, Jim, Kim, limb,
limn, mim, nim, prim, rim,
scrim, shim, skim, slim,
swim, Tim, trim, vim, whim,
bedim, dislimn, forelimb,
passim, prelim, Purim,
Sikkim, slim-jim, snap-brim,
acronym, anonym, antonym,
eponym, homonym,
metonym, paradigm,
paronym, pseudonym,
seraphim, synonym,
tautonym, toponym,
underbrim, ad interim,
heteronym

²**im** \ēm\ see ¹EAM

I'm \īm\ see ¹IME

ima \ē-mə\ see EMA

imable \ī-mə-bəl\ climable,
sublimable, unclimbable

imace \im-əs\ grimace, tzimmes

image \im-ij\ image,
scrimmage, self-image,
afterimage

iman \ē-mən\ see ¹EMON

imate \ī-mət\ climate, primate,
acclimate

¹**imb** \im\ see ¹IM

²**imb** \īm\ see ¹IME

imba \im-bə\ limba, kalimba,
marimba

imbable \ī-mə-bəl\ see IMABLE
imbal \im-bəl\ see IMBLE
imbale \im-bəl\ see IMBLE
imbed \imd\ limbed, rimmed, clean-limbed—*also pasts of verbs listed at* ¹IM
¹imber \im-bər\ limber, timber, sawtimber, unlimber
²imber \ī-mər\ see ¹IMER
imble \im-bəl\ cymbal, gimbal, nimble, symbol, thimble, timbal, timbale, wimble
imbo \im-bō\ bimbo, limbo, akimbo, gumbo-limbo
imbral \am-brəl\ see AMBREL
imbre \am-bər\ see ²AMBAR
imbrel \im-brəl\ timbrel, whimbrel
imbus \im-bəs\ limbus, nimbus
¹ime \īm\ chime, climb, clime, crime, dime, disme, grime, I'm, lime, mime, prime, rhyme, rime, slime, stime, thyme, time, airtime, all-time, bedtime, begrime, big time, birdlime, daytime, downtime, dreamtime, enzyme, flextime, foretime, halftime, lifetime, longtime, lunchtime, Mannheim, Maytime, mealtime, meantime, nighttime, noontime, old-time, onetime, part-time, pastime, peacetime, playtime, quicklime, ragtime, schooltime, seedtime, small-time, sometime, space-time, springtime, sublime, teatime, two-time, uptime, wartime, aftertime, Anaheim, anytime, beforetime, Christmastime, dinnertime, double-time,

harvesttime, Jotunheim, lysozyme, maritime, monorhyme, overtime, pantomime, paradigm, summertime, wintertime, nickel-and-dime
²ime \ēm\ see ¹EAM
imel \im-əl\ gimel, gimmal, kümmel
imeless \īm-ləs\ rhymeless, timeless
imely \īm-lē\ primely, timely, untimely
imen \ī-mən\ flyman, hymen, Hymen, limen, Lyman, Simon
imeon \im-ē-ən\ see IMIAN
imeous \ī-məs\ see IMIS
¹imer \ī-mər\ chimer, climber, dimer, mimer, primer, rhymer, timer, trimer, full-timer, old-timer, small-timer, sublimer, two-timer, wisenheimer
²imer \im-ər\ see IMMER
imerick \im-rik\ see YMRIC
¹imes \īmz\ times, betimes, daytimes, sometimes, betweentimes, oftentimes—*also plurals and possessives of nouns and third person singular presents of verbs listed at* ¹IME
²imes \ēm\ see ¹EAM
imeter \im-ət-ər\ dimeter, limiter, scimitar, trimeter, altimeter, delimiter, perimeter, tachymeter
imetry \im-ə-trē\ symmetry, gravimetry, polarimetry, sypersymmetry
imian \im-ē-ən\ Simeon, simian, Endymion, prosimian

imic \im-ik\ see ²YMIC

imical \im-i-kəl\ inimical, metonymical, synonymical, toponymical

imicry \im-i-krē\ gimmickry, mimicry

imilar \im-ə-lər\ similar, dissimilar

imile \im-ə-lē\ simile, swimmily, facsimile

¹iminal \im-ən-ᵊl\ criminal, liminal, subliminal, supraliminal

²iminal \im-nəl\ see YMNAL

iminy \im-ə-nē\ see IMONY

imis \ī-məs\ primus, thymus, timeous, imprimis, untimeous

imitable \im-ət-ə-bəl\ imitable, illimitable, inimitable

imitar \im-ət-ər\ see IMETER

imiter \im-ət-ər\ see IMETER

imits \im-its\ limits, Nimitz

imity \im-ət-ē\ dimity, proximity, sublimity, anonymity, equanimity, longanimity, magnanimity, pseudonymity, synonymity, unanimity, pusillanimity

imitz \im-its\ see IMITS

imm \im\ see ¹IM

immable \im-ə-bəl\ dimmable, swimmable

immage \im-ij\ see IMAGE

immal \im-əl\ see IMEL

imme \i-mē\ see IMMY

immed \imd\ see IMBED

immer \im-ər\ brimmer, dimmer, glimmer, krimmer, limmer, limner, primer, shimmer, simmer, skimmer, slimmer, swimmer, trimmer—

also comparatives of adjectives listed at ¹IM

immes \im-əs\ see IMACE

immick \im-ik\ see ²YMIC

immickry \im-i-krē\ see IMICRY

immily \im-ə-lē\ see IMILE

immy \im-ē\ gimme, jimmy, limby, shimmy, swimmy

imn \im\ see ¹IM

imner \im-ər\ see IMMER

imo \ē-mō\ primo, sentimo

imon \ī-mən\ see IMEN

imony \im-ə-nē\ simony, niminy-piminy

imothy \im-ə-thē\ timothy, Timothy, polymathy

imp \imp\ blimp, chimp, crimp, gimp, guimpe, imp, limp, pimp, primp, scrimp, shrimp, simp, skimp, wimp, comsymp

impe \imp\ see IMP

imper \im-pər\ limper, shrimper, simper, whimper

imping \im-pən\ see YMPAN

impish \im-pish\ blimpish, impish

imple \im-pəl\ dimple, pimple, simple, wimple, oversimple

imply \im-plē\ dimply, limply, pimply, simply

impy \im-pē\ crimpy, gimpy, scrimpy, shrimpy, skimpy, wimpy

imsy \im-zē\ flimsy, slimsy, whimsy

imulus \im-yə-ləs\ limulus, stimulus

imus \ī-məs\ see IMIS

imy \ī-mē\ grimy, limey, limy, rimy, slimy, stymie, thymy, old-timey

¹in \in\ been, bin, blin, chin,

din, fin, Finn, gin, grin,
Gwyn, hin, in, inn, kin, linn,
Lynn, Lynne, pin, shin, Shin,
sin, skin, spin, thin, tin, twin,
whin, win, wyn, yin, zin,
again, agin, akin, all-in,
backspin, bearskin, begin,
Benin, Berlin, Boleyn,
bowfin, break-in, buckskin,
built-in, burn-in, calfskin,
capeskin, cave-in, chagrin,
check-in, Chongjin, close-in,
clothespin, coonskin, Corinne,
crankpin, cut-in, deerskin,
doeskin, drive-in, drop-in,
duckpin, dustbin, fade-in, fill-
in, foreskin, goatskin, Guilin,
hairpin, Harbin, has-been,
headpin, herein, Jilin, Kerin,
kidskin, kingpin, lambskin,
lead-in, lie-in, linchpin, live-
in, lived-in, lobe-fin, locked-
in, look-in, love-in, moleskin,
munchkin, Nankin, ninepin,
no-win, oilskin, Pekin, phone-
in, pigskin, pinyin, plug-in,
pushpin, redskin, ruin, run-in,
saimin, scarfpin, scarfskin,
sealskin, set-in, sharkskin,
sheepskin, shoo-in, shut-in,
sidespin, sit-in, sleep-in,
snakeskin, stand-in, step-in,
stickpin, swanskin, tailspin,
take-in, tap-in, teach-in,
tenpin, therein, tholepin,
threadfin, throw-in, tie-in,
tiepin, tip-in, toe-in, trade-in,
tuned-in, turn-in, unpin, walk-
in, weigh-in, wherein,
wineskin, within, woolskin,
write-in, candlepin, catechin,
Ha-erh-pin, Ho Chi Minh,

Lohengrin, lying-in,
mandolin, maximin, Mickey
Finn, onionskin, palanquin,
Tianjin, underpin, underspin,
Vietminh, violin, whipper-in,
canthaxanthin

²in \ēn\ see ³INE

³in \an\ see ⁵AN

⁴in \a^n\ Chopin, doyen,
Gauguin, moulin, Petain,
Rodin, serin, coq au vin, coup
de main, fleur de coin,
Mazarin

⁵in \ən\ see ¹UN

¹ina \ī-nə\ china, China, Dina,
Dinah, Heine, Ina, mina,
mynah, Aegina, angina,
Lucina, nandina, piscina,
Regina, salina, shechinah,
vagina, Cochin China,
Carolina, Indochina,
kamaaina, Poland China,
North Carolina, South
Carolina

²ina \ē-nə\ Deena, Dena, kina,
Lena, Nina, plena, Shina,
Tina, vena, vina, arena,
Athena, cantina, catena,
Christina, coquina, corbina,
corvina, czarina, Edwina,
euglena, farina, fontina,
Georgina, hyena, kachina,
Kristina, marina, Marina,
medina, Medina, Messina,
nandina, novena, patina,
piscina, platina, Regina,
retsina, Rowena, salina,
sestina, Shechinah, subpoena,
verbena, Agrippina, amberina,
Angelina, Argentina,
ballerina, casuarina, Carolina,
Catalina, catilena, cavatina,

Chianina, concertina, Filipina,
javelina, Katerina, ocarina,
Palestrina, palomino,
Pasadena, Saint Helena,
semolina, signorina, sonatina,
Taormina, Teresina,
Wilhelminia, Herzegovina,
Pallas Athena, Strait of
Messina

inable \ī-nə-bəl\ minable,
consignable, declinable,
definable, inclinable,
indeclinable, indefinable

inach \in-ich\ Greenwich,
spinach

¹inah \ē-nə\ see ²INA

²inah \ī-nə\ see ¹INA

¹inal \īn-ᵊl\ clinal, final, rhinal,
spinal, trinal, vinyl, matutinal,
officinal, quarterfinal,
semifinal, serotinal

²inal \ēn-ᵊl\ see ENAL

inally \īn-ᵊl-ē\ clinally, finally,
spinally, matutinally

inary \ī-nə-rē\ binary, trinary

¹inas \ī-nəs\ see ¹INUS

²inas \ē-nəs\ see ¹ENUS

inative \in-ət-iv\ see INITIVE

inc \iŋk\ see INK

inca \iŋ-kə\ Dinka, Inca, vinca,
Mandinka

incal \iŋ-kəl\ see INKLE

incan \iŋ-kən\ Incan, Lincoln

¹ince \ins\ blintz, chintz, mince,
prince, quince, rinse, since,
wince, convince, evince,
shinsplints, Port-au-Prince

²ince \ans\ see ³ANCE

incely \in-slē\ princely, tinselly

incer \in-chər\ see INCHER

inch \inch\ chinch, cinch,
clinch, finch, flinch, grinch,

inch, lynch, pinch, squinch,
winch, bullfinch, goldfinch,
greenfinch, hawfinch, unclinch

incher \in-chər\ clincher,
flincher, lyncher, pincer,
pincher, wincher,
affenpinscher, penny-pincher,
Doberman pinscher

inching \in-chiŋ\ unflinching,
penny-pinching

incible \in-sə-bəl\ principal,
principle, vincible, evincible,
invincible, inconvincible

incing \in-siŋ\ ginseng,
mincing, convincing,
unconvincing

incipal \in-sə-bəl\ see INCIBLE

inciple \in-sə-bəl\ see INCIBLE

inck \injk\ see INK

incky \iŋ-kē\ see INKY

incoln \iŋ-kən\ see INCAN

inct \iŋt\ linked, kinked, tinct,
distinct, extinct, instinct,
precinct, succinct, unlinked,
indistinct

inction \iŋ-shən\ distinction,
extinction, contradistinction

inctive \iŋ-tiv\ distinctive,
extinctive, instinctive,
indistinctive

incture \iŋ-chər\ cincture,
tincture

¹ind \īnd\ bind, blind, find,
grind, hind, kind, mind, rind,
signed, spined, tined, wind,
wynd, affined, behind,
confined, inclined, in-kind,
night-blind, purblind, refined,
remind, rewind, sand-blind,
snow-blind, spellbind, stone-
blind, streamlined, unbind,
unkind, unwind, color-blind,

double-blind, gavelkind, gravel-blind, hoodman-blind, humankind, mastermind, nonaligned, single-blind, unaligned, undersigned, well-defined, womankind—*also pasts of verbs listed at* ¹INE

²**ind** \ind\ finned, Ind, Sind, skinned, wind, buckskinned, crosswind, downwind, exscind, prescind, rescind, soft-finned, thick-skinned, thin-skinned, upwind, whirlwind, woodwind, Amerind, spiny-finned, tamarind—*also pasts of verbs listed at* ¹IN

³**ind** \int\ see INT

inda \in-də\ Linda, Lucinda, Melinda, Samarinda

indar \in-dər\ see ²INDER

¹**inded** \īn-dəd\ minded, rinded, broad-minded, fair-minded, high-minded, large-minded, like-minded, low-minded, right-minded, small-minded, strong-minded, tough-minded, weak-minded, absentminded, bloody-minded, civic-minded, evil-minded, feebleminded, narrow-minded, open-minded, simpleminded, single-minded, social-minded, tender-minded—*also regular pasts of verbs listed at* ¹IND

²**inded** \in-dəd\ brinded, long-winded, short-winded, broken-winded—*also pasts of verbs listed at* ²IND

¹**inder** \īn-dər\ binder, blinder, finder, grinder, hinder, minder, winder, bookbinder,

faultfinder, highbinder, netminder, pathfinder, ring binder, self-binder, sidewinder, spellbinder, stem-winder, viewfinder, organ-grinder—*also comparatives of adjectives listed at* ¹IND

²**inder** \in-dər\ cinder, hinder, Pindar, tinder

indful \īn-fəl\ mindful, remindful, unmindful

indhi \in-dē\ see INDY

indi \in-dē\ see INDY

indic \in-dik\ Indic, syndic

indie \in-dē\ see INDY

inding \īn-diŋ\ binding, finding, winding, bookbinding, fact-finding, faultfinding, pathfinding, self-winding, spellbinding, stem-winding

indlass \in-ləs\ see INLESS

indle \in-dᵊl\ brindle, dwindle, kindle, spindle, swindle, enkindle

indless \īn-ləs\ kindless, mindless, spineless

¹**indling** \in-lən\ pindling, spindling

²**indling** \ind-liŋ\ dwindling, kindling, pindling, spindling

¹**indly** \in-lē\ see INLY

²**indly** \īn-lē\ see ¹INELY

indness \īn-nəs\ blindness, fineness, kindness, purblindness, unkindness, loving-kindness

indowed \in-dəd\ see ²INDED

indus \in-dəs\ Indus, Pindus

indy \in-dē\ Cindy, Hindi, indie, lindy, shindy, Sindhi, windy, Rawalpindi

¹**ine** \īn\ bine, brine, chine,

cline, dine, dyne, eyen, fine,
Jain, kine, line, Line, Main,
mine, nine, pine, Rhein,
Rhine, rind, shine, shrine,
sign, spine, spline, stein,
Stein, swine, syne, thine, tine,
trine, twine, vine, whine,
wine, A-line, affine, airline,
align, alkyne, alpine, assign,
balkline, baseline, beeline,
benign, Bernstein, bloodline,
bovine, bowline, branchline,
breadline, buntline, bustline,
byline, canine, caprine,
carbine, carmine, cervine,
clothesline, coastline,
combine, compline, condign,
confine, consign, corvine,
cutline, dateline, deadline,
decline, define, design, divine,
dragline, driveline, earthshine,
Einstein, eiswein, enshrine,
ensign, entwine, equine,
ethyne, feline, ferine, fraulein,
frontline, gantline, grapevine,
guideline, hairline, hard-line,
headline, hemline, hipline,
Holbein, Holstein, incline,
indign, in-line, jawline,
landline, lang syne, lifeline,
longline, lupine, mainline,
malign, midline, moline,
moonshine, off-line, old-line,
opine, outline, outshine,
ovine, Pauline, Pennine,
Petrine, pipeline, piscine,
plotline, pontine, Pontine,
porcine, potline, propine,
quinine, rapine, recline,
redline, refine, reline, repine,
resign, ridgeline, roofline,
Sabine, saline, setline,

shoreline, sideline, Sixtine,
skyline, soft-line, straight-
line, strandline, streamline,
strychnine, subline, sunshine,
supine, syncline, taurine, tie-
line, time-line, topline,
touchline, towline, tramline,
trapline, trephine, trotline,
truckline, tumpline, turbine,
untwine, ursine, vespine,
vulpine, waistline, woodbine,
zayin, zebrine, aerodyne,
alkaline, androgyne,
Angeline, anodyne, anserine,
anticline, aquiline, argentine,
asinine, auld lang syne,
borderline, bottom-line,
Byzantine, calamine,
calcimine, Caroline,
catarrhine, Catiline, celandine,
centerline, cisalpine,
Cisalpine, clandestine,
colubrine, columbine,
Columbine, concubine,
Constantine, countermine,
countersign, crystalline,
cytokine, disincline, eglantine,
endocrine, exocrine,
falconine, fescennine,
Frankenstein, gregarine,
infantine, interline, intertwine,
iodine, Johannine, leonine,
Liechtenstein, monkeyshine,
muscadine, opaline, palatine,
Palestine, passerine,
porcupine, psittacine, realign,
redefine, redesign, riverine,
Rubenstein, saccharine,
sapphirine, saturnine,
serpentine, sibylline, sixty-
nine, subalpine, Theatine,
timberline, turnverein,

turpentine, underline,
undermine, Ursuline, uterine,
valentine, vespertine,
viperine, vulturine, waterline,
zibeline, accipitrine,
adamantine, adulterine,
alexandrine, amaranthine,
Capitoline, elephantine,
Evangeline, Frankfurt am
Main, Rembrandt van Rijn,
Scheswig-Holstein,
nonoxynol-9, Newcastle-upon
Tyne
²**ine** \ē-nā\ fine, wahine
³**ine** \ēn\ bean, clean, dean,
Dean, Deane, dene, e'en,
gene, Gene, glean, green,
Green, greene, jean, Jean,
Jeanne, keen, lean, lien,
mean, mesne, mien, peen,
preen, quean, queen, scene,
screen, seen, sheen, shin, sin,
skean, skene, spean, spleen,
teen, tween, wean, ween,
wheen, yean, Aileen, Arlene,
baleen, beguine, Beguine,
Benin, Bernstein, between,
boreen, bovine, buckbean,
caffeine, canteen, carbine,
careen, Carlene, Cathleen,
Charlene, chlorine, chopine,
chorine, Christine, citrine,
Claudine, codeine, colleen,
Colleen, convene, Coreen,
cotquean, cuisine, Darlene,
dasheen, dauphine, demean,
demesne, dentine, Doreen,
dry-clean, dudeen, eighteen,
Eileen, Essene, Eugene,
fanzine, fascine, fifteen,
fourteen, Francine, gamine,
gangrene, glassine, gyrene,

Helene, Hellene, Hermine,
hoatzin, holstein, Holstein,
horsebean, houseclean,
hygiene, Ilene, Irene,
Jacqueline, Jeanine, Jeannine,
Jolene, Justine, Kathleen,
khamsin, Kristine, Ladin,
lateen, latrine, Lorene, Lublin,
machine, malines, marine,
Marlene, Maureen, Maxine,
moline, moreen, morphine,
Nadine, nankeen, naphthene,
Nicene, nineteen, nongreen,
Noreen, obscene, offscreen,
on-screen, patine, Pauline,
piscine, Pontine, poteen,
praline, preteen, pristine,
propine, protein, quinine,
Rabin, Racine, ratteen, ravine,
routine, saline, saltine,
Salween, sardine, sateen,
scalene, serene, shagreen,
Sharlene, shebeen, siren,
Sistine, sixteen, Slovene,
soybean, spalpeen, strychnine,
subteen, sunscreen, Szczecin,
takin, taurine, terrene, terrine,
thirteen, Tolkien, tontine,
tureen, umpteen, unclean,
undine, unseen, vaccine,
vitrine, windscreen, yestreen,
Yibin, zechin, Aberdeen,
almandine, Angeline,
argentine, Argentine,
Augustine, barkentine,
bengaline, Bernadine,
bombazine, Borodin,
brigandine, brigantine,
brilliantine, Byzantine,
carotene, carrageen,
celandine, clandestine,
columbine, Constantine,

contravene, crepe de chine,
crystalline, damascene,
Dexedrine, Dramamine,
duvetyn, eglantine, endocrine,
Eocene, epicene, Ernestine,
estaurine, evergreen,
fescennine, figurine,
Florentine, fluorine, fukerene,
gabardine, gaberdine,
gadarene, galantine, gasoline,
Geraldine, Ghibelline, go-
between, grenadine, Gretna
Green, guillotine, Halloween,
haute cuisine, Hippocrene,
histamine, Holocene,
Imogene, in-between,
indigene, intervene, Jeraldine,
Josephine, Kalinin, kerosene,
langoustine, legatine,
libertine, limousine, M16,
magazine, mangosteen,
margravine, Medellìn,
melamine, messaline,
Methedrine, mezzanine,
Miocene, mousseline,
Nazarene, nectarine, nicotine,
overseen, opaline, organzine,
palanquin, palatine, pelerine,
percaline, peregrine,
philhellene, Philistine,
plasticene, plasticine,
Pleistocene, Pliocene,
riverine, quarantine, reserpine,
saccharine, Sakhalin, Saladin,
San Joaquin, San Martin,
sapphirine, schizophrene,
serpentine, seventeen,
silkaline, Stelazine,
submarine, subroutine,
supervene, tambourine,
tangerine, Theatine,
tourmaline, trampoline,

transmarine, travertine,
Tridentine, Vaseline,
velveteen, wintergreen,
wolverine, Ursuline,
adamantine, alexandrine,
amphetamine, aquamarine,
Benedictine, bromocriptine,
carbon 13, doxycycline,
elephantine, Evangeline,
internecine, leukotirene,
methylxanthene, mujahideen,
niphedipine, nouvelle cuisine,
Oligocene, Paleocene,
pentamedine, tricothecene,
ultramarine, antihistamine,
benzoapyrene,
diphenhydramine, Mary
Magdalene, NC-17,
polybutadiene, alpha-
fetaprotein, apolipoprotein,
buckminsterfullerene, General
San Martin, oleomargarine
⁴ine \in-ē\ see INNY
⁵ine \ē-nē\ see ¹INI
⁶ine \ən\ see UN
inea \in-ē\ see INNY
ineal \in-ē-əl\ finial, lineal,
   matrilineal, patrilineal,
   unilineal
ined \īnd\ see ¹IND
inee \ī-nē\ see ¹INY
ineless \īn-ləs\ see INDLESS
¹inely \īn-lē\ blindly, finely,
   kindly, affinely, condignly,
   equinely, felinely, purblindly,
   unkindly
²inely \ēn-lē\ see ¹EANLY
inement \īn-mənt\ see IGNMENT
ineness \īn-nəs\ see INDNESS
ineous \in-ē-əs\ gramineous,
   sanguineous, consanguineous,
   ignominious

¹**iner** \ī-nər\ briner, diner, finer, liner, miner, minor, shiner, Shriner, signer, twiner, whiner, airliner, aligner, baseliner, byliner, combiner, confiner, cosigner, definer, designer, diviner, eyeliner, hardliner, headliner, incliner, jetliner, long-liner, moonshiner, one-liner, recliner, refiner, repiner, sideliner, soft-liner, streamliner, Asia Minor, Canis Minor, forty-niner, party-liner, Ursa Minor, superliner

²**iner** \ē-nər\ see EANER

¹**inery** \īn-rē\ finery, pinery, vinery, winery, refinery

²**inery** \ēn-rē\ see EANERY

¹**ines** \ēn\ see ³INE

²**ines** \ēnz\ see EENS

³**ines** \īnz\ Mainz, Appenines—*also plurals and possessives of nouns and third person singular presents of verbs listed at* ¹INE

inest \ī-nəst\ see ¹INIST

inet \in-ət\ see INNET

inew \in-yü\ see INUE

infield \in-fēld\ infield, Winfield

ing \iŋ\ bring, Ching, cling, ding, fling, king, King, ling, Ming, ping, ring, sing, sling, spring, sting, string, swing, thing, wing, wring, zing, backswing, Baoding, bedspring, Beijing, bi-swing, bitewing, bowstring, bullring, Chongqing, clearwing, downswing, drawstring, D ring, earring, first-string, forewing, G-string, greenwing, hairspring, hamstring, handspring, headspring, heartstring, Kunming, lacewing, lapwing, latchstring, mainspring, Nanjing, Nanning, O-ring, offspring, Paoting, plaything, redwing, shoestring, showring, unsling, unstring, upspring, upswing, wellspring, whitewing, windwing, wingding, Xining, à la king, anything, buck-and-wing, ding-a-ling, double-ring, everything, innerspring, Liaoning, pigeonwing, superstring, underwing

inga \iŋ-gə\ anhinga, syringa

inge \inj\ binge, cringe, dinge, fringe, hinge, singe, springe, swinge, tinge, twinge, whinge, impinge, infringe, syringe, unhinge

inged \iŋd\ ringed, stringed, winged, net-winged—*also regular pasts of verbs listed at* ING

ingement \inj-mənt\ impingement, infringement

ingency \in-jən-sē\ stringency, astringency, contingency

ingent \in-jənt\ stringent, astringent, constringent, contingent, refringent

¹**inger** \iŋ-ər\ bringer, clinger, dinger, flinger, pinger, ringer, singer, springer, stinger, stringer, swinger, winger, wringer, zinger, folksinger, gunslinger, humdinger, left-winger, mudslinger, right-

winger, mastersinger,
Meistersinger, minnesinger
²**inger** \iŋ-gər\ finger, linger,
five-finger, forefinger,
malinger, ladyfinger
³**inger** \in-jər\ ginger, Ginger,
injure, singer, swinger
ingery \inj-rē\ gingery, injury
inghy \iŋ-ē\ see ¹INGY
ingi \iŋ-ē\ see ¹INGY
ingian \in-jən\ Thuringian,
Cariovingian, Carolingian,
Merovingian
inging \iŋ-iŋ\ ringing,
springing, stringing, swinging,
folksinging, free-swinging,
gunslinging, handwringing,
mudslinging, upbringing
ingit \iŋ-kət\ see INKET
ingle \iŋ-gəl\ cringle, dingle,
jingle, mingle, shingle, single,
tingle, atingle, commingle,
immingle, Kriss Kringle,
surcingle, intermingle
ingler \iŋ-glər\ jingler, shingler
inglet \iŋ-lət\ kinglet, ringlet,
winglet
ingletree \iŋ-gəl-trē\ singletree,
swingletree
ingli \ing-lē\ see INGLY
inglish \iŋ-glish\ see ENGLISH
ingly \iŋ-glē\ jingly, shingly,
singly, tingly, Zwingli
ingo \iŋ-gō\ bingo, dingo,
gringo, jingo, lingo, pingo,
flamingo, Mandingo, Santo
Domingo
ings \iŋz\ Kings, springs,
eyestrings, Hot Springs,
Colorado Springs—*also
plurals and possessives of
nouns and third person
singular presents of verbs
listed at* ING
ingue \aŋ\ see ²ANG
inguish \iŋ-wish\ distinguish,
extinguish
¹**ingy** \iŋ-ē\ clingy, dinghy,
springy, stringy, swingy,
zingy, shilingi
²**ingy** \in-jē\ dingy, mingy,
stingy
inh \in\ see ¹IN
¹**ini** \ē-nē\ beanie, djinni, genie,
greeny, Jeanie, Jeannie,
meanie, meany, jinni, Meany,
sheeny, spleeny, teeny,
weanie, weeny, wienie,
Alcmene, Athene, Bellini,
Bernini, bikini, Bikini,
Cabrini, Cellini, Eugenie,
linguine, martini, Mazzini,
Mbini, Mycenae, Puccini,
rappini, Rossini, Selene,
tahini, wahine, zucchini,
fantoccini, fettucine,
kundalini, malihini,
Mussolini, Mytilene, nota
bene, scaloppine, spaghettini,
teeny-weeny, tetrazzini,
tortellini
²**ini** \in-ē\ see INNY
inia \in-ē-ə\ zinnia, Bithynia,
Gdynia, gloxinia, Lavinia,
Sardinia, Virginia, Abyssinia,
West Virginia
inial \in-ē-əl\ see INEAL
¹**inian** \in-ē-ən\ dynein,
Arminian, Darwinian,
Latinian, Sardinian, Socinian,
Apollinian, Argentinian,
Augustinian, Carolinian
²**inian** \in-yən\ see INION
¹**inic** \ē-nik\ Enoch, nicotinic

²**inic** \in-ik\ clinic, cynic,
Finnic, platinic, rabbinic,
Jacobinic, mandarinic,
misogynic, muscarinic,
nicotinic, parafinic

inical \in-i-kəl\ binnacle,
clinical, cynical, finical,
pinnacle, dominical,
Jacobinical

inican \in-i-kən\ see INIKIN

inikin \in-i-kən\ minikin,
Dominican

inim \in-əm\ minim,
Houyhnhnm

ining \ī-niŋ\ lining, mining,
shining, declining, designing,
inclining, long-lining,
interlining, undesigning

inion \in-yən\ minion, minyan,
pinion, piñon, champignon,
dominion, Justinian, opinion,
Sardinian, Abyssinian

¹**inis** \in-əs\ finis, pinnace,
Erinys

²**inis** \ī-nəs\ see ¹INUS

inish \in-ish\ finish, Finnish,
thinnish, diminish, refinish

¹**inist** \ī-nəst\ dynast, finest

²**inist** \ē-nəst\ hygienist,
machinist, Orleanist,
Byzantinist, magazinist,
trampolinist

initive \in-ət-iv\ carminative,
definitive, infinitive

inity \in-ət-ē\ trinity, Trinity,
affinity, bovinity, concinnity,
divinity, felinity, feminity,
infinity, latinity, salinity,
sanguinity, vicinity, virginity,
alkalinity, aquitinity,
clandestinity, consanguinity,
crystallinity, femininity,

inconcinnity, masculinity,
saccharinity

inium \in-ē-əm\ delphinium,
triclinium, condominium

injure \in-jər\ see ³INGER

injury \inj-rē\ see INGERY

ink \iŋk\ blink, brink, chink,
Chink, clink, dink, drink, fink,
gink, ink, jink, kink, link,
mink, pink, plink, prink, rink,
shrink, sink, skink, slink,
stink, swink, sync, think,
wink, zinc, bethink, chewink,
cross-link, eyewink,
groupthink, hoodwink,
iceblink, lip-synch, misthink,
outthink, preshrink, rethink,
snowblink, unkink, bobolink,
countersink, distelfink,
doublethink, interlink,
kitchen-sink, Maeterlinck,
rinky-dink

inka \iŋ-kə\ see INCA

inkable \iŋ-kə-bəl\ drinkable,
sinkable, thinkable,
undrinkable, unsinkable,
unthinkable

inkage \iŋ-kij\ linkage,
shrinkage, sinkage

inke \iŋ-kē\ see INKY

inked \iŋt\ see INCT

inker \iŋ-kər\ blinker, clinker,
drinker, pinker, sinker,
skinker, stinker, tinker,
winker, diesinker, freethinker,
headshrinker

inket \iŋ-kət\ Tlingit, trinket

inkey \iŋ-kē\ see INKY

inkgo \iŋ-kō\ see INKO

inki \iŋ-kē\ see INKY

inkie \iŋ-kē\ see INKY

inking \iŋ-kiŋ\ freethinking,
unblinking, unthinking

inkle \iŋ-kəl\ crinkle, inkle,
sprinkle, tinkle, twinkle,
winkle, wrinkle, besprinkle,
periwinkle, Rip van Winkle

inkling \iŋ-kliŋ\ inkling,
sprinkling, twinkling

inkly \iŋ-klē\ crinkly, pinkly,
tinkly, twinkly, wrinkly

inko \iŋ-kō\ ginkgo, pinko

inks \iŋs\ see INX

inky \iŋ-kē\ dinkey, dinky,
inky, kinky, pinkie, pinky,
slinky, stinky, zincky,
Helsinki, Malinke

inland \in-lənd\ Finland, inland,
Vinland

inless \in-ləs\ chinless, sinless,
skinless, spinless, windlass

inley \in-lē\ see INLY

inly \in-lē\ inly, spindly, thinly,
McKinley, Mount McKinley

inn \in\ see ¹IN

innace \in-əs\ see ¹INIS

innacle \in-i-kəl\ see INICAL

inned \ind\ see ²IND

inner \in-ər\ dinner, ginner,
grinner, inner, pinner, sinner,
skinner, spinner, spinor,
thinner, tinner, winner,
beginner, breadwinner,
prizewinner, money-spinner

innet \in-ət\ linnet, minute,
spinet

inney \in-ē\ see INNY

inni \ē-nē\ see ¹INI

innia \in-ē-ə\ see INIA

innic \in-ik\ see ²INIC

innie \in-ē\ see INNY

inning \in-iŋ\ ginning, inning,
spinning, winning, beginning,
breadwinning, prizewinning,
underpinning

innish \in-ish\ see INISH

innity \in-ət-ē\ see INITY

innow \in-ō\ minnow, winnow,
topminnow

inny \in-ē\ cine, finny, ginny,
guinea, Guinea, hinny, mini,
Minnie, ninny, pinny, Pliny,
shinny, skinny, spinney,
squinny, tinny, whinny,
Winnie, ignominy, micromini,
pickaninny, Papua New
Guinea, Equatorial Guinea

¹**ino** \ī-nō\ lino, rhino, Taino,
wino, albino

²**ino** \ē-nō\ beano, chino, fino,
keno, leno, Pinot, vino, Zeno,
bambino, casino, cioppino,
ladino, merino, sordino,
zecchino, andantino,
Angeleno, Bardolino,
campesino, cappuccino,
concertino, Filipino,
maraschino, palomino,
Philipino, San Marino,
pecorino, sopranino, Cape
Mendocino, San Bernardino

³**ino** \ē-nə\ see ²INA

iñon \in-yən\ see INION

¹**inor** \in-ər\ see INNER

²**inor** \ī-nər\ see ¹INER

inos \ī-nəs\ see INNS

inot \ē-nō\ see ²INO

inous \ī-nəs\ see ¹INUS

inscher \in-chər\ see INCHER

inse \ins\ see INCE

inselly \in-slē\ see INCELY

inseng \in-siŋ\ see INCING

insk \insk\ Minsk, Dzerzhinsk,
Semipalatinsk

insky \in-skē\ buttinsky,
kolinsky, Nijinsky, Stravinsky
inster \in-stər\ minster, spinster,
Axminster, Westminster,
Kidderminster
int \int\ bint, Clint, dint, flint,
Flint, glint, hint, lint, mint,
print, quint, skint, splint,
sprint, squint, stint, suint, tint,
blueprint, catmint, footprint,
forint, gunflint, handprint,
hoofprint, horsemint, imprint,
in-print, large-print,
newsprint, offprint, preprint,
remint, reprint, skinflint,
spearmint, thumbprint,
voiceprint, aquatint, calamint,
cuckoopint, fingerprint,
mezzotint, monotint,
overprint, peppermint,
photoprint, wunderkind,
Septuagint
intage \int-ij\ mintage, vintage
intager \int-i-jər\ see INTEGER
intain \int-ᵊn\ see INTON
¹intal \int-ᵊl\ lintel, pintle,
quintal, Septuagintal
²intal \ant-ᵊl\ see ANTLE
integer \int-i-jər\ integer,
vintager
intel \int-ᵊl\ see ¹INTAL
inter \int-ər\ hinter, linter,
minter, printer, sinter,
splinter, sprinter, squinter,
tinter, winter, imprinter,
midwinter, reprinter,
overwinter, teleprinter
intery \int-ə-rē\ printery,
splintery
inth \inth\ plinth, synth,
helminth, colocynth,
labyrinth, terebinth

inthia \in-thē-ə\ Cynthia,
Carinthia
inthian \in-thē-ən\ Corinthian,
labyrinthian
inthine \in-thən\ hyacinthine,
labyrinthine
inting \int-iŋ\ imprinting,
unstinting—*also present
participles of verbs listed at*
INT
intle \int-ᵊl\ see ¹INTAL
¹into \in-tō\ pinto, Shinto,
spinto
²into \in-tü\ thereinto, whereinto
inton \int-ᵊn\ Clinton, quintain,
Winton, badminton
ints \ins\ see INCE
inty \int-ē\ flinty, linty, minty,
squinty, pepperminty
intz \ins\ see INCE
inue \in-yü\ sinew, continue,
discontinue
inuous \in-yə-wəs\ sinuous,
continuous, discontinuous
¹inus \ī-nəs\ dryness, finis,
highness, Minas, Minos,
minus, shyness, sinus,
slyness, spinous, vinous,
wryness, Aquinas, Delphinus,
echinus, Quirinus, Antoninus,
Pontus Euxinus
²inus \ē-nəs\ see ¹ENUS
inute \in-ət\ see INNET
inx \iŋs\ jinx, links, lynx, minx,
sphinx, hijinks, methinks,
tiddledywinks
¹iny \ī-nē\ briny, heinie, liny,
piny, shiny, spiny, tiny,
twiny, viny, whiny, winy,
enshrinee, sunshiny
²iny \in-ē\ see INNY
inya \ē-nyə\ see ²ENIA

inyan \in-yən\ see INION
inyl \īn-ᵊl\ see ¹INAL
inys \in-əs\ see ¹INIS
¹io \ī-ō\ bayou, bio, Clio, Io,
  Lucayo, Ohio
²io \ē-ō\ brio, Cleo, clio, guyot,
  Krio, Leo, Rio, trio,
  caudillo, con brio, Negrillo,
  tornillo, Trujillo, cigarillo,
  Hermosillo, Manzanillo,
  ocotillo
iocese \ī-ə-səs\ see IASIS
iolate \ī-ə-lət\ see ¹IOLET
¹iolet \ī-ə-lət\ triolet, violate,
  violet, Violet, inviolate,
  ultraviolet, near-ultraviolet
²iolet \ē-ə-lət\ see EOLATE
¹ion \ī-ən\ ayin, Brian, Bryan,
  cyan, ion, lion, Lyon, Mayan,
  Ryan, scion, Sion, Zion,
  Amphion, anion, Bisayan,
  Ixion, Orion, Visayan,
  counterion, dandelion,
  zwitterion
²ion \ē-ən\ see ¹EAN
³ion \ē-än\ see ²EON
ior \īr\ see ¹IRE
iory \ī-rē\ see ¹IARY
iot \ī-ət\ see IET
ioter \ī-ət-ər\ see IETER
iouan \ü-ən\ see UAN
ious \ī-əs\ see IAS
ioux \ü\ see ¹EW
ip \ip\ blip, chip, clip, dip, drip,
  flip, grip, grippe, gyp, hip,
  kip, lip, nip, pip, quip, rip,
  scrip, ship, sip, skip, slip,
  snip, strip, tip, trip, whip, yip,
  zip, airship, airstrip, atrip,
  bullwhip, catnip, chiefship,
  clerkship, courtship, cowslip,
  deanship, equip, fieldstrip,

filmstrip, flagship, friendship,
guildship, gunship, half-slip,
handgrip, hardship, harelip,
headship, horsewhip, inclip,
judgeship, kingship, kinship,
landslip, lightship, lordship,
nonslip, outstrip, oxlip, pip-
pip, princeship, Q-ship,
queenship, reship, round-trip,
saintship, sheep-dip, sideslip,
spaceship, steamship,
thaneship, township,
transship, troopship, unship,
unzip, wardship, warship,
airmanship, authorship,
battleship, biochip,
brinkmanship, censorship,
chairmanship, chaplainship,
chieftainship, churchmanship,
coverslip, dealership,
draftsmanship, ego-trip,
externship, fellowship,
fingertip, gamesmanship,
Gaza Strip, grantsmanship,
helmsmanship, horsemanship,
internship, ladyship,
leadership, lectureship,
listenership, marksmanship,
membership, microchip,
oarsmanship, overslip,
ownership, partnership,
penmanship, pogonip,
premiership, readership,
ridership, rulership,
salesmanship, scholarship,
seamanship, showmanship,
skinny-dip, speakership,
sponsorship, sportsmanship,
statesmanship, stewardship,
studentship, swordsmanship,
trusteeship, underlip,
upmanship, viewership,

workmanship, assistantship,
attorneyship, championship,
chancellorship, citizenship,
companionship, containership,
cross-ownership, dictatorship,
directorship, good-fellowship,
guardianship, instructorship,
landownership, laureateship,
governorship, musicianship,
one-upmanship,
outdoorsmanship,
professorship, protectorship,
receivership, relationship,
survivorship, treasurership,
ambassadorship,
associateship, bipartisanship,
entrepreneurship,
librarianship, nonpartisanship,
proprietorship, secretaryship,
solicitorship, interrelationship

ipal \ē-pəl\ see EOPLE

ipari \ip-rē\ see IPPERY

ipatus \ip-ət-əs\ see IPITOUS

ipe \īp\ Cuyp, gripe, hype,
pipe, ripe, slype, snipe, stipe,
stripe, swipe, tripe, type,
wipe, bagpipe, blowpipe,
downpipe, drainpipe,
hornpipe, hosepipe, lead-pipe,
n-type, p-type, panpipe,
pinstripe, rareripe, sideswipe,
standpipe, stovepipe, tintype,
touch-type, unripe, windpipe,
archetype, calotype,
Dutchman's-pipe, guttersnipe,
haplotype, Linotype,
liripipe, logotype,
monotype, overripe,
prototype, stenotype,
Teletype, electrotype,
stereotype, daguerreotype,
anti-idiotype

¹iped \ī-ped\ biped,
parallelepiped

²iped \īpt\ stiped, striped, pin-
striped—*also pasts of verbs
listed at* IPE

ipend \ī-pənd\ ripened, stipend

iper \ī-pər\ diaper, griper,
hyper, piper, riper, sniper,
striper, viper, wiper, bagpiper,
sandpiper, candy-striper,
stereotyper

iperous \ī-prəs\ see YPRESS

ipetal \ip-ət-ᵊl\ basipetal,
bicipital, centripetal, occipital

ipety \ip-ət-ē\ snippety,
peripety, serendipity

iph \if\ see IFF

iphany \if-ə-nē\ see IPHONY

ipher \ī-fər\ cipher, lifer, rifer,
decipher, encipher, pro-lifer,
right-to-lifer

iphery \if-rē\ see IFERY

iphon \ī-fən\ see YPHEN

iphony \if-ə-nē\ tiffany,
Tiffany, antiphony, epiphany,
polyphony

ipi \ē-pē\ see EEPY

ipid \ip-əd\ lipid, insipid

ipience \ip-ē-əns\ incipience,
percipience, impercipience

ipient \ip-ē-ənt\ excipient,
incipient, percipient, recipient,
impercipient

iping \ī-piŋ\ piping, striping,
blood-typing

ipit \ip-ət\ see IPPET

ipital \ip-ət-əl\ see IPETAL

ipitance \ip-ət-əns\ see
IPOTENCE

ipitant \ip-ət-ənt\ see IPOTENT

ipitous \ip-ət-əs\ peripatus,
precipitous, serendipitous

ipity \ip-ət-ē\ see IPETY
¹iple \ip-əl\ see IPPLE
²iple \ī-pəl\ see YPAL
ipless \ip-ləs\ dripless, lipless, zipless
ipling \ip-liŋ\ Kipling, stripling
ipment \ip-mənt\ shipment, equipment, transshipment
ipo \ēp-ō\ see EPOT
ipoli \ip-ə-lē\ see IPPILY
ipotence \ip-ət-əns\ omnipotence, precipitance
ipotent \ip-ət-ənt\ omnipotent, plenipotent, pluripotent, precipitant
¹ippe \ip\ see IP
²ippe \ip-ē\ see IPPY
³ippe \ēp\ see EEP
ipped \ipt\ see IPT
ippee \ip-ē\ see IPPY
ippen \ip-ən\ lippen, pippin
ipper \ip-ər\ chipper, clipper, dipper, dripper, flipper, gripper, hipper, kipper, nipper, ripper, shipper, sipper, skipper, slipper, snipper, stripper, tipper, tripper, whipper, zipper, blue-chipper, day-tripper, mudskipper, Yom-Kippur, double-dipper, gallinipper, lady's slipper, skinny-dipper
ippery \ip-rē\ frippery, Lipari, slippery
ippet \ip-ət\ pipit, sippet, snippet, tippet, trippet, whippet
ippety \ip-ət-ē\ see IPETY
ippi \ip-ē\ see IPPY
ippie \ip-ē\ see IPPY
ippily \ip-ə-lē\ nippily, tripoli, Tripoli, Gallipoli

ippin \ip-ən\ see IPPEN
ipping \ip-iŋ\ chipping, clipping, dripping, lipping, nipping, ripping, shipping, double-dipping, skinny-dipping
ippingly \ip-iŋ-lē\ grippingly, nippingly, trippingly
ipple \ip-əl\ cripple, nipple, ripple, stipple, tipple, triple, participle
ippur \ip-ər\ see IPPER
ippy \ip-ē\ chippy, dippy, drippy, flippy, grippy, hippie, hippy, Lippi, lippy, nippy, slippy, snippy, tippy, trippy, whippy, yippee, yippie, zippy, Xanthippe, Mississippi
ips \ips\ snips, thrips, yips, eclipse, ellipse, midships, amidships, athwartships, fish-and-chips, tidytips, apocalypse—*also plurals and possessives of nouns and third person singular presents of verbs listed at* IP
ipse \ips\ see IPS
ipso \ip-sō\ dipso, calypso, Calypso
ipster \ip-stər\ hipster, quipster, tipster
ipsy \ip-sē\ see YPSY
ipt \ipt\ crypt, hipped, lipped, ripped, script, tipped, conscript, decrypt, encrypt, harelipped, postscript, prescript, rescript, subscript, tight-lipped, transcript, typescript, eucalypt, filter-tipped, manuscript, nondescript, superscript,

swivel-hipped—*also pasts of verbs listed at* IP

ipter \ip-tər\ scripter, lithotripter

iptic \ip-tik\ see YPTIC

iption \ip-shən\ ascription, conniption, conscription, decryption, description, Egyptian, encryption, inscription, prescription, proscription, subscription, transcription, circumscription, nonprescription

iptive \ip-tiv\ ascriptive, descriptive, inscriptive, prescriptive, proscriptive

iptych \ip-tik\ see YPTIC

ipular \ip-yə-lər\ stipular, manipular

ipy \ī-pē\ stripy, typey, stenotypy, daguerrotypy, stereotypy

iquant \ē-kənt\ see ECANT

ique \ēk\ see ¹EAK

iquey \ē-kē\ see EAKY

iquish \ē-kish\ see EAKISH

iquitous \ik-wət-əs\ iniquitous, ubiquitous

iquity \ik-wət-ē\ antiquity, iniquity, obliquity, ubiquity

iquor \ik-ər\ see ¹ICKER

¹ir \ir\ see ²EER

²ir \ər\ see ¹EUR

¹ira \ir-ə\ see ²ERA

²ira \ī-rə\ see YRA

irable \ī-rə-bəl\ wirable, acquirable, desirable, respirable, undesirable

iracle \ir-i-kəl\ see ²ERICAL

irae \īr-ē\ see ¹IRY

iral \ī-rəl\ chiral, gyral, spiral, viral

irant \ī-rənt\ spirant, tyrant, aspirant, retirant

irate \ir-ət\ see IRIT

irby \ər-bē\ see ERBY

irca \ər-kə\ see ¹URKA

irce \ər-sē\ see ERCY

irch \ərch\ see URCH

¹irchen \ər-chən\ see URCHIN

²irchen \ər-kən\ see IRKIN

ircher \ər-chər\ Bircher, lurcher, nurture

irchist \ər-chəst\ Birchist, researchist

ircon \ər-kən\ see IRKIN

ircuit \ər-kət\ circuit, trifurcate, microcircuit

ircular \ər-kyə-lər\ circular, opercular, tubercular, semicircular

ird \ərd\ bird, burred, curd, furred, gird, heard, herd, nerd, spurred, surd, third, turd, word, absurd, begird, bellbird, blackbird, bluebird, buzzword, byword, Cape Verde, catbird, catchword, cowbird, cowherd, crossword, cussword, engird, goatherd, headword, jailbird, jaybird, kingbird, loanword, lovebird, lyrebird, oilbird, password, potsherd, railbird, rainbird, redbird, reword, ricebird, seabird, Sigurd, shorebird, snakebird, snowbird, songbird, sunbird, surfbird, swearword, swineherd, textured, ungird, unheard, watchword, yardbird, afterword, bowerbird, butcher-bird, cedarbird, dollybird, hummingbird,

ladybird, mockingbird,
ovenbird, overheard,
riflebird, tailorbird,
thunderbird, undergird,
wattlebird, weaverbird,
wirlybird—*also pasts of verbs
listed at* [1]EUR

irder \ərd-ər\ see ERDER

irdie \ərd-ē\ see URDY

irdle \ərd-ᵊl\ see URDLE

irdum \ərd-əm\ dirdum,
reductio ad absurdum

[1]ire \īr\ briar, brier, byre, choir,
dire, drier, fire, flier, friar,
fryer, gyre, hire, ire, liar, lyre,
mire, prier, prior, pyre, quire,
shire, sire, Speyer, spier,
spire, squire, tier, tire, trier,
tyer, Tyre, wire, zaire,
acquire, admire, afire, Altair,
aspire, attire, backfire,
balefire, barbed wire,
barbwire, bemire, Blantyre,
blow-dryer, bonfire, brushfire,
bushfire, catbrier, cease-fire,
complier, conspire, defier,
denier, desire, drumfire,
empire, Empire, entire,
esquire, expire, flytier,
grandsire, greenbrier, gunfire,
haywire, hellfire, highflier,
hot-wire, inquire, inspire,
misfire, outlier, perspire,
pismire, prior, quagmire,
require, respire, retire, rimfire,
samphire, sapphire, satire,
Shropshire, spitfire, surefire,
suspire, sweetbrier, tightwire,
transpire, umpire, vampire,
wildfire, amplifier,
Biedermeier, butterflyer,
classifier, fly-by-wire,

fortifier, lammergeier,
magnifier, modifier,
multiplier, nitrifier, nullifier,
pacifier, qualifier, quantifier,
rapid-fire, rectifier, retrofire,
sanctifier, signifier, testifier,
versifier, identifier, intensifier,
Second Empire, down-to-the-
wire—*also nouns formed by
adding* -er *to verbs listed at*
[1]Y

[2]ire \ir\ see [2]EER

[3]ire \ī-rē\ see [1]IARY

[4]ire \ir-ē\ see [1]IRY

[5]ire \ər\ see EUR

ired \īrd\ fired, spired, tired,
wired, hardwired, retired—
also pasts of verbs listed at
[1]IRE

ireless \īr-ləs\ tireless, wireless

ireman \īr-mən\ fireman,
wireman

irement \īr-mənt\ environment,
requirement, retirement

iren \ī-rən\ Byron, gyron,
Myron, siren, environ,
ribavirin

irge \ərj\ see URGE

irgin \ər-jən\ see URGEON

irgo \ər-gō\ see ERGO

iri \ir-ē\ see EARY

iriam \ir-ē-əm\ see ERIUM

iric \ir-ik\ see [2]ERIC

irin \i-rən\ see IREN

irine \ī-rən\ see IREN

iring \īr-iŋ\ firing, wiring,
retiring

irious \ir-ē-əs\ see ERIOUS

iris \ī-rəs\ see IRUS

irish \īr-ish\ Irish, squirish

irit \ir-ət\ Meerut, spirit,

dispirit, emirate, inspirit,
vizierate

irium \ir-ē-əm\ see ERIUM

irius \ir-ē-əs\ see ERIOUS

¹irk \irk\ birk, dirk, Dirk,
kirk

²irk \ərk\ see ¹ORK

irker \ər-kər\ see ¹ORKER

irkie \ər-kē\ see ERKY

irkin \ər-kən\ firkin, gherkin,
jerkin, zircon, Gelsenkirchen

irky \ər-kē\ see ERKY

¹irl \ərl\ birl, burl, churl, curl,
dirl, earl, Earl, Earle, furl,
girl, hurl, knurl, merle, Merle,
pearl, Pearl, purl, skirl,
squirrel, swirl, thirl, thurl, tirl,
twirl, virl, whirl, whorl,
aswirl, awhirl, cowgirl,
impearl, pas seul, playgirl,
salesgirl, schoolgirl, showgirl,
uncurl, unfurl, mother-of-
pearl

²irl \irl\ dirl, skirl

irler \ər-lər\ birler, curler,
pearler, twirler, whirler

irley \ər-lē\ see URLY

irlie \ər-lē\ see URLY

irling \ər-liŋ\ see URLING

irlish \ər-lish\ see URLISH

irly \ər-lē\ see URLY

irm \ərm\ see ¹ORM

irma \ər-mə\ see ERMA

irmary \ərm-rē\ spermary,
infirmary

irmess \ər-məs\ see ERMIS

irmity \ər-mət-ē\ furmity,
infirmity

irmy \ər-mē\ see ERMY

¹irn \irn\ firn, girn, pirn

²irn \ərn\ see URN

¹iro \ir-ō\ see ³ERO

²iro \ē-rō\ see ¹ERO

³iro \ī-rō\ see ¹YRO

¹iron \īrn\ iron, andiron,
environ, flatiron, gridiron

²iron \ī-rən\ see IREN

ironment \īr-mənt\ see
IREMENT

irp \ərp\ see URP

irps \ərps\ stirps, turps—*also
plurals and possessives of
nouns and third person
singular presents of verbs
listed at* URP

irpy \ər-pē\ chirpy, Euterpe

irque \ərk\ see ¹ORK

¹irr \ir\ see ²EER

²irr \ər\ see ¹EUR

irra \ir-ə\ see ²ERA

irrah \ir-ə\ see ²ERA

¹irrel \ərl\ see ¹IRL

²irrel \ər-əl\ see ERRAL

irrely \ər-lē\ see URLY

irrer \ər-ər\ see ERRER

irrhous \ir-əs\ see EROUS

irrhus \ir-əs\ see EROUS

irring \ər-iŋ\ see URRING

irror \ir-ər\ see ²EARER

irrous \ir-əs\ see EROUS

irrup \ər-əp\ chirrup, stirrup,
syrup

irrupy \ər-ə-pē\ chirrupy,
syrupy

irrus \ir-əs\ see EROUS

irry \ər-ē\ see URRY

irs \irz\ see IERS

irsch \irsh\ see IRSH

¹irse \irs\ see IERCE

²irse \ərs\ see ERSE

irsh \irsh\ girsh, kirsch

irst \ərst\ see URST

irsty \ər-stē\ thirsty,
bloodthirsty

irt \ərt\ see ¹ERT
irted \ərt-əd\ see ERTED
irter \ərt-ər\ see ERTER
irth \ərth\ berth, birth, dearth,
earth, firth, girth, mirth,
Perth, worth, childbirth,
Fort Worth, rebirth, self-
worth, stillbirth, unearth,
Wordsworth, afterbirth,
down-to-earth, pennyworth
irthful \ərth-fəl\ mirthful,
worthful
irthless \ərth-ləs\ mirthless,
worthless
irtinent \ərt-nənt\ pertinent,
appurtenant, impertinent
irting \ərt-iŋ\ see ERTING
irtle \ərt-ºl\ see ERTILE
irtually \ərch-lē\ see URCHLY
irtue \ər-chə\ see ERCHA
irty \ərt-ē\ dirty, QWERTY,
shirty, thirty
irus \ī-rəs\ Cyrus, iris, Iris,
Skyros, virus, desirous,
Epirus, Osiris, papyrus,
lentivirus, parvovirus,
rotavirus, papillomavirus
irv \ərv\ see ERVE
irving \ər-viŋ\ see ERVING
irwin \ər-wən\ see ERWIN
¹iry \īr-ē\ eyrie, friary, miry,
spiry, wiry, expiry, inquiry,
venire, praemunire, anno
hegirae
²iry \ī-rē\ see ¹IARY
i's \īz\ see IZE
¹is \is\ see ¹ISS
²is \iz\ see ¹IZ
³is \ē\ see ¹EE
⁴is \ēs\ see IECE
⁵is \ish\ see ¹ISH
¹isa \ē-zə\ see EZA

²isa \ī-zə\ Lisa, Liza, Elisa,
Eliza
isabeth \iz-ə-bəth\ see IZABETH
isable \ī-zə-bəl\ see IZABLE
¹isal \ī-səl\ Faisal, Ijssel,
sisal, skysail, trysail,
radisal
²isal \ī-zəl\ Geisel, incisal,
reprisal, revisal, surprisal,
paradisal
isan \is-ºn\ see ISTEN
isbane \iz-bən\ see ISBON
isbe \iz-bē\ Frisbee, Thisbe
isbee \iz-bē\ see ISBE
isbon \iz-bən\ Brisbane, Lisbon
isc \isk\ see ISK
iscable \is-kə-bəl\ confiscable,
episcopal
iscan \is-kən\ see ISKIN
iscate \is-kət\ see ISKET
isce \is\ see ¹ISS
¹iscean \ī-sē-ən\ Piscean,
Dionysian
²iscean \is-kē-ən\ Piscean,
saurischian, ornithischian
³iscean \is-ē-ən\ see ¹YSIAN
iscence \is-ºns\ puissance,
dehiscence, impuissance,
indehiscence, reminiscence,
reviviscence
iscent \is-ºnt\ puissant,
dehiscent, impuissant,
indehiscent, reminiscent,
reviviscent
isces \ī-sēz\ see ICES
ische \ēsh\ see ²ICHE
ischian \is-kē-ən\ see ²ISCEAN
iscia \ish-ə\ see ITIA
iscible \is-ə-bəl\ see ISSIBLE
iscience \ish-əns\ see ICIENCE
iscient \ish-ənt\ see ICIENT
isco \is-kō\ cisco, disco,

Francisco, Jalisco, Morisco,
San Francisco
iscopal \is-kə-bəl\ see ISCABLE
iscous \is-kəs\ see ISCUS
iscuit \is-kət\ see ISKET
iscus \is-kəs\ discus, viscous,
 viscus, hibiscus, meniscus
¹ise \ēs\ see IECE
²ise \ēz\ see EZE
³ise \īs\ see ¹ICE
⁴ise \īz\ see IZE
¹ised \īst\ see ¹IST
²ised \īzd\ see IZED
isel \iz-əl\ see IZZLE
iseled \iz-əld\ see IZZLED
iseler \iz-lər\ see IZZLER
isement \īz-mənt\ advisement,
 chastisement, despisement,
 disguisement, advertisement,
 disfranchisement,
 enfranchisement,
 disenfranchisement
iser \ī-zər\ see IZER
ises \ī-sēz\ see ICES
¹ish \ish\ dish, fiche, fish,
 flysch, Nis, pish, squish,
 swish, whish, wish, blackfish,
 blowfish, bluefish, bonefish,
 catfish, codfish, crawfish,
 crayfish, dogfish, filefish,
 finfish, flatfish, garfish,
 globefish, goldfish, goosefish,
 Irtysh, kingfish, knish,
 lungfish, lumpfish, monkfish,
 pigfish, pipefish, ratfish,
 redfish, rockfish, sailfish,
 sawfish, shellfish, spearfish,
 starfish, stonefish, sunfish,
 swordfish, tilefish, unwish,
 weakfish, whitefish, angelfish,
 anglerfish, archerfish,
 butterfish, candlefish,

cuttlefish, damselfish,
devilfish, jellyfish, John
Bullish, ladyfish, lionfish,
microfiche, muttonfish,
needlefish, overfish,
paddlefish, ribbonfish,
silverfish, surgeonfish,
triggerfish
²ish \ēsh\ see ²ICHE
isha \ish-ə\ see ITIA
ishable \ish-ə-bəl\ fishable,
 justiciable
ished \isht\ dished, whisht—
 also pasts of verbs listed at
 ¹ISH
isher \ish-ər\ fisher, fissure,
 swisher, ill-wisher, kingfisher,
 well-wisher
ishery \ish-rē\ fishery, Tishri,
 shellfishery
ishi \ē-shē\ chichi, specie,
 maharishi
ishing \ish-iŋ\ bonefishing, fly-
 fishing, sportfishing, well-
 wishing
ishioner \ish-nər\ see ITIONER
ishna \ish-nə\ Krishna,
 Mishnah
ishnah \ish-nə\ see ISHNA
isht \isht\ see ISHED
ishu \ish-ü\ see ¹ISSUE
ishy \ish-ē\ dishy, fishy,
 squishy, swishy
¹isi \ē-zē\ see ¹EASY
²isi \ē-sē\ see EECY
¹isia \izh-ə\ baptisia, Dionysia,
 artemisia
²isia \ē-zhə\ see ²ESIA
¹isian \izh-ən\ see ISION
²isian \ē-zhən\ see ¹ESIAN
isible \iz-ə-bəl\ risible, visible,
 divisible, invisible, indivisible

isin \i-zən\ see ²ISON

ising \ī-ziŋ\ see IZING

ision \izh-ən\ fission, Frisian,
scission, vision, abscission,
collision, concision, decision,
derision, division, elision,
elysian, envision, excision,
incision, misprision, precisian,
precision, prevision,
provision, recision, rescission,
revision, circumcision,
Dionysian, imprecision,
indecision, subdivision,
supervision, television

isional \izh-ə-nəl\ visional,
collisional, decisional,
divisional, excisional,
previsional, provisional

isis \ī-səs\ crisis, Isis, lysis,
nisus, Dionysus, stare decisis

isit \iz-ət\ visit, exquisite,
revisit

isite \iz-ət\ see ISIT

isitive \iz-ət-iv\ acquisitive,
inquisitive

isitor \iz-ət-ər\ visitor,
acquisitor, inquisitor

¹isive \ī-siv\ visive, decisive,
derisive, divisive, incisive,
indecisive

²isive \iz-iv\ visive, derisive,
divisive

isk \isk\ bisque, brisk, disc,
disk, fisc, frisk, risk, whisk,
lutefisk, asterisk, basilisk,
blastodisc, compact disc,
laserdisc, obelisk, odalisque,
tamarisk, videodisc

isker \is-kər\ brisker, frisker,
risker, whisker

isket \is-kət\ biscuit, brisket,
frisket

iskey \is-kē\ see ISKY

iskie \is-kē\ see ISKY

iskin \is-kən\ siskin, Franciscan

isky \is-kē\ frisky, pliskie,
risky, whiskey

island \ī-lənd\ see IGHLAND

islander \ī-lən-dər\ see
IGHLANDER

islands \ī-lənz\ see IGHLANDS

isle \īl\ see ¹ILE

isles \īlz\ see ILES

islet \ī-lət\ see ILOT

isling \iz-liŋ\ brisling, quisling

isly \iz-lē\ see IZZLY

ism \iz-əm\ chrism, chrisom,
ism, prism, schism, abysm,
autism, baalism, baptism,
Birchism, bossism,
Buddhism, casteism, centrism,
charism, Chartism, chemism,
classism, cubism, cultism,
czarism, deism, dwarfism,
faddism, fascism, fauvism,
Gaullism, Grecism, Hobbism,
holism, Jainism, Klanism,
leftism, lyrism, Mahdism,
Maoism, Marxism, monism,
mutism, Nazism, nudism,
Orphism, priggism, purism,
racism, Ramism, rightism,
sadism, Saivism, sapphism,
Scotism, sexism, Shaktism,
Shiism, Sikhism, simplism,
snobbism, sophism, statism,
Sufism, tachism, Tantrism,
Taoism, theism, Thomism,
tourism, tropism, truism,
Turkism, verism, Whiggism,
Yahwism, absurdism,
activism, Adventism,
alarmism, albinism, alpinism,
altruism, amorphism,

anarchism, aneurysm,
anglicism, animism,
aphorism, Arabism, archaism,
asterism, atavism, atheism,
atomism, atticism, Bahaism,
barbarism, Benthamism,
biblicism, blackguardism,
bolshevism, boosterism,
botulism, bourbonism,
Brahmanism, Briticism,
Byronism, cabalism,
Caesarism, Calvinism,
careerism, Castroism,
cataclysm, catechism,
Catharism, centralism,
chauvinism, chimerism,
classicism, colorism,
communism, concretism,
conformism, cretinism,
criticism, cronyism, cynicism,
dadaism, dandyism,
Darwinism, defeatism, de
Gaullism, despotism, die-
hardism, dimorphism,
dirigisme, Docetism, do-
goodism, dogmatism,
Donatism, Don Juanism,
druidism, dualism, dynamism,
egoism, egotism, elitism,
embolism, endemism,
erethism, ergotism, erotism,
escapism, Essenism, etatism,
eunuchism, euphemism,
euphuism, exorcism,
expertism, extremism,
fairyism, familism, fatalism,
feminism, feudalism, fideism,
Fidelism, fogyism,
foreignism, formalism,
futurism, Galenism, gallicism,
galvanism, gangsterism,
genteelism, Germanism,

giantism, gigantism,
globalism, gnosticism,
Gongorism, Gothicism,
gourmandism, gradualism,
grangerism, greenbackism,
Hasidism, heathenism,
Hebraism, hedonism,
Hellenism, helotism,
hermetism, hermitism,
heroism, highbrowism,
Hinduism, hipsterism,
hirsutism, hispanism,
Hitlerism, hoodlumism,
hoodooism, hucksterism,
humanism, Hussitism,
hybridism, hypnotism,
Ibsenism, idealism, imagism,
Irishism, Islamism,
Jansenism, jingoism,
journalism, John Bullism,
Judaism, Junkerism,
kaiserism, Krishnaism, Ku
Kluxism, laconism, laicism,
Lamaism, Lamarckism,
landlordism, Latinism,
legalism, Leninism, lobbyism,
localism, locoism, Lollardism,
luminism, lyricism,
magnetism, mammonism,
mannerism, Marcionism,
masochism, mechanism,
melanism, meliorism,
Menshevism, Mendelism,
mentalism, mesmerism,
methodism, me-tooism,
modernism, Mohockism,
monachism, monadism,
monarchism, mongolism,
Montanism, moralism,
Mormonism, morphinism,
mullahism, mysticism,
narcissism, nationalism,

nativism, nepotism,
neutralism, new dealism,
nihilism, nomadism,
occultism, onanism,
optimism, oralism,
Orangeism, organism,
ostracism, pacifism,
paganism, Pan-Slavism,
pantheism, paroxysm,
Parsiism, passivism,
pauperism, pessimism,
phallicism, pianism, pietism,
plagiarism, Platonism,
pleinairism, Plotinism,
pluralism, pointillism,
populism, pragmatism,
presentism, privatism,
prosaism, Prussianism,
puerilism, pugilism,
Puseyism, Pyrrhonism,
Quakerism, quietism,
rabbinism, racialism,
rationalism, realism,
reformism, rheumatism,
rigorism, robotism,
Romanism, Rousseauism,
rowdyism, royalism, satanism,
savagism, scapegoatism,
schematism, scientism,
sciolism, Scotticism,
Semitism, Shakerism,
Shamanism, Shintoism,
skepticism, socialism,
solecism, solipsism,
Southernism, specialism,
speciesism, Spartanism,
Spinozism, spiritism,
spoonerism, Stalinism,
standpattism, stoicism,
syllogism, symbolism,
synchronism, syncretism,
synergism, talmudism,

tarantism, tectonism,
tenebrism, terrorism,
Teutonism, titanism, Titoism,
tokenism, Toryism, totalism,
totemism, transvestism,
traumatism, tribalism,
tritheism, Trotskyism,
ultraism, unionism, urbanism,
utopism, Vaishnavism,
vampirism, vandalism,
vanguardism, Vedantism,
veganism, verbalism, virilism,
vitalism, vocalism, volcanism,
voodooism, vorticism,
voyeurism, vulcanism,
vulgarism, Wahhabism,
warlordism, welfarism,
Wellerism, witticism,
yahooism, Yankeeism,
Yiddishism, Zionism,
zombiism, absenteeism,
absolutism, abstractionism,
adoptionism, adventurism,
aestheticism, Africanism,
agnosticism, alcoholism,
alienism, amateurism,
amoralism, anabaptism,
anachronism, Anglicanism,
animalism, antagonism,
Arianism, astigmatism,
athleticism, asynchronism,
Atlanticism, atonalism,
Australianism, automatism,
avant-gardism, behaviorism,
Big Brotherism, bilingualism,
biologism, bipedalism,
biracialism, Bonapartism,
bureaucratism, cannibalism,
capitalism, Cartesianism,
catastrophism, Catholicism,
cavalierism, charlatanism,
clericalism, collectivism,

Colonel Blimpism,
commensalism,
commercialism,
communalism, Confucianism,
conservatism, constructivism,
consumerism, corporatism,
creationism, credentialism,
determinism, diabolism,
didacticism, diffusionism,
dilettantism, doctrinairism,
do-nothingism, eclecticism,
ecumenism, egocentrism,
Eleatism, empiricism,
epicenism, epicurism,
epigonism, eremitism,
eroticism, erraticism,
essentialism, ethnocentrism,
eudaemonism, euhemerism,
evangelism, exceptionalism,
exclusivism, exoticism,
expansionism, expressionism,
externalism, Fabianism,
factionalism, factualism,
fanaticism, favoritism,
federalism, Fenianism,
feuilletonism, fifth
columnism, flagellantism,
Fourierism, fraternalism,
freneticism, Freudianism,
funambulism, functionalism,
gallicanism, gutturalism,
henotheism, hermeticism,
Hispanicism, historicism,
hooliganism, Hugenotism,
hypocorism, idiotism,
illiberalism, illuminism,
illusionism, immanentism,
immobilism, impressionism,
indifferentism, Indianism,
infantilism, inflationism,
initialism, insularism,
invalidism, iotacism,

irredentism, Ishmaelitism,
Italianism, Jacobinism,
Jacobitism, jesuitism,
Keynesianism, know-
nothingism, legitimism,
lesbianism, liberalism,
libertinism, literalism,
Lutheranism, Lysenkoism,
Magianism, malapropism,
mandarinism, McCarthyism,
medievalism, mercantilism,
messianism, metabolism,
metamorphism, militarism,
minimalism, misoneism,
monasticism, monetarism,
monotheism, mosaicism,
mutualism, naturalism,
Naziritism, necrophilism,
negativism, neologism, neo-
Nazism, neuroticism, nice-
nellyism, nominalism,
nonconformism, objectivism,
obscurantism, obstructionism,
officialism, opportunism,
organicism, pacificism,
Pantagruelism, parallelism,
parasitism, pastoralism,
paternalism, patriotism,
Peeping Tomism,
perfectionism, personalism,
pharisaism, physicalism,
plebeianism, poeticism,
polyglotism, polytheism,
positivism, postmodernism,
pragmaticism, primitivism,
probabilism, progressivism,
proselytism, protectionism,
Protestantism, provincialism,
pseudomorphism,
psychologism, puritanism,
radicalism, rationalism,
recidivism, reductionism,

refugeeism, regionalism, relativism, restrictionism, revisionism, revivalism, ritualism, romanticism, ruffianism, Sadduceeism, salvationism, sansculottism, sardonicism, scholasticism, secessionism, sectarianism, sectionalism, secularism, sensualism, separatism, serialism, Slavophilism, solidarism, somnambulism, sovietism, Stakhanovism, structuralism, subjectivism, suprematism, surrealism, Sybaritism, sycophantism, systematism, Tammanyism, teetotalism, theocentrism, triumphalism, Uncle Tomism, vagabondism, ventriloquism, vigilantism, voluntarism, volunteerism, Wesleyanism, workaholism, Zwinglianism, abolitionism, academicism, agrarianism, Americanism, analphabetism, anthropomorphism, anthropopathism, anti-Semitism, Arminianism, autoerotism, barbarianism, bibliophilism, bicameralism, biculturalism, biloquialism, bipartisanism, bohemianism, colloquialism, colonialism, conceptualism, confessionalism, constitutionalism, conventionalism, corporativism, cosmopolitism, deviationism, ecumenicism, emotionalism, esotericism, Europocentrism,

evolutionism, exhibitionism, existentialism, expatriatism, fundamentalism, governmentalism, Hegelianism, hermaphroditism, hypercriticism, hyperrealism, hyperurbanism, imperialism, incendiarism, incrementalism, indeterminism, industrialism, instrumentalism, interventionism, introspectionism, irrationalism, isolationism, Malthusianism, Manichaeanism, manorialism, materialism, millennialism, Monarchianism, mongolianism, Monophysitism, Muhammadanism, multilingualism, neoclassicism, Neoplatonism, neorealism, Nestorianism, Occidentalism, operationism, orientalism, Palladianism, parajournalism, parochialism, particularism, pedestrianism, Pelagianism, Pentecostalism, phenomenalism, photojournalism, pictorialism, pococurantism, Postimpressionism, professionalism, pseudoclassicism, reconstructionism, republicanism, Rosicrucianism, sacerdotalism, sacramentalism, self-determinism, sadomasochism, sectarianism, sensationalism, sentimentalism, socinianism, spiritualism, theatricalism, Tractarianism, traditionalism, transcendentalism, transsexualism, trilateralism, ultramontanism, universalism, utopianism, vernacularism, Victorianism, vocationalism, voluntaryism, Albigensianism, anticlericalism, antiquarianism, apocalypticism, assimilationism, associationism, Augustinianism, autoeroticism, ceremonialism, collaborationism, congregationalism, cosmopolitanism, ecclesiasticism, ecumenicalism, environmentalism, Evangelicalism, Hamiltonianism, homoeroticism, epicureanism, experimentalism, immaterialism, individualism, institutionalism, intellectualism, internationalism, libertarianism, middle-of-the-roadism, millenarianism, neo-conservatism, neo-impressionism, operationalism, Pan-Americanism, Peripateticism, photoperiodism, Pre-Raphaelitism, Presbyterianism, Pythegoreanism, Rastafarianism, reactionaryism, Sabbatarianism, supernaturalism, Swedenborgianism, territorialism, Trinitarianism, unitarianism, vegetarianism, Zoroastrianism, Aristotelianism, authoritarianism, egalitarianism, Episcopalianism, humanitarianism, Machiavellianism, neocolonialism, neo-Expressionism, predestinarianism, representationalism, utilitarianism, establishmentarianism, latitudinarianism

isma \iz-mə\ charisma, melisma

ismal \iz-məl\ see YSMAL

[1]isme \īm\ see [1]IME

[2]isme \izᵊm\ see ISM

ismo \ēz-mō\ machismo, verismo, caudillismo

iso \ē-sō\ miso, piso

isom \iz-əm\ see ISM

[1]ison \īs-ᵊn\ bison, hyson, Meissen, streptomycin, Aureomycin, erythromycin

[2]ison \iz-ᵊn\ dizen, mizzen, prison, risen, weasand, wizen, arisen, imprison, Tok Pisin, uprisen

isor \ī-zər\ see IZER

isored \ī-zərd\ guisard, visored

isory \īz-rē\ advisory, provisory, revisory, supervisory

isp \isp\ crisp, lisp, LISP, wisp, will-o-the-wisp

isper \is-pər\ crisper, lisper, whisper

ispy \is-pē\ crispy, wispy

isque \isk\ see ISK

iss \is\ bis, bliss, cis, Chris, cuisse, Dis, hiss, kiss, miss, sis, Swiss, this, vis, wis, abyss, amiss, coulisse, dehisce, dismiss, iwis, koumiss, remiss, submiss, ambergris, hit-and-miss, hit-or-miss, reminisce, verdigris

issa \is-ə\ abscissa, mantissa, Melissa, Orissa, vibrissa

issable \is-ə-bəl\ see ISSIBLE

issal \is-əl\ see ISTLE

issance \is-°ns\ see ISCENCE

issant \is-°nt\ see ISCENT

¹isse \is\ see ISS

²isse \ēs\ see IECE

issed \ist\ see ²IST

issel \is-əl\ see ISTLE

isser \is-ər\ hisser, kisser

issible \is-ə-bəl\ kissable, miscible, admissible, immiscible, municipal, omissible, permissible, remissible, transmissible, impermissible, inadmissible

issile \is-əl\ see ISTLE

¹ission \ish-ən\ see ITION

²ission \izh-ən\ see ISION

issionable \ish-nə-bəl\ fissionable, conditionable

issioner \ish-nər\ see ITIONER

issive \is-iv\ missive, admissive, derisive, dismissive, emissive, permissive, submissive, transmissive

issome \is-əm\ lissome, alyssum

issor \iz-ər\ scissor, whizzer

¹issue \ish-ü\ fichu, issue, tissue, reissue, Mogadishu, overissue

²issue \ish-ə\ see ITIA

issure \ish-ər\ see ISHER

issus \is-əs\ byssus, missus, Mrs., narcissus, Narcissus

issy \is-ē\ hissy, missy, prissy, sissy

¹ist \īst\ Christ, feist, heist, hist, tryst, zeitgeist, Antichrist, black-a-vised, poltergeist— *also pasts of verbs listed at* ¹ICE

²ist \ist\ cist, cyst, fist, gist, grist, kist, list, Liszt, mist, schist, tryst, twist, whist, wist, wrist, assist, backlist, blacklist, checklist, consist, delist, desist, encyst, enlist, entwist, exist, handlist, insist, persist, playlist, protist, Rehnquist, resist, shortlist, subsist, untwist, catechist, coexist, dadaist, exorcist, intertwist, preexist, love-in-a-mist—*also pasts of verbs listed at* ISS

³ist \ēst\ see ¹EAST

¹ista \ē-stə\ turista, camorrista, Fidelista

²ista \is-tə\ crista, vista, arista, ballista, sacahuiste

istaed \is-təd\ see ISTED

istal \is-t°l\ Bristol, crystal, Crystal, distal, listel, pistil, pistol

istan \is-tən\ see ISTON

istance \is-təns\ see ISTENCE

istant \is-tənt\ see ISTENT

¹iste \is-tē\ see ²ICITY

²iste \ēst\ see ¹EAST

³**iste** \is-tə\ see ²ISTA

isted \is-təd\ twisted, vistaed,
closefisted, enlisted, ham-
fisted, hardfisted, limp-
wristed, tightfisted, two-fisted,
unlisted, untwisted, white-
listed, ironfisted, unassisted—
also pasts of verbs listed at
²IST

istel \is-t°l\ see ISTAL

isten \is-°n\ christen, glisten,
listen, Nisan

istenable \is-nə-bəl\ listenable,
medicinable

istence \is-təns\ distance,
assistance, consistence,
existence, insistence,
outdistance, persistence,
resistance, subsistence,
coexistence, inconsistence,
inexistence, nonexistence,
nonresistance, preexistence

istency \is-tən-sē\ consistency,
insistency, persistency,
inconsistency

istent \is-tənt\ distant, assistant,
consistent, existent, insistent,
persistent, resistant,
subsistent, coexistent,
equidistant, inconsistent,
inexistent, nonexistent,
nonpersistent, nonresistant,
preexistent

ister \is-tər\ bister, blister,
clyster, glister, klister, lister,
Lister, mister, sister, twister,
resister, resistor, solicitor,
stepsister, transistor

istery \is-trē\ see ISTORY

istful \ist-fəl\ tristful, wistful

isthmus \is-məs\ see ISTMAS

isti \is-tē\ see ²ICITY

istic \is-tik\ cystic, distich,
fistic, mystic, artistic, autistic,
ballistic, cladistic, cubistic,
eristic, fascistic, faunistic,
floristic, heuristic, holistic,
hubristic, juristic, linguistic,
logistic, meristic, monistic,
patristic, phlogistic, puristic,
sadistic, simplistic, sophistic,
statistic, stylistic, Taoistic,
theistic, Thomistic, touristic,
truistic, veristic, wholistic,
Yahwistic, activistic,
agonistic, alchemistic,
altruistic, amoristic,
anarchistic, animistic,
aphoristic, archaistic,
atavistic, atheistic, atomistic,
belletristic, cabalistic,
Calvinistic, casuistic,
catechistic, Catharistic,
centralistic, chauvinistic,
communistic, crosslinguistic,
dadaistic, dualistic,
dyslogistic, egoistic, egotistic,
essayistic, eucharistic,
eulogistic, euphemistic,
euphuistic, exorcistic,
fabulistic, familistic, fatalistic,
feministic, fetishistic,
feudalistic, fideistic,
formalistic, futuristic,
gongoristic, haggadistic,
Hebraistic, hedonistic,
Hellenistic, humanistic,
humoristic, idealistic,
imagistic, inartistic,
Jansenistic, jingoistic,
journalistic, Judaistic,
Lamaistic, legalistic,
masochistic, mechanistic,
melanistic, mentalistic,

methodistic, modernistic,
moralistic, narcissistic,
nationalistic, nativistic,
nepotistic, nihilistic,
novelistic, onanistic,
optimistic, pantheistic,
pessimistic, pianistic, pietistic,
plagiaristic, Platonistic,
pluralistic, pointillistic,
populistic, pugilistic,
quietistic, realistic,
Romanistic, sciolistic,
shamanistic, shintoistic,
socialistic, solecistic,
solipsistic, specialistic,
surrealistic, syllogistic,
symbolistic, synchronistic,
syncretistic, synergistic,
terroristic, totalistic,
totemistic, ultraistic,
unrealistic, urbanistic,
utopistic, vandalistic,
verbalistic, vitalistic,
voodooistic, voyeuristic,
Zionistic, absolutistic,
adventuristic, anachronistic,
animalistic, anomalistic,
antagonistic, behavioristic,
cannibalistic, capitalistic,
characteristic, collectivistic,
contortionistic, deterministic,
evangelistic, eudaemonistic,
euhemeristic, expansionistic,
expressionistic,
extralinguistic, functionalistic,
Hinayanistic, hypocoristic,
immanentistic,
impressionistic, liberalistic,
literalistic, Mahayanistic,
melioristic, mercantilistic,
militaristic, mediumistic,
metalinguistic, misogynistic,

monopolistic, monotheistic,
naturalistic, negativistic,
neologistic, opportunistic,
paternalistic, physicalistic,
polytheistic, probabilistic,
propagandistic,
psycholinguistic, rationalistic,
recidivistic, reductionistic,
relativistic, revivalistic,
ritualistic, secularistic,
sensualistic, separatistic,
sociolinguistic,
somnambulistic,
ventriloquistic, violinistic,
voluntaristic, colonialistic,
commercialistic,
Deuteronomistic,
emotionalistic, exhibitionistic,
fundamentalistic,
existentalistic, imperialistic,
indeterministic,
introspectionistic,
irrationalistic, materialistic,
oligopolistic,
Postimpressionistic,
sadomasochistic,
sensationalistic,
sociolinguistic, spiritualistic,
traditionalistic, individualistic

istical \is-ti-kəl\ mystical,
deistical, eristical, linguistical,
logistical, monistical,
patristical, sophistical,
statistical, theistical,
alchemistical, atheistical,
casuistical, egoistical,
egotistical, exorcistical,
pantheistical, anomalistical,
hypocoristical, monotheistical,
polytheistical

istich \is-tik\ see ISTIC

istics \is-tiks\ ballistics, ekistics,

linguistics, logistics,
patristics, statistics, stylistics,
futuristics, criminalistics—
*also plurals and possessives
of nouns listed at* ISTIC

istie \is-tē\ see ²ICITY

istil \is-tᵊl\ see ISTAL

istin \is-tən\ see ISTON

istine \is-tən\ see ISTON

istle \is-əl\ bristle, fissile,
gristle, missal, missile,
scissile, thistle, whistle,
abyssal, dickcissel, dismissal,
epistle, pennywhistle

istler \is-lər\ whistler, Whistler,
epistler

istless \ist-ləs\ listless, resistless

istly \is-lē\ bristly, gristly,
thistly, sweet cicely

istmas \is-məs\ Christmas,
isthmus, Kiritimati

isto \is-tō\ aristo, Callisto

istol \is-tᵊl\ see ISTAL

iston \is-tən\ Kristin, piston,
Tristan, Philistine, phlogiston,
amethystine

istor \is-tər\ see ISTER

istory \is-trē\ blistery, history,
mystery, consistory,
prehistory

istral \is-trəl\ mistral, sinistral

istress \is-trəs\ mistress,
headmistress, postmistress,
schoolmistress, sinistrous,
taskmistress, toastmistress

istrophe \is-trə-fē\ antistrophe,
epistrophe

istrous \is-trəs\ see ISTRESS

isty \is-tē\ see ²ICITY

isus \ī-səs\ see ISIS

iszt \ist\ see ²IST

¹it \it\ bit, bitt, brit, Brit, chit,
dit, fit, flit, frit, git, grit, hit,
it, kit, knit, lit, mitt, nit, pit,
Pitt, quit, sit, skit, slit, snit,
spit, split, Split, sprit, teat, tit,
twit, whit, wit, writ, zit,
acquit, admit, armpit, backbit,
backfit, befit, bowsprit,
Brigitte, bushtit, cesspit,
close-knit, cockpit, commit,
culprit, demit, Dewitt, dimwit,
emit, fleapit, gaslit, godwit,
half-wit, henbit, house-sit,
legit, lit crit, misfit, mishit,
moonlit, nitwit, obit, omit,
outfit, outwit, peewit, permit,
pinch-hit, Prakrit, pulpit, refit,
remit, sandpit, Sanskrit,
snakebit, starlit, submit, sunlit,
switch-hit, tidbit, tight-knit,
titbit, tomtit, transmit,
turnspit,twilit, two-bit, unfit,
unknit,well-knit, baby-sit,
benefit,candlelit, counterfeit,
hypocrite, intermit, intromit,
manumit, megahit, recommit,
retrofit, cost-benefit, lickety-
split, overcommit, jack-in-the-
pulpit

²it \ē\ see ¹EE

³it \ēt\ see ¹EAT

¹ita \īt-ə\ vita, baryta, amanita

²ita \ēt-ə\ cheetah, eta, Greta,
Nita, pita, Rita, theta, vita,
zeta, Akita, Anita, Bonita,
bonito, casita, excreta,
Granita, Juanita, Lolita,
mosquito, partita, Suita,
amanita, arboreta, feterita,
incognita, manzanita,
margarita, senhorita, senorita,
Bhagavad Gita

¹itable \īt-ə-bəl\ citable,

writable, excitable, indictable, copyrightable, extraditable

²**itable** \it-ə-bəl\ see ITTABLE

itae \īt-ē\ see ²ITE

itain \it-n\ see ITTEN

¹**ital** \īt-ᵊl\ title, vital, detrital, entitle, nontitle, recital, requital, subtitle, disentitle, intravital, supravital

²**ital** \it-ᵊl\ see ITTLE

italer \it-ᵊl-ər\ whittler, victualler, belittler, Hospitaler

italist \īt-ᵊl-əst\ titlist, vitalist, recitalist

itan \īt-ᵊn\ see IGHTEN

itant \īt-ᵊnt\ mightn't, excitant, incitant, renitent

itany \it-ᵊn-ē\ Brittany, dittany, litany

itch \ich\ ditch, fitch, flitch, glitch, hitch, itch, kitsch, niche, pitch, quitch, rich, snitch, stitch, such, switch, twitch, which, witch, backstitch, bewitch, cross-stitch, enrich, fast-twitch, hemstitch, lockstitch, slow-pitch, slow-twitch, topstitch, unhitch, whipstitch, czarevitch, featherstitch, microswitch

itchen \ich-ən\ kitchen, richen

itchener \ich-nər\ Kitchener, Michener

itcher \ich-ər\ hitcher, pitcher, richer, snitcher, stitcher, switcher, enricher, hemstitcher, Lubavitcher, water witcher

itchery \ich-ə-rē\ bitchery, obituary, stitchery, witchery, bewitchery

itches \ich-əz\ britches, riches, Dutchman's-breeches—*also plurals and possessives of nouns and third person singular presents of verbs listed at* ITCH

itchman \ich-mən\ pitchman, switchman

itchment \ich-mənt\ bewitchment, enrichment

itchy \ich-ē\ bitchy, itchy, kitschy, pitchy, twitchy, witchy

it'd \it-əd\ see ITTED

¹**ite** \īt\ bight, bite, blight, bright, byte, cite, dight, dite, Dwight, fight, flight, fright, height, hight, kite, knight, krait, kyte, light, lite, might, mite, night, plight, quite, right, rite, sight, site, sleight, slight, smite, spite, sprite, tight, trite, white, White, wight, Wight, wite, wright, Wright, write, affright, airtight, albite, alight, all right, all-night, aright, backbite, backlight, bedight, Birchite, birthright, bobwhite, bombsight, bullfight, campsite, cockfight, contrite, Cushite, daylight, deadlight, delight, despite, dogfight, downright, droplight, earthlight, excite, eyebright, eyesight, fanlight, finite, firefight, firelight, fistfight, flashlight, fleabite, floodlight, foresight, forthright, fortnight, frostbite, Gadite, gaslight, gastight, ghostwrite, graphite, gunfight, Gunite, half-light, Hamite, handwrite, headlight,

highlight, hindsight, Hittite,
homesite, hoplite, Hussite,
ignite, illite, infight, in-flight,
incite, indict, indite, insight,
invite, jacklight, jadeite,
lamplight, Levite, lighttight,
lignite, limelight, lintwhite,
lowlight, Lucite, Luddite,
lyddite, Melchite, midnight,
millwright, miswrite,
moonlight, night-light, off-
site, off-white, on-site,
outright, outsight, partite,
penlight, playwright, polite,
prizefight, pyrite, recite,
requite, respite, rushlight,
safelight, searchlight, Semite,
Servite, Shemite, Shiite,
shipwright, sidelight,
skintight, skylight, skywrite,
smectite, snakebite, snow-
white, spaceflight, speedlight,
spotlight, starlight, sticktight,
stoplight, streetlight, sunlight,
Sunnite, taillight, termite,
tonight, torchlight, trothplight,
twilight, twi-night, typewrite,
unite, unsight, upright,
uptight, wainwright,
weeknight, wheelwright,
acolyte, aconite, Ammonite,
Amorite, amosite, anchorite,
anthracite, antiwhite,
apartheid, appetite, Bakelite,
Benthamite, bipartite, black-
and-white, blatherskite,
bleacherite, chalcocite,
Canaanite, Carmelite,
castroite, catamite, cellulite,
copyright, disinvite, disunite,
dynamite, erudite, expedite,
extradite, Fahrenheit,

featherlight, fly-by-night,
gelignite, gesundheit,
gigabyte, Hashemite,
Hepplewhite, Himyarite,
Hitlerite, hug-me-tight,
impolite, Ishmaelite, Israelite,
Jacobite, Josephite,
Kimberlite, laborite, Leninite,
leukocyte, lily-white, localite,
malachite, manganite,
Marcionite, Masonite,
Mennonite, Minorite,
Moabite, muscovite, Nazirite,
out-of-sight, overbite,
overflight, overnight,
oversight, overwrite, parasite,
perovskite, plebiscite,
proselyte, Puseyite, pyrrhotite,
recondite, reunite, satellite,
shergottite, socialite, sodalite,
sodomite, Stagirite, stalactite,
stalagmite, Sybarite, time-of-
flight, transfinite, transvestite,
tripartite, troglodyte,
Trotskyite, ultralight,
underwrite, urbanite,
Wahhabite, watertight,
Wycliffite, yesternight,
adipocyte, anthophyllite,
cosmopolite, exurbanite,
gemütlichkeit, hermaphrodite,
Indo-Hittite, McCarthyite,
multipartite, quadripartite,
suburbanite, theodolite,
Areopagite, Pre-Raphaelite,
Great Australian Bight
²**ite** \īt-ē\ flighty, mighty,
nightie, righty, whitey, whity,
almighty, Almighty, Venite,
Aphrodite, aqua vitae,
arborvitae, lignum vitae
³**ite** \it\ see ¹IT

⁴ite \ēt\ see ¹EAT

ited \īt-əd\ see IGHTED

iteful \īt-fəl\ see IGHTFUL

itely \īt-lē\ see IGHTLY

item \īt-əm\ item, ad infinitum

itement \īt-mənt\ alightment, excitement, incitement, indictment

iten \īt-ᵊn\ see IGHTEN

itener \īt-nər\ see IGHTENER

itent \īt-ᵊnt\ see ITANT

iteor \ēt-ē-ər\ see ETEOR

¹iter \īt-ər\ blighter, fighter, lighter, miter, niter, titer, writer, all-nighter, braillewriter, exciter, first-nighter, lamplighter, nail-biter, one-nighter, prizefighter, screenwriter, scriptwriter, songwriter, speechwriter, sportswriter, states righter, typewriter, copywriter, expediter, fly-by-nighter, Gastarbeiter, underwriter, teletypewriter—*also nouns and comparatives of adjectives formed by adding* -er *to verbs listed at* ¹ITE

²iter \it-ər\ see ITTER

³iter \ēt-ər\ see ¹EATER

iteral \it-ə-rəl\ clitoral, literal, littoral, sublittoral, triliteral

iterally \it-ər-lē\ see ITTERLY

iterate \it-ə-rət\ literate, illiterate, nonliterate, postliterate, preliterate, presbyterate, subliterate, semiliterate

¹ites \īt-ēz\ barytes, sorites, Thersites—*also plurals and possessives of nouns listed at* ²ITE

²ites \īts\ see IGHTS

itey \īt-ē\ see ²ITE

ith \ith\ fifth, frith, grith, kith, myth, pith, sith, smith, Smith, swith, with, withe, blacksmith, forthwith, goldsmith, Goldsmith, gunsmith, herewith, locksmith, songsmith, therewith, tinsmith, tunesmith, wherewith, whitesmith, wordsmith, coppersmith, eolith, Granny Smith, Hammersmith, megalith, metalsmith, microlith, monolith, neolith, silversmith, paleolith

³ith \ēt\ see ¹EAT

⁴ith \ēth\ see ¹EATH

¹ithe \īth\ blithe, kithe, lithe, scythe, tithe, withe, writhe

²ithe \ith\ see ²ITH

³ithe \ith\ see ¹ITH

¹ithee \ith-ē\ see ²ITHY

²ithee \ith-ē\ see ¹ITHY

ither \ith-ər\ blither, cither, dither, hither, slither, swither, thither, whither, wither, zither, come-hither, nowhither, somewhither

itherward \ith-ər-wərd\ thitherward, whitherward

ithesome \īth-səm\ blithesome, lithesome

ithia \ith-ē-ə\ see YTHIA

ithic \ith-ik\ lithic, ornithic, batholithic, Eolithic, granolithic, megalithic, Mesolithic, monolithic, neolithic, Paleolithic

ithing \ī-thiŋ\ tithing, trithing
ithmic \ith-mik\ see YTHMIC
¹ithy \ith-ē\ prithee, withy
²ithy \ith-ē\ mythy, pithy, prithee, smithy, withy
iti \ēt-ē\ see EATY
¹itia \ish-ə\ Lycia, Mysia, wisha, Alicia, Cilicia, comitia, episcia, Galicia, indicia, Letitia, militia, Patricia, Phoenicia, Dionysia
²itia \ē-shə\ see ¹ESIA
itial \ish-əl\ see ICIAL
¹itian \ish-ən\ see ITION
²itian \ē-shən\ see ¹ETION
itiate \ish-ət\ initiate, novitiate, uninitiate
itic \it-ik\ clitic, critic, arthritic, bronchitic, dendritic, enclitic, granitic, graphitic, Hamitic, jaditic, mephitic, proclitic, pruritic, rachitic, Sanskritic, Semitic, Shemitic, Sinitic, anaclitic, analytic, anchoritic, catalytic, cenobitic, copralitic, crystallitic, diacritic, dialytic, dynamitic, eremitic, Himyaritic, hypercritic, jesuitic, paralytic, parasitic, sodomitic, stalactitic, stalagmitic, sybaritic, thallophytic, thrombolytic, troglodytic, cryptanalytic, electrolytic, hermaphroditic, meteoritic, Monophysitic, psychoanalytic
itical \it-i-kəl\ critical, Levitical, political, analytical, apolitical, cenobitical, diacritical, eremitical, hypercritical, hypocritical, impolitical, Jacobitical, jesuitical, parasitical, sodomitical, supercritical, geopolitical, meteoritical, sociopolitical
itics \it-iks\ Semitics, analytics, meteoritics—*also plurals and possessives of nouns listed at* ITIC
itid \it-əd\ see ITTED
itimati \is-məs\ see ISTMAS
itin \īt-ᵊn\ see IGHTEN
iting \īt-iŋ\ biting, flyting, lighting, whiting, writing, backbiting, bullfighting, cockfighting, daylighting, exciting, freewriting, frostbiting, handwriting, infighting, inviting, newswriting, prewriting, prizefighting, skywriting, songwriting, sportswriting, typewriting
ition \ish-ən\ fission, hycian, mission, titian, Titian, addition, admission, ambition, attrition, audition, beautician, clinician, cognition, coition, commission, condition, contrition, demission, dentition, dismission, Domitian, edition, emission, ethician, fruition, ignition, lenition, logician, magician, monition, mortician, munition, musician, nutrition, omission, optician, partition, patrician, perdition, permission, petition, Phoenician, physician, position, punition, remission, rendition, sedition, submission, suspicion, tactician, technician, tradition,

transition, transmission,
tuition, volition, abolition,
acquisition, admonition,
aesthetician, air-condition,
ammunition, apparition,
apposition, coalition,
competition, composition,
cosmetician, decommission,
decondition, definition,
demolition, deposition,
dietitian, Dionysian,
disposition, disquisition,
electrician, erudition,
exhibition, expedition,
exposition, extradition,
imposition, inhibition,
inquisition, intermission,
intromission, intuition,
linguistician, logistician,
malnutrition, malposition,
manumission, mathematician,
mechanician, micturition,
obstetrician, opposition,
Ordovician, parturition,
phonetician, politician,
precognition, precondition,
premonition, preposition,
prohibition, proposition,
recognition, recondition,
repetition, requisition,
rhetorician, statistician,
submunition, superstition,
supposition, transposition,
academician, arithmetician,
decomposition, diagnostician,
dialectician, disinhibition,
geometrician, geriatrician,
indisposition, interposition,
juxtaposition, metaphysician,
onomastician, pediatrician,
presupposition, redefinition,

semiotician, theoretician,
superimposition
itionable \ish-nə-bəl\ see
ISSIONABLE
itional \ish-ə-nəl\ additional,
attritional, cognitional,
coitional, conditional,
nutritional, positional,
traditional, transitional,
tuitional, volitional,
apparitional, appositional,
compositional, definitional,
depositional, expositional,
inquisitional, oppositional,
prepositional, propositional,
repetitional, suppositional,
transpositional, unconditional,
juxtapositional,
presuppositional
itioner \i-shə-nər\ missioner,
commissioner, conditioner,
parishioner, partitioner,
petitioner, practitioner,
exhibitioner, malpractitioner,
nurse-practitioner
itionist \i-shə-nəst\ nutritionist,
partitionist, abolitionist,
coalitionist, demolitionist,
exhibitionist, intuitionist,
oppositionist, prohibitionist
itious \ish-əs\ see ¹ICIOUS
itis \īt-əs\ situs, Titus, arthritis,
botrytis, bronchitis, bursitis,
colitis, cystitis, detritus,
gastritis, iritis, mastitis,
nephritis, neuritis, phlebitis,
dermatitis, enteritis, gingivitis,
hepatitis, Heracleitus, ileitis,
laryngitis, meningitis,
pharyngitis, pneumonitis,
prostatitis, retinitis, sinusitis,
tonsillitis, spondylitis,

tendinitis, urethritis, vaginitis, appendicitis, conjunctivitis, encephalitis, endocarditis, endometritus, folliculitis, Hermaphroditus, peritonitis, analysis situs, diverticulitis, gastroenteritis, poliomyelitis

itish \it-ish\ British, skittish

itius \ish-əs\ see ICIOUS

itle \īt-ᵊl\ see ¹ITAL

it'll \it-ᵊl\ see ITTLE

itment \it-mənt\ fitment, commitment, remitment, recommitment, overcommitment

itness \it-nəs\ fitness, witness, earwitness, eyewitness, unfitness

itney \it-nē\ jitney, Whitney, Mount Whitney

¹ito \ēt-ō\ keto, Leto, Quito, Tito, veto, bonito, burrito, graffito, magneto, Miskito, mosquito, Negrito, Hirohito, incognito, sanbenito

²ito \ēt-ə\ see ²ITA

¹iton \it-ᵊn\ see ITTEN

²iton \īt-ᵊn\ see IGHTEN

itoral \it-ə-rəl\ see ITERAL

itra \ē-trə\ see ²ETRA

itral \ī-trəl\ mitral, nitrile

itrile \ī-trəl\ see ITRAL

it's \its\ see ITS

its \its\ blitz, ditz, Fritz, glitz, grits, it's, its, quits, spitz, Chemnitz, Saint Kitts, slivovitz—*also plurals and possessives of nouns and third person singular presents of verbs listed at* ¹IT

itsail \it-səl\ see ITZEL

itsch \ich\ see ITCH

itschy \ich-ē\ see ITCHY

itsy \it-sē\ see ITZY

itt \it\ see ¹IT

itta \it-ə\ shittah, vitta

ittable \it-ə-bəl\ committable, habitable, hospitable, remittable, transmittable, inhospitable

ittah \it-ə\ see ITTA

ittal \it-ᵊl\ see ITTLE

ittance \it-ᵊns\ pittance, quittance, acquittance, admittance, emittance, immittance, remittance, transmittance, intermittence

ittany \it-ᵊn-ē\ see ITANY

itte \it\ see ¹IT

itted \it-əd\ fitted, it'd, nitid, pitted, teated, witted, committed, dim-witted, half-witted, quick-witted, sharp-witted, slow-witted, thick-witted, unbitted, unfitted, uncommitted—*also pasts of verbs listed at* ¹IT

ittee \it-ē\ see ITTY

itten \it-ᵊn\ bitten, Britain, Briton, Britten, kitten, litten, Lytton, mitten, smitten, witting, written, backbitten, flea-bitten, Great Britain, hard-bitten, New Britain, rewritten, snakebitten, unwritten

ittence \it-ᵊns\ see ITTANCE

ittent \it-ᵊnt\ remittent, intermittent, intromittent

itter \it-ər\ bitter, chitter, critter, fitter, flitter, fritter, glitter, hitter, jitter, knitter, litter, quitter, quittor, sitter, skitter, slitter, spitter, titter, twitter,

aglitter, atwitter, bed-sitter,
embitter, emitter, hairsplitter,
no-hitter, outfitter, rail-
splitter, remitter, shipfitter,
steamfitter, switch-hitter,
transmitter, benefiter,
counterfeiter, intromitter

itterer \it-ər-ər\ fritterer,
litterer, twitterer

itterly \it-ər-lē\ bitterly, literally

ittern \it-ərn\ bittern, cittern,
gittern

ittery \it-ə-rē\ glittery, jittery,
littery, skittery, twittery

ittie \it-ē\ see ITTY

ittier \it-ē-ər\ grittier, prettier,
Whittier, wittier

ittiness \it-ē-nəs\ grittiness,
prettiness, wittiness

¹itting \it-iŋ\ fitting, sitting,
splitting, witting, befitting,
earsplitting, fence-sitting,
formfitting, hairsplitting,
hard-hitting, house-sitting,
resitting, sidesplitting,
unfitting, unwitting,
unremitting

²itting \it-ᵊn\ see ITTEN

ittish \it-ish\ see ITISH

ittle \it-ᵊl\ brittle, it'll, kittle,
little, skittle, spital, spittle,
tittle, victual, whittle, wittol,
acquittal, belittle, committal,
embrittle, hospital, lickspittle,
remittal, transmittal,
noncommittal, recommittal

ittler \it-ᵊl-ər\ see ITALER

ittol \it-ᵊl\ see ITTLE

ittor \it-ər\ see ITTER

ittoral \it-ə-rəl\ see ITERAL

itts \its\ see ITS

itty \it-ē\ bitty, city, ditty,
gritty, kitty, Kitty, pity,
pretty, tittie, witty, committee,
self-pity, itty-bitty, Kansas
City, megacity, nitty-gritty,
Salt Lake City, subcommittee,
supercity, Walter Mitty, Ho
Chi Minh City

itual \ich-ə-wəl\ ritual, habitual

ituary \ich-ə-rē\ see ¹ITCHERY

itum \īt-əm\ see ITEM

itus \īt-əs\ see ITIS

¹ity \it-ē\ see ITTY

²ity \īt-ē\ see ²ITE

itz \its\ see ITS

¹itza \ēt-sə\ pizza, czaritza,
Chichén Itza, Katowice

²itza \it-sə\ czaritza, tamburitza

itzel \it-səl\ schnitzel, spritsail,
Wiener schnitzel

itzi \it-sē\ see ITZY

itzy \it-sē\ bitsy, glitzy, Mitzi,
ritzy, schizy

iu \ü\ see ¹EW

¹ius \ē-əs\ see ¹EUS

²ius \ī-əs\ see ¹IAS

¹iv \iv\ see ²IVE

²iv \ēf\ see ¹IEF

³iv \if\ see IFF

⁴iv \ēv\ see EAVE

¹iva \ī-və\ Saiva, gingiva,
Godiva, saliva

²iva \ē-və\ diva, Eva, kiva,
Shiva, siva, Siva, viva,
geneva, Geneva, yeshiva

³iva \iv-ə\ Shiva, Siva

¹ivable \ī-və-bəl\ drivable,
derivable, revivable,
survivable

²ivable \iv-ə-bəl\ livable,
forgivable

ival \ī-vəl\ rival, archival,
arrival, revival, survival,

adjectival, conjunctival,
genitival, substantival,
infinitival

ivalent \iv-ə-lənt\ ambivalent,
equivalent, unambivalent

ivan \iv-ən\ see IVEN

ivance \ī-vəns\ connivance,
contrivance, survivance

ivative \iv-ət-iv\ privative,
derivative

¹ive \īv\ chive, dive, drive, five,
gyve, hive, I've, jive, live,
rive, shrive, skive, strive,
thrive, wive, alive, archive,
Argive, arrive, beehive,
connive, contrive, deprive,
derive, endive, nosedive,
ogive, revive, self-drive, skin-
dive, survive, test-drive, forty-
five, overdrive, power-dive

²ive \iv\ give, live, sheave, shiv,
sieve, spiv, forgive, misgive,
outlive, relive, unlive,
underactive

³ive \ēv\ see ¹EAVE

ivel \iv-əl\ civil, drivel, frivol,
shrivel, snivel, swivel

iven \iv-ən\ driven, given,
riven, Sivan, striven, thriven,
forgiven, menu-driven

¹iver \ī-vər\ diver, driver, fiver,
arriver, cabdriver, conniver,
contriver, deriver, reviver,
screwdriver, survivor

²iver \iv-ər\ flivver, giver, liver,
quiver, river, shiver, sliver,
almsgiver, aquiver, deliver,
downriver, forgiver, lawgiver,
quicksilver, upriver,
Guadalquivir

¹ivers \ī-vərz\ divers, vivers—

*also plurals and possessives
of nouns listed at* ¹IVER

²ivers \ē-vərz\ see EAVERS

ivery \iv-rē\ livery, shivery,
delivery

ives \īvz\ fives, hives, Ives—
*also plurals and possessives
of nouns and third person
singular presents of verbs
listed at* ¹IVE

ivet \iv-ət\ civet, divot, pivot,
privet, rivet, swivet, trivet

¹ivi \iv-ē\ see IVVY

²ivi \ē-vē\ see EAVEY

ivia \iv-ē-ə\ Bolivia, Olivia

ivial \iv-ē-əl\ trivial, convivial,
quadrivial

ivid \iv-əd\ livid, vivid

ivil \iv-əl\ see IVEL

ivilly \iv-ə-lē\ civilly, privily,
uncivilly

ivily \iv-ə-lē\ see IVILLY

iving \iv-iŋ\ giving, living,
almsgiving, forgiving, free-
living, misgiving,
thanksgiving

ivion \iv-ē-ən\ Vivian, oblivion

ivious \iv-ē-əs\ lascivious,
oblivious

ivir \iv-ər\ see ²IVER

ivity \iv-ət-ē\ privity, acclivity,
activity, captivity, declivity,
festivity, motivity, nativity,
proclivity, absorptivity,
adaptivity, additivity,
affectivity, aggressivity,
coercivity, cognitivity,
collectivity, compulsivity,
conductivity, connectivity,
creativity, destructivity,
diffusivity, directivity,
effectivity, emissivity,

emotivity, exclusivity,
exhaustivity, expansivity,
expressivity, impassivity,
inactivity, infectivity,
negativity, perceptivity,
perfectivity, permittivity,
positivity, primitivity,
productivity, progressivity,
reactivity, receptivity,
reflexivity, relativity,
resistivity, retentivity,
selectivity, sensitivity,
subjectivity, susceptivity,
transitivity, distributivity,
hyperactivity, insensitivity,
overactivity, retroactivity,
radioactivity, hypersensitivity

ivium \iv-ē-əm\ trivium,
quadrivium

iviut \ē-vē-ət\ see EVIATE

ivo \ē-vō\ see EVO

ivocal \iv-ə-kəl\ equivocal,
univocal, unequivocal

ivol \iv-əl\ see IVEL

ivor \ī-vər\ see [1]IVER

ivorous \iv-rəs\ carnivorous,
granivorous, omnivorous,
insectivorous

ivot \iv-ət\ see IVET

ivus \ē-vəs\ see EVOUS

ivver \iv-ər\ see [2]IVER

ivvy \iv-ē\ chivy, civvy, divvy,
Livy, privy, skivvy, tantivy,
divi-divi

ivy \iv-ē\ see IVVY

iw \ef\ see [1]EF

iwi \ē-wē\ see EEWEE

[1]ix \iks\ Brix, Dix, fix, mix, nix,
pyx, six, Styx, admix, affix,
blanc fixe, commix, deep-six,
immix, infix, postfix, prefix,
premix, prix fixe, prolix,

subfix, suffix, transfix, unfix,
antefix, cicatrix, crucifix,
eighty-six, intermix, politics,
six-o-six, superfix,
geopolitics, RU 486—*also
plurals and possessives of
nouns and third person
singular presents of verbs
listed at* ICK

[2]ix \ē\ see [1]EE

ixal \ik-səl\ pixel, affixal,
prefixal, suffixal

[1]ixe \ēks\ breeks, prix fixe, idée
fixe, Macgillicuddy's Reeks—
*also plurals and possessives
of nouns and third person
singular presents of verbs
listed at* [1]EAK

[2]ixe \iks\ see [1]IX

[3]ixe \ēsh\ see [2]ICHE

ixed \ikst\ fixed, mixed, twixt,
betwixt, well-fixed—*also
pasts of verbs listed at* [1]IX

ixel \ik-səl\ see IXAL

ixen \ik-sən\ vixen, Nixon,
Mason-Dixon

ixer \ik-sər\ fixer, mixer, elixir

ixia \ik-sē-ə\ asphyxia,
panmixia

ixie \ik-sē\ Dixie, nixie, Nixie,
pixie, pyxie, tricksy

ixion \ik-shən\ see ICTION

ixir \ik-sər\ see IXER

ixit \ik-sət\ quixote, ipse dixit

ixon \ik-sən\ see IXEN

ixote \ik-sət\ see IXIT

ixt \ikst\ see IXED

ixture \iks-chər\ fixture,
mixture, admixture,
commixture, intermixture

iya \ē-ə\ see [1]IA

iyeh \ē-ə\ see [1]IA

¹**iz** \iz\ biz, fizz, frizz, his, is,
  Ms., phiz, quiz, 'tis, whiz,
  wiz, gee-whiz, show biz
²**iz** \ēz\ see EZE
¹**iza** \ē-zə\ see EZA
²**iza** \ē-thə\ see ETHA
izabeth \iz-ə-bəth\ Elisabeth,
  Elizabeth, Port Elizabeth
izable \ī-zə-bəl\ sizable,
  advisable, cognizable,
  devisable, excisable,
  amortizable, analyzable,
  criticizable, dramatizable,
  exercisable, fertilizable,
  hypnotizable, inadvisable,
  localizable, magnetizable,
  mechanizable, memorizable,
  pulverizable, recognizable,
  vaporizable, computerizable,
  generalizable,
  uncompromisable
izar \ī-zər\ see IZER
izard \iz-ərd\ blizzard, gizzard,
  izzard, lizard, vizard, wizard
¹**ize** \īz\ guise, prise, prize, rise,
  size, wise, abscise, advise,
  apprise, apprize, arise, assize,
  baptize, breadthwise, capsize,
  chastise, clockwise, cognize,
  comprise, crabwise,
  crosswise, demise, despise,
  devise, disguise, disprize,
  downsize, earthrise, edgewise,
  emprise, endwise, excise,
  fanwise, franchise, full-size,
  grecize, high-rise, incise,
  king-size, leastwise,
  lengthwise, Levi's, life-size,
  likewise, low-rise, man-size,
  midsize, misprize, moonrise,
  nowise, outsize, piecewise,
  pint-size, premise, quantize,

  remise, reprise, revise,
  slantwise, streetwise, stylize,
  suffice, sunrise, surmise,
  surprise, twin-size, uprise,
  advertise, aggrandize,
  agonize, alchemize, amortize,
  analyze, anglicize, anywise,
  aphorize, arabize, atomize,
  authorize, autolyze, balkanize,
  barbarize, bastardize,
  bestialize, bolshevize,
  botanize, bowdlerize,
  brutalize, burglarize, canalize,
  canonize, capsulize,
  caramelize, carbonize,
  cartelize, catalyze, catechize,
  cauterize, centralize,
  channelize, Christianize,
  cicatrize, circumcise, civilize,
  classicize, colonize,
  communize, compromise,
  concertize, concretize,
  creolize, criticize, crystalize,
  customize, demonize,
  deputize, dialyze, digitize,
  disfranchise, dogmatize,
  dramatize, elegize, empathize,
  emphasize, energize,
  enfranchise, enterprise,
  equalize, erotize, eternize,
  etherize, eulogize, euphemize,
  exercise, exorcise, factorize,
  fantasize, fascistize, feminize,
  fertilize, feudalize, fictionize,
  finalize, formalize, formulize,
  fossilize, fragmentize,
  fraternize, gallicize, galvanize,
  germanize, ghettoize,
  glamorize, globalize,
  gormandize, gothicize,
  gourmandize, grecianize,
  harmonize, heathenize,

hebraize, hellenize, hierarchize, humanize, hybridize, hypnotize, idolize, immunize, improvise, ionize, ironize, Islamize, itemize, jeopardize, journalize, Judaize, laicize, latinize, legalize, lionize, liquidize, localize, magnetize, marbleize, martyrize, maximize, mechanize, melanize, melodize, memorize, merchandise, mesmerize, methodize, metricize, minimize, mobilize, modernize, moisturize, monetize, mongrelize, moralize, motorize, mythicize, narcotize, nasalize, neutralize, normalize, notarize, novelize, obelize, odorize, optimize, organize, ostracize, otherwise, oversize, oxidize, paganize, paradise, paralyze, pasteurize, patronize, pauperize, penalize, penny-wise, pidginize, plagiarize, plasticize, Platonize, pluralize, pocket-size, poetize, polarize, polemize, pressurize, privatize, prussianize, publicize, pulverize, randomize, realize, recognize, rhapsodize, robotize, romanize, rubberize, sanitize, satirize, scandalize, schematize, schismatize, scrutinize, sensitize, sermonize, signalize, simonize, sinicize, slenderize, sloganize, socialize, sodomize, solarize, sonnetize, specialize, stabilize, Stalinize, standardize, sterilize, stigmatize, strategize, subsidize, summarize, supervise, syllogize, symbolize, sympathize, synchronize, syncretize, synopsize, synthesize, systemize, tantalize, televise, temporize, tenderize, terrorize, tetanize, teutonize, texturize, theorize, thermalize, totalize, tranquilize, traumatize, tyrannize, unionize, unitize, urbanize, utilize, valorize, vandalize, vaporize, verbalize, vernalize, victimize, vitalize, vocalize, vulcanize, vulgarize, weather-wise, weatherize, westernize, winterize, womanize, worldly-wise, accessorize, acclimatize, actualize, allegorize, alphabetize, analogize, anatomize, anesthetize, animalize, annualize, antagonize, anthologize, anticlockwise, apologize, apostatize, apostrophize, arabicize, aromatize, baby blue-eyes, bureaucratize, cannibalize, capitalize, categorize, catholicize, characterize, commercialize, communalize, computerize, conservatize, containerize, contrariwise, conveyorize, cosmeticize, counterclockwise, criminalize, cryptanalize, decentralize, decolonize, de-emphasize, de-energize, dehumanize,

deionize, demagnetize,
demobilize, democratize,
demoralize, deodorize,
depersonalize, depolarize,
desalinize, desensitize,
destabilize, digitalize,
disenfranchise, disorganize,
economize, emotionalize,
epitomize, epoxidize,
eroticize, eternalize,
euthanatize, evangelize,
extemporize, externalize,
familiarize, fanaticize,
federalize, fictionalize,
formularize, gelatinize,
generalize, geologize,
Hispanicize, homogenize,
hospitalize, hypothesize,
idealize, illegalize,
immobilize, immortalize,
impersonalize, Indianize,
indigenize, initialize,
internalize, italicize,
legitimize, liberalize,
literalize, lobotomize,
lysogenize, macadamize,
metabolize, metastasize,
militarize, mineralize,
monopolize, mythologize,
nationalize, naturalize,
parenthesize, philosophize,
politicize, popularize,
proselytize, regularize,
reorganize, revitalize,
romanticize, secularize,
sexualize, sovietize,
subjectivize, suburbanize,
subvocalize, systematize,
temporalize, theologize,
traditionalize, transistorize,
trivialize, ventriloquize,
visualize, Americanize,

apotheosize, colonialize,
compartmentalize,
conceptualize, contextualize,
decriminalize, demilitarize,
denaturalize, departmentalize,
depoliticize, desexualize,
Europeanize, exteriorize,
ideologize, immaterialize,
individualize, industrialize,
internationalize, legitimatize,
materialize, miniaturize,
particularize, politicalize,
phychoanalyze, self-actualize,
sentimentalize, spiritualize,
underutilize, universalize,
constitutionalize,
dematerialize, editorialize,
intellectualize,
deinstitutionalize—*also
plurals and possessives of
nouns and third person
singular presents of verbs
listed at* [1]Y

[2]ize \ēz\ see EZE

ized \īzd\ sized, advised,
outsized, ergotized, ill-
advised, pearlized,
Sanforized, unadvised,
undersized, varisized, well-
advised, elasticized,
modularized, unexercised,
immunocompromised—*also
pasts of verbs listed at* IZE

[1]izen \īz-ᵊn\ bison, dizen,
greisen, bedizen, horizon,
spiegeleisen

[2]izen \iz-ᵊn\ see [2]ISON

izer \ī-zər\ Dreiser, geyser,
kaiser, miser, prizer, riser,
sizar, visor, wiser, adviser,
divisor, incisor, appetizer,
atomizer, energizer,

enterpriser, equalizer,
exerciser, fertilizer, organizer,
oxidizer, stabilizer,
supervisor, synthesizer,
totalizer, tranquilizer,
tyrannizer, vaporizer,
complementizer, deodorizer—
also nouns formed by adding
-er *to verbs listed at* IZE

izing \ī-ziŋ\ rising, sizing,
uprising, appetizing,
enterprising, merchandising,
self-sufficing, unsurprising,
self-sacrificing,
uncompromising

¹izo \ē-zō\ sleazo, chorizo,
mestizo

²izo \ē-sō\ see ISO

izon \īz-ᵊn\ see ¹IZEN

izy \it-sē\ see ITZY

izz \iz\ see ¹IZ

izza \ēt-sə\ see ¹ITZA

izzard \iz-ərd\ see IZARD

izzen \iz-ᵊn\ see ²ISON

izzer \iz-ər\ see ISSOR

izzical \iz-i-kəl\ see YSICAL

izzie \i-zē\ see IZZY

izzle \iz-əl\ chisel, drizzle,
fizzle, frizzle, grizzle, mizzle,
pizzle, sizzle, swizzle

izzled \iz-əld\ chiseled,
grizzled—*also pasts of verbs
listed at* IZZLE

izzler \iz-lər\ chiseler, sizzler,
swizzler

izzly \iz-lē\ drizzly, grisly,
grizzly, mizzly

izzy \iz-ē\ busy, dizzy, fizzy,
frizzy, tizzy, tin lizzie

O

¹o \ü\ see ¹EW

²o \ō\ see ¹OW

³o \ər\ see ¹EUR

¹oa \ō-ə\ boa, Goa, koa, moa,
Noah, proa, stoa, aloha,
balboa, Balboa, jerboa,
Samoa, Krakatoa, Mauna Loa,
Shenandoah, Sinaloa,
Guanabacoa, João Pessoa

²oa \ō\ see ¹OW

oable \ü-ə-bəl\ see UABLE

oach \ōch\ broach, brooch,
coach, loach, poach, roach,
abroach, approach, caroche,
cockroach, encroach,
reproach, stagecoach

oachable \ō-chə-bəl\ coachable,
approachable, inapproachable,
irreproachable,
unapproachable

oacher \ō-chər\ broacher,
coacher, cloture, poacher,
encroacher

¹oad \ōd\ see ODE

²oad \od\ see ¹AUD

oader \ōd-ər\ see ODER

oadie \ōd-ē\ see ²ODY

oady \ōd-ē\ see ²ODY

oaf \ōf\ loaf, oaf, qoph,
meatloaf, witloof, sugarloaf

oafer \ō-fər\ see OFER

oagie \ō-gē\ see OGIE

oah \ō-ə\ see ¹OA

oak \ōk\ see OKE

oaken \ō-kən\ see OKEN

oaker \ō-kər\ see OKER

oakum \ō-kəm\ see OKUM

oaky \ō-kē\ see OKY

oal \ōl\ see ¹OLE

oalie \ō-lē\ see ¹OLY

¹oam \ō-əm\ see ¹OEM

²oam \ōm\ see ¹OME

oamer \ō-mər\ see ¹OMER

oaming \ō-miŋ\ coaming,
combing, gloaming,
Wyoming—*also present
participles of verbs listed at*
¹OME

oamy \ō-mē\ foamy, homey,
loamy, show-me, Suomi,
Dahomey, Naomi, Salome

¹oan \ō-ən\ Owen, roan, rowan,
Minoan, Samoan, waygoing,
Eskimoan, protozoan

²oan \ōn\ see ¹ONE

oaner \ō-nər\ see ¹ONER

oaning \ō-niŋ\ see ²ONING

oap \ōp\ see OPE

oaper \ō-pər\ see OPER

oapy \ō-pē\ see OPI

oar \ōr\ see ¹OR

oard \ōrd\ board, bored, chord,
cord, cored, floored, ford,
Ford, gourd, hoard, horde,
lord, Lord, oared, pored,
poured, sward, sword, toward,
ward, Ward, aboard, accord,
afford, award, backboard,
backsword, baseboard,
billboard, blackboard,
breadboard, broadsword,
buckboard, cardboard,

chalkboard, chessboard,
chipboard, clapboard,
clipboard, concord,
corkboard, dashboard,
discord, duckboard, fjord,
flashboard, floorboard,
footboard, freeboard, garbord,
Gaylord, greensward,
hardboard, headboard,
inboard, keyboard, kickboard,
landlord, lapboard, leeboard,
longsword, matchboard,
moldboard, onboard,
outboard, packboard,
pasteboard, patchboard,
pegboard, pressboard,
punchboard, rearward, record,
reward, sailboard, scoreboard,
seaboard, shipboard,
sideboard, signboard,
skateboard, slumlord,
smallsword, snowboard,
soundboard, splashboard,
springboard, surfboard,
switchboard, tailboard,
untoward, wallboard,
washboard, word-hoard,
warlord, whipcord,
aboveboard, bungee cord,
centerboard, checkerboard,
clavichord, disaccord,
fiberboard, fingerboard,
harpsichord, mortarbord,
motherboard, overboard,
overlord, paddleboard,
paperboard, pinafored,
plasterboard, pompadoured,
shuffleboard, smorgasbord,
storyboard, teeterboard,
tetrachord, untoward,
weatherboard, misericord,

particleboard—*also pasts of
verbs listed at* ¹OR

oarder \ōrd-ər\ boarder,
hoarder, keyboarder,
skateboarder, surfboarder

oarding \ōrd-iŋ\ boarding,
hoarding, skateboarding,
weatherboarding

oared \ōrd\ see OARD

¹oarer \ōr-ər\ see ¹ORER

²oarer \or-ər\ see ¹ORRER

oaring \ōr-iŋ\ see ORING

oarious \or-ē-əs\ see ORIOUS

oarish \or-ish\ see ¹ORISH

¹oarse \ōrs\ see ¹OURSE

²oarse \ors\ see ¹ORSE

oarsen \ōrs-ᵊn\ coarsen,
hoarsen, whoreson

oarsman \ōrz-mən\ oarsman,
outdoorsman

oart \ort\ see ¹ORT

oary \ōr-ē\ see ORY

oast \ōst\ see ²OST

oastal \ōs-tᵊl\ see ¹OSTAL

oaster \ō-stər\ coaster, poster,
roaster, throwster, toaster,
billposter, four-poster, roller-
coaster, roller coaster

oasty \ō-stē\ see OSTY

oat \ōt\ bloat, boat, coat, cote,
dote, float, gloat, goat, groat,
haute, moat, mote, note, oat,
phot, quote, rote, shoat,
smote, stoat, throat, tote, vote,
wrote, afloat, airboat,
bareboat, bluecoat, bumboat,
capote, catboat, compote,
connote, coyote, cutthroat,
demote, denote, devote,
dovecote, eighth note, emote,
endnote, fireboat, fistnote,
flatboat, footnote, greatcoat,

gunboat, half note, headnote,
Hohhot, houseboat,
housecoat, iceboat, keelboat,
keynote, lifeboat, longboat,
one-note, pigboat, promote,
Q-boat, quarter note, raincoat,
Rajkot, redcoat, remote,
rewrote, rowboat, sailboat,
scapegoat, sheepcote,
showboat, speedboat,
steamboat, stoneboat, Sukkot,
Sukkoth, surfboat, tailcoat,
topcoat, towboat, tugboat,
turncoat, U-boat, unquote,
wainscot, whaleboat,
whitethroat, whole note,
woodnote, workboat,
anecdote, antidote, asymptote,
creosote, entrecote, ferryboat,
Huhehot, motorboat, overcoat,
paddleboat, papillote,
petticoat, powerboat,
redingote, riverboat,
rubythroat, Shabuoth, Sialkot,
sugarcoat, symbiote, table
d'hôte, sixteenth note,
undercoat, yellowthroat,
thirty-second note
oate \ō-ət\ see ¹OET
oated \ōt-əd\ coated, noted,
throated, devoted, tailcoated,
petticoated—*also pasts of
verbs listed at* OAT
oaten \ōt-ᵊn\ see OTON
oater \ōt-ər\ bloater, boater,
coater, doter, floater, gloater,
motor, noter, oater, rotor,
scoter, toter, voter,
houseboater, iceboater,
keynoter, promoter, pulmotor,
sailboater, tilt-rotor, trimotor,
locomotor, motorboater

oath \ōth\ see OWTH
oathe \ōth\ see OTHE
oathing \ō-thiŋ\ see OTHING
oating \ōt-iŋ\ boating, coating,
floating, free floating,
sailboating, scapegoating,
speedboating, wainscoting,
motorboating, undercoating—
*also present participles of
verbs listed at* OAT
oatswain \ōs-ᵊn\ see OSIN
oaty \ōt-ē\ see ¹OTE
oax \ōks\ coax, hoax—*also
plurals and possessives of
nouns and third person
singular presents of verbs
listed at* OKE
¹ob \äb\ Ab, blob, bob, Bob,
cob, daub, fob, glob, gob,
hob, job, knob, lob, mob, nob,
Ob, rob, slob, snob, sob,
squab, stob, swab, throb, yob,
bedaub, corncob, demob,
doorknob, heartthrob, hobnob,
kabob, macabre, nabob,
nawab, Punjab, skibob,
memsahib, shish kebab,
thingamabob
²ob \ōb\ see ¹OBE
oba \ō-bə\ arroba, jojoba,
algaroba, Manitoba
obably \äb-lē\ see OBBLY
obal \ō-bəl\ see OBLE
obally \ō-bə-lē\ globally,
primum mobile
obar \ō-bər\ see OBER
obber \äb-ər\ bobber, caber,
clobber, cobber, jobber,
robber, slobber, swabber,
throbber, hobnobber,
Micawber, Skibobber,
stockjobber

obbery \äb-rē\ bobbery,
jobbery, robbery, slobbery,
snobbery, corroboree

obbes \äbz\ Hobbes—*also
possessives and plurals of
nouns and third person
singular presents of verbs
listed at OB*

obbet \äb-ət\ gobbet, probit

obbie \äb-ē\ see OBBY

obbin \äb-ən\ see OBIN

obbish \äb-ish\ slobbish,
snobbish

obble \äb-əl\ see ¹ABBLE

obbler \äb-lər\ cobbler,
gobbler, hobbler, nobbler,
squabbler, wobbler

obbly \äb-lē\ knobbly,
probably, wobbly, Wobbly

obby \äb-ē\ Bobbie, bobby,
Bobby, cobby, dobby, globby,
hobby, knobby, lobby, nobby,
snobby, swabbie, Mesabi,
Punjabi, Wahhabi, Abu
Dhabi, Hammurabi

¹obe \ōb\ daube, globe, Job,
lobe, probe, robe, strobe,
bathrobe, conglobe, disrobe,
earlobe, enrobe, microbe,
wardrobe, Anglophobe,
claustrophobe, Francophobe,
homophobe, negrophobe,
xenophobe, ailurophobe,
computerphobe

²obe \ō-bē\ see OBY

obeah \ō-bē-ə\ see OBIA

obee \ō-bē\ see OBY

obelus \äb-ə-ləs\ see ABILIS

ober \ō-bər\ lobar, sober,
October

obi \ō-bē\ see OBY

obia \ō-bē-ə\ cobia, obeah,

phobia, acrophobia,
algophobia, Anglophobia,
claustrophobia, homophobia,
hydrophobia, negrophobia,
photophobia, technophobia,
xenophobia, agoraphobia,
triskaidekaphobia

obic \ō-bik\ phobic, aerobic,
anaerobic, claustrophobic,
homophobic, hydrophobic,
photophobic, xenophobic

¹obile \ō-bə-lē\ see OBALLY

²obile \ō-bəl\ see OBLE

obin \äb-ən\ bobbin, dobbin,
graben, robin, Robin, Robyn,
round-robin

¹obit \ō-bət\ obit, Tobit, post-
obit

²obit \äb-ət\ see OBBET

oble \ō-bəl\ coble, global,
mobile, noble, airmobile,
ennoble, Grenoble, ignoble,
immobile, San Cristóbal

obo \ō-bō\ gobo, hobo, kobo,
lobo, oboe, adobo

oboe \ō-bō\ see OBO

obol \äb-əl\ see ¹ABBLE

oboree \äb-ə-rē\ see OBBERY

obot \ō-bət\ see ¹OBIT

obra \ō-brə\ cobra, dobra

obster \äb-stər\ lobster, mobster

obular \äb-yə-lər\ globular,
lobular

obule \äb-yül\ globule, lobule

oby \ō-bē\ Gobi, goby, Kobe,
obi, Obie, toby, Toby, adobe,
Nairobi, Okeechobee

obyn \äb-ən\ see OBIN

¹oc \ōk\ see OKE

²oc \äk\ see ¹OCK

³oc \ók\ see ALK

oca \ō-kə\ coca, mocha, oca,

Asoka, carioca, Fukuoka,
mandioca, Shizuoka, tapioca

ocable \ō-kə-bəl\ smokable,
vocable, evocable

ocage \äk-ij\ see OCKAGE

ocal \ō-kəl\ focal, local, socle,
vocal, yokel, bifocal,
subvocal, trifocal, unvocal

ocally \ō-kə-lē\ locally, vocally

ocative \äk-ət-iv\ locative,
vocative, evocative,
provocative

occa \äk-ə\ see ¹AKA

occer \äk-ər\ see OCKER

occie \äch-ē\ see OTCHY

occhi \ó-kē\ see ALKIE

occo \äk-ō\ socko, taco,
cheechako, guanaco,
morocco, Morocco, scirocco,
sirocco

occule \äk-yül\ floccule, locule

occulent \äk-yə-lənt\ flocculent,
inoculant

occulus \äk-yə-ləs\ flocculus,
loculus, oculus

oce \ō-chē\ see ¹OCHE

ocean \ō-shən\ see OTION

ocent \ōs-ᵊnt\ docent, nocent

ocess \äs-əs\ Knossos, process,
colossus, proboscis

¹och \ōk\ see OKE

²och \äk\ see ¹OCK

³och \ósh\ see ²ASH

⁴och \ók\ see ALK

ocha \ō-kə\ see OCA

ochal \äk-əl\ see OCKLE

ochan \ä-k̲ən\ see ACHEN

¹oche \ō-chē\ Kochi, Sochi,
penoche, sotto voce, veloce,
mezza voce

²oche \ōsh\ cloche, gauche,

skosh, brioche, caroche,
guilloche

³oche \ō-kē\ see OKY

⁴oche \ōch\ see OACH

⁵oche \ósh\ see ²ASH

ochee \ō-kē\ see OKY

ocher \ō-kər\ see OKER

ochi \ō-chē\ see ¹OCHE

ochle \ək-əl\ see UCKLE

ochs \äks\ see OX

ochum \ō-kəm\ see OKUM

ocia \ō-shə\ see ¹OTIA

ociable \ō-shə-bəl\ sociable,
associable, dissociable,
insociable, negotiable,
unsociable, indissociable,
renegotiable

ocial \ō-shəl\ social, asocial,
dissocial, precocial, unsocial,
antisocial

ocile \äs-əl\ see OSSAL

ocious \ō-shəs\ atrocious,
ferocious, precocious,
Theodosius

¹ock \äk\ Bach, bloc, block,
bock, brock, chock, clock,
cock, croc, crock, doc, dock,
floc, flock, frock, hock,
Jacque, Jacques, jock, knock,
lakh, loch, lock, Locke,
lough, Mach, moc, mock,
nock, pock, roc, rock,
schlock, shock, smock, sock,
stock, wok, yak, yock, acock,
ad hoc, aftershock, amok,
Arak, backblock, Balzac,
bangkok, Bangkok, baroque,
Bartok, bawcock, bedrock,
bemock, bibcock, bitstock,
blackcock, blesbok,
bloodstock, bois d'arc,
Brecknock, breechblock,

burdock, buttstock, caprock,
coldcock, Comstock,
deadlock, debacle, defrock,
dry dock, duroc, Dvořák,
earlock, en bloc, epoch,
fatstock, feedstock, fetlock,
firelock, flintlock, forelock,
foreshock, gamecock,
gemsbok, gridlock, gunlock,
Hancock, havelock, haycock,
headlock, headstock,
hemlock, Hickock, Iraq, jazz-
rock, Kanak, Kazak, Kazakh,
kapok, kneesock, Langnedoc,
livestock, lovelock,
matchlock, Mohock, Nisroch,
nostoc, o'clock, oarlock,
padlock, peacock, penstock,
petcock, pibroch, picklock,
pinchcock, Polack, post doc,
post hoc, rhebok, rimrock,
roadblock, rootstock,
Rorschach, Rostock, rowlock,
shamrock, Sheetrock,
sherlock, shylock, Sirach,
slick rock, Slovak, springbok,
steenbok, stopcock, Tarlak,
tarok, ticktock, traprock, van
Gogh, warlock, wedlock,
woodcock, wristlock,
zwieback, alpenstock,
Anahuac, antiknock, antilock,
Antioch, Arawak, Ayers
Rock, billycock, chockablock,
hammerlock, hollyhock,
interlock, John Hancock,
lady's-smock, laughingstock,
Little Rock, manioc,
mantlerock, monadnock,
Offenbach, Otomac,
poppycock, Ragnarok,
Sarawak, shuttlecock,
spatterdock, turkey-cock,
weathercock, Czechoslovak,
Bialystok, electroshock,
Inupiaq, Pontianak,
Vladivostok

²ock \ȯk\ see ALK

ockage \äk-ij\ blockage,
brockage, dockage, lockage,
socage

ocke \äk\ see ¹OCK

ocked \äkt\ blocked, crocked,
concoct, decoct, entr'acte,
half-cocked, landlocked,
periproct, entoproct—*also
pasts of verbs listed at* ¹OCK

ocker \äk-ər\ blocker, clocker,
cocker, docker, hocker,
knocker, locker, makar,
mocker, rocker, shocker,
soccer, stocker, footlocker,
appleknocker, beta-blocker,
knickerbocker

ockery \äk-rē\ crockery,
mockery, rockery

ocket \äk-ət\ brocket, crocket,
Crockett, docket, locket,
pocket, rocket, socket,
sprocket, pickpocket,
skyrocket, out-of-pocket,
retro-rocket

ockett \äk-ət\ see OCKET

ockey \äk-ē\ see OCKY

ockian \äk-ē-ən\ Comstockian,
Slovakian, Czechoslovakian

ockiness \äk-ē-nəs\ cockiness,
rockiness, stockiness

ocking \äk-iŋ\ flocking,
shocking, smocking, stocking,
bluestocking, silk-stocking

ockish \äk-ish\ blockish,
stockish

ockle \äk-əl\ coccal, cockle,
  socle, debacle, epochal
ockney \äk-nē\ cockney, Procne
ocko \äk-ō\ see OCCO
ocks \äks\ see OX
ocky \äk-ē\ blocky, cocky,
  hockey, jockey, pocky, rocky,
  Rocky, sake, schlocky,
  stocky, Yaqui, Abnaki, Iraqi,
  Ontake, pea cocky, rumaki,
  jabberwocky, Kawasaki,
  Miyazaki, Nagasaki, Okazaki,
  sukiyaki, teriyaki, Amagasaki,
  enokidake
ocle \ō-kəl\ see OCAL
ocne \äk-nē\ see OCKNEY
oco \ō-kō\ coco, cocoa, loco,
  poco, Bioko, iroko, rococo,
  crème de cacao, locofoco,
  Orinoco, poco a poco
ocoa \ō-kō\ see OCO
ocracy \äk-rə-sē\ autocracy,
  bureaucracy, democracy,
  hypocrisy, mobocracy,
  plutocracy, slavocracy,
  technocracy, theocracy,
  aristocracy, gerontocracy,
  gynecocracy, meritocracy,
  thalassocracy
ocre \ō-kər\ see OKER
ocrisy \äk-rə-sē\ see OCRACY
ocsin \äk-sən\ see OXIN
oct \äkt\ see OCKED
oction \äk-shən\ concoction,
  decoction
octor \äk-tər\ doctor, proctor,
  concocter
oculant \äk-yə-lənt\ see
  OCCULENT
ocular \äk-yə-lər\ jocular,
  locular, ocular, binocular,
  monocular, intraocular

ocule \äk-yül\ see OCCULE
oculus \äk-yə-ləs\ see OCCULUS
ocum \ō-kəm\ see OKUM
ocus \ō-kəs\ crocus, focus,
  hocus, locus, prefocus,
  refocus, soft-focus, hocus-
  pocus
ocused \ō-kəst\ see OCUST
ocust \ō-kəst\ locust, unfocused
ocutor \äk-yət-ər\ prolocutor,
  interlocutor
¹od \äd\ bod, clod, cod, fade,
  Fahd, gaud, god, hod, mod,
  nod, od, odd, plod, pod, prod,
  quad, quod, rod, scrod, shod,
  sod, squad, tod, trod, wad,
  Akkad, amphipod, Arad,
  aubade, ballade, Belgrade,
  Beograde, bipod, Cape Cod,
  couvade, croustade, dry-shod,
  ephod, facade, fantod,
  glissade, hot-rod, jihad,
  lingcod, Nimrod, oeillade,
  pomade, peasecod, ramrod,
  Riyadh, roughshod, roulade,
  saccade, scalade, seedpod,
  slipshod, synod, tie-rod,
  tightwad, tomcod, torsade,
  tripod, accolade, arthropod,
  Ashkhabad, Bacolod,
  bigarade, carbonnade,
  chiffonade, defilade, demigod,
  enfilade, esculade, esplanade,
  fulsillade, gallopade,
  gastropod, goldenrod,
  hexapod, lycopod,
  monkeypod, Novgorod, Novi
  Sad, octopod, promenade,
  pseudopod, Ahmadabad,
  Allahabad, cephalopod,
  Faisalabad, Islamabad,
  ornithopod, prosauropod,

rodomontade, dégringolade, fanfaronade, Upanishad, Scheherazade, Nizhni Novgorod

²**od** \ō\ see ¹OW

³**od** \ōd\ see ODE

⁴**od** \u̇d\ see ¹OOD

⁵**od** \ȯd\ see ¹AUD

o'd \u̇d\ see UDE

oda \ōd-ə\ coda, Rhoda, soda, Baroda, pagoda, sal soda

odal \ōd-ᵊl\ Godel, modal, nodal, yodel, cathodal, intermodal

odden \äd-ᵊn\ sodden, trodden, downtrodden, Ibadan

odder \äd-ər\ dodder, fodder, khaddar, modder, nodder, odder, plodder, prodder, solder, wadder, glissader, hot-rodder—*also comparatives of adjectives listed at* ¹OD

oddery \äd-rē\ see AWDRY

oddess \äd-əs\ bodice, goddess, demigoddess

oddish \äd-ish\ cloddish, kaddish

oddle \äd-ᵊl\ coddle, model, noddle, swaddle, toddle, twaddle, waddle, remodel, mollycoddle

oddler \äd-lər\ coddler, modeler, toddler, twaddler, waddler, mollycoddler

oddly \äd-lē\ see ODLY

oddy \äd-ē\ see ¹ODY

ode \ōd\ bode, bowed, code, goad, load, lode, mode, node, ode, road, rode, Spode, strode, toad, toed, woad, wood, abode, bestrode, boatload, busload, byroad,

carload, cartload, caseload, commode, corrode, crossroad, decode, displode, embowed, encode, epode, erode, explode, forebode, freeload, geode, highroad, implode, inroad, no-load, off-load, outmode, payload, planeload, postcode, railroad, rhapsode, sarod, shipload, square-toed, threnode, trainload, truckload, two-toed, unload, upload, à la mode, antipode, Comstock Lode, discommode, eigenmode, electrode, episode, impastoed, incommode, Kozhikode, Nesselrode, overrode, palinode, pigeon-toed—*also pasts of verbs listed at* ¹OW

odeine \ōd-ē-ən\ see ODIAN

odel \ōd-ᵊl\ see ODAL

odeler \äd-lər\ see ODDLER

oden \ōd-ᵊn\ loden, Odin, Woden

odeon \ōd-ē-ən\ see ODIAN

oder \ōd-ər\ coder, loader, Oder, odor, breechloader, decoder, freeloader, malodor, railroader, unloader, middle-of-the-roader

oderate \äd-rət\ quadrate, moderate, immoderate

odes \ōdz\ Rhodes—*possessives and plurals of nouns and third person singular presents of verbs listed at* ODE

odest \äd-əst\ Mahdist, modest, haggadist, immodest—*also superlatives of adjectives listed at* ¹OD

odesy \äd-ə-sē\ odyssey,
  geodesy, theodicy
odeum \ōd-ē-əm\ see ODIUM
odge \äj\ see ¹AGE
odger \äj-ər\ codger, dodger,
  lodger, roger, Roger, Jolly
  Roger, stinking roger
odgy \äj-ē\ dodgy, podgy,
  stodgy, mistagogy, pedagogy
odian \ōd-ē-ən\ Cambodian,
  custodian, melodeon,
  nickelodeon
odic \äd-ik\ zaddik, cathodic,
  ergodic, melodic, methodic,
  monodic, periodic, prosodic,
  rhapsodic, spasmodic,
  synodic, threnodic, episodic,
  periodic, antismasmodic,
  aperiodic, upanishadic,
  quasiperiodic
odical \äd-i-kəl\ methodical,
  monodical, prosodical,
  synodical, episodical,
  immethodical, periodical
odice \äd-əs\ see ODDESS
odicy \äd-ə-sē\ see ODESY
odie \ō-dē\ see ²ODY
odin \ōd-ᵊn\ see ODEN
odious \ōd-ē-əs\ odious,
  commodious, melodious,
  Methodius, incommodious
odity \äd-ət-ē\ oddity,
  commodity, incommodity
odium \ōd-ē-əm\ odeum,
  odium, podium, rhodium,
  sodium
odius \ō-dē-əs\ see ODIOUS
odless \äd-ləs\ godless, rodless
odling \äd-liŋ\ codling, godling
odly \äd-lē\ godly, oddly,
  ungodly

odo \ōd-ō\ dodo, Komodo,
  Quasimodo
odom \äd-əm\ shahdom, Sodom
odor \ōd-ər\ see ODER
odsk \ätsk\ see ATSK
odular \äj-ə-lər\ modular,
  nodular
odule \äj-ül\ module, nodule
¹ody \äd-ē\ body, cloddy,
  gaudy, Mahdi, noddy, sadhe,
  shoddy, toddy, waddy, wadi,
  anybody, blackbody,
  dogsbody, embody,
  homebody, nobody,
  somebody, wide-body,
  antibody, busybody,
  disembody, everybody,
  Irrawaddy, underbody
²ody \ōd-ē\ Cody, Jodie, Jody,
  roadie, toady, polypody
odyssey \äd-ə-sē\ see ODESY
odz \üj\ see ¹UGE
¹oe \ō\ see ¹OW
²oe \ō-ē\ see OWY
³oe \ē\ see ¹EE
⁴oe \öï\ see OY
¹oea \öi-ə\ see OIA
²oea \ē-ə\ see ¹IA
oeba \ē-bə\ see EBA
oebe \ē-bē\ see ¹EBE
oebel \ā-bəl\ see ABLE
oebus \ē-bəs\ see EBUS
oed \ōd\ see ODE
oehn \ən\ see UN
oeia \ē-ə\ see ¹IA
oeic \ē-ik\ see EIC
oek \ùk\ see ¹OOK
oel \ō-əl\ Joel, Lowell, Noel,
  bestowal, Baden-Powell,
  protozoal
¹oeless \ō-ləs\ see OLUS
²oeless \ü-ləs\ see EWLESS

¹**oem** \ō-əm\ poem, proem,
    jeroboam
²**oem** \ōm\ see ¹OME
³**oem** \óm\ see ¹AUM
oeman \ō-mən\ see OMAN
oena \ē-nə\ see ²INA
¹**oentgen** \en-chən\ see ENSION
²**oentgen** \ən-chən\ see
    UNCHEON
oepha \ē-fə\ see EPHA
¹**o'er** \ōr\ see ¹ORE
²**o'er** \ór\ see ¹OR
¹**oer** \ōr\ see ¹OR
²**oer** \ü-ər\ see ¹EWER
³**oer** \úr\ see ¹URE
⁴**oer** \ō-ər\ blower, knower,
    lower, mower, sewer, shower,
    sower, beachgoer, churchgoer,
    flamethrower, filmgoer,
    foregoer, forgoer,
    mindblower, snowblower,
    snowthrower, winegrower,
    concertgoer, moviegoer,
    cinemagoer, operagoer,
    theatergoer, whistleblower
¹**oes** \əz\ see ¹EUSE
²**oes** \ōz\ see ²OSE
³**oes** \üz\ see ²USE
oesia \ē-shə\ see ¹ESIA
oesn't \əz-ᵊnt\ see ASN'T
oest \ü-əst\ see OOIST
oesus \ē-səs\ see ESIS
¹**oet** \ō-ət\ poet, inchoate, introit
²**oet** \óit\ see ¹OIT
oetess \ō-ət-əs\ coitus, poetess
oeuf \əf\ see UFF
oeur \ər\ see ¹EUR
oeuvre \ərv\ see ERVE
oey \ō-ē\ see OWY
¹**of** \äv\ see ²OLVE
²**of** \əv\ see ¹OVE
³**of** \óf\ see ²OFF

ofar \ō-fər\ see OFER
ofer \ō-fər\ chauffeur, gofer,
    gopher, loafer, Ophir, shofar
¹**off** \äf\ boff, coif, doff, goif,
    kaph, prof, quaff, scoff,
    shroff, taw, toff, carafe, cook-
    off, pilaf, Romanov
²**off** \óf\ cough, doff, off, scoff,
    taw, trough, Azov, beg off,
    blast-off, brush-off, cast-off,
    castoff, checkoff, Chekhov,
    cook-off, cutoff, die-off, drop-
    off, face-off, falloff, far-off,
    goof-off, hands-off, jump-off,
    Khartov, kickoff, Kirov,
    knockoff, Khruschev, layoff,
    leadoff, lift-off, Lvov, one-
    off, Pavlov, payoff, pick-off,
    pickoff, play-off, rake-off,
    rip-off, roll-off, runoff,
    Salchow, sawed-off, sell-off,
    send-off, setoff, show-off,
    shutoff, spin-off, standoff,
    takeoff, Tambov, tap-off, tip-
    off, trade-off, turnoff, well-
    off, Wolof, write-off,
    Wroclaw, better-off, cooling-
    off, damping-off, Gorbachev,
    Molotov, Nabokov,
    philosophe, Pribilof, Rostov,
    beef Stroganoff,
    Rachmaninoff, Rimsky-
    Korsakov
¹**offal** \äf-əl\ see AFEL
²**offal** \ó-fəl\ see AWFUL
offaly \óf-ə-lē\ see AWFULLY
offee \ó-fē\ coffee, toffee
¹**offer** \äf-ər\ coffer, gauffer,
    goffer, offer, proffer, quaffer,
    scoffer, troffer, reoffer
²**offer** \óf-ər\ goffer, offer,
    troffer, reoffer

offin \ȯ-fən\ coffin, dauphin,
  soften, uncoffin
offit \äf-ət\ see OFIT
offle \ȯ-fəl\ see AWFUL
ofit \äf-ət\ profit, prophet, soffit,
  nonprofit, not-for-profit
ofle \ü-fəl\ see UEFUL
¹**oft** \ȯft\ croft, loft, oft, soft,
  toft, aloft, hayloft,
  undercroft—*also pasts of
  verbs listed at* ²OFF
²**oft** \äft\ see ¹AFT
often \ȯ-fən\ see OFFIN
ofty \ȯf-tē\ lofty, softy, toplofty
¹**og** \äg\ bog, clog, cog, flog,
  fog, frog, grog, hog, jog, log,
  nog, Prague, prog, quag,
  shog, slog, smog, tog, wog,
  agog, backlog, bullfrog,
  defog, eclogue, eggnog,
  footslog, groundhog, gulag,
  photog, prologue, putlog,
  quahog, Rolvaag, sandhog,
  stalag, warthog, analog,
  analogue, antilog, apalogue,
  catalog, decalogue,
  demagogue, dialogue,
  golliwog, monologue,
  mummichog, mystagogue,
  nouvelle vague, pedagogue,
  pollywog, semilog, sinologue,
  synagogue, Taganrog,
  theologue, waterlog
²**og** \ȯg\ bog, clog, dog, fog,
  frog, hog, jog, log, smog,
  wog, backlog, bandog, befog,
  bird-dog, bulldog, bullfrog,
  coydog, defog, eclogue,
  firedog, groundhog, hangdog,
  hedgehog, hotdog, lapdog,
  leapfrog, prologue, quahog,
  sandhog, seadog, sheepdog,
  warthog, watchdog, analog,
  analogue, apologue, catalog,
  decalogue, dialogue, dog-eat-
  dog, duologue, epilogue,
  homologue, monologue,
  mummichog, overdog,
  pettifog, pollywog, sinologue,
  theologue, Tagalog,
  travelogue, underdog,
  waterlog, yellow-dog,
  ideologue
³**og** \ōg\ see ¹OGUE
oga \ō-gə\ toga, yoga,
  Conestoga
ogamous \äg-ə-məs\
  endogamous, exogamous,
  monogamous, heterogamous
ogamy \äg-ə-mē\ endogamy,
  exogamy, homogamy,
  misogamy, monogamy
ogan \ō-gən\ brogan, Mount
  Logan, shogun, slogan
ogany \äg-ə-nē\ see OGONY
ogative \äg-ət-iv\ derogative,
  prerogative, interrogative
¹**oge** \ōj\ doge, gamboge,
  horologe
²**oge** \ōzh\ loge, Limoges
³**oge** \ō-jē\ see OJI
⁴**oge** \üzh\ see ²UGE
ogel \ō-gəl\ see ¹OGLE
ogenous \äj-ə-nəs\
  androgynous, erogenous,
  homogenous, monogynous,
  heterogenous
ogeny \äj-ə-nē\ progeny,
  androgeny, autogeny,
  homogeny, misogyny,
  monogyny, ontogeny,
  phylogeny, heterogeny
¹**oger** \äj-ər\ see ODGER
²**oger** \ȯg-ər\ see ²OGGER

oges \ōzh\ see ²OGE
¹ogey \ō-gē\ see OGIE
²ogey \ùg-ē\ see OOGIE
oggan \äg-ən\ see OGGIN
oggar \äg-ər\ see ¹OGGER
¹ogger \äg-ər\ agar, clogger,
　flogger, Hoggar, jogger,
　laager, lager, logger, slogger,
　Ahaggar, defogger,
　footslogger, agar-agar,
　cataloger, pettifogger
²ogger \òg-ər\ auger, augur,
　clogger, jogger, logger,
　maugre, sauger, defogger,
　hotdogger, cataloger,
　pettifogger
¹oggery \äg-rē\ toggery,
　demagoguery
²oggery \ò-gə-rē\ augury,
　doggery
oggin \äg-ən\ noggin, toboggan,
　Copenhagen
oggle \äg-əl\ boggle, goggle,
　joggle, ogle, toggle,
　boondoggle, hornswoggle,
　synagogal
¹oggy \äg-ē\ boggy, foggy,
　groggy, moggy, quaggy,
　smoggy, soggy, yagi,
　demagogy
²oggy \òg-ē\ foggy, soggy
¹ogh \ōg\ see ¹OGUE
²ogh \ōk\ see OKE
³ogh \äk\ see ¹OCK
⁴ogh \ō\ see OW
ogi \ō-gē\ see OGIE
ogian \ō-jən\ see OJAN
ogic \äj-ik\ logic, choplogic,
　illogic, anagogic, analogic,
　biologic, chronologic,
　cryptologic, cytologic,
　demagogic, dendrologic,
dialogic, ecologic, ethnologic,
　geologic, histologic,
　horologic, hydrologic,
　mythologic, neurologic,
　nosologic, oncologic,
　pathologic, pedagogic,
　pedologic, petrologic,
　phonologic, proctologic,
　psychologic, serologic,
　technologic, theologic,
　virologic, zoologic,
　dermatologic, etiologic,
　gerontologic, gynecologic,
　hagiologic, hematologic,
　ideologic, immunologic,
　ophthalmologic, ornithologic,
　pharmacologic, physiologic,
　roentgenologic, sociologic,
　teleologic, teratologic,
　toxicologic, volcanologic,
　bacteriologic, endocrinologic,
　meteorologic, paleontologic,
　parasitologic, sedimentologic,
　symptomologic,
　epidemiologic
ogical \äj-i-kəl\ logical,
　alogical, illogical, anagogical,
　analogical, biological,
　Christological, chronological,
　cosmological, cryptological,
　cytological, dendrological,
　ecological, enological,
　ethnological, ethological,
　extralogical, gemological,
　geological, graphological,
　histological, horological,
　hydrological, limnological,
　morphological, mycological,
　mythological, necrological,
　neurological, nomological,
　oncological, pathological,
　pedagogical, pedological,

penological, petrological,
philological, phonological,
phrenological, phycological,
proctological, psephological,
psychological, scatological,
seismological, serological,
sinological, tautological,
technological, theological,
topological, typological,
ufological, virological,
zoological, abiological,
anthropological,
archaeological, cardiological,
climatological, criminological,
demonological,
dermatological,
embryological, entomological,
eschatological, etiological,
etymological, futurological,
genealogical, gerontological,
gynecological, hagiological,
hematological, herpetological,
ichthyological, iconological,
ideological, immunological,
Mariological, methodological,
mineralogical, musicological,
numerological,
ophthalmological,
ornithological,
pharmacological,
phraseological, physiological,
primatological,
roentgenological,
selenological, semiological,
sociological, teleological,
teratological, terminological,
thanatological, toxicological,
volcanological,
bacteriological,
characterological,
dialectological,
ecclesiological,

endocrinological,
epistemological,
geomorphological,
meteorological,
paleontological,
parasitological,
phenomenological,
sedimentological,
symptomatological,
epidemiological,
gastroenterological

ogie \ō-gē\ bogey, bogie, dogie,
fogy, hoagie, logy, pogy,
stogie, vogie, yogi, pirogi

¹ogle \ō-gəl\ Gogel, ogle

²ogle \äg-əl\ see OGGLE

oglio \ōl-yō\ see ¹OLLO

¹ogna \ō-nə\ see ONA

²ogna \ō-nē\ see ¹ONY

³ogna \ōn-yə\ see ²ONIA

ogne \ōn\ see ¹ONE

ogned \ōnd\ see ¹ONED

ogo \ō-gō\ go-go, logo, Logo,
Togo, a-go-go

ogony \äg-ə-nē\ cosmogony,
mahogany, theogony

ographer \äg-rə-fər\
biographer, cartographer,
chorographer, cryptographer,
demographer, discographer,
ethnographer, geographer,
lithographer, mythographer,
phonographer, photographer,
pornographer, stenographer,
typographer, bibliographer,
choreographer, hagiographer,
heliographer, iconographer,
lexicographer, oceanographer,
paleographer, autobiographer,
biogeographer,
chromatographer,

cinematographer,
historiographer

ography \äg-rə-fē\ aerography,
autography, biography,
cacography, cartography,
chorography, chronography,
cosmography, cryptography,
demography, discography,
ethnography, filmography,
geography, holography,
hydrography, hypsography,
lithography, lymphography,
mammography, mythography,
nomography, orthography,
phonography, photography,
pictography, planography,
pornography, reprography,
sonography, stenography,
thermography, tomography,
topography, typography,
venography, xerography,
xylography, angiography,
aortography, bibliography,
cardiography, choreography,
chromatography,
crystallography, hagiography,
heliography, iconography,
lexicography, metallography,
oceanography, paleography,
physiography, radiography,
roentgenography,
videography, arteriography,
autobiography,
cinematography,
encephalography,
historiography,
psychobiography,
electroencephalography

ogress \ō-grəs\ ogress, progress

ogrom \äg-rəm\ grogram,
pogrom

¹ogue \ōg\ brogue, drogue,
rogue, togue, vogue, yogh,
collogue, crannog, pirogue,
prorogue, Krivoy Rog,
disembogue

²ogue \äg\ see ¹OG

³ogue \ȯg\ see ²OG

oguery \äg-rē\ see ¹OGGERY

oguish \ō-gish\ roguish,
voguish

ogun \ō-gən\ see OGAN

ogynous \äj-ə-nəs\ see
OGENOUS

ogyny \äj-ə-nē\ see OGENY

oh \ō\ see ¹OW

oha \ō-ə\ see ¹OA

ohl \ōl\ see ¹OLE

ohm \ōm\ see ¹OME

ohn \än\ see ¹ON

ohns \änz\ see ONZE

ohn's \onz\ see ONZE

ohnson \än-sən\ Johnson,
Jonson, Wisconsin

ohr \ōr\ see ¹OR

¹oi \ä\ see ¹A

²oi \ȯi\ see OY

oia \ȯi-ə\ cholla, Goya, Hoya,
olla, toea, Nagoya, sequoia,
Sequoya, atemoya,
cherimoya, paranoia

oian \ȯi-ən\ see OYEN

oic \ō-ik\ stoic, azoic, bistroic,
echoic, heroic, anechoic,
Cenozoic, Mesozoic, mock-
heroic, vetinoic, antiheroic,
Paleozoic

oice \ȯis\ choice, Joyce, Royce,
voice, devoice, Du Bois,
invoice, pro-choice, rejoice,
unvoice, sailor's-choice

oiced \ȯist\ see OIST

oicer \ȯi-sər\ choicer, voicer,
pro-choicer, rejoicer

¹**oid** \ȯid\ Boyd, Floyd, Freud,
void, android, avoid,
chancroid, colloid, conoid,
cuboid, cycloid, deltoid,
dendroid, devoid, discoid,
factoid, fungoid, globoid,
hydroid, hypnoid, keloid,
mucoid, Negroid, ovoid,
percoid, prismoid, pygmoid,
rhizoid, rhomboid, schizoid,
scombroid, sigmoid, spheroid,
steroid, styloid, tabloid,
thalloid, thyroid, toroid,
toxoid, trochoid, typhoid,
Veddoid, viroid, adenoid,
alkaloid, amoeboid, aneroid,
anthropoid, arachnoid,
asteroid, Australoid,
carcinoid, Caucasoid,
celluloid, crystalloid,
ellipsoid, embryoid,
eunuchoid, helicoid,
hemorrhoid, hominoid,
humanoid, hysteroid,
metalloid, Mongoloid,
myeloid, nautiloid, nucleoid,
obovoid, opioid, osteoid,
overjoyed, paranoid,
philanthropoid, planetoid,
Polaroid, retinoid,
rheumatoid, solenoid,
Stalinoid, trapezoid,
unalloyed, unemployed,
cannabinoid, carotenoid,
eicosanoid, meteoroid,
tuberculoid, underemployed,
Neanderthaloid—*also pasts of
verbs listed at* OY
²**oid** \ä\ see ¹A
oidal \ȯid-ᵊl\ chancroidal,
choroidal, colloidal,
conchoidal, cuboidal,
cycloidal, discoidal,
spheroidal, toroidal,
adenoidal, asteroidal,
ellipsoidal, emulsoidal,
hemorrhoidal, metalloidal,
planetoidal, saccharoidal,
trapezoidal, paraboloidal
oider \ȯid-ər\ broider, voider,
avoider, embroider,
reembroider
oie \ä\ see ¹A
oif \äf\ see ¹OFF
oign \ȯin\ see ¹OIN
oil \ȯil\ boil, Boyle, broil, coil,
Doyle, foil, hoyle, moil, loyal,
noil, oil, roil, royal, Royal,
soil, spoil, toil, voile, aboil,
airfoil, assoil, charbroil,
cinquefoil, despoil, embroil,
entoil, garboil, gargoyle,
gumboil, hard-boil, Isle
Royal, langue d'oïl, milfoil,
non-oil, parboil, recoil,
subsoil, supercoil, tinfoil,
topsoil, trefoil, turmoil,
counterfoil, disloyal,
hydrofoil, quatrefoil, rhyme
royal, surroyal, pennyroyal
oilage \ȯi-lij\ soilage, spoilage
¹**oile** \äl\ see ¹AL
²**oile** \ȯil\ see OIL
oiled \ȯild\ foiled, oiled, hard-
boiled, soft-boiled, uncoiled,
well-oiled—*also pasts of
verbs listed at* OIL
oiler \ȯi-lər\ boiler, broiler,
moiler, oiler, spoiler, toiler,
charbroiler, despoiler, Free-
Soiler, subsoiler, potboiler
oiling \ȯi-liŋ\ boiling, moiling
oilless \ȯil-ləs\ soilless,
recoilless

oilsman \ȯilz-mən\ foilsman,
spoilsman

oilus \ȯi-ləs\ see OYLESS

oily \ȯi-lē\ doily, oily, roily

¹oin \ȯin\ coin, foin, groin,
groyne, join, loin, quoin,
adjoin, Burgoyne, conjoin,
Des Moines, disjoin, eloign,
enjoin, essoin, purloin, recoin,
rejoin, sainfoin, sirloin,
subjoin, tenderloin,
Assiniboin

²oin \aⁿ\ see ⁴IN

oine \än\ see ¹ON

oined \ȯind\ conjoined,
uncoined—*also pasts of verbs
listed at* ¹OIN

oiner \ȯi-nər\ coiner, joiner

oines \ȯin\ see ¹OIN

o-ing \ō-iŋ\ see ¹OING

¹oing \ō-iŋ\ bowing, going,
knowing, rowing, sewing,
showing, churchgoing, deep-
going, foregoing, free-
flowing, glassblowing,
ingrowing, mind-blowing,
ongoing, outgoing, seagoing,
waygoing, concertgoing,
easygoing, moviegoing,
oceangoing, operagoing,
theatergoing, thoroughgoing,
whistle-blowing, to-ing and
fro-ing—*also present
participles of verbs listed at*
¹OW

²oing \ü-iŋ\ bluing, doing,
Ewing, misdoing, undoing,
wrongdoing, evildoing—*also
present participles of verbs
listed at* ¹EW

³oing \ō-ən\ see ¹OAN

oings \ō-iŋz\ outgoings—*also*

*possessives and plurals of
nouns and third person
singular presents of verbs
listed at* ¹OING

¹oint \ȯint\ joint, point, adjoint,
anoint, appoint, aroint,
ballpoint, bluepoint,
checkpoint, conjoint, disjoint,
drypoint, eyepoint, gunpoint,
knifepoint, midpoint,
nonpoint, outpoint, pinpoint,
pourpoint, standpoint, tuck-
point, viewpoint,
counterpoint, disappoint,
needlepoint, petit point,
silverpoint

²oint \ant\ see ⁵ANT

ointe \ant\ see ⁵ANT

ointed \ȯint-əd\ jointed,
pointed, lap-jointed, loose-
jointed, double-jointed, well-
appointed —*also pasts of
verbs listed at* ¹OINT

ointer \ȯint-ər\ jointer, pointer,
anointer

ointing \ȯin-tiŋ\ finger-
pointing—*present participles
of verbs listed at* ¹OINT

ointment \ȯint-mənt\ ointment,
anointment, appointment,
disappointment

¹oir \īr\ see ¹IRE

²oir \är\ see ³AR

³oir \ȯir\ see OYER

⁴oir \ȯr\ see ¹OR

¹oire \är\ see ³AR

²oire \ȯir\ see OYER

³oire \ȯr\ see ¹OR

¹ois \ä\ see ¹A

²ois \ȯi\ see OY

³ois \ō-əs\ Lois, Powys

⁴ois \ȯis\ see OICE

¹oise \äz\ poise, 'twas, vase, was, Ahwaz, bourgeoise, Lamaze, Shiraz, vichyssoise, The Afars and the Isas—*also plurals and possessives of nouns and third person singular presents of verbs listed at* ¹A

²oise \óiz\ hoise, noise, Noyes, poise, turquoise, counterpoise, equipoise, avoirdupois—*also plurals and possessives of nouns and third person singular presents of verbs listed at* OY

³oise \oi-zē\ see OISY

oison \óiz-°n\ foison, poison, empoison

oist \óist\ foist, hoist, joist, moist, voiced, unvoiced, semimoist—*also pasts of verbs listed at* OICE

oister \ói-stər\ cloister, moister, oyster, roister

oisterous \ói-strəs\ see OISTRESS

oistral \ói-strəl\ cloistral, coistrel

oistrel \ói-strəl\ see OISTRAL

oistress \ói-strəs\ cloistress, boisterous, roisterous

oisy \ói-zē\ Boise, noisy, cramoisie

¹oit \óit\ doit, droit, poet, quoit, adroit, Detroit, exploit, maladroit, Massasoit

²oit \āt\ see ¹ATE

³oit \ō-ət\ see ¹OET

⁴oit \ä\ see ¹A

oite \ät\ see ¹OT

oiter \ói-tər\ goiter, loiter, exploiter, reconnoiter

oitus \ō-ət-əs\ see OETESS

oivre \äv\ see ¹OLVE

¹oix \ä\ see ¹A

²oix \ói\ see OY

oiz \óis\ see ²OISE

ojan \ō-jən\ Trojan, theologian

oje \ō-jē\ see OJI

oji \ō-jē\ Moji, shoji, anagoge, Hachioje

¹ok \äk\ see ¹OCK

²ok \ək\ see UCK

³ok \ók\ see ALK

oka \ō-kə\ see OCA

okable \ō-kə-bəl\ see OCABLE

¹oke \ōk\ bloke, broke, choke, cloak, coke, Coke, croak, folk, hoke, joke, moke, oak, oke, poke, Polk, roque, smoke, soak, soke, spoke, stoke, stroke, toke, toque, woke, yogh, yoke, yolk, ad hoc, awoke, backstroke, baroque, bespoke, breaststroke, chain-smoke, convoke, cowpoke, downstroke, evoke, heatstroke, housebroke, in-joke, invoke, keystroke, kinfolk, kinsfolk, menfolk, Nisroch, outspoke, presoak, provoke, revoke, she-oak, sidestroke, slowpoke, sunchoke, sunstroke, townsfolk, uncloak, unyoke, upstroke, workfolk, artichoke, equivoque, fisherfolk, gentlefolk, herrenvolk, masterstroke, okeydoke, Roanoke, thunderstroke, womenfolk, Mount Revelstoke

²oke \ō-kē\ see OKY

³**oke** \ō\ see ¹OW

⁴**oke** \ůk\ see ¹OOK

oked \ōkt\ stoked, yolked

okee \ō-kē\ see OKY

okel \ō-kəl\ see OCAL

oken \ō-kən\ broken, oaken,
spoken, token, woken,
awoken, bespoken, betoken,
fair-spoken, foretoken, free-
spoken, heartbroken,
housebroken, outspoken,
plainspoken, short-spoken,
soft-spoken, unbroken, well-
spoken, wind-broken

oker \ō-kər\ broker, choker,
croaker, joker, ocher, poker,
soaker, smoker, stoker,
stroker, chain-smoker,
invoker, pawnbroker,
provoker, revoker,
stockbroker, mediocre

okey \ō-kē\ see OKY

oki \ō-kē\ see OKY

okie \ō-kē\ see OKY

oking \ō-kiŋ\ broking, choking

oko \ō-kō\ see OCO

okum \ō-kəm\ Bochum,
hokum, locum, oakum

oky \ō-kē\ choky, croaky,
folkie, hokey, Loki, Okie,
pokey, poky, smoky, troche,
trochee, yolky, enoki, Great
Smoky, hokeypokey, karaoke,
Okefenokee

¹**ol** \ōl\ see ¹OLE

²**ol** \äl\ see ¹AL

³**ol** \ȯl\ see ALL

ola \ō-lə\ bola, cola, Kola, Lola,
tola, Zola, Angola, boffola,
Canola, gondola, granola,
mandola, payola, pergola,
plugola, scagliola, Savanarola,
viola, Viola, acerola,
ayatollah, braciola, Española,
gladiola, Gorgonzola,
hemiola, Hispaniola, moviola,
Osceola, roseola, Victrola

olable \ō-lə-bəl\ see OLLABLE

olace \äl-əs\ see OLIS

olan \ō-lən\ see OLON

oland \ō-lənd\ see OWLAND

olander \əl-ən-dər\ colander,
Julunder

¹**olar** \ō-lər\ see OLLER

²**olar** \äl-ər\ see OLLAR

olas \ō-ləs\ see OLUS

olater \äl-ət-ər\ bardolater,
idolater, bibliolater,
Mariolater

olatrous \äl-ə-trəs\ idolatrous,
bibliolatrous, heliolatrous

olatry \äl-ə-trē\ bardolatry,
idolatry, statolatry, zoolatry,
bibliolatry, heliolatry,
iconolatry, Mariolatry

¹**old** \ōld\ bold, bowled, cold,
fold, gold, hold, mold, mould,
old, polled, scold, sold, soled,
souled, told, wold, acold, age-
old, ahold, behold, billfold,
blindfold, controlled,
Cotswold, cuckold, enfold,
fanfold, foothold, foretold,
freehold, gatefold, handhold,
household, ice-cold, infold,
leasehold, pinfold, potholed,
roothold, scaffold, sheepfold,
stone-cold, stronghold,
threshold, toehold, twice-told,
unfold, unmold, untold,
uphold, whole-souled,
withhold, centerfold,
copyhold, fingerhold,
manifold, manyfold,

marigold, multifold, oversold,
petioled, severalfold,
stranglehold, throttlehold—
also pasts of verbs listed at
¹OLE

²**old** \ōld\ see ALD

oldan \ōl-dən\ see OLDEN

olden \ōl-dən\ golden, holden,
olden, soldan, beholden,
embolden

¹**older** \ōl-dər\ boulder, folder,
holder, molder, polder,
shoulder, smolder,
bondholder, cardholder,
householder, jobholder,
landholder, placeholder,
shareholder, slaveholder,
stadtholder, stakeholder,
stallholder, stockholder,
toolholder, officeholder,
titleholder, policyholder—
also comparatives of
adjectives listed at ¹OLD

²**older** \äd-ər\ see ODDER

oldi \ōl-dē\ see ALDI

oldie \ōl-dē\ see OLDY

olding \ōl-diŋ\ folding, holding,
molding, hand-holding,
inholding, landholding,
slaveholding

oldster \ōl-stər\ see OLSTER

oldt \ōlt\ ¹OLT

oldy \ōl-dē\ moldy, oldie

¹**ole** \ōl\ bole, boll, bowl, coal,
cole, Cole, dhole, dole, droll,
foal, goal, hole, knoll, kohl,
Kohl, mole, ole, pole, Pole,
poll, prole, role, roll, scroll,
Seoul, shoal, skoal, sol, sole,
soul, stole, stroll, thole, tole,
toll, troll, vole, whole,
armhole, atoll, bankroll,

beanpole, bedroll, blowhole,
bolthole, borehole, bunghole,
cajole, catchpole, charcoal,
chuckhole, condole, console,
control, creole, Creole,
drumroll, enroll, ensoul, extol,
eyehole, fishbowl, flagpole,
foxhole, frijol, hellhole,
Huichol, inscroll, insole,
keyhole, kneehole, knothole,
logroll, loophole, manhole,
maypole, midsole, Mongol,
Nicole, outsole, parole, patrol,
payroll, peephole, pesthole,
pinhole, pistole, pitchpole,
porthole, posthole, pothole,
redpoll, resole, ridgepole,
Sheol, sinkhole, sotol,
stokehole, tadpole, taphole,
thumbhole, top-hole,
touchhole, turnsole, unroll,
Walpole, washbowl,
wormhole, amatol, aureole,
banderole, bannerol,
barcarole, buttonhole,
cabriole, camisole, capriole,
caracole, carmagnole,
casserole, croquignole,
cubbyhole, decontrol,
Demerol, escarole, farandole,
fumarole, girandole, grand
guignol, innersole, methanol,
oriole, oversoul, petiole, pick-
and-roll, pigeonhole, protocol,
rigmarole, Seminole,
cholesterol, Costa del Sol

²**ole** \ō-lē\ see ¹OLY

³**ole** \ōl\ see ALL

olean \ō-lē-ən\ see ¹OLIAN

oled \ōld\ see ¹OLD

oleful \ōl-fəl\ doleful, soulful

olely \ō-lē\ see ¹OLY

¹**olem** \ō-ləm\ golem, solum
²**olem** \ā-ləm\ see ALAAM
olemn \äl-əm\ see OLUMN
¹**oleon** \ō-lē-ən\ see ¹OLIAN
²**oleon** \ōl-yən\ see ²OLIAN
¹**oler** \ō-lər\ see OLLER
²**oler** \äl-ər\ see OLLAR
olery \ōl-rē\ see OLLERY
olesome \ōl-səm\ dolesome,
   Folsom, wholesome
oless \ō-ləs\ see OLUS
oleum \ō-lē-əm\ see OLIUM
oleus \ō-lē-əs\ coleus, soleus
oley \ō-lē\ see ¹OLY
¹**olf** \älf\ golf, Rolf, Adolph,
   Randolph, Rudolph, Lake
   Rudolf
²**olf** \əlf\ see ULF
olfing \óf-iŋ\ see OFFING
olga \äl-gə\ Olga, Volga
oli \ō-lē\ see ¹OLY
olia \ō-lē-ə\ Mongolia, pignolia,
   Anatolia, melancholia, Inner
   Mongolia, Outer Mongolia
olian \ō-lē-ən\ aeolian, Aeolian,
   eolian, Mongolian, napoleon,
   Napoleon, simoleon,
   Tyrolean, Anatolian
¹**olic** \äl-ik\ colic, frolic, Gaelic,
   rollick, Aeolic, bucolic,
   carbolic, embolic, Mongolic,
   symbolic, systolic, alcoholic,
   anabolic, apostolic, catabolic,
   diabolic, hyperbolic,
   melancholic, metabolic,
   parabolic, vitriolic,
   workaholic
²**olic** \ō-lik\ colic, fumarolic,
   bibliopolic
olicking \ä-lik-iŋ\ frolicking,
   rollicking
olicy \äl-ə-sē\ policy, Wallasey

olid \äl-əd\ solid, squalid,
   stolid—*also pasts of verbs
   listed at* ²ALA
¹**olin** \äl-ən\ see ⁵OLLEN
²**olin** \ō-lən\ see OLON
olis \äl-əs\ braless, Hollis, polis,
   solace, tallith, Wallace,
   Wallis, Cornwallis,
   Manizales, torticollis
olish \äl-ish\ polish, abolish,
   demolish, apple-polish
olitan \äl-ət-ⁿn\ cosmopolitan,
   megapolitan, metropolitan,
   Neapolitan, megalopolitan
olity \äl-ət-ē\ see ¹ALITY
olium \ō-lē-əm\ scholium,
   linoleum, petroleum, trifolium
olivar \äl-ə-vər\ see OLIVER
¹**olk** \elk\ see ¹ELK
²**olk** \ōk\ see OKE
³**olk** \əlk\ see ULK
⁴**olk** \ók\ see ALK
olked \ōkt\ see OKED
olkie \ō-kē\ see OKY
olky \ō-kē\ see OKY
¹**oll** \ōl\ see ¹OLE
²**oll** \äl\ see ¹AL
³**oll** \ól\ see ALL
¹**olla** \äl-ə\ see ²ALA
²**olla** \ói-ə\ see OIA
ollable \ō-lə-bəl\ controllable,
   inconsolable, uncontrollable
ollack \äl-ək\ see OLOCH
¹**ollah** \ō-lə\ see OLA
²**ollah** \äl-ə\ see ²ALA
³**ollah** \əl-ə\ see ¹ULLAH
ollands \äl-ənz\ see OLLINS
ollar \äl-ər\ choler, collar,
   dollar, dolor, haler, holler,
   Mahler, scholar, squalor,
   taler, thaler, blue-collar,
   brass-collar, half-dollar,

white-collar, Emmentaler,
Eurodollar, petrodollar
ollard \äl-ərd\ bollard, collard,
collered, hollered, Lollard,
pollard
olled \ōld\ see ¹OLD
ollee \ō-lē\ see ¹OLY
ollege \äl-ij\ see OWLEDGE
¹**ollen** \ō-lən\ see OLON
²**ollen** \əl-ə\ see ¹ULLAH
³**ollen** \əl-ən\ see ULLEN
⁴**ollen** \ȯ-lən\ see ALLEN
⁵**ollen** \äl-ən\ Colin, pollen,
Rollin, Nordrhein-Westfalen
oller \ō-lər\ bowler, choler,
dolor, droller, molar, polar,
poler, poller, roller, solar,
stroller, troller, bankroller,
cajoler, comptroller,
controller, extoller, patroller,
premolar, steamroller,
antisolar, buttonholer,
logroller, Maryknoller,
pigeonholer
ollery \ōl-rē\ drollery, cajolery
ollet \äl-ət\ collet, Smollett,
tallith, wallet,
whatchamacallit
ollett \äl-ət\ see OLLET
olley \äl-ē\ see ¹OLLY
ollick \äl-ik\ see ¹OLIC
ollicking \ä-lik-iŋ\ see
OLICKING
ollie \äl-ē\ see ¹OLLY
ollin \äl-ən\ see ⁵OLLEN
olling \ō-liŋ\ bowling,
logrolling—*also present
participles of verbs listed at*
¹OLE
ollins \äl-ənz\ collins, Hollands,
Tom Collins
ollis \äl-əs\ see OLIS

ollity \äl-ət-ē\ see ¹ALITY
¹**ollo** \ōl-yō\ imbroglio, arroz
con pollo
²**ollo** \ō-yō\ yo-yo, criollo
³**ollo** \äl-ō\ see ¹OLLOW
ollop \äl-əp\ collop, dollop,
lollop, polyp, scallop, scollop,
trollop, wallop, codswallop,
escallop
¹**ollow** \äl-ō\ follow, hollo,
hollow, swallow, wallow,
Apollo, robalo, Leoncavallo
²**ollow** \äl-ə\ see ²ALA
ollower \äl-ə-wər\ follower,
swallower, wallower
ollster \ōl-stər\ see OLSTER
¹**olly** \äl-ē\ Bali, Cali, brolly,
collie, colly, dolly, folly,
golly, Halle, holly, Holly,
jolly, Lally, lolly, Mali,
Mollie, molly, Molly, Ollie,
Pali, poly, Polly, quale,
Raleigh, trolley, volley,
Denali, finale, Kigali,
loblolly, Nepali, petrale,
Somali, Svengali, tamale,
melancholy, pastorale, teocalli
²**olly** \ȯ-lē\ see AWLY
olm \ōm\ see ¹OME
olman \ōl-mən\ dolman,
dolmen, patrolman
olmen \ōl-mən\ see OLMAN
olmes \ōmz\ Holmes—*also
possessives and plurals of
nouns and third person
singular presents of verbs
listed at* ¹OME
olo \ō-lō\ bolo, kolo, nolo, polo,
solo, Barolo, Marco Polo
oloch \äl-ək\ Moloch, pollack,
rowlock
ologer \äl-ə-jər\ astrologer,

chronologer, horologer,
mythologer

ologist \äl-ə-jəst\ anthologist,
biologist, cetologist,
conchologist, cosmologist,
cryptologist, cytologist,
dendrologist, ecologist,
enologist, ethnologist,
ethologist, fetologist,
gemologist, geologist,
graphologist, histologist,
horologist, hydrologist,
Indologist, limnologist,
mixologist, morphologist,
mycologist, mythologist,
necrologist, nephrologist,
neurologist, oncologist,
ontologist, oologist,
pathologist, pedologist,
penologist, petrologist,
philologist, phonologist,
phrenologist, phycologist,
psychologist, seismologist,
serologist, sexologist,
sinologist, technologist,
topologist, typologist,
ufologist, virologist,
zoologist, anthropologist,
archaeologist, audiologist,
cardiologist, climatologist,
cosmetologist, criminologist,
dermatologist, Egyptologist,
embryologist, entomologist,
enzymologist, escapologist,
etymologist, futurologist,
genealogist, gerontologist,
gynecologist, hematologist,
herpetologist, ichthyologist,
ideologist, immunologist,
kremlinologist, lexicologist,
martyrologist, methodologist,
mineralogist, musicologist,

nematalogist, numerologist,
oceanologist, ophthalmologist,
ornithologist, osteologist,
papyrologist, pharmacologist,
phraseologist, physiologist,
planetologist, primatologist,
rheumatologist,
roentgenologist, semiologist,
sociologist, speleologist,
teleologist, teratologist,
thanatologist, toxicologist,
urbanologist, volcanologist,
bacteriologist, diabetologist,
dialectologist,
endocrinologist,
epistemologist, liturgiologist,
meteorologist, neonatologist,
paleontologist, parasitologist,
phenomenologist,
sedimentologist,
anesthesiologist,
epidemiologist,
gastroenterologist,
otolaryngologist

ologous \äl-ə-gəs\ heterologous,
homologous, tautologous

ology \äl-ə-jē\ anthology,
apology, astrology, biology,
bryology, cetology,
Christology, chronology,
conchology, cosmology,
cryptology, cytology,
dendrology, doxology,
ecology, enology, ethnology,
ethology, fetology, gemology,
geology, graphology,
haplology, histology,
homology, horology,
hydrology, hymnology,
Indology, limnology,
lithology, mixology,
morphology, mycology,

myology, mythology,
necrology, nephrology,
neurology, nosology,
oncology, ontology, oology,
pathology, pedology,
penology, petrology,
philology, phlebology,
phonology, phrenology,
phycology, proctology,
psychology, scatology,
seismology, serology,
sexology, sinology,
symbology, tautology,
technology, tetralogy,
theology, topology,
trichology, typology, ufology,
urology, virology, zoology,
angelology, anthropology,
archaeology, audiology,
axiology, cardiology,
climatology, codicology,
cohomology, cosmetology,
craniology, criminology,
dactylology, demonology,
deontology, dermatology,
Egyptology, embryology,
entomology, enzymology,
escapology, eschatology,
etiology, etymology,
futurology, genealogy,
gerontology, gynecology,
hematology, herpetology,
ichthyology, iconology,
ideology, immunology,
kremlinology, laryngology,
lexicology, lichenology,
Mariology, martyrology,
methodology, mineralogy,
museology, musicology,
narratology, nematology,
numerology, oceanology,
opthalmology, ornithology,
osteology, pharmacology,
phraseology, physiology,
planetology, primatology,
radiology, reflexology,
rheumatology, roentgenology,
semiology, sociology,
speleology, sumerology,
teleology, teratology,
terminology, thanatology,
toxicology, urbanology,
volcanology, vulcanology,
bacteriology, chronobiology,
cryptozoology, dialectology,
ecclesiology, endocrinology,
epistemology, liturgiology,
metapsychology,
meteorology, microbiology,
micromorphology,
neonatology, onomatology,
paleontology, parapsychology,
parasitology, phenomenology,
sedimentology,
symptomatology,
anesthesiology, epidemiology,
ethnomusicology,
gastroenterology,
otolaryngology, paleobiology,
paleopathology,
periodontology,
otorhinolaryngology

olon \ō-lən\ bowline, Colin,
colon, Nolan, solon, stolen,
stollen, stolon, swollen,
eidolon, semicolon

olonel \ərn-ᵊl\ see ERNAL

olonist \äl-ə-nəst\ colonist,
Stalinist

¹olor \əl-ər\ color, cruller,
culler, muller, sculler, bicolor,
discolor, off-color, three-
color, tricolor, Technicolor,
watercolor

²olor \ō-lər\ *see* OLLER
³olor \äl-ər\ *see* OLLAR
olored \əl-ərd\ colored, dullard,
  bicolored, rose-colored,
  varicolored
olp \ōp\ *see* OPE
olpen \ō-pən\ *see* OPEN
olph \älf\ *see* OLF
ols \älz\ hols, Casals
olsom \ōl-səm\ *see* OLESOME
olster \ōl-stər\ bolster, holster,
  oldster, pollster, upholster
¹olt \ōlt\ bolt, colt, dolt, holt,
  jolt, molt, poult, smolt, volt,
  eyebolt, Humboldt, kingbolt,
  revolt, ringbolt, unbolt,
  thunderbolt
²olt \olt\ *see* ALT
olta \äl-tə\ *see* ALTA
olter \ōl-tər\ bolter, coulter
oltish \ōl-tish\ coltish, doltish
oluble \äl-yə-bəl\ soluble,
  voluble, dissoluble, insoluble,
  irresoluble, resoluble,
  indissoluble
olum \ō-ləm\ *see* OLEM
olumn \äl-əm\ column, slalom,
  solemn, Malayalam
olus \ō-ləs\ bolas, bolus, solus,
  snowless, toeless, Coriolus,
  electroless, gladiolus, holus-
  bolus
olvable \äl-və-bəl\ solvable,
  dissolvable, evolvable,
  insolvable, resolvable,
  revolvable, irresolvable
¹olve \älv\ salve, solve, absolve,
  au poivre, convolve, devolve,
  dissolve, evolve, involve,
  resolve, revolve, coevolve
²olve \äv\ grave, of, salve, Slav,
  suave, taw, waw, moshav,

thereof, whereof, Zouave,
  Tishah-b'Ab, unheard-of,
  well-thought-of
olvement \älv-mənt\
  evolvement, involvement,
  noninvolvement
olvent \äl-vənt\ solvent,
  dissolvent
olver \äl-vər\ solver, absolver,
  dissolver, involver, revolver
¹oly \ō-lē\ goalie, holey, holy,
  lowly, mole, moly, pollee,
  slowly, solely, aioli, amole,
  anole, cannoli, frijole, pinole,
  unholy, guacamole, ravioli,
  roly-poly
²oly \äl-ē\ *see* ¹OLLY
olyp \äl-əp\ *see* OLLOP
¹om \äm\ balm, bomb, bombe,
  calm, from, gaum, Guam,
  glom, malm, mom, palm,
  Pom, pram, prom, psalm,
  qualm, rhomb, ROM, tom, A-
  bomb, aplomb, ashram,
  becalm, Ceram, cheongsam,
  coulomb, Coulomb, dive-
  bomb, embalm, EPROM,
  firebomb, grande dame, H-
  bomb, imam, Islam, Long
  Tom, napalm, nizam,
  noncom, phenom, pogrom,
  pom-pom, reclame, rhabdom,
  salaam, seram, sitcom,
  Songnam, tam-tam,
  therefrom, tom-tom,
  wherefrom, wigwam,
  cardamom, diatom, intercom,
  Peeping Tom, Uncle Tom,
  Vietnam, Dar es Salaam,
  Omar Kayyam
²om \ōm\ *see* ¹OME
³om \üm\ *see* ¹OOM

⁴om \əm\ see ¹UM
⁵om \u̇m\ see ²UM
⁶om \ȯm\ see ¹AUM
oma \ō-mə\ chroma, coma,
  Roma, soma, aroma, diploma,
  glaucoma, sarcoma, Tacoma,
  carcinoma, granuloma,
  melanoma, Oklahoma,
  glioblastoma, neurofibroma
omac \ō-mik\ see ²OMIC
¹omace \äm-əs\ see OMISE
²omace \əm-əs\ see UMMOUS
omach \əm-ək\ see UMMOCK
omache \äm-ə-kē\ see OMACHY
omachy \äm-ə-kē\
  Andromache, logomachy
omal \ō-məl\ domal, stomal,
  prodromal, chromosomal
omaly \äm-ə-lē\ balmily,
  homily, anomaly
oman \ō-mən\ bowman,
  foeman, gnomon, nomen,
  omen, Roman, showman,
  snowman, yeoman, agnomen,
  cognomen, crossbowman,
  longbowman, praenomen,
  Sertoman
omany \äm-ə-nē\ see OMINY
omas \äm-əs\ see OMISE
omathy \äm-ə-thē\
  chrestomathy, stichomythy
¹omb \ōm\ see ¹OME
²omb \u̇m\ see ¹OOM
³omb \äm\ see ¹OM
⁴omb \əm\ see ¹UM
omba \äm-bə\ see AMBA
¹ombe \ōm\ see ¹OME
²ombe \u̇m\ see ¹OOM
³ombe \äm\ see ¹OM
ombed \u̇md\ see OOMED
¹omber \äm-ər\ bomber,
  calmer, palmar, palmer,

Palmer, dive-bomber,
  embalmer, fighter-bomber
²omber \äm-bər\ ombre,
  sambar, somber
³omber \ō-mər\ see ¹OMER
ombic \ō-mik\ see ²OMIC
ombical \ō-mi-kəl\ see ²OMICAL
ombie \äm-bē\ zombie,
  Abercrombie
ombing \ō-miŋ\ see OAMING
¹ombo \äm-bō\ combo, mambo,
  sambo
²ombo \əm-bō\ see UMBO
¹ombre \äm-brē\ hombre,
  ombre
²ombre \äm-bər\ see ²OMBER
³ombre \əm-brē\ see UMBERY
ombus \äm-bəs\ rhombus,
  thrombus
¹ome \ōm\ brougham, chrome,
  comb, combe, dome, foam,
  gloam, gnome, holm, home,
  loam, mome, nome, ohm, om,
  poem, pome, roam, Rom,
  Rome, tome, airdrome, at-
  home, bichrome, cockscomb,
  coulomb, coxcomb, defoam,
  down-home, Jerome,
  Nichrome, ogham, seadrome,
  shalom, sholom, Stockholm,
  syndrome, aerodrome,
  astrodome, catacomb,
  chromosome, currycomb,
  double-dome, gastronome,
  halidrome, hecatomb,
  hippodrome, honeycomb,
  metronome, monochrome,
  motordrome, palindrome,
  ribosome, stay-at-home,
  Styrofoam
²ome \ō-mē\ see OAMY
³ome \əm\ see ¹UM

omedy \äm-əd-ē\ comedy,
  psalmody, tragicomedy
omely \əm-lē\ see ²UMBLY
omen \ō-mən\ see OMAN
omenal \äm-ən-ᵊl\ see OMINAL
omene \äm-ə-nē\ see OMINY
¹**omer** \ō-mər\ comber, foamer,
  homer, Homer, omer, roamer,
  vomer, beachcomber,
  Reaumur, Lag b'Omer,
  misnomer
²**omer** \əm-ər\ see UMMER
omery \əm-ə-rē\ see UMMERY
omet \äm-ət\ comet, grommet,
  vomit
ometer \äm-ət-ər\ barometer,
  chronometer, cyclometer,
  drunkometer, ergometer,
  gasometer, geometer,
  hydrometer, hygrometer,
  kilometer, manometer,
  micrometer, odometer,
  pedometer, photometer,
  pulsometer, pyrometer,
  rheometer, seismometer,
  spectrometer, speedometer,
  tachometer, thermometer,
  anemometer, audiometer,
  diffractometer, electrometer,
  magnetometer, alcoholometer
ometry \äm-ə-trē\ astrometry,
  barometry, chronometry,
  cytometry, geometry,
  isometry, micrometry,
  optometry, photometry,
  psychometry, seismometry,
  thermometry, craniometry,
  sociometry, trigonometry
omey \ō-mē\ see OAMY
omi \ō-mē\ see OAMY
omia \ō-mē-ä\ peperomia,
  Utsunomia

¹**omic** \äm-ik\ comic, anomic,
  atomic, coelomic, Islamic,
  tsunamic, agronomic,
  anatomic, antinomic,
  autonomic, economic,
  ergonomic, gastronomic,
  metronomic, subatomic,
  taxonomic, tragicomic,
  Deuteronomic, heroicomic,
  physiognomic, polyatomic,
  seriocomic, macroeconomic,
  microeconomic,
  socioeconomic
²**omic** \ō-mik\ gnomic,
  oghamic, Potomac, rhizomic,
  catacombic, monochromic,
  palindromic
¹**omical** \äm-i-kəl\ comical,
  domical, agronomical,
  anatomical, astronomical,
  economical, gastronomical,
  metronomical, tragicomical,
  heroicomical, physiognomical
²**omical** \ō-mi-kəl\ domical,
  coxcombical
omics \äm-iks\ atomics,
  Islamics, tectonics,
  bionomics, economics,
  ergonomics, macroeconomics,
  microeconomics—*also
  plurals and possessives of
  nouns listed at* ¹OMIC
omily \äm-ə-lē\ see OMALY
ominal \äm-ən-ᵊl\ nominal,
  abdominal, cognominal,
  phenomenal, epiphenomenal
ominance \äm-nəns\
  dominance, prominence,
  predominance
ominant \äm-nənt\ dominant,
  prominent, predominant,

semidominant, subdominant, superdominant

ominate \äm-ə-nət\ innominate, prenominate

omine \äm-ə-nē\ see OMINY

ominence \äm-nəns\ see OMINANCE

ominent \äm-nənt\ see OMINANT

¹**oming** \əm-iŋ\ coming, plumbing, becoming, forthcoming, homecoming, incoming, oncoming, shortcoming, upcoming, unbecoming, up-and-coming—*also present participles of verbs listed at* ¹UM

²**oming** \ō-miŋ\ see OAMING

omini \äm-ə-nē\ see OMINY

ominous \äm-ə-nəs\ ominous, prolegomenous

ominy \äm-ə-nē\ hominy, Romany, Melpomene, anno Domini, eo nomine

omise \äm-əs\ pomace, promise, shammes, shamus, Thomas, Saint Thomas, doubting Thomas

omish \ō-mish\ gnomish, Romish

omit \äm-ət\ see OMET

omium \ō-mē-əm\ chromium, holmium, encomium, prostomium

¹**omma** \äm-ə\ see ²AMA

²**omma** \əm-ə\ see UMMA

¹**ommel** \äm-əl\ pommel, Jamil, Rommel, trommel

²**ommel** \əm-əl\ pommel, pummel, Beau Brummell

ommet \äm-ət\ see OMET

ommie \äm-ē\ see ¹AMI

ommon \äm-ən\ Amon, Brahman, common, shaman, yamen, Roscommon, Tutankhamen

ommoner \äm-ə-nər\ almoner, commoner, gewürztraminer

¹**ommy** \äm-ē\ see ¹AMI

²**ommy** \əm-ē\ see UMMY

omo \ō-mō\ bromo, Como, homo, Pomo, promo, Oromo, majordomo

omon \ō-mən\ see OMAN

¹**omp** \ämp\ champ, chomp, clomp, comp, pomp, romp, stamp, stomp, swamp, tramp, tromp, whomp

²**omp** \əmp\ see UMP

ompany \əmp-nē\ company, accompany, intracompany

ompass \əm-pəs\ compass, rumpus, encompass, gyrocompass

omper \äm-pər\ romper, stamper, stomper, swamper, wafflestomper

ompers \äm-pərz\ Gompers—*also possessives and plurals of nouns listed at* OMPER

ompey \äm-pē\ see OMPY

omplement \äm-plə-mənt\ complement, compliment

ompliment \äm-plə-mənt\ see OMPLEMENT

ompo \äm-pō\ campo, compo

ompous \äm-pəs\ see ¹OMPASS

ompson \äm-sən\ see AMSUN

ompt \aůnt\ see ²OUNT

ompy \äm-pē\ Pompey, swampy

omythy \äm-ə-thē\ see OMATHY

¹**on** \än\ ban, Bonn, chon, con,

conn, dawn, don, Don, Donn, drawn, Fan, faun, fawn, gone, guan, Han, John, Jon, khan, maun, mon, on, pan, pawn, phon, prawn, Ron, Shan, spawn, swan, Vaughn, wan, yawn, yon, yuan, aeon, add-on, agon, agone, Akan, alençon, Amman, ancon, anon, Anshan, Anton, archon, argon, Argonne, Aswan, atman, Avon, axon, barchan, baton, blouson, bon ton, bonbon, boron, boson, bouillon, Brython, bygone, caisson, Calgon, canton, capon, Ceylon, chaconne, chiffon, chignon, Chiron, chiton, chrismon, cistron, clip-on, codon, come-on, cordon, coupon, crampon, crayon, crepon, cretonne, crouton, Dacron, dead-on, Dear John, dewan, doggone, doggoned, Dogon, Don Juan, eon, exon, far-gone, flacon, foregone, Freon, fronton, Fujian, Garonne, Gibran, gluon, gnomon, Golan, Gosplan, guidon, hadron, Hainan, hazan, Henan, hogan, Huainan, Hunan, icon, Inchon, intron, Ivan, Jinan, Kanban, kaon, Kashan, Kazan, Kerman, Khoisan, Kirman, koan, krypton, kurgan, Kurgan, lauan, Leon, lepton, liman, log on, Luzon, macron, Massan, Medan, Memnon, meson, micron, Milan, mod con, moron, mouton, Multan, muon,

natron, neon, nephron, neuron, neutron, ninon, nylon, odds-on, Oman, Oran, Orlon, outgone, pacon, parton, Pathan, pavane, pecan, peon, Phaethon, photon, phyton, pion, pinon, piton, plankton, pluton, pompon, prion, proton, Pusan, put-on, pylon, python, Qur'an, radon, rayon, recon, rhyton, run-on, Saint John, Saipan, salon, San Juan, Schumann, Shaban, shaman, shaitan, Shingon, Simplon, Sjoelland, slip-on, snap-on, solon, soupçon, soutane, Stefan, stolon, Suwon, Szechuan, Szechwan, Tainan, Taiwan, taipan, tampon, taxon, Teflon, teston, Tétouan, Tetuán, thereon, tisane, torchon, toucan, toyon, trigon, Tristan, triton, trogon, Tucson, Typhon, tzigane, uhlan, Ulsan, upon, walk-on, witan, whereon, Wonsan, wonton, Wuhan, xenon, Xi'an, yaupon, Yukon, Yunnan, Yvonne, zircon, Abadan, Abijan, Acheron, Ahriman, aileron, amazon, Amazon, amnion, Aragon, autobahn, Avalon, Babylon, Bakhtaran, Balaton, balmacaan, Bantustan, Barbizon, baryon, Basilan, betatron, biathlon, cabochon, calutron, carillon, carryon, celadon, chorion, colophon, Culiacàn, cyclotron, decagon, decathlon, demijohn, deuteron, dipteron, echelon, electron, elevon, epsilon, etymon, fermion, follow-on, Fujisan, Genghis Khan, goings-on, gonfalon, Grand Teton, graviton, harijan, helicon, heptagon, hexagon, hopping John, Huascaràn, Ilion, Irian, Isfahan, Kazakhstan, Kublai Khan, Kyrgyzstan, Lake Huron, Lebanon, leprechaun, lexicon, liaison, Lipizzan, logion, macédoine, marathon, Marathon, marzipan, mastodon, Mazatlàn, Mbabane, Mellotron, Miquelon, morion, myrmidon, negatron, nonagon, noumenon, nucleon, Oberon, octagon, omicron, Oregon, organon, ostracon, Pakistan, Palawan, pantheon, paragon, Parmesan, parmigiana, Parthenon, pentagon, Percheron, Phaethon, Phlegethon, polygon, positron, Procyon, put-upon, Rajasthan, Ramadan, Rubicon, silicon, Suleiman, tachyon, Taiyuan, talkathon, Teheran, telamon, telethon, thereupon, Tian Shan, Tucuman, undergone, upsilon, virion, walkathon, whereupon, woebegone, Yerevan, Zahedan, abutilon, Agamemnon, archenteron, arrière-ban, asyndeton, automaton, Azerbaijan, Bellerophon, bildungsroman, carrying-on, Diazenon, dimetrodon, dodecagon, encephalon, ephemeron, himation, interferon, kakiemon, Laocoön, mesenteron, Michoacàn, millimicron, oxymoron, phenomenon, protozoon, Saskatchewan, septentrion, sine qua non, t'ai chi ch'uan, Taklimakan, Vientiane, West Irian, Xiangtan, anacoluthon, diencephalon, ferrosilicon, mesencephalon, metencephalon, prolegomenon, prothalamion, prosencephalon, pteranodon, spermatozoon, telencephalon, ultramarathon, epiphenomenon, myelencephalon, kyrie eleison, San Miguel de Tucumàn

²**on** \ō^n\ fond, ton, ballon, baton, bouillon, Dijon, flacon, fourgon, frisson, Gabon, garçon, lorgnon, Lyons, maçon, marron, Marron, mouflon, soupçon, Toulon, Villon, Aubusson, bourguignon, feuilleton, Ganelon, gueridon, limaçon, papillon, filet mignon, Saint Emilion

³**on** \ȯn\ awn, Bonn, bonne, brawn, dawn, Dawn, drawn, faun, fawn, gone, lawn, maun, on, pawn, prawn, Sean, spawn, Vaughn, won, yawn, add-on, agon, agone, begone, bygone, chaconne, clip-on, come-on, dead-on, doggone, far-gone, foregone, hands-on, hard-on, head-on, hereon,

impawn, indrawn, Kherson,
odds-on, outgone, Puchon,
put-on, Quezon, run-on, slip-
on, snap-on, Taejon, thereon,
turned-on, upon, walk-on,
whereon, wiredrawn,
withdrawn, bourguignonne,
carryon, follow-on, goings-on,
hanger-on, hereupon, looker-
on, put-upon, thereupon,
undergone, whereupon,
woebegone, carrying-on

⁴on \ōn\ see ¹ONE

⁵on \ən\ see UN

¹ona \ō-nə\ dona, Dona, Jonah,
krone, Mona, Nona, Rhona,
Rona, Shona, trona, Ancona,
Bellona, bologna, Bologna,
cinchona, corona, kimono,
Leona, madrona, Pamplona,
persona, Ramona, Verona,
Arizona, Barcelona,
Desdemona, in propria
persona

²ona \än-ə\ see ¹ANA

oña \ōn-yə\ see ³ONIA

onachal \än-i-kəl\ see ONICAL

onae \ō-nē\ see ¹ONY

onah \ō-nə\ see ONA

¹onal \ōn-ᵊl\ clonal, tonal,
zonal, atonal, coronal,
hormonal, baritonal,
microtonal, polyclonal,
polytonal, semitonal

²onal \än-ᵊl\ Donal, Ronal

onald \än-ᵊld\ Donald, Ronald,
MacDonald

onant \ō-nənt\ see ONENT

onas \ō-nəs\ see ²ONUS

onative \ō-nət-iv\ conative,
donative

onc \äŋk\ see ¹ONK

¹once \äns\ see ²ANCE

²once \əns\ see UNCE

¹onch \äŋk\ see ¹ONK

²onch \änch\ see ¹AUNCH

oncha \äŋ-kə\ see ANKA

oncho \än-chō\ honcho, poncho,
rancho

onchus \äŋ-kəs\ bronchus,
rhonchus

onco \äŋ-kō\ bronco, Franco

¹ond \änd\ blond, bond, fond,
frond, Gond, pond, rand,
sonde, wand, yond, abscond,
Armand, beau monde,
beyond, despond, fishpond,
Gironde, gourmand, haut
monde, millpond, neoned,
pair-bond, respond,
allemande, towmond,
correspond, demimonde,
Eurobond, Trebizond,
Trobriand, vagabond,
radiosonde, slough of
despond—*also pasts of verbs
listed at* ¹ON

²ond \ōⁿ\ see ²ON

³ond \ont\ see ¹AUNT

onda \än-də\ Lahnda, Rhonda,
Rhondda, Ronda, Wanda,
Golconda, Luganda, Ruanda,
Rwanda, Uganda, anaconda,
Campo Grande

ondam \än-dəm\ see ¹ONDOM

ondant \än-dənt\ see ONDENT

onday \ən-dē\ see UNDI

ondays \ən-dēz\ see UNDAYS

ondda \än-də\ see ONDA

onde \änd\ see ¹OND

ondeau \än-dō\ see ONDO

ondel \än-dᵊl\ condyle, fondle,
rondel

ondence \än-dəns\
    correspondence, despondence
ondency \än-dən-sē\
    despondency, correspondency
ondent \än-dənt\ fondant,
    despondent, respondent,
    corespondent, correspondent
¹onder \än-dər\ bonder, condor,
    maunder, ponder, squander,
    wander, yonder, zander,
    absconder, responder,
    transponder—*also*
    comparatives of adjectives
    listed at ¹OND
²onder \ən-dər\ see UNDER
ondly \än-lē\ see ¹ANLY
ondness \än-nəs\ see ANNESS
ondo \än-dō\ condo, Hondo,
    rondeau, rondo, secondo,
    tondo, forzando, glissando,
    lentando, parlando,
    scherzando, sforzando,
    allargando, rallentando,
    ritardando, accelerando
¹ondom \än-dəm\ condom,
    quondam
²ondom \ən-dəm\ see UNDUM
ondor \än-dər\ see ¹ONDER
ondrous \ən-drəs\ see
    UNDEROUS
ondyle \än-dᵊl\ see ONDEL
¹one \ōn\ blown, bone, clone,
    cone, crone, drone, flown,
    groan, grown, hone, Joan,
    known, loan, lone, moan,
    Mon, mown, none, own,
    phone, pone, prone, Rhone,
    roan, Saône, scone, sewn,
    shone, shoon, shown, sone,
    sown, stone, throne, thrown,
    tone, trone, won, zone, agon,
    aitchbone, alone, atone,

backbone, bemoan, birthstone,
Blackstone, breastbone,
brimstone, brownstone,
capstone, cheekbone,
chinbone, cogon, cologne,
Cologne, colon, Coloón,
condone, curbstone, cyclone,
daimon, debone, depone,
dethrone, disown, drystone,
earphone, enthrone,
fieldstone, flagstone,
flyblown, freestone, full-
blown, gallstone, gemstone,
Gijón, Gladstone, gravestone,
grindstone, hailstone,
halftone, handblown,
headphone, headstone, high-
flown, hipbone, homegrown,
hormone, impone, ingrown,
inkstone, intone, jawbone,
keystone, León, leone,
limestone, lodestone, Mount
Mayon, milestone, millstone,
misknown, moonstone,
oilstone, outgrown, outshown,
ozone, peon, pinbone,
pinecone, pinon, pinyon,
postpone, propone, Ramon,
rezone, rhinestone, sandstone,
shade-grown, shinbone,
Shoshone, soapstone, T-bone,
tailbone, thighbone,
tombstone, touchstone,
Touch-Tone, tritone,
trombone, turnstone, twelve-
tone, two-tone, Tyrone,
unknown, unthrone, well-
known, whalebone, wheel-
thrown, whetstone,
windblown, wishbone,
Yangon, allophone,
anglophone, anklebone,

barbitone, Barbizon, barytone,
Bayamon, bombardon, Canal
Zone, chaperon, cherrystone,
cobblestone, collarbone,
cornerstone, cortisone,
cuttlebone, diaphone,
Dictaphone, epigone,
francophone, free-fire zone,
Gaborone, gramophone,
herringbone, homophone,
ironstone, knucklebone,
marrowbone, megaphone,
mellophone, methadone,
microphone, microtone,
minestrone, monotone,
overblown, overflown,
overgrown, overthrown,
overtone, Picturephone,
polyphone, rottenstone,
sacaton, saxophone, semitone,
shacklebone, silicone,
sousaphone, speakerphone,
stepping-stone, telephone,
Toreón, undertone,
vibraphone, xylophone,
Yellowstone, anticyclone,
Asunción, bred-in-the-bone,
Concepción, eau de cologne,
mesocyclone, norethindrone,
Nuevo Leon, radiophone, sine
qua non, testosterone,
videophone, Darby and Joan,
Ponce de Leon, Sierra Leone,
radiotelephone
²one \ō-nē\ see ¹ONY
³one \än\ see ¹ON
⁴one \ən\ see UN
⁵one \ȯn\ see ³ON
onean \ō-nē-ən\ see ¹ONIAN
¹oned \ōnd\ boned, stoned,
toned, cologned, high-toned,
pre-owned, rawboned,

rhinestoned, two-toned,
cobblestoned—*also pasts of
verbs listed at* ¹ONE
²oned \än\ see ¹ON
oneless \ōn-ləs\ boneless,
toneless
onely \ōn-lē\ lonely, only,
pronely
onement \ōn-mənt\ atonement,
cantonment, dethronement,
disownment, enthronement
oneness \ən-nəs\ dunness,
doneness, oneness, rotundness
onent \ō-nənt\ sonant,
component, deponent,
exponent, opponent,
proponent, bicomponent
oneous \ō-nē-əs\ see ONIOUS
¹oner \ō-nər\ boner, donor,
droner, groaner, honer, loaner,
loner, stoner, toner, zoner,
condoner, dethroner, intoner,
landowner, shipowner,
telephoner
²oner \ȯn-ər\ see ¹AWNER
onerous \än-ə-rəs\ onerous,
sonorous
ones \ōnz\ Jones, nones,
sawbones, Davy Jones,
lazybones, skull and
crossbones—*also plurals and
possessives of nouns and
third person singular presents
of verbs listed at* ¹ONE
onest \än-əst\ honest, dishonest,
Hinayanist, Mahayanist
¹oney \ō-nē\ see ¹ONY
²oney \ən-ē\ see UNNY
³oney \ü-nē\ see OONY
¹ong \äŋ\ Chang, Fang, gong,
hong, Huang, prong, Shang,
Tang, tong, yang, Anyang,

barong, biltong, Da Nang,
dugong, Guiyang, Hanyang,
Heng-yang, Hong Kong,
kiang, liang, Mah-Jongg,
Malang, Padang, satang,
Wuchang, Zhejiang,
Zhenjiang, billabong,
Chittagong, Liaoyang, Pyong-
yang, Semarang,
scuppernong, Shenyang,
Sturm und Drang, Vietcong,
Shijiazhuang, Ujung Pandang,
Wollongong, ylang-ylang,
Heilongjiang

²ong \ȯŋ\ bong, dong, gong,
long, prong, song, strong,
thong, throng, tong, wrong,
agelong, along, Armstrong,
barong, belong, biltong,
birdsong, chaise longue,
daylong, dingdong,
diphthong, dugong, endlong,
erelong, furlong, Geelong,
Haiphong, headlong,
headstrong, Kaesong,
kampong, lifelong, livelong,
Mekong, monthlong,
Nanchang, nightlong, oblong,
oolong, part-song, ping-pong,
Ping-Pong, plainsong,
prolong, sarong, Shandong,
sidelong, singsong, so long,
souchong, weeklong, yard-
long, yearlong, billabong,
Chittagong, cradlesong,
evensong, Palembang,
scuppernong, sing-along,
summerlong, tagalong,
Vietcong

³ong \əŋ\ see ¹UNG

⁴ong \u̇ng\ see ²UNG

onga \äŋ-gə\ conga, panga,

tonga, Tonga, Kananga,
mridanga, Alba Longa,
Zamboanga, Bucaramanga

onge \ənj\ see UNGE

onged \ȯŋd\ pronged, thonged,
multipronged—*also pasts of
verbs listed at* ²ONG

¹onger \əŋ-gər\ hunger,
monger, younger, fellmonger,
fishmonger, ironmonger,
newsmonger, phrasemonger,
scaremonger, warmonger,
whoremonger, wordmonger,
costermonger, fashionmonger,
gossipmonger, rumormonger,
scandalmonger

²onger \ən-jər\ see ¹UNGER

ongery \əŋ-grē\ hungry,
fellmongery, ironmongery

ongful \ȯŋ-fəl\ wrongful,
songful

ongin \ən-jən\ see UNGEON

ongish \ȯŋ-ish\ longish,
strongish

ongo \äŋ-gō\ bongo, Congo,
congou, Kongo, mongo,
Niger-Congo, Pago Pago

ongous \əŋ-gəs\ see UNGOUS

¹ongue \əŋ\ see ¹UNG

²ongue \ȯŋ\ see ²ONG

ongued \əŋd\ lunged, tongued

ongy \ən-jē\ see UNGY

onhomous \än-ə-məs\ see
ONYMOUS

oni \ō-nē\ see ¹ONY

¹onia \ō-nē-ə\ bignonia,
clintonia, Estonia, Laconia,
Livonia, mahonia, paulownia,
Polonia, Slavonia,
Snowdonia, tithonia, valonia,
zirconia, Amazonia,

Caledonia, Catalonia,
Macedonia
²**onia** \ō-nyə\ Konya, Sonia,
Sonja, Sonya, ammonia,
Bologna, pneumonia, Polonia,
tithonia, valonia, anhedonia,
Caledonia, Macedonia, New
Caledonia, Patagonia
³**onia** \ōn-yə\ doña, begonia
onial \ō-nē-əl\ baronial,
colonial, ceremonial,
matrimonial, testimonial
¹**onian** \ō-nē-ən\ chthonian,
aeonian, Antonian, Baconian,
Clactonian, demonian,
Devonian, draconian,
Estonian, Etonian, favonian,
gorgonian, Ionian, Jacksonian,
Oxonian, plutonian,
Samsonian, Shoshonean,
Slavonian, Amazonian,
Apollonian, Arizonian,
Babylonian, calypsonian,
Chalcedonian, Hamiltonian,
parkinsonian
²**onian** \ō-nyən\ Zonian,
Amazonian, Babylonian,
Estonian, Macedonian
onic \än-ik\ chronic, chthonic,
conic, dornick, phonic, sonic,
tonic, Aaronic, agonic, atonic,
benthonic, bionic, Brittonic,
Brythonic, bubonic, Byronic,
canonic, carbonic, cryonic,
cyclonic, daimonic, demonic,
draconic, euphonic,
gnomonic, harmonic, hedonic,
ionic, Ionic, ironic, laconic,
Masonic, mnemonic,
planktonic, platonic, plutonic,
pneumonic, Puranic,
Pythonic, sardonic, Saronic,

sermonic, Slavonic,
symphonic, synchronic,
tectonic, Teutonic, ultrasonic,
zirconic, catatonic,
diachronic, diatonic,
disharmonic, electronic,
embryonic, hegemonic,
histrionic, homophonic,
hydroponic, inharmonic,
isotonic, macaronic,
megaphonic, microphonic,
monophonic, monotonic,
nonionic, pharaonic,
Philharmonic, polyphonic,
quadraphonic, semitonic,
Solomonic, supersonic,
supertonic, telephonic,
thermionic, architectonic,
chameleonic, cardiotonic,
electrotonic, geotectonic,
Neoplatonic, stereophonic,
extraembryonic
onica \än-i-kə\ Monica,
harmonica, japonica,
Salonika, veronica, Veronica,
Thessalonica
onical \än-i-kəl\ chronicle,
conical, monachal, monocle,
canonical, demonical,
ironical, deuterocanonical
onicals \än-i-kəlz\ Chronicles,
canonicals
onicker \ä-ni-kər\ see
ONNICKER
onicle \än-i-kəl\ see ONICAL
onicles \än-i-kəlz\ see ONICALS
onics \än-iks\ onyx, phonics,
bionics, cryonics, mnemonics,
Ovonics, photonics, sardonyx,
tectonics, avionics,
electronics, histrionics,
hydroponics, microphonics,

nucleonics, quadriphonics,
radionics, supersonics,
thermionics, architectonics—
*also plurals and possessives
of nouns listed at* ONIC
onika \än-i-kə\ see ONICA
oniker \ä-ni-kər\ see ONNICKER
¹oning \än-iŋ\ awning,
couponing
²oning \ō-niŋ\ loaning,
jawboning, landowning
onion \ən-yən\ see UNION
onious \ō-nē-əs\ erroneous,
euphonious, felonious,
harmonious, Polonius,
Suetonius, symphonious,
acrimonious, ceremonious,
disharmonious, inharmonious,
parsimonious, sanctimonious,
Marcus Antonius,
unceremonious
¹onis \ō-nəs\ see ²ONUS
²onis \än-əs\ see ¹ONUS
onish \än-ish\ donnish, monish,
admonish, astonish,
premonish, leprechaunish
onishment \än-ish-mənt\
admonishment, astonishment
onium \ō-nē-əm\ euphonium,
harmonium, plutonium,
pandemonium, Pandemonium
onius \ō-nē-əs\ see ONIOUS
onja \ō-nyə\ see ²ONIA
onjon \ən-jən\ see UNGEON
onjure \än-jər\ conjure, rondure
¹onk \äŋk\ ankh, bronc, clonk,
conch, conk, Franck, honk,
Planck, plonk, zonk,
honkytonk
²onk \əŋk\ see UNK
onker \äŋ-kər\ conker, conquer,
honker

¹onkey \äŋ-kē\ see ONKY
²onkey \əŋ-kē\ see UNKY
onkian \äŋ-kē-ən\ conquian,
Algonkian
onky \äŋ-kē\ conkey, donkey,
honkie, wonky, yanqui
onless \ən-ləs\ see UNLESS
only \ōn-lē\ see ONELY
onment \ōn-mənt\ see
ONEMENT
¹onn \än\ see ¹ON
²onn \ón\ see ³ON
¹onna \ón-ə\ donna, Donna,
fauna, prima donna,
megafauna
²onna \än-ə\ see ¹ANA
onnage \ən-ij\ see UNNAGE
¹onne \än\ see ¹ON
²onne \ən\ see UN
³onne \ón\ see ³ON
onner \än-ər\ see ¹ONOR
onnet \än-ət\ bonnet, sonnet,
bluebonnet, sunbonnet,
warbonnet
onnicker \ä-ni-kər\ donnicker,
doniker, monicker, moniker
onnie \än-ē\ see ¹ANI
onnish \än-ish\ see ONISH
onnor \än-ər\ see ¹ONOR
¹onny \än-ē\ see ¹ANI
²onny \ən-ē\ see UNNY
¹ono \ō-nō\ phono, cui bono,
kimono, pro bono, kakemono,
makimono
²ono \ō-nə\ see ONA
³ono \än-ō\ see ¹ANO
onocle \än-i-kəl\ see ONICAL
onomer \än-ə-mər\ monomer,
astronomer, comonomer
onomist \än-ə-məst\
agronomist, autonomist,
economist, ergonomist,

gastronomist, synonymist, taxonomist, Deuteronomist

onomous \än-ə-məs\ see ONYMOUS

onomy \än-ə-mē\ agronomy, antonymy, astronomy, autonomy, economy, eponymy, gastronomy, homonomy, metonymy, synonymy, taphonomy, taxonomy, toponymy, Deuteronomy, diseconomy, heteronomy, teleonomy

¹onor \än-ər\ Bonner, fawner, goner, honor, dishonor, O'Connor, Lipizzaner, marathoner, Afrikaner, weimaraner

²onor \ō-nər\ see ¹ONER

onorous \än-ə-rəs\ see ONEROUS

onquer \äŋ-kər\ see ONKER

onquian \äŋ-kē-ən\ see ONKIAN

¹ons \änz\ see ONZE

²ons \ōⁿ\ see ²ON

onsil \än-səl\ see ONSUL

onsin \än-sən\ see OHNSON

onson \än-sən\ see OHNSON

onsor \än-sər\ panzer, sponsor

onsul \än-səl\ consul, tonsil

on't \ōnt\ don't, won't

¹ont \ənt\ blunt, brunt, bunt, front, grunt, hunt, lunt, punt, runt, shunt, strunt, stunt, want, wont, affront, beachfront, bowfront, breakfront, confront, forefront, housefront, lakefront, manhunt, out-front, seafront, shirtfront, shorefront, storefront, swellfront, up-front, witch-hunt, battlefront, oceanfront, riverfront, waterfront

²ont \änt\ see ²ANT

³ont \ȯnt\ see ¹AUNT

¹ontal \änt-ᵊl\ pontil, fontal, quantal, horizontal, periodontal

²ontal \ənt-ᵊl\ see UNTLE

ontan \änt-ⁿ\ see ONTON

ontas \änt-əs\ see ONTUS

¹onte \änt-ē\ see ¹ANTI

²onte \än-tā\ see ¹ANTE

onted \ȯnt-əd\ vaunted, wonted, undaunted—*also pasts of verbs listed at* ¹AUNT

onter \ənt-ər\ see UNTER

onth \ənth\ month, billionth, millionth, trillionth, twelvemonth

ontian \änt-ē-ən\ Zontian, post-Kantian

ontic \änt-ik\ ontic, deontic, Vedantic, orthodontic, anacreontic

ontil \änt-ᵊl\ see ¹ONTAL

ontinent \änt-ⁿ-ənt\ continent, incontinent, subcontinent, supercontinent

ontis \än-təs\ see ²ANTOS

ontist \änt-əst\ Vedantist, orthodontist, prosthodontist

onto \än-tō\ see ¹ANTO

onton \änt-ⁿn\ ponton, wanton, Lahontan

ontra \än-trə\ contra, mantra, tantra, per contra

ontre \änt-ər\ see ¹AUNTER

ontus \änt-əs\ Pontus, Pocahontas

onty \änt-ē\ see ¹ANTI

¹onus \än-əs\ Cronus, Faunus, Adonis

²onus \ō-nəs\ bonus, Cronus,
Jonas, onus, slowness,
Adonis, colonus

¹ony \ō-nē\ bony, coney, crony,
phony, pony, stony, Toni,
tony, Tony, yoni, baloney,
Benoni, bologna, canzone,
Marconi, Moroni, Oenone,
padrone, spumoni, tortoni,
abalone, acrimony, agrimony,
alimony, antimony,
cannelloni, ceremony,
chalcedony, colophony,
macaroni, mascarpone,
matrimony, minestrone,
palimony, parsimony,
patrimony, pepperoni,
provolone, rigatoni,
sanctimony, telephony,
testimony, zabaglione, con
espressione, conversazione,
dramatis personae

²ony \än-ē\ see ¹ANI

onya \ō-nyə\ see ²ONIA

onymist \än-ə-məst\ see
ONOMIST

onymous \än-ə-məs\
bonhomous, anonymous,
antonymous, autonomous,
eponymous, homonymous,
pseudonymous, synonymous,
heteronomous

onymy \än-ə-mē\ see ONOMY

¹onyon \än-yən\ ronyon,
wanion

²onyon \ən-yən\ see UNION

onyx \än-iks\ see ONICS

onze \änz\ bonze, bronze, pons,
long johns, Saint John's,
Afrikaans, solitons, islet of
Langerhans—*also plurals and
possessives of nouns and*

*third person singular presents
of verbs listed at* ¹ON

onzi \än-zē\ see ONZY

onzy \än-zē\ bronzy, Ponzi

¹oo \ü\ see ¹EW

²oo \ō\ see ¹OW

oob \üb\ see UBE

oober \ü-bər\ see UBER

ooby \ü-bē\ booby, looby, ruby,
Ruby

¹ooch \üch\ brooch, hooch,
mooch, pooch, smooch,
capuche, scaramouch

²ooch \ōch\ see OACH

oocher \ü-chər\ see UTURE

oochy \ü-chē\ smoochy,
Baluchi, penuche, Vespucci,
Kawaguchi

¹ood \ud\ good, hood, pud,
rudd, should, stood, wood,
would, yod, basswood,
bentwood, blackwood,
boxwood, brushwood,
childhood, cordwood,
deadwood, do-good,
dogwood, driftwood,
Ellwood, Elwood, falsehood,
fatwood, feel-good, firewood,
fruitwood, girlhood, godhood,
greasewood, greenwood,
groundwood, gumwood,
hardwood, ironwood,
kingwood, knighthood,
maidhood, manhood,
monkhood, monkshood,
Mount Hood, no-good,
pinewood, plywood,
priesthood, pulpwood,
redwood, rosewood,
sainthood, selfhood,
Sherwood, softwood,
sonhood, statehood,

stinkwood, Talmud,
teakwood, unhood,
Wedgwood, wifehood,
withstood, wormwood,
arrowwood, bachelorhood,
brotherhood, buttonwood,
candlewood, cedarwood,
cottonwood, fatherhood,
hardihood, Hollywood,
likelihood, livelihood,
maidenhood, motherhood,
nationhood, neighborhood,
parenthood, peckerwood,
personhood, Robin Hood,
sandalwood, scattergood,
servanthood, sisterhood,
spinsterhood, toddlerhood,
tulipwood, understood,
widowhood, womanhood,
misunderstood, unlikelihood,
widowerhood

²**ood** \ōd\ see ODE

³**ood** \üd\ see UDE

⁴**ood** \əd\ see ¹UD

¹**ooded** \əd-əd\ blooded, cold-
blooded, full-blooded, half-
blooded, hot-blooded, pure-
blooded, red-blooded,
star-studded, warm-blooded—
also pasts of verbs listed at
¹UD

²**ooded** \ùd-əd\ hooded,
wooded, hard-wooded, soft-
wooded

¹**ooder** \üd-ər\ see UDER

²**ooder** \əd-ər\ see UDDER

ooding \ùd-iŋ\ pudding, do-
gooding

oodle \üd-ºl\ boodle, doodle,
feudal, noodle, poodle,
strudel, caboodle, flapdoodle,
paludal, Yankee-Doodle

oodman \ùd-mən\ goodman,
woodman

oodoo \üd-ü\ doo-doo, hoodoo,
kudu, voodoo

oods \ùdz\ backwoods, dry
goods, piney woods—*also
plurals and possessives of
nouns and third person
singular presents of verbs
listed at* ¹OOD

oodsman \ùdz-mən\ woodsman,
backwoodsman, ombudsman

¹**oody** \üd-ē\ broody, Judi,
Judie, Judy, moody, Rudy,
Trudy

²**oody** \ùd-ē\ cuddy, goody,
hoody, woody, goody-goody

³**oody** \əd-ē\ see ¹UDDY

ooer \ü-ər\ see ¹EWER

ooey \ü-ē\ see EWY

¹**oof** \üf\ goof, kloof, poof,
pouf, proof, roof, spoof,
woof, aloof, behoof, disproof,
fireproof, foolproof, forehoof,
rustproof, shadoof,
soundproof, sunroof, Tartuffe,
unroof, bulletproof, opera
bouffe, shatterproof,
waterproof, weatherproof

²**oof** \ùf\ hoof, poof, roof, woof,
forehoof, Tartuffe

³**oof** \ōf\ see OAF

⁴**oof** \üv\ see ³OVE

oofah \ü-fə\ see UFA

¹**oofer** \ü-fər\ proofer, roofer,
twofer, waterproofer

²**oofer** \ùf-ər\ hoofer, woofer

oofy \ü-fē\ goofy, spoofy, Sufi

ooga \ü-gə\ see UGA

ooge \üj\ see ¹UGE

ooger \ùg-ər\ see UGUR

oogie \ùg-ē\ bogey, boogie,
  boogie-woogie
oo-goo \ü-gü\ see UGU
ooh \ü\ see ¹EW
ooh-pooh \ü-pü\ hoopoe, pooh-
  pooh
ooi \ü-ē\ see EWY
ooist \ü-əst\ doest, tattooist,
  voodooist—*also superlatives
  of adjectives listed at* ¹EW
¹ook \ùk\ book, brook, Brooke,
  chook, cook, Cook, crook,
  gook, hook, look, nook, rook,
  schnook, shook, snook, stook,
  took, bankbook, betook,
  billhook, caoutchouc,
  chapbook, checkbook,
  Chinook, cookbook, forsook,
  fishhook, guidebook,
  handbook, hornbook,
  hymnbook, Insbruck, Kobuk,
  logbook, matchbook, mistook,
  Mount Cook, notebook,
  outlook, partook, passbook,
  Pembroke, playbook,
  pothook, promptbook,
  psalmbook, retook,
  schoolbook, scrapbook,
  sketchbook, skyhook,
  songbook, studbook,
  textbook, unhook, Windhoek,
  workbook, yearbook,
  buttonhook, copybook,
  donnybrook, gerenuk,
  inglenook, Leeuwenhoek,
  overbook, overlook, overtook,
  pocketbook, storybook,
  tenterhook, undertook,
  Volapuk, gobbledygook
²ook \ük\ see UKE
ooka \ü-kə\ yuca, bazooka,

felucca, palooka, Toluca,
  verruca, Juan de Fuca
ookah \ùk-ə\ hookah, sukkah
ooke \ùk\ see ¹OOK
ooker \ùk-ər\ booker, cooker,
  hooker, Hooker, looker,
  snooker, good-looker,
  onlooker
ookery \ùk-ə-rē\ crookery,
  rookery
ookie \ùk-ē\ bookie, brookie,
  cookie, cooky, hooky, nooky,
  rookie, rooky, Takatsuki,
  walkie-lookie
ooking \ùk-iŋ\ booking,
  cooking, good-looking,
  onlooking
ooklet \ùk-lət\ booklet,
  brooklet, hooklet
¹ooks \üks\ deluxe, gadzooks—
  *also plurals and possessives
  of nouns and third person
  singular presents of verbs
  listed at* UKE
²ooks \ùks\ Brooks, crux, luxe,
  zooks, deluxe, gadzooks—
  *also plurals and possessives
  of nouns and third person
  singular presents of verbs
  listed at* ¹OOK
¹ooky \ü-kē\ kooky, spooky,
  bouzouki, Kabuki, saluki,
  tanuki
²ooky \ùk-ē\ see OOKIE
¹ool \ül\ boule, boulle, buhl,
  cool, drool, fool, fuel, ghoul,
  gul, joule, mewl, mule, pool,
  Poole, pul, pule, rule, school,
  spool, stool, tool, tulle, you'll,
  yule, air-cool, ampoule,
  babul, Banjul, befool,
  Blackpool, carpool, cesspool,

curule, Elul, faldstool,
footstool, hangul, Kabul,
Kurnool, misrule, Mosul,
preschool, retool, self-rule,
synfuel, toadstool, tomfool,
uncool, vanpool, whirlpool,
Barnaul, fascicule, gallinule,
graticule, groupuscule,
Hartlepool, Istanbul, lenticule,
Liverpool, majuscule,
minuscule, molecule,
monticule, overrule, reticule,
ridicule, vestibule, water-cool,
biomolecule

²**ool** \úl\ see ¹UL

oola \ü-lə\ see ULA

oole \ül\ see ¹OOL

oolean \ü-lē-ən\ see ULEAN

ooled \üld\ bejeweled,
unschooled, vestibuled—*also
pasts of verbs listed at* ¹OOL

ooler \ü-lər\ cooler, gular,
puler, ruler, carpooler, grade-
schooler, high schooler,
preschooler, ridiculer,
watercooler

oolie \ü-lē\ see ULY

oolish \ü-lish\ coolish, foolish,
ghoulish, mulish, pound-
foolish

¹**oolly** \ü-lē\ see ULY

²**oolly** \úl-ē\ see ²ULLY

¹**oom** \üm\ bloom, boom,
broom, brougham, brume,
combe, cwm, doom, flume,
fume, gloom, glume, groom,
Hume, khoum, loom, neume,
plume, rheum, room, spume,
tomb, toom, vroom, whom,
womb, zoom, abloom,
assume, backroom, ballroom,
barroom, bathroom, bedroom,

boardroom, bridegroom,
broadloom, checkroom,
classroom, cloakroom,
coatroom, consume, costume,
courtroom, darkroom,
dayroom, entomb, enwomb,
exhume, foredoom,
greenroom, guardroom,
headroom, heirloom,
homeroom, houseroom,
illume, inhume, jibboom,
Khartoum, legroom, legume,
lunchroom, mudroom,
mushroom, newsroom,
perfume, playroom,
poolroom, pressroom,
presume, proofroom, relume,
resume, salesroom,
schoolroom, showroom,
sickroom, simoom, stateroom,
stockroom, storeroom,
subsume, taproom, Targum,
tearoom, toolroom,
wardroom, washroom,
workroom, anteroom,
checkerbloom, dyer's broom,
elbowroom, impostume,
locker-room, miniboom, nom
de plume, smoke-filled room,
witches'-broom

²**oom** \úm\ see ²UM

oomed \ümd\ groomed, plumed,
wombed, well-groomed—*also
pasts of verbs listed at* ¹OOM

oomer \ü-mər\ see UMER

oomily \ü-mə-lē\ gloomily,
contumely

¹**ooming** \ü-mən\ see UMAN

²**ooming** \ü-miŋ\ see UMING

oomlet \üm-lət\ boomlet,
plumelet

oomy \ü-mē\ bloomy, boomy,

doomy, fumy, gloomy,
plumy, rheumy, roomy,
spumy, costumey

¹**oon** \ün\ boon, Boone, coon,
croon, dune, goon, hewn,
June, loon, lune, moon, noon,
prune, rune, shoon, soon,
spoon, swoon, strewn, toon,
tune, aswoon, attune, baboon,
balloon, bassoon, buffoon,
Calhoun, cardoon, cartoon,
cocoon, commune, doubloon,
dragoon, festoon, fine-tune,
forenoon, gaboon, gadroon,
galloon, Gudrun, half-moon,
harpoon, immune, impugn,
jargoon, jejune, Kowloon,
Kunlun, lagoon, lampoon,
lardoon, maroon, monsoon,
Neptune, oppugn, Pashtun,
patroon, platoon, poltroon,
pontoon, premune, puccoon,
quadroon, raccoon, ratoon,
repugn, rockoon, rough-hewn,
saloon, shalloon, soupspoon,
spittoon, spontoon, teaspoon,
Torun, tribune, triune, tuchun,
tycoon, typhoon, untune,
Walloon, afternoon,
barracoon, Brigadoon,
Cameroon, demilune,
dessertspoon, honeymoon,
importune, macaroon,
octoroon, opportune,
pantaloon, picaroon,
picayune, rigadoon,
saskatoon, Saskatoon,
tablespoon, contrabassoon,
inopportune

²**oon** \ōn\ see ¹ONE

oona \ü-nə\ see UNA

oonal \ün-ᵊl\ see UNAL

oone \ün\ see ¹OON

ooner \ü-nər\ crooner, crowner,
lunar, pruner, schooner,
sooner, swooner, tuner,
harpooner, lacunar,
lampooner, oppugner,
honeymooner, semilunar

¹**oonery** \ün-rē\ buffoonery,
lampoonery, poltroonery

²**oonery** \ü-nə-rē\ see UNARY

ooney \ü-nē\ see OONY

oonie \ü-nē\ see OONY

ooning \ü-niŋ\ nooning,
ballooning, cartooning,
gadrooning

oonish \ü-nish\ moonish,
buffoonish, cartoonish,
picayunish

oonless \ün-ləs\ moonless,
tuneless, woundless

oons \ünz\ lunes, zounds,
eftsoons, afternoons—*also
plurals and possessives of
nouns and third person
singular presents of verbs
listed at* ¹OON

oony \ü-nē\ gooney, loony,
luny, Moonie, moony, muni,
puisne, puny, spoony, Zuni,
Mulroney

o-op \üp\ see ¹OOP

oop \üp\ bloop, coop, croup,
droop, drupe, dupe, goop,
group, hoop, loop, loupe,
poop, roup, scoop, sloop,
snoop, soup, stoop, stoup,
stupe, swoop, troop, troupe,
whoop, age-group, in-group,
out-group, recoup, regroup,
subgroup, T-group, alley-oop,
cock-a-hoop, Guadalupe,

Guadeloupe, nincompoop, paratroop, supergroup

ooped \üpd\ looped—*pasts of verbs listed at* OOP

oopee \ü-pē\ see OOPY

ooper \ü-pər\ blooper, cooper, Cooper, Cowper, duper, grouper, looper, scooper, snooper, stupor, swooper, super, trooper, trouper, party pooper, paratrooper, pooper-scooper, super-duper

ooping \ü-piŋ\ grouping, trooping, trouping

oopoe \ü-pü\ see OOH-POOH

oops \ùps\ hoops, oops, whoops, woops

oopy \ü-pē\ croupy, droopy, groupie, Kewpie, loopy, snoopy, soupy, Tupi, whoopee

¹oor \ōr\ see ¹OR

²oor \ùr\ see ¹URE

¹oorage \ùr-ij\ moorage, sewerage

²oorage \ōr-ij\ see ²ORAGE

³oorage \òr-ij\ see ³ORAGE

¹oore \ōr\ see ¹ORE

²oore \ùr\ see ¹URE

oored \ōrd\ see OARD

oorer \ōr-ər\ see ¹ORER

oori \ùr-ē\ see ¹URY

¹ooring \ōr-iŋ\ see ¹ORING

²ooring \ùr-iŋ\ see URING

¹oorish \ùr-ish\ boorish, Moorish, poorish

²oorish \òr-ish\ see ¹ORISH

oorly \ùr-lē\ see URELY

oorman \ōr-mən\ see OREMAN

oors \ōrz\ Bors, yours, drawers, indoors, outdoors, underdrawers, withindoors,

withoutdoors, Louis Quatorze—*also plurals and possessives of nouns and third person singular presents of verbs listed at* ¹ORE

oorsman \ōrz-mən\ see OARSMAN

oort \òrt\ see ¹ORT

oosa \ü-sə\ see ¹USA

¹oose \üs\ see ¹USE

²oose \üz\ see ²USE

¹ooser \ü-sər\ see UCER

²ooser \ü-zər\ see USER

oosey \ü-sē\ see UICY

¹oosh \üsh\ see OUCHE

²oosh \ùsh\ see ²USH

oost \üst\ boost, juiced, Proust, roost, langouste, produced, self-induced, Zlatoust—*also pasts of verbs listed at* ¹USE

oosy \ü-zē\ see OOZY

¹oot \ùt\ foot, put, root, Root, soot, afoot, barefoot, bigfoot, bird's-foot, Blackfoot, clubfoot, crow's-foot, enroot, flatfoot, forefoot, hotfoot, input, kaput, outfoot, output, Rajput, snakeroot, splayfoot, taproot, throughput, uproot, acre-foot, arrowroot, bitterroot, cajeput, candle-foot, gingerroot, orrisroot, pussyfoot, tenderfoot, underfoot

²oot \üt\ see UTE

³oot \ət\ see ¹UT

¹ootage \üt-ij\ fruitage, rootage, scutage

²ootage \ùt-ij\ footage, rootage

¹ooted \üt-əd\ booted, fruited, muted, suited, abluted, deep-rooted, jackbooted, pantsuited, voluted—*also pasts of verbs listed at* UTE

²**ooted** \ut-əd\ footed, barefooted, clubfooted, deep-rooted, duckfooted, fleet-footed, four-footed, light-footed, slow-footed, splayfooted, surefooted, web-footed, wing-footed, cloven-footed—*also pasts of verbs listed at* ¹OOT

¹**ooter** \ut-ər\ footer, putter, shot-putter, pussyfooter

²**ooter** \üt-ər\ see UTER

¹**ooth** \ü<u>th</u>\ smooth, soothe, tooth

²**ooth** \üth\ booth, Booth, couth, crwth, routh, ruth, Ruth, scouth, sleuth, sooth, tooth, truth, Truth, youth, bucktooth, Duluth, eyetooth, forsooth, half-truth, sawtooth, selcouth, tollbooth, uncouth, untruth, vermouth, snaggletooth

oothe \ü<u>th</u>\ see ¹OOTH

oothed \ütht\ toothed, gap-toothed, snaggletoothed

oothless \üth-ləs\ see UTHLESS

oothly \üth-lē\ soothly, uncouthly

oothy \ü-thē\ couthie, toothy

ootie \üt-ē\ see ¹OOTY

¹**ooting** \ut-iŋ\ footing, off-putting

²**ooting** \üt-iŋ\ see UTING

ootle \üt-ᵊl\ see UTILE

ootless \üt-ləs\ bootless, fruitless

ootlet \üt-lət\ fruitlet, rootlet

oots \üts\ boots, firstfruits, grassroots, slyboots, Vaduz, shoot-the-chutes—*also*

plurals and possessives of nouns and third person singular presents of verbs listed at UTE

ootsie \ut-sē\ footsie, tootsie

¹**ooty** \üt-ē\ beauty, booty, Clootie, cootie, cutie, duty, footy, fluty, fruity, hooty, rooty, snooty, sooty, tutti, zooty, agouti, Djibouti, Funafuti, heavy-duty, persecutee, tutti-frutti

²**ooty** \ut-ē\ rooty, sooty, tutti

³**ooty** \ət-ē\ see UTTY

oove \üv\ see ³OVE

oover \ü-vər\ see ³OVER

oovy \ü-vē\ groovy, movie

ooze \üz\ see ²USE

oozer \ü-zər\ see USER

oozle \ü-zəl\ see ²USAL

oozy \ü-zē\ bluesy, boozy, choosy, floozy, newsy, oozy, Susie, woozy, Jacuzzi

¹**op** \äp\ bop, chap, chop, clop, cop, crop, drop, flop, fop, glop, hop, knop, lop, mop, op, plop, pop, prop, scop, shop, slop, sop, stop, strop, swap, top, whop, wop, Aesop, airdrop, atop, backdrop, backstop, bakeshop, barhop, bebop, bellhop, blacktop, bookshop, carhop, cartop, chop-chop, clip-clop, clop-clop, coin-op, cooktop, co-op, desktop, dewdrop, doorstop, dramshop, Dunlop, eardrop, eavesdrop, ESOP, estop, f-stop, fire-stop, flattop, flip-flop, foretop, grogshop, gumdrop, hardtop, hedgehop, high-top, hilltop, hip-hop,

hockshop, housetop, joypop,
maintop, milksop, nonstop,
one-stop, outcrop, pawnshop,
pop-top, ragtop, raindrop,
redtop, ripstop, rooftop,
sharecrop, shortstop, skin-
pop, slipslop, snowdrop,
soursop, stonecrop,
sweatshop, sweetshop,
teardrop, tip-top, treetop,
unstop, workshop, agitprop,
barbershop, carrottop,
countertop, double-crop,
double-stop, Ethiop, island-
hop, lollipop, malaprop,
mom-and-pop, mountaintop,
overtop, table-hop, tabletop,
techno-pop, teenybop,
turboprop, whistle-stop,
window-shop, Babelthuap

²op \ō\ see ¹OW

opa \ō-pə\ opa, opah, Europa

opah \ō-pə\ see OPA

opal \ō-pəl\ copal, nopal, opal,
Opal, Simferopol,
Constantinople

ope \ōp\ cope, coup, dope,
grope, holp, hope, Hope, lope,
mope, nope, ope, pope, Pope,
rope, scop, scope, slope, soap,
stope, taupe, tope, trope,
aslope, borescope, downslope,
elope, gantlope, gantelope,
Good Hope, myope,
nightscope, pyrope, sandsoap,
soft-soap, tightrope, towrope,
antelope, antipope, calliope,
cantaloupe, chronoscope,
envelope, epitope, Ethiope,
gyroscope, horoscope,
interlope, isotope, kinescope,
microscope, misanthrope,

periscope, phalarope,
radarscope, sniperscope,
snooperscope, stethoscope,
telescope, heliotrope,
kaleidoscope, stereoscope

opean \ō-pē-ən\ see OPIAN

opee \ō-pē\ see OPI

open \ō-pən\ holpen, open,
reopen, wide-open

opence \əp-əns\ see UPPANCE

openny \əp-nē\ threepenny,
twopenny

oper \ō-pər\ coper, doper,
groper, loper, moper, roper,
soaper, toper, eloper, no-
hoper, soft-soaper, interloper

opera \äp-rə\ see OPRA

opery \ō-prē\ popery, ropery

opey \ō-pē\ see OPI

oph \ōf\ see OAF

ophagous \äf-ə-gəs\
coprophagous, esophagus,
necrophagous, sarcophagus,
zoophagous, anthropophagous

ophagy \äf-ə-jē\ geophagy,
coprophagy, anthropophagy

¹ophe \ō-fē\ see OPHY

²ophe \òf\ see ²OFF

opher \ō-fər\ see OFER

ophet \äf-ət\ see OFIT

¹ophic \äf-ik\ strophic,
antistrophic, apostrophic,
catastrophic

²ophic \ō-fik\ strophic, trophic,
atrophic

ophical \äf-i-kəl\ philosophical,
theosophical

ophie \ō-fē\ see OPHY

ophir \ō-fər\ see OFER

ophonous \äf-ə-nəs\
cacophonous, homophonous

ophony \äf-ə-nē\ cacophony,

colophony, homophony,
monophony, theophany,
heterophony, stereophony

ophy \ō-fē\ Sophie, sophy,
strophe, trophy

opi \ō-pē\ dopey, Hopi, mopey,
ropy, soapy, topee, topi

opia \ō-pē-ə\ dystopia, myopia,
sinopia, utopia, cornucopia,
Ethiopia

opian \ō-pē-ən\ Aesopian,
cyclopean, dystopian, utopian,
Ethiopian, cornucopian

¹opic \äp-ik\ topic, tropic,
Aesopic, anthropic, ectopic,
Ethiopic, subtropic,
gyroscopic, hygroscopic,
macroscopic, microscopic,
misanthropic, periscopic,
philanthropic, semitropic,
stethoscopic, telescopic,
kaleidoscopic, stereoscopic

²opic \ō-pik\ tropic, myopic,
Ethiopic, psychotropic

opical \äp-i-kəl\ topical,
tropical, anthropical,
subtropical, microscopical,
philanthropical, semitropical,
Neotropical

oplar \äp-lər\ see OPPLER

ople \ō-pəl\ see OPAL

opol \ō-pəl\ see OPAL

¹opolis \äp-ə-ləs\ propolis,
acropolis, cosmopolis,
necropolis, Heliopolis,
megalopolis, metropolis,
Florianopolis

²opolis \äp-ləs\ see OPLESS

opolist \äp-ə-ləst\ monopolist,
bibliopolist

opoly \äp-ə-lē\ choppily,
floppily, sloppily, duopoly,
monopoly, vox populi,
oligopoly, Tiruchchirappalli

oppa \äp-ə\ see ¹APA

opped \äpt\ see OPT

oppel \äp-əl\ see OPPLE

opper \äp-ər\ bopper, chopper,
copper, cropper, dropper,
flopper, hopper, lopper,
mopper, popper, proper,
shopper, stopper, swapper,
topper, whopper, yapper,
clodhopper, eavesdropper,
eyedropper, eyepopper,
grasshopper, hedgehopper,
improper, job-hopper,
joypopper, leafhopper,
namedropper, rockhopper,
sharecropper, showstopper,
skin-popper, table-hopper,
teenybopper, treehopper,
woodchopper, window-
shopper

oppery \äp-rē\ coppery, foppery

oppet \äp-ət\ moppet, poppet

oppily \äp-ə-lē\ see OPOLY

oppiness \äp-ē-nəs\ choppiness,
floppiness, sloppiness

opping \äp-iŋ\ hopping,
sopping, topping, whopping,
clodhopping, eye-popping,
job-hopping, name-dropping,
outcropping

opple \äp-əl\ popple, stopple,
topple, estoppel

oppler \äp-lər\ Doppler, poplar

oppy \äp-ē\ choppy, copy,
crappie, floppy, gloppy,
hoppy, kopje, poppy, sloppy,
soppy, stroppy, jalopy, okapi,
serape, microcopy, Nahuel
Huapi, photocopy

opra \äp-rə\ copra, opera

ops \äps\ chops, copse, Ops, tops, beechdrops, cyclops, eyedrops, Pelops, pinedrops, sundrops, muttonchops, triceratops—*also plurals and possessives of nouns and third person singular presents of verbs listed at* ¹OP

opse \äps\ see OPS

opsy \äp-sē\ dropsy, autopsy, biopsy, necropsy

opt \äpt\ Copt, knopped, opt, topped, adopt, close-cropped, co-opt, end-stopped—*also pasts of verbs listed at* ¹OP

opter \äp-tər\ copter, adopter, helicopter, ornithopter

optic \äp-tik\ Coptic, optic, panoptic, synoptic, electro-optic

optimist \äp-tə-məst\ optimist, Optimist, Soroptimist

option \äp-shən\ option, adoption, co-option

optric \äp-trik\ catoptric, dioptric

opula \äp-yə-lə\ copula, scopula

opulace \äp-yə-ləs\ populace, populous

opulate \äp-yə-lāt\ copulate, populate, over-populate

opuli \äp-ə-lē\ see OPOLY

opulous \äp-yə-ləs\ see OPULACE

opus \ō-pəs\ opus, Canopus, magnum opus, pithecanthropus

¹**opy** \ō-pē\ see OPI

²**opy** \äp-ē\ see OPPY

¹**oque** \ōk\ see OKE

²**oque** \äk\ see ¹OCK

³**oque** \ȯk\ see ALK

oquial \ō-kwē-əl\ colloquial, ventriloquial

¹**or** \ȯr\ boar, Boer, Bohr, bore, chore, core, corps, crore, door, drawer, floor, for, fore, four, frore, gore, Gore, hoar, hoer, kor, lore, Moore, mor, more, More, nor, o'er, oar, or, ore, poor, pore, pour, roar, score, shore, snore, soar, sore, splore, spoor, spore, store, swore, Thor, tor, tore, torr, war, whore, wore, yore, your, you're, abhor, actor, adore, afore, and/or, ashore, backdoor, bailor, bandore, Beardmore, bedsore, before, bezoar, bookstore, candor, captor, centaur, claymore, closed-door, condor, decor, deplore, dime-store, donor, downpour, drugstore, encore, ephor, explore, Exmoor, eyesore, feoffor, fetor, Fillmore, folklore, footsore, forebore, forswore, forscore, galore, hardcore, ichor, ignore, implore, Indore, indoor, inpour, inshore, Lahore, lakeshore, Lenore, lessor, memoir, mentor, Mysore, nearshore, Nestor, offshore, onshore, outdoor, outpour, outsoar, outwore, pastor, psywar, rancor, rapport, raptor, Realtor, restore, rhetor, savior, seafloor, seashore, sector, seignior, senhor, señor, sensor, settlor, Seymour, signor, smoothbore,

sophomore, stentor, stertor,
stressor, stridor, subfloor,
temblor, tensor, therefor,
therefore, threescore, Timor,
trapdoor, turgor, uproar,
vendor, wherefore, woodlore,
albacore, alongshore, anaphor,
anymore, archosaur,
Baltimore, Bangalore,
Barrymore, brontosaur,
carnivore, CD4, Coimbatore,
commodore, comprador,
confessor, consignor, corridor,
cuspidor, devisor, dinosaur,
door-to-door, Ecuador, either-
or, Eleanor, Eleanore, elector,
Elinor, en rapport, evermore,
franchisor, furthermore,
guarantor, Gwalior,
hackamore, hadrosaur,
hellebore, herbivore,
heretofore, humidor,
Labrador, louis d'or, man-of-
war, manticore, matador,
metaphor, meteor, millepore,
Minotaur, mirador, Mount
Rushmore, nevermore,
omnivore, out-of-door, petit
four, picador, pinafore,
pompadour, predator,
promisor, pterosaur, reservoir,
sagamore, Salvador,
Salvatore, semaphore,
Singapore, stegosaur,
stevedore, superstore,
sycamore, Theodore,
theretofore, troubador, tug-of-
war, two-by-four, uncalled-
for, underscore, vavasor,
warrantor, alienor,
ambassador, ankylosaur,
conquistador, conservator,
Corregidor, de Pompadour, El
Salvador, esprit de corps,
forevermore, hereinbefore,
ichthyosaur, insectivore,
legislator, plesiosaur, San
Salvadore, toreador,
tyrannosaur, Ulan Bator,
administrator, lobster
thermidor, Talleyrand-
Perigord

²or \ər\ see ¹EUR

ora \ōr-ə\ aura, bora, Cora,
Dora, flora, Flora, hora,
Laura, Lora, mora, Nora, sora,
Torah, Andorra, angora,
aurora, Aurora, begorra,
camorra, fedora, gemara,
Gomorrah, Lenora, Masora,
menorah, pandora, Pandora,
remora, senhora, señora,
signora, Sonora, grandiflora,
Juiz de Fora, Leonora,
Simchas Torah, Tuscarora,
Lomas de Zamora

orable \ōr-ə-bəl\ horrible,
pourable, storable, adorable,
deplorable, restorable

orace \ȯr-əs\ see AURUS

oracle \ȯr-ə-kəl\ coracle, oracle

orage \ōr-ij\ borage, floorage,
forage, porridge, storage

orah \ōr-ə\ see ORA

¹oral \ōr-əl\ aural, choral, coral,
Coral, floral, laurel, Laurel,
moral, oral, quarrel, sorrel,
aboral, amoral, auroral,
balmoral, binaural, immoral,
monaural, peroral, restoral,
sororal

²oral \ȯrl\ schorl, whorl, ceorl

oram \ōr-əm\ see ORUM

orate \ōr-ət\ see ORET

orative \ōr-ət-iv\ explorative,
pejorative, restorative

oray \ə-rē\ see URRY

orb \órb\ forb, orb, sorb, Sorb,
absorb, adsorb, desorb, resorb

orbate \ór-bət\ see ORBIT

orbeil \ór-bəl\ see ORBEL

orbel \ór-bəl\ corbeil, corbel,
warble

orbent \ór-bənt\ absorbent,
immunosorbent

orbet \ór-bət\ see ORBIT

orbit \ór-bət\ orbit, sorbet,
adsorbate

orc \órk\ see ²ORK

orca \ór-ka\ orca, Majorca,
Minorca, Palma de Mallorca

orcas \ór-kəs\ Dorcas, orchis

orce \ōrs\ see ¹OURSE

orced \órst\ see ¹ORST

¹orceful \ōrs-fəl\ forceful,
resourceful

²orceful \órs-fəl\ see ORSEFUL

¹orcement \ōr-smənt\
deforcement, divorcement,
enforcement, reinforcement

²orcement \ór-smənt\ see
ORSEMENT

orcer \ōr-sər\ courser, enforcer,
reinforcer—*also comparatives
of adjectives listed at* ¹OURSE

orch \órch\ porch, scorch, torch,
blowtorch, sunporch

orcher \ór-chər\ scorcher,
torture

orchid \ór-kəd\ forked, orchid,
cryptorchid, monorchid

orchis \ór-kəs\ see ORCAS

¹ord \ōrd\ see OARD

²ord \ərd\ see IRD

³ord \ór\ see ¹OR

ordan \órd-ⁿn\ see ²ARDEN

ordancy \órd-ⁿn-sē\ mordancy,
discordancy

ordant \órd-ⁿnt\ mordant,
mordent, accordant,
concordant, discordant

orde \ōrd\ see OARD

orded \órd-əd\ see ²ARDED

ordent \órd-ⁿnt\ see ORDANT

order \órd-ər\ boarder, border,
corder, order, warder,
awarder, disorder, recorder,
reorder, rewarder, made-to-
order

ordered \órd-ərd\ bordered,
ordered—*also pasts of verbs
listed at* ORDER

orders \órd-ərz\ Borders—*also
possessives and plurals of
nouns and third person
singular presents of verbs
listed at* ORDER

ordial \órd-ē-əl\ exordial,
primordial

ordid \órd-əd\ see ²ARDED

¹ording \órd-iŋ\ lording,
recording, rewarding—*also
present participles of verbs
listed at* ²OARD

²ording \ərd-iŋ\ see ERDING

ordingly \órd-iŋ-lē\
accordingly, rewardingly

ordion \órd-ē-ən\ accordion,
Edwardian

ordist \órd-əst\ recordist,
clavichordist, harpsichordist

ordon \órd-ⁿn\ see ²ARDEN

ordure \ór-jər\ see ORGER

¹ordy \órd-ē\ Geordie, Lordy,
awardee

²ordy \ərd-ē\ see URDY

¹ore \ór-ē\ see ORY

²ore \úr\ see ¹URE

³**ore** \ər-ə\ see ¹OROUGH

⁴**ore** \ōr\ see ¹OR

oreal \ōr-ē-əl\ see ORIAL

orean \ȯr-ē-ən\ see ORIAN

oreas \ȯr-ē-əs\ see ORIOUS

ored \ōrd\ see OARD

oredom \ōrd-əm\ boredom,
    whoredom

orehead \ȯr-əd\ see ORRID

¹**oreign** \är-ən\ see ¹ORIN

²**oreign** \ȯr-ən\ see ²ORIN

oreigner \ȯr-ə-nər\ see ORONER

orem \ōr-əm\ see ORUM

oreman \ōr-mən\ corpsman,
    doorman, foreman,
    longshoreman

orence \ȯr-ən(t)s\ see AWRENCE

oreous \ȯr-ē-əs\ see ORIOUS

orer \ōr-ər\ borer, corer, floorer,
    pourer, roarer, scorer,
    schnorrer, snorer, soarer,
    adorer, deplorer, explorer—
    *also comparatives of
    adjectives listed at* ¹ORE

¹**ores** \ōr-əs\ see ¹ORUS

²**ores** \ōrz\ Azores, indoors,
    outdoors—*also possessives
    and plurals of nouns and
    third person singular presents
    of verbs listed at* ¹ORE

³**ores** \ȯr-əs\ see AURUS

oreson \ōrs-ᵊn\ see OARSEN

orest \ȯr-əst\ see ¹ORIST

orester \ȯr-ə-stər\ see ORISTER

oret \ōr-ət\ floret, sororate

oreum \ōr-ē-əm\ see ORIUM

oreward \ōr-wərd\ see
    OREWORD

oreword \ōr-wərd\ foreword,
    shoreward

orey \ȯr-ē\ see ORY

orf \ȯrf\ see ORPH

¹**org** \ȯrg\ morgue, cyborg

²**org** \ȯr-ē\ see ORY

organ \ȯr-gən\ gorgon, morgan,
    Morgan, organ, Glamorgan,
    Demogorgon, Mid
    Glamorgan, South
    Glamorgan, West Glamorgan

orge \ȯrj\ forge, George, gorge,
    scourge, disgorge, drop-forge,
    engorge, Lloyd George,
    reforge, Olduvai Gorge

orger \ȯr-jər\ bordure, forger,
    gorger, ordure

orgi \ȯr-gē\ see ORGY

orgia \ȯr-jə\ Borgia, Georgia,
    Strait of Georgia

orgian \ȯr-jən\ Georgian,
    Swedenborgian

orgon \ȯr-gən\ see ORGAN

orgue \ȯrg\ see ORG

orgy \ȯr-gē\ corgi, porgy

ori \ȯr-ē\ see ORY

oria \ȯr-ē-ə\ gloria, Gloria,
    noria, scoria, centaurea,
    euphoria, Peoria, Pretoria,
    victoria, Victoria, Vitoria,
    phantasmagoria

orial \ōr-ē-əl\ boreal, oriel,
    oriole, arboreal, armorial,
    auctorial, authorial, cantorial,
    censorial, corporeal, cursorial,
    factorial, fossorial, manorial,
    marmoreal, memorial,
    pictorial, praetorial,
    proctorial, raptorial, rectorial,
    sartorial, seignorial, sensorial,
    sponsorial, tonsorial, tutorial,
    uxorial, vectorial,
    conductorial, consistorial,
    curatorial, dictatorial,
    directorial, editorial,
    equatorial, immemorial,

incorporeal, janitorial,
monitorial, monsignorial,
natatorial, piscatorial,
preceptorial, professorial,
purgatorial, reportorial,
senatorial, territorial,
ambassadorial, conservatorial,
combinatorial, conspiratorial,
extracorporeal, gladiatorial,
gubernatorial, imperatorial,
inquisitorial, legislatorial,
procuratorial, propriatorial,
prosecutorial, extraterritorial,
improvisatorial
oriam \ōr-ē-əm\ see ORIUM
orian \òr-ē-ən\ Dorian, saurian,
Taurean, aurorean, Gregorian,
historian, Nestorian,
praetorian, stentorian,
victorian, dinosaurian,
hyperborean, Oratorian,
prehistorian, senatorian,
terpsichorean, salutatorian,
valedictorian
oriant \ōr-ē-ənt\ see ORIENT
oriat \òr-ē-ət\ see ²AUREATE
oric \òr-ik\ auric, choric, Doric,
toric, Armoric, caloric,
clitoric, dysphoric, euphoric,
folkloric, historic, phosphoric,
plethoric, pyloric, anaphoric,
cataphoric, metaphoric,
meteoric, paregoric,
prehistoric, sophomoric,
aleatoric, phantasmagoric
orical \òr-i-kəl\ auricle,
historical, rhetorical,
ahistorical, allegorical,
categorical, metaphorical,
oratorical, transhistorical,
sociohistorical
orics \òr-iks\ see ORYX

orid \òr-əd\ see ORRID
oriel \ōr-ē-əl\ see ORIAL
orient \ōr-ē-ənt\ orient, Orient,
euphoriant
¹orin \òr-ən\ florin, foreign,
Lauren, Orrin, sarin, sporran,
warren, Warren, Gagarin,
cyclosporine
²orin \ōr-ən\ see ¹ORINE
¹orine \ōr-ən\ chlorine, florin,
cephalosporin
²orine \òr-ən\ see ¹ORIN
oring \ōr-iŋ\ boring, flooring,
roaring, shoring, inpouring,
longshoring, outpouring, rip-
roaring—*also present
participles of verbs listed at*
¹OR
öring \ər-iŋ\ see URRING
oriole \ōr-ē-əl\ see ORIAL
orious \òr-ē-əs\ aureus, Boreas,
glorious, arboreous,
censorious, inglorious,
laborious, notorious, sartorius,
uproarious, uxorious,
vainglorious, victorious,
meritorious
¹oris \ōr-əs\ see ¹ORUS
²oris \òr-əs\ see AURUS
¹orish \òr-ish\ boarish, poorish,
whorish, folklorish
²orish \ùr-ish\ see ¹OORISH
orist \òr-əst\ florist, forest,
Forrest, sorest, afforest, Black
Forest, deforest, folklorist,
reforest, allegorist, Petrified
Forest—*also superlatives of
adjectives listed at* ¹OR
orister \òr-ə-stər\ chorister,
forester
ority \òr-ət-ē\ authority,
majority, minority, priority,

seniority, sonority, apriority,
exteriority, inferiority,
interiority, posteriority,
superiority

orium \ōr-ē-əm\ castoreum,
ciborium, emporium,
pastorium, scriptorium,
sensorium, auditorium,
crematorium, in memoriam,
moratorium, natatorium,
sanitorium, sudatorium

¹ork \ərk\ burke, Burke, chirk,
cirque, clerk, dirk, Dirk, irk,
jerk, kirk, Kirk, lurk, murk,
perk, quirk, shirk, smirk,
stirk, Turk, work, yerk, zerk,
artwork, berserk, breastwork,
brickwork, bridgework,
brightwork, brushwork,
capework, casework,
clockwork, coachwork, de
Klerk, ductwork, Dunkirk,
earthwork, falsework,
fieldwork, firework, flatwork,
footwork, formwork,
framework, goldwork,
groundwork, guesswork,
hackwork, handwork,
headwork, homework,
housework, ironwork, knee-
jerk, legwork, lifework, make-
work, meshwork, millwork,
network, outwork, paintwork,
patchwork, piecework,
presswork, quillwork, rework,
roadwork, salesclerk,
schoolwork, Selkirk,
Southwark, spadework,
steelwork, stickwork,
stonework, teamwork,
timework, topwork, waxwork,
webwork, woodwork,

basketwork, busywork,
crewelwork, donkeywork,
fancywork, handiwork,
journeywork, laquerwork,
masterwork, needlework,
openwork, overwork,
paperwork, plasterwork, soda
jerk, wonderwork,
cabinetwork

²ork \ork\ cork, Cork, dork,
fork, pork, quark, stork,
torque, York, bulwark, Cape
York, futhorc, hayfork, New
York, North York, pitchfork,
uncork

¹orked \orkt\ corked, forked,
uncorked

²orked \or-kəd\ see ORCHID

¹orker \ər-kər\ jerker, lurker,
shirker, worker, berserker,
caseworker, dockworker,
fieldworker, handworker,
ironworker, outworker,
pieceworker, steelworker,
tearjerker, wageworker,
woodworker, autoworker,
metalworker, needleworker,
wonderworker

²orker \or-kər\ corker,forker,
porker, torquer

orkie \or-kē\ see ORKY

orking \ər-kiŋ\ hardworking,
tear-jerking, woodworking,
wonder-working

orky \or-kē\ corky, dorky,
forky, Gorky, porky, Yorkie

¹orl \ərl\ see ¹IRL

²orl \orl\ see ³ORAL

orld \ərld\ burled, knurled,
whorled, world, dreamworld,
New World, old-world,
demiworld, microworld,

netherworld, otherworld, underworld—*also pasts of verbs listed at* [1]IRL

orled \ərld\ see ORLD

[1]**orm** \ərm\ berm, firm, germ, herm, perm, Perm, sperm, squirm, term, therm, worm, affirm, bookworm, budworm, confirm, cutworm, deperm, deworm, earthworm, flatworm, glowworm, heartworm, hookworm, hornworm, inchworm, infirm, long-term, lugworm, lungworm, midterm, pinworm, ringworm, roundworm, sandworm, screwworm, short-term, silkworm, tapeworm, woodworm, angleworm, armyworm, caddis worm, disaffirm, disconfirm, gymnosperm, pachyderm, reconfirm, angiosperm, echinoderm

[2]**orm** \ȯrm\ corm, dorm, form, norm, storm, swarm, warm, aswarm, barnstorm, brainstorm, conform, deform, Delorme, firestorm, free-form, hailstorm, inform, L-form, landform, life-form, lukewarm, perform, planform, platform, postform, preform, rainstorm, re-form, reform, sandstorm, snowstorm, transform, triform, windstorm, chloroform, cruciform, dendriform, dentiform, disciform, fungiform, funnelform, fusiform, letterform, microform,

multiform, nonconform, thunderstorm, uniform, vermiform

ormable \ȯr-mə-bəl\ formable, conformable, performable, transformable

ormal \ȯr-məl\ formal, normal, abnormal, conformal, informal, subnormal, paranormal, semiformal, supernormal

ormally \ȯr-mə-lē\ formally, formerly, normally, stormily, abnormally, informally, subnormally, paranormally, supernormally

orman \ȯr-mən\ corpsman, Mormon, Norman, Anglo-Norman

ormance \ȯr-məns\ conformance, performance, nonconformance

ormant \ȯr-mənt\ dormant, formant, informant

ormative \ȯr-mət-iv\ formative, normative, informative, performative, reformative, transformative

orme \ȯrm\ see [2]ORM

ormed \ȯrmd\ formed, normed, informed, malformed, unformed—*also pasts of verbs listed at* [2]ORM

[1]**ormer** \ȯr-mər\ dormer, former, swarmer, warmer, barnstormer, benchwarmer, brainstormer, conformer, heart-warmer, informer, performer, reformer, transformer

[2]**ormer** \ər-mər\ see URMUR

ormerly \ȯr-mə-lē\ see
  ORMALLY
ormie \ȯr-mē\ see ¹ORMY
ormily \ȯr-mə-lē\ see ORMALLY
orming \ȯr-miŋ\ brainstorming,
  heartwarming, housewarming,
  habit-forming, nonperforming
ormist \ȯr-məst\ warmest,
  conformist, reformist,
  nonconformist
ormity \ȯr-mət-ē\ conformity,
  deformity, enormity,
  nonconformity, uniformity
ormless \ȯrm-ləs\ formless,
  gormless
ormon \ȯr-mən\ see ORMAN
¹**ormy** \ȯr-mē\ stormy, dormie
²**ormy** \ər-mē\ see ERMY
¹**orn** \ȯrn\ born, borne, bourn,
  corn, horn, lorn, morn,
  mourn, Norn, porn, scorn,
  shorn, sworn, thorn, torn,
  warn, worn, acorn, adorn,
  airborne, alphorn, althorn,
  baseborn, bicorne, bighorn,
  blackthorn, boxthorn,
  broomcorn, buckthorn,
  bullhorn, Cape Horn,
  careworn, Christ's-thorn,
  Dearborn, dehorn, earthborn,
  einkorn, firethorn, firstborn,
  foghorn, foreborn, foresworn,
  forewarn, forlorn, forworn,
  freeborn, greenhorn,
  hartshorn, hawthorn,
  Hawthorne, highborn, inborn,
  inkhorn, krummhorn, leghorn,
  longhorn, lovelorn, lowborn,
  newborn, outworn, popcorn,
  pronghorn, reborn, seaborne,
  shipborne, shoehorn,
  shopworn, shorthorn,
skyborne, soilborne, staghorn,
  stillborn, stinkhorn, suborn,
  timeworn, tinhorn, tricorne,
  trueborn, twice-born, unborn,
  unworn, wayworn, wellborn,
  well-worn, wind-borne,
  alpenhorn, barleycorn,
  Capricorn, flügelhorn,
  foreign-born, Golden Horn,
  Matterhorn, peppercorn,
  unicorn, waterborne,
  waterworn, weatherworn,
  winterbourne
²**orn** \ərn\ see URN
ornament \ȯr-nə-mənt\
  ornament, tournament
¹**orne** \ōrn\ see ¹ORN
²**orne** \ȯrn\ see ²ORN
orned \ȯrnd\ horned, thorned,
  unadorned—*also pasts of
  verbs listed at* ²ORN
orner \ȯr-nər\ warner, Warner,
  Cape Horner, dehorner,
  suborner
ornery \än-rē\ see ¹ANNERY
orney \ər-nē\ see ¹OURNEY
ornful \ȯrn-fəl\ mournful,
  scornful
ornice \ȯr-nəs\ cornice, ornice,
  notornis
orning \ȯr-niŋ\ morning,
  mourning, warning, aborning
ornis \ȯr-nəs\ see ORNICE
ornment \ərn-mənt\ see
  ERNMENT
orny \ȯr-nē\ corny, horny,
  porny, thorny, tourney
¹**oro**\ ər-ə\ see ¹OROUGH
²**oro** \ō-rō\ Chamorro, Mindoro,
  Rio de Oro
oroner \ȯr-ə-nər\ coroner,
  foreigner, warrener

¹**orough** \ər-ə\ borough, burgh, burro, burrow, curragh, furrow, ore, thorough, Gainsborough, Greensboro, Roxborough, Scarborough, Yarborough, Edinburgh, kookaburra, Peterborough, Soke of Peterborough, Huntingdon and Peterborough

²**orough** \ər-ō\ see ¹URROW

¹**orous** \ōr-əs\ see ¹ORUS

²**orous** \ór-əs\ see AURUS

orp \órp\ dorp, gorp, thorp, warp, Australorp, Krugersdorp, octothorp, Oglethorpe

orpe \órp\ see ORP

orper \ór-pər\ dorper, torpor

orph \órf\ corf, dwarf, morph, Düsseldorf, anthropomorph

orphan \ór-fən\ orphan, endorphin, beta-endorphin

orpheus \ór-fē-əs\ Morpheus, Orpheus

orphic \ór-fik\ orphic, ectomorphic, endomorphic, mesomorphic, pseudomorphic, metamorphic, anthropomorphic

orphin \ór-fən\ see ORPHAN

orphous \ór-fəs\ amorphous, isomorphous

orphrey \ór-frē\ orphrey, porphyry

orphyrin \ór-fə-rən\ see ARFARIN

orphyry \ór-frē\ see ORPHREY

orpoise \ór-pəs\ see ORPUS

orpor \ór-pər\ see ORPER

orps \ōr\ see ¹OR

¹**orpsman** \ōr-mən\ see OREMAN

²**orpsman** \ór-mən\ see ORMAN

orpus \ór-pəs\ corpus, porpoise, habeas corpus

orque \órk\ see ²ORK

orquer \ór-kər\ see ²ORKER

¹**orra** \är-ə\ see ¹ARA

²**orra** \ór-ə\ see ²ORA

³**orra** \ō-rə\ see ¹ORA

orrader \är-əd-ər\ see ORRIDOR

¹**orrah** \ōr-ə\ see ORA

²**orrah** \är-ə\ see ¹ARA

¹**orran** \är-ən\ see ¹ORIN

²**orran** \ór-ən\ see ²ORIN

orrence \ór-əns\ see AWRENCE

orrel \ór-əl\ see ²ORAL

orrent \ór-ənt\ horrent, torrent, warrant, abhorrent

¹**orrer** \ór-ər\ borer, horror, roarer, schnorrer, sorer, abhorrer, explorer

²**orrer** \ōr-ər\ see ¹ORER

orres \ór-əs\ see AURUS

orrest \ór-əst\ see ¹ORIST

orrible \ór-ə-bəl\ see ²ORABLE

orrid \ór-əd\ florid, horrid, torrid

¹**orridge** \är-ij\ see ¹ORAGE

²**orridge** \ór-ij\ see ³ORAGE

orridor \är-əd-ər\ corridor, forrader

¹**orrie** \är-ē\ see ¹ARI

²**orrie** \ór-ē\ see ORY

orrier \ór-ē-ər\ see ARRIOR

orrin \ór-ən\ see ²ORIN

¹**orris** \är-əs\ charas, Juárez, Maurice, morris, Morris, Norris, orris, Banaras, Benares, Polaris, Ciudad Juárez

²**orris** \ōr-əs\ see ¹ORUS

³**orris** \ór-əs\ see AURUS

orro \ō-rō\ see ²ORO

orror \ór-ər\ see ¹ORRER
¹**orrow** \är-ō\ borrow, claro,
  morrow, sorrow, taro, Pizarro,
  saguaro, tomorrow,
  Catanzaro, Kilimanjaro,
  Mohenjo-Daro
²**orrow** \är-ə\ see ¹ARA
¹**orry** \är-ē\ see ¹ARI
²**orry** \ər-ē\ see URRY
ors \ōrz\ see OORS
orsal \ór-səl\ see ORSEL
¹**orse** \órs\ coarse, corse, course,
  force, gorse, hoarse, horse,
  Morse, Norse, source,
  clotheshorse, concourse,
  deforce, discourse, divorce,
  endorse, enforce, extrorse,
  introrse, midcourse,
  packhorse, perforce, post-
  horse, racecourse, racehorse,
  recourse, remorse, retrorse,
  sawhorse, stringcourse,
  unhorse, war-horse,
  Whitehorse, workhorse,
  charley horse, Crazy Horse,
  hobbyhorse, nonrecourse,
  stalking-horse, reinforce,
  watercourse
²**orse** \ərs\ see ERSE
orseful \órs-fəl\ forceful,
  remorseful, resourceful
orsel \ór-səl\ dorsal, morsel
orseman \ór-smən\ horseman,
  Norseman
orsement \ór-smənt\
  endorsement, reinforcement
orsen \ərs-ᵊn\ see ERSON
orser \ər-sər\ see URSOR
orset \ór-sət\ corset, Dorset
orsey \ór-sē\ see ORSY
orsion \ór-shən\ see ²ORTION

¹**orst** \órst\ forced, horst—*also
  pasts of verbs listed at* ¹ORSE
²**orst** \ərst\ see URST
orsted \ər-stəd\ see ERSTED
orsum \ór-səm\ dorsum,
  foursome
orsy \ór-sē\ gorsy, horsey
¹**ort** \órt\ boart, bort, court, fort,
  forte, mort, Oort, ort, port,
  Porte, quart, short, snort, sort,
  sport, swart, thwart, tort,
  torte, wart, wort, abort,
  airport, amort, aport, assort,
  athwart, backcourt, bellwort,
  birthwort, bistort, Bridgeport,
  cavort, cohort, colewort,
  comport, consort, contort,
  crosscourt, deport, disport,
  distort, downcourt, effort,
  escort, exhort, export, extort,
  forecourt, frontcourt,
  glasswort, gosport, half-court,
  homeport, milkwort, Newport,
  outport, passport, presort,
  purport, ragwort, report, resort, resort, retort, seaport,
  Shreveport, spaceport,
  spoilsport, Stockport, support,
  transport, bladderwort,
  davenport, life-support,
  nonsupport, pennywort, Saint-
  John's wort, teleport,
  ultrashort, worrywart,
  pianoforte, underreport
²**ort** \ōr\ see ¹OR
³**ort** \ərt\ see ¹ERT
ortable \ōrt-ə-bəl\ portable,
  deportable, exportable,
  importable, reportable,
  supportable, transportable,
  insupportable

ortage \órt-ij\ portage, shortage, colportage

ortal \órt-ᵊl\ chortle, mortal, portal, quartile, immortal

ortar \órt-ər\ see ORTER

ortative \órt-ət-iv\ hortative, portative, assortative, exhortative

¹**orte** \órt\ see ¹ORT

²**orte** \órt-ē\ see ORTY

orted \órt-əd\ warted, assorted, ill-sorted—*also pasts of verbs listed at* ¹ORT

ortedly \órt-əd-lē\ purportedly, reportedly

orten \órt-ᵊn\ quartan, shorten, foreshorten

orter \órt-ər\ mortar, porter, Porter, quarter, snorter, sorter, colporteur, distorter, exhorter, exporter, extorter, headquarter, importer, lambsquarter, reporter, resorter, ripsnorter, transporter—*also comparatives of adjectives listed at* ¹ORT

orteur \órt-ər\ see ORTER

¹**orth** \órth\ forth, Forth, fourth, north, North, thenceforth, Firth of Forth

²**orth** \ərth\ see IRTH

orthful \ərth-fəl\ see IRTHFUL

orthless \ərth-ləs\ see IRTHLESS

orthy \ər-thē\ earthy, worthy, airworthy, blameworthy, Galsworthy, newsworthy, noteworthy, praiseworthy, seaworthy, trustworthy, creditworthy

ortic \órt-ik\ see ²ARTIC

ortical \órt-i-kəl\ cortical, vortical

ortie \órt-ē\ see ORTY

orting \órt-iŋ\ sporting, selfsupporting

ortion \ór-shən\ portion, torsion, abortion, apportion, contortion, distortion, extorsion, extortion, proportion, retortion, disproportion, proabortion, reapportion, antiabortion

ortionate \ór-shnət\ extortionate, proportionate, disproportionate

ortionist \ór-shnəst\ abortionist, contortionist, extortionist

ortis \órt-əs\ fortis, mortise, tortoise, aquafortis, rigor mortis

ortise \órt-əs\ see ORTIS

ortive \órt-iv\ sportive, abortive, contortive, extortive

ortle \órt-ᵊl\ see ORTAL

ortly \órt-lē\ courtly, portly, shortly, thwartly

ortment \órt-mənt\ assortment, comportment, deportment, disportment

ortoise \órt-əs\ see ORTIS

orton \órt-ᵊn\ Morton, Norton, Wharton

orts \órts\ quartz, shorts, sports, undershorts—*also plurals and possessives of nouns and third person singular presents of verbs listed at* ¹ORT

ortunate \órch-nət\ fortunate, importunate, unfortunate

orture \ór-chər\ see ORCHER

orty \órt-ē\ forty, shorty, sortie, sporty, warty, mezzo forte, pianoforte

orum \ōr-əm\ foram, forum,

jorum, quorum, decorum,
Mizoram, ad valorem,
cockalorum, indecorum,
Karakoram, variorum, pons
asinorum, sanctum sanctorum,
schola cantorum

¹orus \ōr-əs\ Boris, chorus,
Doris, Horus, loris, porous,
sorus, torus, canorous,
decorous, Delores, Dolores,
pelorus, phosphorus,
sonorous, deoch an doris,
doch-an-dorris

²orus \ȯr-əs\ see AURUS

orward \ȯr-wərd\ forward,
shoreward, flash-forward,
henceforward, carryforward

ory \ȯr-ē\ Corey, corrie, dory,
glory, gory, hoary, Laurie,
Lori, lorry, lory, nori, quarry,
saury, sorry, story, Tory, zori,
centaury, clerestory, John
Dory, outlawry, satori,
vainglory, a priori, allegory,
amatory, auditory, cacciatore,
castratory, category, con
amore, crematory, damnatory,
decretory, desultory, dilatory,
dormitory, expletory,
feudatory, fumitory,
Goteborg, gustatory, gyratory,
hortatory, hunky-dory,
inventory, laudatory, lavatory,
mandatory, migratory,
minatory, monitory,
Montessori, nugatory,
offertory, oratory, overstory,
predatory, prefatory,
probatory, promissory,
promontory, purgatory,
repertory, Ruwenzori,
signatory, statutory, sudatory,

territory, transitory,
understory, vibratory,
vomitory, yakitori,
accusatory, admonitory,
adulatory, a fortiori, aleatory,
ambulatory, amendatory,
applicatory, approbatory,
celebratory, circulatory,
combinatory, commendatory,
compensatory, condemnatory,
confirmatory, confiscatory,
conservatory, consolatory,
contributory, copulatory,
cosignatory, declamatory,
declaratory, dedicatory,
defamatory, denigratory,
depilatory, depository,
derogatory, designatory,
dispensatory, divinatory,
escalatory, excitatory,
exclamatory, exculpatory,
excusatory, exhibitory,
exhortatory, expiatory,
expiratory, explanatory,
explicatory, exploratory,
expository, expurgatory,
incantatory, incubatory,
indicatory, inflammatory,
informatory, innovatory,
inspiratory, inundatory,
invitatory, judicatory,
laboratory, Lake Maggiore,
masticatory, masturbatory,
memento mori, millefiori,
modulatory, obfuscatory,
obligatory, observatory,
performatory, persecutory,
predicatory, premonitory,
preparatory, prohibitory,
reformatory, regulatory,
repository, retributory,
revelatory, respiratory,

salutatory, stipulatory,
supplicatory, transmigratory,
undulatory, adjudicatory, a
posteriori, annihilatory,
annunciatory, anticipatory,
appreciatory, assimilatory,
circumlocutory, classificatory,
concilliatory, confabulatory,
congratulatory, de-escalatory,
denunciatory, depreciatory,
discriminatory, ejaculatory,
hallucinatory, improvisatore,
improvisatory, interrogatory,
intimidatory, investigatory,
participatory, propitiatory,
recommendatory,
recriminatory, renunciatory,
reverberatory, viola d'amore,
amelioratory,
overcompensatory,
reconciliatory, supererogatory,
immunoregulatory

oryx \ȯr-iks\ oryx, Armorics,
combinatorics

orze \ȯrz\ see OORS

¹os \äs\ boss, doss, dross, floss,
fosse, gloss, joss, Maas, os,
pross, stoss, toss, Argos,
bathos, benthos, bugloss,
chaos, Chios, cosmos, Delos,
demos, Ellás, emboss, Eos,
epos, Eros, ethos, Hyksos,
kaross, kudos, kvass, Lagos,
Laplace, Lemnos, Lesbos,
Logos, Madras, Melos,
mythos, nol-pros, nonpros,
Paros, pathos, peplos, pharos,
ringtoss, Samos, telos, topos,
tripos, coup de grace,
demitasse, extrados, gravitas,
intrados, isogloss, omphalos,

reredos, semigloss, Thanatos,
underboss, volte-face

²os \ō\ see ¹OW

³os \ōs\ see ¹OSE

⁴os \ȯs\ see ¹OSS

¹osa \ō-sə\ Xhosa, Formosa,
mimosa, Reynosa, curiosa,
virtuosa, anorexia nervosa

²osa \ō-zə\ mimosa, mucosa,
serosa, Spinoza, sub rosa,
curiosa, virtuosa, Zaragoza

¹osable \ō-zə-bəl\ closable,
disposable, erosible,
explosible, opposable,
reclosable, supposable,
decomposable, superposable,
indecomposable,
superimposable

²osable \ü-zə-bəl\ see USABLE

osal \ō-zəl\ hosel, losel,
deposal, disposal, proposal,
reposal, supposal

osan \ōs-ᵊn\ see OSIN

osch \äsh\ see ²ASH

¹oschen \ō-shən\ see OTION

²oschen \ȯ-shən\ see AUTION

oscible \äs-ə-bəl\ see OSSIBLE

osco \äs-kō\ see OSCOE

oscoe \äs-kō\ Bosco, roscoe,
Roscoe, fiasco

oscopy \äs-kə-pē\ arthroscopy,
microscopy, spectroscopy,
sigmoidoscopy

¹ose \ōs\ close, dose, gross, os,
arkose, Carlos, cosmos,
crustose, cymose, dextrose,
engross, erose, fructose,
globose, glucose, jocose,
lactose, maltose, mannose,
megadose, morose, mythos,
nodose, pappose, pathos,
pentose, pilose, plumose,

ramose, rhamnose, ribose,
rugose, scapose, schistose,
setose, spinose, strigose,
sucrose, Sukkoth, triose,
vadose, ventricose, verbose,
viscose, adios, adipose,
bellicose, calvados, cellulose,
comatose, diagnose,
grandiose, granulose, Helios,
lachrymose, otiose, overdose,
racemose, Shabuoth, tuberose,
varicose, inter alios, inter
vivos, metamorphose,
religiose
²ose \ōz\ brose, Broz, chose,
close, clothes, cloze, doze,
froze, gloze, hose, nose, pose,
prose, rose, Rose, Ambrose,
appose, aros, bedclothes,
bluenose, brownnose,
bulldoze, Burroughs,
compose, depose, dextrose,
disclose, dispose, enclose,
expose, foreclose, fructose,
glucose, hardnose, impose,
nightclothes, oppose,
plainclothes, primrose,
propose, quickfroze, repose,
rockrose, suppose, transpose,
tuberose, unclose, uprose,
viscose, wind rose, Berlioz,
counterpose, decompose,
diagnose, discompose,
indispose, interpose,
juxtapose, letters close,
pettitoes, predispose,
presuppose, pussytoes,
recompose, shovelnose,
superpose, underclothes,
anastomose, metamorphose,
overexpose, superimpose,
underexpose—*also plurals*

*and possessives of nouns and
third person singular presents
of verbs listed at* ¹OW
³ose \üz\ see ²USE
osed \ōzd\ closed, nosed,
composed, exposed, hard-
nosed, opposed, pug-nosed,
snub-nosed, stenosed,
supposed, unclosed,
indisposed, shovel-nosed,
toffee-nosed, well-disposed—
also pasts of verbs listed at
²OSE
osee \ō-zē\ see OSY
osel \ō-zəl\ see OSAL
osen \ōz-ᵊn\ chosen, frozen,
quickfrozen, lederhosen
¹oser \ō-zər\ closer, dozer,
poser, proser, brownnoser,
bulldozer, composer,
discloser, disposer, exposer,
imposer, opposer, proposer,
decomposer, interposer,
photocomposer
²oser \ü-zər\ see USER
¹oset \ō-zət\ see ²OSIT
²oset \äz-ət\ see ¹OSIT
³oset \äs-ət\ see OSSET
osey \ō-zē\ see OSY
¹osh \ósh\ see ²ASH
²osh \ōsh\ see ²OCHE
¹oshed \äsht\ sloshed,
galoshed—*also pasts of verbs
listed at* ¹ASH
²oshed \ósht\ see ¹ASHED
oshen \ō-shən\ see OTION
osher \äsh-ər\ see ¹ASHER
osia \ō-shə\ see ¹OTIA
osible \ō-zə-bəl\ see ¹OSABLE
osier \ō-zhər\ see OSURE
osily \ō-zə-lē\ cozily, nosily,
rosily

osin \ōs-ᵊn\ boatswain, Mosan, pocosin

osing \ō-ziŋ\ closing, nosing, disclosing, imposing, supposing

osion \ō-zhən\ plosion, corrosion, displosion, erosion, explosion, implosion

osis \ō-səs\ gnosis, hypnosis, narcosis, necrosis, neurosis, orthosis, osmosis, prognosis, psychosis, sclerosis, thrombosis, brucellosis, cyanosis, dermatosis, diagnosis, halitosis, heterosis, psittacosis, scoliosis, silicosis, symbiosis, anaplasmosis, autohypnosis, coccidiosis, hyperhidrosis, pediculosis, psychoneurosis, tuberculosis, mononucleosis, immunodiagnosis, neurofibromatosis

¹osit \äz-ət\ closet, posit, composite, deposit, exposit

²osit \ō-zət\ prosit, roset

osite \äz-ət\ see ¹OSIT

ositive \äz-ət-iv\ positive, appositive, seropositive

ositor \äz-ət-ər\ compositor, depositor, expositor

osius \ō-shəs\ see OCIOUS

osive \ō-siv\ plosive, corrosive, erosive, explosive, implosive, purposive

osk \äsk\ mosque, kiosk, abelmosk

¹oso \ō-sō\ proso, maestoso, rebozo, arioso, furioso, gracioso, grandioso, mafioso, Mato Grosso, oloroso, spiritoso, vigoroso, virtuoso, concerto grosso

²oso \ō-zō\ bozo, rebozo, furioso, gracioso, grandioso, spiritoso, vigoroso

³oso \ü-sō\ see USOE

osophy \äs-ə-fē\ philosophy, theosophy, anthroposophy

osque \äsk\ see OSK

¹oss \òs\ boss, cross, crosse, floss, gloss, loss, moss, Ross, sauce, toss, across, bugloss, crisscross, emboss, Kinross, kouros, lacrosse, outcross, pathos, ringtoss, topcross, uncross, albatross, applesauce, autocross, double-cross, intercross, motocross, semigloss

²oss \ōs\ see ¹OSE

³oss \äs\ see ¹OS

ossa \äs-ə\ see ¹ASA

ossable \äs-ə-bəl\ see OSSIBLE

ossal \äs-əl\ docile, dossal, fossil, glossal, jostle, tassel, throstle, warsle, wassail, apostle, colossal, indocile, isoglossal

¹osse \äs\ see ¹OS

²osse \äs-ē\ see ¹OSSY

³osse \òs\ see ¹OSS

ossed \òst\ see ³OST

osser \ò-sər\ Chaucer, crosser, saucer, double-crosser

osset \äs-ət\ cosset, faucet, Osset, posset, Samoset

ossible \äs-ə-bəl\ possible, cognoscible, embossable, impossible

ossic \äs-ik\ see OSSICK

ossick \äs-ik\ fossick, isoglossic

ossil \äs-əl\ see OSSAL

ossity \äs-ət-ē\ adiposity, atrocity, callosity, ferocity, gibbosity, monstrosity, pomposity, porosity, precocity, velocity, viscosity, zygosity, animosity, bellicosity, curiosity, generosity, grandiosity, hideosity, luminosity, nebulosity, preciosity, reciprocity, scrupulosity, sensuosity, sinuosity, strenuosity, tortuosity, tuberosity, varicosity, virtuosity, impetuosity, religiosity, voluminosity, impecuniosity

ossly \ós-lē\ costly, crossly

osso \ō-sō\ see ¹OSO

ossos \äs-əs\ see OCESS

ossular \äs-ə-lər\ grossular, wassailer

ossum \äs-əm\ blossom, passim, possum, opossum

ossus \äs-əs\ see OCESS

¹ossy \äs-ē\ Aussie, bossy, dassie, drossy, flossy, glossy, posse, quasi, dalasi, Kumasi, Likasi, sannyasi

²ossy \ó-sē\ Aussie, bossy, lossy, mossy

¹ost \äst\ sol-faist, Pentecost, teleost—*also pasts of verbs listed at* ¹OS

²ost \ōst\ boast, coast, ghost, host, most, oast, post, roast, toast, almost, bedpost, compost, doorpost, endmost, foremost, gatepost, goalpost, Gold Coast, guidepost, headmost, hindmost, impost, inmost, midmost, milepost, Milquetoast, outmost, outpost, provost, rearmost, riposte, seacoast, signpost, sternmost, sternpost, topmost, upcoast, upmost, utmost, aftermost, ante-post, bottommost, coast-to-coast, easternmost, farthermost, fingerpost, furthermost, headforemost, hithermost, innermost, Ivory Coast, lowermost, nethermost, northernmost, outermost, rudderpost, southernmost, sternforemost, undermost, uppermost, uttermost, westernmost

³ost \óst\ cost, frost, lost, accost, defrost, exhaust, hoarfrost, star-crossed, holocaust, Pentecost, permafrost—*also pasts of verbs listed at* ¹OSS

⁴ost \əst\ see ¹UST

osta \äs-tə\ costa, pasta

¹ostal \ōs-tᵊl\ coastal, postal, bicoastal, intercostal

²ostal \äs-tᵊl\ see OSTEL

ostasy \äs-tə-sē\ apostasy, isostasy

oste \ōst\ see ²OST

ostel \äs-tᵊl\ hostel, hostile, Pentecostal

¹oster \äs-tər\ coster, foster, Foster, roster, impostor, piaster, Double Gloucester, paternoster, snollygoster

²oster \ós-tər\ foster, Foster, roster, Double Gloucester

³oster \ō-stər\ see OASTER

ostic \äs-tik\ Gnostic, acrostic, agnostic, prognostic, diagnostic ostile \äs-t°l\ see OSTEL

ostle \äs-əl\ see OSSAL

¹ostly \ōst-lē\ ghostly, hostly, mostly

²ostly \ós-lē\ see OSSLY

ostomy \äs-tə-mē\ ostomy, colostomy, enterostomy

oston \ós-tən\ Austin, Boston, Godwin Austen

ostor \äs-tər\ see ¹OSTER

¹ostral \ós-trəl\ austral, rostral

²ostral \äs-trəl\ see OSTREL

ostrel \äs-trəl\ austral, costrel, nostril, rostral, wastrel, colostral

ostril \äs-trəl\ see OSTREL

ostrum \äs-trəm\ nostrum, rostrum, colostrum

osty \ō-stē\ ghosty, toasty

osure \ō-zhər\ closure, crosier, osier, composure, disclosure, disposure, enclosure, exclosure, exposure, foreclosure, discomposure, overexposure, underexposure

osy \ō-zē\ cozy, dozy, mosey, nosy, Osee, posy, prosy, rosy, ring-around-a-rosy

osyne \äs-°n-ē\ Euphrosyne, Mnemosyne

osz \ósh\ see ²ASH

oszcz \ósh\ see ²ASH

¹ot \ät\ aught, baht, blot, boite, bot, chott, clot, cot, dot, ghat, got, grot, hot, jat, jot, khat, knot, kyat, lot, Lot, lotte, motte, naught, not, plot, pot, rot, scot, Scot, Scott, shot, skat, slot, snot, sot, spot, squat, swat, swot, tot, trot, watt, Watt, what, wot, yacht, allot, ascot, begot, besot, big

shot, bloodshot, bowknot, boycott, buckshot, bullshot, cachepot, calotte, cannot, Connacht, crackpot, Crockpot, culotte, dashpot, despot, dreadnought, earshot, ergot, escot, eyeshot, eyespot, feedlot, fiat, firepot, fleshpot, forgot, fox-trot, fusspot, fylfot, garrote, gavotte, grapeshot, gunshot, half-knot, have-not, highspot, hotchpot, hotshot, ikat, jackpot, Korat, kumquat, long shot, loquat, marplot, mascot, motmot, nightspot, one-shot, Pequot, potshot, Rabat, red-hot, robot, Sadat, sandlot, sexpot, Shabbat, shallot, Shebat, sheepcote, slingshot, slipknot, slungshot, snapshot, somewhat, stinkpot, stockpot, subplot, sunspot, teapot, tin-pot, topknot, tosspot, try-pot, upshot, wainscot, whatnot, white-hot, woodlot, aeronaut, aliquot, apparat, apricot, aquanaut, argonaut, astronaut, bergamot, cachalot, Camelot, caveat, carry-cot, coffeepot, cosmonaut, counterplot, diddley-squat, doodley-squat, flowerpot, gallipot, guillemot, Gujarat, Hottentot, Huguenot, kilowatt, Lancelot, megawatt, microdot, Nouakchott, ocelot, overshot, paraquat, patriot, Penobscot, peridot, polka dot, polyglot, samizdat, sansculotte, scattershot, terawatt, tommyrot, touch-me-not, underplot, undershot,

Willemstadt, Wyandot, wyandotte, compatriot, forget-me-not, immunoblot, Inupiat, requiescat, Johnny-on-the-spot

²ot \ō\ see ¹OW

³ot \ōt\ see OAT

⁴ot \ȯt\ see ¹OUGHT

ôt \ō\ see ¹OW

ota \ōt-ə\ bota, flota, lota, quota, rota, biota, Dakota, iota, Lakota, pelota, Toyota, Minnesota, North Dakota, South Dakota

otable \ōt-ə-bəl\ notable, potable, quotable

otage \ōt-ij\ dotage, flotage, anecdotage

otal \ōt-ᵊl\ dotal, motile, scrotal, total, immotile, subtotal, teetotal, anecdotal, antidotal, sacerdotal

otalist \ōt-ᵊl-əst\ teetotalist, anecdotalist, sacerdotalist

otamus \ät-ə-məs\ see OTOMOUS

otany \ät-ᵊn-ē\ botany, cottony, monotony

otarist \ōt-ə-rəst\ motorist, votarist

otary \ōt-ə-rē\ coterie, rotary, votary, locomotory, prothonotary

otas \ō-təs\ see OTUS

otch \äch\ blotch, botch, crotch, hotch, notch, scotch, Scotch, splotch, swatch, watch, bird-watch, deathwatch, debauch, dogwatch, hopscotch, hotchpotch, Sasquatch, stopwatch, top-notch, wristwatch, butterscotch

otchet \äch-ət\ crotchet, rochet

otchman \äch-mən\ Scotchman, watchman

otchy \äch-ē\ blotchy, boccie, botchy, splotchy, hibachi, huarache, huisache, Karachi, vivace, mariachi

¹ote \ōt-ē\ dhoti, floaty, loti, roti, throaty, cenote, coyote, chayote, peyote, quixote

²ote \ōt\ see OAT

³ote \ät\ see ¹OT

otea \ōt-ē-ə\ protea, scotia

oted \ōt-əd\ see OATED

otem \ōt-əm\ see OTUM

oten \ōt-ᵊn\ see OTON

oter \ōt-ər\ see OATER

oterie \ōt-ə-rē\ see OTARY

¹oth \äth\ broth, cloth, froth, Goth, moth, sloth, swath, troth, wroth, betroth, breechcloth, broadcloth, cheesecloth, dishcloth, facecloth, floorcloth, loincloth, Naboth, oilcloth, sackcloth, sailcloth, washcloth, Alioth, behemoth, tablecloth, Ustrogoth, Visigoth

²oth \ōs\ see ¹OSE

³oth \ōt\ see OAT

⁴oth \ōth\ see OWTH

othal \ȯth-əl\ see OTHEL

othe \ōth\ clothe, loathe, betroth, unclothe

othel \ȯth-əl\ brothel, betrothal

¹other \əth-ər\ brother, mother, nother, other, rather, smother, tother, another, foremother, godmother, grandmother, housemother, stepbrother, stepmother

²other \äth-ər\ see ¹ATHER

otherly \ə<u>th</u>-ər-lē\ brotherly,
motherly, southerly,
grandmotherly

othes \ōz\ see ²OSE

othesis \äth-ə-səs\ prothesis,
hypothesis

othic \äth-ik\ gothic, neo-
Gothic, Ostrogothic,
Visigothic

othing \ō-<u>th</u>iŋ\ clothing,
loathing, underclothing

otho \ō-tō\ see ¹OTO

¹oti \ōt-ē\ see ¹OTE

²oti \ȯt-ē\ see AUGHTY

¹otia \ō-shə\ scotia, Scotia,
agnosia, dystocia,
Cappadocia, Nova Scotia

²otia \ōt-ē-ə\ see OTEA

otiable \ō-shə-bəl\ see OCIABLE

otiant \ō-shənt\ see OTIENT

¹otic \ät-ik\ Scotic, aquatic,
biotic, chaotic, demotic,
despotic, erotic, exotic,
hypnotic, narcotic, necrotic,
neurotic, Nilotic, osmotic,
psychotic, quixotic, robotic,
sclerotic, semiotic, abiotic,
anecdotic, asymptotic,
bibliotic, embryotic,
epiglottic, homeotic,
Huguenotic, idiotic,
macrobiotic, melanotic,
patriotic, posthypnotic,
sansculottic, symbiotic,
antibiotic, autoerotic,
compatriotic, homoerotic

²otic \ōt-ik\ lotic, photic,
aphotic, aprotic, dichotic,
robotic

³otic \ȯt-ik\ see AUTIC

otica \ät-i-kə\ erotica, exotica

otice \ōt-əs\ see OTUS

otics \ät-iks\ robotics,
astronautics, bibliotics—*also
plurals and possessives of
nouns listed at* ¹OTIC

otid \ät-əd\ see OTTED

otient \ō-shənt\ quotient,
negotiant

otile \ōt-ᵊl\ see OTAL

¹oting \ōt-iŋ\ see OATING

²oting \ät-iŋ\ see OTTING

¹otinous \ät-nəs\ see OTNESS

²otinous \ät-ᵊn-əs\ see
¹OTONOUS

otion \ō-shən\ Goshen,
groschen, lotion, motion,
notion, ocean, potion,
commotion, demotion,
devotion, emotion, Laotian,
promotion, slow-motion,
locomotion

otional \ō-shnəl\ motional,
notional, devotional,
emotional, promotional,
unemotional

otis \ōt-əs\ see OTUS

otist \ōt-əst\ protist, Scotist,
anecdotist

otive \ōt-iv\ motive, votive,
emotive, promotive,
automotive, locomotive

otl \ät-ᵊl\ see OTTLE

otle \ät-ᵊl\ see OTTLE

otley \ät-lē\ see OTLY

otly \ät-lē\ Atli, hotly, motley

otment \ät-mənt\ allotment,
ballottement

otness \ät-nəs\ hotness,
squatness

oto \ō-tō\ koto, photo, roto,
Sotho, Basotho, con moto, de
Soto, ex-voto, in toto, Kyoto,

Lesotho, Mosotho, Sesotho, Kumamoto, telephoto

otomous \ät-ə-məs\ dichotomous, hippopotamus

otomy \ät-ə-mē\ dichotomy, lobotomy, tracheotomy, episiotomy

oton \ōt-ᵊn\ croton, Jotun, oaten, Lofoten, verboten

¹otonous \ät-ᵊn-əs\ rottenness, monotonous, serotinous

²otonous \ät-nəs\ see OTNESS

otor \ōt-ər\ see OATER

otorist \ōt-ə-rəst\ see OTARIST

otory \ōt-ə-rē\ see OTARY

ots \äts\ Graz, hots, lots, Scots, Spaatz, swats, ersatz, Galati—*also plurals and possessives of nouns and third person singular presents of verbs listed at* ¹OT

otsk \ätsk\ see ATSK

otsman \ät-smən\ Scotsman, yachtsman

ott \ät\ see ¹OT

otta \ät-ə\ see ¹ATA

ottage \ät-ij\ cottage, plottage, pottage, wattage

ottal \ät-ᵊl\ see OTTLE

¹otte \ät\ see ¹OT

²otte \ȯt\ see ¹OUGHT

otted \ät-əd\ knotted, potted, spotted, carotid, proglottid, polka-dotted—*also pasts of verbs listed at* ¹OT

ottement \ät-mənt\ see OTMENT

otten \ät-ᵊn\ cotton, gotten, gratin, ratton, rotten, shotten, au gratin, begotten, forgotten, guncotton, ill-gotten, misbegotten, sauerbraten

ottenness \ät-ᵊn-əs\ see ¹OTONOUS

otter \ät-ər\ blotter, cotter, dotter, knotter, otter, plotter, potter, Potter, Qatar, rotter, spotter, squatter, swatter, Tatar, totter, trotter, water, alotter, boycotter, flyswatter, garroter, globe-trotter, pinspotter, sandlotter, alma mater, imperator, teeter-totter—*also comparatives of adjectives listed at* ¹OT *and words ending in* -water *listed at* ¹ATER

ottery \ät-ə-rē\ lottery, pottery, Tatary, tottery, watery

ottic \ät-ik\ see ¹OTIC

ottid \ät-əd\ see OTTED

ottie \ät-ē\ see ATI

otting \ät-iŋ\ jotting, wainscoting

ottis \ät-əs\ glottis, clematis, epiglottis, literatus

ottische \ät-ish\ see OTTISH

ottish \ät-ish\ hottish, schottische, Scottish, sottish, sanculottish

ottle \ät-ᵊl\ bottle, dottle, glottal, mottle, pottle, ratel, rotl, throttle, wattle, atlatl, bluebottle, Aristotle, monocotyl, Nahuatl, epiglottal, Quetzalcoatl

¹otto \ät-ō\ see ¹ATO

²otto \ȯt-ō\ see ¹AUTO

ottom \ät-əm\ see ¹ATUM

otty \ät-ē\ see ATI

otum \ōt-əm\ notum, scrotum, totem, factotum, teetotum

otun \ōt-ᵊn\ see OTON

oture \ō-chər\ see OACHER

otus \ōt-əs\ lotus, notice, Otis,
   denotice, Pelotas
oty \ȯt-ē\ see ¹AUGHTY
otyl \ät-ᵊl\ see OTTLE
¹ou \ō\ see ¹OW
²ou \ü\ see ¹EW
³ou \au̇\ see ²OW
oubled \ə-bəld\ see UBBLED
ouble \əb-əl\ see UBBLE
oubler \əb-lər\ doubler,
   bubbler, troubler
oubly \əb-lē\ see UBBLY
oubt \au̇t\ see ³OUT
oubted \au̇t-əd\ see OUTED
oubter \au̇t-ər\ see ²OUTER
¹ouc \ü\ see ¹EW
²ouc \ük\ see UKE
³ouc \u̇k\ see ¹OOK
ouce \üs\ see ¹USE
¹oucester \äs-tər\ see ¹OSTER
²oucester \ȯs-tər\ see ²OSTER
¹ouch \üch\ see ¹OOCH
²ouch \üsh\ see OUCHE
³ouch \əch\ see ¹UTCH
⁴ouch \au̇ch\ couch, crouch,
   grouch, ouch, pouch, slouch,
   vouch, avouch, debouch,
   scaramouch, retort pouch
ouche \üsh\ douche, louche,
   ruche, squoosh, swoosh,
   whoosh, barouche, capuche,
   cartouche, debouch, farouche,
   kurus, tarboosh, scaramouch
¹ouchy \əch-ē\ see UCHY
²ouchy \au̇-chē\ grouchy,
   pouchy, slouchy
ou'd \üd\ see UDE
¹oud \üd\ see UDE
²oud \au̇d\ boughed, bowed,
   cloud, crowd, loud, proud,
   shroud, stroud, aloud,
   becloud, enshroud,

highbrowed, house-proud,
purse-proud, Red Cloud,
unbowed, overcrowd,
thundercloud—*also pasts of
verbs listed at* ²OW
ouda \üd-ə\ see UDA
oudy \au̇d-ē\ see OWDY
oue \ü\ see ¹EW
ouf \üf\ see ¹OOF
ouffe \üf\ see ¹OOF
oug \əg\ see UG
¹ouge \üj\ see ¹UGE
²ouge \üzh\ see ²UGE
³ouge \au̇j\ gouge, scrouge
¹ough \ō\ see ¹OW
²ough \ü\ see ¹EW
³ough \au̇\ see ²OW
⁴ough \äk\ see ¹OCK
⁵ough \əf\ see UFF
⁶ough \ȯf\ see ²OFF
¹ougham \ōm\ see ¹OME
²ougham \üm\ see ¹OOM
oughed \au̇d\ see ²OUD
oughen \əf-ən\ see UFFIN
ougher \əf-ər\ see UFFER
oughie \əf-ē\ see UFFY
oughish \əf-ish\ see UFFISH
oughly \əf-lē\ see UFFLY
oughs \ōz\ see ²OSE
¹ought \ȯt\ aught, bought,
   brought, caught, dot, fought,
   fraught, ghat, lotte, naught,
   nought, ought, sought, taught,
   taut, thought, wrought,
   besought, distraught,
   dreadnought, forethought,
   handwrought, high-wrought,
   onslaught, self-taught, store-
   bought, unthought, aeronaut,
   aforethought, afterthought,
   aquanaut, argonaut, astronaut,

cosmonaut, juggernaut,
overbought, overwrought

²**ought** \aut\ see ³OUT

oughten \ȯt-ᵊn\ see AUTEN

oughty \aut-ē\ doughty,
droughty, gouty, pouty,
snouty, trouty

¹**oughy** \ō-ē\ see OWY

²**oughy** \ü-ē\ see EWY

ouie \ü-ē\ see EWY

ouille \ü-ē\ see EWY

¹**ouis** \ü-ē\ see EWY

²**ouis** \ü-əs\ see EWESS

ouk \ük\ see UKE

ouki \ü-kē\ see ¹OOKY

¹**oul** \ōl\ see ¹OLE

²**oul** \ül\ see ¹OOL

³**oul** \aul\ see ²OWL

¹**ould** \ōld\ see ¹OLD

²**ould** \ud\ see ¹OOD

oulder \ōl-dər\ see ¹OLDER

ouldered \ōl-dərd\ bouldered,
shouldered, round-shouldered,
square-shouldered—*also pasts
of verbs listed at* ¹OLDER

ouldest \ud-əst\ couldest,
shouldest, wouldest,
Talmudist

ouldn't \ud-ᵊnt\ shouldn't,
wouldn't

¹**oule** \ü-lē\ see ULY

²**oule** \ül\ see ¹OOL

ouled \ōld\ see ¹OLD

oulee \ü-lē\ see ULY

¹**ouleh** \ü-lə\ see ULA

²**ouleh** \ü-lē\ see ULY

ouli \ü-lē\ see ULY

oulie \ü-lē\ see ULY

ouling \au-liŋ\ see ²OWLING

oulish \ü-lish\ see OOLISH

¹**ou'll** \ül\ see ¹OOL

²**ou'll** \ul\ see ¹UL

oulle \ül\ see ¹OOL

oulli \ü-lē\ see ULY

oully \au-lē\ see ²OWLY

oult \ōlt\ see ¹OLT

oulter \ōl-tər\ see OLTER

oum \üm\ see ¹OOM

oumenal \ü-mən-ᵊl\ see UMINAL

¹**oun** \aun\ see ²OWN

²**oun** \ün\ see ¹OON

ounce \auns\ bounce, flounce,
jounce, ounce, pounce,
trounce, announce, denounce,
enounce, pronounce,
renounce, mispronounce

ouncement \aun-smənt\
announcement,
denouncement,
pronouncement

ouncer \aun-sər\ bouncer,
announcer

ouncil \aun-səl\ see OUNSEL

ouncy \aun-sē\ bouncy, flouncy,
jouncy, viscountcy

¹**ound** \ünd\ stound, swound,
wound—*also pasts of verbs
listed at* ¹OON

²**ound** \aund\ bound, crowned,
found, ground, hound, mound,
pound, Pound, round, sound,
stound, swound, wound,
abound, aground, all-round,
around, astound, background,
black-crowned, bloodhound,
campground, chowhound,
compound, confound,
coonhound, dachshund,
deerhound, deskbound,
earthbound, eastbound,
elkhound, expound,
fairground, fogbound, foot-
pound, foreground, foxhound,
go-round, greyhound,

hardbound, hellhound, hidebound, homebound, horehound, housebound, icebound, impound, inbound, newfound, newshound, northbound, outbound, playground, pot-bound, profound, propound, rebound, redound, resound, rockbound, snowbound, softbound, southbound, spellbound, stone-ground, stormbound, strikebound, surround, unbound, well-found, westbound, white-crowned, wolfhound, year-round, aboveground, all-around, belowground, battleground, decompound, go-around, muscle-bound, outward-bound, paperbound, Puget Sound, runaround, turnaround, ultrasound, underground, weather-bound, wraparound, merry-go-round, superabound—*also pasts of verbs listed at* ²OWN

oundal \aun-d°l\ poundal, roundel

oundary \aun-drē\ see OUNDRY

ounded \aun-dəd\ drownded, rounded, confounded, unbounded, unfounded, well-founded, well-grounded

oundel \aun-d°l\ see OUNDAL

ounder \aun-dər\ bounder, flounder, founder, grounder, pounder, rounder, sounder, all-rounder, backgrounder, dumbfounder, tenpounder

ounding \aun-diŋ\ drownding, grounding, sounding, astounding, high-sounding, rockhounding

¹oundless \ün-ləs\ see OONLESS

²oundless \aun-ləs\ groundless, soundless

oundlet \aun-lət\ see OWNLET

oundling \aun-liŋ\ foundling, groundling

oundly \aund-lē\ roundly, soundly

oundness \aun-nəs\ roundness, unsoundness

oundry \aun-drē\ boundary, foundry

¹ounds \ünz\ see OONS

²ounds \aunz\ hounds, zounds, inbounds, Barren Grounds, out-of-bounds—*also plurals and possessives of nouns and third person singular presents of verbs listed at* ²OUND

oundsel \aun-səl\ see OUNSEL

oundsman \aunz-mən\ see OWNSMAN

ounge \aunj\ lounge, scrounge, chaise lounge

¹ounger \aun-jər\ lounger, scrounger

²ounger \əŋ-gər\ see ¹ONGER

ounker \əŋ-kər\ see UNKER

ounsel \aun-səl\ council, counsel, groundsel

¹ount \änt\ see ²ANT

²ount \aunt\ count, fount, mount, account, amount, demount, discount, dismount, high-count, miscount, recount, remount, seamount, surmount, viscount, catamount, paramount, rediscount, tantamount, undercount

ountable \aunt-ə-bəl\

countable, accountable,
demountable, discountable,
surmountable,
insurmountable,
unaccountable

ountain \aůnt-ᵊn\ fountain,
mountain, transmountain, cat-
a-mountain, Riding Mountain

ountcy \aůn-sē\ see OUNCY

ounter \aůnt-ər\ counter,
discounter, encounter,
recounter, rencounter

ountess \aůnt-əs\ countess,
viscountess

ountie \aůnt-ē\ see OUNTY

ounting \aůnt-iŋ\ mounting,
accounting

ounty \aůnt-ē\ bounty, county,
Mountie, viscounty

¹oup \ōp\ see OPE

²oup \ü\ see ¹EW

³oup \üp\ see ¹OOP

¹oupe \ōp\ see OPE

²oupe \üp\ see ¹OOP

ouper \ü-pər\ see OOPER

oupie \ü-pē\ see OOPY

ouping \ü-piŋ\ see OOPING

ouple \əp-əl\ see ¹UPLE

ouplet \əp-lət\ see ¹UPLET

oupous \ü-pəs\ see UPUS

oupy \ü-pē\ see OOPY

¹our \ōr\ see ¹OR

²our \ůr\ see ¹URE

³our \aůr\ see ²OWER

⁴our \är\ see ³AR

⁵our \ər\ see ¹EUR

oura \ůr-ə\ see URA

ourable \ōr-ə-bəl\ see ¹ORABLE

ourage \ər-ij\ courage,
demurrage, discourage,
encourage

¹ourbon \ər-bən\ see ¹URBAN

²ourbon \ůr-bən\ see ²URBAN

¹ource \ōrs\ see ¹OURSE

²ource \órs\ see ¹ORSE

¹ourceful \ōrs-fəl\ see
¹ORCEFUL

²ourceful \órs-fəl\ see ORSEFUL

ourcing \ōr-siŋ\ outsourcing—
*also present participles of
verbs listed at* ¹OURSE

ourd \ōrd\ see OARD

ourde \ůrd\ see ¹URED

¹ou're \ōr\ see ¹OR

²ou're \ü-ər\ see ¹EWER

³ou're \ůr\ see ¹URE

⁴ou're \ər\ see ¹EUR

oured \ōrd\ see OARD

¹ourer \ōr-ər\ see ¹ORER

²ourer \ůr-ər\ see ¹URER

³ourer \aůr-ər\ flowerer,
scourer, deflowerer,
devourer—*also comparatives
of adjectives listed at* ²OWER

¹ourg \ůr\ see ¹URE

²ourg \ərg\ see ERG

¹ourge \ərj\ see URGE

²ourge \órj\ see ORGE

ourger \ər-jər\ see ERGER

ouri \ůr-ē\ see ¹URY

¹ourier \ůr-ē-ər\ courier,
couturier, couturiere, vaunt-
courier

²ourier \ər-ē-ər\ see URRIER

¹ouring \ōr-iŋ\ see ORING

²ouring \ůr-iŋ\ see URING

ourish \ər-ish\ currish, flourish,
nourish, amateurish

ourist \ůr-əst\ see URIST

ourly \aůr-lē\ dourly, hourly,
sourly

¹ourn \ōrn\ see ¹ORN

²ourn \ərn\ see URN

³ourn \órn\ see ²ORN

ournal \ərn-ᵊl\ see ERNAL

ournament \ȯr-nə-mənt\ see ORNAMENT

ourne \ōrn\ see ¹ORN

¹ourney \ər-nē\ Bernie, Ernie, ferny, gurney, journey, tourney, attorney

²ourney \ȯr-nē\ see ORNY

ourneyer \ər-nē-ər\ journeyer, vernier

ournful \ȯrn-fəl\ see ORNFUL

ourning \ȯr-niŋ\ see ORNING

ournment \ərn-mənt\ see ERNMENT

¹ours \ōrz\ see ¹OORS

²ours \ärz\ see ARS

³ours \ȯrz\ see ²OORS

⁴ours \aȯrz\ ours, after-hours— *also plurals and possessives of nouns and third singular presents of verbs listed at* ²OWER

⁵ours \ȯr\ see ¹URE

¹ourse \ōrs\ coarse, course, force, hoarse, source, concourse, deforce, discourse, divorce, enforce, perforce, racecourse, recourse, resource, intercourse, reinforce, telecourse, tour de force, watercourse

²ourse \ȯrs\ see ¹ORSE

oursome \ȯr-səm\ see ORSUM

¹ourt \ȯrt\ see ¹ORT

²ourt \ȯrt\ see ¹URT

ourtesy \ərt-ə-sē\ courtesy, curtesy, discourtesy

ourth \ȯrth\ see ¹ORTH

ourtier \ȯr-chər\ see ORCHER

¹ourtly \ōrt-lē\ see ¹ORTLY

²ourtly \ȯrt-lē\ see ²ORTLY

oury \aȯr-ē\ see OWERY

¹ous \ü\ see ¹EW

²ous \üs\ see ¹USE

¹ousa \ü-sə\ see ¹USA

²ousa \ü-zə\ see ²USA

ousal \aȯ-zəl\ housel, spousal, tousle, arousal, carousal

ousand \aȯz-ᵊn\ see OWSON

¹ouse \üs\ see ¹USE

²ouse \aȯs\ blouse, chiaus, chouse, douse, Gauss, grouse, house, Klaus, Laos, louse, mouse, scouse, souse, spouse, Strauss, baghouse, bathhouse, Bauhaus, birdhouse, blockhouse, bughouse, bunkhouse, cathouse, chophouse, clubhouse, cookhouse, courthouse, deckhouse, degauss, delouse, doghouse, dollhouse, dormouse, espouse, farmhouse, firehouse, flophouse, gashouse, gatehouse, glasshouse, greenhouse, guardhouse, henhouse, hothouse, icehouse, in-house, jailhouse, lighthouse, lobscouse, longhouse, madhouse, Manaus, nuthouse, outhouse, penthouse, playhouse, poorhouse, roadhouse, roughhouse, roundhouse, schoolhouse, smokehouse, springhouse, statehouse, storehouse, teahouse, titmouse, tollhouse, warehouse, washhouse, wheelhouse, White House, whorehouse, workhouse, boardinghouse, clearinghouse, coffeehouse, countinghouse,

customhouse, house-to-house,
meetinghouse, Mickey
Mouse, overblouse,
pilothouse, porterhouse,
powerhouse, slaughterhouse,
sugarhouse, summerhouse,
treasure-house, Westinghouse

³**ouse** \aůz\ blouse, bouse,
bowse, browse, douse, dowse,
drowse, house, mouse, rouse,
spouse, touse, arouse,
carouse, delouse, doss-house,
espouse, rehouse, roughhouse,
warehouse—*also plurals and
possessives of nouns and
third person singular presents
of verbs listed at* ²ow

⁴**ouse** \üz\ see ²USE

ousel \aů-zəl\ see OUSAL

ouser \aů-zər\ dowser, houser,
mouser, schnauzer, trouser,
wowser, warehouser, rabble-
rouser

ousin \əz-ᵊn\ see ¹OZEN

ousinage \əz-ᵊn-ij\ cousinage,
cozenage

ousing \aů-ziŋ\ housing,
rousing, rabble-rousing

¹**ousle** \ü-zəl\ see ²USAL

²**ousle** \aů-zəl\ see OUSAL

ousse \üs\ see ¹USE

ousseau \ü-sō\ see USOE

¹**oust** \aůst\ Faust, joust, oust,
roust—*also pasts of verbs
listed at* ²OUSE

²**oust** \üst\ see OOST

ouste \üst\ see OOST

¹**ousy** \aů-zē\ see OWSY

²**ousy** \aů-sē\ mousy, Firdawsi

¹**out** \ü\ see ¹EW

²**out** \üt\ see UTE

³**out** \aůt\ bout, clout, doubt,
drought, flout, glout, gout,
grout, knout, kraut, lout, out,
pout, rout, route, scout, shout,
snout, spout, sprout, stout,
tout, trout, ablaut, about, all-
out, bailout, blackout, blissed-
out, blowout, breakout,
breechclout, brownout,
burned-out, burnout,
checkout, clapped-out,
closeout, cookout, cop-out,
cutout, devout, dishclout,
downspout, dropout, dugout,
eelpout, fade-out, fallout, far-
out, flameout, flat-out,
foldout, force-out, freak-out,
freeze out, full-out, gross-out,
groundout, handout, hangout,
hideout, holdout, ice-out,
knockout, layout, lights-out,
lockout, lookout, misdoubt,
payout, phaseout, pitchout,
printout, psych-out, pullout,
punch-out, putout, rainspout,
readout, redoubt, rollout,
sellout, setout, shakeout,
shoot-out, shutout, sick-out,
sold-out, spaced-out, speak-
out, spinout, stakeout,
standout, straight-out,
stressed-out, stretch-out,
strikeout, takeout, thought-
out, throughout, throw out,
time-out, tryout, turnout,
umlaut, veg out, walkout,
washed-out, washout, way-
out, whacked-out, whiteout,
wigged-out, wipeout, without,
workout, worn-out, zonked-
out, all get-out, carryout,
diner-out, down-and-out,
falling-out, gadabout,

hereabout, knockabout, layabout, out-and-out, roundabout, rouseabout, roustabout, runabout, sauerkraut, stirabout, thereabout, turnabout, walkabout, waterspout

¹oute \üt\ see UTE

²oute \aủt\ see ³OUT

outed \aủt-əd\ snouted, spouted, undoubted—*also pasts of verbs listed at* ³OUT

¹outer \üt-ər\ see UTER

²outer \aủt-ər\ doubter, flouter, grouter, outer, pouter, router, scouter, shouter, spouter, touter, come-outer, down-and-outer, out-and-outer

¹outh \üth\ see ²OOTH

²outh \aủth\ mouth, routh, scouth, south, bad-mouth, goalmouth, loudmouth, poor-mouth, blabbermouth, cottonmouth, hand-to-mouth, motormouth, word-of-mouth

outerly \əth-ər-lē\ see OTHERLY

outhey \aủ-thē\ see OUTHY

outhful \üth-fəl\ see UTHFUL

outhie \ü-thē\ see OOTHY

outhly \üth-lē\ see OOTHLY

outhy \aủ-thē\ mouthy, Southey

outi \üt-ē\ see ¹OOTY

outing \aủt-iŋ\ outing, scouting

outish \aủt-ish\ loutish, snoutish

outre \üt-ər\ see UTER

outrement \ü-trə-mənt\ see UTRIMENT

outs \aủts\ hereabouts, ins and outs, thereabouts, whereabouts

outy \aủt-ē\ see OUGHTY

ou've \üv\ see ³OVE

ouver \ü-vər\ see ³OVER

oux \ü\ see ¹EW

ouy \ē\ see ¹EE

ouyhnhnm \in-əm\ see INIM

ouzel \ü-zəl\ see ²USAL

¹ov \äf\ see ¹OFF

²ov \óf\ see ²OFF

ova \ō-və\ nova, Cralova, Jehovah, Moldova, bossa nova, Casanova, Czestochowa, Kemerovo, supernova

ovable \ü-və-bəl\ movable, provable, approvable, disprovable, immovable, improvable, removable, irremovable

ovah \ō-və\ see OVA

oval \ü-vəl\ approval, removal, disapproval

ovat \əv-ət\ see OVET

¹ove \əv\ dove, glove, love, of, shove, above, foxglove, hereof, kid-glove, ringdove, thereof, truelove, whereof, ladylove, light-o'-love, roman-fleuve, turtledove, unheard of, well-thought-of, hereinabove

²ove \ōv\ clove, cove, dove, drove, fauve, grove, hove, Jove, mauve, rove, stove, strove, throve, trove, wove, alcove, behove, cookstove, mangrove, woodstove, Garden Grove, interwove, treasure trove

³ove \üv\ groove, move, poof, poove, prove, you've, approve, behoove, commove, disprove, improve, remove, reprove, disapprove

¹**ovel** \äv-əl\ grovel, novel, antinovel, Yaroslavl

²**ovel** \əv-əl\ grovel, hovel, shovel

ovement \üv-mənt\ movement, improvement

¹**oven** \əv-ən\ coven, oven, sloven

²**oven** \ō-vən\ cloven, coven, woven, Beethoven, handwoven, interwoven

¹**over** \əv-ər\ cover, glover, hover, lover, plover, bedcover, discover, dustcover, hardcover, re-cover, recover, slipcover, softcover, uncover, windhover, undercover

²**over** \ō-vər\ clover, Dover, drover, Grover, over, plover, rover, stover, trover, allover, changeover, crossover, cutover, flashover, flopover, flyover, hangover, Hannover, Hanover, holdover, layover, leftover, makeover, moreover, once-over, Passover, popover, pullover, pushover, rollover, runover, slipover, spillover, stopover, strikeover, takeover, turnover, voice-over, walkover, warmed-over, carryover, crossing-over, going-over, Strait of Dover

³**over** \ü-vər\ groover, Hoover, louver, mover, prover, earthmover, improver, maneuver, remover, reprover, Vancouver, disapprover

⁴**over** \äv-ər\ see ¹AVER

overable \əv-rə-bəl\ discoverable, recoverable, irrecoverable

overly \əv-ər-lē\ loverly, Sir Roger de Coverley

overt \ō-vərt\ covert, overt

overy \əv-rē\ discovery, recovery

ovet \əv-ət\ covet, lovat

ovey \ə-vē\ covey, lovey-dovey

ovian \ō-vē-ən\ Jovian, Markovian, Pavlovian, Varsovian

ovie \ü-vē\ see OOVY

ovo \ō-vō\ Provo, ab ovo, de novo, Porto Novo

ovost \äv-əst\ see AVIST

ovsk \òfsk\ Dnepropetrovsk, Petropavlovsk

¹**ow** \ō\ beau, blow, bow, bro, Chou, crow, do, doe, dough, ewe, floe, flow, foe, fro, froe, frow, glow, go, grow, ho, hoe, jo, Jo, joe, Joe, know, lo, low, mho, mot, mow, no, No, O, oh, owe, Po, Poe, pow, pro, rho, roe, row, schmo, sew, shew, show, sloe, slow, snow, so, sow, stow, Stowe, strow, though, throe, throw, toe, tow, trow, whoa, woe, yo, aglow, ago, airflow, airglow, alow, although, backflow, backhoe, bandeau, Baotou, barlow, bateau, below, bestow, bon mot, Bordeaux, bravo, by-blow, cachepot, caló, Carlow, chapeau, chateau, Chi-Rho, cockcrow, cornrow, crossbow, Day-Glo, dayglow, Defoe, de trop, deathblow, deco, downbow, elbow, escrow,

fencerow, flambeau, flyblow,
fogbow, forego, foreknow,
forgo, Fuzhou, galop, Gateau,
genro, gigot, go-slow,
Gounod, Guangzhou, gung
ho, hallo, Hangzhou,
Hankow, heave-ho, hedgerow,
heigh-ho, hello, hollo, hullo,
inflow, jabot, Jane Doe, jim
crow, Jinzhou, John Doe,
Hounslow, kayo, KO,
Kwangchow, Lanzhou,
longbow, low-low, macho,
mahoe, maillot, manteau,
Marlowe, matelot, merlot,
Meursault, Miró, misknow,
Moho, mojo, Monroe,
morceau, Moscow, mucro,
mudflow, nightglow, no-no,
no-show, nouveau, outflow,
outgo, outgrow, oxbow,
Paot'ou, Pernod, picot, Pinot,
plateau, pronto, Quanzhou,
rainbow, reflow, regrow, repo,
reseau, rondeau, rondo,
Roseau, rouleau, Rousseau,
sabot, salchow, scarecrow,
self-sow, serow, shadblow,
Shantou, sideshow, skid row,
Soho, so-so, sourdough,
sunbow, Suzhou, tableau,
Taizhou, tiptoe, Thoreau,
tonneau, trousseau, Trudeau,
uh-oh, unsew, up-bow,
upthrow, van Gogh, Watteau,
windrow, windthrow,
Xuzhou, Zhangzhou,
Zhengzhou, Zhuzhon, Zibo,
afterglow, aikido, alpenglow,
Angelo, apropos, art deco, art
nouveau, audio, Baguio,
Bamako, barrio, Bergamo,

bibelot, Bilbao, bordereau,
Borneo, buffalo, Buffalo,
bungalow, Bushido, buteo,
calico, cameo, cachalot,
cembalo, centimo, CEO,
chassepot, cheerio, Cicero,
Clemenceau, cogito, comedo,
comme il faut, Comoro,
counterflow, curaçao,
Curaçao, curassow, curio,
daimyo, danio, dataflow,
Delano, Diderot, do-si-do,
domino, dynamo, embryo,
entrepôt, Erato, escargot,
Eskimo, extrados, fabliau,
folio, fricandeau, furbelow,
gigolo, go-no-go, guacharo,
hammertoe, haricot, heel-and-
toe, hetero, HMO, Holy Joe,
Idaho, indigo, Jericho,
kakapo, Kosciuszko, latigo,
long-ago, Maceió,
Manchukuo, Mario, massicot,
medico, Mexico, mistletoe,
modulo, Monaco, Navaho,
Navajo, NCO, nuncio, oleo,
olio, overflow, overgrow,
overthrow, ovolo, Pamlico,
Papago, patio, peridot, picaro,
piccolo, Pierrot, polio,
pomelo, pompano, portico,
PPO, Prospero, proximo, quid
pro quo, radio, raree-show,
ratio, Richard Roe,
Rochambeau, rococo, rodeo,
Romeo, saddlebow, Sapporo,
sapsago, Scorpio, semipro,
sloppy joe, so-and-so, SRO,
standing O, status quo, stereo,
stop-and-go, studio, subito,
tallyho, tangelo, Taranto,
ticktacktoe, tic-tac-toe, tit-tat-

toe, TKO, to-and-fro, Tokyo,
tombolo, touch-and-go,
touraco, tournedos, tremolo,
tuckahoe, tupelo, UFO,
ultimo, undergo, undertow,
Veneto, vertigo, vibrio,
virago, vireo, zydeco,
Antonio, Arapaho, centesimo,
con spirito, continuo, DMSO,
Etobicoke, ex nihilo,
fantastico, fellatio, Fernando
Póo, fortissimo, Geronimo,
get-up-and-go, Guantanamo,
hereinbelow, in utero, in
vacuo, La Rochfoucauld,
lentissimo, lothario,
magnifico, malapropos,
milesimo, New Mexico,
oregano, politico, portfolio,
presidio, prestissimo,
punctilio, Querétaro, Quintana
Roo, Rosario, quo warranto,
Sarajevo, scenario, simpatico,
Zhangjiakou, ab initio,
archipelago, braggadocio,
duodecimo, ex officio,
generalissimo, impresario,
internuncio, oratorio,
Paramaribo, pianissimo, rose
of Jericho

²**ow** \aů\ bough, bow, brow,
chiao, chow, ciao, cow, dhow,
Dou, dow, Dow, Frau, hao,
how, howe, Howe, jow, Lao,
mow, now, ow, plow, pow,
prau, prow, row, scow,
slough, sough, sow, Tao, tau,
thou, vow, wow, Yao, allow,
avow, Belau, Bissau,
bowwow, cacao, cahow,
Callao, Davao, chowchow,
chow chow, Cracow, Donau,
endow, enow, erenow,
eyebrow, gangplow, Haikou,
Hankow, hausfrau, haymow,
highbrow, hoosegow,
Jungfrau, know-how, kowtow,
Krakow, landau, lowbrow,
luau, Lucknow, Macao,
meow, miaow, Moscow,
Niihau, nohow, Pelau,
powwow, Qing-dao,
snowplow, somehow,
Zwickau, anyhow, curaçao,
Curaçao, disallow, disavow,
disendow, middlebrow,
Guinea-Bissau, Marianao,
Mindanao, holier-than-thou

³**ow** \òv\ see ²OFF

owa \ō-vᵊ\ see OVA

¹**owable** \ō-ə-bəl\ knowable,
sewable, unknowable

²**owable** \aů-ə-bəl\ plowable,
allowable, disavowable

owage \ō-ij\ flowage, stowage,
towage

¹**owal** \ō-əl\ see OEL

²**owal** \aůl\ see ²OWL

¹**owan** \ō-ən\ see ¹OAN

²**owan** \aů-ən\ Gawain, gowan,
rowan, rowen, Bandar Seri
Begawan

¹**oward** \ōrd\ see OARD

²**oward** \aůrd\ see OWERED

¹**owd** \üd\ see UDE

²**owd** \aůd\ see ²OUD

owdah \aůd-ə\ see ³AUDE

owder \aůd-ər\ chowder,
powder, gunpowder, five-
spice powder—*also
comparatives of adjectives
listed at* ²OUD

owdown \ō-daůn\ blowdown,

lowdown, showdown,
slowdown

owdy \aừd-ē\ cloudy, dowdy,
howdy, rowdy, cum laude,
pandowdy, magna cum laude,
summa cum laude

owe \ō\ see ¹OW

¹owed \ōd\ see ODE

²owed \aừd\ see ²OUD

owedly \aừ-əd-lē\ allowedly,
avowedly

owel \aừl\ see ²OWL

oweling \aừ-liŋ\ see ²OWLING

¹owell \aừl\ see ²OWL

²owell \ō-əl\ see OEL

¹owen \aừ-ən\ see ²OWAN

²owen \ō-ən\ see ¹OAN

¹ower \ōr\ see ¹OR

²ower \aừr\ bower, cower, dour,
dower, flour, flower, gaur,
giaour, glower, hour, lower,
our, plower, power, scour,
shower, sour, tour, tower,
vower, avower, cornflower,
deflower, devour, embower,
empower, firepower, high-
power, man-hour, mayflower,
moonflower, off-hour,
pasqueflower, Peshawar,
repower, safflower, sunflower,
wallflower, watchtower,
wildflower, willpower,
candlepower, cauliflower,
disendower, Eisenhower,
overpower, passionflower,
person-hour, Schopenhauer,
superpower, sweet-and-sour,
thundershower, waterpower,
womanpower

³ower \ō-ər\ see ⁵OER

owered \aừrd\ coward,
flowered, powered, towered,

high-powered, ivory-towered,
superpowered,
underpowered—*also pasts of
verbs listed at* ²OWER

owerer \aừr-ər\ see ³OURER

owerful \aừr-fəl\ flowerful,
powerful

owering \aừ-riŋ\ lowering,
nonflowering

owery \aừr-ē\ bowery, cauri,
dowry, floury, flowery, kauri,
Maori, showery

owff \aừf\ howff, langlauf

owhee \ō-ē\ see OWY

owie \aừ-ē\ Maui, zowie

owing \ō-iŋ\ see ¹OING

¹owl \ōl\ see ¹OLE

²owl \aừl\ bowel, cowl, dowel,
foul, fowl, growl, Howell,
howl, jowl, owl, prowl, rowel,
scowl, towel, trowel, vowel,
yowl, avowal, batfowl,
befoul, embowel, peafowl,
seafowl, wildfowl, disavowal,
disembowel, waterfowl

owland \ō-lənd\ lowland,
Poland, Roland

owledge \äl-ij\ college,
knowledge, acknowledge,
foreknowledge

¹owler \ō-lər\ see OLLER

²owler \aừ-lər\ growler, howler,
waterfowler

owless \ō-ləs\ see OLUS

owline \ō-lən\ see OLON

¹owling \ō-liŋ\ see OLLING

²owling \aừ-liŋ\ cowling,
growling, howling, toweling,
antifouling, biofouling,
waterfowling

owlock \äl-ək\ see OLOCH

¹owly \ō-lē\ see ¹OLY

²**owly** \aủ-lē\ foully, growly,
  haole, jowly
¹**owman** \ō-mən\ see OMAN
²**owman** \aủ-mən\ bowman,
  cowman, plowman
ow-me \ō-mē\ see OAMY
¹**own** \ōn\ see ¹ONE
²**own** \aủn\ brown, Brown,
  clown, crown, down, Down,
  drown, frown, gown, lown,
  noun, town, blowdown,
  boomtown, breakdown,
  Bridgetown, bringdown,
  Capetown, clampdown,
  closedown, comedown,
  cooldown, countdown,
  crackdown, crosstown,
  downtown, drawdown,
  embrown, facedown,
  Freetown, Georgetown,
  George Town, godown,
  hoedown, hometown,
  Jamestown, knockdown,
  letdown, lockdown,
  lookdown, lowdown,
  markdown, meltdown,
  nightgown, pastedown,
  phasedown, pronoun,
  pushdown, put-down, renown,
  rubdown, rundown, scale-
  down, shakedown,
  showdown, shutdown, sit-
  down, slowdown, Southdown,
  splashdown, stand-down,
  step-down, stripped-down,
  sundown, thumbs-down, tie-
  down, top-down, touchdown,
  turndown, uncrown, uptown,
  Von Braun, write-down,
  Youngstown, Allentown,
  broken-down, buttondown,
  Charlottetown, Chinatown,

dressing-down, eiderdown,
  Germantown, hand-me-down,
  reach-me-down, shantytown,
  tumbledown, upside down,
  watered-down, man-about-
  town
ownded \aủn-dəd\ see OUNDED
ownding \aủn-diŋ\ see
  OUNDING
¹**owned** \ōnd\ see ¹ONED
²**owned** \aủnd\ see ²OUND
¹**owner** \ō-nər\ see ¹ONER
²**owner** \ü-nər\ see OONER
³**owner** \aủ-nər\ browner,
  crowner, downer, sundowner
owness \ō-nəs\ see ²ONUS
ownia \ō-nē-ə\ see ¹ONIA
ownie \aủ-nē\ see OWNY
¹**owning** \ō-niŋ\ see ²ONING
²**owning** \aủ-ning\ Browning—
  *also present participles of
  verbs listed at* ²OWN
ownish \aủ-nish\ brownish,
  clownish
ownlet \aủn-lət\ roundlet,
  townlet
ownsman \aủnz-mən\
  gownsman, groundsman,
  roundsman, townsman
owny \aủ-nē\ brownie, browny,
  downy, townie
owper \ü-pər\ see OOPER
owry \aủr-ē\ see OWERY
owse \aủz\ see ²OUSE
owser \aủ-zər\ see OUSER
owson \aủz-ᵊn\ thousand,
  advowson
owster \ō-stər\ see OASTER
owsy \aủ-zē\ blousy, blowsy,
  drowsy, lousy
owth \ōth\ both, growth, loath,
  loth, oath, quoth, sloth, troth,

wroth, betroth, outgrowth,
upgrowth, Alioth,
intergrowth, overgrowth,
undergrowth

owy \ō-ē\ blowy, Chloe,
doughy, joey, Joey, showy,
snowy, towhee, echoey,
kalanchoe

owys \ō-əs\ see ³OIS

ox \äks\ box, cox, fox, Fox,
gox, Knox, lox, ox, pax,
phlox, pox, aurochs, bandbox,
boondocks, cowpox, detox,
dreadlocks, firebox, Fort
Knox, gearbox, gravlax,
hatbox, hotbox, icebox,
jukebox, lockbox, mailbox,
matchbox, musk-ox, outfox,
pillbox, postbox, redox,
saltbox, sandbox, skybox,
smallpox, snuffbox, soapbox,
strongbox, sweatbox, toolbox,
unbox, volvox, witness-box,
workbox, Xerox, chatterbox,
equinox, orthodox, Orthodox,
paradox, pillar-box,
shadowbox, Skinner box,
tinderbox, econobox, Greek
Orthodox, heterodox,
homeobox, jack-in-the-box,
unorthodox, neoorthodox,
dementia praecox—*also
plurals and possessives of
nouns and third person
singular presents of verbs
listed at* ¹OCK

oxen \äk-sən\ oxen,
Niedersachsen

oxer \äk-sər\ boxer, Boxer,
bobby-soxer

oxie \äk-sē\ see OXY

oxin \äk-sən\ coxswain, tocsin,

toxin, dioxin, aflatoxin,
mycotoxin

oxswain \äk-sən\ see OXIN

oxy \äk-sē\ boxy, doxy, foxy,
moxie, oxy, proxy, epoxy,
orthodoxy, Orthodoxy,
heterodoxy, neoorthodoxy

oy \ȯi\ boy, buoy, cloy, coy,
foy, goy, hoy, joy, Joy, koi,
ploy, poi, Roy, soy, strawy,
toy, troy, Troy, ahoy, alloy,
Amoy, annoy, batboy,
bellboy, bok choy, borzoi,
busboy, callboy, carboy,
charpoy, choirboy, convoy,
cowboy, decoy, deploy,
destroy, doughboy, employ,
enjoy, envoy, fly-boy,
footboy, Hanoi, hautbois,
highboy, houseboy, killjoy,
Khoikhoi, Leroy, linkboy,
lowboy, McCoy, newsboy,
pak choi, playboy, plowboy,
po'boy, postboy, potboy,
Quemoy, Rob Roy, Saint
Croix, Savoy, schoolboy,
sepoy, tallboy, teapoy,
Tolstoy, tomboy, travois,
viceroy, Adonai, attaboy,
bullyboy, copyboy, corduroy,
hoi polloi, Illinois, Iroquois,
Kawagoe, maccaboy, Niterói,
overjoy, paperboy, redeploy,
reemploy, Tinkertoy, Helen of
Troy

oya \ȯi-ə\ see OIA

oyable \ȯi-ə-bəl\ deployable,
employable

¹oyal \īl\ see ¹ILE

²oyal \ȯil\ see OIL

oyalist \ȯi-ə-ləst\ loyalist,
royalist

oyalty \ȯil-tē\ loyalty, royalty,
  disloyalty, viceroyalty
oyance \ȯi-əns\ buoyance,
  joyance, annoyance,
  chatoyance, clairvoyance,
  flamboyance
oyancy \ȯi-ən-sē\ buoyancy,
  chatoyancy, flamboyancy
oyant \ȯi-ənt\ buoyant,
  chatoyant, clairvoyant,
  flamboyant
oyce \ois\ see OICE
oyd \ȯid\ see ¹OID
oyden \ȯi-dᵊn\ Croydon,
  hoyden
oydon \ȯi-dᵊn\ see OYDEN
oyed \ȯid\ see ¹OID
oyen \ȯi-ən\ doyen, Goyen,
  Iroquoian
oyer \ȯir\ coir, foyer, moire,
  caloyer, destroyer
oyes \oiz\ see ²OISE
oying \ȯiŋ\ see AWING
oyle \ȯil\ see OIL
oyless \ȯi-ləs\ joyless, Troilus

oyment \ȯi-mənt\ deployment,
  employment, enjoyment,
  unemployment
oyne \ȯin\ see ¹OIN
¹oyo \ȯi-ō\ boyo, arroyo
²oyo \ȯi-ə\ see OIA
o-yo \ō-yō\ see ²OLLO
oyster \ȯi-stər\ see OISTER
¹oz \əz\ see ¹EUSE
²oz \ȯz\ see ¹AUSE
³oz \ōz\ see ²OSE
oza \ō-zə\ see ²OSA
oze \ōz\ see ²OSE
¹ozen \əz-ᵊn\ cousin, cozen,
  dozen, cater-cousin
²ozen \ōz-ᵊn\ see OSEN
ozenage \əz-ᵊn-ij\ see
  OUSINAGE
ozer \ō-zər\ see ¹OSER
ozily \ō-zə-lē\ see OSILY
¹ozo \ō-sō\ see ¹OSO
²ozo \ō-zō\ see ²OSO
ozy \ō-zē\ see OSY
ozzer \äz-ər\ rozzer, alcazar
ozzle \äz-əl\ Basel, Basil,
  nozzle, schnozzle

u

¹**u** \ü\ see ¹EW

²**u** \ə\ Chang-de, hao-tzu

¹**ua** \ü-ə\ skua, Karlsruhe, lehua, Quechua, Timucua

²**ua** \ä\ see ¹A

uable \ü-ə-bəl\ chewable, doable, suable, viewable, accruable, construable, renewable

ual \ü-əl\ see ¹UEL

uan \ü-ən\ bruin, ruin, Siouan, yuan

uancy \ü-ən-sē\ see UENCY

uant \ü-ənt\ see UENT

uart \ürt\ see ¹URT

ub \əb\ blub, chub, club, cub, drub, dub, flub, grub, hub, nub, pub, rub, scrub, shrub, slub, snub, stub, sub, tub, bathtub, flubdub, hubbub, nightclub, washtub, overdub, Beelzebub

uba \ü-bə\ Cuba, juba, scuba, tuba, Aruba, Santiago de Cuba

ubal \ü-bəl\ Jubal, nubile, ruble, tubal

uban \ü-bən\ see EUBEN

ubbard \əb-ərd\ cupboard, Mother Hubbard

ubber \əb-ər\ blubber, clubber, drubber, dubber, grubber, lubber, rubber, scrubber, slubber, snubber, tubber, landlubber, nightclubber, money-grubber

ubbery \əb-rē\ blubbery, rubbery, shrubbery

ubbily \əb-ə-lē\ bubbly, chubbily, grubbily

ubbin \əb-ən\ dubbin, nubbin

ubbing \əb-iŋ\ drubbing, rubbing, slubbing, landlubbing

ubble \əb-əl\ bubble, double, nubble, rubble, stubble, trouble, abubble, redouble, undouble, hubble-bubble

ubbled \ə-bəld\ bubbled, doubled, troubled, redoubled

ubbler \əb-lər\ see OUBLER

¹**ubbly** \əb-lē\ bubbly, doubly, nubbly, stubbly

²**ubbly** \əb-ə-lē\ see UBBILY

ubby \əb-ē\ chubby, clubby, cubby, grubby, hubby, nubby, Rabi, scrubby, shrubby, snubby, stubby, tubby

ube \üb\ boob, cube, lube, rube, tube, blowtube, Danube, flashcube, haboob, jujube, hypercube

uben \ü-bən\ see EUBEN

ubens \ü-bənz\ Rubens—*also possessives and plurals of nouns listed at* EUBEN

uber \ü-bər\ Buber, cuber, goober, tuber

uberance \ü-brəns\ exuberance, protuberance

uberant \ü-brənt\ exuberant, protuberant

uberous \ü-brəs\ see UBRIS

ubic \ü-bik\ cubic, pubic, cherubic

ubile \ü-bəl\ see UBAL

ubious \ü-bē-əs\ dubious, rubious

ubis \ü-bəs\ pubis, rubus, Anubis

uble \ü-bəl\ see UBAL

ublic \əb-lik\ public, republic

ublican \əb-li-kən\ publican, republican

ubman \əb-mən\ clubman, Tubman

ubric \ü-brik\ lubric, rubric

ubrious \ü-brē-əs\ lugubrious, salubrious, insalubrious

ubris \ü-brəs\ hubris, tuberous

ubtile \ət-ᵊl\ see UTTLE

ubus \ü-bəs\ see UBIS

uby \ü-bē\ see OOBY

uca \ü-kə\ see OOKA

ucal \ü-kəl\ ducal, nuchal, archducal

ucan \ü-kən\ glucan, kuchen, Lucan, interleukin

ucat \ək-ət\ see UCKET

¹ucca \ü-kə\ see OOKA

²ucca \ək-ə\ see UKKA

uccal \ək-əl\ see UCKLE

ucci \ü-chē\ see OOCHY

ucco \ək-ō\ see UCKO

uccor \ək-ər\ see UCKER

uccory \ək-rē\ see UCKERY

ucculence \ək-yə-ləns\ see UCULENCE

uce \üs\ see ¹USE

uced \üst\ see OOST

ucement \ü-smənt\ inducement, seducement

ucence \üs-ᵊns\ nuisance, translucence

ucer \ü-sər\ juicer, looser, adducer, Bull Mooser, inducer, lime-juicer, producer, transducer, introducer, reproducer

¹uch \ich\ see ITCH

²uch \ük\ see UKE

³uch \əch\ see ¹UTCH

uchal \ü-kəl\ see UCAL

¹uche \ü-chē\ see OOCHY

²uche \üch\ see ¹OOCH

³uche \üsh\ see OUCHE

uchen \ü-kən\ see UCAN

ucher \ü-chər\ see UTURE

uchin \ü-shən\ see UTION

uchsia \ü-shə\ see UTIA

uchy \əch-ē\ duchy, smutchy, touchy, archduchy

ucia \ü-shə\ see UTIA

ucial \ü-shəl\ crucial, fiducial

ucian \ü-shən\ see UTION

ucible \ü-sə-bəl\ crucible, deducible, educible, inducible, producible, protrusible, irreducible, reproducible, irreproducible

ucid \ü-səd\ deuced, lucid, pellucid, Seleucid

ucifer \ü-sə-fər\ crucifer, Lucifer

ucity \ü-sət-ē\ abstrusity, caducity

ucive \ü-siv\ see USIVE

¹uck \ək\ buck, Buck, chuck, cluck, cruck, duck, guck, huck, luck, muck, pluck, puck, Puck, ruck, schmuck, shuck, snuck, struck, stuck, suck, truck, Truk, tuck, yech, yuck, amok, awestruck, bushbuck, Canuck, dumbstruck, Kalmuck, lame-

duck, light-struck,
moonstruck, mukluk, muktuk,
potluck, reedbuck, roebuck,
sawbuck, shelduck,
stagestruck, starstruck,
sunstruck, unstuck, upchuck,
woodchuck, geoduck,
Keokuk, Habakkuk,
megabuck, muckamuck, nip
and tuck, high-muck-a-muck

²uck \úk\ see ¹OOK

ukar \ək-ər\ see UCKER

ucker \ək-ər\ bucker, chukar,
chukker, ducker, mucker,
plucker, pucker, shucker,
succor, sucker, trucker,
tucker, bloodsucker,
sapsucker, seersucker

uckery \ək-rē\ puckery, succory

ucket \ək-ət\ bucket, ducat,
tucket, gutbucket, Nantucket

uckle \ək-əl\ buccal, buckle,
chuckle, knuckle, suckle,
truckle, Arbuckle, bare-
knuckle, parbuckle, pinochle,
swashbuckle, turnbuckle,
unbuckle, honeysuckle

uckled \ək-əld\ cuckold,
knuckled, bare-knuckled—
also pasts of verbs listed at
UCKLE

uckler \ək-lər\ buckler,
knuckler, swashbuckler

uckling \ək-liŋ\ duckling,
suckling, swashbuckling

ucko \ək-ō\ bucko, stucco

uckold \ək-əld\ see UCKLED

uckoo \ü-kü\ cuckoo, Maluku

ucks \əks\ see ¹UX

uckus \úk-əs\ ruckus, Sukkoth

ucky \ək-ē\ ducky, lucky,
mucky, plucky, yucky,
Kentucky, unlucky, happy-go-
lucky

uco \ü-kō\ pachuco, osso buco

ucre \ü-kər\ euchre, lucre

uct \əkt\ duct, abduct, adduct,
conduct, construct, deduct,
destruct, eruct, induct,
instruct, obstruct, aqueduct,
deconstruct, reconstruct,
usufruct, viaduct—*also pasts
of verbs listed at* UCK

uctable \ək-tə-bəl\ see UCTIBLE

uctal \ək-t°l\ ductal, ductile

uctance \ək-təns\ conductance,
inductance, reluctance

uctible \ək-tə-bəl\ conductible,
constructible, deductible,
destructible, indestructible,
ineluctable, reconstructible

uctile \ək-t°l\ see UCTAL

ucting \ək-tiŋ\ ducting,
semiconducting

uction \ək-shən\ fluxion,
ruction, suction, abduction,
adduction, conduction,
construction, deduction,
destruction, eduction,
effluxion, induction,
instruction, obstruction,
production, reduction,
seduction, deconstruction,
introduction, reconstruction,
reproduction,
photoreproduction

uctive \ək-tiv\ adductive,
conductive, constructive,
deductive, destructive,
inductive, instructive,
productive, reductive,
seductive, reconstructive,
reproductive, self-destructive,
counterproductive

uctor \ək-tər\ abductor,
adductor, conductor,
constructor, destructor,
eductor, inductor, instructor,
reconstructor, semiconductor

uctress \ək-trəs\ conductress,
instructress, seductress

uculence \ək-yə-ləns\
succulence, truculence

ucy \ü-sē\ see UICY

¹ud \əd\ blood, bud, crud, cud,
dud, flood, fud, Judd, mud,
rudd, scud, spud, stud, sudd,
thud, coldblood, disbud, full-
blood, half-blood, hotblood,
lifeblood, oxblood, redbud,
rosebud, warmblood, stick-in-
the-mud

²ud \üd\ see UDE

³ud \u̇d\ see ¹OOD

uda \üd-ə\ Buddha, Gouda,
Judah, Barbuda, Bermuda,
remuda, barracuda,
Buxtehude, Gautama Buddha

udable \üd-ə-bəl\ excludable,
extrudable, includable,
ineludible

udah \üd-ə\ see UDA

udal \üd-ᵊl\ see OODLE

udas \üd-əs\ Judas, Santa
Gertrudis

¹udd \u̇d\ see ¹OOD

²udd \əd\ see ¹UD

udded \əd-əd\ see ¹OODED

udder \əd-ər\ budder, flooder,
judder, rudder, shudder, udder

uddha \üd-ə\ see UDA

uddhist \üd-əst\ see ¹UDIST

uddie \əd-ē\ see ¹UDDY

¹udding \əd-iŋ\ budding,
studding

²udding \u̇d-iŋ\ see OODING

uddle \əd-ᵊl\ buddle, cuddle,
fuddle, huddle, muddle,
puddle, ruddle, befuddle

uddly \əd-lē\ cuddly, Dudley,
muddly, studly

¹uddy \əd-ē\ bloody, buddy,
Buddy, cruddy, cuddy,
duddie, muddy, ruddy, study,
fuddy-duddy, understudy

²uddy \u̇d-ē\ see ²OODY

¹ude \üd\ brood, crowd, crude,
dude, feud, food, hued, Jude,
lewd, mood, nude, oud, pood,
prude, pseud, rood, rude,
shrewd, snood, stewed,
who'd, wood, wud, you'd,
allude, collude, conclude,
delude, denude, elude, etude,
exclude, extrude, exude, fast-
food, Gertrude, include,
intrude, obtrude, occlude,
postlude, preclude, prelude,
protrude, quaalude, Quaalude,
seafood, seclude, subdued,
transude, unglued, altitude,
amplitude, aptitude, attitude,
certitude, consuetude,
crassitude, desuetude,
finitude, fortitude, gratitude,
habitude, hebetude, interlude,
lassitude, latitude, longitude,
magnitude, mansuetude,
multitude, negritude,
platitude, plenitude,
plentitude, promptitude,
pulchritude, quietude,
rectitude, seminude, servitude,
solitude, turpitude, vastitude,
beatitude, correctitude,
decrepitude, exactitude,
inaptitude, incertitude,
ineptitude, infinitude,

ingratitude, inquietude,
similitude, solicitude,
vicissitude, dissimilitude,
inexactitude, verisimilitude

²ude \üd-ə\ see UDA

udel \üd-ᵊl\ see OODLE

udence \ü-dᵊn(t)s\ Prudence,
students, imprudence,
jurisprudence

udeness \üd-nəs\ see UDINOUS

udent \üd-ᵊnt\ prudent,
imprudent, student,
jurisprudent

udents \ü-dᵊn(t)s\ see UDENCE

uder \üd-ər\ brooder, Tudor,
concluder, deluder, excluder,
extruder, intruder, obtruder,
preluder—*also comparatives
of adjectives listed at* UDE

¹udge \əj\ budge, drudge,
fudge, grudge, judge, nudge,
sludge, smudge, trudge,
adjudge, begrudge, forejudge,
misjudge, prejudge

²udge \üj\ see ¹UGE

udgeon \əj-ən\ bludgeon,
dudgeon, gudgeon,
curmudgeon

udget \əj-ət\ budget, fussbudget

udgie \əj-ē\ see UDGY

udging \əj-iŋ\ drudging,
grudging

udgy \əj-ē\ budgie, pudgy,
sludgy, smudgy

udible \üd-ə-bəl\ see UDABLE

udi \ü-dē\ see ¹OODY

udie \ü-dē\ see ¹OODY

udinal \üd-nəl\ altitudinal,
aptitudinal, attitudinal,
latitudinal, longitudinal,
platitudinal

udinous \üd-nəs\ crudeness,
lewdness, rudeness,
shrewdness, altitudinous,
multitudinous, platitudinous,
plenitudinous, pulchritudinous

udis \üd-əs\ see UDAS

udish \üd-ish\ dudish, prudish

¹udist \üd-əst\ Buddhist,
feudist, nudist—*also
superlatives of adjectives
listed at* UDE

²udist \ùd-əst\ see OULDEST

udity \üd-ət-ē\ crudity, nudity

udley \əd-lē\ see UDDLY

udly \əd-lē\ see UDDLY

udo \üd-ō\ judo, kudo, pseudo,
scudo, escudo, Matsudo,
testudo

udor \üd-ər\ see UDER

udsman \ùdz-mən\ see
OODSMAN

udson \əd-sən\ Hudson, Judson

udu \üd-ü\ see OODOO

¹udy \ü-dē\ see ¹OODY

²udy \əd-ē\ see ¹UDDY

¹ue \ü\ see ¹EW

²ue \ā\ see ¹AY

ued \üd\ see UDE

ueful \ü-fəl\ rueful, pantofle

ueghel \ü-gəl\ see UGAL

ueil \əi\ Arauil, Argentueil

¹uel \ü-əl\ crewel, cruel, dual,
duel, gruel, jewel, Jewel,
Jewell, newel, Newell,
accrual, eschewal, refuel,
renewal, Pantagruel

²uel \ül\ see ¹OOL

uely \ü-lē\ see ULY

uement \ü-mənt\ see EWMENT

uence \ü-əns\ affluence,
confluence, congruence,

effluence, influence,
pursuance, refluence,
incongruence
uency \ü-ən-sē\ fluency,
truancy, affluency,
congruency, nonfluency
ueness \ü-nəs\ see EWNESS
uenster \ən-stər\ see UNSTER
uent \ü-ənt\ fluent, suint, truant,
affluent, confluent, congruent,
effluent, influent, incongruent
uer \ü-ər\ see ¹EWER
uerdon \ərd-ᵊn\ see URDEN
uerile \ùr-əl\ see URAL
ues \üz\ see ²USE
uesman \üz-mən\ see EWSMAN
uesome \ü-səm\ gruesome,
twosome
uesy \ü-zē\ see OOZY
uet \ü-ət\ bluet, cruet, peewit,
suet, conduit, intuit
uette \et\ see ¹ET
uey \ü-ē\ see EWY
ufa \ü-fə\ loofah, tufa, opera
buffa
uff \əf\ bluff, buff, chough,
chuff, cuff, duff, fluff, gruff,
guff, huff, luff, muff, puff,
rough, ruff, scruff, scuff,
slough, snuff, sough, stuff,
tough, tuff, dyestuff, earmuff,
enough, foodstuff, handcuff,
rebuff, oeil-de-boeuf,
overstuff
uffa \ü-fə\ see UFA
¹uffe \üf\ see ¹OOF
²uffe \ùf\ see ²OOF
uffed \əft\ chuffed, ruffed, tuft,
candytuft—*also pasts of verbs
listed at* UFF
uffel \əf-əl\ see ¹UFFLE

uffer \əf-ər\ bluffer, buffer,
duffer, puffer, rougher,
snuffer, stuffer, suffer,
candlesnuffer—*also
comparatives of adjectives
listed at* UFF
uffet \əf-ət\ buffet, tuffet
uffin \əf-ən\ muffin, puffin,
roughen, toughen, ragamuffin
uffish \əf-ish\ huffish, roughish
¹uffle \əf-əl\ duffel, muffle,
ruffle, scuffle, shuffle, snuffle,
truffle, kerfuffle, reshuffle,
unmuffle
²uffle \ü-fəl\ see UEFUL
uffled \əf-əld\ truffled,
unruffled—*also pasts of verbs
listed at* UFFLE
uffler \əf-lər\ muffler, shuffler,
snuffler
uffly \əf-lē\ bluffly, gruffly,
roughly, ruffly
uffy \əf-ē\ chuffy, fluffy, huffy,
puffy, scruffy, snuffy, stuffy,
toughie
ufi \ü-fē\ see OOFY
ufous \ü-fəs\ rufous, Rufus
uft \əft\ see UFFED
ufti \əf-tē\ mufti, tufty
ufty \əf-tē\ see UFTI
ufus \ü-fəs\ see UFOUS
ug \əg\ bug, chug, Doug, drug,
dug, fug, hug, jug, lug, mug,
plug, pug, rug, shrug, slug,
smug, snug, thug, trug, tug,
ugh, vug, bedbug, billbug,
debug, earplug, firebug,
fireplug, goldbug, humbug,
lovebug, stinkbug, unplug,
antidrug, chugalug,
doodlebug, jitterbug, ladybug,

litterbug, mealybug,
shutterbug

uga \ü-gə\ beluga, Cayuga,
Kaluga, Sevruga, Tortuga,
Chattanooga

ugal \ü-gəl\ Brueghel, bugle,
frugal, fugal, fugle, kugel,
conjugal

ugar \úg-ər\ see UGUR

¹uge \üj\ huge, kludge, Lodz,
scrooge, scrouge, stooge,
deluge, centrifuge, subterfuge

²uge \üzh\ Bruges, luge, rouge,
deluge, gamboge, refuge,
Baton Rouge

ugel \ü-gəl\ see UGAL

uges \üzh\ see ²UGE

uggaree \əg-rē\ see ¹UGGERY

¹ugger \əg-ər\ bugger, chugger,
lugger, mugger, plugger,
rugger, slugger, Bavagar,
Jamnagar, Srinagar, hugger-
mugger, Navanagar

²ugger \úg-ər\ see UGUR

¹uggery \əg-rē\ buggery,
puggaree, snuggery, thuggery,
skulduggery

²uggery \úg-rē\ see UGARY

ugget \əg-ət\ drugget, nugget

uggie \əg-ē\ see UGGY

uggish \əg-ish\ sluggish,
thuggish

uggle \əg-əl\ guggle, juggle,
smuggle, snuggle, struggle

uggler \əg-lər\ juggler,
smuggler, struggler

uggy \əg-ē\ buggy, druggie,
druggy, fuggy, luggie, muggy

¹ugh \əg\ see UG

²ugh \ü\ see ¹EW

ughes \üz\ see ²USE

ugle \ü-gəl\ see UGAL

ugli \ə-glē\ see UGLY

uglia \úl-yə\ see ULIA

ugly \əg-lē\ smugly, Ugli, ugly,
plug-ugly

ugn \ün\ see ¹OON

ugner \ü-nər\ see OONER

ugric \ü-grik\ tugrik, Ugric,
Finno-Ugric

ugrik \ü-grik\ see UGRIC

ugu \ü-gü\ fugu, goo-goo

ugur \úg-ər\ booger, bugger,
sugar

uhe \ü-ə\ see UA

uhl \ül\ see ¹OOL

¹uhr \ər\ see ¹EUR

²uhr \úr\ see ¹URE

ührer \úr-ər\ see ¹URER

¹ui \ā\ see ¹AY

²ui \ē\ see ¹EE

uice \üs\ see ¹USE

uiced \üst\ see OOST

uiceless \ü-sləs\ see USELESS

uicer \ü-sər\ see UCER

uicy \ü-sē\ goosey, juicy, Lucy,
sluicy, sprucy, Brancusi,
Watsui, acey-deucey,
Arginusae, loosey-goosey

uid \ü-id\ Clwyd, druid, fluid

uidable \īd-ə-bəl\ see ¹IDABLE

uidance \īd-ᵊns\ see IDANCE

uide \īd\ see ¹IDE

uided \īd-əd\ see IDED

uider \īd-ər\ see ¹IDER

uidon \īd-ᵊn\ see IDEN

uiker \ī-kər\ see IKER

uild \ild\ see ILLED

uilder \il-dər\ see ILDER

uilding \il-diŋ\ see ILDING

uile \īl\ see ¹ILE

uileless \īl-ləs\ see ILELESS

uiler \ī-lər\ see ILAR

uilleann \i-lən\ see ILLON

uilt \ilt\ see ILT
uimpe \amp\ see ³AMP
¹uin \ü-ən\ see UAN
²uin \ən\ see UN
³uin \aⁿ\ see ⁴IN
uing \ü-iŋ\ see ²OING
uint \ü-ənt\ see UENT
uir \ur\ see ¹URE
uirdly \ur-lē\ see URELY
uis \ü-əs\ see EWESS
uisance \üs-ᵊns\ see UCENCE
uisard \ī-zərd\ see ISORED
¹uise \üz\ see ²USE
²uise \īz\ see IZE
uiser \ü-zər\ see USER
uish \ü-ish\ see EWISH
uisne \ü-nē\ see OONY
uiste \is-tē\ see ²ICITY
¹uit \ü-ət\ see UET
²uit \üt\ see UTE
uitable \üt-ə-bəl\ see UTABLE
uitage \üt-ij\ see ¹OOTAGE
uite \üt\ see UTE
uited \üt-əd\ see ¹OOTED
uiter \üt-ər\ see UTER
uiterer \üt-ər-ər\ fruiterer,
  pewterer
uiting \üt-iŋ\ see UTING
uitless \üt-ləs\ see OOTLESS
uitlet \üt-lət\ see OOTLET
uitor \üt-ər\ see UTER
uitous \ü-ə-təs\ circuitous,
  fortuitous, gratuitous
uits \üts\ see OOTS
¹uittle \üt-ᵊl\ see UTILE
²uittle \ət-ᵊl\ see UTTLE
¹uity \ü-ət-ē\ acuity, annuity,
  circuity, congruity, fatuity,
  fortuity, gratuity, vacuity,
  ambiguity, assiduity,
  conspicuity, contiguity,
  continuity, incongruity,

ingenuity, perpetuity,
promiscuity, superfluity,
discontinuity
²uity \üt-ē\ see ¹OOTY
¹uk \ük\ see UKE
²uk \uk\ see ¹OOK
³uk \ək\ see UCK
ukar \ə-kər\ see UCKER
uke \ük\ cuke, duke, fluke,
  gook, juke, kook, Luke, nuke,
  puke, snook, souk, spook,
  suq, tuque, uke, yeuk,
  archduke, Baruch,
  caoutchouc, Chinook, Kirkuk,
  Mamluk, rebuke, Heptateuch,
  Hexateuch, Pentateuch
¹uki \ü-kē\ see ¹OOKY
²uki \u-kē\ see OOKIE
ukka \ək-ə\ chukka, pukka,
  yucca, felucca
ukkah \uk-ə\ see OOKAH
ukker \ək-ər\ see UCKER
ukkoth \uk-əs\ see UCKUS
uku \ü-kü\ see UCKOO
¹ul \ul\ bull, Bull, full, pull,
  shul, wool, you'll, armful,
  bagful, bellpull, brimful,
  bulbul, canful, capful, carful,
  cheekful, chestful, chock-full,
  cupful, drawerful, earful,
  eyeful, fistful, forkful,
  glassful, handful, houseful,
  jarful, John Bull, jugful, leg-
  pull, mouthful, outpull,
  pailful, panful, pipeful,
  plateful, potful, push-pull,
  rackful, roomful, sackful,
  scoopful, shelfful, skinful,
  spoonful, stickful, tankful,
  tinful, topful, trainful, trayful,
  trunkful, tubful, barrelful,
  basketful, bellyful,

teaspoonful, dyed-in-the-
wool, tablespoonful

²**ul** \ül\ see ¹OOL

³**ul** \əl\ see ¹ULL

ula \ü-lə\ Beulah, Fula, hula,
moola, pula, Tula, ampulla,
tabbouleh, Ashtabula, San
Pedro Sula

ular \ü-lər\ see OOLER

ulcent \əl-sənt\ see ULSANT

ulcer \əl-sər\ see ULSER

ulch \əlch\ cultch, gulch, mulch

¹**ule** \ü-lē\ see ULY

²**ule** \ül\ see ¹OOL

ulean \ü-lē-ən\ Boolean,
Acheulean, cerulean

uled \üld\ see OOLED

ulep \ü-ləp\ see ULIP

uler \ü-lər\ see OOLER

ules \ülz\ Jules—*also
possessives and plurals of
nouns and third person
singular presents of verbs
listed at* ¹OOL

ulet \əl-ət\ see ¹ULLET

¹**uley** \ü-lē\ see ULY

²**uley** \ül-ē\ see ²ULLY

ulf \əlf\ golf, gulf, Gulf, engulf,
Beowulf, Saronic Gulf

ulgar \əl-gər\ see ULGUR

ulge \əlj\ bulge, divulge,
indulge, overindulge

¹**ulgence** \əl-jəns\ divulgence,
indulgence, refulgence

²**ulgence** \úl-jəns\ effulgence,
refulgence

ulgent \əl-jənt\ fulgent,
indulgent

ulgur \əl-gər\ bulgur, vulgar

ulhas \əl-əs\ see ULLUS

uli \úl-ē\ see ²ULLY

ulia \ül-yə\ Julia, Puglia,
Apulia, Friuli-Venezia Guilia

ulie \ü-lē\ see ULY

ulip \ü-ləp\ julep, tulip

ulish \ü-lish\ see OOLISH

ulity \ü-lət-ē\ credulity,
garrulity, sedulity, incredulity

ulk \əlk\ bulk, hulk, skulk, sulk,
yolk

ulky \əl-kē\ bulky, sulky

¹**ull** \əl\ cull, dull, gull, hull,
Hull, lull, mull, null, scull,
skull, stull, trull, annul,
Choiseul, mogul, numskull,
pas seul, monohull, multihull,
Sitting Bull, Solihull,
Kingston upon Hull

²**ull** \úl\ see ¹UL

¹**ulla** \úl-ə\ bulla, mullah, Sulla,
ampulla

²**ulla** \ü-lə\ see ULA

³**ulla** \əl-ə\ see ¹ULLAH

ullage \əl-ij\ sullage, ullage

¹**ullah** \əl-ə\ Gullah, mullah,
nullah, stollen, medulla,
ayatollah

²**ullah** \úl-ə\ see ¹ULLA

ullan \əl-ən\ see ULLEN

ullard \əl-ərd\ see OLORED

ullate \əl-ət\ see ¹ULLET

ulle \ül\ see ¹OOL

ullein \əl-ən\ see ULLEN

ullen \əl-ən\ mullein, stollen,
sullen, Lucullan

¹**uller** \úl-ər\ fuller, puller

²**uller** \əl-ər\ see ¹OLOR

ulles \əl-əs\ see ULLUS

¹**ullet** \əl-ət\ culet, cullet, gullet,
mullet, cucullate

²**ullet** \úl-ət\ bullet, Bullitt,
pullet

ulley \úl-ē\ see ²ULLY

ullion \əl-yən\ cullion, mullion,
 scullion, slumgullion

ullis \əl-əs\ see ULLUS

ullitt \úl-ət\ see ²ULLET

ullman \úl-mən\ fulmine,
 Pullman

ullus \əl-əs\ Dulles, Agulhas,
 Catullus, portcullis, Cape
 Agulhas

¹ully \əl-ē\ cully, dully, gully,
 sully

²ully \úl-ē\ bully, fully, gully,
 muley, puli, pulley, woolly

ulmine \úl-mən\ see ULLMAN

ulp \əlp\ gulp, pulp, insculp

ulsant \əl-sənt\ pulsant,
 convulsant, demulcent

ulse \əls\ dulse,pulse, avulse,
 convulse, expulse, impulse,
 repulse

ulser \əl-sər\ pulser, ulcer

ulsion \əl-shən\ pulsion,
 avulsion, compulsion,
 convulsion, emulsion,
 evulsion, expulsion,
 impulsion, propulsion,
 repulsion, revulsion

ulsive \əl-siv\ compulsive,
 convulsive, emulsive,
 expulsive, impulsive,
 propulsive, repulsive

ult \əlt\ cult, adult, consult,
 exult, incult, indult, insult,
 occult, penult, result, tumult,
 catapult, antepenult

ultancy \əlt-ᵊn-sē\ consultancy,
 exultancy

ultant \əlt-ᵊnt\ consultant,
 exultant, resultant

ultch \əlch\ see ULCH

ulter \əl-tər\ consultor, insulter,
 occulter

ultery \əl-trē\ see ULTRY

ultor \əl-tər\ see ULTER

ultry \əl-trē\ sultry, adultery

ulture \əl-chər\ culture,
 multure, vulture, subculture,
 agriculture, apiculture,
 aquaculture, aviculture,
 counterculture, floriculture,
 horticulture, mariculture,
 monoculture, silviculture,
 viniculture, arboriculture

ulty \əl-tē\ see ¹ALTI

ulu \ü-lü\ lulu, Sulu, Zulu,
 Bangweulu, Honolulu

ulunder \əl-ən-dər\ see
 OLANDER

ulva \əl-və\ ulva, vulva

ulvar \əl-vər\ see ULVER

ulver \əl-vər\ culver, vulvar

uly \ü-lē\ bluely, boule, coolie,
 coolly, coulee, duly, ghoulie,
 Julie, muley, newly, puli,
 ruly, stoolie, Thule, truly,
 tule, Bernoulli, guayule,
 patchouli, tabbouleh, unduly,
 unruly, ultima Thule

¹um \əm\ bum, chum, come,
 crumb, cum, drum, dumb,
 from, glum, gum, hum, lum,
 mum, numb, plum, plumb,
 rhumb, rum, scrum, scum,
 slum, some, strum, sum,
 swum, them, thrum, thumb,
 alum, aplomb, become,
 benumb, degum, dim sum,
 dumdum, eardrum, ho-hum,
 humdrum, income, outcome,
 subgum, succumb, therefrom,
 Tom Thumb, tom-tom,

wherefrom, yum-yum,
bubblegum, kettledrum,
overcome, sugarplum, hop-
o'my-thumb

²**um** \ům\ cum, groom, Qom,
Targum, mare librum

³**um** \üm\ see ¹OOM

uma \ü-mə\ duma, pneuma,
puma, satsuma, Ancohuma,
Montezuma

umable \ü-mə-bəl\ assumable,
consumable, presumable,
subsumable, inconsumable

umage \əm-ij\ see UMMAGE

uman \ü-mən\ blooming,
crewman, human, lumen,
Newman, numen, Truman,
Yuman, acumen, albumen,
albumin, bitumen, ichneumon,
illumine, inhuman, panhuman,
subhuman, antihuman,
catechumen, protohuman,
superhuman

umanist \ü-mə-nəst\ see
UMENIST

umanous \ü-mə-nəs\ see
UMINOUS

umb \əm\ see ¹UM

umbar \əm-bər\ see ¹UMBER

umbed \əmd\ green-thumbed,
unplumbed

umbel \əm-bəl\ see UMBLE

umbency \əm-bən-sē\
incumbency, recumbency

umbent \əm-bənt\ decumbent,
incumbent, procumbent,
recumbent, superincumbent

¹**umber** \əm-bər\ cumber,
Humber, lumbar, lumber,
number, slumber, umber,
cucumber, encumber,
outnumber, renumber,

disencumber, Reynolds
number, Avogadro's number

²**umber** \əm-ər\ see UMMER

umbered \əm-bərd\
unnumbered,
unencumbered—*also pasts of
verbs listed at* ¹UMBER

umberland \əm-bər-lənd\
Cumberland, Northumberland

umberous \əm-brəs\ see
UMBROUS

umbery \əm-brē\ ombre,
slumbery

umbing \əm-iŋ\ see OMING

umble \əm-bəl\ bumble,
crumble, fumble, grumble,
humble, jumble, mumble,
rumble, scumble, stumble,
tumble, umbel, rough-and-
tumble

umbler \əm-blər\ bumbler,
fumbler, grumbler, mumbler,
rumbler, stumbler, tumbler

umbling \əm-bliŋ\ rumbling,
tumbling

¹**umbly** \əm-blē\ crumbly,
grumbly, humbly, mumbly,
rumbly

²**umbly** \əm-lē\ comely,
dumbly, dumly, numbly

umbness \əm-nəs\ dumbness,
glumness, numbness, alumnus

umbo \əm-bō\ gumbo, jumbo,
umbo, Colombo, mumbo
jumbo

umbra \əm-brə\ umbra,
penumbra

umbral \əm-brəl\ see UMBRIL

umbria \əm-brē-ə\ Cumbria,
Umbria, Northumbria

umbril \əm-brəl\ tumbril,
umbral, penumbral

umbrous \əm-brəs\ cumbrous,
  slumberous
ume \üm\ see ¹OOM
umed \ümd\ see OOMED
umedly \ü-məd-lē\ consumedly,
  presumedly
umelet \üm-lət\ see OOMLET
umely \ü-mə-lē\ see OOMILY
umen \ü-mən\ see UMAN
umenist \ü-mə-nəst\ humanist,
  luminist, ecumenist,
  illuminist, phillumenist
umer \ü-mər\ bloomer,
  Bloomer, groomer, humor,
  roomer, rumor, Sumer, tumor,
  consumer, costumer,
  exhumer, perfumer, presumer,
  schussboomer
umeral \üm-rəl\ humeral,
  humoral, numeral
umerous \üm-rəs\ see
  UMOROUS
umerus \üm-rəs\ see UMOROUS
umey \ü-mē\ see OOMY
umf \əmf\ see UMPH
umi \ü-mē\ see OOMY
umice \əm-əs\ see UMMOUS
umid \ü-məd\ humid, tumid
¹umin \əm-ən\ cumin, summon
²umin \ü-mən\ see UMAN
uminal \ü-mən-əl\ luminal,
  noumenal
uminate \ü-mə-nət\ acuminate,
  illuminate
umine \ü-mən\ see UMAN
uming \ü-miŋ\ blooming,
  consuming, everblooming,
  time-consuming,
  unassuming—*also present
  participles of verbs listed at*
  ¹OOM

uminist \ü-mə-nəst\ see
  UMENIST
uminous \ü-mə-nəs\ luminous,
  numinous, albuminous,
  aluminous, bituminous,
  leguminous, quadrumanous,
  voluminous
umma \əm-ə\ gumma, momma,
  summa
ummage \əm-ij\ rummage,
  West Brumage
¹ummary \əm-rē\ see ²UMMERY
²ummary \əm-ə-rē\ see
  ¹UMMERY
ummate \əm-ət\ see UMMET
ummel \əm-əl\ see ²OMMEL
ummell \əm-əl\ see ²OMMEL
ummer \əm-ər\ bummer,
  comer, drummer, gummer,
  hummer, mummer, plumber,
  rummer, slummer, strummer,
  summer, latecomer,
  midsummer, newcomer,
  overcomer, up-and-comer—
  *also comparatives of
  adjectives listed at* ¹UM
ummery \əm-ə-rē\ flummery,
  mummery, summary,
  summery, Montgomery
ummet \əm-ət\ grummet,
  plummet, summit,
  consummate
ummie \əm-ē\ see UMMY
ummit \əm-ət\ see UMMET
ummock \əm-ək\ hummock,
  stomach
ummon \əm-ən\ see ¹UMIN
ummoner \əm-nər\ see UMNAR
ummous \əm-əs\ gummous,
  hummus, pomace, pumice
ummox \əm-əks\ flummox,

hummocks, lummox,
stomachs

ummus \əm-əs\ see UMMOUS

ummy \əm-ē\ chummy,
crummie, crummy, dummy,
gummy, mommy, mummy,
plummy, rummy, scummy,
slummy, tummy, yummy

umnar \əm-nər\ summoner,
Sumner, columnar

umner \əm-nər\ see UMNAR

umness \əm-nəs\ see UMBNESS

umnus \əm-nəs\ see UMBNESS

umor \ü-mər\ see UMER

umoral \üm-rəl\ see UMERAL

umorous \üm-rəs\ humerus,
humorous, numerous,
tumorous, innumerous

umous \ü-məs\ brumous,
humus, spumous, posthumous

ump \əmp\ bump, chump,
clomp, clump, comp, crump,
dump, flump, frump, grump,
hump, jump, lump, mump,
plump, pump, rump, slump,
stump, sump, thump, trump,
tump, ump, whump,
mugwump, no-trump, tub-
thump, callithump, overtrump

umper \əm-pər\ bumper,
dumper, jumper, lumper,
plumper, pumper, stumper,
thumper, tub-thumper, Bible-
thumper

umph \əmf\ bumf, humph,
galumph, harrumph

umpish \əm-pish\ dumpish,
frumpish, lumpish, plumpish

umpkin \əŋ-kən\ see UNKEN

umple \əm-pəl\ crumple,
rumple

umply \əm-plē\ crumply,
plumply, rumply

umps \əms\ dumps, mumps—
*also plurals and possessives
of nouns and third person
singular presents of verbs
listed at* UMP

umption \əm-shən\ gumption,
assumption, consumption,
presumption, resumption,
subsumption

umptious \əm-shəs\ bumptious,
scrumptious, presumptuous

umptive \əm-tiv\ assumptive,
consumptive, presumptive

¹**umptuous** \əm-chəs\
sumptuous, presumptuous

²**umptuous** \əm-shəs\ see
UMPTIOUS

umpus \əm-pəs\ see ²OMPASS

umpy \əm-pē\ bumpy, clumpy,
dumpy, frumpy, grumpy,
humpy, jumpy, lumpy,
stumpy

umulous \ü-myə-ləs\ see
UMULUS

umulus \ü-myə-ləs\ cumulous,
cumulus, tumulus

umus \ü-məs\ see UMOUS

umy \ü-mē\ see OOMY

¹**un** \ən\ bun, done, Donne, dun,
fen, foehn, fun, gun, hon,
Hun, jun, maun, none, nun,
one, pun, run, shun, son,
spun, stun, sun, sunn, ton,
tonne, tun, won, A-1, begun,
blowgun, chaconne, Chang-
chun, Chaplin, finespun, first-
run, flashgun, forerun,
godson, grandson, handgun,
hard-won, homespun, long

run, outdone, outgun, outrun, popgun, pressrun, rerun, sea-run, shotgun, six-gun, stepson, undone, V-1, well-done, Acheron, Algonquin, allemande, all-or-none, Balzacian, hit-and-run, kiloton, machine-gun, megaton, one-on-one, one-to-one, overdone, overrun, PL/1, Sally Lunn, scattergun, tommy gun, twenty-one, underdone, underrun, Xiamen, alexandrine

²un \ün\ see ¹OON

³un \ u̇n\ Fushun, Lushun, tabun

una \ü-nə\ Buna, Cunha, Luna, Poona, puna, tuna, Altoona, kahuna, lacuna, laguna, vicuña, Tristan da Cunha

¹uña \ü-nə\ see UNA

²uña \ün-yə\ see UNIA

unal \ün-ᵊl\ communal, jejunal, lagoonal, monsoonal, tribunal

unar \ü-nər\ see OONER

unary \ü-nə-rē\ unary, festoonery, sublunary, superlunary

unate \ü-nət\ unit, lacunate, tribunate

unc \ənk\ see UNK

uncan \əŋ-kən\ see UNKEN

unce \əns\ dunce, once—*also plurals and possessives of nouns and third person singular presents of verbs listed at* ¹ONT

unch \ənch\ brunch, bunch, Bunche, crunch, hunch, lunch, munch, punch, scrunch, keypunch, ploughman's lunch

unche \ənch\ see UNCH

uncheon \ən-chən\ luncheon, puncheon, truncheon

uncher \ən-chər\ cruncher, luncher, muncher, cowpuncher, keypuncher, counterpuncher

unchy \ən-chē\ bunchy, crunchy, punchy

uncial \ən-sē-əl\ uncial, internuncial

uncle \əŋ-kəl\ nuncle, uncle, carbuncle, caruncle, furuncle, granduncle, peduncle

¹unco \əŋ-kō\ bunco, junco, unco

²unco \əŋ-kə\ see UNKAH

unct \əŋt\ trunked, adjunct, conjunct, defunct, disjunct—*also pasts of verbs listed at* UNK

unction \əŋ-shən\ function, junction, unction, compunction, conjunction, disjunction, dysfunction, injunction, malfunction, extreme unction

unctional \əŋ-shnəl\ functional, junctional, dysfunctional

unctious \əŋ-shəs\ compunctious, rambunctious

unctory \əŋ-trē\ emunctory, perfunctory

uncture \əŋ-chər\ juncture, puncture, acupuncture, conjuncture, disjuncture

uncular \əŋ-kyə-lər\ avuncular, carbuncular, peduncular

unculus \əŋ-kyə-ləs\ homunculus, ranunculus

¹und \ənd\ bund, fund, gunned,

defund, obtund, refund,
rotund, secund, cummerbund,
orotund, pudibund, rubicund,
underfund—*also pasts of
verbs listed at* UN
²**und** \und\ bund, dachshund
³**und** \unt\ see ¹UNT
⁴**und** \aund\ see ²OUND
unda \ən-də\ Munda, Sunda,
osmunda, rotunda,
barramunda, floribunda
undae \ən-dē\ see UNDI
undant \ən-dənt\ abundant,
redundant, superabundant
unday \ən-dē\ see UNDI
undays \ən-dēz\ Mondays,
Sundays, undies—*also
plurals and possessives of
nouns listed at* UNDI
undem \ən-dəm\ see UNDUM
under \ən-dər\ Bandar, blunder,
plunder, sunder, thunder,
under, wonder, asunder,
hereunder, thereunder
underous \ən-drəs\ plunderous,
wondrous, thunderous
¹**undi** \ən-dē\ Monday, sundae,
Sunday, Whitmonday,
Whitsunday, barramundi, Bay
of Fundy, jaguarundi, Mrs.
Grundy, salmagundi,
coatimundi
²**undi** \ün-dē\ Burundi, Ruanda-
Urundi
undies \ən-dēz\ see UNDAYS
undity \ən-dət-ē\ fecundity,
profundity, rotundity,
moribundity, orotundity,
rubicundity
undle \ən-dᵊl\ bundle, rundle,
trundle, unbundle
undness \ən-nəs\ see ONENESS

undum \ən-dəm\ corundum, ad
eundem, Carborundum
undy \ən-dē\ see UNDI
une \ün\ see ¹OON
uneau \ü-nō\ see UNO
uneless \ün-ləs\ see OONLESS
uner \ü-nər\ see OONER
unes \ünz\ see OONS
¹**ung** \əŋ\ bung, clung, dung,
flung, hung, lung, pung, rung,
slung, sprung, strung, stung,
sung, swung, tongue, tung,
wrung, young, Young,
among, bee-stung, far-flung,
high-strung, Kaifeng, low-
slung, unstrung, unsung, well-
hung, adder's-tongue,
double-hung, double-tongue,
triple-tongue, overhung,
overstrung, underslung
²**ung** \uŋ\ Jung, Kung, Sung,
Antung, Bandung, Dandong,
Dadong, Hamhung, Tatung,
Kaohsiung, Zigong, Nibelung,
geländesprung,
Götterdämmerung
ungal \ən-gəl\ see UNGLE
unge \ənj\ lunge, plunge,
sponge, expunge
unged \ənjd\ see ONGUED
ungeon \ən-jən\ donjon,
dungeon, spongin
¹**unger** \ən-jər\ lunger, plunger,
sponger, expunger
²**unger** \əŋ-gər\ see ¹ONGER
ungible \ən-jə-bəl\ fungible,
inexpungible
ungle \əŋ-gəl\ bungle, fungal,
jungle, pungle
ungo \əŋ-gō\ fungo, mungo
ungous \əŋ-gəs\ fungous,
fungus, humongous

ungry \ən-grē\ see ONGERY
ungus \əŋ-gəs\ see UNGOUS
ungy \ən-jē\ grungy, spongy
unha \ü-nə\ see UNA
uni \ü-nē\ see OONY
unia \ün-yə\ petunia, vicuña
unic \ü-nik\ eunuch, Munich, Punic, runic, tunic
unicate \ü-ni-kət\ tunicate, excommunicate
unich \ü-nik\ see UNIC
union \ən-yən\ bunion, grunion, onion, ronyon, trunnion, Paul Bunyan
unis \ü-nəs\ see EWNESS
¹unish \ən-ish\ Hunnish, punish
²unish \ü-nish\ see OONISH
unit \ü-nət\ see UNATE
unitive \ü-nət-iv\ punitive, unitive
unity \ü-nət-ē\ unity, community, disunity, immunity, impunity, importunity, opportunity, European Community
unk \əŋk\ bunk, chunk, clunk, drunk, dunk, flunk, funk, gunk, hunk, junk, monk, plunk, punk, shrunk, skunk, slunk, spunk, stunk, sunk, thunk, trunk, bohunk, chipmunk, debunk, Podunk, punch-drunk, quidnunc
unkah \əŋ-kə\ punkah, unco
unkard \əŋ-kərd\ bunkered, drunkard, Dunkard, hunkered
unked \əŋt\ see UNCT
unken \əŋ-kən\ Duncan, drunken, pumpkin, shrunken, sunken
unker \əŋ-kər\ bunker, Bunker, clunker, Dunker, flunker, hunker, junker, lunker, plunker, punker, younker, debunker, spelunker
unkie \əŋ-kē\ see UNKY
unkin \əŋ-kəm\ see UNCAN
unks \əŋs\ hunks, quincunx— *also plurals and possessives of nouns and third singular presents of verbs listed at* UNK
unky \əŋ-kē\ chunky, clunky, donkey, flunky, funky, gunky, hunky, Hunky, junkie, junky, monkey, punkie, punky, spunkie, spunky
unless \ən-ləs\ runless, sonless, sunless
unn \ən\ see UN
unnage \ən-ij\ dunnage, tonnage, megatonnage
unned \ənd\ see ¹UND
unnel \ən-ᵊl\ funnel, gunnel, gunwale, runnel, trunnel, tunnel
unner \ən-ər\ cunner, gunner, runner, scunner, stunner, tonner, forerunner, front-runner, gunrunner, roadrunner, rumrunner
unnery \ən-rē\ gunnery, nunnery
unness \ən-nəs\ see ONENESS
unning \ən-iŋ\ cunning, running, stunning
unnion \ən-yən\ see UNION
unnish \ən-ish\ see ¹UNISH
unny \ən-ē\ bunny, funny, gunny, honey, money, runny, sonny, sunny, tunny, Ballymoney
uno \ü-nō\ Bruno, Juneau, Juno, numero uno

unster \ən-stər\ Meunster,
  punster
¹unt \ùnt\ dachshund,
  Dortmund, exeunt
²unt \ənt\ see ¹ONT
untal \ənt-ᵊl\ see UNTLE
unter \ənt-ər\ blunter, bunter,
  chunter, grunter, hunter,
  punter, shunter, confronter,
  foxhunter, headhunter,
  pothunter, witch-hunter
unting \ənt-iŋ\ bunting,
  foxhunting, head-hunting,
  witch-hunting—*also present
  participles of verbs listed at*
  ¹ONT
untle \ənt-ᵊl\ frontal, gruntle,
  confrontal, disgruntle,
  contrapuntal
unty \ənt-ē\ punty, runty
unwale \ən-ᵊl\ see UNNEL
unx \əŋs\ see UNKS
uny \ü-nē\ see OONY
unyan \ən-yən\ see UNION
uoth \ü-əs\ see EWESS
¹uoy \ü-ē\ see EWY
²uoy \òi\ see OY
uoyance \ü-əns\ see OYANCE
uoyancy \òi-ən-sē\ see OYANCY
uoyant \òi-ənt\ see OYANT
up \əp\ cup, dup, hup, pup,
  scup, sup, tup, up, yup,
  backup, balls-up, bang-up,
  beat-up, blowup, breakup,
  brush up, buildup, built-up,
  call-up, catch-up, change-up,
  checkup, chin-up, cleanup,
  close-up, cock-up, crack-up,
  cutup, dried-up, dustup,
  eggcup, eyecup, faceup, fill-
  up, flare-up, foul-up, frame-
  up, fry-up, getup, giddap,
  grown-up, hang-up, heads-up,
  hepped up, het up, holdup,
  hookup, hopped-up, jack-up,
  jam-up, kickup, kingcup,
  lash-up, lay-up, lead-up,
  letup, line up, linkup, lockup,
  lookup, louse up, made-up,
  makeup, markup, matchup,
  mix-up, mixed-up, mock-up,
  mop-up, mug up, nip-up, one-
  up, pasteup, pickup, pileup,
  pinup, pop-up, pull-up,
  punch-up, push-up, put-up, re-
  up, roundup, run-up, scaleup,
  screwup, send-up, setup,
  shack up, shake-up, shape-up,
  shook-up, shoot up, sign up,
  sit-up, slap-up, slipup,
  smashup, speedup, stand-up,
  start-up, step up, stepped-up,
  stickup, stuck-up, sum-up,
  sunup, take-up, teacup,
  thumbs-up, tie-up, toss-up,
  touch-up, trumped-up, tune-
  up, turnup, walk-up,
  warm-up, washed-up, washup,
  windup, wised-up, workup,
  wrap-up, write-up, belly up,
  buttercup, button-up, cover-
  up, dial-up, follow-up, higher-
  up, hurry-up, pick-me-up,
  pony up, runner-up, seven-up,
  shoot-em-up, summing-up,
  up-and-up, wickiup, winding-
  up, Johnny-jump-up, sunny-
  side up
upa \ü-pə\ pupa, stupa
upas \ü-pəs\ see UPUS
upboard \əb-ərd\ see UBBARD
upe \üp\ see ¹OOP
upel \ü-pəl\ see ²UPLE
upelet \ü-plət\ see ²UPLET

uper \ü-pər\ see OOPER
upi \ü-pē\ see OOPY
upid \ü-pəd\ Cupid, stupid
upil \ü-pəl\ see ²UPLE
¹uple \əp-əl\ couple, supple,
    decouple
²uple \ü-pəl\ cupel, duple,
    pupil, scruple, quadruple,
    quintuple, sextuple
³uple \üp-ᵊl\ supple, quadruple,
    quintuple, sextuple
¹uplet \əp-lət\ couplet,
    gradruplet, quintuplet,
    sextuplet
²uplet \ü-plət\ drupelet,
    quadruplet
uplicate \ü-pli-kət\ duplicate,
    quadruplicate, quintuplicate,
    sextuplicate
upor \ü-pər\ see OOPER
uppance \əp-əns\ threepence,
    twopence, comeuppance
upper \əp-ər\ crupper, scupper,
    supper, upper, stand-upper
uppie \əp-ē\ see UPPY
¹upple \üp-əl\ see ³UPLE
²upple \əp-əl\ see ¹UPLE
uppy \əp-ē\ cuppy, guppy,
    puppy,yuppie
upt \əpt\ abrupt, corrupt,
    disrupt, erupt, irrupt,
    developed, incorrupt,
    interrupt—*also pasts of verbs
    listed at* UP
upter \əp-tər\ corrupter,
    disrupter, interrupter
uptible \əp-tə-bəl\ corruptible,
    eruptible, irruptible,
    incorruptible, interruptible
uption \əp-shən\ abruption,
    corruption, disruption,

eruption, irruption,
    interruption
uptive \əp-tiv\ corruptive,
    disruptive, eruptive, irruptive,
    interruptive
upus \ü-pəs\ croupous, lupus,
    upas
uq \ük\ see UKE
uque \ük\ see UKE
¹ur \ōr\ see ¹ORE
²ur \u̇r\ see ¹URE
³ur \ər\ see ¹EUR
ura \u̇r-ə\ dura, durra, Jura,
    sura, surah, Agoura, bravura,
    caesura, datura, Madura,
    tamboura, tempura, aqua pura,
    Arafura, Bujumbura,
    appoggiatura, Bonaventura,
    coloratura, Telanaipura,
    Anuradhapura, camera
    obscura
urable \u̇r-ə-bəl\ curable,
    durable, thurible, endurable,
    incurable, insurable,
    perdurable
uracy \u̇r-ə-sē\ curacy,
    obduracy
urae \u̇r-ē\ see ¹URY
urah \ür-ə\ see URA
ural \u̇r-əl\ crural, jural, mural,
    neural, plural, puerile, rural,
    Ural, caesural, commissural,
    extramural, intramural
uralist \u̇r-ə-ləst\ muralist,
    pluralist, ruralist
uran \ü-rən\ see ²URIN
urance \u̇r-əns\ durance,
    assurance, endurance,
    insurance, coinsurance,
    reassurance, reinsurance
urate \u̇r-ət\ curate, turret,
    obdurate, barbiturate

urative \úr-ə-tiv\ curative,
  durative
urb \ərb\ see ERB
¹urban \ər-bən\ bourbon,
  Durban, rurban, turban,
  turbine, urban, Urban,
  exurban, suburban, interurban
²urban \úr-bən\ bourbon,
  Bourbon, rurban
urber \ər-bər\ Berber, Ferber,
  Thurber, disturber
urbia \ər-bē-ə\ Serbia, exurbia,
  suburbia
urbid \ər-bəd\ turbid, verbid
urbine \ər-bən\ see ¹URBAN
urbit \ər-bət\ burbot, sherbet,
  turbit, turbot
urble \ər-bəl\ see ERBAL
urbot \ər-bət\ see URBIT
urcate \ər-kət\ see IRCUIT
urch \ərch\ birch, church,
  Church, curch, lurch, perch,
  search, smirch, besmirch,
  Christchurch, research,
  unchurch
urchin \ər-chən\ birchen,
  urchin
urchly \ərch-lē\ churchly,
  virtually
urcia \ər-shə\ see ERTIA
¹urd \úrd\ see ¹URED
²urd \ərd\ see IRD
urdane \ərd-ᵊn\ see URDEN
urden \ərd-ᵊn\ burden, guerdon,
  lurdane, verdin, disburden,
  unburden, overburden
urder \ərd-ər\ see ERDER
urderer \ərd-ər-ər\ murderer,
  verderer
urdle \ərd-ᵊl\ curdle, girdle,
  hurdle, engirdle
urdu \ər-dü\ see ERDU

urdum \ərd-əm\ see IRDUM
urdy \ərd-ē\ birdie, sturdy,
  wordy, hurdy-gurdy, Mesa
  Verde, Monteverdi
¹ure \ür\ Boer, boor, bourg,
  cure, dour, ewer, fewer, lure,
  moor, Moor, Moore, Muir,
  poor, pure, Ruhr, sewer,
  skewer, spoor, stour, sure,
  tour, Tours, your, you're,
  abjure, adjure, Adour, allure,
  amour, Ashur, assure,
  brochure, ceinture, cocksure,
  coiffure, conjure, contour,
  couture, demure, detour, dirt-
  poor, endure, ensure, Exmoor,
  faubourg, Fraktur, grandeur,
  gravure, guipure, hachure,
  immure, impure, insure, inure,
  kultur, land-poor, langur,
  ligure, manure, mature,
  mohur, obscure, parure,
  perdure, procure, secure,
  siddur, tambour, tandoor,
  tenure, Uighur, unmoor,
  velour, velure, amateur,
  aperture, armature,
  blackamoor, carrefour, carte
  du jour, coinsure,
  commissure, confiture,
  connoisseur, coverture,
  cubature, curvature, cynosure,
  debouchure, embouchure,
  epicure, filature, forfeiture,
  garniture, geniture, green-
  manure, haute couture,
  immature, insecure, ligature,
  manicure, overture, paramour,
  pedicure, plat du jour,
  portraiture, prelature,
  premature, quadrature,
  reassure, Reaumur, reinsure,

saboteur, sepulture, sequitur,
signature, simon-pure,
sinecure, soup du jour,
tablature, temperature,
troubadour, white amur,
vavasour, Yom Kippur,
candidature, caricature,
discomfiture, distemperature,
divestiture, entablature,
entrepreneur, expenditure,
imprimatur, investiture,
literature, miniature,
musculature, nomenclature,
nonsequitur, primogeniture,
ultraminiature
²ure \ür-ē\ see ¹URY
urean \ür-ē-ən\ see URIAN
ureau \ür-ō\ see URO
¹ured \ürd\ gourde, Kurd, urd,
assured, steward,
underinsured—*also pasts of
verbs listed at* ¹URE
²ured \ərd\ see IRD
urely \ür-lē\ buirdly, poorly,
purely, surely, cocksurely,
demurely, impurely, maturely,
obscurely, immaturely,
insecurely, prematurely
urement \ür-mənt\ allurement,
immurement, inurement,
procurement, securement
uren \ür-ən\ see ²URIN
ureous \ür-ē-əs\ see URIOUS
¹urer \ür-ər\ curer, führer,
furor, furore, juror, lurer,
tourer, abjurer, assurer,
insurer, manurer, procurer,
tambourer, coinsurer,
reinsurer—*also comparatives
of adjectives listed at* ¹URE
²urer \ər-ər\ see ERRER
¹urety \ür-ət-ē\ see URITY

²urety \ürt-ē\ see URTI
urey \ür-ē\ see ¹URY
urf \ərf\ kerf, scurf, serf, surf,
turf, enserf, bodysurf
urfy \ər-fē\ Murphy, scurfy,
turfy
urg \ərg\ see ERG
urgative \ər-gə-tiv\ see
URGATIVE
urge \ərj\ dirge, merge, purge,
scourge,serge, splurge,
spurge, surge, urge, verge,
converge, deterge, diverge,
emerge, immerge, resurge,
submerge, upsurge,
dramaturge
urgence \ər-jəns\ see ERGENCE
urgency \ər-jən-sē\ see
ERGENCY
urgent \ər-jənt\ urgent,
assurgent, convergent,
detergent, divergent,
emergent, insurgent,
resurgent, preemergent
urgeon \ər-jən\ burgeon,
sturgeon, surgeon, virgin
¹urger \ər-gər\ burgher, turgor,
cheeseburger, hamburger,
Limburger
²urger \ər-jər\ see ERGER
urgery \ərj-rē\ see ERJURY
¹urgh \ər-ə\ see ¹OROUGH
²urgh \ər-ō\ see ¹URROW
³urgh \ərg\ see ERG
urgher \ər-gər\ see ¹URGER
urgic \ər-jik\ see ERGIC
urgical \ər-ji-kəl\ surgical,
liturgical, theurgical,
dramaturgical
urgid \ər-jəd\ turgid, synergid
urgle \ər-gəl\ burgle, gurgle
urgor \ər-gər\ see ¹URGER

urgy \ər-jē\ clergy, dramaturgy, metallurgy

uri \ūr-ē\ see ¹URY

¹urial \ūr-ē-əl\ curial, urial, Uriel, mercurial, seigneurial, tenurial, entrepreneurial

²urial \er-ē-əl\ see ARIAL

urian \ūr-ē-ən\ durian, Hurrian, Arthurian, centurion, epicurean

uriance \ūr-ē-əns\ see URIENCE

uriant \ūr-ē-ənt\ see URIENT

¹urible \ūr-ə-bəl\ see URABLE

²urible \ər-ə-bəl\ see ERABLE

uric \ūr-ik\ uric, mercuric, sulfuric

urid \ūr-əd\ lurid, murid

urie \ūr-ē\ see ¹URY

uriel \ūr-ē-əl\ see ¹URIAL

urience \ūr-ē-əns\ prurience, luxuriance

urient \ūr-ē-ənt\ esurient, luxuriant, parturient

¹urier \er-ē-ər\ see ERRIER

²urier \ūr-ē-ər\ see ¹OURIER

uriere \ūr-ē-ər\ see ¹OURIER

¹urin \ər-ən\ burin, murrain

²urin \ūr-ən\ burin, Huron, urine, Belgian Tervuren

urine \ūr-ən\ see ²URIN

uring \ūr-iŋ\ during, mooring, touring

urion \ūr-ē-ən\ see URIAN

urious \ūr-ē-əs\ curious, furious, spurious, incurious, injurious, luxurious, penurious, perjurious, sulfureous, usurious

uris \ūr-əs\ see URUS

urist \ūr-əst\ purist, tourist, manicurist, pedicurist, caricaturist, chiaroscurist,

miniaturist—*also superlatives of adjectives listed at* ¹URE

urity \ūr-ət-ē\ purity, surety, futurity, impurity, maturity, obscurity, security, immaturity, insecurity, prematurity

urk \ərk\ see ¹ORK

¹urka \ər-kə\ charka, circa, Gurkha, mazurka

²urka \ūr-kə\ Gurkha, mazurka

urke \ərk\ see ¹ORK

urker \ər-kər\ see ¹ORKER

urkey \ər-kē\ see ERKY

¹urkha \ūr-kə\ see ²URKA

²urkha \ər-kə\ see ¹URKA

urki \ər-kē\ see ERKY

urky \ər-kē\ see ERKY

url \ərl\ see ¹IRL

urled \ərld\ see ORLD

urlew \ərl-ü\ curlew, purlieu

urlieu \ərl-ü\ see URLEW

urlin \ər-lən\ see ERLIN

urling \ər-liŋ\ curling, hurling, sterling—*also present participles of verbs listed at* ¹IRL

urlish \ər-lish\ churlish, girlish

urly \ər-lē\ burley, burly, curly, early, girlie, hurly, knurly, pearly, squirrely, surly, swirly, twirly, whirly, hurly-burly

urman \ər-mən\ see ERMAN

urmity \ər-mət-ē\ see IRMITY

urmur \ər-mər\ firmer, infirmer, murmur, termer, wormer

urn \ərn\ burn, churn, curn, earn, erne, fern, kern, learn, pirn, quern, spurn, stern, tern, terne, turn, urn, yearn,

adjourn, astern, attorn, casern,
concern, discern, downturn,
epergne, eterne, extern,
heartburn, intern, lucerne,
nocturn, nocturne, outturn,
return, sauternes, secern,
sojourn, sunburn, unlearn,
upturn, U-turn, windburn,
Comintern, overturn, taciturn,
unconcern

urnable \ər-nə-bəl\ burnable,
discernible, returnable,
indiscernible

urnal \ərn-ᵊl\ see ERNAL

urne \ərn\ see URN

urned \ərnd\ burned, durned,
concerned, unearned,
unlearned, well-turned,
windburned—*also pasts of
verbs listed at* URN

urner \ər-nər\ burner, earner,
turner, discerner, returner,
afterburner

urnery \ər-nə-rē\ see ERNARY

urney \ər-nē\ see ¹OURNEY

urnian \ər-nē-ən\ see ERNIAN

urnish \ər-nish\ burnish,
furnish

urnt \ərnt\ see EARNT

urnum \ər-nəm\ sternum,
alburnum, laburnum,
viburnum

uro \ur-ō\ bureau, duro, euro,
enduro, maduro, politburo,
chiaroscuro

uron \ur-ən\ see ²URIN

uror \ur-ər\ see ¹URER

urore \ur-ər\ see ¹URER

urous \ur-əs\ see URUS

urp \ərp\ burp, chirp, slurp,
stirp, twerp, usurp

urphy \ər-fē\ see URFY

urple \ər-pəl\ purple, empurple

urplice \ər-pləs\ see URPLUS

urplus \ər-pləs\ surplice,
surplus

urps \ərps\ see IRPS

urr \ər\ see ¹EUR

¹urra \ur-ə\ see URA

²urra \ər-ə\ see ¹OROUGH

urrage \ər-ij\ see OURAGE

urragh \ər-ə\ see ¹OROUGH

urrain \ər-ən\ see ¹URIN

urral \ər-əl\ see ERRAL

urrant \ər-ənt\ see URRENT

urray \ər-ē\ see URRY

urre \ər\ see ¹EUR

urred \ərd\ see IRD

urrence \ər-əns\ concurrence,
conference, deterrence,
incurrence, occurrence,
transference,
countertransference

urrent \ər-ənt\ currant, current,
weren't, concurrent,
crosscurrent, decurrent,
deterrent, occurrent, recurrent,
susurrant, countercurrent,
undercurrent, supercurrent

urrer \ər-ər\ see ERRER

urret \ur-ət\ see URATE

urrey \ər-ē\ see URRY

urrian \ur-ē-ən\ see URIAN

urrie \ər-ē\ see URRY

urrier \ər-ē-ər\ courier, currier,
furrier, hurrier, worrier—*also
comparatives of adjectives
listed at* URRY

urring \ər-iŋ\ furring, shirring,
stirring, skiöring—*also
present participles of verbs
listed at* ¹EUR

urrish \ər-ish\ see OURISH

¹urro \ər-ə\ see ¹OROUGH

²**urro** \ər-ō\ see ¹URROW
¹**urrow** \ər-ō\ borough, burgh, burro, burrow, furrow, thorough
²**urrow** \ər-ə\ see ¹OROUGH
urry \ər-ē\ blurry, burry, curry, flurry, furry, dhurrie, gurry, hurry, Moray, Murray, murrey, scurry, slurry, spurrey, surrey, Surrey, whirry, worry, hurry-scurry
ursa \ər-sə\ see ERSA
ursal \ər-səl\ see ¹ERSAL
ursar \ər-sər\ see URSOR
ursary \ərs-rē\ bursary, cursory, mercery, nursery, anniversary
urse \ərs\ see ERSE
ursed \ərst\ see URST
ursement \ər-smənt\ see ERCEMENT
urser \ər-sər\ see URSOR
ursery \ərs-rē\ see URSARY
ursion \ər-zhən\ see ¹ERSION
ursionist \ərzh-nəst\ see ERSIONIST
ursive \ər-siv\ see ERSIVE
ursor \ər-sər\ bursar, cursor, mercer, nurser, purser, worser, disburser, disperser, precursor, rehearser, reverser, traverser
ursory \ərs-rē\ see URSARY
urst \ərst\ burst, cursed, durst, erst, first, Hearst, thirst, verst, worst, wurst, accursed, airburst, Amherst, athirst, cloudburst, downburst, emersed, feetfirst, groundburst, headfirst, outburst, sunburst, liverwurst, microburst—*also pasts of verbs listed at* ERSE

ursus \ər-səs\ see ERSUS
¹**ursy** \ər-sē\ see ERCY
²**ursy** \əs-ē\ see USSY
¹**urt** \ûrt\ yurt, Erfurt, Frankfurt, Betancourt
²**urt** \ərt\ see ¹ERT
urtain \ərt-ᵊn\ see ERTAIN
urtal \ərt-ᵊl\ see ERTILE
urtenance \ərt-ᵊn-əns\ see ERTINENCE
urtenant \ərt-nənt\ see IRTINENT
urter \ərt-ər\ see ERTER
urtesy \ərt-ə-sē\ see OURTESY
urthen \ər-thən\ burthen, earthen
urther \ər-thər\ further, murther
urti \ûrt-ē\ pretty, surety, Trimurti
urtium \ər-shəm\ nasturtium, sestertium
urtive \ərt-iv\ see ERTIVE
urtle \ərt-ᵊl\ see ERTILE
urton \ərt-ᵊn\ see ERTAIN
urture \ər-chər\ see IRCHER
uru \ûr-ü\ guru, kuru, Nauru
urus \ûr-əs\ urus, Arcturus, mercurous, sulfurous, Epicurus, sui juris, tinea cruris
urve \ərv\ see ERVE
urved \ərvd\ see ERVED
urviness \ər-vē-nəs\ see ERVINESS
urvy \ər-vē\ curvy, nervy, scurvy, topsy-turvy
¹**ury** \ûr-ē\ curie, Curie, fleury, fury, houri, Jewry, jury, Kure, Urey, Bhojpuri, de jure, Missouri, tandoori, lusus naturae
²**ury** \er-ē\ see ¹ARY

urze \ərz\ see ERS
urzy \ər-zē\ see ERSEY
¹us \əs\ bus, buss, crus, cuss,
　fuss, Gus, Huss, muss, plus,
　pus, Russ, suss, thus, truss,
　us, airbus, concuss, cost-plus,
　discuss, nonplus, percuss,
　railbus, untruss, autobus,
　blunderbuss, microbus,
　minibus
²us \ü\ see ¹EW
³us \üs\ see ¹USE
⁴us \üsh\ see OUCHE
⁵us \üz\ see ²USE
¹usa \ü-sə\ Sousa, Azusa,
　Medusa, Appaloosa, Gebel
　Musa, Jebel Musa
²usa \ü-zə\ Sousa, Susa,
　Medusa, Arethusa
usable \ü-zə-bəl\ fusible,
　losable, usable, abusable,
　diffusible, excusable,
　infusible, reusable,
　transfusible, inexcusable,
　irrecusable
usae \ü-sē\ see UICY
¹usal \ü-səl\ streusel, occlusal
²usal \ü-zəl\ foozle, fusil, ouzel,
　snoozle, streusel, accusal,
　bamboozle, occlusal, perusal,
　refusal
usc \əsk\ see USK
uscan \əs-kən\ buskin, Ruskin,
　Tuscan, Etruscan, molluscan
uscat \əs-kət\ see USKET
uscle \əs-əl\ see USTLE
uscular \əs-kyə-lər\ muscular,
　corpuscular, crepuscular,
　majuscular
uscule \əs-kyül\ crepuscule,
　opuscule
¹use \üs\ Bruce, crouse, crus,

cruse, deuce, douce, goose,
juice, loose, moose, mousse,
noose, nous, puce, rhus, ruse,
Russ, schuss, sluice, spruce,
truce, use, Zeus, Aarhus,
abstruse, abuse, adduce,
Arhus, Atreus, burnoose,
caboose, Cayuse, Cepheus,
ceruse, conduce, couscous,
deduce, diffuse, disuse, educe,
effuse, excuse, footloose,
induce, Lanús, misuse,
mongoose, Morpheus, negus,
obtuse, Orpheus, papoose,
Peleus, Perseus, prepuce,
produce, profuse, Proteus,
Purus, recluse, reduce, refuse,
retuse, reuse, Sanctus, seduce,
Tereus, Theseus, traduce,
transduce, unloose, vamoose,
Belarus, Betelgeuse,
calaboose, charlotte russe,
introduce, mass-produce,
Odysseus, Prometheus,
reproduce, self-abuse,
Syracuse, Typhoeus,
hypotenuse, Sancti Spiritus
²use \üz\ blues, booze, bruise,
choose, cruise, cruse, Druze,
flews, fuse, Hughes, lose,
Meuse, muse, news, ooze,
roose, ruse, schmooze,
snooze, trews, use, whose,
abuse, accuse, amuse,
Andrews, bemuse, berceuse,
chanteuse, chartreuse,
coiffeuse, confuse, contuse,
danseuse, defuse, diffuse,
diseuse, disuse, effuse,
Elbrus, enthuse, excuse, ill-
use, infuse, masseuse, misuse,
perfuse, peruse, recluse,

recuse, refuse, reuse, suffuse, Toulouse, transfuse, vendeuse, Betelgeuse, disabuse, interfuse, mitrailleuse, Newport News, p's and q's, Santa Cruz, Vera Cruz, Goody Two-shoes

used \üzd\ used, confused, underused—*also pasts of verbs listed at* ²USE

useless \ü-sləs\ juiceless, useless

user \ü-zər\ boozer, bruiser, chooser, cruiser, doozer, loser, snoozer, user, abuser, accuser, amuser, diffuser, excuser, infuser, peruser, multiuser

¹ush \əsh\ blush, brush, crush, flush, gush, hush, Cush, lush, mush, plush, rush, shush, slush, squush, thrush, tush, airbrush, bulrush, bum's rush, hairbrush, hush-hush, inrush, nailbrush, onrush, paintbrush, sagebrush, toothbrush, uprush, bottlebrush, Hindu Kush, underbrush

²ush \ush\ bush, Bush, mush, push, shush, squoosh, swoosh, tush, whoosh, ambush, Hindu Kush, rosebush, thornbush

ushabel \ə-shə-bəl\ crushable, flushable

¹usher \əsh-ər\ blusher, brusher, crusher, gusher, musher, rusher, usher, four-flusher, goldrusher—*also comparatives of adjectives listed at* ¹USH

²usher \ush-ər\ pusher, ambusher

ushi \ush-ē\ see ²USHY

ushing \əsh-iŋ\ onrushing, toothbrushing, unblushing— *also present participles of verbs listed at* ¹USH

ushu \ü-shü\ Kyushu, Kitakyushu

¹ushy \əsh-ē\ brushy, gushy, mushy, plushy, rushy, slushy

²ushy \ush-ē\ bushy, cushy, mushy, pushy, sushi

usi \ü-sē\ see UICY

usian \ü-zhən\ see USION

¹usible \ü-sə-bəl\ see UCIBLE

²usible \ü-zə-bəl\ see USABLE

usic \ü-zik\ music, Tungusic

usie \ü-zē\ see OOZY

usil \ü-zəl\ see ²USAL

using \əs-iŋ\ busing, trussing, antibusing

usion \ü-zhən\ fusion, affusion, allusion, Carthusian, collusion, conclusion, confusion, contusion, delusion, diffusion, effusion, elusion, exclusion, extrusion, illusion, inclusion, infusion, intrusion, Malthusian, obtrusion, occlusion, perfusion, prelusion, profusion, prolusion, protrusion, reclusion, seclusion, transfusion, Venusian, Andalusian, disillusion, malocclusion, autotransfusion

usionist \üzh-nəst\ fusionist, diffusionist, exclusionist, illusionist, perfusionist

usity \ü-sət-ē\ see UCITY

usive \ü-siv\ abusive, allusive, amusive, collusive,

conclusive, conducive,
delusive, diffusive, effusive,
elusive, exclusive, extrusive,
illusive, inclusive, intrusive,
obtrusive, occlusive,
prelusive, protrusive,
reclusive, inconclusive

usk \əsk\ brusque, cusk, dusk,
husk, musk, rusk, tusk,
subfusc

usker \əs-kər\ busker, husker,
tusker

usket \əs-kət\ muscat, musket

uskie \əs-kē\ see USKY

uskin \əs-kən\ see USCAN

usky \əs-kē\ dusky, husky,
muskie, musky

usly \əs-lē\ pussley, thusly

uso \ü-sō\ see USOE

usoe \ü-sō\ trousseau, whoso,
Caruso, Robinson Crusoe

usory \üs-ə-rē\ delusory,
prolusory, illusory

usque \əsk\ see USK

¹uss \u̇s\ puss, Russ, schuss,
chartreuse, sea puss, sourpuss,
glamour-puss, octopus,
platypus

²uss \üs\ see ¹USE

³uss \əs\ see ¹US

ussant \əs-ᵊnt\ mustn't,
discussant

ussate \əs-ət\ see USSET

usse \üs\ see ¹USE

ussel \əs-əl\ see USTLE

ussell \əs-əl\ see USTLE

usset \əs-ət\ gusset, russet,
decussate

ussia \əsh-ə\ Prussia, Russia,
Belorussia

ussian \əsh-ən\ see USSION

ussing \əs-iŋ\ see USING

ussion \əsh-ən\ Prussian,
Russian, concussion,
discussion, percussion,
Belorussian, repercussion

ussive \əs-iv\ jussive, tussive,
concussive, percussive,
repercussive

ussle \əs-əl\ see USTLE

ussley \əs-lē\ see USLY

ussy \əs-ē\ fussy, hussy, mussy,
pursy, pussy

¹ust \əst\ bust, crust, dost, dust,
gust, just, lust, must, musth,
rust, thrust, trust, wast, adjust,
adust, august, combust,
degust, disgust, distrust,
encrust, entrust, mistrust,
moondust, piecrust, robust,
stardust, upthrust, antitrust,
dryasdust, unitrust,
wanderlust—*also pasts of
verbs listed at* ¹US

²ust \əs\ see ¹US

³ust \üst\ see OOST

ustable \əs-tə-bəl\ see USTIBLE

ustard \əs-tərd\ bustard,
custard, mustard—*also pasts
of verbs listed at* USTER

usted \əs-təd\ busted, disgusted,
maladjusted, well-adjusted—
also pasts of verbs listed at
¹UST

uster \əs-tər\ bluster, buster,
cluster, Custer, duster, fluster,
luster, muster, thruster,
adjuster, blockbuster,
combustor, deluster,
gangbuster, lackluster,
sodbuster, trustbuster,
antitruster, filibuster

ustful \əst-fəl\ lustful, thrustful,
trustful, distrustful

usth \əst\ see ¹UST
ustian \əs-chən\ see USTION
ustible \əs-tə-bəl\ adjustable,
combustible, incombustible
ustin \əs-tən\ Justin, Augustine
ustine \əs-tən\ see USTIN
ustic \əs-tik\ fustic, rustic
ustion \əs-chən\ fustian,
combustion
ustious \əs-chəs\ robustious,
rumbustious
ustive \əs-tiv\ adjustive,
combustive, maladjustive
ustle \əs-əl\ bustle, hustle,
muscle, mussel, Russell,
rustle, trestle, tussle,
corpuscle, crepuscle, Jack
Russell
ustn't \əs-ᵊnt\ see USSANT
ustom \əs-təm\ custom,
frustum, accustom,
disaccustom
ustor \əs-tər\ see USTER
ustrious \əs-trē-əs\ illustrious,
industrious
ustrous \əs-trəs\ blustrous,
lustrous
ustule \əs-chül\ frustule, pustule
ustum \əs-təm\ see USTOM
ustus \əs-təs\ Justus, Augustus
usty \əs-tē\ busty, crusty, dusty,
fusty, gusty, lusty, musty,
rusty, trusty
usy \iz-ē\ see IZZY
¹ut \ət\ but, butt, cut, glut, gut,
hut, jut, mutt, nut, putt, rut,
scut, shut, slut, smut, soot,
strut, tut, ut, what, abut,
beechnut, catgut, chestnut,
clean-cut, clear-cut, cobnut,
cockshut, crosscut, groundnut,

haircut, locknut, offcut,
peanut, pignut, rebut, recut,
rotgut, shortcut, somewhat,
tut-tut, uncut, walnut,
woodcut, butternut,
congregate, hazelnut, overcut,
scuttlebutt, undercut,
uppercut, open-and-shut
²ut \ü\ see ¹EW
³ut \üt\ see UTE
⁴ut \u̇t\ see ¹OOT
uta \üt-ə\ Baruta, likuta, valuta
utable \üt-ə-bəl\ mutable,
scrutable, suitable,
commutable, computable,
disputable, immutable,
inscrutable, permutable,
statutable, executable,
incommutable, incomputable,
indisputable, irrefutable,
prosecutable, substitutable
utage \üt-ij\ see ¹OOTAGE
utal \üt-ᵊl\ see UTILE
utan \üt-ᵊn\ cutin, gluten,
Luton, mutine, Newton,
Teuton, Laputan, rambutan,
Rasputin, highfalutin
utant \üt-ᵊnt\ mutant, disputant,
pollutant
utative \üt-ət-iv\ putative,
commutative, imputative
¹utch \əch\ clutch, crutch,
cutch, dutch, Dutch, grutch,
hutch, much, scutch, smutch,
such, touch, nonesuch,
retouch, double-clutch,
overmuch
²utch \u̇ch\ butch, putsch
utcher \əch-ər\ scutcher,
retoucher
utchy \əch-ē\ see UCHY

ute \üt\ boot, bruit, brut, brute, bute, Bute, butte, chute, cloot, coot, cute, flute, fruit, glout, hoot, jute, Jute, loot, lute, moot, mute, newt, pood, root, Root, rout, route, scoot, scute, shoot, snoot, soot, suit, suite, toot, tout, ut, Ute, acute, astute, Asyût, beetroot, Beirut, birthroot, bloodroot, breadfruit, butut, cahoot, Canute, cheroot, clubroot, commute, compute, confute, crapshoot, deaf-mute, depute, dilute, dispute, elute, en route, enroot, folkmoot, freeboot, galoot, grapefruit, hardboot, hirsute, imbrute, impute, jackboot, jackfruit, jumpsuit, kashruth, lawsuit, minute, nonsuit, offshoot, outshoot, Paiute, pantsuit, permute, playsuit, pollute, pursuit, recruit, refute, repute, salute, seaboot, snowsuit, solute, sunsuit, swimsuit, taproot, tracksuit, transmute, uproot, volute, absolute, Aleut, arrowroot, Asyût, attribute, autoroute, bandicoot, bitterroot, bodysuit, boilersuit, bumbershoot, constitute, convolute, Denver boot, destitute, disrepute, dissolute, evolute, execute, gingerroot, institute, involute, kiwifruit, malamute, overshoot, parachute, persecute, prosecute, prostitute, qiviut, resolute, restitute, revolute, subacute, substitute, troubleshoot, undershoot, electrocute, Hardecanute, Inuktitut, irresolute, reconstitute

uted \üt-əd\ see ¹OOTED

utee \üt-ē\ see ¹OOTY

utely \üt-lē\ cutely, mutely, accutely, astutely, minutely, absolutely, dissolutely, irresolutely

uten \üt-ᵊn\ see UTAN

uteness \üt-nəs\ cuteness, glutenous, glutinous, muteness, mutinous, acuteness, diluteness, hirsuteness, absoluteness, destituteness, dissoluteness, irresoluteness

utenist \üt-ᵊn-əst\ lutenist, Teutonist

utenous \üt-nəs\ see UTENESS

uteous \üt-ē-əs\ beauteous, duteous, gluteus, luteous

uter \üt-ər\ cooter, neuter, fluter, hooter, looter, pewter, rooter, router, scooter, shooter, souter, suiter, suitor, tooter, tutor, accoutre, commuter, computer, confuter, crapshooter, diluter, disputer, freebooter, peashooter, recruiter, saluter, sharpshooter, six-shooter, trapshooter, two-suiter, zoot-suiter, coadjutor, executor, instituter, persecutor, prosecutor, prostitutor, troubleshooter, microcomputer, minicomputer, superminicomputer—*also*

*comparatives of adjectives
listed at* UTE

utes \üts\ see OOTS

uteus \üt-ē-əs\ see UTEOUS

¹uth \üt\ see UTE

²uth \üth\ see ²OOTH

¹uther \ü-thər\ Luther, Uther

²uther \ə-ther\ see ¹OTHER

uthful \üth-fəl\ ruthful, truthful,
youthful, untruthful

uthless \üth-ləs\ ruthless,
toothless

uti \üt-ē\ see ¹OOTY

utia \ü-shə\ fuchsia, minutia,
Saint Lucia

utian \ü-shən\ see UTION

utic \üt-ik\ maieutic, scorbutic,
toreutic, hermeneutic,
parachutic, propaedeutic,
therapeutic

utical \üt-i-kəl\ cuticle,
hermeneutical, pharmaceutical

uticle \üt-i-kəl\ see UTICAL

utie \üt-ē\ see ¹OOTY

utiful \üt-i-fəl\ beautiful, dutiful

utile \üt-°l\ brutal, cuittle,
footle, futile, tootle, utile,
inutile, Kwakiutl

utin \üt-°n\ see UTAN

utine \üt-°n\ see UTAN

uting \üt-iŋ\ fluting, luting,
suiting, hip-shooting,
sharpshooting, trapshooting

¹utinous \üt-°n-əs\ glutinous,
mutinous

²utinous \üt-nəs\ see UTENESS

utiny \üt-°n-ē\ mutiny, scrutiny

ution \ü-shən\ Lucian, ablution,
Aleutian, capuchin,
Confucian, dilution, elution,
locution, pollution, solution,
absolution, allocution,

attribution, comminution,
consecution, constitution,
contribution, convolution,
destitution, devolution,
diminution, dissolution,
distribution, elocution,
evolution, execution,
exsolution, institution,
involution, lilliputian,
persecution, prosecution,
prostitution, resolution,
restitution, retribution,
revolution, Rosicrucian,
substitution, antipollution,
circumlocution, electrocution,
irresolution, maldistribution,
reconstitution, redistribution

utionary \ü-shə-ner-ē\
illocutionary, revolutionary

utionist \ü-shnəst\
devolutionist, elocutionist,
evolutionist, revolutionist,
redistributionist

utish \üt-ish\ brutish, Vutish

utist \üt-əst\ chutist, flutist,
absolutist, parachutist,
therapeutist—*also
superlatives of adjectives
listed at* UTE

utive \üt-iv\ dilutive,
constitutive, persecutive,
substitutive

utl \ü-t°l\ see UTILE

utland \ət-lənd\ Jutland,
Rutland

utlass \ət-ləs\ cutlass, gutless

utler \ət-lər\ butler, Butler,
cutler, sutler

utless \ət-ləs\ see UTLASS

utlet \ət-lət\ cutlet, nutlet

utment \ət-mənt\ hutment,
abutment

utney \ət-nē\ chutney, gluttony,
  Ascutney
uto \üt-ō\ Bhutto, Pluto, putto,
  Basuto, cornuto, Maputo,
  tenuto, sostenuto
uton \üt-ⁿ\ see UTAN
utor \üt-ər\ see UTER
utriment \ü-trə-mənt\
  nutriment, accoutrement
uts \əts\ see UTZ
utsch \ùch\ see ²UTCH
utsi \üt-sē\ see ²UZZI
utsk \ütsk\ Irkutsk, Yakutsk
utsy \ət-sē\ gutsy, klutzy
utt \ət\ see ¹UT
uttack \ət-ək\ see UTTOCK
uttal \ət-ᵊl\ see UTTLE
utte \üt\ see UTE
uttee \ət-ē\ see UTTY
¹utter \ət-ər\ butter, clutter,
  cutter, flutter, gutter, mutter,
  nutter, putter, scutter, shutter,
  splutter, sputter, strutter,
  stutter, utter, abutter, aflutter,
  haircutter, price-cutter,
  rebutter, stonecutter,
  unclutter, woodcutter
²utter \ùt-ər\ see ¹OOTER
uttery \ət-ə-rē\ buttery, fluttery,
  spluttery
¹utti \üt-ē\ see ¹OOTY
²utti \ùt-ē\ see ²OOTY
utting \ùt-iŋ\ see ¹OOTING
uttish \ət-ish\ ruttish, sluttish
uttle \ət-ᵊl\ cuittle, scuttle,
  shuttle, subtile, subtle,
  rebuttal
utto \üt-ō\ see UTO
uttock \ət-ək\ buttock, Cuttack,
  futtock
utton \ət-ᵊn\ button, glutton,

mutton, Sutton, keybutton,
  unbutton, leg-of-mutton
uttony \ət-nē\ see UTNEY
utty \ət-ē\ butty, gutty, jutty,
  nutty, puttee, putty, rutty,
  smutty
utum \üt-əm\ scutum, sputum
uture \ü-chər\ blucher, future,
  moocher, suture
uty \üt-ē\ see ¹OOTY
utz \əts\ futz, klutz, lutz, nuts,
  blood-and-guts—*also plurals
  and possessives of nouns and
  third person singular presents
  of verbs listed at* ¹UT
utzy \ət-sē\ see UTSY
uu \ü\ see ¹EW
uvial \ü-vē-əl\ fluvial, pluvial,
  alluvial, colluvial, diluvial,
  eluvial
uvian \ü-vē-ən\ alluvion,
  diluvian, Peruvian, vesuvian,
  Vesuvian, postdiluvian,
  antediluvian
uvion \ü-vē-ən\ see UVIAN
uvium \ü-vē-əm\ alluvium,
  colluvium, effluvium, eluvium
¹ux \əks\ crux, flux, lux, tux,
  afflux, aw-shucks, conflux,
  deluxe, efflux, influx, redux,
  reflux, Benelux—*also plurals
  and possessives of nouns and
  third person singular presents
  of verbs listed at* UCK
²ux \ùks\ see ²OOKS
¹uxe \üks\ see ¹OOKS
²uxe \ùks\ see ²OOKS
³uxe \əks\ see ¹UX
uxion \ək-shən\ see UCTION
uy \ī\ see ¹Y
uygur \ē-gər\ see EAGER
uyot \ē-ō\ see ²IO

uyp \īp\ see IPE
¹uz \üts\ see OOTS
²uz \úz\ see ²USE
uze \üz\ see ²USE
uzz \əz\ see ¹EUSE
¹uzzi \ü-zē\ see OOZY
²uzzi \üt-sē\ Tutsi, Abruzzi

uzzle \əz-əl\ guzzle, muzzle,
nuzzle, puzzle
uzzler \əz-lər\ guzzler, puzzler,
gas-guzzler
uzzy \əz-ē\ fuzzy, muzzy,
scuzzy

y

¹y \ī\ ai, ay, aye, bi, buy, by, bye, chi, cry, die, dry, dye, eye, fie, fly, fry, guy, Guy, hi, hie, high, i, I, lie, lye, my, nigh, phi, pi, pie, ply, pry, psi, rye, scythe, sei, shy, sigh, sky, sly, spry, spy, sty, Tai, Thai, thigh, thy, tie, try, vie, why, wry, wye, xi, Y , aby, agley, air-dry, ally, Altai, anti, apply, assai, awry, aye-aye, Bacchae, Baha'i, banzai, barfly, Belgae, belie, bigeye, birds-eye, blackfly, blow-dry, blowby, blowfly, blue-sky, Bottai, bone-dry, bonsai, botfly, Brunei, buckeye, bugeye, bulls-eye, bye-bye, canaille, catchfly, cat's-eye, cockeye, cockshy, comply, cross-eye, deadeye, decry, deep-fry, deep-sky, deerfly, defy, Delphi, deny, descry, drip-dry, Dubai, elhi, Eli, espy, firefly, fish-eye, flyby, forby, freeze-dry, frogeye, gadfly, gallfly, GI, good-bye, greenfly, grisaille, gun-shy, Haggai, Hawkeye, hereby, hi-fi, hog-tie, horsefly, housefly, imply, jai alai, July, Katmai, Kaui, Kenai, knee-high, lanai, Lanai, lay-by, Levi, magpie, mao-tai, Masai, medfly, Moirai, mooneye, nearby, necktie, nisi, outbye, outcry, oxeye, Panay, panfry, Parcae, piece-dye, pigsty, pinkeye, Po Hai, pop eye, potpie, Qinghai, quasi, rabbi, re-try, red-eye, rely, reply, rocaille, rough-dry, Sakai, sci-fi, semi, Sendai, serai, shanghai, Shanghai, shoofly, shut-eye, Sinai, sky-high, small-fry, sockeye, stand by, standby, stir-fry, supply, swing-by, terai, test-fly, thereby, tie-dye, titi, tongue-tie, two-ply, untie, Versailles, walleye, watcheye, well-nigh, whereby, whitefly, wise guy, worms-eye, Adonai, alibi, alkali, amplify, apple-pie, argufy, basify, beautify, butterfly, by-and-by, calcify, certify, Chou En-lai, citify, clarify, classify, cockneyfy, codify, crucify, cut-and-dry, DIY, damnify, damselfly, dandify, deify, densify, dignify, dobsonfly, do-or-die, dragonfly, edify, falsify, fancify, fortify, frenchify, fructify, gasify, Gemini, gentrify, glorify, goggle-eye, goldeneye, gratify, Haggai, hexerei, horrify, Iceni, justify, lignify, liquefy, lithify, Lorelei, lullaby, Madurai, magnify, Malachi, Maracay, modify, mollify, Molokai, Mordecai, mortify, multi-ply,

multiply, mummify, mystify,
nazify, nitrify, notify, nullify,
occupy, Olduvai, ossify,
overbuy, overfly, overlie,
pacify, Paraguay, passerby,
peccavi, petrify, PPI,
preachify, prettify, prophesy,
purify, putrefy, qualify,
quantify, ramify, rarefy,
ratify, RBI, rectify, reify, res
gestae, resupply, Russify,
samurai, sanctify, satisfy,
scarify, semidry, signify,
simplify, sine die, specify,
speechify, stratify, stultify,
stupefy, Tenebrae, terrify,
testify, tigereye, typify,
uglify, ultrahigh, underlie,
unify, Uruguay, Veneti,
verify, versify, vilify, vinify,
vitrify, vivify, zombify,
acetify, acidify, a priori,
beatify, decertify, declassify,
demystify, denazify, detoxify,
Dioscuri, disqualify,
dissatisfy, diversify, electrify,
exemplify, facetiae, Helvetii,
humidify, identify, indemnify,
intensify, objectify, personify,
preoccupy, reliquiae, reunify,
revivify, rigidify, saponify,
solemnify, solidify, syllabify,
transmogrify, undersupply,
vox populi, a fortiori,
caravanserai, corpus delicti,
deacidify, dehumidify, ex
hypothesi, modus vivendi,
nolle prosequi, oversimplify,
amicus curiae, curriculum
vitae, modus operandi
²y \ē\ see ¹EE
ya \ē-ə\ see ¹IA

yable \ī-ə-bəl\ see ¹IABLE
yad \ī-əd\ dryad, dyad, naiad,
   sayyid, triad, hamadryad,
   jeremiad
yan \ī-ən\ see ¹ION
yant \ī-ənt\ see IANT
yatt \ī-ət\ see IET
ybe \īb\ see ¹IBE
ybele \ib-ə-lē\ Cybele,
   ambiboly
yber \ī-bər\ see IBER
ybia \i-bē-ə\ see IBIA
ybris \ī-brəs\ see IBROUS
ycad \ī-kəd\ cycad, spiked
ycan \ī-kən\ see ¹ICHEN
yean \ī-cən\ see ¹ICHEN
yce \īs\ see ¹ICE
¹ych \ik\ see ICK
²ych \īk\ see ²IKE
yche \ī-kē\ see ¹IKE
ychnis \ik-nəs\ see ICKNESS
ycia \ish-ə\ see ¹ITIA
ycian \ish-ən\ see ITION
ycin \īs-ᵊn\ see ¹ISON
¹ycle \ī-kəl\ cycle, Michael,
   recycle, Calvin cycle,
   epicycle, Exercycle,
   hemicycle, kilocycle,
   motorcycle, unicycle, Wanne-
   Eickel
²ycle \ik-əl\ see ICKLE
ycler \ik-lər\ see ICKLER
yd \ü-id\ see UID
yde \īd\ see ¹IDE
ydia \i-dē-ə\ see IDIA
ydian \id-ē-ən\ see IDIAN
ydice \id-ə-sē\ see IDICE
ydney \id-nē\ see IDNEY
ye \ī\ see ¹Y
yeable \ī-ə-bəl\ see ¹IABLE
yed \īd\ see ¹IDE
yer \īr\ see ¹IRE

yeth \ī-əth\ see ¹IATH

yfe \īf\ see IFE

yfed \ər-əd\ see OVED

yg \ig\ see IG

ygamous \ig-ə-məs\ see
   IGAMOUS

ygamy \ig-ə-mē\ see IGAMY

ygia \ī-jə\ see IJAH

ygian \ij-ən\ Phrygian, pidgin,
   pigeon, smidgen, stygian,
   wigeon, religion,
   Cantabrigian, irreligion,
   callipygian

ygiene \ī-jēn\ see AIJIN

ygma \ig-mə\ see IGMA

ygnet \ig-nət\ cygnet, signet

ygnus \ig-nəs\ see IGNESS

ygos \ī-gəs\ see YGOUS

ygous \ī-gəs\ gigas, azygos,
   callipygous, hemizygous,
   homozygous, steatopygous

ygrapher \ig-rə-fər\ see
   IGRAPHER

ygraphist \ig-rə-fəst\ see
   IGRAPHIST

ygyny \ij-ə-nē\ see IGINE

ying \ī-iŋ\ crying, flying, lying,
   trying, high-flying, low-lying,
   outlying, undying, nitrifying,
   terrifying, underlying

yke \īk\ see ²IKE

yked \īkt\ see ¹IKED

yl \ēl\ see ²EAL

ylan \il-ən\ see ILLON

ylar \ī-lər\ see ILAR

yle \īl\ see ¹ILE

ylem \ī-ləm\ see ILUM

yler \ī-lər\ see ILAR

ylet \ī-lət\ see ILOT

yley \ī-lē\ see YLY

yli \ē-lē\ see EELY

ylic \il-ik\ see ILIC

ylie \ī-lē\ see YLY

yling \ī-liŋ\ see ¹ILING

yll \īl\ see ¹ILE

ylla \il-ə\ see ²ILLA

yllable \il-ə-bəl\ see ILLABLE

yllary \il-ə-rē\ see ILLARY

yllic \il-ik\ see ILIC

yllis \il-əs\ see ILLUS

yllium \il-ē-əm\ see ILIUM

¹yllo \ē-lō\ see ²ILO

²yllo \ī-lō\ see ¹ILO

ylum \ī-ləm\ see ILUM

ylus \ī-ləs\ see ILUS

yly \ī-lē\ dryly, highly, maile,
   Philae, riley, shyly, slyly,
   smiley, Wiley, wily, Wyley,
   wryly, life of Riley

ym \im\ see ¹IM

yma \ī-mə\ Chaima, cyma

yman \ī-mən\ see IMEN

ymathy \im-ə-thē\ see IMOTHY

ymbal \im-bəl\ see IMBLE

ymbalist \im-bə-ləst\ cymbalist,
   symbolist

ymbol \im-bəl\ see IMBLE

ymbolist \im-bə-ləst\ see
   YMBALIST

yme \īm\ see ¹IME

ymeless \īm-ləs\ see IMELESS

ymen \ī-mən\ see IMEN

ymer \ī-mər\ see ¹IMER

¹ymic \ī-mik\ thymic, enzymic

²ymic \im-ik\ gimmick, mimic,
   bulimic, acronymic,
   antonymic, eponymic,
   homonymic, matronymic,
   metonymic, patronymic,
   synonymic, toponymic

ymical \im-i-kəl\ see IMICAL

ymie \ī-mē\ see IMY

ymion \im-ē-ən\ see IMIAN

ymity \im-ət-ē\ see IMITY

ymmetry \im-ə-trē\ see IMETRY
ymn \im\ see ¹IM
ymp \imp\ see IMP
ymph \imf\ lymph, nymph
ymric \im-rik\ Cymric, limerick
ymry \əm-rē\ see ²UMMERY
ymus \ī-məs\ see IMIS
ymy \ī-mē\ see IMY
yn \in\ see ¹IN
ynah \ī-nə\ see ¹INA
ynast \ī-nəst\ see ¹INIST
¹ynch \inch\ see INCH
²ynch \iŋk\ see INK
yncher \in-chər\ see INCHER
ynd \īnd\ see ¹IND
yndic \in-dik\ see INDIC
yne \īn\ see ¹INE
ynein \in-ē-ən\ see ¹INIAN
yness \ī-nəs\ see ¹INUS
ynia \in-ē-ə\ see INIA
ynic \in-ik\ see ²INIC
ynical \in-i-kəl\ see INICAL
ynn \in\ see ¹IN
ynne \in\ see ¹IN
ynth \inth\ see INTH
ynthia \in-thē-ə\ see INTHIA
ynx \iŋs\ see INX
yon \ī-ən\ see ¹ION
yone \ī-ə-nē\ see YONY
yony \ī-ə-nē\ bryony, Alcyone
yp \ip\ see IP
ypal \ī-pəl\ typal, disciple,
    archetypal, prototypal
ype \īp\ see IPE
yper \ī-pər\ see IPER
ypey \ī-pē\ see IPY
yph \if\ see IFF
yphen \ī-fən\ hyphen, siphon
yphic \if-ik\ see IFIC
yphony \if-ə-nē\ see IPHONY
ypic \ip-ik\ typic, philippic,

genotypic, holotypic,
    stereotypic
yping \ī-piŋ\ see IPING
ypo \ī-pō\ hypo, typo
ypress \ī-prəs\ cypress, Cyprus,
    viperous
yprus \ī-prəs\ see YPRESS
ypse \ips\ see IPS
ypso \ip-sō\ see IPSO
ypsy \ip-sē\ gypsy, Gypsy, tipsy
ypt \ipt\ see IPT
yptian \ip-shən\ see IPTION
yptic \ip-tik\ cryptic, diptych,
    styptic, triptych, ecliptic,
    elliptic, apocalyptic
ypy \ī-pē\ see IPY
yr \ir\ see ²EER
yra \ī-rə\ Ira, Lyra, Myra, naira,
    bell-lyra, hegira, hetaira,
    palmyra, spirogyra
yral \ī-rəl\ see IRAL
yrant \ī-rənt\ see IRANT
yre \īr\ see ¹IRE
yreal \ir-ē-əl\ see ERIAL
yria \ir-ē-ə\ see ¹ERIA
yriad \ir-ē-əd\ see ERIOD
yrian \ir-ē-ən\ see ¹ERIAN
yric \ī-rik\ pyric, oneiric,
    panegyric, see ²ERIC
yrical \ir-i-kəl\ see ²ERICAL
¹yrie \ir-ē\ see EARY
²yrie \ī-rē\ see ¹IARY
yril \ir-əl\ see ¹ERAL
yrist \ir-əst\ see ¹ERIST
yrium \ir-ē-əm\ see ERIUM
yrna \ər-nə\ see ERNA
¹yro \ī-rō\ biro, Cairo, gyro,
    Gyro, tyro
²yro \ir-ō\ see ³ERO
yron \īr-ən\ see IREN
yros \ī-rəs\ see IRUS

yrrh \ər\ see ¹EUR

yrrha \ir-ə\ see ²ERA

yrrhic \ir-ik\ see ²ERIC

yrrhus \ir-əs\ see EROUS

yrse \ərs\ see ERSE

yrsus \ər-səs\ see ERSUS

yrtle \ərt-°l\ see ERTILE

yrup \ər-əp\ see IRRUP

yrupy \ər-ə-pē\ see IRRUPY

yrus \ī-rəs\ see IRUS

ysail \ī-səl\ see ¹ISAL

ysch \ish\ see ¹ISH

yse \īs\ see ¹ICE

ysh \ish\ see ¹ISH

¹ysia \ish-ə\ see ITIA

²ysia \izh-ə\ see ISIA

¹ysian \is-ē-ən\ Piscean, Odyssean, Dionysian

²ysian \ish-ən\ see ITION

³ysian \izh-ən\ see ISION

⁴ysian \ī-sē-ən\ see ¹ISCEAN

ysical \iz-i-kəl\ physical, quizzical, metaphysical

ysis \ī-səs\ see ISIS

ysm \iz-əm\ see ISM

ysmal \iz-məl\ dismal, abysmal, baptismal, cataclysmal, catechismal

yson \īs-°n\ see ¹ISON

yss \is\ see ¹ISS

yssal \is-əl\ see ISTLE

yssean \is-ē-ən\ see ¹YSIAN

ysseus \ish-əs\ see ¹ICIOUS

yssum \is-əm\ see ISSOME

yssus \is-əs\ see ISSUS

yst \ist\ see ²IST

ystal \is-t°l\ see ISTAL

¹yster \is-tər\ see ISTER

²yster \ī-stər\ see ¹EISTER

ystery \is-trē\ see ISTORY

ystic \is-tik\ see ISTIC

ystical \is-ti-kəl\ see ISTICAL

ystine \is-tən\ see ISTON

¹ysus \ē-səs\ see ESIS

²ysus \ī-səs\ see ISIS

yta \īt-ə\ see ¹ITA

yte \īt\ see ¹ITE

yterate \it-ə-rət\ see ITERATE

ytes \īt-ēz\ see ITES

¹ythe \ī\ see ¹Y

²ythe \īt͟h\ see ¹ITHE

ythia \it͟h-ē-ə\ lithia, Scythia, forsythia, stichomythia

ythian \it͟h-ē-ən\ Pythian, Scythian

ythmic \it͟h-mik\ rhythmic, arrhythmic, eurythmic, logarithmic

ythy \i-t͟hē\ see ITHY

ytic \it-ik\ see ITIC

ytical \it-i-kəl\ see ITICAL

ytics \it-iks\ see ITICS

yting \īt-iŋ\ see ITING

ytis \ī-təs\ see ITIS

ytton \it-°n\ see ITTEN

yve \īv\ see ¹IVE

yx \iks\ see ¹IX

yxia \ik-sē-ə\ see IXIA

yxie \ik-sē\ see IXIE

yze \īz\ see IZE